THE PENGUIN BOOK OF

·

TWENTIETH-CENTURY PROTEST

·

EDITED BY BRIAN MacARTHUR

PENGUIN BOOKS

For Georgie MacArthur

PENGUIN BOOKS

Published by the Penguin Group
Penguin Books Ltd, 27 Wrights Lane, London W8 5TZ, England
Penguin Putnam Inc., 375 Hudson Street, New York, New York 10014, USA
Penguin Books Australia Ltd, Ringwood, Victoria, Australia
Penguin Books Canada Ltd, 10 Alcorn Avenue, Toronto, Ontario, Canada M4V 3B2
Penguin Books (NZ) Ltd, Private Bag 102902, NSMC, Auckland, New Zealand

Penguin Books Ltd, Registered Offices: Harmondsworth, Middlesex, England

First published by Viking 1998
Published in Penguin Books 1999
1 3 5 7 9 10 8 6 4 2

Set in Monotype Garamond
Typeset by Rowland Phototypesetting Ltd, Bury St Edmunds, Suffolk
Printed in England by Clays Ltd, St Ives plc

TWENTIETH-CENTURY PROFILES

Brian Macarthur is associate editor of *The Times*. He was founder editor of *Today* and *The Times Higher Education Supplement*, editor of the *Western Morning News* and former deputy editor of the *Sunday Times*. He has written *Eddy Shah, Today* and the *Newspaper Revolution*, and *Deadline Sunday*, and edited *Despatches from the Gulf War*. He has been interested in the power of oratory since first hearing Aneurin Bevan on the hustings in 1950 and has edited both *The Penguin Book of Historic Speeches* and *The Penguin Book of Twentieth-Century Speeches*.

Brian Macarthur lives in London and has two daughters.

There is nothing more baffling to the reformer than the patience of the people with wrongs, except their impatience when they are roused to a sense of their wrongs. You find the people enduring injustice, oppression, fraud, generation after generation, and without a murmur – just a groan – for centuries. The patience of the people is a marvel of all time. Then suddenly they are stirred up to a sense of the injustice that has been inflicted on them, and when they rise in their might there is nothing which is more baffling than their impatience. They can hardly wait for the counsels of prudence in their efforts to redress wrongs which they have endured for centuries.

David Lloyd George

Some men see things as they are and say why? I dream of things that never were and say why not?

George Bernard Shaw

When Hitler attacked the Jews I was not a Jew, therefore, I was not concerned. And when Hitler attacked the Catholics, I was not a Catholic and therefore I was not concerned. And when Hitler attacked the unions and the industrialists, I was not a member of the unions and I was not concerned. Then Hitler attacked me and the Protestant church – and there was nobody left to be concerned.

Martin Niemoller

CONTENTS

ACKNOWLEDGEMENTS

I could not have researched this anthology without the help of many friends, experts, historians and libraries.

My major debts are to Barry Turner and Mary Fulton for their hospitality and their library in Gascony, Georgie and Tessa MacArthur, Lynette Carr and Sandra Bourne, Anthony Howard, Tony Lacey of Penguin Books, my agent Hilary Rubinstein, but above all to my partner Maureen Waller who endured the past three years of absorption in this anthology with hardly a squeak of protest.

I have ransacked the incomparable London Library as well as *The Times* Library, the British Library Newspaper Library, the Fawcett, TUC and *Irish Times* libraries and the *London Review of Books* Archive and am grateful to them all. Our libraries are one of the unsung glories of Britain.

Allison Bozniak in the United States and Peter Rose, Edward Wild and Guy Penman in London helped with research.

Others who have willingly offered advice include Tariq Ali, David Alton, Michael Aris, Alan Bell, Tony Benn, Rose Billington, Alastair Brett, John Byford, Vernon Coleman, Bela Cunha, Malcolm Dean, Brian Doherty, Lisa Gallagher, Richard Gott, Janet Griffin, John Grigg, Liz Halsall, Robin Hanbury Tenison, Nigel Hawkes, Mark Henderson, Peter Hennessy, Simon Jenkins, Robert Kaiser, Anthony Lewis, Joanna Mackle, Tom McNally, Brenda Maddox, Ann Mallalieu, Alison Menzies, Merrick, Dan Mills, George Monbiot, Terri Natale, John Naughton, Joyce D'Silva, Ursula Owen, Maggie van Reenen, Peter Riddell, Manuel Riesco, Salman Rushdie, Frank B. Shaw, Victoria Solomonides, Peter Stothard, John Vidal, James Walsh, Geoffrey Whitfield and Hugo Young.

A particular debt should be acknowledged to the work of several historians, notably A. J. P. Taylor, Peter Clarke, Robert Ensor, Kenneth O. Morgan and Robert Blake on Britain, Roy Foster on Ireland, Hugh Brogan and Esmond Wright on the United States, Orlando Figes on Russia and to Lawrence James, Thomas Pakenham and David Caute, Sheila Rowbotham and William Safire.

Sources

Among the most useful reference works were the Penguin dictionaries of
history, Chambers *Biographical Dictionary*, Chambers *British Biographies of the
Twentieth Century* and *The Companion to British History* (with *History Today*).
William Safire's *Lend Me Your Ears* is a superb chronicle of great speeches as
Sheila Rowbotham's *A Century of Women* is of feminism. *Protest, Politics, Cause
Groups and Campaigns*, Eds F. F. Ridley and Grant Jordan (OUP) is a useful
guide to contemporary single-issue protest campaigns.

PERMISSIONS

Grateful thanks are also due to the following for permission to reprint copyright material in this book:

Kingsley Amis: to Jonathan Clowes Ltd, London, on behalf of the Literary Estate of Sir Kingsley Amis; **John Arlott**: to the Guardian Syndication Department; **James Baldwin**: to Penguin Books Ltd; **Stanley Baldwin**: to Earl Baldwin of Bewdley; **Tony Benn**: to the author; **Aneurin Bevan**: to the Labour Party; **Robert Blatchford**: to the Labour Party; **Niels Bohr**: to News International Syndication; **Nikolai Bukharin**: to Macmillan Ltd; **Rachel Carson**: to Laurence Pollinger Ltd and the Estate of Rachel Carson; **'Cassandra' (William Connor)**: to Mirror Group plc; **Whittaker Chambers**: to Random House Inc; **Charter 88**: to the publisher; **The Church of England**: to Church House Publishing, © The Central Board of Finance of the Church of England 1985; **Eldridge Cleaver**: to Random House UK Ltd (Jonathan Cape Ltd); **Coalition Against Runway Two**: to the authors; **Vernon Coleman**: to the author; **Alex Comfort**: to Corinne M. Reed Comfort on behalf of the author; **Compassion in World Farming**: to the authors; **Anthony Crosland**: to Susan Crosland; *Daily Mail*: to Solo Syndication Ltd; **Richard Davenport-Hines**: to the author; **Simone de Beauvoir**: to Random House UK Ltd (Jonathan Cape Ltd) and Rosica Colin Ltd; **Bernadette Devlin**: to the Controller of Her Majesty's Stationery Office on behalf of Parliament; **Earth First!**: to the authors; **Albert Einstein**: to *The Atlantic Monthly*; **Frantz Fanon**: to HarperCollins Publishers Ltd; **Michael Foot**: to the author; **Paul Foot**: to the author; **Betty Friedan**: to Penguin Books Ltd; **Friends of the Earth**: to the authors; **Peter Fryer**: to Dobson Books Ltd; **J. K. Galbraith**: to Penguin Books Ltd; **John Galsworthy**: to Mr Alan A. Meyer; **Mahatma Gandhi**: to Mrs Sonia Gandhi; **G. E. R. Gedye**: to Victor Gollancz Ltd; **David Lloyd George**: to Express Newspapers plc; **André Gide**: to Penguin Books Ltd; **Victor Gollancz**: to Victor Gollancz Ltd; **Germaine Greer**: to Gillon Aitken Associates Ltd, © 1970 Germaine Greer; **John Grigg**: to the author c/o The Society of Authors; **Robert Harris**: to the author; **Graham Harvey**: to Little, Brown & Company (UK); **Vaclav Havel**: to the Tanja Howarth Literary Agency; **F. A. Hayek**: to Routledge Ltd; **Sarah Hipperson**:

to the author and The Working Press; **Ho Chi Minh**: to Gioi Publishers; **J. A. Hobson**: to Routledge Ltd; **Richard Hoggart**: to the author; **Geoffrey Howe**: to the Controller of her Majesty's Stationery Office on behalf of Parliament; **Trevor Huddleston**: to Bantam Doubleday Dell Publishing Group; **Will Hutton**: to the author; *Irish Times*: to the publisher; **Simon Jenkins**: to The Times Syndication Department, © *The Times*/Simon Jenkins; **Wei Jingsheng**: to the author; **Josiah Mwangi Kariuki**: to Oxford University Press; **John Keegan**: to the author; **Jomo Kenyatta**: to Random House UK Ltd (Secker & Warburg Ltd); **John Maynard Keynes**: to Macmillan Press Ltd; **Martin Luther King**: to The Heirs to the Estate of Martin Luther King, Jr., c/o Writer's House Inc. as agent for the proprietor © 1963 by Martin Luther King, Jr., copyright renewed 1991 by Coretta Scott King; **Arthur Koestler**: to The Peters Fraser & Dunlop Group Ltd; **Victor Kravchenko**: to Andrew Kravchenko, Executor of the Estate of Victor Kravchenko; **Milan Kundera**: to Faber & Faber Ltd; **Aung San Suu Kyi**: to Penguin Books Ltd; **Jean-Jacques Lebel**: to Bloomsbury Publishing plc and Tariq Ali; **V. I. Lenin**: to Progress Publishers; **Primo Levi**: to Penguin Books Ltd and Giulio Einaudi Editore; **Bernard Levin**: to the author and Curtis Brown Ltd, © Bernard Levin; **Sinclair Lewis**: to the Nobel Foundation, Stockholm; **Mario Vargas Llosa**: to the author c/o Agencia Literaria Carmen Balcells SA, Barcelona; **Mary McCarthy**: to Orion Publishing Group; **Iain Macleod**: to the Rt Hon. Baroness Macleod of Borve; **Norman Mailer**: to A. M. Heath & Company; **The Baroness Mallalieu**: to the author; **Nelson Mandela**: to Meer Care & Desai (Solicitors); **George Mangakis**: to *Index on Censorship*; **W. Somerset Maugham**: to A. P. Watt Ltd on behalf of The Royal Literary Fund; **Merrick**: to the author; **Rosalind Miles**: to the author; **George Monbiot**: to the Guardian Syndication Department, © the *Guardian*; **Charles Moore**: to the author; **Keith Murdoch**: to News Limited & Associated Companies; **Edward R. Murrow**: to Casey Murrow, for the Estate of Edward R. Murrow; **Ferenc Nagy**: to Simon & Schuster Inc; **Edward Norman**: to the author; *The Observer*: to the Observer Syndication Department; **Viktor Orban**: to Richard Scott Simon Ltd; **George Orwell**: to Mark Hamilton as the Literary Executor of the Estate of the late Sonia Brownell Orwell and Martin Secker & Warburg Ltd; **John Osborne**: © Helen Osborne, to Gordon Dickerson on behalf of the author's estate; **Sylvia Pankhurst**: to Richard Pankhurst; **Melanie Phillips**: to the author and Little, Brown & Company UK; **John Pilger**: to the author; **Dennis Potter**: to Faber & Faber Ltd; **Enoch Powell**: to the Controller of Her Majesty's Stationery Office on behalf of Parliament; **Evadne Price**: to A. M. Heath & Company; **J. B. Priestley**: to the New Statesman & Society; **RSPCA**: to the RSPCA Publications

Department; **A. Philip Randolph**: to the A. Philip Randolph Institute; **Lord Rees-Mogg**: to the author; **Michael Rosen**: to The Peters Fraser & Dunlop Group Ltd; **Seebohm Rowntree**: to Macmillan Ltd; **Bertrand Russell**: to The Bertrand Russell Peace Foundation Ltd; **Stephen Sackur**: to the author and the *London Review of Books*; **Edward Said**: to the author and *The Nation*; **Ken Saro-Wiwa**: to the Executors of the Estate of Ken Saro-Wiwa; **Siegfried Sassoon**: to George Sassoon, copyright Siegfried Sassoon; **Arthur Scargill**: to the National Union of Mineworkers; **Arthur M. Schlesinger**: to W. W. Norton & Company Inc, © Arthur M. Schlesinger, Jr., 1991, 1992; **Inge Scholl**: to John Murray (Publishers) Ltd; **E. F. Schumacher**: to Random House Inc; **Haidar Abdul Shafi**: to the author; **George Bernard Shaw**: to the Society of Authors on behalf of the Bernard Shaw Estate; **Alexander Solzhenitsyn**: to The Harvill Press, © Alexander I. Solzhenitsyn, 1974, © in the English translation Harper & Row, Publishers, Inc., 1975; **Earl Spencer**: to the author; **Helen Steel and Dave Morris**: to the authors; **Gloria Steinem**: to the author, © Gloria Steinem, 1978; **I. F. Stone**: to *The Nation*; *The Sunday Times*: to News International Syndication, © Times Newspapers Ltd; **Rabindranath Tagore**: to Visva-Bharati; **Peter Tatchell**: to the author; **R. H. Tawney**: to John Murray (Publishers) Ltd and the Estate of R. H. Tawney; **E. P. Thompson**: to The Merlin Press Ltd; *The Times*: to News International Syndication, © Times Newspapers Ltd; **David Tinker**: to Penguin Books Ltd; **Kenneth Tynan**: to the Observer Syndication Department; **George Vlachos**: to the Melina Mercouri Foundation; **Colin Welch**: to Mrs Frances Brown; **Peter Wildeblood**: to Orion Publishing Group (Weidenfeld & Nicolson Ltd); **Ellen Wilkinson**: to Victor Gollancz Ltd; **August Wilson**: to the author; **Donald Woods**: to Penguin Books Ltd; **Martin Woollacott**: to the Guardian Syndication Department, © the *Guardian*; **Malcolm X**: to Random House UK Ltd; **Liu Xiaobo, Zhou Duo, Hou Dejian, Gao Xin**: to Liu Xiaobo; **Hugo Young**: to the Guardian Syndication Department, © the *Guardian*.

Every effort has been made to contact or trace all copyright holders. Penguin would be glad to rectify any omissions or errors brought to their notice at the earliest opportunity.

INTRODUCTION

At the turn of a century, almost one hundred years on, we listen to their voices and wonder at their power.

One was the son of a Scottish carpenter in a family of ten children. He started work at the age of seven and was sent down the mine at ten. After being victimized for championing the miners, he went to night school, became a journalist and was the inspiration of the Independent Labour Party. He was the first Labour candidate to the British Parliament. As a Labour MP in 1901 he delivered the first major speech on Socialism to the House of Commons.

As Keir Hardie denounced – in terms that would still be recognized ninety-seven years later – the shame brought upon Britain by allowing the wealthy to corrupt the press, silence the pulpit and degrade national life, he declared: 'We are called upon at the beginning of the twentieth century to decide the question propounded in the Sermon on the Mount as to whether we will worship God or Mammon. The present day is a Mammon-worshipping age.'

Another, the first black American to be awarded a Ph.D by Harvard, dared to challenge the Uncle Tom of his generation, Booker T. Washington. Washington advocated accommodation with the whites and was willing to agree to segregation. William Du Bois disagreed.

'The problem of the twentieth century,' he wrote in 1903, 'is the problem of the color-line, the relationship of the darker to the lighter races of men in Asia and Africa, America and the islands of the sea.'

Another was a middle-class Englishwoman who in the same year founded the Women's Social and Political Union – the suffragettes. When their protests at the subjugation of women were ignored by politicians, Sylvia Pankhurst led them in smashing shop windows and breaking up political meetings to attract attention to the cause of women's liberation.

A fourth was a British economist who in the same year published his classic analysis of imperialism. 'Imperialism,' J. A. Hobson wrote, 'is a depraved choice of national life ... Its adoption as a policy implies a deliberate renunciation of the higher inner qualities which for a nation as for an individual constitute the ascendancy of reason over brute impulse.'

As they denounced capitalism, imperialism and segregation of women and blacks, Hardie and Hobson, Du Bois and Pankhurst were voices in the wilderness, speaking for the silent, small people ranged against mighty forces. In Britain the Labour Party had still to be constituted, much of the map of the world was painted in British red and women did not even have the vote. In the United States, as the first protest in this anthology describes, 200 Negroes a year were being roasted alive by lynch mobs. Yet each rebel demonstrated the power of protest and why protest matters. When they articulate ideas whose time is coming, voices in the wilderness have a habit of becoming the voices of the masses.

When the British statesman David Lloyd George was fighting the House of Lords over his People's Budget in 1909, he marvelled at the patience of the people. There was nothing more baffling to the reformer, he declared, than their patience with wrongs – except when they were raised to a sense of their wrongs. 'When they are stirred up to a sense of the injustice that has been inflicted on them and when they rise in their might there is nothing which is more baffling than their impatience. They can hardly wait for the counsels of prudence in their efforts to redress wrongs which they have endured for centuries.' He added: 'We are in for a protracted fight but if we stand together we can win.'

The fight by Du Bois was indeed protracted but Hardie, Hobson and Pankhurst achieved success within years. The first Labour government was formed in 1924. Women were given the vote in 1918 and fully enfranchised in 1928. Lenin was so impressed by Hobson's analysis of the economic motive for imperialism that it became the basis of Communist foreign policy (an achievement he may not have wished) – and within fifty years India, the jewel in the British Crown, had its freedom. Each of them also inspired succeeding generations. Du Bois was joint founder of the National Association for the Advancement of Colored People and there is a direct line from him to A. Philip Randolph and Martin Luther King, as there is from Pankhurst to Simone de Beauvoir and Betty Friedan and from Hobson to Lenin, Gandhi and Jomo Kenyatta.

As the British political philosopher Harold Laski observed, the wicked heresies of today are the sober commonplaces of tomorrow. If the poor are no longer dumped in the workhouses described by Beatrice Webb, if the abject poverty that so enraged Seebohm Rowntree and Jack London no longer exists to the same degree, if Negroes are no longer lynched, most women go out to work and Britain is no longer an imperial power, it is because those early voices in the wilderness stirred the people to a sense of the wrongs inflicted upon them.

Protest is the stuff of everyday life. Study newspaper front pages or television news bulletins and they are crowded with dissenting and protesting voices. Search for protest on the Internet and there are more than 360,000 items. That is because we all utter protests every day whether about bosses, bureaucrats and politicians, our taxes or our neighbours, new bypasses and new airport runways or the destruction of tropical rainforest and urban traffic jams. We rage briefly, decide there is nothing we can do apart from casting an apathetic vote every few years and opt for the quiet life. The men and women represented in this anthology (which can be complemented by *The Penguin Book of Twentieth-Century Speeches*) opted instead for the life of struggle. They invited scorn, derision and hatred. Some (Gandhi, Trotsky, Martin Luther King) were assassinated. Some were imprisoned (Clifford Allen, Mandela, Havel). One – Steve Biko – was beaten to death in his prison cell. Several, including Solzhenitsyn, were exiled. Even when their action seemed futile, the students of Tiananmen Square made their protest and the men and women in Stalin's gulags made their mental notes for posterity. A few (Emily Hobhouse, Northcliffe, Keith Murdoch) were simply outraged by the complacency they witnessed around them and won instant results – a new regime in Boer concentration camps, a new Ministry of Munitions, the sacking of the British general at Gallipoli.

Only a small number of the hundreds of thousands of protests made during the turmoil of the twentieth century are chronicled in this anthology. That is inevitable given that any book has a finite number of pages and that any editor's choice will be personal and eclectic. My choices are mainly from the tradition of political pamphleteering in speeches, manifestos and charters, books, political magazines and angry articles in newspapers (where they reach audiences of thousands) – and deliberately exclude songs, poetry and literature. The songs of Bob Dylan and Alex Glasgow or the First World War poetry of Wilfred Owen belong in other anthologies.

The selection has obviously been influenced by my own experience of sixty years of the century as the son of parents who left school at fourteen but who if they had been born thirty years later would have gone to university. Where their potential went unfulfilled, my generation profited from the Education Act of 1944 and the advocacy of such political thinkers as R. H. Tawney. We were the first generation to go to redbrick universities, only to be dismissed as scum by Somerset Maugham.

The voices of protest which spoke to the students of my small northern grammar school were the *Manchester Guardian* on Cyprus and Suez (an issue represented in this anthology by the *Observer* although the *Guardian* was equally if not more courageous) and the despair of John Osborne's Jimmy

Porter in *Look Back in Anger* at the small-mindedness of British life. Jimmy Porter's impotent rage was certainly appreciated and understood up north. There were no good, brave causes left, he raged. But there were. We went on to university and marched against apartheid, won easy headlines by shouting 'Macmillan Out!' when the British prime minister arrived in Yorkshire to shoot grouse with the Duke of Devonshire, meanwhile fighting the university authorities for the right to live where we wished instead of where they dictated (an unarticulated demand for the sexual freedom that was coming in the sixties and an early harbinger of the student protest of 1968).

There were mightier causes beyond our own provincial world. As Jimmy Porter lamented the lack of good brave causes, Stalin was crushing the Hungarian uprising, Trevor Huddleston was alerting the world to the denial of Christianity of South Africa's apartheid and Arthur Koestler was describing how murderers were hanged and creating the moral climate for the abolition of capital punishment in Britain. And a British government led by a politician whose career had peaked in the 1930s and 1940s was staging its last and doomed imperial adventure.

Brave causes? Still to come were the overthrowing of segregation in the United States, the Soviet tyranny in Europe and the dismantling of the British empire. Still to come were women's liberation, student revolt, Vietnam, Pol Pot, banning the bomb and threats to the global environment. Still to come were smaller causes – the right of a man to love a man without its being a criminal act or the simple right to read *Lady Chatterley's Lover*. Still to emerge were such leaders as Castro, Fanon, Mandela, Martin Luther King, Vaclav Havel or Germaine Greer. 'We shall overcome', sang the students with Pete Seeger. Over the next forty years they did. And still now, at the turn of a new century, there are brave causes such as animal rights or the protection of the environment, or the fights against 'Frankenstein' food created from genetically modified crops or the omnipotent power of the global multinational companies. The manifestos can be found on the Internet, often expressed in the language of agitprop rather than the measured prose of Keir Hardie and William Du Bois or J. A. Hobson and Sylvia Pankhurst, but which speak equally eloquently and powerfully to new generations. They can be shared and read by millions across the world and create global protest movements.

Given the ascendancy of the right in the politics of the West over the past century, it is inevitable that much of the protest in this anthology is from the left. But there are tides in the affairs of men and women and what this book also demonstrates is that the pendulum of protest is always swinging. The Lenin who denounced the autocratic methods and brutality of the Tsar set up a dictatorship of the proletariat which became equally brutal and autocratic, as Bukharin and Solzhenitsyn testify. An overdose of British socialism in the late 1970s created the climate for Margaret Thatcher, who was influenced by F. A. Hayek's *The Road to Serfdom* of 1944 – and an overdose of Thatcherism created the climate for Tony Blair and New Labour's Third Way. The success of black power in the United States now creates the conditions in which Arthur J. Schlesinger mourns the disuniting of America. And Primo Levi bears eloquent witness that if another holocaust is to be avoided new generations must constantly be reminded of the horrors of the past, lest they forget.

'Some men see things as they are and say why?' said George Bernard Shaw. 'I dream of things that never were and say why not?' Commemorated within this anthology are the men and women who asked 'Why?' and 'Why not?' Most helped to improve the human lot. When they set out to change the world around them, most protesters are dismissed as nuisances, cranks or dangerous threats to the status quo. Yet this anthology demonstrates that there is no progress without protest. 'For years,' Martin Luther King wrote from Birmingham Jail, 'I have heard the word "Wait!" It rings in the ear of every Negro with piercing familiarity. This "Wait" has almost always meant "Never".' Martin Luther King had dreams, decided not to wait and died for them – but his protests provoked great improvements in the legal status of America's blacks. There have been few more satisfying, more moving or more noble sights in the last half of the twentieth century than King leading the great march on Washington, or Nelson Mandela walking erect and unbowed from jail or the students of East Germany tearing down the Berlin Wall. Unless we protest we stay as we are. Protest is the engine of democracy.

IDA B. WELLS
1900

'Roasted to death'

Ida B. Wells (1862–1931) was born a slave but became a journalist, social activist and advocate of civil rights. At the turn of the century, white mobs were putting 200 blacks to death by lynching every year. They were 'roasted to death', as she wrote in this article for Arena *magazine on 'The White Man's Problem', where she argued that violence was a political tool to keep African Americans enslaved.*

Our country's national crime is *lynching*. It is not the creature of an hour, the sudden outburst of uncontrolled fury, or the unspeakable brutality of an insane mob. It represents the cool, calculating deliberation of intelligent people who openly avow that there is an 'unwritten law' that justifies them in putting human beings to death without complaint under oath, without trial by jury, without opportunity to make defense, and without right of appeal . . .

The sentiment of the country has been appealed to, in describing the isolated condition of white families in thickly populated Negro districts; and the charge is made that these homes are in as great danger as if they were surrounded by wild beasts. And the world has accepted this theory without let or hindrance. In many cases there has been open expression that the fate meted out to the victim was only what he deserved. In many other instances there has been a silence that says more forcibly than words can proclaim it that it is right and proper that a human being should be seized by a mob and burned to death upon the unsworn and the uncorroborated charge of his accuser. No matter that our laws presume every man innocent until he is proved guilty; no matter that it leaves a certain class of individuals completely at the mercy of another class; no matter that it encourages those criminally disposed to blacken their faces and commit any crime in the calendar so long as they can throw suspicion on some Negro, as is frequently done, and then lead a mob to take his life; no matter that mobs make a farce of the law and a mockery of justice; no matter that hundreds of boys are being hardened in crime and schooled in vice by the repetition of such scenes before their eyes – if a white woman declares herself insulted or assaulted, some life must pay the penalty, with all the horrors of the Spanish Inquisition and all the barbarism of the Middle Ages. The world looks on and says it is well.

Not only are 200 men and women put to death annually, on the average, in this country by mobs, but these lives are taken with the greatest publicity. In many instances the leading citizens aid and abet by their presence when they do not participate, and the leading journals inflame the public mind to the lynching point with scare-head articles and offers of rewards. Whenever a burning is advertised to take place, the railroads run excursions, photographs are taken, and the same jubilee is indulged in that characterized the public hangings of 100 years ago. There is, however, this difference: in those old days the multitude that stood by was permitted only to guy or jeer. The nineteenth-century lynching mob cuts off ears, toes and fingers, strips off flesh, and distributes portions of the body as souvenirs among the crowd. If the leaders of the mob are so minded, coal-oil is poured over the body and the victim is then roasted to death.

No scoffer at our boasted American civilization could say anything more harsh of it than does the American white man himself who says he is unable to protect the honor of his women without resort to such brutal, inhuman and degrading exhibitions as characterize 'lynching bees.' The cannibals of the South Sea Islands roast human beings alive to satisfy hunger. The red Indian of the Western plains tied his prisoner to the stake, tortured him, and danced in fiendish glee while his victim writhed in the flames. His savage, untutored mind suggested no better way than that of wreaking vengeance upon those who had wronged him. These people knew nothing about Christianity and did not profess to follow its teachings; but such primary laws as they had they lived up to. No nation, savage or civilized, save only the United States of America, has confessed its inability to protect its women save by hanging, shooting and burning alleged offenders.

•

KEIR HARDIE
1901

'Socialism'

James Keir Hardie (1856–1915), who began work at the age of seven, became the first Independent Labour MP when he was elected for West Ham in 1892. A century later, he remains Labour's acknowledged folk hero. Hardie, a pacifist, supporter of the temperance movement and fierce champion of the miners, went down the mines himself when he was only ten. He was the first (defeated) Labour candidate in Mid-Lanark in 1888, the main inspiration of the Independent Labour Party and, in 1900, the Labour Representation Committee, which became the Labour Party in 1906.

When he delivered this protest against capitalism, he had become MP for Merthyr Tydfil, a mining community in South Wales. It was the first complete Socialist declaration made in the House of Commons.

I make no apology for bringing the question of Socialism before the House of Commons. It has long commanded the attention of the best minds in the country. It is a growing force in the thought of the world, and whether men agree or disagree with it, they have to reckon with it, and may as well begin by understanding it.

I begin by pointing out that the growth of our national wealth instead of bringing comfort to the masses of the people is imposing additional burdens on them. We are told on high authority that some 300 years ago the total wealth of the English nation was a 100 millions sterling. At the beginning of the last century it had increased to 2,000 millions, and this year it is estimated to be 13,000 millions. While our population during the last century increased three and a half times, the wealth of the community increased over six times. But one factor in our national life remained with us all through the century, and is with us still, and that is that at the bottom of the social scale there is a mass of poverty and misery equal in magnitude to that which obtained 100 years ago. I submit that the true test of progress is not the accumulation of wealth in the hands of a few, but the elevation of a people as a whole. I admit frankly that a considerable improvement was made in the condition of the working people during the last century. At the beginning of the nineteenth century the nation industrially was sick almost unto death. It was at that time passing from the old system of handicraft, under which every man was his own employer and his own capitalist, and traded direct with his customer, to the factory system which the introduction of machinery brought into existence. During these 100 years the wealth of the nation accumulated, and the condition of the working classes as compared with the early years of the century improved, but I respectfully submit to the House that there was more happiness, more comfort and more independence before machinery began to accumulate wealth.

The high standard of comfort reached by the labouring classes at the end of the last century has not brought them that happiness which obtained in England 300 years ago, when there was no machinery, no large capitalists, no private property in land, as we know it today, and when every person had the right to use the land for the purpose of producing food for himself and his family. I said that an improvement was made during the last century, but I would qualify that statement in this respect – that practically the whole of that improvement was made during the first seventy-five years. During the last quarter of the century the condition of the working classes has been practically stationary. There have been slight increases of wages here and reductions of hours there, but the landlord with his increased rent has more than absorbed any advantage that may have been gained.

We are rapidly approaching a point when the nation will be called upon to decide between an uncontrolled monopoly, conducted for the benefit and in the interests of its principal shareholders, and a monopoly owned, controlled and manipulated by the state in the interests of the nation as a whole. I do not require to go far afield for arguments to support that part of my statement concerning the danger which the aggregation of wealth in a few hands is bringing upon us. This House and the British nation know to their cost the danger which comes from allowing men to grow rich and permitting them to use their wealth to corrupt the press, to silence the pulpit, to degrade our national life, and to bring reproach and shame upon a great people, in order that a few unscrupulous scoundrels might be able to add to their ill-gotten gains. The war in South Africa is a millionaires' war. Our troubles in China are due to the desire of the capitalists to exploit the people of that country as they would fain exploit the people of South Africa. Much of the jealousy and bad blood existing between this country and France is traceable to the fact that we went to war in Egypt to suppress a popular uprising, seeking freedom for the people, in order that the interest of our bondholders might be secured. Socialism, by placing land and the instruments of production in the hands of the community, eliminates only the idle, useless class at both ends of the scale. Half a million of the people of this country benefit by the present system; the remaining millions of toilers and business men do not. The pursuit of wealth corrupts the manhood of men. We are called upon at the beginning of the twentieth century to decide the question propounded in the Sermon on the Mount as to whether we will worship God or Mammon. The present day is a Mammon-worshipping age. Socialism proposes to dethrone the brute-god Mammon and to lift humanity into its place. I beg to submit in this very imperfect fashion the resolution on the Paper, merely promising that the last has not been heard of the Socialist movement either in the country or on the floor of this House, but that, just as sure as Radicalism democratized the system of government politically in the last century so will Socialism democratize the country industrially during the century upon which we have just entered.

•

EMILY HOBHOUSE
1901

'Concentration camps'

Lord Kitchener adopted a scorched-earth policy after he became commander-in-chief of the British forces in South Africa during the Boer War. Boer women and children were herded into concentration camps, where more than 20,000 died.

Emily Hobhouse went to South Africa to visit the camps. She was horrified by the plight of the Boers and lobbied the government to alleviate conditions in the camps. She kept a diary, published at length in the Guardian *(where her brother L. T. Hobhouse was a leader-writer), and wrote letters home, including this open letter to St John Brodrick, Secretary for War. She made her humanitarian protest so eloquently that Joseph Chamberlain, Colonial Secretary, had the camps transferred to his control and conditions were speedily transformed.*

Mrs Pienaar is so brave and calm. She has six children ranging in age from fifteen down to two years, *and she does not know where one of them is.* She was taken right away from them. Her husband is in detention of some kind in Bloemfontein but not allowed to see her. She expects her confinement in about three weeks, yet has to lie on the bare hard ground till she is stiff and sore, and she has had nothing to sit on for over two months, but must squat on a rolled-up blanket. All her baby linen was in readiness at her home, but all is lost. This is but one case, quite ordinary, among hundreds and hundreds.

The women are wonderful: they cry very little and never complain. The very magnitude of their sufferings, indignities, loss and anxiety seems to lift them beyond tears, and these people, who have had comfortable, even luxurious homes, just set themselves to quiet endurance and to make the best of their bare and terrible lot. Only when it cuts afresh at them through their children do their feelings flash out. Mrs Reintjes, for instance, has six children in camp, all ill – two in the hospital with typhoid and four sick in the tent. She also expects her confinement soon. Her husband is in Ceylon. She has means and would gladly provide for herself either in town or in the Colony, where she has relatives, or by going back to her farm. It was not burnt, only the furniture was destroyed. Yet there she has to stay, watching her children droop and sicken. For their sakes she did plead with tears that she might go and fend for herself. It is such a wholesale cruelty and one of which England must be ashamed. And it presses hardest on the children. They droop in the terrible heat and with the insufficient unsuitable food. Whatever you do, whatever the military authorities may do, it is all only a miserable patch upon a very great wrong. Whatever you do is only temporary alleviation and can touch only a very few. The whole system is a mistake and has placed thousands physically unfit in conditions of life which they have not strength to endure. In front of them is blank ruin – and whole families are severed and scattered they don't know where. Will you try somehow to make the British public understand the position and force it to ask itself what is going to be done with these people. There must be already full 50,000 of them, and I should not wonder if there were not more.

If only the British people would try to exercise a little imagination – picture the whole miserable scene, and answer how long such a cruelty is to be tolerated.

•

SEEBOHM ROWNTREE
1901

'Poverty'

Seebohm Rowntree's Poverty: A Study of Town Life *became a classic and influenced the 1906 Liberal and 1945 Labour governments. Rowntree (1871–1954), a Quaker, labour director and then chairman of the chocolate factory, introduced an eight-hour working day in 1896. His study did for York what Charles Booth had done for London by showing that 30 per cent of York citizens were living in poverty and that neither idleness nor drinking was to blame.*

Allowing for broken time, the average wage for a labourer in York is from 18s[hillings]. to 21s.; whereas, according to the figures given earlier in this chapter, the minimum expenditure necessary to maintain in a state of physical efficiency a family of two adults and three children is 21s. 8d., or, if there are four children, the sum required would be 26s.

It is thus seen that *the wages paid for unskilled labour in York are insufficient to provide food, shelter and clothing adequate to maintain a family of moderate size in a state of bare physical efficiency.* It will be remembered that the above estimates of necessary minimum expenditure are based upon the assumption that the diet is even less generous than that allowed to able-bodied paupers in the York

Workhouse, and that *no allowance is made for any expenditure other than that absolutely required for the maintenance of merely physical efficiency.*

And let us clearly understand what 'merely physical efficiency' means. A family living upon the scale allowed for in this estimate must never spend a penny on railway fare or omnibus. They must never go into the country unless they walk. They must never purchase a halfpenny newspaper or spend a penny to buy a ticket for a popular concert. They must write no letters to absent children, for they cannot afford to pay the postage. They must never contribute anything to their church or chapel, or give any help to a neighbour. The following table will be recognized when we consider the effect of inadequate nutrition upon the general health and vitality of the worker.

Comparison with Prison and Workhouse Diets

If we compare the diets of the families in Class 1 with the diets provided in prisons and workhouses, the serious inadequacy of the former is again disclosed.

An examination of this table shows that the diet of the labourers in York compares very unfavourably, as regards nutritive value, and even more unfavourably as regards supply of protein, with the diet given to the inmates of prisons and workhouses.

It is evident that the diet of the servant-keeping class is, upon the whole, in excess of that required for the maintenance of health.

Secondly, it is probably safe to assume that, in the case of average families of the artisan class, the food supply is adequate, although it is clear that in many cases it can only continue so by abstention from wasteful expenditure upon drink, etc.

On the other hand, the labouring classes, upon whom the bulk of the muscular work falls, and who form so large a proportion of the industrial population, are *seriously underfed.* The average energy value of the diet in the case of the fourteen families selected for study being no less than 23 per cent below standard, while the average deficiency in proteins amounts to as much as 29 per cent. The inquiry, it is true, has shown that the money available for the purchase of food is not always spent in the most economical way, but the fact remains that unless an unreasonably stringent diet be adopted, the means to purchase a sufficient supply of nourishing food are not possessed by the labourers and their families.

The serious physiological effects of inadequate food have already been pointed out, and they are powerfully attested by health statistics, but it may be doubted if the English public has yet recognized their economic importance.

Dietaries	Protein (per man per day)	Energy Value (per man per day)
	Grams	Calories
Workhouses –		
English Class 1..................	136	3702
Prisons –		
English:		
Class B	134	3038
Convict (hard labour)	177	4159
Scotch:		
Rate IV	134	3115
Convict (Rate VII)	173	3717
Munich	104	2915
Brandenburg	127	3410
York average of 14 families, wages under 26s.	89	2685
Standard requirements for moderate work		
(Atwater)	125	3500

The relation of food to industrial efficiency is so obvious and so direct as to be a commonplace among students of political economy. 'What an employer will get out of his workman,' as a well-known economist has reminded us, 'will depend very much on what he first gets into him. Not only are bone and muscle to be built up and kept up by food, but every stroke of the arm involves an expenditure of nervous energy which is to be supplied only through the alimentary canal. What a man can do in twenty-four hours will depend very much on what he can have to eat in those twenty-four hours; or, perhaps, it would be more correct to say, what he has had to eat the twenty-four hours previous. If his diet be liberal, his work may be mighty. If he be underfed, he must underwork.'

These facts, always important, have now acquired an urgency that it is not easy to exaggerate in consequence of the stress and keenness of international competition; and, at a time when increasing thought is being given to the conditions of commercial success, it is not inappropriate to direct attention to a most serious and depressing fact in the present social situation. If adequate nourishment be necessary to efficiency, the highest commercial success will be impossible so long as large numbers even of the most sober and industrious of the labouring classes receive but three-fourths of the necessary amount of food.

•

JACK LONDON
1903

'The People of the Abyss'

Jack London, pseudonym of John Griffith Chaney (1876–1916), had already published The God of His Fathers *and* The Son of the Wolf *about life in the Klondike when he arrived in London in 1902 at the age of twenty-six. He went straight to an old-clothes shop, rigged himself out in a second-hand suit and went to live in the East End around the notorious London docks. He encountered what he described as a 'chronic condition of misery'. The workhouses were full and were forced to turn away starving crowds.*

The result was The People of the Abyss *and what follows is its final chapter. 'For the English, so far as manhood and womanhood and health and happiness go, I see a broad and smiling future,' London wrote in his preface. 'But for a great deal of the political machinery, which at present mismanages for them, I see nothing else than the scrapheap.'*

Has Civilization bettered the lot of man? 'Man' I use in its democratic sense, meaning the average man. So the question re-shapes itself: *Has Civilization bettered the lot of the average man?*

Let us see. In Alaska, along the banks of the Yukon River, near its mouth, live the Innuit folk. They are a very primitive people, manifesting but mere glimmering adumbrations of that tremendous artifice, Civilization. Their capital amounts possibly to £2 per head. They hunt and fish for their food with bone-headed spears and arrows. They never suffer from lack of shelter. Their clothes, largely made from the skins of animals, are warm. They always have fuel for their fires, likewise timber for their houses, which they build partly underground, and in which they lie snugly during the periods of intense cold. In the summer they live in tents, open to every breeze, and cool. They are healthy, and strong, and happy. Their one problem is food. They have their times of plenty and times of famine. In good times they feast; in bad times they die of starvation. But starvation, as a chronic condition, present with a large number of them all the time, is a thing unknown. Further, they have no debts.

In the United Kingdom, on the rim of the Western Ocean, live the English folk. They are a consummately civilized people. Their capital amounts to at least £300 per head. They gain their food, not by hunting and fishing, but by toil at colossal artifices. For the most part, they suffer from lack of shelter. The greater number of them are vilely housed, do not have enough fuel to keep them warm, and are insufficiently clothed. A constant number never have any houses at all, and sleep shelterless under the stars. Many are to be found, winter and summer, shivering on the streets in their rags. They have good times and bad. In good times most of them manage to get enough to eat, in bad times they die of starvation. They are dying now, they were dying yesterday and last year, they will die tomorrow and next year, of starvation; for they, unlike the Innuit, suffer from a chronic condition of starvation. There are 40,000,000 of the English folk, and 939 out of every 1,000 of them die in poverty, while a constant army of 8,000,000 struggles on the ragged edge of starvation. Further, each babe that is born, is born in debt to the sum of £22. This is because of an artifice called the National Debt.

In a fair comparison of the average Innuit and the average Englishman, it will be seen that life is less rigorous for the Innuit; that while the Innuit suffers only during bad times from starvation, the Englishman suffers during good times as well; that no Innuit lacks fuel, clothing or housing, while the Englishman is in perpetual lack of these three essentials . . .

The creature comforts man enjoys are the products of man's labour. Since Civilization has failed to give the average Englishman food and shelter equal to that enjoyed by the Innuit, the question arises: *Has Civilization increased the producing power of the average man?* If it has not increased man's producing power, then Civilization cannot stand.

But, it will be instantly admitted, Civilization *has* increased man's producing power. Five men can produce bread for 1,000. One man can produce cotton cloth for 250 people, woollens for 300, and boots and shoes for 1,000. Yet it has been shown that English folk by the millions do not receive enough food, clothes and boots. Then arises the third and inexorable question: *If Civilization has increased the producing power of the average man, why has it not bettered the lot of the average man?*

There can be one answer only – MISMANAGEMENT. Civilization has made possible all manner of creature comforts and heart's delights. In these the average Englishman does not participate. If he shall be for ever unable to participate, then Civilization falls. There is no reason for the continued existence of an artifice so avowed a failure. But it is impossible that men should have reared this tremendous artifice in vain. It stuns the intellect. To acknowledge so crushing a defeat is to give the death-blow to striving and progress.

One other alternative, and one other only, presents itself. *Civilization must be compelled to better the lot of the average man.* This accepted, it becomes at once a question of business management. Things profitable must be continued; things unprofitable must be eliminated. Either the Empire is a profit to England, or it is a loss. If it is a loss, it must be done away with. If it is a profit, it must be managed so that the average man comes in for a share of the profit.

If the struggle for commercial supremacy is profitable, continue it. If it is not, if it hurts the worker and makes his lot worse than the lot of a savage, then fling foreign markets and industrial empire overboard. For it is a patent fact that if 40,000,000 people, aided by Civilization, possess a greater individual producing power than the Innuit, then those 40,000,000 people should enjoy more creature comforts and heart's delights than the Innuits enjoy.

If the 400,000 English gentlemen, 'of no occupation', according to their own statement in the census of 1881, are unprofitable, do away with them. Set them to work ploughing game preserves and planting potatoes. If they are profitable, continue them by all means, but let it be seen to that the average Englishman shares somewhat in the profits they produce by working at no occupation.

In short, society must be reorganized, and a capable management put at the head. That the present management is incapable, there can be no discussion. It has drained the United Kingdom of its life-blood. It has enfeebled the stay-at-home folk till they are unable longer to struggle in the van of the competing nations. It has built up a West End and an East End as large as the kingdom is large, in which one end is riotous and rotten, the other end sickly and underfed.

A vast empire is foundering on the hands of this incapable management. And by empire is meant the political machinery which holds together the English-speaking people of the world outside the United States. Nor is this charged in a pessimistic spirit. Blood empire is greater than political empire, and the English of the New World and the Antipodes are strong and vigorous as ever. But the political empire under which they are nominally assembled is perishing. The political machine known as the British Empire is running down. In the hands of its management it is losing momentum every day.

It is inevitable that this management, which has grossly and criminally mismanaged, shall be swept away. Not only has it been wasteful and inefficient, but it has misappropriated the funds. Every worn-out, pasty-faced pauper, every blind man, every prison babe, every man, woman and child whose belly is gnawing with hunger pangs, is hungry because the funds have been misappropriated by the management.

Nor can one member of this managing class plead not guilty before the judgement bar of Man. 'The living in their houses, and in their graves the dead,' are challenged by every babe that dies of innutrition, by every girl that flees the sweater's den to the nightly promenade of Piccadilly, by every worked-out toiler that plunges into the canal. The food this managing class eats, the wine it drinks, the shows it makes, and the fine clothes it wears, are challenged by 8 million mouths which have never had enough to fill them, and by twice 8 million bodies which have never been sufficiently clothed and housed.

There can be no mistake. Civilization has increased man's producing power a hundredfold, and through mismanagement the men of Civilization live worse than the beasts, and have less to eat and wear and protect them from the elements than the savage Innuit in a frigid climate who lives today as he lived in the stone age 10,000 years ago.

•

WILLIAM DU BOIS
1903

'Black folk'

Booker T. Washington had been the acknowledged leader of America's blacks since his Atlanta Exposition address in 1885. He believed in accommodation with the whites and was willing to agree to segregation. William Du Bois (1868–1963), whose doctoral thesis at Harvard was on the suppression of the African slave trade, became the leader of the opposition to Washington. 'The problem of the twentieth century,' Du Bois wrote prophetically in The Souls of Black Folk, *'is the problem of the color-line, the relation of the darker to the lighter races of men in Asia and Africa, in America and the islands of the sea.' His book demolished Washington's policy of 'submission' to the whites.*

It has been claimed that the Negro can survive only through submission. Mr Washington distinctly asks that black people give up, at least for the present, three things:

    first, political power;

    second, insistence on civil rights;

    third, higher education of Negro youth;

and concentrate all their energies on industrial education, the accumulation of wealth, and the conciliation of the South. This policy has been courageously and insistently advocated for over fifteen years, and has been triumphant for perhaps ten years. As a result of this tender of the palm-branch, what has been the return? In these years there have occurred:

1. The disfranchisement of the Negro.

2. The legal creation of a distinct status of civil inferiority for the Negro.

3. The steady withdrawal of aid from institutions for the higher training of the Negro.

These movements are not, to be sure, direct results of Mr Washington's teachings; but his propaganda has, without a shadow of doubt, helped their speedier accomplishment. The question then comes: Is it possible, and probable, that 9 millions of men can make effective progress in economic lines if they are deprived of political rights, made a servile caste, and allowed only the most meager chance for developing their exceptional men? If history and reason give any distinct answer to these questions, it is an emphatic *No.* And Mr Washington thus faces the triple paradox of his career:

1. He is striving nobly to make Negro artisans business men and property-owners; but it is utterly impossible, under modern competitive methods, for working-men and property-owners to defend their rights and exist without the right of suffrage.

2. He insists on thrift and self-respect, but at the same time counsels a silent submission to civic inferiority such as is bound to sap the manhood of any race in the long run.

3. He advocates common-school and industrial training, and deprecates institutions of higher learning; but neither the Negro common-schools, nor Tuskegee itself, could remain open a day were it not for teachers trained in Negro colleges, or trained by their graduates.

This triple paradox in Mr Washington's position is the object of criticism by two classes of colored Americans. One class is spiritually descended from Toussaint the Savior, and they represent the attitude of revolt and revenge; they hate the white South blindly and distrust the white race generally, and so far as they agree on definite action, think that the Negro's only hope lies in emigration beyond the borders of the United States. And yet, by the irony of fate, nothing has more effectually made this program seem hopeless than the recent course of the United States toward weaker and darker peoples in the West Indies, Hawaii, and the Philippines – for where in the world may we go and be safe from lying and brute force?

The other class of Negroes who cannot agree with Mr Washington have hitherto said little aloud. They deprecate the sight of scattered counsels, of internal disagreement; and especially they dislike making their just criticism of a useful and earnest man an excuse for a general discharge of venom from small-minded opponents. Such men feel in conscience bound to ask of this nation three things:

1. The right to vote.
2. Civic equality.
3. The education of youth according to ability.

They acknowledge Mr Washington's invaluable service in counseling patience and courtesy in such demands; they do not ask that ignorant black men vote when ignorant whites are debarred, or that any reasonable restrictions in the suffrage should not be applied; they know that the low social level of the mass of the race is responsible for much discrimination against it, but they also know, and the nation knows, that relentless color-prejudice is more often a cause than a result of the Negro's degradation; they seek the abatement of this relic of barbarism, and not its systematic encouragement and pampering by all agencies of social power from the Associated Press to the Church of Christ.

This group of men honor Mr Washington for his attitude of conciliation toward the white South; they accept the 'Atlanta Compromise' in its broadest interpretation; they recognize, with him, many signs of promise, many men of high purpose and fair judgment, in this section; they know that no easy task has been laid upon a region already tottering under heavy burdens. But, nevertheless, they insist that the way to truth and right lies in straightforward honesty, not in indiscriminate flattery; in praising those of the South who do well and criticizing uncompromisingly those who do ill; in taking advantage of the opportunities at hand and urging their fellows to do the same, but at the same time in remembering that only a firm adherence to their higher ideals and aspirations will ever keep those ideals within the realm of possibility. They do not expect that the free right to vote, to enjoy civic rights, and to be educated, will come in a moment; they do not expect to see the bias and prejudices of years disappear at the blast of a trumpet; but they are absolutely certain that the way for a people to gain their reasonable rights is not by voluntarily throwing them away and insisting that they do not want them; that the way for a people to gain respect is not by continually belittling and ridiculing themselves; that, on the contrary, Negroes must insist continually, in season and out of season, that voting is necessary to modern manhood, that color discrimination is barbarism, and that black boys need education as well as white boys.

In failing thus to state plainly and unequivocally the legitimate demands of their people, even at the cost of opposing an honored leader, the thinking classes of American Negroes would shirk a heavy responsibility – a responsibility to themselves, a responsibility to the struggling masses, a responsibility to the darker races of men whose future depends so largely on this American experiment, but especially a responsibility to this nation – this common

Fatherland. It is wrong to encourage a man or a people in evil-doing; it is wrong to aid and abet a national crime simply because it is unpopular not to do so. The growing spirit of kindliness and reconciliation between the North and South after the frightful differences of a generation ago ought to be a source of deep congratulation to all, and especially to those whose mistreatment caused the war; but if that reconciliation is to be marked by the industrial slavery and civic death of those same black men, with permanent legislation into a position of inferiority, then those black men, if they are really men, are called upon by every consideration of patriotism and loyalty to oppose such a course by all civilized methods, even though such opposition involves disagreement with Mr Booker T. Washington. We have no right to sit silently by while the inevitable seeds are sown for a harvest of disaster to our children, black and white.

•

J. A. HOBSON
1903

'Imperialism'

'Ideas live longer than men, and the writer who can attach his name to an idea is safe for immortality,' the historian A. J. P. Taylor wrote fifty years after the first publication of Imperialism *by J. A. Hobson (1858–1940). 'No survey of the international history of the twentieth century can be complete without the name of J. A. Hobson. He it was who found an economic motive for imperialism. Lenin took over Hobson's explanation, which thus became the basis for Communist foreign policy . . .' Hobson showed, Taylor added, that the capitalist, however pacific, must seek foreign investment and therefore be driven into imperialist rivalry with the capitalists of other states.*

The spirit of imperialism poisons the springs of democracy in the mind and character of the people. As our free self-governing colonies have furnished hope, encouragement and leadership to the popular aspirations in Great Britain, not merely by practical successes in the arts of popular government, but by the wafting of a spirit of freedom and equality, so our despotically ruled dependencies have ever served to damage the character of our people by feeding the habits of snobbish subservience, the admiration of wealth and rank, the corrupt survivals of the inequalities of feudalism. This process began with the advent of the East Indian nabob and the West Indian planter into English society and politics, bringing back with his plunders of the slave trade and the gains of corrupt and extortionate officialism the acts of vulgar ostentation, domineering demeanour and corrupting largesse to dazzle and degrade the life of our people. Cobden, writing in 1860 of our Indian Empire, put this pithy question: 'Is it not just possible that we may become corrupted at home by the reaction of arbitrary political maxims in the East upon our domestic politics, just as Greece and Rome were demoralized by their contact with Asia?'

The rise of a money-loaning aristocracy in Rome, composed of keen, unscrupulous men from many nations, who filled the high offices of state with their creatures, political 'bosses' or military adventurers, who had come to the front as usurers, publicans or chiefs of police in the provinces, was the most distinctive feature of later imperial Rome. This class was continually recruited from returned officials and colonial millionaires. The large incomes drawn in private official plunder, public tribute, usury and official incomes from the provinces had the following reactions upon Italy. Italians were no longer wanted for working the land or for manufactures, or even for military service. 'The later campaigns on the Rhine and the Danube,' it is pointed out, 'were really slave-hunts on a gigantic scale.'

The Italian farmers, at first drawn from rural into military life, soon found themselves permanently ousted from agriculture by the serf labour of the *latifundia*, and they and their families were sucked into the dregs of town life, to be subsisted as a pauper population upon public charity. A mercenary colonial army came more and more to displace the home forces. The parasitic city life, with its lowered vitality and the growing infrequency of marriage, to which Gibbon draws attention, rapidly impaired the physique of the native population of Italy, and Rome subsisted more and more upon immigration of raw vigour from Gaul and Germany. The necessity of maintaining powerful mercenary armies to hold the provinces heightened continually the peril, already manifest in the last years of the Republic, arising from the political ambitions of great pro-consuls conspiring with a moneyed interest at Rome against the Commonwealth. As time went on, this moneyed oligarchy became an hereditary aristocracy, and withdrew from military and civil service, relying more and more upon hired foreigners: themselves sapped by luxury and idleness and tainting by mixed servitude and licence the Roman populace, they so enfeebled the state as to destroy the physical and moral vitality required to hold in check and under government the vast repository of forces in the exploited Empire. The direct cause of Rome's decay and fall is expressed politically by the term 'over-centralization', which conveys in brief the real essence of imperialism as distinguished from national growth on the one hand and colonialism upon the other. Parasitism practised through taxation and usury, involved a constantly increasing centralization of the instruments of government, and a growing strain upon this government as the prey became more impoverished by the drain and showed signs of restiveness. 'The evolution of this centralized society was as logical as every other work of nature. When force reached the stage where it expressed itself exclusively through money the governing class ceased to be chosen because they were valiant or eloquent, artistic, learned or devout, and were selected solely because they had the faculty of acquiring and keeping wealth. As long as the weak retained enough vitality to produce something which could be absorbed, this oligarchy was invariable; and, for very many years after the native peasantry of Gaul and Italy had perished from the land, new blood, injected from more tenacious races, kept the dying civilization alive. The weakness of the moneyed class lay in this very power, for they not only killed the producer, but in the strength of their acquisitiveness they failed to propagate themselves.'

This is the largest, plainest instance history presents of the social parasitic process by which a moneyed interest within the state, usurping the reins of government, makes for imperial expansion in order to fasten economic suckers into foreign bodies so as to drain them of their wealth in order to support domestic luxury. The new imperialism differs in no vital point from this old example. The element of political tribute is now absent, or quite subsidiary, and the crudest forms of slavery have disappeared: some elements of more genuine and disinterested government serve to qualify and mask the distinctively parasitic nature of the later sort. But nature is not mocked: the laws which, operative throughout nature, doom the parasite to atrophy, decay, and final extinction, are not evaded by nations any more than by individual organisms. The greater complexity of the modern process, the endeavour to escape the parasitic reaction by rendering some real but quite unequal and inadequate services to 'the host', may retard but cannot finally avert the natural consequences of living upon others. The claim that an imperial state forcibly subjugating other peoples and their lands does so for the purpose of rendering services to the conquered equal to those which she exacts is notoriously false: she neither intends equivalent services nor is capable of rendering them, and the pretence that such benefits to the governed form a leading motive or result of imperialism implies a degree of moral or intellectual obliquity so grave as itself to form a new peril for any nation fostering so false a notion of the nature of its conduct. 'Let the motive be in the deed, not in the event,' says a Persian proverb. . .

Imperialism is a depraved choice of national life, imposed by self-seeking interests which appeal to the lusts of quantitative acquisitiveness and of forceful domination surviving in a nation from early centuries of animal struggle for existence. Its adoption as a policy implies a deliberate renunciation of that cultivation of the higher inner qualities which for a nation as for an individual constitutes the ascendency of reason over brute impulse. It is the besetting sin of all successful states, and its penalty is unalterable in the order of nature.

•

GEORGE BERNARD SHAW
1905

'Women at the opera'

George Bernard Shaw (1856–1950) was dramatist, essayist, critic, pamphleteer – and also a writer of letters to the editor of The Times, *as on this occasion after an irritating night at the opera.*

Sir,

The opera management at Covent Garden regulates the dress of its male patrons. When is it going to do the same to the women?

On Saturday night I went to the opera. I wore the costume imposed on me by the regulations of the house. I fully recognize the advantage of those regulations. Evening dress is cheap, simple, durable, prevents rivalry and extravagance on the part of male leaders of fashion, annihilates class distinctions, and gives men who are poor and doubtful of their social position (that is, the great majority of men) a sense of security and satisfaction that no clothes of their own choosing could confer, besides saving a whole sex the trouble of considering what they should wear on state occasions. The objections to it are as dust in the balance in the eyes of the ordinary Briton. These objections are that it is colourless and characterless; that it involves a whitening process which makes the shirt troublesome, slightly uncomfortable and seriously unclean; that it acts as a passport for undesirable persons; that it fails to guarantee sobriety, cleanliness and order on the part of the wearer; and that it reduces to a formula a very vital human habit which should be the subject of constant experiment and active private enterprise. All such objections are thoroughly un-English. They appeal only to an eccentric few, and may be left out of account with the fantastic objections of men like Ruskin, Tennyson, Carlyle and Morris to tall hats.

But I submit that what is sauce for the gander is sauce for the goose.

Every argument that applies to the regulation of the man's dress applies equally to the regulation of the woman's. Now let me describe what actually happened to me at the opera. Not only was I in evening dress by compulsion, but I voluntarily added many graces of conduct as to which the management made no stipulation whatever. I was in my seat in time for the first chord of the overture. I did not chatter during the music nor raise my voice when the opera was too loud for normal conversation. I did not get up and go out when the statue music began. My language was fairly moderate considering the number and nature of the improvements on Mozart volunteered by Signor Caruso, and the respectful ignorance of the dramatic points of the score exhibited by the conductor and the stage manager – if there is such a functionary at Covent Garden. In short, my behaviour was exemplary.

At nine o'clock (the opera began at eight) a lady came in and sat down very conspicuously in my line of sight. She remained there until the beginning of the last act. I do not complain of her coming late and going early; on the contrary, I wish she had come later and gone earlier. For this lady, who had very black hair, had stuck over her right ear the pitiable corpse of a large white bird, which looked exactly as if someone had killed it by stamping on its breast, and then nailed it to the lady's temple, which was presumably of sufficient solidity to bear the operation. I am not, I hope, a morbidly squeamish person; but the spectacle sickened me. I presume that if I had presented myself at the doors with a dead snake round my neck, a collection of black beetles pinned to my shirtfront, and a grouse in my hair, I should have been refused admission. Why, then, is a woman to be allowed to commit such a public outrage? Had the lady been refused admission, as she should have been, she would have soundly berated the tradesman who imposed the disgusting head-dress on her under the false pretence that 'the best people' wear such things, and withdrawn her custom from him; and thus the root of the evil would be struck at; for your fashionable woman generally allows herself to be dressed according to the taste of a person whom she would not let sit down in her presence. I once, in Drury Lane Theatre, sat behind a *matinée* hat decorated with the two wings of a seagull, artificially reddened at the joints so as to produce an illusion of being freshly plucked from a live bird. But even that lady stopped short of the whole seagull. Both ladies were evidently regarded by their neighbours as ridiculous and vulgar; but that is hardly enough when the offence is one which produces a sensation of physical sickness in persons of normal humane sensibility.

I suggest to the Covent Garden authorities that, if they feel bound
to protect their subscribers against the danger of my shocking them
with a blue tie, they are at least equally bound to protect me against the
danger of a woman shocking me with a dead bird.

Yours truly,
G. Bernard Shaw

•

ROBERT BLATCHFORD
1908

'The shadow of fear'

Merrie England, *published by Robert Blatchford (1851–1943) in 1894, sold 2 million
copies and was reprinted well into the twentieth century. 'My work,' Blatchford declared,
'is to teach socialism, to get recruits for the Socialist army . . . I am a recruiting sergeant.'
He was described as 'the People's Plato' and compared with Isaiah, Amos and Micah:
for every British convert made by Marx's* Das Kapital, *declared the* Manchester
Guardian, *there were 100 made by* Merrie England.

Blatchford founded the campaigning newspaper, The Clarion, *which published some
of its articles as Pass On Pamphlets, that sold for a penny. This extract is from* The
New Religion.

While women are weeping and children starving; while industrious men and
women are herding like beasts in filthy and fever-haunted hovels, to build
art galleries and churches, town halls and colleges, is like putting on a muslin
shirt over a filthy skin, a diamond crown upon a leprous head.

The religion and the culture which demand riches and blazonry while vice
and misery are at their side are like painted harlots, hiding their debaucheries
with rouge and their shame with satin and spices.

The cant and affectation of piety and culture which lisp sentiment and
chant hymns in drawing rooms and chapels while flesh and blood are perishing
in the streets, and while the souls of our sisters creep shuddering to hell –
this religion and this culture, these maudlin, sickening things, with their poems
and sonatas, their chants and benedictions, are things false and vain and
nothing else but *lies.*

There can be no true culture, there can be no true art, there can be no
true progress, there can be no true religion without sincerity. I have seen in
Manchester a noble picture of Greek women at the fountain, hung up to

instil into the minds of the citizens of that sordid, sooty, vulgar and hideous town a love of beauty, and outside the art gallery I have seen a grey-headed old Englishwoman staggering along, bent double under a sack of cinders . . .

A gulf parts the masses from the classes. This gulf is the gulf of ignorance, and only knowledge can bridge it. It is astounding, the utter ignorance of the lives of the poor, the complete misapprehension of their conditions, their trials, their hopes and their ideals, which the rich manifest in their words and deeds . . .

Even if we accept wages as the one thing needful; even if we go as far as the man in *Our Mutual Friend*, and consider the labour question simply as 'a question of so many pounds of beef and so many pints of porter', can we say that the masses have as much beef and porter as they need?

What of the wages of the tailors, the shirt-makers, the match-makers, the dockers, the sailors, the railway men, the farm labourers, the lead-workers, the slipper-makers, the shop assistants, the domestic servants, the canal-boat workers, the chain and nail makers, the old soldiers, the match hawkers, the feather dressers, the silk dyers, the artificial-flower makers, the fishermen, the costers, the news boys? What of *all* the workers' *wives*?

But wages are not all. We have to ask how hard and how long these people work; we have to ask what their homes are like, what health they enjoy, how much rest and culture, and fresh air, and wholesome recreation they obtain.

And we find that their homes are dismal and mean, that their labour is long and hard, that they have scarcely any fresh air, or sweet rest, or pure amusements . . .

Consider again the dangers, the hardships and the sickness incidental to the work of the sailors, the fishermen, the colliers, the chemical workers, the match-makers. Go among the cotton operatives and *see* how factory work in factory towns deteriorates the people mentally and physically.

It is not of the submerged tenth we are thinking only. It is of the English people. Over all is the shadow of fear – the fear of failure and the workhouse. But I could not in a volume so much as enumerate all the evils of our present English civilization. There is a whole library of Blue-books filled with the statistics and the evidence of the hardships and labours and sufferings of those who create the wealth of this rich miserable country. Not the least of the wrongs of the poor is one of which Blue-books take no cognizance, the denial to the best brain and bone and sinew of the nation of the respect due to all men by virtue of their manhood. Our workers are honoured and loved too little; they are governed and patronized and lectured overmuch.

What, then, do we demand? We demand that national co-operation shall displace individual competition; we demand to this end the nationalization of the land and all the instruments of production and of distribution. We demand that our industry be organized, and that production be for use and not for sale.

We demand that our agricultural resources be developed because agriculture is more pleasant and more healthy than manufactures, because in an agricultural nation the towns would be cleaner and handsomer and more wholesome, and because the destruction of our agriculture renders us dependent upon foreign countries for our food, and so exposes us to certain defeat and ruin in case of war.

At present the people of the manufacturing towns have not only ceased to possess their own country: they have ceased to know it. They never see England. They see only brick walls, chimneys, smoke and cinder heaps. They are unable to so much as conceive the fairness and sweetness of England. They are strangers and aliens in their own land.

We say, then, give the British people their own country. But we do not stop there. We demand that they shall not only be made the free possessors of their own country, but also of their own earnings, of their own lives, of their own bodies and their own souls.

We regard work as a means and not as an end: men should work to live; they should not live to work. We demand for the people as much leisure, as full and sweet and noble a life, as the world can give. We want labour to have its own; not merely the price of its sweat, but its due meed of love and honour. In our eyes the lifeboat-man is a hero, and the African machine-gun soldier 'opening up new markets' is a brigand and assassin. In our eyes the skilled craftsman or farmer is a man of learning, and the Greek-crammed pedant is a dunce. In our eyes an apple orchard is more beautiful and precious than a ducal palace. In our eyes the worth of a nation depends on the worthiness of its people's lives, and not upon the balance at the national bank. We want a religion of justice and charity and love. We do not want pious cant on Sundays and chicanery and lust all the rest of the week. We want a God who is fit for business, and a business that is worthy of God. We want the code of private honour and the bonds of domestic love carried into all our public affairs. We want a realization, in fact, of the brotherhood we hear so much about in theory. Because we know the meaning of heredity and environment, because we believe that men are what their surroundings make them, we want justice for all, love for all, mercy for all.

We are the party of humanity. Our religion is the religion of humanity. 'The black with his woolly head, the felon, the diseased, the illiterate are not denied.' The thief on the cross, the Magdalen at the well, are our brother and our sister; bone of our bone, flesh of our flesh. If you persecute these, if you insult them, if you rob them, you rob and persecute and insult us. Without the love, and the counsel, and the aid of our fellow-creatures, the best of us were savages – little more than brutes. What we are they made us; what we know they taught us; what we have they gave us: we are theirs, and they are ours, and for them we speak and write, with all the power God gave us . . .

•

NATIONAL ASSOCIATION FOR THE ADVANCEMENT OF COLORED PEOPLE
1909

'Civil liberty'

Scores of Negroes were killed or wounded and thousands driven from Springfield, Illinois in the summer of 1908 when a mob raged through Abraham Lincoln's home town for two days.

Six months later Mary White Ovington, who wanted to revive the spirit of the abolitionists, met Southern journalist William English Walling, who had asked in the Independent *whether any powerful body of citizens was ready to aid the Negroes.*

The NAACP was born at that meeting. Working with Dr Henry Kowitz, they decided to open their campaign on Lincoln's birthday – 12 February. They turned to Oswald Garrison Villard, president of the New York Evening Post, *who drafted and publicized their call for supporters. Ovington, Villard and William Du Bois were among the major signatories when the Association was incorporated in 1911.*

The celebration of the Centennial of the birth of Abraham Lincoln, widespread and grateful as it may be, will fail to justify itself if it takes no note of and makes no recognition of the colored men and women for whom the great Emancipator labored to assure freedom. Besides a day of rejoicing, Lincoln's birthday in 1909 should be one of taking stock of the nation's progress since 1865.

How far has it lived up to the obligations imposed upon it by the Emancipation Proclamation? How far has it gone in assuring to each and every citizen, irrespective of color, the equality of opportunity and equality before the law, which underlie our American institutions and are guaranteed by the Constitution?

If Mr Lincoln could revisit this country in the flesh, he would be disheartened and discouraged. He would learn that on January 1, 1909, Georgia had rounded out a new confederacy by disfranchising the Negro, after the manner of all the other Southern states. He would learn that the Supreme Court of the United States, supposedly a bulwark of American liberties, had refused every opportunity to pass squarely upon this disfranchisement of millions, by laws avowedly discriminatory and openly enforced in such manner that the white men may vote and that black men be without a vote in their government; he would discover, therefore, that taxation without representation is the lot of millions of wealth-producing American citizens, in whose hands rests the economic progress and welfare of an entire section of the country.

He would learn that the Supreme Court, according to the official statement of one of its own judges in the Berea College case, has laid down the principle that if an individual state chooses, it may 'make it a crime for white and colored persons to frequent the same market place at the same time, or appear in an assemblage of citizens convened to consider questions of a public or political nature in which all citizens, without regard to race, are equally interested.'

In many states Lincoln would find justice enforced, if at all, by judges elected by one element in a community to pass upon the liberties and lives of another. He would see the black men and women, for whose freedom 100,000 soldiers gave their lives, set apart in trains, in which they pay first-class fares for third-class service, and segregated in railway stations and in places of entertainment; he would observe that state after state declines to do its elementary duty in preparing the Negro through education for the best exercise of citizenship.

Added to this, the spread of lawless attacks upon the Negro, North, South and West – even in the Springfield made famous by Lincoln – often accompanied by revolting brutalities, sparing neither sex nor age nor youth, could but shock the author of the sentiment that 'government of the people, by the people, for the people; should not perish from the earth.'

Silence under these conditions means tacit approval. The indifference of the North is already responsible for more than one assault upon democracy, and every such attack reacts as unfavorably upon whites as upon blacks. Discrimination once permitted cannot be bridled; recent history in the South shows that in forging chains for the Negroes the white voters are forging chains for themselves. 'A house divided against itself cannot stand'; this government cannot exist half-slave and half-free any better today than it could in 1861.

Hence we call upon all the believers in democracy to join in a national conference for the discussion of present evils, the voicing of protests, and the renewal of the struggle for civil and political liberty.

•

SYLVIA PANKHURST
1909

'Force-feeding'

The Women's Social and Political Union was founded by Emmeline Pankhurst in 1903 to seek votes for women. The Daily Mail *described its members as suffragettes. When the Union was ignored by politicians and the press, it decided to become more militant and started interrupting major political meetings and breaking shop windows. Suffragettes refused to pay fines and were sent to prison where they staged hunger strikes.*

In her book The Suffragettes, *Sylvia Pankhurst (1882–1960) described how four protesting members of the WSPU were treated.*

Mrs Leigh explained that on arriving at Winson Green gaol on Wednesday, 22 September, she had broken her cell windows as a protest against the prison treatment. As a punishment she was thrust that evening into a cold dimly lit punishment cell. A plank bed was brought in and she was forcibly stripped and handcuffed with the hands behind during the day, except at meal times when the palms were placed together in front. At night the hands were fastened in front with the palms out. Potatoes, bread and gruel were brought into her cell on Thursday but she did not touch them and in the afternoon she was taken, still handcuffed, before the magistrates who sentenced her to a further nine days in the punishment cell. At midnight on Thursday, her wrists being terribly swollen and painful, the handcuffs were removed.

She still refused food and on Saturday she was taken to the doctor's room. Here is her account of the affair:

> The doctor said: 'You must listen carefully to what I have to say. I have my orders from my superior officers' (he had a blue official paper in his hand to which he referred) 'that you are not to be released even on medical grounds. If you still refrain from food I must take other measures to compel you to take it.' I then said: 'I refuse, and if you force food on me, I want to know how you are going to do it.' He said: 'That is a matter for me to decide.' I said that he must prove that I was insane; that the Lunacy Commissioners would have to be summoned to prove that I was insane. I declared that forcible feeding was an operation, and therefore could not be performed without a sane patient's consent. He merely bowed and said: 'Those are my orders.'

She was then surrounded and held down, while the chair was tilted backwards. She clenched her teeth but the doctor pulled her mouth away to form a pouch and the wardress poured in milk and brandy, some of which trickled in through the crevices. Later in the day the doctors and wardresses again appeared. They forced her down on to the bed, and held her there. One of the doctors then produced a tube two yards in length with a glass junction in the centre and a funnel at one end. He forced the other end of the tube up her nostril, hurting her so terribly that the matron and two of the wardresses burst into tears and the second doctor interfered. At last the tube was pushed down into the stomach. She felt the pain of it to the end of the breastbone. Then one of the doctors stood upon a chair holding the funnel end of the tube at arm's length and poured food down while the wardresses and the other doctor all gripped her tight. She felt as though she would suffocate. There was a rushing, burning sensation in her head, the drums of her ears seemed to be bursting. The agony of pain in the throat and breastbone continued. The thing seemed to go on for hours. When at last the tube was withdrawn, she felt as though all the back of her nose and throat were being torn out with it.

Then almost fainting she was carried back to the punishment cell and put to bed. For hours the pain in the chest, nose and ears continued and she felt terribly sick and faint. Day after day the struggle continued; she used no violence but each time resisted and was overcome by force of numbers. Often she vomited during the operation. When the food did not go down quickly enough the doctor pinched her nose with the tube in it causing her even greater pain.

On Tuesday afternoon she heard Miss Edwards, one of her fellow prisoners, cry from an open doorway opposite, 'Locked in a padded cell since Sunday.' Then the door was shut. She applied to see the visiting magistrates, and appealed to them on behalf of her comrade, saying that she knew her to have a weak heart, but was told that no prisoner could interfere on another's behalf. She protested by breaking the windows of the hospital cell to which, owing to her weakness, she had now been taken, and was then thrust into the padded cell as Miss Edwards was taken from it, the bed which she had occupied being still warm. The padded cell was lined with some India rubber-like stuff, and she felt as though she would suffocate for want of air. She was kept there till Wednesday, still being fed by force.

On Saturday she felt that she could endure the agony of it no longer, and determined to barricade her cell. She piled up her bed and chair, but after three hours men warders forced the door open with spades. Then the chief warder threatened and abused her and she was dragged back to the padded cell.

In Miss Ainsworth's case the feeding was done through the mouth. Her jaws were prised open with a steel instrument to allow the gag to be placed between her teeth. She experienced great sickness, especially when the tube was being withdrawn.

Miss Hilda Burkitt's experiences were very dreadful. She had already fasted four days and was extremely weak when she was seized by two doctors, four wardresses and the matron, who tried for more than half an hour to force her to swallow from the feeding cup. Then a tube was forced up her nose, but she succeeded in coughing it back twice and at last, very near collapse, she was carried to her cell and put to bed by the wardresses. 'This will kill me sooner than starving,' she said. 'I cannot stand much more of it, but I am proud you have not beaten me yet.' Still suffering greatly in head, nose and throat, she was left alone for half an hour and the matron and wardresses then returned to persuade her to take food. On her refusal they said, 'Well, you will have to come again; they are waiting.' 'Oh, surely not the torture chamber again,' she cried; but they lifted her out of bed and carried her back to the doctors, who again attempted to force her to drink from the feeding cup. Still she was able to resist and then one of them said, 'The Home Office has given me every power to use what force I like. I am going to use the stomach pump.' 'It is illegal and an assault; I shall prosecute you,' was her reply, but as she spoke a gag was forced into her mouth and the tube followed. She had almost fainted and felt as if she were going to die, and now for some reason the tube was withdrawn without having been used, but in her great weakness the officials were now able to overcome her resistance and to pour liquid into her mouth with the feeding cup.

This sort of thing went on day after day. On Thursday morning she was unconscious when they came into her cell, and they succeeded in feeding her. During the night she was in agony. She told the doctor he had given her too much food and cried: 'For mercy's sake, let me be, I am too tired,' but brandy and Benger's food were forcibly administered. During the whole month she only slept four nights.

•

BEATRICE WEBB
1909

'*The workhouse*'

Beatrice (1858–1943) and Sidney Webb (1859–1947) were married in 1892 and formed a partnership which helped to create the British welfare state.

In 1894 they founded the London School of Economics. Beatrice, who came from a wealthy background, had a strong social conscience and worked with Charles Booth on his studies of poverty in London. She was a member of the Royal Commission on the Poor Laws. When it published its conclusions, she signed a dissenting minority report. This section describes the general mixed workhouse.

We have to report that there exists in all parts of the kingdom, among all classes, the greatest dislike and distrust of this typical Poor Law institution. The respectable poor, we are told, 'have a horror of it', and they will not go 'into the house at all unless they are compelled'. The whole institution, reports our medical investigator, 'is abhorred . . . The Workhouse and everything within its walls is anathema excepting to the very dregs of the population.' It is, said one of our witnesses, 'the supreme dread of the poor'. 'Life in the Workhouse,' sum up our investigators, 'does not build character up. It breaks down what little independence or alertness of mind is left . . . It is too good for the bad and too bad for the good.'

This 'evil reputation' of the General Mixed Workhouse among the respectable poor is, reports our medical investigator, 'partly traditional or historical, and partly due to the curious and objectionable agglomeration of purposes which it now serves. It is a home for imbeciles, an almshouse for the destitute poor, a refuge for deserted children, a lying-in hospital for dissolute women, a winter resort for the ill-behaved casual labourer or summer beggar, a lodging for tramps and vagrants as well as a hospital for the sick.'

'Being gathered into one establishment,' says the vice-chairman of the Manchester Board of Guardians, 'all must be subject to the same regulations – framed to be deterrent to the lazily disposed, and to prevent preference of the workhouse to labour. The day-rooms and dormitories are necessarily shared by good and bad, and close association is inevitable. The cost of separation into small groups in a Workhouse is prohibitive of attempts to place like-minded inmates together. This aggregation of inmates is not at all unpleasant or irksome to the loafer, to the vicious, to the drunkard seeking the safety and rest of the Workhouse after a debauch, and to the careless idler, who is ever preying upon the labour of others.

'Their chief objection to the Workhouse is the curtailment of liberty and the absence of opportunity of self-indulgence. But to the reputable clean-minded inmate this association with the depraved is the bitterest and most humiliating experience of life.'

It is to be noted that this condemnation applies alike to the five or six hundred smaller Workhouses or Poorhouses of rural districts of the United Kingdom, as well as to the two or three hundred larger establishments. These latter have terrors of their own. 'The mere size of the Great House' may, indeed, as has been suggested, be in itself 'a strong deterrent to the honest poor. Accustomed to live in a single room, they are appalled at the size of the Workhouse, and as terrified to go into it as a child into the sea. It can seldom be possible . . . for any one man to grasp all the details of our largest Workhouses, and where he cannot do so there must be great danger of neglect and bad under-management.' But the smallest rural Workhouses exhibit, in some respects, the greatest mixture.

'A small country Workhouse with fifty or sixty inmates,' testifies a well-known and experienced county administrator in the North of England, 'is a shame to our Christian civilization. There may be found collected in it perhaps ten old men and ten old women, drunken, idle blackguards, the outcasts of society; and, compelled to live among them, perhaps five or six respectable old people who, through absolutely no fault of their own, having worked hard all their inoffensive lives, have come to poverty. There will probably be three or four imbeciles of each sex, sometimes harmless and amusing, very often vicious and annoying to the inmates; two or three single women waiting for their confinements – in many cases an annual visit; three or four loafing "ins and outs", able-bodied men; three or four feeble persons; and eight or ten illegitimate children – all practically living together, and too often under a master who is tyrannical in his treatment and careless of his duties. It is a life absolutely repugnant to the respectable poor. Surely the time has come when, for the sake of not only the aged poor, but of the sick, the imbeciles and the children, a drastic reform should be made, which would, at all events, bring us to a level with Denmark and other European countries.' It is in the wards of such small country Workhouses that the visitor may see – to use the words of an experienced lady Guardian of the Poor in a southern county – 'all the inmates under lock and key, good characters and bad classed together, imbeciles and epileptics among them, all dressed in ill-fitting Work-house clothes of old-fashioned clumsy make, all sitting on hard benches round the long tables or the walls of the ward, while the building with its

bare stone floors, curtainless windows, and harshly clanging locks seemed
more like a prison for criminals than a last home for aged men and women'.

•

DAVID LLOYD GEORGE
1909

'Lords and landlords'

*The historic budget introduced in 1909 by David Lloyd George (1863–1945) proposed
a modest supertax on the very rich and new taxes on land so that the Liberals could wage
'implacable warfare' against poverty and squalor, especially by the provision of old age
pensions which he had proposed a year earlier. After a momentous national controversy,
the budget was thrown out by the House of Lords – an action which provoked the conflict
between Lords and Commons that led to the Parliament Act of 1911 curbing the power
of hereditary peers.*

*Lloyd George, one of the greatest orators of the century, once said, 'My platform is the
country.' As the Lords resisted his budget he delivered a series of speeches on platforms
around Britain. His denunciation of the Lords was made at the National Liberal Club
in London. He also excoriated landlords in a speech at the Edinburgh Castle public house
at Limehouse in London's East End – the most famous and most effective speech of his
life.*

LORDS

The sinister assembly which is more responsible than any other power for
wrecking popular hopes has, in my judgement, perpetrated its last act of
destructive fury.

They have slain the Budget. In doing so they have killed the bill, which if
you will permit me to say so, had in it more promise of better things for the
people of this country than most bills that have been submitted to the House
of Commons. It made provision against the inevitable evils which befall such
large masses of our poor population – their old age, infirmity, sickness and
unemployment. The schemes of which it was the foundation would, in my
judgement, if they had been allowed to fructify, have eliminated at least
hunger from the terrors that haunt the workman's cottage.

And yet here you have an order of men blessed with every fortune which
providence can bestow on them grudging a small pittance out of their
super-abundance in order to protect those who have built up their wealth

against the haunting terrors of misery and despair. They have thrown out the Budget, and, in doing so, have initiated one of the greatest, gravest and most promising struggles of the time. Liberty owes as much to the foolhardiness of its foes as it does to the sapience and wisdom of its friends. I wish for no better illustration of that than this incident.

For years, for generations, Liberal statesmen have striven to bring to an issue these great forces. Their bills were mutilated, torn and devitalized by this machine, and they were never able to bring the cause to any sort of decision. It has been done at last, and I am proud that I have had a small share in it. At last the cause between the peers and the people has been set down for trial in the great assize of the people, and the verdict will soon come. The assembly which has delayed, denied and mutilated justice for so long has at last been brought to justice . . .

Here are you, a nation of nearly 45 million, one of the greatest nations the world has ever seen, a nation whose proficiency in the art of government is unrivalled, a nation which has no superior in commerce or in industry. It has established the greatest merchant fleets that ever rode the waves. It has got the greatest international commerce in the world. It has founded the greatest and most extensive empire the world has ever witnessed.

And yet we are told that this great nation, with such a record of splendid achievements in the past and in the present, is unfit to make its own laws, is unfit to control its own finance, and that it is to be placed as if it were a nation of children or lunatics, under the tutelage and guardianship of some other body – and what body? Who are the guardians of this mighty people? Who are they?

They are men who have neither the training, the qualifications nor the experience which would fit them for such a gigantic task.

At last with all their cunning, their greed has overborne their craft, and we have got them at last. And we do not mean to let them go until all the accounts in the ledger have been settled. Ah! Why did they do it on the Budget? This is simply the fulfilment of the measure of their iniquity. Nay, more than that. Mr Balfour said, 'This is merely your pet vanity.' What? The right of the Commons to grant supplies a pet vanity! It is a franchise won through generations of sacrifice and of suffering. The Commons of England stormed the heights after many repulses, many a failure, with heavy losses, but they captured them, and the plain of government was at their feet.

Now, when we are beginning to realize the possibilities of that position, when we have discovered – I won't say for the first time – but discovered in real earnest what the power of finance means in the repression of wrongs, the House of Lords come along and say, 'We will share the garrisoning of that position.' All I can say is if that position, if that rampart, is surrendered it will be the greatest act of folly any democracy has ever perpetrated. Every grain of freedom is more precious than radium, and the nation that throws it away is the most wanton of prodigals. Think of the most commonplace public right we enjoy. What an incident of our everyday life! Yet it has cost generations of pleading and of pain to wring it out of the grip of tyranny.

Here we are this afternoon, at a public meeting, discussing urgent matters of vital public importance, and think nothing of it – nothing of it! But you know that this commonplace right has cost centuries of strife, of suffering, of struggling to our forefathers. And the rights of the Commons of England to grant supplies and to make the redress of grievances the condition of that grant drenched England with blood. That right is the proud possession of Englishmen. They were pre-eminent in the conflict that won it. It is their noblest tradition, and I do not believe that the dauntless national spirit which won that liberty has become so degenerate that at the call of an effete oligarchy, without striking a blow, Englishmen of today mean to surrender one of the finest and fairest provinces of freedom won by their ancestors.

LANDLORDS

Who is the landlord? The landlord is a gentleman – I have not a word to say about him in his personal capacity – the landlord is a gentleman who does not earn his wealth. He does not even take the trouble to receive his wealth. He has a host of agents and clerks to receive it for him. He does not even take the trouble to spend his wealth. He has a host of people around him to do the actual spending for him. He never sees it until he comes to enjoy it. His sole function, his chief pride is stately consumption of wealth produced by others. What about the doctor's income? How does the doctor earn his income? The doctor is a man who visits our homes when they are darkened with the shadow of death: who, by his skill, his trained courage, his genius, wrings hope out of the grip of despair, wins life out of the fangs of the Great Destroyer. All blessings upon him and his divine art of healing that mends bruised bodies and anxious hearts. To compare the reward which he gets for that labour with the wealth which pours into the pockets of the landlord purely owing to the possession of his monopoly is a piece – if they will forgive me for saying so – of insolence which no intelligent man would tolerate.

I went down to a coalfield the other day, and they pointed out to me many collieries there. They said: 'You see that colliery? The first man who went there spent a quarter of a million in sinking shafts, in driving mains and levels. He never got coal, and he lost his quarter of a million. The second man who came spent £100,000 – and he failed. The third man came along and he got the coal.' What was the landlord doing in the meantime? The first man failed; but the landlord got his royalty, the landlord got his dead-rent – and a very good name for it. The second man failed, but the landlord got his royalty.

These capitalists put their money in, and I asked, 'When the cash failed, what did the landlord put in?' He simply put in the bailiffs. The capitalist risks, at any rate, the whole of his money; the engineer puts his brains in; the miner risks his life. Have you been down a coal mine? I went down one the other day. We sank down into a pit half a mile deep. We then walked underneath the mountain, and we had about three-quarters of a mile of rock and shale above us. The earth seemed to be straining – around us and above us – to crush us in. You could see the pit-props bent and twisted and sundered, their fibres split in resisting the pressure. Sometimes they give way, and then there is mutilation and death. Often a spark ignites, the whole pit is deluged in fire, and the breath of life is scorched out of hundreds of breasts by the consuming flame. In the very next colliery to the one I descended, just a few years ago, 300 people lost their lives in that way; and yet when the Prime Minister and I knock at the doors of these great landlords, and say to them: 'Here, you know these poor fellows who have been digging up royalties at the risk of their lives, some of them are old, they have survived the perils of their trade, they are broken, they can earn no more. Won't you give something towards keeping them out of the workhouse?' they scowl at us. We say, 'Only a ha'penny, just a copper.' They retort, 'You thieves!' And they turn their dogs on to us, and you can hear their bark every morning. If this is an indication of the view taken by these great landlords of their responsibility to the people who, at the risk of life, create their wealth, then I say their day of reckoning is at hand.

The ownership of land is not merely an enjoyment, it is a stewardship. It has been reckoned as such in the past, and if the owners cease to discharge their functions in seeing to the security and defence of the country, in looking after the broken in their villages and in their neighbourhoods, the time will come to reconsider the conditions under which land is held in this country. No country, however rich, can permanently afford to have quartered upon its revenue a class which declines to do the duty which it was called upon to perform since the beginning.

•

KEIR HARDIE
1910

'The coronation'

George V succeeded Edward VII in 1910. His accession meant still more of the adulation of royalty that sickened Keir Hardie (1856–1915) and which he attacked repeatedly in the House of Commons. He wrote this philippic in the Pioneer.

The most desperate efforts are being made to popularize the coming Coronation. Public authorities have been given power to spend the ratepayers' money illegally on decorations and festivities. Poor little half-starved children are to be presented with Coronation mugs or medals to commemorate the event. The workers are to be shut out from their employment for two whole days to show how heartily their loyal hearts rejoice over the Coronation of the King. Two holidays on full pay would not be amiss, but an empty pocket is not an incentive to loyalty.

Thus, despite all the efforts of the astute stage managers, royalty is being found out. It is a huge imposture. The atmosphere of a court is surcharged with hypocrisy, insincerity, flattery and immorality.

The Coronation, with its pomp and show, its make-believe, its glorification of militarism, and its mockery of the solemnities of religion, is an affront to all that is true and self-respecting in our national life.

Wales is to have an 'Investiture' as a reminder that an English king and his robber barons strove for ages to destroy the Welsh people, and finally succeeded in robbing them of their lands, driving them into the mountain fastnesses of their native land like hunted beasts, and then had the insolence to have his son 'invested' in their midst. The King is to make a Coronation tour in Ireland to view the miles of lonely waste from which the persecution of his royal forebears has driven the Irish people into exile in other lands. And, crowning infamy, one million pounds is to be spent on a Coronation Durbar at Delhi, in the district round which *20,000 people are dying every week* of plague and hunger.

The *Daily Chronicle* explains why the patient, long-suffering people of India are thus to be mocked in their misery. Here is what it says: 'One can safely say that, following the visit of the King, we shall see a boom in India, particularly on the commercial side. To those who are looking to our Dominions to provide either an outlet for capital or a future for their sons, India should receive the consideration to which it is entitled.'

There we have 'loyalty' of the monied ruling classes in all its shameless nakedness. The King is to be used to provide an 'outlet for the capital' of the rich or more soft jobs for their sons.

Half a century ago Republicanism was the creed of Radicalism and Nonconformity. But the corrupting influences of wealth and a debased newspaper press have eaten the soul out of the manhood of the nation.

If we cannot set our heel upon the thing, we can at least show our contempt for it and preserve our own self-respect by refusing to participate in any of the foolery connected with this Coronation.

•

JOHN GALSWORTHY
1911

'Air war'

The English novelist John Galsworthy (1867–1933) is mostly remembered for The Forsyte Saga *(especially after it was dramatized by BBC Television), his account of life upstairs and below stairs in Edwardian England.*

The aeroplane had suddenly burst into existence when he sent this protest in a letter to The Times.

Of all the varying symptoms of madness in the life of modern nations, the most dreadful is this prostitution of the conquest of the air to the ends of warfare.

If ever men presented a spectacle of sheer inanity it is now – when, having at long last triumphed in their struggle to subordinate to their welfare the unconquered element, they have straightaway commenced to defile that element, so heroically mastered, by filling it with engines of destruction. If ever the gods were justified of their ironic smile – by the gods, it is now! Is there any thinker alive watching this still utterly preventable calamity without horror and despair? Horror at what must come of it, if not promptly stopped; despair that men can be so blind, so hopelessly and childishly the slaves of their own marvellous inventive powers. Was there ever so patent a case for scotching at birth a hideous development of the black arts of warfare; ever such an occasion for the Powers in conference to ban once and for all a new and ghastly menace?

A little reason, a grain of common sense, a gleam of sanity before it is too late – before vested interests and the chains of a new habit have enslaved us too hopelessly. If this fresh devilry be not quenched within the next few years it will be too late. Water and earth are wide enough for men to kill each other on. For the love of the sun, and stars, and the blue sky, that have given us all our aspirations since the beginning of time, let us leave the air to innocence! Will not those who have eyes to see goodwill towards men, and the power to put that goodwill into practice, bestir themselves while there is yet time, and save mankind from this last and worst of all its follies?

•

EMILIANO ZAPATA
1911

'End the tyranny'

Emiliano Zapata (1879–1919) was the legendary popular hero of the 1910–17 Mexican revolution who defended the rights of poor peasants to seize land from wealthy farm owners. His revolutionary manifesto, The Plan of Ayala, *was drawn up after Francisco Madero returned in triumph to Mexico City after the resignation of the dictator Porfirio Díaz. Madero refused Zapata's request that land be returned to the Indians, insisting on the disarmament of the Zapatistas.*

The Ayala manifesto, most of which is included in this extract, declared Madero incapable of fulfilling the goals of the revolution and vowed to return stolen land to the Indians. The slogan was 'Land and Liberty'.

We who undersign, constituted in a revolutionary junta to sustain and carry out the promises which the revolution of 20 November 1910, just past, made to the country, declare solemnly before the face of the civilized world which judges us and before the nation to which we belong and which we love, propositions which we have formulated to end the tyranny which oppresses us and redeem the fatherland from the dictatorships which are imposed on us.

Taking into consideration that the Mexican people led by Don Francisco I. Madero went to shed their blood to reconquer liberties and recover their rights which had been trampled on, and not for a man to take possession of power, violating the sacred principles which he took an oath to defend under the slogan 'Effective Suffrage and No Reelection', outraging thus the faith, the cause, the justice, and the liberties of the people: taking into consideration that that man to whom we refer is Don Francisco I. Madero, the same who initiated the above-cited revolution, who imposed his will and influence as a governing norm on the Provisional Government of the ex-President of the Republic Attorney Francisco L. de Barra, causing with this deed repeated sheddings of blood and multiplicate misfortunes for the fatherland in a manner deceitful and ridiculous, having no intentions other than satisfying his personal ambitions, his boundless instincts as a tyrant, and his profound disrespect for the fulfilment of the pre-existing laws emanating from the immortal code of '57, written with the revolutionary blood of Ayutla.

Taking into account that the so-called Chief of the Liberating Revolution of Mexico, Don Francisco I. Madero, through lack of integrity and the highest weakness, did not carry to a happy end the revolution which gloriously he initiated with the help of God and the people, since he left standing most of the governing powers and corrupted elements of oppression of the dictatorial government of Porfirio Díaz, which are not nor can in any way be the representation of National Sovereignty, and which, for being most bitter adversaries of ours and of the principles which even now we defend, are provoking the discomfort of the country and opening new wounds in the bosom of the fatherland, to give it its own blood to drink; taking also into account that the aforementioned Sr Francisco I. Madero, present President of the Republic, tries to avoid the fulfilment of the promises which he made to the Nation in the Plan of San Luis Potosí, restricting the above-cited promises to the agreements of Ciudad Juárez, by means of false promises and numerous intrigues against the Nation nullifying, pursuing, jailing, or killing revolutionary elements who helped him to occupy the high post of President of the Republic.

Taking into consideration that the so-often-repeated Francisco I. Madero has tried with the brute force of bayonets to shut up and to drown in blood the pueblos who ask, solicit, or demand from him the fulfilment of the promises of the revolution, calling them bandits and rebels, condemning them to a war of extermination without conceding or granting a single one of the guarantees which reason, justice, and the law prescribe; taking equally into consideration that the President of the Republic Francisco I. Madero has made of Effective Suffrage a bloody trick on the people, already against the will of the same people imposing Attorney José M. Pino Suárez in the Vice-Presidency of the Republic, or [imposing as] Governors of the States [men] designated by him, like the so-called General Ambrosio Figueroa, scourge and tyrant of the people of Morelos, or entering into scandalous cooperation with the científico party, fuedal landlords, and oppressive bosses, enemies of the revolution proclaimed by him, so as to forge new chains and follow the pattern of a new dictatorship more shameful and more terrible than that of Porfirio Díaz, for it has been clear and patent that he has outraged the sovereignty of the States, trampling on the laws without any respect for lives or interests, as has happened in the State of Morelos, and others, leading them to the most horrendous anarchy which contemporary history registers.

For these considerations we declare the aforementioned Francisco I. Madero inept at realizing the promises of the revolution of which he was the author, because he has betrayed the principles with which he tricked the will of the people and was able to get into power: incapable of governing, because he has no respect for the law and justice of the pueblos, and a traitor to the fatherland, because he is humiliating in blood and fire Mexicans who want liberties, so as to please the científicos, landlords, and bosses who enslave us, and from today on we begin to continue the revolution begun by him, until we achieve the overthrow of the dictatorial powers which exist.

We give notice: that [regarding] the fields, timber, and water which landlords, científicos, or bosses have usurped, the pueblos or citizens who have the titles corresponding to those properties will immediately enter into possession of that real estate of which they have been despoiled by the bad faith of our oppressors, maintaining at any cost with arms in hand the mentioned possession; and the usurpers who consider themselves with a right to them [those properties] will deduce it before the special tribunals which will be established on the triumph of the revolution.

In virtue of the fact that the immense majority of Mexican pueblos and citizens are owners of no more than the land they walk on, suffering the horrors of poverty without being able to improve their social condition in any way or to dedicate themselves to Industry or Agriculture, because lands, timber, and water are monopolized in a few hands, for this cause there will be expropriated the third part of those monopolies from the powerful proprietors of them, with prior indemnization, in order that the pueblos and citizens of Mexico may obtain ejidos, colonies, and foundations for pueblos, or fields for sowing or labouring, and the Mexicans' lack of prosperity and well-being may improve in all and for all.

[Regarding] The landlords, científicos, or bosses who oppose the present plan directly or indirectly, their goods will be nationalized and the two third parts which [otherwise would] belong to them will go for indemnizations of war, pensions for widows and orphans of the victims who succumb in the struggle for the present plan.

In order to execute the procedures regarding the properties aforementioned, the laws of disamortization and nationalization will be applied as they fit, for serving us as norm and example can be those laws put in force by the immortal Juárez on ecclesiastical properties, which punished the despots and conservatives who in every time have tried to impose on us the ignominious yoke of oppression and backwardness.

The insurgent military chiefs of the Republic who rose up with arms in hand at the voice of Don Francisco I. Madero to defend the plan of San Luis Potosí, and who oppose with armed force the present plan, will be judged traitors to the cause which they defended and to the fatherland, since at present many of them, to humour the tyrants, for a fistful of coins, or for bribes or connivance, are shedding the blood of their brothers who claim the fulfilment of the promises which Don Francisco I. Madero made to the nation.

Mexicans: consider that the cunning and bad faith of one man is shedding blood in a scandalous manner, because he is incapable of governing; consider that his system of government is choking the fatherland and trampling with the brute force of bayonets on our institutions; and thus, as we raised up our weapons to elevate him to power, we again raise them up against him for defaulting on his promises to the Mexican people and for having betrayed the revolution initiated by him, we are not personalists, we are partisans of principles and not of men!

Mexican people, support this plan with arms in hand and you will make the prosperity and well-being of the fatherland.

•

DAILY HERALD
1912

'The Titanic'

The sinking of the Titanic *was the first news story in the* Daily Herald, *the new British national newspaper founded by George Lansbury. The* Herald *was a supporter of the Labour Party and was instantly on its mettle, analysing the figures and showing that 121 steerage women and children were saved and 134 drowned but that 246 first- and second-class women and children were saved and only twenty drowned. Its comment columns were fiercely critical of the White Star Line.*

They have paid 30 per cent to their shareholders and they have sacrificed 51 per cent of the steerage children. They have gone to sea criminally under-equipped with the means of life saving, they have neglected boat drill, they have filled their boat with cooks and valets, with pleasure gardens and luxurious lounges; they have done all this to get big profits and please the first-class passengers. And when the catastrophe came they hastened to get their first-class passengers and their chairman safely away. Fifty-three children remained to die. They were steerage passengers! One hundred and thirty-four women and children slain. They were steerage passengers!

We are oppressed by a feeling of helplessness in the clutch of blind forces, forces we have held in check and made use of for our own purposes, but which have now got their revenge on us in a sudden breaking loose. Catastrophes in a mine do not affect us in this way; we are angry and not overwhelmed, for we know that with better precautions on the part of mine owners the majority of accidents could be avoided. It may be that when we know more we shall have the same feeling with regard to the sinking of the *Titanic*. It may be these 1,500 lives are a sacrifice to the lust for quick passages, that it was a short cut across the Atlantic that found this short cut to death. We are told that other transatlantic ships have lately found many icebergs on their route. One may ask, then, why they kept it, when the danger from submerged peaks is so plain? Why have not all ships kept, and why did not the *Titanic* keep, south out of the way of the danger? The reason is plain: liners must not get behind their scheduled time. If humanly possible, they must get in front of it. We withhold our opinion until an inquiry has been made, but if the facts are as we may well suspect, then the death of 1,500 of our fellows lies at the shipping company's door.

•

OBSERVER
1912

'The Titanic'

The Observer *was equally critical.*

A great wrong has been committed in the world. Safety can never be absolute. But we are not dealing with the inevitable in this case. We are dealing with a preventable disaster, for which no man upon the *Titanic* was mainly to blame. By error and inadequacy on shore, by unimaginative routine and official inertia, by the decay of national interest in mercantile seamanship 1,600 souls have been sacrificed. She had been warned that ice was thicker in the path than usual. Well, vigilance at look-out and on the bridge would perceive it. At evening the *Titanic* – following, remember, the route of possible death deliberately chosen by the shipping companies in concert as against the slightly longer path of assured safety to the south – was in the region which can only be called the great ship-trap of the seas. The companies have ordered in the last few days that the route shall be changed. Why did they not change it before? Why was the *Titanic* sent into the ship-trap when it is certain that by making the course only a few hours longer the 1,600 lives now sacrificed would never have been lost?

There are other issues not less urgent. It would surpass the sombre power of a Dantesque imagination to enforce the horror of this commonplace of ocean traffic: that the modern ocean liner with two or three thousand souls on board provides enough boat accommodation for only about a third of her passengers and crew. There is no technical reason why the proportion should not be largely increased or why other devices should not be employed, giving every man a chance for life.

Behind the grief for the *Titanic* is a sense of bitter waste. There will be a cloud upon the conscience of England and America until the lessons of the saddest tragedy wrought amidst the peaceful nations in the whole history of the seas, shall be so applied that the lives of those who died on the *Titanic* shall not have been offered in vain.

•

AMERICAN SOCIALIST PARTY
1912

'A yoke of bondage'

The American Socialist Party first contested a national election in 1892. Its history was closely identified with the career of Eugene V. Debs (1855–1926), founder of the Railway Union and one of the most charismatic men thrown up by the American labour movement. Debs stood for president in 1904, 1908 and 1912, when his platform was outright opposition to capitalism. He polled 900,000 votes in the contest with Wilson, Roosevelt and Taft.

The Socialist Party declares that the capitalist system has outgrown its historical function, and has become utterly incapable of meeting the problems now confronting society. We denounce this outgrown system as incompetent and corrupt and the source of unspeakable misery and suffering to the whole working class.

Under this system the industrial equipment of the nation has passed into the absolute control of a plutocracy which exacts an annual tribute of hundreds of millions of dollars from the producers. Unafraid of any organized resistance, it stretches out its greedy hands over the still undeveloped resources of the nation – the land, the mines, the forests and the water powers of every state of the Union.

In spite of the multiplication of labor-saving machines and improved methods in industry which cheapen the cost of production, the share of the producers grows ever less, and the prices of all the necessities of life steadily increase. The boasted prosperity of this nation is for the owning class alone. To the rest it means only greater hardship and misery. The high cost of living is felt in every home. Millions of wage-workers have seen the purchasing power of their wages decrease until life has become a desperate battle for mere existence.

Multitudes of unemployed walk the streets of our cities or trudge from state to state awaiting the will of the masters to move the wheels of industry.

The farmers in every state are plundered by the increasing prices exacted for tools and machinery and by extortionate rents, freight rates and storage charges.

Capitalist concentration is mercilessly crushing the class of small businessmen and driving its members into the ranks of propertyless wage-workers. The overwhelming majority of the people of America are being forced under a yoke of bondage by this soulless industrial despotism.

It is this capitalist system that is responsible for the increasing burden of armaments, the poverty, slums, child labor, most of the insanity, crime and prostitution, and much of the disease that afflicts mankind.

Under this system the working class is exposed to poisonous conditions, to frightful and needless perils to life and limb, is walled around with court decisions, injunctions and unjust laws, and is preyed upon incessantly for the benefit of the controlling oligarchy of wealth. Under it also, the children of the working class are doomed to ignorance, drudging toil and darkened lives.

We declare, therefore, that the longer sufferance of these conditions is impossible, and we purpose to end them all. We declare them to be the product of the present system in which industry is carried on for private greed, instead of for the welfare of society. We declare, furthermore, that for these evils there will be and can be no remedy and no substantial relief except through Socialism under which industry will be carried on for the common good and every worker receive the full social value of the wealth he creates.

Society is divided into warring groups and classes, based upon material interests. Fundamentally, this struggle is a conflict between the two main classes, one of which, the capitalist class, owns the means of production, and the other, the working class, must use these means of production, on terms dictated by the owners.

The capitalist class, though few in numbers, absolutely controls the government, legislative, executive and judicial. This class owns the machinery of gathering and disseminating news through its organized press. It subsidizes seats of learning – the colleges and schools – and even religious and moral agencies. It has also the added prestige which established customs give to any order of society, right or wrong.

The working class, which includes all those who are forced to work for a living whether by hand or brain, in shop, mine or on the soil, vastly outnumbers the capitalist class. Lacking effective organization and class solidarity, this class is unable to enforce its will. Given such a class solidarity and effective organization, the workers will have the power to make all laws and control all industry in their own interest. All political parties are the expression of economic class interests. All other parties than the Socialist Party represent one or another group of the ruling capitalist class. Their political conflicts reflect merely superficial rivalries between competing capitalist groups. However they result, these conflicts have no issue of real value to the workers. Whether the Democrats or Republicans win politically, it is the capitalist class that is victorious economically.

The Socialist Party is the political expression of the economic interests of the workers. Its defeats have been their defeats and its victories their victories. It is a party founded on the science and laws of social development. It proposes that, since all social necessities today are socially produced, the means of their production and distribution shall be socially owned and democratically controlled.

In the face of the economic and political aggressions of the capitalist class, the only reliance left the workers is that of their economic organizations and their political power. By the intelligent and class conscious use of these, they may resist successfully the capitalist class, break the fetters of wage slavery, and fit themselves for the future society, which is to displace the capitalist system. The Socialist Party appreciates the full significance of class organization and urges the wage-earners, the working farmers and all other useful workers to organize for economic and political action, and we pledge ourselves to support the toilers of the fields as well as those in the shops, factories and mines of the nation in their struggles for economic justice.

In the defeat or victory of the working-class party in this new struggle for freedom lies the defeat or triumph of the common people of all economic groups, as well as the failure or triumph of popular government. Thus the

Socialist Party is the party of the present-day revolution which makes the transition from economic individualism to Socialism, from wage slavery to free co-operation, from capitalist oligarchy to industrial democracy.

•

THE SOLEMN COVENANT
1912

'Home rule'

When Asquith introduced the Home Rule Bill in 1912, Ulster was not excluded and the question of whether Ireland was one nation or two was raised. Ulster's Protestants were encouraged in their resistance to Home Rule by Andrew Bonar Law, leader of the Unionists. Sir Edward Carson, leader of the Irish Unionists in the Commons, used the device of the Ulster Covenant, signed by nearly 250,000 people, to prevent riots in Belfast.

Being convinced in our consciences that Home Rule would be disastrous to the material well-being of Ulster as well as of the whole of Ireland, subversive of our civil and religious freedom, destructive of our citizenship, and perilous to the unity of the Empire, we, whose names are underwritten, men of Ulster, loyal subjects of His Gracious Majesty King George V, humbly relying on the God whom our fathers in days of stress and trial confidently trusted, hereby pledge ourselves in Solemn Covenant throughout this our time of threatened calamity to stand by one another in defending, for ourselves and our children, our cherished position of equal citizenship in the United Kingdom, and in using all means which may be found necessary to defeat the present conspiracy to set up a Home Rule Parliament in Ireland; and, in the event of such a Parliament being forced upon us, we further solemnly and mutually pledge ourselves to refuse to recognize its authority. In sure confidence that God will defend the right, we hereto subscribe our names, and, further, we individually declare that we have not already signed this Covenant.

•

BERTRAND RUSSELL
1914

'Barbarism'

As well as being one of the century's greatest philosophers and mathematicians, Bertrand Russell (1872–1970) was also one of its great protesters, with a record of eloquent protest stretching from the First World War to Vietnam in the 1960s. He was a fellow of Trinity College, Cambridge, and had published Principia Mathematica *(with A. N. Whitehead) when he sent this letter to* The Nation, *the prominent Liberal weekly.*

Against the vast majority of my countrymen, even at this moment, in the name of humanity and civilization, I protest against our share in the destruction of Germany.

A month ago, Europe was a peaceful comity of nations; if an Englishman killed a German, he was hanged. Now, if an Englishman kills a German, or if a German kills an Englishman, he is a patriot, who has deserved well of his country. We scan the newspapers with greedy eyes for news of slaughter, and rejoice when we read of innocent young men, blindly obedient to the word of command, mown down in thousands by the machine-guns of Liège. Those who saw the London crowds, during the nights leading up to the Declaration of War, saw a whole population, hitherto peaceable and humane, precipitated in a few days down the steep slope to primitive barbarism, letting loose, in a moment, the instincts of hatred and blood-lust against which the whole fabric of society has been raised. 'Patriots' in all countries acclaim this brutal orgy as a noble determination to vindicate the right; reason and mercy are swept away in one great flood of hatred; dim abstractions of unimaginable wickedness – Germany to us and the French, Russia to the Germans – conceal the simple fact that the enemy are men, like ourselves, neither better nor worse – men who love their homes and the sunshine, and all the simple pleasures of common lives; men now mad with terror in the thought of their wives, their sisters, their children, exposed, with our help, to the tender mercies of the conquering Cossack.

And all this madness, all this rage, all this flaming death of our civilization and our hopes, has been brought about because a set of official gentlemen, living luxurious lives, mostly stupid, and all without imagination or heart, have chosen that it should occur rather than that any one of them should suffer some infinitesimal rebuff to his country's pride. No literary tragedy can approach the futile horror of the White Paper. The diplomatists, seeing from the first the inevitable end, mostly wishing to avoid it, yet drifted from hour to hour of the swift crisis, restrained by punctilio from making or accepting the small concessions that might have saved the world, hurried on at last by blind fear to loose the armies for the work of mutual butchery.

And behind the diplomatists, dimly heard in the official documents, stand vast forces of national greed and national hatred – atavistic instincts, harmful to mankind at its present level, but transmitted from savage and half-animal ancestors, concentrated and directed by governments and the press, fostered by the upper class as a distraction from social discontent, artificially nourished by the sinister influence of the makers of armaments, encouraged by a whole foul literature of 'glory', and by every textbook of history with which the minds of children are polluted.

England, no more than other nations which participate in this war, can be absolved either as regards its national passions or as regards its diplomacy.

For the past ten years, under the fostering care of the government and a portion of the press, a hatred of Germany has been cultivated and a fear of the German Navy. I do not suggest that Germany has been guiltless; I do not deny that the crimes of Germany have been greater than our own. But I do say that whatever defensive measures were necessary should have been taken in a spirit of calm foresight, not in a wholly needless turmoil of panic and suspicion. It is this deliberately created panic and suspicion that produced the public opinion by which our participation in the war has been rendered possible.

•

DAILY MAIL
1915

'The tragedy of the shells'

Although both Sir John French, the British Commander-in-chief in France, and Lord Kitchener, Secretary for War, had expressed concern about the shortage of high-explosive shells to fight the Germans, Prime Minister Herbert Asquith denied that there was any problem. The owner of the Daily Mail, *Lord Northcliffe, knew from letters sent to him by soldiers at the front that the shortage of munitions was severely hampering their fighting power. On 21 May 1915, he published the most influential leading article of the war. The* Mail *was burnt at the Stock Exchange and sales of the paper fell from 1.3 million to 238,000 – but five days later Lloyd George was moved from the Exchequer to a newly created Ministry of Munitions to sort out the crisis.*

In the dark days when Lord Haldane – who, we can definitely say, is going – showed signs of renewed tinkering with the army, the *Daily Mail* suggested that Lord Kitchener should take charge of the raising of the new troops. Lord Kitchener at once saw the size of that part of his job, and that part of the work was done as well as anyone could do it. We have never liked, and the public have never liked, Lord Kitchener's use of his own name – instead of the King's – in connection with these armies; and the public has greatly disliked some of the advertising methods employed by Lord Kitchener, but it has pardoned him in the urgent need of the moment, and the soldiers are there. How many, nobody knows. German estimates place them at 2,000,000, though they say that these men are largely unprovided with arms. Whether the Germans are right or wrong we do not know. *What we do know is that Lord Kitchener has starved the army in France of high-explosive shells.* The German aeroplanes which hover over our positions all day long know how we stand at the front in regard to numbers of men, and the work of the German spies at the ports of departure in England and those of arrival in France adds to their information.

A Liberal newspaper which is in very close touch with the government spoke yesterday of 'the quarrel between Lord Kitchener and Sir John French'. There should be no such quarrel. It has never been pretended that Lord Kitchener is a soldier in the sense that Sir John French is a soldier. Lord Kitchener is a gatherer of men – and a very fine gatherer too. But his record in the South African War as a fighting general – apart from his excellent organizing work as Chief of the Staff – was not brilliant. The opinion which Lord Roberts expressed as to his handling of troops at Paardeberg is well known, and we have never met a soldier who held any other opinion. Nothing in Lord Kitchener's experience suggests that he has the qualifications required for conducting a European campaign in the field, and we can only hope that no such misfortune will befall this nation as that he should be permitted to interfere with the actual strategy of this gigantic war.

The admitted fact is that Lord Kitchener *ordered the wrong kind of shell* – the same kind of shell which he used largely against the Boers in 1900. He persisted in sending shrapnel – a useless weapon in trench warfare. He was warned repeatedly that the kind of shell required was a violently explosive bomb which would dynamite its way through the German trenches and entanglements and enable our brave men to advance in safety. The kind of shell our poor soldiers have had has caused the death of thousands of them.

Incidentally, it has brought about a Cabinet crisis and the formation of what we hope is going to be a National Government.

We are not a military nation, and therefore do not understand the difference between soldiers and soldiers. Sir John Cowans is a great soldier – one of the greatest soldiers in the world. It is to him we owe the superb arrangements for the feeding of our troops. Sir William Robertson, Sir John French's Chief of Staff, is a great soldier. To him is due the fine staff work of the British Army in France. Lord Kitchener is a great soldier. To him is due the idea of advertising for an army. Sir John French is a great soldier. We owe to Sir John French the leadership which has enabled a handful of men from the British Islands, the Dominions, and India to hold back the mightiest army in the world, the remorseless horde that has been preparing for this particular struggle for forty-four years. Not being a military nation, we do not know how to discriminate between various types of soldiers. If, by any mischance, Lord Kitchener went to France to conduct the campaign, we should probably have a costly object lesson in the difference between African and European warfare. It is to be hoped that Lord Kitchener – with proper and necessary assistance – will remain at the War Office, though when compulsory service comes his sphere of usefulness will, of course, be greatly diminished. That compulsion is coming, and coming soon, is proved by the extremities to which Lord Kitchener is reduced. The advertisement he published yesterday urging the enlistment of men of forty – married men – which we greatly regret having printed and which the *Daily Mail* will decline to print again – is proof of it. Men of forty should not be used until the recruiting powers of the country are exhausted. The expenditure that is coming upon this nation in the near future in the matter of the dependents of married men who have been advertised into the army is one that nobody thinks of in this moment of extravagance. The expense, however, is a small part of it; there are also to be considered the break up of homes, the break up of businesses which follow the enlistment of married men, and the sorrow and grief of wives and children.

It is no testimony to Lord Kitchener's organizing ability that this gross unfairness should continue. Rather is it an indication that his life in India and Egypt has made him unacquainted with British conditions. We invite him on Sunday to take a stroll down Oxford Street to the City and return by the Strand. He will meet some thousands of capable young 'slackers' who are staying at home, and, as one of our correspondents said yesterday, 'stealing the businesses of married men who have gone to the front'.

In the midst of all the confusion of Cabinet making, the vital questions of the navy, the shortage of high-explosive shells, and the sending of men to France are being forgotten. True, it may only be a matter of a few days, but, as someone has remarked recently, things happen at such a pace in 1915 that the events which would fill six months of an ordinary year are crowded into a single week.

Our little army cannot wait.

•

WOODROW WILSON
1915

'*The sinking of the* Lusitania'

More than 1,100 passengers and crew, including 124 Americans, were killed when a German submarine torpedoed and sank the British passenger ship Lusitania *on 7 May 1915. It was an act that brought the United States and Germany to the brink of war and provoked the President, Woodrow Wilson (1856–1924), to send this diplomatic note to Germany via its ambassador in Washington.*

The Government of the United States has been apprised that the Imperial German Government considered themselves obliged by the extraordinary circumstances of the present war and the measures adopted by their adversaries in seeking to cut Germany off from all commerce, to adopt methods of retaliation which go much beyond the ordinary methods of warfare at sea, in the proclamation of a war zone from which they have warned neutral ships to keep away. This Government has already taken occasion to inform the Imperial German Government that it cannot admit the adoption of such measures or such a warning of danger to operate as in any degree an abbreviation of the rights of American shipmasters or of American citizens bound on lawful errands as passengers on merchant ships of belligerent nationality; and that it must hold the Imperial German Government to a strict accountability for any infringement of those rights, intentional or incidental. It does not understand the Imperial German Government to question those rights. It assumes, on the contrary, that the Imperial Government accept, as of course, the rule that the lives of noncombatants, whether they be of neutral citizenship or citizens of one of the nations at war, cannot lawfully or rightfully be put in jeopardy by the capture or destruction of an unarmed merchantman, and recognize also, as all other nations do, the obligation to take the usual precaution of visit and search to ascertain whether a suspected merchantman is in fact of belligerent nationality or is in fact carrying contraband of war under a neutral flag.

The Government of the United States, therefore, desires to call the attention of the Imperial German Government with the utmost earnestness to the fact that the objection to their present method of attack against the trade of their enemies lies in the practical impossibility of employing submarines in the destruction of commerce without disregarding those rules of fairness, reason, justice and humanity which all modern opinion regards as imperative. It is practically impossible for the officers of a submarine to visit a merchantman at sea and examine her papers and cargo. It is practically impossible for them to make a prize of her; and, if they cannot put a prize crew on board of her, they cannot sink her without leaving her crew and all on board of her to the mercy of the sea in her small boats. These facts it is understood the Imperial German Government frankly admit. We are informed that in the instances of which we have spoken time enough for even that poor measure of safety was not given, and in at least two of the cases cited not so much as a warning was received. Manifestly submarines cannot be used against merchantmen, as the last few weeks have shown, without an inevitable violation of many sacred principles of justice and humanity.

American citizens act within their indisputable rights in taking their ships and in traveling wherever their legitimate business calls them upon the high seas, and exercise those rights in what should be the well-justified confidence that their lives will not be endangered by acts done in clear violation of universally acknowledged international obligations, and certainly in the confidence that their own Government will sustain them in the exercise of their rights.

There was recently published in the newspapers of the United States, I regret to inform the Imperial German Government, a formal warning, purporting to come from the Imperial German Embassy at Washington addressed to the people of the United States and stating, in effect, that any citizen of the United States who exercised his right of free travel upon the seas would do so at his peril if his journey should take him within the zone of waters within which the Imperial German Navy was using submarines against the commerce of Great Britain and France, notwithstanding the respectful but very earnest protest of his Government, the Government of the United States. I do not refer to this for the purpose of calling the attention of the Imperial German Government at this time to the surprising irregularity of a communication from the Imperial German Embassy at Washington addressed to the people of the United States through the newspapers, but only for the purpose of pointing out that no warning that an unlawful and inhumane act will be committed can possibly be accepted as an excuse or palliation for that act or as an abatement of the responsibility for its commission.

Long acquainted as this Government has been with the character of the Imperial German Government and with the high principles of equity by which they have in the past been actuated and guided, the Government of the United States cannot believe that the commanders of the vessels which committed these acts of lawlessness did so except under a misapprehension of the orders issued by the Imperial German naval authorities. It takes it for granted that, at least within the practical possibilities of every such case, the commanders even of submarines were expected to do nothing that would involve the lives of noncombatants or the safety of neutral ships, even at the cost of failing in their object of capture or destruction. It confidently expects, therefore, that the Imperial German Government will disavow the acts of which the Government of the United States complains, that they will make reparation so far as reparation is possible for injuries which are without measure, and that they will take immediate steps to prevent the recurrence of anything so obviously subversive of the principles of warfare for which the Imperial German Government have in the past so wisely and so firmly contended.

•

DAILY MAIL
1915

'The sinking of the Lusitania'

There were anti-German riots in England. In Liverpool troops were called in after three days of general destruction. The German Knights of the Garter were struck off the roll. The Daily Mail *spoke for England.*

We chronicle today the foulest of the many foul crimes that have stained the German arms. The great Cunard liner *Lusitania*, the pride of two continents and a household word among Britons and Americans all over the earth, was torpedoed yesterday off the Irish coast. She sank rapidly and with a loss of life that must, we fear, inevitably prove heavy.

There is but one word for such an infamy. It is not an act of war; it is a case of sheer, cowardly murder. Before she sailed from New York the German Embassy in Washington advertised in the American papers that all travellers crossing the Atlantic would embark at their own risk. Many of the 1,200 passengers who had booked their berths in the *Lusitania* were warned by mysterious telegrams that she would be sunk. The warning was disregarded. It seemed incredible that even the German pirates would attack a liner that served no military purpose and was known to be carrying hundreds of neutral non-combatants, women and children as well as men. But the Americans and ourselves have still to learn the character of our German foe. He is free from all the restraints of humanity. He is a stabbing, slashing, trampling, homicidal maniac, dead to all sense of respect for the laws of God and man, a wild and cunning beast that has broken loose and must be caught and killed before there can again be any peace or security in the world. The premeditation of his latest atrocity merely adds to its fiendishness.

To the American people who have suffered from this felon's blow equally with ourselves we address no words of impertinent counsel. But we do venture to offer them from the bottom of our hearts a message of the profoundest sympathy. It is at such times as these that the essential kinship of the English-speaking peoples is made unmistakably manifest. We share their indignation, their loathing and contempt for the assassins who sneak under the waters and wage a campaign of murder against unarmed and defenceless passenger ships, merchant vessels, and fishing trawlers; and we promise them that, so far as in us lies, the deaths of these American citizens shall be avenged.

For the British Government and the British people there is one clear moral to be drawn from what has happened. It is that we must fall upon Germany tooth and nail, fight her with her own weapons, decline any longer to be bound by restrictions that she herself repudiates, and gather up all our resources to crush this brood of vipers into impotence. We shall suffer much, we shall lose men by the thousands, and ships, it may be, by the score; but in the end, please God, we shall have cleansed Europe and the world of a venomous pest.

•

KEITH MURDOCH
1915

'*Gallipoli*'

The British naval attacks on the Dardanelles, aimed at conquering the Gallipoli peninsula and seizing Constantinople, went disastrously wrong. The Australian, New Zealand and British troops were pinned down by the Turks and stuck in trenches for nearly a year. The Australian journalist Keith Murdoch (1886–1952) was outraged by what he saw

in Gallipoli, where thousands of soldiers were being sacrificed by incompetent British
commanders.

On his arrival in London, where he was to head an Australian newspaper group's
cable office, he showed Geoffrey Dawson, editor of The Times, *an 8,000-word account*
he had written for the Australian prime minister about the situation he had uncovered at
Gallipoli. Dawson sent him to Lord Northcliffe, who suggested he showed his report to
Lloyd George, then prime minister. Even though it was not published in his lifetime,
Murdoch's report, declassified by the Australian government only in 1980, had an almost
instant effect. The British General Sir Ian Hamilton was relieved of his command and
within days Lord Kitchener, Secretary for War, agreed to evacuation.

For the general staff, and I fear for Hamilton the British Commander, officers
and men have nothing but contempt. They express it fearlessly. That, however,
is not peculiar to Anzac. Sedition is talked round every tin of bully beef on
the peninsula, and it is only loyalty that holds the forces together. Every
returning troopship, every section of the line of communications, is full of
the same talk. I like General Hamilton and found him exceedingly kindly. I
admire him as a journalist. But as a strategist he has completely failed.
Undoubtedly, the essential and first step to restore the morale of the shaken
forces is to recall him and his Chief of Staff, a man more cordially detested
in our forces than Enver Pasha. What the army here wants is a young leader,
a man who has had no past, and around whom the officers can rally . . .

I cannot see any solution which does not begin with the recall of
Hamilton . . .

It is not for me to judge Hamilton, but it is plain that when an army has
completely lost faith in its general, and he has on numerous occasions proved
his weaknesses, only one thing can be done. He has very seldom been at
Anzac. He lives at Imbros. The French call him 'the General who lives on
an Island'. The story may not be true, but the army believes that Hamilton
left Suvla on 21 August remarking, 'Everything hangs in the balance, the
Yeomanry are about to charge.' Of course the army laughs at a general who
leaves the battlefield when everything hangs in the balance.

What I want to say to you now very seriously is that the continuous and
ghastly bungling over the Dardanelles enterprise was to be expected from
such a general staff as the British Army possesses, so far as I have seen it.
The conceit and complacency of the red feather men are equalled only by
their incapacity. Along the lines of communications, and especially at Mudros,
are countless high officers and conceited young cubs who are plainly only
playing at war. What can you expect of men who have never worked
seriously, who have lived for their appearance and for social distinction and

self-satisfaction, and who are now called on to conduct a gigantic war? Kitchener has a terrible task in getting pure work out of these men, whose motives can never be pure, for they are unchangeably selfish. I want to say frankly that it is my opinion, and that without exception of Australian officers, that appointments to the general staff are made from motives of friendship and special influence. Australians now loathe and detest any Englishman wearing red . . . I could tell you of many scandals, but the instance that will best appeal to you is that of the staff ship *Aragon*. She is a magnificent and luxurious South American liner, anchored in Mudros harbour as a base for the Inspector-General of Communications. I can give you no idea of how the Australians – and the new British officers too – loathe the *Aragon*. Heaven knows what she is costing, but certainly the staff lives in luxury. And nothing can exceed the rudeness of these chocolate general staff soldiers to those returning from the front. The ship's adjutant is the worst instance of rude and disgusting snobbishness and incapacity I have come across. With others, plain downright incapacity is the main characteristic. I must say this of them also, that whereas at our 3rd Australian General Hospital on shore we had 134 fever cases, including typhus, with only a few mosquito nets, and *no ice*, and few medical comforts, the *Aragon* staff was wallowing in ice. Colonel Stawell – you know him as Melbourne's leading consultant – and Sir Alex McCormick are not sentimentalists. But they really wept over the terrible hardships of the wounded, due to the incapacity of the *Aragon*. One concrete case is that of 150 wounded men landed in dead of night, with no provisions and no instructions, at the hospital beach, to make their way as best they could to the hospital, which had no notice of their arrival. While I was at the hospital a beautiful general and his staff rode in to make an inspection. Despite their appearance as perfect specimens of the general staff, I thought we shall now get the ice from the *Aragon* on to the brows of our unfortunate men. But no ice appeared next day.

I have great faith still in the Englishman . . . But this unfortunate expedition has never been given a chance. It required large bodies of seasoned troops. It required a great leader. It required self-sacrifice on the part of the staff as well as that sacrifice so wonderfully and liberally made on the part of the soldiers. It has had none of these things. Its troops have been second class, because (they were) untried before their awful battles and privations of the peninsula. And behind it all is the gross selfishness and complacency on the part of the staff.

•

C. E. MONTAGUE
1915

'The British regular officer'

The novelist and essayist C. E. Montague (1867–1928) was a writer on the Manchester Guardian *for thirty-five years until 1925. He is now remembered for* Disenchantment, *a collection of essays published in 1922, which were a scathing indictment of the complacency of the British regular officers. As he recalls how idealism perished in the trenches after the Battle of Loos, Montague cannot conceal his contempt.*

The winter after the battle of Loos a sentry on guard at one part of our line could always see the prostrate skeletons of many English dead. They lay outside our wire, picked clean by the rats, so that the khaki fell in on them loosely – little heaps of bone and cloth half hidden now by nettles and grass. If the sentry had been a year in the army he knew well enough that they had gone foredoomed into a battle lost before a shot was fired. After the Boer War, you remember, England, under the first shock of its blunders, had tried to find out why the staff work was so bad. What it found, in the words of a famous report, was that the fashion in sentiment in our Regular Army was to think hard work 'bad form'; a subaltern was felt to be a bit of a scrub if he worried too much about discovering how to support an attack when he might be more spiritedly employed in playing polo.

And so the swathes of little brown bundles, with bones showing through, lay in the nettles and grass.

Consider the course of the life of the British Regular officer as you had known him in youth – not the pick, the saving few, the unconquerably sound and keen, but the average, staple article made by a sleek, complacent, snobbish, safe, wealth-governed England after her own image. Think of his school; of the mystic aureole of quasi-moral beauty attached by authority there to absorption in the easy thing – in play; the almost passionate adoration of all those energies and dexterities which, in this world of evolution towards the primacy of the acute, full brain, are of the least possible use as aids to survival in men and to victory in armies. Before he first left home for school he may have been a normal child who only craved to be given some bit, any odd bit, of 'real work', as an experience more thrilling than games. Like most children, he may have had a zestful command of fresh, vivid, personal speech, his choice of words expressing simply and gaily the individual working of his mind and his joy in its work. Through easy contact with gardeners, gamekeepers and village boys he often had established a quite natural, unconscious friendliness with people of different social grades. He was probably born of the kind that pries young, that ask, when they play on sea sands, why there are tides, and what goes on in the sky that there should be rain. And then down came the shades of the prison-house. To make this large, gay book of fairy tales, the earth, dull and stale to a child importunately fingering at its covers might seem a task to daunt the strongest. But many of the teachers of our youth are indomitable men. They can make earth's most ardent small lover learn from a book what a bore his dear earth can be, with her strings of names of towns, rivers and lakes, her mileages *à faire mourir*, and her insufferable tale of flax and jute. With an equal firmness your early power of supple and bright-coloured speech may be taken away and a rag-bag of feeble stock phrases, misfits for all your thoughts, and worn dull and dirty by everyone else, be forced upon you instead of the treasure you had.

You may leave school unable to tell what stars are about you at night or to ask your way to a journey's end in any country but your own. Between your helpless mind and most of your fellow-countrymen thick screens of divisions are drawn, so that when you are fifteen you do not know how to speak to them with a natural courtesy; you have a vague idea that they will steal your watch if you leave it about. Above all, you have learned that it is still 'bad form' to work; that the youth with brains and no money may well be despised by the youth with money and no brains; that the absorbed student or artist is ignoble or grotesque; that to be able to afford yourself 'a good time' is a natural title to respect and regard; and that to give yourself any 'good time' that you can is an action of spirit. So it went on at prep school, public school, Sandhurst, Camberley. That was how Staff College French came to be what it was. And as it was what it was, you can guess what Staff College tactics and strategy were, and why all the little brown bundles lay where they did in the nettles and grass . . .

These apprehensions were particularly apt to arise if you had spent an hour that day in seeing herds of the English 'common people' ushered down narrowing corridors of barbed wire into some gap that had all the German machine-guns raking its exit, the nature of Regular officers' pre-war education in England precluding the prompt evolution of any effectual means on our side to derange the working of this ingenious abattoir. We had asked for it all. We had made the directing brains of our armies the poor things that they were. Small blame to them if in this season of liquidation they failed to produce assets which we had never equipped them to earn – mental nimbleness, powers of individual observation, quickness to cap with counterstrokes of invention each new device of the fertile specialists opposite. Being as we had moulded them, they had probably done pretty well in doing no worse.

> What's *done* we partly may compute,
> But know not what's *resisted*.

Who shall say what efforts it may have cost some of those poor custom-ridden souls not to veto, for good and all, an engine of war so far from 'smart' as the tank, or to accept any help at all from such folk as the new-fangled, untraditional airmen, some of whom took no shame to go forth to the fray in pyjamas. Not they alone, but all of ourselves, with our boastful chatter about the 'public school spirit', our gallant, robust contempt for 'swats' and 'smugs' and all who invented new means to new ends and who trained and used their brains with a will – we had arranged for these easy battues of thousands of Englishmen, who, for their part, did not fail. Tomorrow you would see it all again – a few hundred square yards of ground gained by the deaths, perhaps, of 20,000 men who would

> Go to their graves like beds, fight for a plot
> Which is not tomb enough and continent
> To hide the slain.

So it would go on, week after week, sitting after sitting of the dismal court that liquidated in the Flanders mud our ruling classes' wasted decades, until we either lost the war outright or were saved from utter disaster by clutching at aid from French brains and American numbers. Like Lucifer when he was confronted with the sky at night, you 'looked and sank'.

> Around the ancient track marched, rank on rank,
> The army of unalterable law.

What had we done, when we could, that the stars in their courses should fight for us now? Or left undone, of all that could provoke this methodical universe of swinging and returning forces to shake off such dust from its constant wheels?

•

BERTRAND RUSSELL
1916

'Savage punishment'

Bertrand Russell (1872–1970) gave the title 'Two Years Hard Labour for refusing to disobey the "Dictates of Conscience"' to a pamphlet he wrote on 15 April 1916. Six men were arrested for distributing it – some 250,000 copies had been sent out. Russell then announced in a letter to The Times *that he was the author: if anybody was to be persecuted it should be him. He was arrested, tried and fined £100. When he did not pay the fine, his goods in Cambridge were seized and sold to make up the sum. Another result of his protest was that he was deprived of his lectureship at Trinity College, Cambridge.*

This was the sentence passed on Ernest F. Everett, of 222 Denton's Green Lane, St Helens, by a court martial held on 10 April.

Everett was a teacher at St Helens, and had been opposed to all war since the age of sixteen. He appealed as a conscientious objector before the Local and Appeal Tribunals, both of which treated him very unfairly, going out of their way to recommend his dismissal from school. They recognized his conscientious claim only so far as to award him non-combatant service. But as the purpose of such service is to further the prosecution of the war and to release others for the trenches, it was impossible for him to accept the decision of the tribunals.

On 31 March he was arrested as an absentee, brought before the magistrates, fined £2, and handed over to the military authorities. By them he was taken under escort to Warrington Barracks, where he was compelled to put on uniform. On 1 April he was taken to Abergele, where he was placed in the Non-Combatant Corps, which is part of the army.

He adopted consistently a policy of passive resistance to all military orders. The first morning, 2 April, when the men were ordered to fall in for fatigue duty, he refused, saying: 'I refuse to obey any order given by any military authority.' According to the corporal who gave the order, Everett 'said it in quite a nice way'.

The corporal informed the lieutenant, who repeated the order, and warned Everett of the seriousness of his conduct. Everett still answered politely, but explained why he could not obey. The lieutenant ordered the conscientious objector to the guard-room, where he remained all night.

The captain visited the prisoner, who stated that 'he was not going to take orders'. The captain ordered him to be brought before the commanding officer on a charge of disobedience.

Everett was next brought before the colonel, who read aloud to him Section 9 of the Army Act, and explained the serious consequences of disobedience. But Everett remained firm, saying, 'He could not and would not obey any military order.'

The result was that he was tried by court martial on 10 April. He stated in evidence in his own defence: 'I am prepared to do work of national importance which does not include military service, so long as I do not thereby release some other man to do what I am not prepared to do myself.'

The sentence was two years' hard labour. Everett is now suffering this savage punishment solely for refusal to go against his conscience. He is fighting the old fight for liberty and against religious persecution in the same spirit in which martyrs suffered in the past. Will you join the persecutors? Or will you stand for those who are defending conscience at the cost of obloquy and pain of mind and body?

Forty other men are suffering persecution for conscience sake in the same way as Mr Everett. Can *you* remain silent while this goes on?

•

PROCLAMATION OF THE IRISH REPUBLIC
1916

'Ireland summons her children to the flag'

The Easter Rising, a rebellion in Dublin from 24 to 29 April 1916 seeking immediate independence for Ireland, was led by Patrick Pearse and James Connolly of Sinn Féin. The proclamation was mainly the work of Pearse, who proclaimed a provisional government of the Irish Republic, as its president, from the General Post Office which served as the rebel headquarters.

Pearse, Connolly and twelve other rebel leaders were court-martialled and executed.

Irishmen and Irishwomen: In the name of God and of the dead generations from which she receives her old tradition of nationhood, Ireland, through us, summons her children to her flag and strikes for her freedom.

Having organized and trained her manhood through her secret revolutionary organization, the Irish Republican Brotherhood, and through her open military organizations, the Irish Volunteers, and the Irish Citizen Army, having patiently perfected her discipline, having resolutely waited for the right moment to reveal itself, she now seizes that moment, and, supported by her exiled children in America and by gallant allies in Europe, but relying in the first on her own strength, she strikes in full confidence of victory.

We declare the right of the people of Ireland to the ownership of Ireland, and to the unfettered control of Irish destinies, to be sovereign and indefeasible. The long usurpation of that right by a foreign people and government has not extinguished the right, nor can it ever be extinguished except by the destruction of the Irish people. In every generation the Irish people have asserted their right to national freedom and sovereignty; six times during the past 300 years they have asserted it in arms. Standing on that fundamental right and again asserting it in arms in the face of the world, we hereby proclaim the Irish Republic as a sovereign independent state, and we pledge our lives and the lives of our comrades-in-arms to the cause of its freedom, of its welfare, and of its exaltation among the nations.

The Irish republic is entitled to, and hereby claims, the allegiance of every Irishman and Irishwoman. The republic guarantees religious and civil liberty, equal rights and equal opportunities to all its citizens, and declares its resolve to pursue the happiness and prosperity of the whole nation and of all its parts, cherishing all the children of the nation equally, and oblivious of the differences carefully fostered by an alien government, which have divided a minority from the majority in the past.

Until our arms have brought the opportune moment for the establishment of a permanent national government, representative of the whole people of Ireland, and elected by the suffrages of all her men and women, the provisional government, hereby constituted, will administer the civil and military affairs of the republic in trust for the people. We place the cause of the Irish republic under the protection of the Most High God, whose blessing we invoke upon our arms, and we pray that no one who serves that cause will dishonour it by cowardice, inhumanity or rapine. In this supreme hour the Irish nation must, by its valour and discipline, and by the readiness of its children to sacrifice themselves for the common good, prove itself worthy of the august destiny to which it is called.

Signed on behalf of the provisional government,
Thomas J. Clarke, Sean MacDiarmada, Thomas MacDonagh, P. H. Pearse, Eamonn Ceannt, James Connolly, Joseph Plunkett

•

CLIFFORD ALLEN
1917

'The denial of liberty'

Clifford Allen (1889–1939), who helped found the Daily Citizen, *was also one of the founders of the No-Conscription Fellowship in November 1914, and its first chairman. He was granted exemption, conditional on undertaking work of national importance. He did not comply, and was arrested on 31 July 1916. After serving 112 days' hard labour and six months' labour, he was sentenced to a further two years' hard labour and returned to prison.*

This extract is from his defence at his third court martial.

I am not a Christian in the accepted sense of any denomination. I am a Socialist. I have before previous courts martial stated my belief that the method of warfare is socially and morally wrong, whatever the pretext for which it may be adopted.

But in addition to this belief I wish to make it clear that I cannot take any share in military work in this war, because I believe there is no substantial reason to prevent peace negotiations being entered upon at once. I believe that you sitting here and the *peoples* of all nations on both sides are yearning for peace. I believe that the *governments* of all nations are too afraid of releasing their peoples to make peace.

A Cabinet minister has stated officially that so far in this war 7 million human beings have been killed in all the nations and 45 million wounded. The question every citizen has to consider is:

'*Will there be such a supreme difference between peace now and peace in, say, two years' time as to justify the supreme sacrifice of say another 7 million lives?*'

I submit that the difference will prove so trivial in comparison with the sacrifice involved that the peoples of all the nations will look back with amazement when they come to realize how the governments permitted and instigated this sacrifice to achieve so small a result.

The issue of territorial adjustment could be settled round a table tomorrow. The only other problem is the crushing of German military tyranny. On this point I am, as a Socialist, united with my own nation and government in desiring to overthrow German autocracy, but I differ from my government in contending that the only way of securing this object is through the medium of peace. While the war continues and the German nation thinks itself in danger, the German Government will be successful in persuading the people to support it. Remove this menace by the establishment of peace, and the German democracy will at once assert itself, and, remembering the example of Russia, overthrow Kaiserism and all that it stands for.

Thus it seems to me that the postponement of peace, with the consequent certainty of enormous sacrifice of life, will not make any appreciable difference in territorial and similar peace terms, but will, in fact, delay the achievement of the really important object of the Allied Powers, namely, the overthrow of German militarism and Prussian autocracy.

I will not take any part in a war which I believe could be brought to so immediate and satisfactory a conclusion.

Such being my attitude to all war, and to this war, I can, of course, in no way acquiesce in conscription, which is designed to equip the nation for war. I have an additional reason for this. I shall continue in prison to refuse every offer of release which demands from me any sort of acceptance of conditions which originate in conscription, even though they may be of a civil character. I resist war because I love liberty. Conscription is the denial of liberty.

If I hold that war and militarism are evils which will only cease when men have the courage to stand apart from them, I should be false to my own belief if I avoided the dangers of military service only to accept some safe civil work as a condition of exemption from such service.

This country is faced with the most insidious danger that can confront a free people in the claim of the state to dispose of a man's life against his will, and what is worse, against his moral convictions, and of his service without his consent. A war which you can only win by the compulsion of unwilling men and the persecution of those who are genuine will ultimately achieve the ruin of the very ideals for which you are fighting.

You can shut me up in prison over and over again, but you cannot imprison my free spirit. The duty of every citizen is to serve his fellow-men. In all humility I believe I am being faithful to this obligation of citizenship by pursuing my present policy.

•

FRANCIS MEYNELL
1917

'Starving at the Ritz'

The Daily Herald *did not identify the writer who dined at the Ritz on 20 November 1917 and whose report, with the menu in full, was splashed across the front page as part of the paper's campaign against the inequality of sacrifice between the rich and the poor. The writer was Francis Meynell (1891–1975), one of the* Herald's *brightest talents. 'The words "No Tea", "No Sugar", "No Margarine", "No Butter" have become quite familiar to the soldiers' wives and children,' said a* Herald *editorial comment. 'They know that the rich and well-to-do are not compelled to wait in queues for hours on end. No, their supplies arrive regularly, like manna from on high.'*

A *Herald* representative dined at the Ritz on 20 November. His job was to see for himself, and for the readers of this paper, how the patriotic rich had 'tightened their belts', how thin the fare had become, how the grim tragedy of the war had affected the proudest heritage of our race – or, as the proverb says, an 'Englishman's kitchen is his castle'.

The menu tells a story, but not the full story. Those of our readers whose hearts go out in sympathy to the Fat Man on account of these deplorably short commons will be relieved to hear that it is possible to supplement the menu almost at will. The *Herald* representative, having heard some nonsense about the shortage of milk, is now able to reassure the world living east of — that the whole thing is a myth – invented no doubt by the crafty Germans or the pacifist Bolos. For we demanded whipped cream to add to our soup – and a bowl was produced; a cream sauce was served with the fish; cream flowed plentifully over the *macédoine de fruits*; and a jug of cream came with our coffee. Moreover, that providence which puts us all in our places has made wheat to grow accordingly. The *Herald* representative managed to eat four rolls himself – and there would have been no difficulty in obtaining more if he could have swallowed more.

The first course was *hors d'œuvres* – little dishes of sardines, shelled shrimps, eggs mayonnaise, olives, etc. – *a sufficient meal by itself.* The second, a rich soup, for which he ordered – and obtained – the bowl of cream – *almost a meal by itself.* The third course was a generous helping of exquisitely cooked sole, lobster and white wine joining with the cream for its dressing – *an ample meal by itself.* The fourth course was chicken, cooked to a turn. Half a fowl (less

RITZ HOTEL

Carte du Jour – Diner du 20 Novembre 1917

Hors-d'Oeuvre 1/6 p.p.
Saumon Fumé 1/6 p.p.

Natives 4/6 per doz.
Caviar 4/- p.p.

POTAGES.

Petite Marmite 2/- p.p.
Consommé Tapioca 1/- p.p.
Croûte au Pot 1/- p.p.

Crème de Volaille Du Barry 1/6 p.p.
Crème de Petits Pois Frais 1/- p.p.
Julienne au Consommé 1/-

POISSONS.

Suprême de Sole Tout Paris 3/6 p.p.
Turbot Poché, Beurre Fondu 3/ – 5/-
Filet de Sole Murat 3/6 p.p.
Whitebait Diablé 1/6 p.p.
Sole Braisée Bonne Femme 7/-

Mousseline de Merlan au Champagne
2/6 p.p.
Timbale de Homard Américaine
4/ – 7/-
Eperlan à l'Anglaise 2/- p.p.

ENTRÉES.

Suprême de Poulet Jeannette 3/6 p.p.
Jambon d'York au Porto et Epinards
au Velouté 2/6 p.p.
Médaillon de Volaille Gratiné Saint-
Georges 4/6 p.p.
Perdreau à la Crème 10/-

Poulet Reine Poëlé Mascotte
4/6 – 7/-
Ris de Veau Braisé aux Petits Pois
Française 6/-
Tournedos Sauté Madère et Champignons
3/6 p.p.
Double Caille aux Muscats 4/6 p.p.

RÔTIS.

Poulet Reine 12/-
Aylesbury 12/ – 15/-
Bécassine 4/6
Poularde 16/-
Pigeon 5/-

Cailles 4/6 each
Selle d'Agneau,
Faisan 12/-
Perdreaux 8/-
Canard Sauvage 8/-

Bécasse 8/-

LÉGUMES.

Gnocchi 1/6 p.p.
Petits Pois 2/- p.p.
Laitues 1/6 p.p.
Nouilles Fraîches 1/6 p.p.
Haricots Verts 2/- p.p.

Chicorée 1/- p.p.
Tomates 1/6 p.p.
Macaroni 1/- p.p.
Spaghetti 1/- p.p.
Choux-fleurs 1/6 p.p.

Epinards 1/- p.p.

ENTREMETS.

Coeur Glacé Tortoni 2/6 p.p.
Macédoine de Fruits Vendôme 2/6 p.p.
Coupe Jacques 2/- p.p.

Comice Cardinal 2/6 p.p.
Pomme Marguerite 2/- p.p.
Compote Assortie 2/- p.p.

GLACES.
Vanille, Framboises, Cassis 3/6 p.p.

FRUITS

RITZ HOTEL, Piccadilly, W.

its leg, which is, as everyone knows, quite impossible to eat) is served for two persons – *a substantial meal by itself.* To test whether another course of meat would be served and whether one might go outside the narrow limits of the menu, bacon with tomatoes was then ordered. The choice may sound a little odd. Its aesthetic justification, our readers need not be reminded, is as a jerk, a strong division, a contrast between the delicately cooked chicken of the previous course and the charm of the sweet to follow.

Moreover, in other places is there not supposed to be a shortage of bacon? Clearly a mistake. The *Herald* representative had three rashers and three tomatoes to his share – again, *a meal in itself.* Then the *macédoine de fruits.* One did not need sugar, for the Muscat grapes and the Maraschino were effective, if a trifle expensive, substitutes. Here, too, the cream flowed. Coffee, cream and liqueur rounded off a dinner which, with the cheaper champagne (only 14s. a bottle, against the average £1 1s.), fed two people quite respectably for £3 – and paid the tip into the bargain.

These notes will, we hope, put an end to the miserable suspicions entertained by the lower orders that the rich are better off than themselves in wartime. The war, we know, has levelled everyone. If prices are high and food is short down your way, why not 'pig it' at the Ritz?

As we were bowed out of the door we saw, under the arches at the front of the hotel, three old women huddled up in their rags for the night.

•

SIEGFRIED SASSOON
1917

'A soldier's declaration'

As an officer who had won the Military Cross for his bravery at the front in hauling back his wounded men under German fire, the poet Siegfried Sassoon (1886–1967) made the most famous protest of the First World War when he signed his soldier's declaration which Bertrand Russell and John Middleton Murry, the writer and critic, helped him to draft. The second and fourth paragraphs most clearly represent Sassoon's own views. After being treated as a psychiatric patient at Craiglockhart Hospital, Sassoon returned to the front.

I am making this statement as an act of wilful defiance of military authority, because I believe the war is being deliberately prolonged by those who have the power to end it.

I am a soldier, convinced that I am acting on behalf of soldiers. I believe that this war, upon which I entered as a war of defence and liberation, has now become a war of aggression and conquest. I believe that the purposes for which I and my fellow soldiers entered upon this war should have been so clearly stated as to have made it impossible to change them, and that, had this been done, the objects which actuated us would now be attainable by negotiation.

I have seen and endured the suffering of the troops, and I can no longer be a party to prolong these sufferings for ends which I believe to be evil and unjust.

I am not protesting against the conduct of the war, but against the political errors and insincerities for which the fighting men are being sacrificed.

On behalf of those who are suffering now I make this protest against the deception which is being practised on them; also I believe that I may help to destroy the callous complacence with which the majority of those at home regard the continuance of agonies which they do not share, and which they have not sufficient imagination to realize.

•

V. I. LENIN
1917

'Democracy'

The State and the Revolution *was written by Vladimir Ilyich Lenin (1870–1924) in the months immediately preceding the October revolution which swept the Bolsheviks to power and made him the dictator of Russia. The existing state machinery must be 'crushed, smashed to bits, wiped off the face of the earth', Lenin argued, as he emphasized the need for a strong, repressive party state – a dictatorship of the proletariat during the transition to the Communist utopia when the bourgeois state was smashed. There would be no room for capitalistic democracy.*

In capitalist society, providing it develops under the most favourable conditions, we have a more or less complete democracy in the democratic republic. But this democracy is always hemmed in by the narrow limits set by capitalist exploitation, and consequently always remains, in essence, a democracy for the minority, only for the propertied classes, only for the rich. Freedom in capitalist society always remains about the same as it was in the ancient Greek republics: freedom for the slave-owners. Owing to the conditions of capitalist exploitation the modern wage slaves are so crushed by want and poverty that 'they cannot be bothered with democracy', 'they cannot be bothered with politics'; in the ordinary, peaceful course of events the majority of the population is debarred from participation in public and political life . . .

Democracy for an insignificant minority, democracy for the rich – that is the democracy of capitalist society. If we look more closely into the machinery of capitalist democracy, we shall see everywhere, in the 'petty' – supposedly petty – details of the suffrage (residential qualification, exclusion of women, etc.), in the technique of the representative institutions, in the actual obstacles to the right of assembly (public buildings are not for 'beggars'!), in the purely capitalist organization of the daily press, etc., etc. – we shall see restriction after restriction upon democracy. These restrictions, exceptions, exclusions, obstacles for the poor seem slight, especially in the eyes of one who has never known want himself and has never been in close contact with the oppressed classes in their mass life (and nine-tenths, if not ninety-nine hundredths, of the bourgeois publicists and politicians are of this category); but in their sum total these restrictions exclude and squeeze out the poor from politics, from active participation in democracy.

Marx grasped this *essence* of capitalist democracy splendidly, when, in analysing the experience of the Commune, he said that the oppressed are allowed once every few years to decide which particular representatives of the oppressing class shall represent and repress them in parliament!

But from this capitalist democracy – that is inevitably narrow and stealthily pushes aside the poor, and is therefore hypocritical and false to the core – forward development does not proceed simply, directly and smoothly towards 'greater and greater democracy', as conceived by the liberal professors and petty-bourgeois opportunists. No, forward development, i.e. development towards communism, proceeds through the dictatorship of the proletariat, and cannot do otherwise, for the *resistance* of the capitalist exploiters cannot be *broken* by anyone else or in any other way.

And the dictatorship of the proletariat, i.e. the organization of the vanguard of the oppressed as the ruling class for the purpose of suppressing the oppressors, cannot result merely in an expansion of democracy. *Alongside* an immense expansion of democracy, which *for the first time* becomes democracy for the poor, democracy for the people, and not democracy for the moneybags, the dictatorship of the proletariat brings about a series of restrictions on the freedom of the oppressors, the exploiters, the capitalists. We must suppress them in order to free humanity from wage slavery, their resistance must be crushed by force; it is clear that where there is suppression, where there is violence, there is no freedom and no democracy.

Democracy for the vast majority of the people, and suppression by force, i.e. exclusion from democracy, of the exploiters and oppressors of the people – this is the change democracy undergoes during the *transition* from capitalism to communism.

Only in communist society, when the resistance of the capitalists has already been completely crushed, when the capitalists have disappeared, when there are no classes (i.e. when there is no difference between the members of society as regards their relation to the social means of production), *only* then the state 'ceases to exist', and it *'becomes possible to speak of freedom'*. Only then will a really complete democracy become possible and be achieved, a democracy really without any exceptions. And only then will democracy begin to *wither away*, owing to the simple fact that, freed from capitalist slavery, from the untold horrors, savagery, absurdities and infamies of capitalist exploitation, people will gradually *become accustomed* to observing the elementary rules of community life that have been known for centuries and repeated for thousands of years in all copybook maxims; they will become accustomed to observing them without force, without coercion, without subordination, *without the special apparatus* of coercion which is called the state.

The expression 'the state *withers away*' is very well chosen, for it indicates both the gradualness of the process and its spontaneous nature. Only habit can, and undoubtedly will, have such an effect; for we see around us on millions of occasions how readily people become accustomed to observing the rules of community life that are indispensable to them when there is no exploitation, when there is nothing that rouses indignation, evokes protest and revolt and creates the need for *suppression*.

Thus, in capitalist society we have a democracy that is curtailed, wretched, false, a democracy only for the rich, for the minority. The dictatorship of the proletariat, the period of transition to communism, will for the first time create democracy for the people, for the majority, along with the necessary suppression of the minority – the exploiters. Communism alone is capable of giving really complete democracy, and the more complete it is the more quickly will it become unnecessary and wither away of itself.

•

EVADNE PRICE
1918

'Forgive me, Mother'

The parents of the young women – 'England's Splendid Daughters' – who worked at the French front as ambulance drivers had no idea of the horror they experienced nor any wish to know. One of those young women was Winifred Constance Young, who kept a diary which was used by Evadne Price (1896–1985) when she wrote Not So Quiet *under the pseudonym Helen Zenna Smith in 1930. It was intended to be a parody of Erich Remarque's* All Quiet on the Western Front, *but became a memorial to the dead, a pacifist denunciation of the futility of war, based on Winifred Young's experiences in 1918 – which a mother simply could not comprehend.*

Oh, come with me, Mother and Mrs Evans-Mawnington. Let me show you the exhibits straight from the battlefield. This will be something original to tell your committees, while they knit their endless miles of khaki scarves . . . something to spout from the platform at your recruiting meetings. Come with me. Stand just there.

Here we have the convoy gliding into the station now, slowly, so slowly. In a minute it will disgorge its sorry cargo. My ambulance doors are open, waiting to receive. See, the train has stopped. Through the occasionally drawn blinds you will observe the trays slotted into the sides of the train. Look closely, Mother and Mrs Evans-Mawnington, and you shall see what you shall see. Those trays each contain something that was once a whole man . . . the heroes who have done their bit for king and country . . . the heroes who marched blithely through the streets of London town singing 'Tipperary', while you cheered and waved your flags hysterically. They are not singing now, you will observe. Shut your ears, Mother and Mrs Evans-Mawnington, lest their groans and heart-rending cries linger as long in your memory as in the memory of the daughter you sent out to help win the war.

See the stretcher-bearers lifting the trays one by one, slotting them deftly into my ambulance. Out of the way quickly, Mother and Mrs Evans-Mawnington – lift your silken skirts aside . . . a man is spewing blood, the moving has upset him, finished him . . . He will die on the way to hospital if he doesn't die before the ambulance is loaded. I know . . . All this is old history to me. Sorry this has happened. It isn't pretty to see a hero spewing up his life's blood in public, is it? Much more romantic to see him in the picture papers being awarded the VC, even if he is minus a limb or two. A most unfortunate occurrence!

That man strapped down? That raving, blaspheming creature screaming filthy words you don't know the meaning of . . . words your daughter uses in everyday conversation, a habit she has contracted from vulgar contact of this kind. Oh, merely gone mad, Mother and Mrs Evans-Mawnington. He may have seen a headless body running on and on, with blood spurting from the trunk. The crackle of the frost-stiff dead men packing the duck-boards watertight may have gradually undermined his reason. There are many things the sitters tell me on our long night rides that could have done this.

No, not shell-shock. The shell-shock cases take it more quietly as a rule, unless they are suddenly startled. Let me find you an example. Ah, the man they are bringing out now. The one staring straight ahead at nothing . . . twitching, twitching, twitching, each limb working in a different direction, like a Jumping Jack worked by a jerking string. Look at him, both of you. Bloody awful, isn't it, Mother and Mrs Evans-Mawnington? That's shell-shock. If you dropped your handbag on the platform, he would start to rave as madly as the other. What? You won't try the experiment? You can't watch him? Why not? *Why not?* I have to, every night. Why the hell can't you do it for once? Damn your eyes.

Forgive me, Mother and Mrs Evans-Mawnington. That was not the kind of language a nicely-brought-up young lady from Wimbledon Common uses. I forget myself. We will begin again.

See the man they are fitting into the bottom slot. He is coughing badly. No, not pneumonia. Not tuberculosis. Nothing so picturesque. Gently, gently, stretcher-bearers . . . he is about done. He is coughing up clots of pinky-green filth. Only his lungs, Mother and Mrs Evans-Mawnington. He is coughing well tonight. That is gas. You've heard of gas, haven't you? It burns and shrivels the lungs to . . . to the mess you see on the ambulance floor there. He's about the age of Bertie, Mother. Not unlike Bertie, either, with his gentle brown eyes and fair curly hair. Bertie would look up pleadingly like that in between coughing up his lungs . . . The son you have so generously given to the war. The son you are so eager to send out to the trenches before Roy Evans-Mawnington, in case Mrs Evans-Mawnington scores over you at the next recruiting meeting . . . 'I have given my only son.'

Cough, cough, little fair-haired boy. Perhaps somewhere your mother is thinking of you . . . boasting of the life she has so nobly given . . . the life you thought was your own, but which is hers to squander as she thinks fit. 'My boy is not a slacker, thank God.' Cough away, little boy, cough away.

What does it matter, providing your mother doesn't have to face the shame of her son's cowardice?

•

R. H. TAWNEY
1918

'Keep the workers' children in their place'

After 1918 all children received full-time education in free day schools to the age of fourteen. Yet when the Education Bill was passed, the Federation of British Industries objected to the proposal that eight hours a week should be taken within working hours for further education. In this article for the Daily News, *R. H. Tawney (1880–1962) attacked 'the Master Class theory of society' held by those he called 'the Bourbons of industry'.*

While well-known leaders of the cotton industry have been at pains to suggest how the circumstances of their particular trade might be adapted to meet the principle of the Education Bill, the attitude adopted in the Memorandum of the Federation of British Industries is one of frigid opposition to the whole policy of universal continued education. Education, it states, ought not to be extended beyond fourteen, 'until . . . the labour market has adjusted itself to the new conditions'. Of any consciousness, as is felt by an increasing number of employers, that there is an obligation upon those who organize industry to take pains to adapt it to the requirements of education, of any suspicion that fifty-five-and-a-half to sixty hours' labour a week may actually be excessive for children who have just left school, or that to stop education abruptly at fourteen is to stop it when it is just beginning to be most fruitful, or that there is a duty to the higher education to build a better world for all, there is, in this precious document, not a trace. The Bourbons of industry who drafted it have learned nothing and forgotten nothing. Europe is in ruins; and out of the sea of blood and tears the Federation of British Industries emerges jaunty and unabashed, clamouring that whatever else is shaken, the vested interest of employers in the labour of children of fourteen must not be disturbed by so much as eight hours a week.

But it is not merely for economic reasons that the Federation is opposed to higher education for all young persons. It is absolved from the necessity of proving that universal higher education is impossible because it does not really believe that universal higher education is desirable. Behind the objection based on the convenience of industry lies another objection based on the theory that all except a small minority of children are incapable of benefiting by education beyond the age of fourteen. It is not actually stated, indeed, that working-class children, like anthropoid apes, have fewer convolutions in their brains than the children of captains of industry. But the authors of the Memorandum are evidently sceptical as to either the possibility or the desirability of offering higher education to more than a small proportion of them.

In the manner of a European traveller describing a race which is too backward to count up to more than ten, it draws a sharp distinction between 'the more promising' child who is mentally capable of benefiting by higher education, and 'the less promising' child who is not. For the former there is to be full-time secondary education. For the latter there is to be elementary education up to fourteen, part of which, in the last two years of school life – a sinister suggestion – 'might be directly vocational and intended to fit the child for the particular industry which he will enter at fourteen'; and then full-time work in the factory. Nor is it contemplated that the children who are 'mentally capable of profiting by secondary education' will be more than a select minority. In a charming sentence, which reveals in a flash the view which it takes both of the function of the working classes in society and of the meaning of education, the Memorandum enters a solemn caveat against the dangers of excessive education. 'They would very strongly advise that in selecting children for higher education, care should be taken to avoid creating, as was done, for example, in India, a large class of persons *whose education is unsuitable for the employment which they eventually enter.'*

There it is, the whole Master Class theory of society in a sentence! One cannot refute it by argument, as one can refute the Federation's particular prophecies of the industrial disaster which would be caused by a more general diffusion of higher education. For this is not a question of fact, but of ultimate belief, and those who think that men are first of all men have no premise in common with those who think, like the authors of the Federation's Memorandum, that they are first of all servants, or animals, or tools.

One cannot, I say, disprove such a doctrine, any more than one can disprove a taste for militarism, or for drugs, or for bad novels. But one can expose its consequences. And its consequences are simple. They are some new form of slavery. Stripped of its decent draperies of convention, what it means is that education is to be used, not to enable human beings to become themselves through the development of their personalities, nor to strengthen the spirit of social solidarity, nor to prepare men for the better service of their fellows, nor to raise the general level of society; but to create a new commercial aristocracy, based on the selection for higher education of 'the more promising' children of working-class parents from among the vulgar mass, who are fit only to serve as the cannon-fodder of capitalist industry.

•

JOHN MAYNARD KEYNES/
COUNT BROCKDORFF-RANTZAU
1919

'Reparations'

John Maynard Keynes (1883–1946), one of the greatest economists of the century, represented the British Treasury at the 1919 Versailles Peace Conference. He resigned over the issue of German reparations and made his case against the Versailles settlement in the prophetic work The Economic Consequences of the Peace. *It was his view that neither Lloyd George nor Woodrow Wilson understood that the perils of the future lay not in frontiers or sovereignties but in food, coal and transport. The economic burden on Germany was impossibly high, would ensure economic privation and social upheaval and even prevent lasting peace in Europe.*

   This extract incorporates the protest delivered on behalf of Germany at the conference by Count Brockdorff-Rantzau.

The policy of reducing Germany to servitude for a generation, of degrading the lives of millions of human beings, and of depriving a whole nation of happiness should be abhorrent and detestable – abhorrent and detestable, even if it were possible, even if it enriched ourselves, even if it did not sow the decay of the whole civilized life of Europe. Some preach it in the name of justice. In the great events of man's history, in the unwinding of the complex fates of nations, justice is not so simple. And if it were, nations are not authorized, by religion or by natural morals, to visit on the children of their enemies the misdoings of parents or of rulers . . .

   The essential facts of the situation, as I see them, are expressed simply. Europe consists of the densest aggregation of population in the history of the world. This population is accustomed to a relatively high standard of life, in which, even now, some sections of it anticipate improvement rather than deterioration. In relation to other continents Europe is not self-sufficient; in particular it cannot feed itself. Internally the population is not evenly distributed, but much of it is crowded into a relatively small number of dense industrial centres. This population secured for itself a livelihood before the war, without much margin of surplus, by means of a delicate and immensely complicated organization, of which the foundations were supported by coal, iron, transport, and an unbroken supply of imported food and raw materials from other continents. By the destruction of this organization and the interruption of the stream of supplies, a part of this population is deprived of its means of livelihood. Emigration is not open to the redundant surplus. For it would take years to transport them overseas, even, which is not the case, if countries could be found which were ready to receive them. The danger confronting us, therefore, is the rapid depression of the standard of life of the European populations to a point which will mean actual starvation for some (a point already reached in Russia and approximately reached in Austria). Men will not always die quietly. For starvation, which brings to some lethargy and a helpless despair, drives other temperaments to the nervous instability of hysteria and to a mad despair. And these in their distress may overturn the remnants of organization, and submerge civilization itself in their attempts to satisfy desperately the overwhelming needs of the individual. This is the danger against which all our resources and courage and idealism must now co-operate.

On 13 May 1919 Count Brockdorff-Rantzau addressed to the Peace Conference of the Allied and Associated Powers the report of the German Economic Commission charged with the study of the effect of the conditions of peace on the situation of the German population. 'In the course of the last two generations,' the commission reported, 'Germany has become transformed from an agricultural state to an industrial state. So long as she was an agricultural state, Germany could feed 40 million inhabitants. As an industrial state she could ensure the means of subsistence for a population of 67 million: and in 1913 the importation of food-stuffs amounted, in round figures, to 12 million tons. Before the war a total of 15 million persons in Germany provided for their existence by foreign trade, navigation, and the use, directly or indirectly, of foreign raw material.' After rehearsing the main relevant provisions of the Peace Treaty the report continues: 'After this diminution of her products, after the economic depression resulting from the loss of her colonies, her merchant fleet and her foreign investments, Germany will not be in a position to import from abroad an adequate quantity of raw material. An enormous part of German industry will, therefore, be condemned inevitably to destruction. The need of importing food-stuffs will increase considerably at the same time that the possibility of satisfying this demand is as greatly diminished. In a very short time, therefore, Germany will not be in a position to give bread and work to her numerous millions of inhabitants, who are prevented from earning their livelihood by navigation and trade. These persons should emigrate, but this is a material impossibility, all the more because many countries and the most important ones will oppose any German immigration. To put the peace conditions into execution would logically involve, therefore, the loss of several millions of persons in Germany. This catastrophe would not be long in coming about, seeing that the health of the population has been broken down during the war by the blockade, and during the armistice by the aggravation of the blockade of famine. No help, however great, or over however long a period it were continued, could prevent these deaths *en masse*.

'We do not know, and indeed we doubt,' the report concludes, 'whether the delegates of the Allied and Associated Powers realize the inevitable consequences which will take place if Germany, an industrial state, very thickly populated, closely bound up with the economic system of the world, and under the necessity of importing enormous quantities of raw material and food-stuffs, suddenly finds herself pushed back to the phase of her development which corresponds to her economic condition and the numbers of her population as they were half a century ago. Those who sign this treaty will sign the death sentence of many millions of German men, women and children.'

I know of no adequate answer to these words. The indictment is at least as true of the Austrian, as of the German, settlement. This is the fundamental problem in front of us, before which questions of territorial adjustment and the balance of European power are insignificant. Some of the catastrophes of past history, which have thrown back human progress for centuries, have been due to the reactions following on the sudden termination, whether in the course of nature or by the act of man, of temporarily favourable conditions which have permitted the growth of population beyond what could be provided for when the favourable conditions were at an end.

•

RABINDRANATH TAGORE
1919

'A degradation not fit for human beings'

The massacre at Amritsar in 1919 when General Dyer opened fire on an unarmed Indian crowd and killed 379 people was the decisive moment when Indians were alienated from British rule. Mahatma Gandhi responded with a new political weapon: civil disobedience – but was so shocked by the violence it provoked that he suspended the campaign.

The poet and philosopher Rabindranath Tagore (1861–1941), the first Asian to win the Nobel Prize (for literature) in 1913, felt that he had to act. He travelled to Calcutta but found that no politician was prepared to risk his career by chairing a public meeting. So he made his own solitary protest in this letter to the viceroy, Lord Chelmsford – the first public protest by a prominent Indian against the massacre that ended the Raj.

The enormity of the measures taken by the Government in the Punjab for quelling some local disturbances has, with a rude shock, revealed to our minds the helplessness of our position as British subjects in India. The disproportionate severity of the punishments inflicted upon the unfortunate people and the methods of carrying them out, we are convinced, are without parallel in the history of civilized governments, barring some conspicuous exceptions, recent and remote. Considering that such treatment has been meted out to a population, disarmed and resourceless, by a power which has the most terribly efficient organization for destruction of human lives, we must strongly assert that it can claim no political expediency, far less moral justification. The accounts of insults and sufferings undergone by our brothers in the Punjab have trickled through the gagged silence, reaching every corner of India, and the universal agony of indignation roused in the hearts of our people has been ignored by our rulers – possibly congratulating themselves for what they imagine as salutary lessons. This callousness has been praised by most of the Anglo-Indian papers, which have in some cases gone to the brutal length of making fun of our sufferings, without receiving the least check from the same authority – relentlessly careful in smothering every cry of pain and expression of judgement from the organs representing the sufferers. Knowing that our appeals have been in vain and that the passion of vengeance is blinding the nobler vision of statesmanship in our Government, which could so easily afford to be magnanimous as befitting its physical strength and moral tradition, the very least I can do for my country is to take all consequences upon myself in giving voice to the protest of millions of my countrymen, surprised into a dumb anguish of terror. The time has come when badges of honour make our shame glaring in their incongruous context of humiliation, and I for my part wish to stand, shorn of all special distinctions, by the side of those of my countrymen, who, for their so-called insignificance, are liable to suffer a degradation not fit for human beings.

These are the reasons which have painfully compelled me to ask Your Excellency, with due deference and regret, to relieve me of my title of Knighthood, which I had the honour to accept from His Majesty the King

at the hands of your predecessor, for whose nobleness of heart I still entertain
great admiration.

•

THE NATION
1920

'The "Black and Tans"'

*The British response to the guerrilla struggle waged by the Irish Republican Army in 1920
was the recruitment of the equally deadly paramilitary force, the 'Black and Tans', brutal
mercenaries who became a terror squad. Their tactics were endorsed by the Lloyd George
government. 'Things are being done in Ireland,' said Asquith, 'which would disgrace the
blackest annals of the lowest despotism in Europe.' The brutality of the 'Black and Tans'
alienated liberal opinion from Lloyd George, as is shown in this denunciation of him in*
The Nation, *Britain's most influential weekly journal of liberal opinion.*

Is the British Government to lose its place among the civilized governments
of the world, and to sink under their odium and contempt? That and nothing
less is the question on which the British people have to make up their minds.

For every hour this barbarian force remains in existence, the British
Government remains outside the civilized order. It can say nothing about
Lenin's Chinese executioners. It can call in the famous report on the Belgian
atrocities, and ask Lord Bryce to make a public apology to Germany for the
rude things he said about her soldiers. For it has come to this, that we have
raised a mercenary force in England – it being no longer possible to recruit
for the RIC in Ireland – among demobilized officers out of a job, that we
give these men a sovereign a day with their keep, and let them understand,
by one kind of *sous-entendu* or another, that as soon as they find themselves
on the other side of the Irish Sea they may kill, wound, burn and loot as they
please.

It needs no special insight to tell us that men recruited under these
circumstances for such a job are the last men in the world to be trusted with
this horrible discretion over the lives of men and women. Among the millions
who went through the war there are left idle at this moment a number of
reckless and desperate men, accustomed to its excitement and barbarism,
who find settled life forbidding, and for such men paid lawlessness in Ireland
has greater attractions than any prospects of adventure that offer themselves
at home. The government have deliberately recruited for service in Ireland

a body of men to whom Ireland means nothing more than the opportunity for violence presented in any occupied enemy country, and having recruited such a body they allow it or encourage it to become what such a force became in Russia. They are called the 'Black and Tans'. But their real name is the 'Black Hundreds'.

This is nothing less than the deliberate overthrow of the civilized order and the proclamation of anarchy as God and law. It is a return to primitive times and primitive habits. If we do not owe the Irish people over whom we assert our rule this elementary security, what in heaven's name do we owe them? Is there any obligation of government more simple in any society that pretends to civilization? Thucydides, who did not write yesterday, remarked as an interesting fact that even in his day there were parts of Greece where men kept arms because their homes were not safe. In this year of grace, six years after we went to war to strike one last victorious blow for liberty and the rights of man, the Irishman's home is in such danger night and day, from men enlisted by the government whose wages he is taxed to pay, that he has every reason for sleeping with a revolver under his pillow. Within four hours' sail of London, England rules after the manner of the conquering hordes of the East who held by the sword and the sword alone. There is a great deal of horror-stricken talk about revolutionaries and Bolshevism, but no preacher of direct action ever asserted a doctrine that challenges, as this does, the fundamental character of our society and all civilized society. For the personal rights of the citizen, guaranteed and upheld by impartial law, are more important and more elementary than any political rights exercised through Parliament. A man might want to get rid of Parliament and yet deny altogether this doctrine that a ruler owes no allegiance to the common law, and that he can make as free with the lives and property of his subjects as any Eastern despot. Such is the lesson that our rulers are teaching those revolutionaries of whom they profess such fear. Lenin himself is not a more eloquent apostle of the law that those persons only have rights who have the power to enforce them.

This state of things has a special significance for us because of one thing over which Englishmen have been more jealous in the past than the people of any other country, and that is the claim of the official to override or escape the common law. *Le droit administratif* has never been acclimatized here. Whereas in most continental countries the legality of official acts is tested in administrative courts, in England minister and official take their chance with the private citizen in the ordinary courts. The supremacy of the civil law is acknowledged in text-books on martial law, and this is regarded as a special recognition of a general doctrine held of great account by Englishmen.

Therefore we take a full stride towards anarchy when we allow a government to declare that men may commit criminal acts, if they belong to this force, without liability in the civil court and without the risk of punishment in a military one. This is to claim a greater and more barbarous latitude for the RIC than the worst claim made by Germany and hotly denied by us. Germany claimed the right to shoot civilians in occupied Belgium and France in punishment for the acts of individual Frenchmen or Belgians, or as a piece of frightfulness to terrorize. Germany was at war with France and Belgium. The government claim the right to act in Ireland precisely as Germany acted in Belgium and France. But they have never proclaimed war on Ireland or asked Parliament to sanction such an enterprise. If this claim is tolerated now, where is it to stop? Today it is the peasants of Balbriggan or Fermoy who watch their homes burn, while their children cry in the street from terror of bayonet and bomb. Whose turn will it be tomorrow? There is no reason why Mr George's government, seizing the occasion of an unpopular or a violent strike, should not let loose such a force in this country.

Where are our public men today? Mr Asquith and his colleagues are men with great responsibilities not only by reason of their standing in the country but also because they have all played a part in the problem of Irish liberty, and none of them is free from blame for its utter discomfiture.

It is plain humanity in which the Liberal leaders are wanting. Were Sir Henry Campbell-Bannerman alive, a single speech on the methods of barbarism would rally the conscience of the nation. Were Mr Gladstone alive, the country would ring with his indictment, and no government could maintain this nefarious course for twenty-four hours. Today the British people have no taste for their bloody work, but the leaders, Labour and Liberal, give no expression to the indignation and concern of the majority of the people.

Are the murders and burnings of Fermoy, Tuam, Balbriggan, Trim, Mallow, and scores of towns and villages, are the midnight raids on houses from which men and boys are taken to be bayoneted and shot at the caprice of this or that scoundrel in uniform, are the evictions of hundreds of peasants at the point of the bayonet, are all the hideous methods of terrorism and espionage known to a political police bidden by its employers to forget the law – are these methods repugnant or not to 'the humanity and the justice and the democratic principles of the English people'? If they are, let public men speak out, for at present it looks as if we were bent on bringing on ourselves a worse reproach than Germany earned in 1914 when she went into a great crime almost without a protest. The German politicians had at least the excuse that their country was at war. That is a bad excuse, but it is better than any that Englishmen will find for their silence today.

•

EDWIN MONTAGU
1920

'Racial humiliation'

The massacre at Amritsar in 1919, when General Dyer opened fire on an unarmed Indian crowd and killed 379 people, was the decisive moment when Indians were alienated from British rule. Mahatma Gandhi responded with a new political weapon: civil disobedience.

The British Secretary for India was Edwin Montagu (1879–1924). When Dyer was effectively dismissed from the army, his British champions raised his case in Parliament. They wanted Montagu's head. Supported by Winston Churchill, Secretary for War, Montagu refused to yield to his critics and castigated Dyer for the 'racial humiliation' he had inflicted at Amritsar.

The real issue can be stated in one sentence, and I will content myself by asking the House one question. If an officer justifies his conduct, no matter how gallant his record is – and everybody knows how gallant General Dyer's record is – by saying that there was no question of undue severity, that if his means had been greater the casualties would have been greater, and that the motive was to teach a moral lesson to the whole of the Punjab, I say without hesitation, and I would ask the Committee to contradict me if I am wrong, because the whole matter turns upon this, that it is the doctrine of terrorism.

If you agree to that, you justify everything that General Dyer did. Once you are entitled to have regard neither to the intentions nor to the conduct of a particular gathering, and to shoot and to go on shooting, with all the horrors that were here involved, in order to teach somebody else a lesson, you are embarking upon terrorism, to which there is no end. I say, further, that when you pass an order that all Indians, whoever they may be, must crawl past a particular place, when you pass an order to say that all Indians, whoever they may be, must forcibly or voluntarily salaam any officer of His Majesty the King, you are enforcing racial humiliation. I say, thirdly, that when you take selected schoolboys from a school, guilty or innocent, and whip them publicly, when you put up a triangle, where an outrage which we all deplore and which all India deplores has taken place, and whip people who have not been convicted, when you flog a wedding party, you are indulging in frightfulness, and there is no other adequate word which could describe it. If the Committee follows me on these three assertions, this is the choice and this is the question which the Committee has put to it today before coming to an answer. Dismiss from your mind, I beg of you, all personal questions. I have been pursued for the last three months, I have been pursued throughout my association by some people and by some journals with personal attack. I do not propose to answer them today. Are you going to keep your hold upon India by terrorism, racial humiliation and subordination, and frightfulness, or are you going to rest it upon the goodwill, and the growing goodwill, of the people of your Indian Empire?

I believe that to be the whole question at issue. If you decide in favour of the latter course, well, then you have got to enforce it. It is no use one session passing a great Act of Parliament which, whatever its merits or demerits proceeded on the principle of partnership for India in the British Commonwealth, and then allowing your administration to depend upon terrorism. You have got to act in every department, civil and military, unintermittently upon a desire to recognize India as a partner in your Commonwealth. You have got to safeguard your administration on the principles of that order passed by the British Parliament. You have got to revise any obsolete ordinance or law which infringes the principles of liberty which you have inculcated into the educated classes in India. That is your one chance – to adhere to the decision that you put into your legislation when you are criticizing administration. There is the other choice – to hold India by the sword, to recognize terrorism as part of your weapon, as part of your armament, to guard British honour and British life with callousness about Indian honour and Indian life. India is on your side in enforcing order. Are you on India's side in ensuring that order is enforced in accordance with the canons of modern love of liberty in the British democracy? There has been no criticism of any officer, however drastic his action was, in any province outside the Punjab. There were thirty-seven instances of firing during the terribly dangerous disturbances of last year. The Government of India and His Majesty's Government have approved thirty-six cases and only censured one. They censured one because, however good the motive, they believe that it infringed the principle which has always animated the British Army.

The great objection to terrorism, the great objection to the rule of force, is that you pursue it without regard to the people who suffer from it, and that having once tried it you must go on. Every time an incident happens you are confronted with the increasing animosity of the people who suffer, and there is no end to it until the people in whose name we are governing India, the people of this country, and the national pride and sentiment of the Indian people rise together in protest and terminate your rule in India as being impossible on modern ideas of what an empire means. There is an alternative policy which I assumed office to commend to this House and which this House has supported until today. It is to put the coping stone on the glorious work which England has accomplished in India by leading India to a complete free partnership in the British Commonwealth, to say to India: 'We hold British lives sacred, but we hold Indian lives sacred, too. We want to safeguard British honour by protecting and safeguarding Indian honour, too. Our institutions shall be gradually perfected while protection is afforded to you and ourselves against revolution and anarchy in order that they may commend themselves to you.'

There is a theory abroad on the part of those who have criticised His Majesty's Government upon this issue that an Indian is a person who is tolerable so long as he will obey your orders, but if once he joins the educated classes, if once he thinks for himself, if once he takes advantage of the educational facilities which you have provided for him, if once he imbibes the ideas of individual liberty which are dear to the British people, why then you class him as an educated Indian and as an agitator. What a terrible and cynical verdict on the whole!

There is another theory, that of partnership, and I am trying to justify the theory endorsed by this House last year. I am suggesting to this Committee that the Act of Parliament is useless unless you enforce it both in the keeping of order and in administration. I am trying to avoid any discussion of details which do not, to my mind, affect that broad issue. I am going to submit to this House this question, on which I would suggest with all respect they should vote: Is your theory of domination or rule in India the ascendancy of one race over another, of domination and subordination – [HON. MEMBERS: 'No!'] – or is your theory that of partnership? If you are applying domination as your theory, then it follows that you must use the sword with increasing severity – [HON. MEMBERS: 'No!'] – until you are driven out of the country by the united opinion of the civilized world. [*Interruption*. An HON. MEMBER: 'Bolshevism!'] If your theory is justice and partnership, then you will condemn a soldier, however gallant, who says that there was no question of undue severity, and that he was teaching a moral lesson to the whole Punjab. That condemnation, as I said at the beginning, has been meted out by everybody, civil and military, who has considered this question. Nobody ever suggested, no Indian has suggested, as far as I know, no reputable Indian has suggested, any punishment, any vindictiveness, or anything more than the repudiation of the principles upon which General Dyer acted. I invite this House to choose, and I believe that the choice they make is fundamental to a continuance of the British Empire, and vital to the continuation, permanent as I believe it can be, to the connection between this country and India.

•

HO CHI MINH
1920

'Oppression'

The Vietnamese political leader Ho Chi Minh (1892–1969) worked in London and the United States from 1912 until he moved to France in 1918. At the eighteenth National Congress of the French Socialist Party at Tours in December 1920, speaking as the delegate from Indo-China, he sided with the left wing and approved the resolution to found the French Communist Party and join the Third International.

I come here with deep sadness to speak as a member of the Socialist Party, against the imperialists who have committed abhorrent crimes on my native land.

French imperialism entered Indo-China half a century ago. In its selfish interests, it conquered our country with bayonets. Since then we have not only been oppressed and exploited shamelessly, but also tortured and poisoned pitilessly. We have been poisoned with opium, alcohol, etc. I cannot, in some minutes, reveal all the atrocities that the predatory capitalists have inflicted on Indo-China. Prisons outnumber schools and are always overcrowded with detainees. Any natives having socialist ideas are arrested and sometimes murdered without trial. Such is the so-called justice in Indo-China. In that country, the Vietnamese are discriminated against, they do not enjoy safety like Europeans or those having European citizenship. We have neither freedom of press nor freedom of speech. Even freedom of assembly and freedom of association do not exist. We have no right to live in other countries or to go abroad as tourists. We are forced to live in utter ignorance and obscurity because we have no right to study. In Indo-China the colonialists find all ways and means to force us to smoke opium and drink alcohol to poison and exploit us. Thousands of Vietnamese have been led to a slow death or massacred to protect other people's interests.

Comrades, such is the treatment inflicted upon more than 20 million

Vietnamese, that is more than half the population of France. And they are said to be under French protection! The Socialist Party must act practically to support the oppressed natives.

•

MARIE STOPES
1921

'*Birth control*'

Married Love, *published in 1918, was the product of Marie Stopes's mission to free women from the ignorance of sex which had made her own first marriage so unhappy. It was an instant success. By 1924, 400,000 copies had been sold, as well as 300,000 of its successor,* Wise Parenthood, *a guide to contraception. Stopes (1880–1958) transformed British attitudes to sex. Although attacked by churches, politicians and the press, she opened her Mothers' Clinic for Constructive Birth Control, which gave free contraceptive advice, in north London in 1921.*

When Stopes sought the backing of Lloyd George, he urged her to show she had the support of the public: 'Hold great meetings. There has never been a really respectable great meeting on the subject.' She made this speech at the meeting she organized at London's Queen's Hall. It was packed.

Sometimes those who feel intensely with me, yet shrink from doing anything for the poor mothers, because they think that by so helping them young girls and others will learn methods of birth control and may thus be sent downhill on a life they ought not to embark upon. So I want to make it clear once and for all that such an idea must not be allowed to hinder us. One of the very first experiences in the Birth Control Clinic was a strong case to show how misguided that would be. The second person who came to my clinic when it was first opened came on behalf of a girl of twenty who was pregnant for the sixth time! And every previous time she had had an abortion performed by her own mother! We, of course, had no help for that girl. We cannot deal with such cases. Yet it shows that in that terrible underworld of misery and anguish which we selfish, self-centred, lazy people so seldom visualize and understand, there *is* already 'knowledge' of a kind. 'Knowledge' is going round which is utterly detrimental, utterly unwholesome and tragic in its effects. The true knowledge which we are bringing to counteract that is clean and wholesome, and is pure physiological information to replace the miserable half-knowledge which already exists.

Then, too, another aspect of my Birth Control Clinic is lit up by the fact that by the word 'control' I mean CONTROL. It is extraordinary how the words 'birth control' have become associated with a negative and repressive movement. Now, in my opinion, control consists in being able to go uphill just as well as to go downhill; to turn to the right as well as to the left. I will tell you the story of one woman who came a fortnight ago.

She was one of the type that certain clergymen in their pulpits would refer to as 'those wicked women who refuse maternity'. All through her marriage she had openly declared she did not want children. But to me she came for help and said: 'I have been married seventeen years and have not had a child.' I asked her whether she wished she had one and she said: 'Of course, *of course* I want a child, but I've never told anyone; I pretend that I do not want one because I can't get it,' and then she cried, and exclaimed: 'I would give my life, and suffer any torture to have a child.' We gave her information which I think will help, and I hope that in about nine months there may be a clinic baby in that home . . .

Another incredible thing is the general lack of knowledge about sex and all the wonderful and beautiful mysteries of marriage. The extent of this ignorance is extraordinary. Do you know we had five cases of people married for years, and in each case the husband has not known how to play his part, and the wife is still a virgin and she wonders why she does not have a child! . . .

We have already today sufficient sound physiological knowledge to, from this moment (if one could only get everyone to know of it), check the birth of every diseased, unhealthy, unprepared-for child. We really can stem at the source this incessant stream of misery which is always greater than our resources can deal with.

How great this misery, and how great the expense of it is to our race, can be found by reading a few of these Blue-books. You could very advantageously spend a few shillings at Imperial House, Kingsway, buying reports in regard to prisons, costs of maintenance of schools of detention for the feeble-minded, asylums for the blind, schools for the defective, and so forth. Surely it is far better to spend the money on healthy, happy children who cost us far less per head than the wastrels! [*Applause.*] To get rid of the wastrels in a Christian way we must see that they are not born.

Beyond this, this ideal which I present is not *merely* that we shall be simply healthy people and have only healthy children born; it is further that we shall consciously step forward to a greater potentiality of health, beauty, happiness and understanding of life. An old false idea, which early got incorporated into Christianity, is that the enjoyment of beauty and a sex life in marriage was a wrong, or at any rate a lesser thing than the ascetic and repressed life.

That idea is now doing us infinite harm. It is a lower and baser ideal which was suited to the earlier stages of evolution, but we have now passed through the stages of human evolution, when that idea is of any further use. The ideal which humanity today needs is the ideal of a full joyous life of real understanding, coupled with control, and with the full use of every beautiful aspect of the life of man and woman together . . .

I absolutely deny that the so-called 'self-control' which consists of the ascetic repressing of mutual love between man and woman is a high ideal. It was a temporary ideal suited to a phase of life in which there was no scientific knowledge. I now say quite clearly that the truest and a far higher ideal is for a man and woman to love each other profoundly as a pair of individuals, and to benefit by that love and interchange which each needs from the other. And at the same time, but as a separate conscious act, to create only those children for which they have sufficient means, sufficient love and sufficient health. That is to say, that married lovers should play the part of parents *only* when they can add individuals of value to the race.

•

MAHATMA GANDHI
1922

'Non-violence'

Still regarded in India as a saint and martyr, Mahatma Gandhi (1869–1948) was a miracle worker, says Lawrence James, the historian of the British Raj: 'He took on the Goliath of the British Raj and overcame it through his own interior moral strength: humility and rectitude proved more than a match for arrogance and armed might.'

Gandhi became leader of the Indian National Congress in 1920 and the party adopted his programme of Satyagraha, non-violent non-cooperation. As he travelled through India in support of his campaign, often addressing meetings of more than 100,000 people, he was constantly shadowed by the police. But it was not until 1922 that he was arrested and charged with sedition for three articles in his magazine Young India.

At his trial at Ahmadabad Gandhi pleaded guilty. When asked if he wished to speak on the question of his sentence, Gandhi said he would make a statement which he read to the court after making a few introductory remarks.

Non-violence is the first article of my faith. It is also the last article of my creed. But I had to make my choice. I had either to submit to a system which I considered had done an irreparable harm to my country, or incur the risk of the mad fury of my people bursting forth, when they understood the truth from my lips. I know that my people have sometimes gone mad. I am deeply sorry for it and I am therefore here to submit not to a light penalty but to the highest penalty. I do not ask for mercy. I do not plead any extenuating act. I am here, therefore, to invite and cheerfully submit to the highest penalty that can be inflicted upon me for what in law is a deliberate crime and what appears to me to be the highest duty of a citizen. The only course open to you, the judge, is, as I am just going to say in my statement, either to resign your post, or inflict on me the severest penalty, if you believe that the system and law you are assisting to administer are good for the people. I do not expect that kind of conversion, but by the time I have finished with my statement, you will perhaps have a glimpse of what is raging within my breast to run this maddest risk which a sane man can run.

Gandhi then read his statement to the court:

I owe it perhaps to the Indian public and to the public in England to placate which this prosecution is mainly taken up that I should explain why from a staunch loyalist and cooperator I have become an uncompromising disaffec-tionist and non-cooperator. To the court too I should say why I plead guilty to the charge of promoting disaffection towards the government established by law in India.

My public life began in 1893 in South Africa, in troubled weather. My first contact with British authority in that country was not of a happy character. I discovered that as a man and an Indian I had no rights. More correctly, I discovered that I had no rights as a man, because I was an Indian.

But I was not baffled. I thought that this treatment of Indians was an excrescence upon a system that was intrinsically and mainly good. I gave the government my voluntary and hearty co-operation, criticizing it freely where I felt it was faulty but never wishing its destruction.

Consequently when the existence of the empire was threatened in 1899 by the Boer challenge, I offered my services to it, raised a volunteer ambulance corps and served at several actions that took place for the relief of Ladysmith. Similarly in 1906, at the time of the Zulu revolt, I raised a stretcher-bearer party and served till the end of the 'rebellion'. On both these occasions I received medals and was even mentioned in dispatches. For my work in South Africa I was given by Lord Hardinge a Kaisar-i-Hind Gold Medal. When the war broke out in 1914 between England and Germany, I raised a volunteer ambulance corps in London consisting of the then resident Indians in London, chiefly students. Its work was acknowledged by the authorities to be valuable. Lastly, in India, when a special appeal was made at the War

Conference in Delhi in 1918 by Lord Chelmsford for recruits, I struggled at the cost of my health to raise a corps in Kheda and the response was being made when the hostilities ceased and orders were received that no more recruits were wanted. In all these efforts at service I was actuated by the belief that it was possible by such services to gain a status of full equality in the empire for my countrymen.

The first shock came in the shape of the Rowlatt Act, a law designed to rob the people of all real freedom. I felt called upon to lead an intensive agitation against it. Then followed the Punjab horrors beginning with the massacre at Jallianwala Bagh and culminating in crawling orders, public floggings and other indescribable humiliations. I discovered too that the plighted word of the Prime Minister to the Mussulmans of India regarding the integrity of Turkey and the holy places of Islam was not likely to be fulfilled. But in spite of the forebodings and the grave warnings of friends, at the Amritsar Congress in 1919, I fought for cooperation in working the Montagu-Chelmsford reforms, hoping that the Prime Minister would redeem his promise to the Indian Mussulmans, that the Punjab wound would be healed and that the reforms, inadequate and unsatisfactory though they were, marked a new era of hope in the life of India.

But all that hope was shattered. The Khilafar promise was not to be redeemed. The Punjab crime was whitewashed and most culprits went not only unpunished but remained in service and in some cases continued to draw pensions from the Indian revenue, and in some cases were even rewarded. I saw too that not only did the reforms not mark a change of heart, but they were only a method of further draining India of her wealth and of prolonging her servitude.

I came reluctantly to the conclusion that the British connection had made India more helpless than she ever was before, politically and economically. A disarmed India has no power of resistance against any aggressor if she wanted to engage in armed conflict with him. So much is this the case that some of our best men consider that India must take generations before she can achieve Dominion status. She has become so poor that she has little power of resisting famines. Before the British advent, India spun and wove in her millions of cottages just the supplement she needed for adding to her meagre agricultural resources. This cottage industry, so vital for India's existence, has been ruined by incredibly heartless and inhuman processes as described by English witnesses. Little do town-dwellers know how the semi-starved masses of India are slowly sinking to lifelessness. Little do they know that their miserable comfort represents the brokerage they get for the work they do for the foreign exploiter, that the profits and the brokerage are sucked from the masses. Little do they realize that the government established by law in British India is carried on for this exploitation of the masses. No sophistry, no jugglery in figures can explain away the evidence that the skeletons in many villages present to the naked eye. I have no doubt whatsoever that both England and the town-dwellers of India will have to answer, if there is a God above, for this crime against humanity which is perhaps unequalled in history. The law itself in this country has been used to serve the foreign exploiter. My unbiased examination of the Punjab Martial Law cases has led me to believe that at least 95 per cent of convictions were wholly bad. My experience of political cases in India leads me to the conclusion that in nine out of ten the condemned men were totally innocent. Their crime consisted in love of their country. In ninety-nine cases out of a hundred justice has been denied to Indians as against Europeans in the courts of India. This is not an exaggerated picture. It is the experience of almost every Indian who has had anything to do with such cases. In my opinion, the administration of the law is thus prostituted consciously or unconsciously for the benefit of the exploiter.

The greatest misfortune is that Englishmen and their Indian associates in the administration of the country do not know that they are engaged in the crime I have attempted to describe. I am satisfied that many Englishmen and Indian officials honestly believe that they are administering one of the best systems devised in the world and that India is making steady though slow progress. They do not know that a subtle but effective system of terrorism and an organized display of force on the one hand, and the deprivation of all powers of retaliation or self-defence on the other, have emasculated the people and induced in them the habit of simulation. This awful habit has added to the ignorance and the self-deception of the administrators. Section 124a under which I am happily charged is perhaps the prince among the political sections of the Indian Penal Code designed to suppress the liberty of the citizen. Affection cannot be manufactured or regulated by law. If one has no affection for a person or system, one should be free to give the fullest expression to his disaffection, so long as he does not contemplate, promote or incite to violence. But the section under which Mr Banker and I are charged is one under which mere promotion of disaffection is a crime. I have studied some of the cases tried under it, and I know that some of the most loved of India's patriots have been convicted under it. I consider it a privilege, therefore, to be charged under that section. I have endeavoured to give in their briefest outline the reasons for my disaffection. I have no personal ill-will against any single administrator, much less can I have any disaffection towards the King's person. But I hold it to be a virtue to be disaffected towards a government which in its totality has done more harm to India than any previous system. India is less manly under the British rule than she ever was before. Holding such a belief, I consider it to be a sin to have affection for the system. And it has been a precious privilege for me to be able to write what I have in the various articles, tendered in evidence against me.

In fact, I believe that I have rendered a service to India and England by showing in non-cooperation the way out of the unnatural state in which both are living. In my humble opinion, non-cooperation with evil is as much a duty as is cooperation with good. But in the past, non-cooperation has been deliberately expressed in violence to the evil doer. I am endeavouring to show to my countrymen that violent non-cooperation only multiplies evil and that as evil can only be sustained by violence, withdrawal of support of evil requires complete abstention from violence. Non-violence implies voluntary submission to the penalty for non-cooperation with evil. I am here, therefore, to invite and submit cheerfully to the highest penalty that can be inflicted upon me for what in law is a deliberate crime and what appears to me to be the highest duty of a citizen. The only course open to you, the judge, is either to resign your post and thus dissociate yourself from evil, if you feel that the law you are called upon to administer is an evil and that in reality I am innocent; or to inflict on me the severest penalty if you believe that the system and the law you are assisting to administer are good for the people of this country and that my activity is therefore injurious to the public weal.

•

V. I. LENIN
1923

'Stalin is too rude'

While Lenin (1870–1924) recovered from his stroke in 1922, he became increasingly suspicious of Josef Stalin, the General Secretary who was Leon Trotsky's rival to succeed Lenin. He started dictating notes for the forthcoming Party Congress, some by telephone to a stenographer in the next room. The notes, written a year before he died, became known as 'Lenin's Testament'.

He began debating the claims of Trotsky and Stalin on 24 December 1922, but reserved his most devastating – and prophetic – criticisms for Stalin in a postscript added on 4 January 1923.

I intend to examine here a number of considerations of a purely personal character.

I think that from this point of view the basic factor in the problem of stability are such members of the Central Committee as Stalin and Trotsky. In my view the relationship between them constitutes a good half of the danger of a split which could be avoided and the avoidance of which, in my opinion, should be served, among other things, by increasing the numbers of the Central Committee to fifty or one hundred persons.

Having become General Secretary, Comrade *Stalin* has acquired immense power in his hands, and I am not certain he will always know how to use this power with sufficient caution. On the other hand, Comrade *Trotsky*, as his struggle against the Central Committee over the question of the Commissariat of Railways has already shown, is distinguished not only by his remarkable abilities. Personally he is, no doubt, the most able person in the present Central Committee, but he also has excessive self-confidence and is overly attracted by the purely administrative aspect of affairs.

These two qualities of the two most prominent leaders of the present Central Committee might inadvertently lead to a split, and if our party does not take measures to prevent this, the split might arise unexpectedly . . .

Postscript: Stalin is too rude, and this fault, quite tolerable in our midst or in relations among communists, becomes intolerable for one who holds the office of General Secretary. Therefore I propose to the comrades that they consider a means of removing Stalin from that post and appointing to it another person who in all other respects differs from Stalin in one advantage alone, namely, that he is more patient, more loyal, more polite, and more considerate to comrades, less capricious, and so forth. This circumstance may seem to be an insignificant trifle. But I think that from the point of view of preventing a split and from the point of view of the relations between Stalin and Trotsky which I discussed above, this is not a trifle, or it is a trifle that may acquire decisive significance.

Dictated, 4 January 1923

ADOLF HITLER
1924

'The eternal court of history'

Adolf Hitler (1889–1945) was put on trial in 1924 after attempting to overthrow the Bavarian government and then staging a march through Munich which was machine-gunned by police. Sixteen storm troopers were killed. He treated the court with contempt. Afterwards, in prison, he wrote Mein Kampf *(My Struggle). It demonstrated his ambition to be taken as an original thinker, and is described by historian Alan Bullock as 'remarkably interesting' for anybody trying to understand Hitler's mind.*

The first extract is from Hitler's speech at his trial, the second, describing the end of the First World War, is from Mein Kampf.

The army we have formed is growing from day to day . . . I nourish the proud hope that one day the hour will come when these rough companies will grow to battalions, the battalions to regiments, the regiments to divisions, that the old cockade will be taken from the mud, that the old flags will wave again, that there will be a reconciliation at the last great divine judgement which we are prepared to face . . . For it is not you, gentlemen, who pass judgement on us. That judgement is spoken by the eternal court of history. What judgement you will hand down, I know. But that court will not ask us: 'Did you commit high treason, or did you not?' That court will judge us, the Quartermaster-General of the old Army [Ludendorff], his officers and soldiers, as Germans who wanted only the good of their own people and Fatherland; who wanted to fight and die. You may pronounce us guilty a thousand times over, but the goddess of the eternal court of history will smile and tear to tatters the brief of the state prosecutor and the sentence of this court. For she acquits us.

By the end of September my division, for the third time, arrived at the positions we had stormed as a young volunteer regiment.

What a memory.

Now, in the autumn of 1918, the men had become different, there was political discussion among the troops. The poison from home was beginning to have its effect here, as everywhere. The young drafts succumbed to it altogether. They had come straight from home.

During the night of 13–14 October the British began to throw gas-shells on to the southern front before Ypres. We were still on a hill south of Werwick on the evening of 13 October, when we came under a drum-fire lasting several hours, which continued throughout the night with more or less violence. About midnight a number of us dropped out – some for ever. Towards morning I felt a pain which got worse with every quarter hour that passed, and at about seven o'clock I tottered rearwards with scorching eyes, reporting myself for the last time in that war.

A few hours later my eyes had turned into burning coals, and it was all dark around me. I was sent to hospital at Pasewalk in Pomerania, and while there I was destined to see the revolution.

Bad rumours kept on coming in from the navy, which was said to be in a ferment, but this seemed to me to be something born of the excited imagination of a few youths rather than a matter affecting large numbers of men. In hospital everyone talked of the end of the war, which they hoped was swiftly approaching, but no one imagined it was to come immediately. I was unable to read the newspapers.

In November the general tension increased. Then one day the disaster came upon us suddenly and without warning. Sailors arrived in lorries and called on all to revolt, a few Jewish youths being the leaders in that struggle for the 'freedom, beauty and dignity' of our national life. Not one of them had ever been to the front.

The following days brought with them the worst realization of my life. The rumours grew more and more definite. What I had imagined to be a local affair was apparently a general revolution. In addition to all this, distressing news came back from the front. They wanted to capitulate. Yes – was such a thing possible?

On 10 November the aged pastor came to the hospital for a short address; then we heard everything.

I was present and was profoundly affected. The good old man seemed to be trembling when he told us that the House of Hohenzollern was to wear the German imperial crown no more – that the Fatherland had become a republic.

So all had been in vain. In vain all the sacrifices and privations, in vain the starvation and thirst for many endless months, in vain the hours we spent doing our duty, gripped by the fear of death, and in vain the death of 2 million men!

And our country?

But – was this the only sacrifice we should be called on to endure? Was the Germany of the past worth less than we thought? Had she no obligation owing to her own history? Were we worthy to clothe ourselves in the glory of the past? In what light could this act be presented for justification to future generations?

Miserable, depraved criminals!

The more I tried in that hour to get clear ideas about that tremendous event, the more did I blush with burning rage and shame. What was all the pain of my eyes in comparison with this misery?

There were horrible days and worse nights to follow. I knew that all was lost. In those nights my hatred arose against the originators of that act.

The Emperor William had been the first German Emperor to offer the hand of friendship to the leaders of Marxism, little guessing that scoundrels are without honour. While they held the imperial hand in theirs, their other hand was already feeling for the dagger.

With Jews there is no bargaining – there is merely the hard 'Either – or'.

I resolved to become a politician.

•

MARCUS GARVEY
1925

'One God! One aim! One destiny!'

The Black Pride movement launched by Marcus Garvey (1887–1940) in Harlem in 1918 spread throughout America's black world. Nearly a thousand divisions of the United Negro Improvement Association were formed with 500,000 members. It awakened a race consciousness that made Harlem known around the world.

Garvey's movement collapsed when he was convicted of swindling. He wrote this front-page editorial for Negro World *in Atlanta Federal Penitentiary.*

The time has come for the Negro to forget and cast behind him his hero worship and adoration of other races, and to start out immediately to create and emulate heroes of his own.

We must canonize our own saints, create our own martyrs, and elevate to positions of fame and honor black men and women who have made their distinct contributions to our racial history. Sojourner Truth is worthy of the place of sainthood alongside of Joan of Arc; Crispus Attucks and George William Gordon are entitled to the halo of martyrdom with no less glory than that of the martyrs of any other race. Toussaint L'Ouverture's brilliancy as a soldier and statesman outshone that of a Cromwell, Napoleon and Washington; hence, he is entitled to the highest place as a hero among men.

Africa has produced countless numbers of men and women, in war and in peace, whose lustre and bravery outshine that of any other people. Then why not see good and perfection in ourselves?

We must inspire a literature and promulgate a doctrine of our own without any apologies to the powers that be. The right is ours and God's. Let contrary sentiment and cross opinions go to the winds. Opposition to race independence is the weapon of the enemy to defeat the hopes of an unfortunate people. We are entitled to our own opinions and not obligated to or bound by the opinions of others.

If others laugh at you, return the laughter to them; if they mimic you, return the compliment with equal force. They have no more right to dishonor, disrespect and disregard your feeling and manhood than you have in dealing with them. Honor them when they honor you; disrespect and disregard them when they vilely treat you. Their arrogance is but skin deep and an assumption that has no foundation in morals or in law. They have sprung from the same family tree of obscurity as we have; their history is as rude in its primitiveness as ours; their ancestors ran wild and naked, lived in caves and in the branches of trees, like monkeys, as ours; they made human sacrifices, ate the flesh of their own dead and the raw meat of the wild beast for centuries even as they accuse us of doing; their cannibalism was more prolonged than ours; when we were embracing the arts and sciences on the banks of the Nile their ancestors were still drinking human blood and eating out of the skulls of their conquered dead; when our civilization had reached the noonday of progress they were still running naked and sleeping in holes and caves with rats, bats and other insects and animals. After we had already unfathomed the mysteries of the stars and reduced the heavenly constellations to minute and regular calculus they were still backwoodsmen, living in ignorance and blatant darkness.

The world today is indebted to us for the benefits of civilization. They stole our arts and sciences from Africa. Then why should we be ashamed of ourselves? Their MODERN IMPROVEMENTS are but DUPLICATES of a grander civilization that we reflected thousands of years ago, without the advantage of what is buried and still hidden, to be resurrected and reintroduced by the intelligence of our generation and our prosperity. Why should we be discouraged because somebody laughs at us today? Who is to tell what tomorrow will bring forth? Did they not laugh at Moses, Christ and Mohammed? Was there not a Carthage, Greece and Rome? We see and have changes every day, so pray, work, be steadfast and be not dismayed.

As the Jew is held together by his RELIGION, the white races by the assumption and the unwritten law of SUPERIORITY, and the Mongolian by the precious tie of BLOOD, so likewise the Negro must be united in one GRAND RACIAL HIERARCHY. Our UNION MUST KNOW NO CLIME, BOUNDARY, or NATIONALITY. Like the great Church of Rome, Negroes the world over MUST PRACTICE ONE FAITH, that of confidence in themselves, with one God! One aim! One destiny! Let no religious scruples, no political machination divide us, but let us hold together under all climes and in every country, making among ourselves a Racial Empire upon which 'the sun shall never set.'

Let no voice but your own speak to you from the depths. Let no influence but your own raise you in time of peace and time of war. Hear all, but attend only that which concerns you.

Your first allegiance shall be to your God, then to your family, race and country. Remember always that the Jew in his political and economic urge is always first a Jew; the white man is first a white man under all circumstances, and you can do no less than being first and always a Negro, and then all else will take care of itself. Let no one inoculate you for their own conveniences. There is no humanity before that which starts with yourself. 'Charity begins at home.' First to thyself be true, and 'thou canst not then be false to any man.'

God and nature first made us what we are, and then out of our own creative genius we make ourselves what we want to be. Follow always that great law.

Let the sky and God be our limit, and eternity our measurement. There is no height to which we cannot climb by using the active intelligence of our own minds. Mind creates, and as much as we desire in nature we can have through the creation of our own minds. Being at present the scientifically weaker race, you shall treat others only as they treat you; but in your homes and everywhere possible you must teach the higher development of science to your children; and be sure to develop a race of scientists *par excellence*, for in science and religion lies our only hope to withstand the evil designs of modern materialism. Never forget your God. Remember, we live, work and pray for the establishing of a great and binding RACIAL HIERARCHY, the founding of a RACIAL EMPIRE whose only natural, spiritual and political limits shall be God and 'Africa, at home and abroad.'

•

R. H. TAWNEY
1926

'Material riches'

R. H. Tawney (1880–1962), who was to become president of the Workers Educational Association and professor of economic history at the London School of Economics, was a Christian socialist and critic of the corrupting effect of capitalism. When Tawney died the Labour leader Hugh Gaitskell said that his books combined 'learning with passion'. Tawney's passionate beliefs were deployed in the conclusion to his influential book Religion and the Rise of Capitalism.

The most obvious facts are the most easily forgotten. Both the existing economic order, and too many of the projects advanced for reconstructing it, break down through their neglect of the truism that, since even quite common men have souls, no increase in material wealth will compensate them for arrangements which insult their self-respect and impair their freedom. A reasonable estimate of economic organization must allow for the fact that, unless industry is to be paralysed by recurrent revolts on the part of outraged human nature, it must satisfy criteria which are not purely economic. A reasonable view of its possible modifications must recognize that natural appetites may be purified or restrained, as, in fact, in some considerable measure they already have been, by being submitted to the control of some larger body of interests. The distinction made by the philosophers of classical antiquity between liberal and servile occupations, the medieval insistence that riches exist for man, not man for riches, Ruskin's famous outburst, 'there is no wealth but life,' the argument of the Socialist who urges that production should be organized for service, not for profit, are but different attempts to emphasize the instrumental character of economic activities, by reference to an ideal which is held to express the true nature of man.

Of that nature and its possibilities the Christian Church was thought, during the greater part of the period discussed in these pages, to hold by definition a conception distinctively its own. It was therefore committed to the formulation of a social theory, not as a philanthropic gloss upon the main body of its teaching, but as a vital element in a creed concerned with the destiny of men whose character is formed, and whose spiritual potentialities are fostered or starved, by the commerce of the market-place and the institutions of society. Stripped of the eccentricities of period and place, its philosophy had as its centre a determination to assert the superiority of moral principles over economic appetites, which have their place, and an important place, in the human scheme, but which, like other natural appetites, when flattered and pampered and overfed, bring ruin to the soul and confusion to society. Its casuistry was an attempt to translate these principles into a code of practical ethics, sufficiently precise to be applied to the dusty world of warehouse and farm. Its discipline was an effort, too often corrupt and pettifogging in practice, but not ignoble in conception, to work the Christian virtues into the spotted texture of individual character and social conduct. That practice was often a sorry parody on theory is a truism which should need no emphasis. But in a world where principles and conduct are unequally mated, men are to be judged by their reach as well as by their grasp – by the ends at which they aim as well as by the success with which they attain them. The prudent critic will try himself by his achievement rather than by his ideals, and his neighbours, living and dead alike, by their ideals not less than by their achievement.

Circumstances alter from age to age, and the practical interpretation of moral principles must alter with them. Few who consider dispassionately the facts of social history will be disposed to deny that the exploitation of the weak by the powerful, organized for purposes of economic gain, buttressed by imposing systems of law, and screened by decorous draperies of virtuous sentiment and resounding rhetoric, has been a permanent feature in the life of most communities that the world has yet seen. But the quality in modern societies, which is most sharply opposed to the teaching ascribed to the Founder of the Christian Faith, lies deeper than the exceptional failures and abnormal follies against which criticism is most commonly directed. It consists in the assumption, accepted by most reformers with hardly less *naïveté* than by the defenders of the established order, that the attainment of material riches is the supreme object of human endeavour and the final criterion of human success. Such a philosophy, plausible, militant, and not indisposed, when hard pressed, to silence criticism by persecution, may triumph or may decline. What is certain is that it is the negation of any system of thought or morals which can, except by a metaphor, be described as Christian. Compromise is as impossible between the Church of Christ and the idolatry of wealth, which is the practical religion of capitalist societies, as it was between the Church and the State idolatry of the Roman Empire.

'Modern capitalism,' writes Mr Keynes, 'is absolutely irreligious, without internal union, without much public spirit, often, though not always, a mere congeries of possessors and pursuers.' It is that whole system of appetites and values, with its deification of the life of snatching to hoard, and hoarding to snatch, which now, in the hour of its triumph, while the plaudits of the crowd still ring in the ears of the gladiators and the laurels are still unfaded on their brows, seems sometimes to leave a taste as of ashes on the lips of a civilization which has brought to the conquest of its material environment resources unknown in earlier ages, but which has not yet learned to master itself.

•

A MINER'S WIFE
1926

'One slice or two?'

When the General Strike began in 1926 over the issue of a living wage for miners, even the Daily Herald *was stopped since the Trades Union Congress had called out the printers. Winston Churchill, then Chancellor of the Exchequer, sponsored the* British Gazette, *an official government newspaper, which denounced the workers as 'the enemy'. The TUC responded with a strike sheet, the* British Worker. *On 6 May it published this article on how the coal struggle affected a miner's wife.*

No section of the community is carrying a heavier burden than the miner's wife.

At the best of times her toil is hard. She has not only all the work of other housewives; the conditions of the mining industry and the housing in colliery villages make her task specially heavy.

Nowhere is housing worse. Sometimes she has little better than a one-room hovel without any of the ordinary comforts of life, and not even a scrap of garden round it.

Water supply is bad, sanitary conveniences intolerable, and the dirt of the pit is constantly carried into her home. Every man comes back from his shift covered with coal dust and with wet clothes, which have to be dried and mended.

All day long she is occupied with her children and with caring for the men going out or coming in. In addition to all her toil she has constant anxiety while her men folk are away at their dangerous task underground.

In recent years her work and anxiety has been increased by low wages and unemployment.

She is faced each week with the terrible business of making a starvation wage cover the family's needs, and a man who works underground must be well fed and well cared for. Hungry children must have their meals even if boots and clothes are lacking.

Every woman will know that in such conditions the mother's needs come last. The miner's wife says: 'Wage-earners and children first.' She is well satisfied if she can give them enough. What is left over is her share.

The possibility of lower wages in the mining industry is sheer tragedy for the women of the coalfields.

When there is talk of equal sacrifices by employers and employed the human needs of the miner's family are forgotten. Any reduction in the level of wages for them would mean falling below the hunger line.

It would not be a case of going without luxuries, of taking bread instead of cake; it would mean giving a hungry child one slice of bread instead of two, and water when it needs milk.

Nor could a more prosperous time in the future make up for the privation of the present. To reduce the children's food today means so to stunt their growth as to leave ill-effects for the rest of their lives.

Therefore, this struggle is for the women of the coalfields one of desperate need, and they turn confidently to their sisters in other industries, asking them to stand beside them now and so save their children for the future.

•

LIBERAL PARTY
1928

'We Can Conquer Unemployment'

Asquith dictated the preface and Lloyd George funded the inquiry which led to the publication of the 'Yellow Book' by the Liberal Party in 1928, whose members included Keynes, Lloyd George and Seebohm Rowntree. A year later, under the direction of Rowntree, it was published as a manifesto with the title 'We Can Conquer Unemployment', a pledge which was affirmed by Lloyd George to Liberal candidates. 'This was a dramatic event,' says A. J. P. Taylor, 'the moment when the new ideas towards which economists were fumbling first broke into public consciousness . . .' Lloyd George's programme repudiated the system of balanced budgets. Instead there were to be great public works paid for by a deliberate deficit.

Liberalism stands for liberty; but it is an error to think that a policy of liberty must be always negative, that the state can help liberty only by abstaining from action, that invariably men are freest when their government does least. Withdraw the police from the streets of the towns, and you will, it is true, cease to interfere with the liberty of the criminal, but the law-abiding citizens will soon find that they are less free than before. Abolish compulsory education: the child, and perhaps his parent, will no longer be forced to do what they may perhaps not wish to do; but the adults of the next generation will be denied the power to read, to think, to succeed, which is essential to a real freedom. Repeal, to take one more example, the Shops Acts: short-sighted shopkeepers will be allowed to trade for longer hours, but other shopkeepers and the whole class of shop-assistants will be robbed of their proper share of the leisure without which life is a servitude. Often more law may mean more liberty.

But not of course always. The principle may be pushed too far. There is such a thing as a meddlesome, unjustified officious interference, against which we have to be on our guard. The fact remains that there is much positive work that the state can do which is not merely consistent with liberty, but essential to it. The idea of the extreme individualist, that in proportion as state action expands freedom contracts, is false.

Equally false is the idea that because state action on the widest scale is favoured by Socialists, those who are not Socialists must oppose any and every extension of state action. It will lead, it is said, to Socialism in the long run. It is a partial surrender to false and flimsy theories.

True that the Socialist is inclined to welcome extensions of state activity for their own sakes; he regards them all as stages on the road to an ideal which he cherishes. But the fact that we do not share his ideal, and do not favour particular measures merely because they might be steps towards it, is no reason why, out of prejudice, we should close our eyes to whatever merits those measures may possess in themselves. If no one had ever generalized about Socialism, or used the word, or made it the rallying cry for a party, these measures might have been universally welcomed. It would be folly to reject what is right because some would have it lead to what is wrong.

A further great change, that goes far to decide the character of the modern world, is the establishment of political democracy. When individualism took its rise, political rights were still confined to a comparatively narrow class, so that there was no glaring contrast between the industrial status of the manual worker and his political status, between the economic autocracy exercised by the individual employer in farm or factory and the political oligarchy of the 'privileged classes' in the government of the state. Universal franchise and the democratization of political parties have changed all that. There is now felt to be something inconsistent between the industrial status of the worker as a factory 'hand', subject to strict discipline and holding his employment on the most precarious of tenures, and his political status as a free and equal citizen and a maker and unmaker of governments.

To a certain extent this inconsistency is inherent in the necessities of industrial organization. No good can come, as even the controllers of Soviet Russia have had to recognize, of blurring the distinction between those whose function is to conceive and to plan and those whose function is to execute their plans. Nor is there anything to be gained by applying blindly the political devices of the public meeting and the ballot-box to the quite different problems of industrial life. It would, we think, be wrong and dishonest to hold out hopes to the ordinary man that he will ever be in a position to choose at each moment of the day whether he will do this thing or that, or even to take a direct part in the election or dismissal of those from whom he receives his immediate instructions. But it is not unreasonable to hope and to plan both that he shall take a direct part in framing and administering the code of discipline under which his daily work must be done, and also that, through the organizations which he has built and the leaders in whom he has confidence, he shall come to exercise an increasing influence on the wider government both of the business unit and of the whole industry of which he forms part.

The state here, from the nature of the case, can do little; but it can do something, and the nation should resolve that something shall be done. In the main, however, we must look, on the one hand, to a spread of the statesmanlike and pioneering spirit which has already found expression in the best practice of individual firms; on the other, to a growing determination on the part of the great Labour organizations to do their share in promoting, and indeed enforcing, efficiency in the conduct of business enterprise – to make their weight felt as powerfully in the constructive work of organizing industry for the tasks of peace as they have made it felt on occasions in the conduct of industrial warfare.

Our conclusion, then, is not the rough-and-ready rule that, since so much already has been done in the direction of state action, the simple course is to do the rest and to nationalize everything. Individual management and the competition on which it is based still work reasonably well within a wide range of miscellaneous industries. They are an unrivalled method for ensuring the decentralization of management – that is, for securing that power and responsibility should be exercised as near as possible to the act to be performed, and not through a long line of intermediaries. They are an excellent means for securing a variety of experiment, and for trying out the comparative efficiency both of methods and of men. They provide, though with some friction and inequality, the only practicable method which has yet been suggested of evaluating the various goods and services which it is the function of industry to supply. We regard, therefore, the direct management of industries by departments of state, or agencies analogous to them, as prima facie undesirable and likely to remain the exception rather than the rule.

Faced by these conditions in modern industry, convinced that our present social order denies a real liberty to a great proportion of the population, anxious to effect the reforms that are necessary without at the same time injuring the springs of such efficiency (and it is not small) as that order retains, we have framed the constructive proposals, touching the many parts of the one great problem, which this book contains. Financial and industrial reforms, international trade and national development, the juster distribution of wealth, the worker's right to be a citizen, and not merely a subject, in the world of production – the measures we advocate in relation to all these things spring from one clear purpose. We believe with a passionate faith that the end of all political and economic action is not the perfecting or the perpetuation of this or that piece of mechanism or organization, but that individual men and women may have life, and that they may have it more abundantly.

•

LABOUR PARTY
1929

'Labour and the Nation'

Under Ramsay MacDonald, the Labour Party fought the general election of 1929 with a manifesto called 'Labour and the Nation.' 'The Party is essentially one of action and it asks for power both in order to lay the foundations of a new social order and to relieve immediate distress,' MacDonald wrote in a foreword. Labour won the election and he became prime minister of the first government elected by universal suffrage.

The manifesto, notably well written, was the work of R. H. Tawney, and was a popular version of his famous book The Acquisitive Society.

After four years of Conservative Government the Labour Party renews its appeal to the people of Great Britain. Its opponents have had their opportunity. They asked the nation for a crushing majority, and, thanks to the exploitation of a fraudulent conspiracy – a conspiracy of which many honest Conservatives are now heartily ashamed – the majority was accorded them. The consequences today are patent to all. Of the electors who complied with the exhortation to forget England and remember Russia there are now, it is probable, comparatively few who regard the results of their altruism with unmixed satisfaction.

The Chancellor of the Exchequer, in a characteristic speech, has claimed that the Cabinet has 'given a period of stability to the country'. It has indeed. In its determination to make the world safe for the plutocracy which, it affects to believe, is the only conceivable form of civilization, it has fastened on the nation a stability more alarming than many crises – the stability of aimlessness, of torpor, and, should it continue, of decay. It has stabilized luxury and squalor, private waste and public parsimony, idleness and the disorganization of productive industry, an expenditure upon armaments which, in spite of trifling reductions, is still extravagant, and a not less extravagant economy upon the services which fortify the health and enrich the spirit of the whole community. It has even contemplated the stabilization in perpetuity of the supremacy of property and the Tory Party, by the creation of a new House of Lords with a permanent Conservative majority, and with powers even greater than those of which it was deprived by the Parliament Act. The only detail it has forgotten to stabilize is a civilized standard of life for the workers of Great Britain.

Whether they are workers who initiate and organize and plan, or who execute and manipulate and construct; whether they labour in the mine, in the factory and on the farm, or in the laboratory of the scientist and the office of the administrator, it is by their energy and their skill, their intelligence and their devotion that the fabric of civilization has been reared in the past and is maintained today. It is to them, in the first place, that the Labour Party addresses its appeal. It speaks, not as the agent of this class or that, but as the political organ created to express the needs and voice the aspirations of all who share in the labour which is the lot of mankind. They know, and it knows, that the force which sustains society is not passive property, but creative effort, and that, by science, co-operation and the spirit of service, the world can be made a more tolerable abode for future generations. It calls upon them with confidence to aid it in its task.

The Labour Party, since it holds that creed, is a Socialist party. Its aim is the organization of industry, and the administration of the wealth which industry produces, in the interest, not of the small minority (less than 10 per cent of the population) who own the greater part of the land, the plant and the equipment without access to which their fellow-countrymen can neither work nor live, but of all who bring their contribution of useful service to the common stock. Its Socialism, therefore, is neither a sentimental aspiration for an impossible utopia, nor a blind movement of revolt against poverty and oppression. It is the practical recognition of the familiar commonplace that 'morality is in the nature of things', and that men are all, in very truth, members one of another. It is a conscious, systematic and unflagging effort to use the weapons forged in the victorious struggle for political democracy to end the capitalist dictatorship in which democracy finds everywhere its most insidious and most relentless foe.

What has made industrial civilization, with all its horrors, less intolerable today than the nightmare of squalor and greed which shocked the conscience of mankind a century ago – what alone, indeed, has enabled industrial civilization to survive and expand – is precisely the tentative, doctrineless Socialism, which, amid cries of impending ruin from the more thoughtless members of the privileged classes, has found tardy and imperfect recognition in the care for public health and public education, in Factory Acts and Mines Regulation Acts and Minimum Wage Acts, in the development of local government and the expansion of municipal enterprise, in the growth of public expenditure upon social services, and in the provision of the financial resources by which such services may be maintained. The Labour Party believes that the time has come when principles should be deduced from experience, and the teaching of history should be turned to practical account. It stands for the deliberate establishment, by experimental methods, without violence or disturbance, with the fullest utilization of scientific knowledge and administrative skill, of a social order in which the resources of the community shall be organized and administered with a single eye to securing for all its members the largest possible measure of economic welfare and personal freedom.

The nation has been deafened with warnings from the press and from politicians of the horrors which the triumph of the Socialist idea must bring in its train, and that venerable bogey will be resuscitated, no doubt – skull and crossbones, clanking chains, bloody dagger and all – at the next election. The Labour Party is concerned with grave realities, not with picturesque fairy tales. If its opponents care to rehearse once more a time-honoured fiction, in which even the most ignorant of them no longer believe, they are welcome to such tainted profits as mendacity can bring to their bankrupt exchequer. Practical men and women will consider, not fables regarding tomorrow, but the facts of today. They will not be argued into submitting to present miseries because the future contains problems that only the future can solve. They will refuse to be deterred from coping with pressing evils and initiating urgent reforms by hypothetical terrors brandished before them by interests which cling to the former for the profits which they yield, and dread the latter for the personal loss which may be involved to themselves. They will judge the present government, as governments should be judged, not by its words, but by its deeds – by its achievements, its actions and its omissions.

The Labour Party accepts that criterion. When once again it assumes office, it not only will be willing, but will desire, that the nation should judge it by its works. But, if it demands to be tried by its record itself, it demands no less that the same just measure should be applied to its opponents. It is not Socialism which today is in the dock, but the policy of parties to whom Socialism is anathema. With one short interval of eight months, Conservatives, or Conservatives and Liberals in coalition – for, though they are sparring today, they are old allies – have governed Great Britain since the day when they hailed, with outward enthusiasm and inward terror, the dawn of the new era of social justice which, as both of them so often and so eloquently explained, the return of peace was to usher in. How have these masters of statecraft used the power entrusted them by the confidence of their fellow-countrymen in the traditional wisdom of the governing classes? What sort of world have they created as an alternative to the Socialist Commonwealth?

It is, on the whole, a pleasant enough world for them and their friends – though even they, if only they knew it, have more to gain than to lose by the reconstruction of a social system which surrounds affluence with insistent spectres of want and despair, and condemns a minority to purchase ease and luxury for itself by the degradation of its fellow-men. But the welfare of a nation and the wisdom of its rulers are to be judged, not by the riches enjoyed by a handful of property-owners, but by the comfort and independence of the masses whose labours maintain it, and by its success in applying the resources of science to bring within the reach of all the conditions of a dignified and civilized existence.

Custom blinds the eye and deadens the ear. Poverty and exploitation no longer appear shocking when their victims are numbered, not by units, but by millions. A visitor from another planet, however, who surveyed the condition of Great Britain in 1928, might be pardoned if he felt that even the blessings of a Conservative Government had been purchased at a price which was somewhat excessive. He would recognize, indeed, as the Labour Party recognizes, that order cannot be produced from chaos by a stroke of the pen, and he would not impute to the government responsibility for the continuance of evils which can yield only to patient effort consistently applied over a period of years. But he would ask whether it had begun, at least, a serious attack upon them, or whether it had abandoned the task in apathetic indifference. The electors who are uninterested, and rightly uninterested, in the small change of political controversy, will ask the same. They will consider whether the direction, the tendency, the spirit, of the government's policy has been of a kind to leave the affairs of the nation in a better position than when it assumed office, or whether they have been such as to aggravate existing maladies and to render confusion worse confounded. The answer to that question, the Labour Party submits, is not in doubt.

The parties of privilege of birth and privilege of wealth have – so they tell us – done their best. They have conspicuously failed. The desolation of the mining areas, the queues outside the Employment Exchanges, the mounting debts of Poor Law Guardians are their condemnation and their epitaph. The time has come for the people, who have been the victims of their incompetence, to assume the direction of their own economic destinies, and to create a society in which security and culture shall be, not the privilege of a minority, but the heritage of all. In the bankruptcy of capitalism – a bankruptcy revealed, not only by its failure to offer a tolerable livelihood to the mass of the population, but by its inability to harness for the service of man the new resources which the progress of science has revealed, or even to administer existing resources with the efficiency which was once its special boast – Labour alone can lead the nation to a prosperity established on the secure foundations of knowledge, good will, and the comradeship of all in the service of all.

•

ANEURIN BEVAN
1929

'Bedwellty workhouse'

Aneurin Bevan (1897–1960), one of thirteen children of a miner who went down the pits at the age of thirteen, ranks with Keir Hardie as one of the greatest British Socialists of the twentieth century. He was elected to Parliament in 1929 for the Welsh mining town of Ebbw Vale and brought with him, in the words of his biographer Michael Foot, a fiery message of protest from one of the most impoverished areas of the country.

In his maiden speech, Bevan took on Winston Churchill. In his second, he took on another Tory lion, Neville Chamberlain, who as Minister of Health had amended the Poor Law so that it was administered by Chamberlain's nominees instead of elected local Guardians. Bevan had led the revolt in South Wales. Chamberlain objected when the new Labour government proposed to revoke his bill. Bevan rose to the attack and made his parliamentary reputation.

I know cases of colliers who had to walk four or five miles in the morning to do work connected with building walls, cracking stones and weeding turnips. In some cases these men worked from 7.30 in the morning to five p.m.; in one case a man was paid 16s. a week for doing that kind of work, out of which he had to pay 4s. 6d. per week rent, and he had a wife and two children to maintain. In face of these facts, how can the right hon. Gentleman the Member for Edgbaston expect hon. Members on this side of the House to listen to his remarks with patience? The wonder is that the right hon. Gentleman's merciless administration was tolerated so long. I never thought it possible that any man from a detached position in this House could encourage an administration so inhuman, but after listening to the speech which has been made by the right hon. Gentleman I am not at all surprised.

Three weeks before I came to this House a medical officer of health, representing a Poor Law authority, asked that a man suffering from asthma should be taken into the infirmary. The man was almost in a dying condition. He was taken into the infirmary at Bedwellty, and he was scarcely able to sit on a chair which was provided for him. That man was kept for hours sitting in a chair without any refreshment and without anybody seeing him at all, and he received no attention whatsoever. As a matter of fact, it is now admitted in the Bedwellty district that if you go into the Bedwellty Workhouse you had better shuffle off this mortal coil as quickly as possible. In the Bedwellty Workhouse the inmates get up at eight o'clock and they are given for breakfast a chunk of bread and margarine; at twelve o'clock they have a cooked dinner, and the tea is a repetition of the breakfast. It is a fact that from five o'clock in the evening to eight o'clock the following morning they receive no food at all – I am speaking of people between seventy and eighty years of age. I have known them during the winter months being driven out of the rest room into the yards to walk around in the perishing cold.

•

STANLEY BALDWIN
1930

'The prerogative of the harlot'

The press baron Lord Beaverbrook launched the United Empire Party in 1930 and began putting up candidates. The first, at a by-election in London, succeeded in splitting the vote and the seat was won by Labour. As Stanley Baldwin (1867–1947), leader of the Conservative Party, contemplated resignation, he was stung by an anonymous personal attack in the Daily Mail *describing him as unfit to lead the party. He responded with the twentieth-century's most famous attack on the power of press barons – and went on to become prime minister in 1935.*

I have no idea of the name of that gentleman. I would only observe that he is well qualified for the post which he holds. The first part of that statement is a lie and the second part of the statement, by its implication, is untrue. The paragraph itself could only have been written by a cad. I have consulted a very high legal authority and I am advised that an action for libel would lie. I shall not move in the matter, and for this reason: I should get an apology and heavy damages. The first is of no value, the second I would not touch with a bargepole. What the proprietorship of these papers is aiming at is power, and power without responsibility – the prerogative of the harlot throughout the ages.

•

SINCLAIR LEWIS
1930

'The New Humanism'

There was a storm of criticism when Sinclair Lewis (1885–1951) became the first American to win the Nobel Prize for Literature in 1930. Once, said the Rev. Henry Van Dyke, Americans were taught to honour traditions. Now they only scoffed at them. Lewis had upset middle America by satirizing the materialism, philistinism and intolerance of small-town life in his novels Main Street, Babbitt *and* Elmer Gantry. *When he received the award in Stockholm, Lewis took revenge on his critics.*

Oh, socially our universities are close to the mass of our citizens, and so are they in the matter of athletics. A great college football game is passionately witnessed by 80,000 people, who have paid five dollars apiece and motored anywhere from ten to a thousand miles for the ecstasy of watching twenty-two men chase one another up and down a curiously marked field. During the football season, a capable player ranks very nearly with our greatest and most admired heroes – even with Henry Ford, President Hoover and Colonel Lindbergh.

And in one branch of learning, the sciences, the lords of business who rule us are willing to do homage to the devotees of learning. However bleakly one of our trader aristocrats may frown upon poetry or the visions of a painter, he is graciously pleased to endure a Millikan, a Michelson, a Banting, a Theobald Smith.

But the paradox is that in the arts our universities are as cloistered, as far from reality and living creation, as socially and athletically and scientifically they are close to us. To a true-blue professor of literature in an American university, literature is not something that a plain human being, living today, painfully sits down to produce. No; it is something dead; it is something magically produced by superhuman beings who must, if they are to be regarded as artists at all, have died at least one hundred years before the diabolical invention of the typewriter. To any authentic don, there is something slightly repulsive in the thought that literature could be created by any ordinary human being, still to be seen walking the streets, wearing quite commonplace trousers and coat and looking not so unlike a chauffeur or a farmer. Our American professors like their literature clear and cold and pure and very dead.

I do not suppose that American universities are alone in this. I am aware that to the dons of Oxford and Cambridge, it would seem rather indecent to suggest that Wells and Bennett and Galsworthy and George Moore may, while they commit the impropriety of continuing to live, be compared to anyone so beautifully and safely dead as Samuel Johnson. I suppose that in the universities of Sweden and France and Germany there exist plenty of professors who prefer dissection to understanding. But in the new and vital and experimental land of America, one would expect the teachers of literature to be less monastic, more human, than in the traditional shadows of old Europe.

They are not.

There has recently appeared in America, out of the universities, an astonishing circus called 'the New Humanism.' Now of course 'humanism' means so many things that it means nothing. It may infer anything from a belief that Greek and Latin are more inspiring than the dialect of contemporary peasants to a belief that any living peasant is more interesting than a dead Greek. But it is a delicate bit of justice that this nebulous word should have been chosen to label this nebulous cult.

Insofar as I have been able to comprehend them – for naturally in a world so exciting and promising as this today, a life brilliant with Zeppelins and Chinese revolutions and the Bolshevik industrialization of farming and ships and the Grand Canyon and young children and terrifying hunger and the lonely quest of scientists after God, no creative writer would have time to follow all the chilly enthusiasms of the New Humanists – this newest of sects reasserts the dualism of man's nature. It would confine literature to the fight between man's soul and God, or man's soul and evil.

But, curiously, neither God nor the devil may wear modern dress, but must retain Grecian vestments. Oedipus is a tragic figure for the New Humanists; man, trying to maintain himself as the image of God under the menace of dynamos, in a world of high-pressure salesmanship, is not. And the poor comfort which they offer is that the object of life is to develop self-discipline – whether or not one ever accomplishes anything with this self-discipline. So this whole movement results in the not particularly novel doctrine that both art and life must be resigned and negative. It is a doctrine of the blackest reaction introduced into a stirringly revolutionary world.

Strangely enough, this doctrine of death, this escape from the complexities and danger of living into the secure blankness of the monastery, has become widely popular among professors in a land where one would have expected only boldness and intellectual adventure, and it has more than ever shut creative writers off from any benign influence which might conceivably have come from the universities.

But it has always been so. America has never had a Brandes, a Taine, a Goethe, a Croce.

With a wealth of creative talent in America, our criticism has most of it been a chill and insignificant activity pursued by jealous spinsters, ex-baseball-reporters, and acid professors. Our Erasmuses have been village schoolmistresses. How should there be any standards when there has been no one capable of setting them up?

•

DEMOCRATIC PARTY
1932

'Our covenant'

By the time Franklin Delano Roosevelt (1882–1945) defeated Herbert Hoover in the 1932 presidential election, the nation was in despair. The economy had collapsed and one in four workers was unemployed. Roosevelt pledged a new deal for America. This was the introduction to the Democratic platform.

In this time of unprecedented economic and social distress the Democratic Party declares its conviction that the chief causes of this condition were the disastrous policies pursued by our government since the world war, of economic isolation, fostering the merger of competitive businesses into monopolies and encouraging the indefensible expansion and contraction of credit for private profit at the expense of the public.

Those who were responsible for these policies have abandoned the ideals on which the war was won and thrown away the fruits of victory, thus rejecting the greatest opportunity in history to bring peace, prosperity and happiness to our people and to the world.

They have ruined our foreign trade; destroyed the values of our commodities and products, crippled our banking system, robbed millions of our people of their life savings, and thrown millions more out of work, produced widespread poverty and brought the government to a state of financial distress unprecedented in time of peace.

The only hope for improving present conditions, restoring employment, affording permanent relief to the people, and bringing the nation back to the proud position of domestic happiness and of financial, industrial, agricultural and commercial leadership in the world lies in a drastic change in economic governmental policies.

We believe that a party platform is a covenant with the people to be faithfully kept by the party when entrusted with power, and that the people are entitled to know in plain words the terms of the contract to which they are asked to subscribe. We hereby declare this to be the platform of the Democratic Party:

The Democratic Party solemnly promises by appropriate action to put into effect the principles, policies and reforms herein advocated, and to eradicate the policies, methods and practices herein condemned. We advocate an immediate and drastic reduction of governmental expenditures by abolishing useless commissions and offices, consolidating departments and bureaus, and eliminating extravagance, to accomplish a saving of not less than 25 per cent in the cost of federal government, and we call upon the Democratic Party in the states to make a zealous effort to achieve a proportionate result.

•

STEPHEN S. WISE
1933

'Stop Hitler now'

Rabbi Stephen S. Wise was born in Budapest in 1874, moved to the United States as a child and became a prominent liberal writer and lecturer. He helped found the Jewish Institute of Religion, the American Jewish Congress, the Federation of American Zionists and New York's Free Synagogue, and represented Zionist interests at the 1919 Versailles Peace Conference. When Hitler became German chancellor in 1933 and started his attack on the Jews, Rabbi Wise was one of the first to warn of the danger Hitler posed to the world. He gave this speech to an anti-Nazi rally at Madison Square Garden in March 1933.

Not out of the bitterness of anger but out of the deepest of sorrow and the spirit of compassion do we speak tonight. For Germany we have asked and we continue to ask justice and even magnanimity from her erstwhile foes. We demand in the sight of humanity the right for Germany from the nations and the right from Germany for the Jewish people. No wrong under the heavens could be greater than to make German Jews scapegoats because Germany has grievances against the nations. We who would secure justice from the nations for Germany and justice to Jews from Germany affirm tonight that Germany cannot hope to secure justice through injustice to its Jewish people.

This protest is not against the German people whom we honor and revere and cherish. How could we, of the household of Israel, fail to cherish and honor the German people, one of the great peoples of earth, a people that has made monumental, indeed eternal, contributions to human well being in the domains of religion, literature and the arts. How could we fail to cherish and to revere the people of Goethe and Schiller, Immanuel Kant and Hegel, Beethoven and Wagner, Heine and Einstein.

This protest is not against the political program of Germany, for Germany is master within her own household, but solely against the present anti-Jewish policy of the Nazi Government. There is no need for our German-born neighbors in America nor for our fellow Jews in Germany to appeal to us to avoid an anti-Jewish demonstration. We are not against Germany, and it is an unforgivable calumny to declare that we are '*Deutschfeindlich.*' We are the friends of, and believers in, Germany. Germany at its highest. Germany at its truest, the German nation at its noblest. Because we are the friends of Germany, because we have inextinguishable faith in the basic love for righteousness of the German people, we appeal to Germany representing as this meeting does Protestants, Catholics, Jews in the name of America, which has been stirred as rarely before against wrongs perpetrated upon Jews.

We know that it is not easy to cancel the Nazi program of thirteen years, and still we know that it can be done. A dictatorship is omnipotent and, above all, the German people at its best will support the government in every honest effort to avert the shame on the medievalization of German Jewry. If the Nazi Government will use for the suppression of the anti-Semitic campaign in Germany 1/100 or 1/1000 part of the vigor and rigor with which it has suppressed differing or, as it believes, dangerous political parties, anti-Semitism will perish in Germany.

We understand the plea and the plaint of our brother Jews in Germany. They are German patriots who love their Fatherland and have had reason to love it. Some of their leaders are under the impact of panic and terror, others under some form of compulsion, in any event the compulsion of a great fear if not actual coercion. Do they appeal to the Nazi Government to bring about a cessation of its anti-Jewish campaign as they have appealed to us to end our protest? We have no quarrel with our Jewish brothers in Germany and their leaders, but their policy of uncomplaining assent and of super-cautious silence has borne evil fruit. They who have virtually been silent through the years of anti-Jewish propaganda cannot be followed by us as the wisest of counselors. And if things are to be worse because of our protest, if there are to be new penalties and new reprisals in Germany, which I cannot bring myself to believe, then humbly and sorrowfully we bow our heads in the presence of the tragic fate that threatens and once again appeal to the public opinion of mankind and to the conscience of Christendom to save civilization from the shame that may be imminent.

To those leaders of German Jewry who declare the present anti-Jewish situation in Germany is a local German question, we call attention to the words of Abraham Lincoln. Defenders of slavery urged and excused slavery on the ground that it was local. Lincoln's answer was, SLAVERY IS LOCAL BUT FREEDOM IS NATIONAL. The conscience of humanity has made a world problem of the present situation of the Jews. We lay down no conditions tonight, we make no stipulations, we do not even urge demands. But we do affirm certain elementary axioms of civilization. The Jews of the world, no more than the Jews of Germany, do not demand exceptional treatment or privileged position or favored status for themselves. We do not even ask for rights. We ask only for the right. We demand the right.

What are these elementary maxims of civilization as we call them? The immediate cessation of anti-Semitic activities and propaganda in Germany, including an end to the policy of racial discrimination against and of economic exclusion of Jews from the life of Germany. That is Jewish life, and the human rights of Jews must be safeguarded. One other absolutely reasonable and just axiom rather than demand: The revocation of all special measures already taken against Jewish non-nationals and their equal treatment with all other non-nationals in Germany. Which of these demands shall we abate? Whatever be the threat of reprisal, none of these can be withdrawn or altered or moderated without insult to Germany and without tragic self-stultification on the part of Jews.

But it must be made clear in the hearing of men that even if life and human rights are to be safeguarded, there must not be a substitution of the status of helotry for violence. Such substitution will not satisfy us nor satisfy the aroused conscience of humankind even though Jews in Germany must sink into the horror of seeming acquiescence. Every economic discrimination is a form of violence. Every racial exclusion is violence. To say that there will be no pogroms is not enough. A dry and bloodless economic pogrom remains violence and force.

Hear the word of a great English statesman, of one who did as much as any other Englishman of his day to make England mighty: 'Providence would deal good or ill fortune to nations according as they dealt well or ill by the Jews.' This is not a warning but a prophecy. May the German people merit the fulfillment of this prophecy of good fortune by dealing well and justly and as a Christian nation by the Jews.

I close as I began. We are not met in the spirit of bitterness, hatred or revenge. We do not desire that the German people be punished because of the unwisdom of the measures and the injustice of some practices of its government. Whatever nations may ask in the spirit of reparation and reprisal, we who are Jews know that our spirit must be in consonance with the high tradition of Jewish forbearance and Jewish forgiveness. But there must be no further reprisals against our fellow Jews, no penalizing them as German hostages because the conscience of the world utters its mighty protest. God help the German people to be equal to themselves.

•

HAILE SELASSIE
1936

'Death-dealing rain'

Haile Selassie (1892–1975), the last emperor of Ethiopia, took his country into the League of Nations in 1923. When the Italian dictator Mussolini invaded Ethiopia in 1935, the emperor went in person to protest to the League of Nations in Geneva. Selassie described Mussolini's methods of waging war, and was the first head of state to appeal to the League to rescue his nation, but he was spurned. Mussolini won the war, proclaimed a new Roman empire, and Haile Selassie settled as an exile in England. The League, exposed as a sham, died.

It is my duty to inform the governments assembled in Geneva, responsible as they are for the lives of millions of men, women and children, of the deadly peril which threatens them, by describing to them the fate which has been suffered by Ethiopia.

It is not only upon warriors that the Italian Government has made war. It has, above all, attacked populations far removed from hostilities, in order to terrorize and exterminate them.

At the beginning, towards the end of 1935, Italian aircraft hurled upon my armies bombs of tear-gas. Their effects were but slight. The soldiers learned to scatter, waiting until the wind had rapidly dispersed the poisonous gases.

The Italian aircraft then resorted to mustard gas. Barrels of liquid were hurled upon armed groups. But this means also was not effective; the liquid only affected a few soldiers, and barrels upon the ground were themselves a warning to troops and to the population of the danger.

It was at the time when the operations for the encircling of Makale were taking place that the Italian command, fearing a rout, followed the procedure which it is now my duty to denounce to the world. Special sprayers were installed on board aircraft so that they could vaporize, over vast areas of territory, a fine, death-dealing rain. Groups of nine, fifteen, eighteen aircraft followed one another so that the fog issuing from them formed a continuous sheet. It was thus that, as from the end of January 1936, soldiers, women, children, cattle, rivers, lakes and pastures were drenched continually with this deadly rain. In order to kill off systematically all living creatures, in order the more surely to poison waters and pastures, the Italian command made its aircraft pass over and over again. That was its chief method of warfare.

The very refinement of barbarism consisted in carrying ravage and terror into the most densely populated parts of the territory – the points farthest removed from the scene of hostilities. The object was to scatter fear and death over a great part of the Ethiopian territory.

These fearful tactics succeeded. Men and animals succumbed. The deadly rain that fell from the aircraft made all those whom it touched fly shrieking with pain. All those who drank the poisoned water or ate the infected food also succumbed in dreadful suffering. In tens of thousands the victims of the Italian mustard gas fell. It is in order to denounce to the civilized world the tortures inflicted upon the Ethiopian people that I resolved to come to Geneva . . .

In October 1935, the fifty-two nations who are listening to me today gave me an assurance that the aggressor would not triumph, that the resources of the Covenant would be employed in order to ensure the reign of right and the failure of violence.

I ask the fifty-two nations not to forget today the policy upon which they embarked eight months ago, and in faith of which I directed the resistance of my people against the aggressor whom they had denounced to the world. Despite the inferiority of my weapons, the complete lack of aircraft, artillery, munitions, hospital services, my confidence in the League was absolute. I thought it to be impossible that fifty-two nations, including the most powerful in the world, should be successfully opposed by a single aggressor. Counting on the faith due to treaties, I had made no preparation for war, and that is the case with certain small countries in Europe . . .

War then took place in the atrocious conditions which I have laid before the assembly.

What real assistance was given to Ethiopia by the fifty-two nations who had declared the Rome Government guilty of a breach of the Covenant and had undertaken to prevent the triumph of the aggressor? Has each of the member states, as it was its duty to do in virtue of its signature appended to Article 16 of the Covenant, considered the aggressor as having committed an act of war personally directed against itself? I had placed all my hopes in the execution of these undertakings. My confidence had been confirmed by the repeated declaration made in the council to the effect that aggression must not be rewarded and that force would be compelled to bow before right.

In December 1935, the council made it quite clear that its feelings were in harmony with those of hundreds of millions of people who, in all parts of the world, had protested against the proposal to dismember Ethiopia. It was constantly repeated that there was not merely a conflict between the Italian Government and Ethiopia but also a conflict between the Italian Government and the League of Nations, and that is why I personally refused all proposals to my personal advantage made to me by the Italian Government if only I would betray my people and the Covenant of the League of Nations. I was defending the cause of all small peoples who are threatened with aggression.

What has become of the promises made to me?

The Ethiopian Government never expected other governments to shed their soldiers' blood to defend the Covenant when their own immediate personal interests were not at stake. Ethiopian warriors asked only for means to defend themselves. On many occasions I have asked for financial assistance for the purchase of arms. That assistance has been constantly refused me. What, then, in practice, is the meaning of Article 16 and of collective security?

Apart from the Kingdom of the Lord there is not on this earth any nation that is superior to any other. Should it happen that a strong government finds it may, with impunity, destroy a weak people, then the hour strikes for that weak people to appeal to the League of Nations to give its judgement in all freedom. God and history will remember your judgement . . .

Representatives of the world, I have come to discharge in your midst the most painful of the duties of the head of a state. What reply shall I have to take back to my people?

•

THE TIMES
1936

'Morganatic marriage'

The abdication crisis was provoked when Edward VIII, who had succeeded George V in January 1936, made it clear to Stanley Baldwin, the prime minister, that he intended to marry his American mistress, Wallis Simpson, as soon as she was divorced. She obtained her divorce on 27 October. As the King was Supreme Governor of the Church of England, which did not recognize divorce, Baldwin, the Archbishop of Canterbury and the leaders of all the major political parties agreed that the King could not marry Mrs Simpson.

Urged on by Geoffrey Dawson, editor of The Times, *Baldwin advised the King that he should renounce Mrs Simpson or abdicate. Eager to compromise and with the support of the two major press barons, Beaverbrook and Rothermere, the King proposed some form of morganatic marriage – Mrs Simpson to become his wife but not Queen.*

On 8 December, The Times, *often described as 'The Thunderer', protested in its main leading article at the very idea of morganatic marriage. Two days later, the King abdicated.*

Mr Baldwin's further statement to the House yesterday has left little occasion for any genuine or involuntary misunderstanding of the relations between the King and his ministers in respect of the marriage which His Majesty wishes to make. It completely satisfied the House of Commons, as it showed by a blunt refusal to tolerate the efforts of Mr Churchill and one or two others to improve upon it with suggestions or conditions of their own. In such a statement, as the House was well aware, the Prime Minister was speaking for the King as well as for his advisers, and there was good reason to resent unofficial attempts to go behind it.

Mr Baldwin has now made it clear to the world that ministers are as reluctant as any of the King's subjects to hurry a momentous decision. It concerns, as Mr Baldwin said, the King's 'own future happiness'. It also concerns the interests of all his subjects. On the other hand, the King himself is quite as fully aware as his Ministers that prolonged suspense would risk disaster to the interests of the country and the Empire. Nor is this all that has to be said of light-minded, though always unconvincing, allegations that the Cabinet has intervened abruptly in the King's private affairs, forced unwelcome advice upon him, and importuned him for instant compliance. The allegations were too bad to be true. They were in fact not true. And no more ought to be heard of them, or will be heard of them from anyone who has the King's prestige and the political security of the realm at heart. Mr Baldwin was able to inform the House that no advice at all has been tendered by the Cabinet to His Majesty except in the matter of the morganatic marriage on which he expressly consulted them. Nor, even then, did Ministers raise the question of the marriage. It was raised by the King himself. The Cabinet, and the Cabinets and peoples of the Empire, can only await quietly and sympathetically whatever conclusion His Majesty may reach on a subject which has been in his mind, as Mr Baldwin said, for some time past. Nor are its intrinsic embarrassments and absurdities the only reason for condemning its resurrection at this stage. Those who purport to be advancing it in His Majesty's interest are doing so in the face of the considered and unanimous decision of the five Empire Governments. In the form of advocacy which they have chosen, it is an unpleasantly significant recrudescence of the same movement – in the same quarter – which threatened not long ago to depict the Sovereign as in conflict with his elected and appointed ministerial advisers. It is also an attempt to force upon the King a decision which is his and his only, and which he may be trusted to take in his own time with full regard for the Constitution of which he is a custodian and for the hereditary trust, written and unwritten, that came into his hands from his father ten months ago.

•

CASSANDRA (WILLIAM CONNOR)
1936

'I accuse'

As 'Cassandra' in the Daily Mirror, *William Connor (1909–67) was the most controversial newspaper columnist of his era. 'Even the casual "Good Morning" was accompanied by the awful din of screeching mental brakes,' said one of his editors, Hugh Cudlipp.*

As The Times *protested at the idea of a morganatic marriage for the King, the* Daily Mirror *joined the* Daily Express *and* Daily Mail *in a rearguard action for the King against the Church and the Cabinet, in which Cassandra played the role of striker.*

I am writing about what I regard as the biggest mistake of all time.

I accuse leaders of the Church of England of placing our King in a position from which it is almost impossible to retreat.

I accuse the Prime Minister and his Government of failing to take a loyal nation into its confidence at an early date, thereby permitting a desperate situation in which humiliation is the only answer.

Why was the country faced with an ultimatum?
The destiny of our King ultimately belongs not to himself, not to his ministers, but to us his people.

The first thing we hear of the disagreement is that the Cabinet is waiting for an answer to the most menacing threat that a government can make.

The situation developed long ago.

But it took time to arrange things.

The strength of the monarch had to be gauged.

Why weren't the Dominions told the truth?
Mr Baldwin has said that the government is not prepared to introduce legislation whereby Mrs Simpson could be debarred from becoming the legal Queen of England.

He has further stated that such a change could not be effective without the consent of all the Dominions.

He has satisfied himself that their assent would not be forthcoming.

I say: How can the people of the Dominions express their views on the situation?

What have they had to go by? A few American magazines and newspapers based on a thin and unreliable structure of conjecture.

They have had no advice from their leaders.

They have had no facts.

No details.

Only wild rumours from the other side of the Atlantic.

What does the Canadian, working in far Alberta, say?

What does the New Zealander feel?

The peoples of the Dominions have NOT been consulted.

How can we expect their Parliaments to have the courage to decide on an outcome the issue of which the Mother of Parliaments has dexterously dodged?

The future of the Empire cannot be decided by the result of a few hasty telephone conversations among politicians.

This is an issue so great that it has to be put to the test – the people themselves have to be consulted.

Things have been rushed through.

There has been no time and so far there has been no opportunity.

What are the objections?
I will tell you.

Mrs Wallis Simpson has divorced not one husband, but two.

I read from an inspired source that –

'The Church, the West End of London and the aristocracy generally object strongly to the marriage of a divorced person, innocent or guilty. They say that the marriage obligation is a solemn binding of two people for life.'

I will pass over the Church.

There is more corruption, there is more spiritual rottenness in the West End of London than in any other place in the country.

And the aristocracy? First cast out the beam that is in thine own eye! The sorry pageant of adultery and divorce is an unceasing spectacle from this elevated class.

What are the consequences of abdication?
Simply the greatest tragedy that could befall England.

We are a humane and sympathetic people.

Foreigners regard us as a cold and puritanical race.

That is not so.

No nation is so tolerant on so wide a scale.

But our laws on divorce are medieval and unjust. As a body, the Church – though there are notable exceptions – supports these outdated laws as they stand. The attitude of the country is in fierce opposition to them and has been actively so for the last ten years.

But the King will be the first man to be denied even the merits of the law such as they are.

Take away our King from us and the monarchy suffers the greatest blow that has been struck for centuries.

Abroad people will regard us with derision and contempt. It is possible that the King is not doing a wise thing. But he believes in it with all his heart. For thirty years he has served us. Since he was a mere boy he has worked as few people ever have.

The war was fought on the cry of 'King and Country'.

Edward VIII wasn't King then, but he was no child. He knew the strains of the Royal Family.

He helped his father bear his burden. And now, when at last he wishes to make the foremost and greatest decision of his life – the government desert him and give no help.

Is this England?

More than ever we need personality on the throne.

We've got it.

The world is divided into people and powerful rulers.

What leadership will England have if our King abdicates?

A monarchy brought into disrepute.

What is the position of America?

America desires this marriage – fervently and with deep sincerity.

Upton Sinclair has stated: 'I urge the common people of Britain to realize what the Cabinet's action will do to Anglo–American friendship. This story has been thrashed out here for months. American sympathy is overwhelmingly with Mrs Simpson and the King's democratic attitude.'

What is wrong with an American lady?

Isn't she as good as a Swede or a Greek or an Albanian?

Why try to preserve the old tradition of royalty marrying royalty?

If political significance is attached to the proposed bride's country of origin, then America compares favourably with every other country outside of Great Britain.

Our interests are in common.

We both desire peace.

We both respect democracy.

We both abhor dictatorship.

This is a chance to extend our friendship – or damage it to an incalculable extent . . .

What of the Royal Family?

By its action the government has placed the members of the Royal Family in an ugly position.

There is no other word for it.

The Heir to the Throne is in an unenviable circumstance. Should he accede he is bound to find the country split in two.

Not a theoretical division, but a strong, bitter clash of views, in which the merits and demerits of the monarchical system are fiercely fought.

And Queen Mary?

If ever a woman deserves our sympathy she does. A better Queen has never ruled this country.

Whatever her views on the case, it is a sad and melancholy thing that she should witness this strife.

She above all people knows that happiness in marriage is important above all things.

She knows that the people wish to see her son blessed with it. She knows that we are pleased with his democracy and his unrivalled courage.

She knows what it is to uphold royal traditions in the face of relentless opposition.

The loss of her husband was immeasurable in its resultant grief to her.

Let us hope that the outcome of present state affairs adds no more to that burden.

The people of this country and our Empire are shocked and stunned by this crisis.

They have been kept in suspense.

They have been barred from the truth.

The cancer of rumour has undermined their confidence, and it will not be restored until the happiness of the King they have learned to love is apparent and obvious in every action that he does.

•

WINSTON CHURCHILL
1936

'The locust years'

By 1936 Winston Churchill (1874–1965), abandoned by his party, betrayed by his friends and stripped of office, was convinced that Germany was stronger in air power than Britain and France combined. He urged Stanley Baldwin to allow a House of Commons debate on defence, during which he delivered this speech, one of the greatest of his career. It was the day that Churchill spoke for all who knew that sooner or later Britain must confront Hitler and he worked on the speech through the night, dictating and revising passages to hone one of his finest philippics – aimed directly at Baldwin.

'He drives his points home with a sledgehammer,' Harold Nicolson recorded as he watched Churchill deliver the speech, which ended with a remarkable peroration in which he damned the House of Commons.

The First Lord of the Admiralty in his speech the other night went even farther. He said, 'We are always reviewing the position.' Everything, he assured us, is entirely fluid. I am sure that that is true. Anyone can see what the position is. The government simply cannot make up their minds, or they cannot get the Prime Minister to make up his mind. So they go on in strange paradox, decided only to be undecided, resolved to be irresolute, adamant for drift, solid for fluidity, all-powerful to be impotent. So we go on preparing more months and years – precious, perhaps vital to the greatness of Britain – for the locusts to eat. They will say to me, 'A Minister of Supply is not necessary, for all is going well.' I deny it. 'The position is satisfactory.' It is not true. 'All is proceeding according to plan.' We know what that means . . .

Owing to past neglect, in the face of the plainest warnings, we have now entered upon a period of danger greater than has befallen Britain since the U-boat campaign was crushed; perhaps, indeed, it is a more grievous period than that, because at that time at least we were possessed of the means of securing ourselves and of defeating that campaign. Now we have no such assurance. The era of procrastination, of half-measures, of soothing and baffling expedients, of delays, is coming to its close. In its place we are entering a period of consequences. We have entered a period in which for more than a year, or a year and a half, the considerable preparations which are now on foot in Britain will not, as the Minister clearly showed, yield results which can be effective in actual fighting strength; while during this very period Germany may well reach the culminating point of her gigantic military preparations, and be forced by financial and economic stringency to contemplate a sharp decline, or perhaps some other exit from her difficulties. It is this lamentable conjunction of events which seems to present the danger of Europe in its most disquieting form. We cannot avoid this period; we are in it now. Surely, if we can abridge it by even a few months, if we can shorten this period when the German Army will begin to be so much larger than the French Army, and before the British Air Force has come to play its complementary part, we may be the architects who build the peace of the world on sure foundations.

Two things, I confess, have staggered me, after a long parliamentary experience, in these debates. The first has been the dangers that have so swiftly come upon us in a few years, and have been transforming our position and the whole outlook of the world. Secondly, I have been staggered by the failure of the House of Commons to react effectively against those dangers. That, I am bound to say, I never expected. I never would have believed that we should have been allowed to go on getting into this plight, month by month and year by year, and that even the government's own confessions of error would have produced no concentration of parliamentary opinion and force capable of lifting our efforts to the level of emergency. I say that unless the House resolves to find out the truth for itself it will have committed an act of abdication of duty without parallel in its long history.

•

ARTHUR KOESTLER/JOSÉ ORTEGA Y GASSET
1936

'Civil war'

Within days of the start of the Spanish Civil War, reports began to circulate of the atrocities being committed by General Franco's Nationalists as they attempted to overthrow the Spanish Second Republic. José Ortega y Gasset (1883–1955), president of the law faculty at the University of Madrid, published a memorandum drawn up by the faculty's governing body on rebel terror.

Arthur Koestler went as a journalist to report the war and afterwards wrote Spanish Testament, *in which he quoted Ortega y Gasset's report to which he added his own commentary.*

Civil wars, that divide families and breed hatred, have always been prosecuted in a particularly ruthless manner; the crimes that are being committed by the insurgents at the moment, however, surpass anything that has hitherto been known in the way of organized savagery. The spirit that inspires these retrograde hordes is that of the Carlist wars, the spirit that existed under the fanatical and intolerant regime of Ferdinand VII. Once more the red caps of the 'Requetes' have risen up from the blood-drenched Spanish soil; once more bishops and priests play their part in dastardly guerrilla warfare. They give their blessing to the Moors, who have been called in to strangle the Spanish people, and hang round their necks medallions of the crucifixion, telling them that they are magic amulets.

It is impossible to include in this document all the atrocities which the insurgents are perpetrating on the martyred Spanish people. Every day that passes brings new scenes of horror. We will quote only a few of them here which illustrate graphically the criminal methods against which we appeal to international opinion.

The rebels, in all the districts occupied by them, systematically shoot workers carrying a trade union card. The corpses are left lying on view in the streets or heaped up in the cemeteries, each with the card of a trade union tied to leg or arm, in order to show the reason for the execution.

In the town of Seville alone, and independently of any military action, more than 9,000 workers and peasants were executed. The Moors and Foreign Legionaries went through the streets of humble one-storey houses in the working-class districts throwing hand grenades through the windows, killing women and children. The Moorish troops gave themselves up to sacking and plundering. General Queipo de Llano describes scenes of rape on the wireless with a coarse relish that is an indirect incitement to a repetition of such scenes.

At this point I shall interrupt the memorandum of the Faculty of Law in order to supplement its description of the incidents in Seville.

During the Civil War I was twice in Seville; the first time from 27 to 29 August 1936, as a journalist, the second time from 12 February to 12 May 1937, as a prisoner. Both what I heard in Seville and, to some extent, my own experiences there serve to confirm the authenticity of the above document. I should like to quote another eye-witness account, that of Jesús Corrales of Algeciras, a hotel employee.

Corrales fled from Algeciras eight days after the insurrection, when he found that the rebels, failing to find him at home, had shot his twenty-one-year-old wife, Gertrudis Sarmiento, his two-year-old son, Ricardo, and his eight-month-old daughter, Carmen. His flight took him via Seville to Portugal, and from there via Corunna, Vigo and San Sebastián to France. I met him at the end of October in Paris, where I had an opportunity of examining his documents and checking his statements by my own personal knowledge of Seville. Here follows his sworn statement, for which I take full responsibility:

> In Seville, in a small street of the district of San Bernardo, I saw with my own eyes the shooting of a group of about 150 prisoners, among whom there were some women. In order to keep the refractory population in a constant state of terror, General Queipo de Llano gave orders that the prisoners should not be shot, as at first, in the barracks, in the prison or the cemetery, but in the streets of working-class districts, and that the corpses should be left lying in the streets for from twelve to sixteen hours, after oil had been poured on them so as to avoid the possibility of epidemics. Mass executions had therefore been carried out since the last few days of July, according to a systematic plan, in the districts of Macarena, San Lorenzo, San Bernardo and Triana alternately. The total number of those shot when I arrived in Seville was estimated at 7,000, i.e. a daily average of 100 to 150 people. The usual procedure was for the delinquents to be transported in lorries to the street chosen for the execution, where they were made to get out of the lorries in groups of ten and were then shot. Such horrible scenes took place, however, that the procedure was later on simplified and the prisoners were shot one by one in the back of the head with revolvers as they got out of the lorries.

This account shows that the memorandum of the Faculty of Law in no way exaggerates, but rather falls short of the full truth. 'In Algeciras,' continues the memorandum,

> 'the pregnant wife of a Trade Union official who had fled to Gibraltar was forced to drink a mixture of castor oil and petrol and then sent to join her husband. She died the following day. A large number of other women were forced to drink the same mixture. The Moorish troops amused themselves by throwing bombs at bakers' shops where working-class women were standing in queues.

Here again some amplification is necessary. The author stayed in Algeciras on 30 August on the way from Seville to Gibraltar. He was told that in this little port, where the Foreign Legion and Moors from Africa first touched

Spanish soil, about 400 people had been murdered, among them a particularly large number of infants and children.

The lawyers' report continues:

> In Granada more than 5,000 workers were shot; similarly all the free-masons were arrested, after the card-index of the local lodge had been discovered. The prisoners were taken to the cemetery and compelled to dig a common grave for themselves, in which they were then shot.
>
> Among those murdered was the poet García Lorca, the leading spirit of the younger generation of Spanish writers.
>
> In the hamlets of Pedro Abad, El Carpio and Espejo, after the shooting of the militiamen, their wives were violated and their breasts cut off.
>
> In the little town of El Carpio, near Córdoba, which was recaptured by the government troops, 200 workers had previously been shot in the cemetery; the members of their families were marched to the cemetery accompanied by the village drummer, to take their last farewell of their husbands; and when assembled there, they were shot down by machine-guns on the orders of a captain of the Foreign Legion.
>
> Six members of the F A I (Iberian Anarchist Federation) were locked up by Phalangists in a hut, which was soaked with petrol and set alight. All that was found of them was their charred corpses.
>
> In Baena (Córdoba), according to the testimony of Antonio Moreno Benavente, of the Socialist Group, who managed to escape when the rebels took the town, the rebels shot everyone whose name appeared on the files of the workers' organizations. Their cruelty, as in other places, took the form of compelling the victims to dig their own graves. They took the Presidents of the Socialist Group and the Socialist Youth Party, Gregorio Lonzo and Manuel Sevillano, and the Secretary of the Socialist Youth, Eduardo Cortés, tied them together and shot them, while the families of the three men were made to look on. On 29 August 296 out of the 375 members of the parties mentioned were shot. On 9 August, thirty workmen were forced to repair the fortifications of the historic castle of the town, and after forty-eight hours of incessant work without rest and without food, during which they were urged on with whips, they were thrown from the castle rock into the depths below. Three of them had already gone mad.

•

ANDRÉ GIDE
1936

'The God That Failed'

The French novelist André Gide (1869–1951) was one of the most famous living European writers when he went to the Soviet Union in 1936. He had become an enthusiastic convert to Communism. 'Why do I long for Communism?' he wrote. 'Because it is Communism which can – indeed must – promote a new and better form of civilization.'

This report, compiled from the two books he wrote on his return and used in 1960 in The God That Failed *(with contributions from, among others, Arthur Koestler, Stephen Spender and Richard Wright), shows that he was quickly disillusioned.*

Among all workers and artisans in the Soviet Union it is the writer who is most favoured and indulged. The immense privileges that I was offered amazed and terrified me and I was afraid of being seduced and corrupted. I did not go to the Soviet Union for the sake of benefits and those that I saw were glaring. But that did not prevent my criticism since the most favoured position enjoyed by writers in Russia – better than in any other country in the world – was granted only to the right-thinking. That was a danger signal to me and I was immediately on my guard. The price exacted is the total surrender of all opposition, and opposition in the Soviet Union is merely the exercise of free criticism. I discovered that a certain distinguished member of the Academy of Sciences had just been released from prison, whose sole crime had been independence of judgement, and when foreign scientists tried to get in touch with him, they were always told that he was indisposed. Another was dismissed from his professorship and denied laboratory facilities for having expressed scientific opinions which did not tally with current Soviet doctrine, and he was obliged to write a public letter of recantation to avoid deportation. It is a characteristic trait of despotism to be unable to suffer independence and to tolerate only servility. However just his brief, woe betide the Soviet lawyer who rises to defend an accused whom the authorities wish to see convicted. Stalin allows only praise and approbation and soon he will be surrounded only by those who cannot put him in the wrong since they have no opinions whatsoever. His portrait is seen everywhere, his name is on everyone's lips and praise of him occurs in every public speech. Is all this the result of worship, love or fear? Who can say?

I remember, on the way to Tiflis, as we went through Gori – the little village where he was born – I thought it would be a kind and courteous attention to send him a personal message as an expression of gratitude for the warm welcome we had received in the Soviet Union where we had been treated everywhere with lavish hospitality. I thought that no better opportunity would occur again, so I had the car stop at the post office and I handed in a telegram which began: 'Passing through Gori on our wonderful trip I feel the impulse to send you' – but here the translator paused and said that he could not transmit such a message, that 'you', when addressed to Stalin, was not sufficient. It was not decent, he declared, and something must be added. He suggested 'You leader of the workers' or else 'You Lord of the people'. It seemed to me absurd and I said that Stalin must surely be above such flattery, but all in vain. Nothing would budge him and he would not transmit the telegram unless I agreed to the emendation. I reflected sadly that such formalities contribute to erect an insuperable barrier between Stalin and his subjects. I was also frequently obliged to make additions or alterations in the speeches I delivered in the course of my visit. They explained to me that a word like 'destiny' must always be preceded by the epithet 'glorious' when it referred to the destiny of the Soviet Union; on the other hand, they requested me to delete the adjective 'great' when it qualified a king, since a monarch can never be 'great'!

As long as man is oppressed and downtrodden, as long as the compulsion of social injustice keeps him in subjection, we are at liberty to hope much from what has not yet had opportunity to burgeon, from all the latent fertility in the fallow classes. Just as we hope much from children who may eventually grow up into quite commonplace people, in the same way we often have the illusion that the masses are composed of men of a finer clay than the rest of disappointing humanity.

In Marxist doctrine there is no such thing as truth – at least not in any absolute sense – there is only relative truth. I believe, however, that in so serious a matter it is criminal to lead others astray, and urgent to see matters as they are, not as we would wish them to be – or had hoped that they might be. The Soviet Union has deceived our fondest hopes and shown us tragically in what treacherous quicksand an honest revolution can founder. The same old capitalist society has been re-established, a new and terrible despotism crushing and exploiting man, with all the abject and servile mentality of serfdom. Russia, like Demophoon, has failed to become a God and she will never now arise from the fires of the Soviet ordeal.

•

ISABEL BROWN
1937

'A martyred city'

The support of Hitler's Nazi Germany and Mussolini's Fascist Italy was crucial to the success of General Franco's Nationalists in defeating the Republicans in the Spanish Civil War (1936–9). On behalf of Franco, the German Condor Legion started in 1937 the first saturation bombing of civilians in history. The most notorious bombardment, made known to the world by Picasso, was at Guernica, which was razed to the ground on 26 April.

Yet another city had earlier suffered the same fate. The bombardment of Durango caused the death of 300 people, mostly women and children, as well as a priest celebrating Mass and many monks and nuns. Another 2,500 were wounded. A delegation of British church-people visited Durango two hours after the bombardment. The report written by Isabel Brown was published by the British Relief Committee for Victims of Fascism. The chief signatories were Dr Hewlett Johnson, Dean of Canterbury, and John MacMurray, professor of philosophy at London University.

Durango is a little provincial town of 10,000 people, increased to 15,000 by refugees driven there from the various battle fronts in Northern Spain. With its houses springing from the chalk, its churches and convents, its streets planted with tamarisk, its old market, this fair little town was peaceful and smiling, despite the revolt. Thirty-five miles from the front, the centre of an agricultural district, it is an important market town.

Calm, industrious and deeply religious the population carried on as though far from the trenches. Almost all the men had gone to the front, few were left to work in the factories and fields, so one saw hardly anyone except women and children. Here and there were groups of abandoned children, ill-fed and in distress, arriving from other parts of the Basque country to seek refuge in this provincial centre. It was not a military town nor was it being used for any military purpose. What could such a peaceful city have to fear from war? Of what should the people be afraid? They did nothing but work.

While their brothers, sons and husbands were away fighting to preserve their little country from Fascism and foreign invasion, the women of Durango continued to work and pray. They continued their religious observances as of old and the churches attracted large congregations at the time for prayers. Who would dream that one day Junker planes would attack such inoffensive people? There was surely nothing to fear, the rebels were human like themselves, they had mothers and children, they would never drop bombs on an undefended town.

THE BOMBERS COME

Everybody in Durango was convinced that there was no danger, even when they heard the noise of motors in the sky. There was none of the terrified reaction which is natural when a squadron of aeroplanes appears over a military town in Aragon, Estremadura, Asturias or Catalonia. In these places at the first warning the inhabitants leave their houses, rush through the streets into the fields or else find shelter in a cellar, but this is by no means frequent. Generally, led by unexplained instinct, they feel more safe in open country. After all, a meadow or a coppice is no target for an airman.

In silence the crowds await the end of the bombardment. Then when the danger has passed, after an interval of some duration, the people return to their homes feeling desperate and anxious. Will they find the young child who ran in another direction or the old grandmother who would insist on remaining in the house? Will their home be still standing? Will ruins and worst of all, a corpse meet their frightened eyes? The relief, when all is well!

DEATH FROM THE SKIES

But at Durango nothing like this occurred, for the people thought the aeroplanes were not concerned with them. When they came the population did not move, in fact some of them continued their way to the churches, sure in the knowledge that they would find asylum in the consecrated buildings. How little they knew the purpose of those forty German planes.

31 March 1937 – a fateful day for Durango. The women were in church, in the home or at the market. The few men in their workshops or fields, children playing in the streets and squares.

Suddenly! Unexpectedly! The most violent aerial bombardment yet experienced in the Spanish war was upon them.

First of all bombs weighing one or two cwts fell from the planes on the Parish Church of Santa Maria. At the moment Abbé Morilla was raising the sacrament for consecration a bomb fell at the foot of the altar. Later, under a mass of wreckage, the body of the priest was found clad in his sacerdotal vestments, his hand still grasping the sacrament.

At the same time ten bombs fell upon the College of the Jesuits, the walls were blown in, entombing Father Villalabeitia, who was administering communion to a large number of the faithful. All were killed, including the choir boy who was assisting the minister.

On that morning three churches, chapels and a number of working-class houses were completely destroyed.

In the afternoon of the same day there was a second raid of German planes. This time the inhabitants of the town started a despairing flight into the countryside. Alas! it was too late, the first bombs were already falling. The convent of the Augustinians was demolished and fifteen nuns perished. When their bodies were recovered from the debris all were terribly mutilated.

Yet this was not enough. Flying very low, the German aircraft rained heavy machine-gun fire on a number of nuns in the cloister gardens, seriously wounding these and many other unhappy people.

As for the inhabitants of the town who, terrified by the events of the morning, had fled to the countryside, they did not escape. The Germans, having finished their horrible mission in the town, followed the women and children and old men and mowed them down with machine-guns and grenades.

This fearful carnage of a Catholic town's people by the 'Aryan' exponents of 'Culture' shows the hatred that the Nazis have for all organized ideas which may counter their own. The Basque Catholic Nationalists are solidly standing out against Fascism and in support of the democratic regime in Spain. It is doubtful if the rebel Spanish pilots could have been persuaded to make such a barbaric attack upon fellow Catholics. It needed Hitler's picked men to do that.

There is something of stark desperation when they resort to this kind of warfare.

THE RAIDS CONTINUE

The motorized police came in from Bilbao, along with forces of militia and the Bilbao fire brigade, to bring help to the people. Fire had broken out and made rescue work difficult, though nothing was spared to try and help the wounded and dying. Their sad work was not finished when, two days later, the German squadrons came again and once more made a special mark of religious buildings. In one convent the nuns were present at Mass and several perished with the priest who was conducting the service.

Two other villages, Elorrio and Ochandoano, then suffered the same fate as Durango. Again Hitler's target was churches, women, children and old men. Then again to Durango for the third time in four days. After these bombardments the town is now a heap of ruins with 300 dead and 2,500 wounded. The little Basque town of Durango has disappeared.

The Dean of Canterbury was in the Basque country with a delegation of

church-people. Here are some of the comments he made to the press on 8
April:

> We heard on our arrival in Bilbao of the bombardment of Durango in
> which we were informed that the first figures, which have nearly doubled
> since, were 800 casualties of which 180 were killed. Among them were
> several priests and nuns. One of the priests was actually saying Mass
> when he was killed. We decided to go to Durango to see for ourselves,
> and did so on Friday afternoon, 2 April.
>
> When we were a short distance from the town we saw six enemy
> bombers, accompanied by a large number of fighting planes, appear
> over Durango and drop bombs on it. We saw the explosions of the
> bombs. After the planes had disappeared we proceeded to Durango
> and inspected the damage. Durango was largely destroyed. The bombing
> must have been of terrific intensity. The churches and the convents
> suffered in particular, and it was quite clear, even to an inexperienced
> eye, that the damage could only have been done from the air.

Durango is now no more than a name, but that name spells Fascism in
action with all its savagery and its violence.

It is a pleading symbol of what Fascism means – that Fascism against
which the Spanish people are fighting with such heroism. There is a sacred
duty imposed upon us, men and women throughout the whole world, to do
everything possible to prevent the establishment of such a Fascist regime in
Spain – a regime which is the shame of our modern civilization.

•

NIKOLAI BUKHARIN
1937

'My drop of blood'

*Lenin described the Bolshevik Nikolai Bukharin (1888–1938) as the biggest and most
valuable theorist in the Communist Party. Yet when Stalin started the Moscow show trials
in the 1930s, he was one of many veterans of the 1917 Revolution who were liquidated.
He was expelled from the Party in 1937, put on trial and shot.*

*A few days before his arrest, he had written a letter, 'To a Future Generation of Party
Leaders', and had asked his wife A. M. Larina to memorize it. After she returned from
confinement she put it in writing and, when Bukharin's rehabilitation was being arranged*

in 1961, she sent it to the Committee of Party Control. The letter is quoted in the Soviet historian Roy Medvedev's Let History Judge.

I am leaving life. I am lowering my head not before the proletarian axe, which must be merciless but also virginal. I feel my helplessness before a hellish machine, which, probably by the use of medieval methods, has acquired gigantic power, fabricates organized slander, acts boldly and confidently.

Dzerzhinsky is gone; the remarkable traditions of the Cheka have gradually faded into the past, when the revolutionary idea guided all its actions, justified cruelty to enemies, guarded the state against any kind of counterrevolution. That is how the Cheka earned special confidence, special respect, authority and esteem. At present, most of the so-called organs of the NKVD are a degenerate organization of bureaucrats, without ideas, rotten, well paid, who use the Cheka's bygone authority to cater to Stalin's morbid suspiciousness (I fear to say more) in a scramble for rank and fame, concocting their slimy cases, not realizing that they are at the same time destroying themselves – history does not put up with witnesses of foul deeds.

Any member of the Central Committee, any member of the Party can be rubbed out, turned into a traitor, terrorist, diversionist, spy, by these 'wonder-working organs'. If Stalin should ever get any doubts about himself, confirmation would instantly follow.

Storm clouds have risen over the Party. My one head, guilty of nothing, will drag down thousands of guiltless heads. For an organization must be created, a Bukharinite organization, which is in reality not only nonexistent now, the seventh year that I have had not a shadow of disagreement with the Party, but was also nonexistent then, in the years of the right opposition.

I have been in the Party since I was eighteen, and the purpose of my life has always been to fight for the interests of the working class, for the victory of socialism. These days the paper with the sacred name *Pravda* prints the filthiest lie, that I, Nikolai Bukharin, have wished to destroy the triumphs of October, to restore capitalism. That is unexampled insolence, that is a lie that could be equalled in insolence, in irresponsibility to the people, only by such a lie as this: it has been discovered that Nikolai Romanov devoted his whole life to the struggle against capitalism and monarchy, to the struggle for the achievement of a proletarian revolution. If, more than once, I was mistaken about the methods of building socialism, let posterity judge me no more harshly than Vladimir Ilyich did. We were moving toward a single goal for the first time, on a still unblazed trail. Other times, other customs, *Pravda* carried a discussion page, everyone argued, searched for ways and means, quarrelled and made up and moved on together.

I appeal to you, a future generation of Party leaders, whose historical mission will include the obligation to take apart the monstrous cloud of crimes that is growing ever huger in these frightful times, taking fire like a flame and suffocating the Party.

I appeal to all Party members! In these days, perhaps the last of my life, I am confident that sooner or later the filter of history will inevitably sweep the filth from my head. I was never a traitor; without hesitation I would have given my life for Lenin's. I loved Kirov, started nothing against Stalin. I ask a new young and honest generation of Party leaders to read my letter at a Party Plenum, to exonerate me, and to reinstate me in the Party.

Know, comrades, that on that banner, which you will be carrying in the victorious march to Communism, is also my drop of blood.

•

LEON TROTSKY
1937

'The Revolution Betrayed'

Leon Trotsky (1879–1940) ranks with Lenin as the inspiration of the Russian Revolution. After the Bolsheviks seized power, he led the negotiations at Brest-Litovsk, organized the Red Army and crushed the Kronstadt rebellion. Stalin, however, beat Trotsky to the succession when Lenin died and Trotsky was expelled from the Communist Party in 1927.

The Moscow trials confirmed Trotsky in his belief that Stalin had undermined all that the revolution stood for. He finished The Revolution Betrayed *in 1936, shortly before the start of the trial of the Party stalwarts, Zinoviev and Kamenev, both accused of organizing terrorism. Stalin denounced 'Trotskyist wreckers and spies', hounded Trotsky from exile in Norway and had him assassinated in Mexico three years later.*

The basis of bureaucratic rule is the poverty of society in objects of consumption, with the resulting struggle of each against all. When there are enough goods in a store, the purchasers can come whenever they want to. When there are few goods, the purchasers are compelled to stand in a queue. When the queues are very long, it is necessary to appoint a policeman to keep order. Such is the starting point of the power of the Soviet bureaucracy. It 'knows' who is to get something and who has to wait.

A raising of the material and cultural level ought, at first glance, to lessen the necessity of privileges, narrow the sphere of application of 'bourgeois law', and thereby undermine the standing ground of its defenders, the bureaucracy. In reality the opposite thing has happened: the growth of the productive forces has been so far accompanied by an extreme development of all forms of inequality, privilege, and advantage, and therewith of bureaucratism. That too is not accidental.

In its first period, the Soviet regime was undoubtedly far more egalitarian and less bureaucratic than now. But that was an equality of general poverty. The resources of the country were so scant that there was no opportunity to separate out from the masses of the population any broad privileged strata. At the same time the 'equalizing' character of wages, destroying personal interestedness, became a brake upon the development of the productive forces. The Soviet economy had to lift itself from its poverty to a somewhat higher level before fat deposits of privilege became possible. The present state of production is still far from guaranteeing all necessities to everybody. But it is already adequate to give significant privileges to a minority, and convert inequality into a whip for the spurring on of the majority. That is the first reason why the growth of production has so far strengthened not the socialist, but the bourgeois features of the state.

But that is not the sole reason. Alongside the economic factor dictating capitalistic methods of payment at the present stage, there operates a parallel political factor in the person of the bureaucracy itself. In its very essence it is the planter and protector of inequality. It arose in the beginning as the bourgeois organ of a workers' state. In establishing and defending the advantages of a minority, it of course draws off the cream for its own use. Nobody who has wealth to distribute ever omits himself. Thus out of a social necessity there has developed an organ which has far outgrown its socially necessary function and become an independent factor and therewith the source of great danger for the whole social organism.

The social meaning of the Soviet Thermidor now begins to take form before us. The poverty and cultural backwardness of the masses have again become incarnate in the malignant figure of the ruler with a great club in his hand. The deposed and abused bureaucracy, from being a servant of society, has again become its lord. On this road it has attained such a degree of social and moral alienation from the popular masses that it cannot now permit any control over either its activities or its income.

The bureaucracy's seemingly mystic fear of 'petty speculators, grafters and gossips' thus finds a wholly natural explanation. Not yet able to satisfy the elementary needs of the population, the Soviet economy creates and resurrects at every step tendencies to graft and speculation. On the other side, the privileges of the new aristocracy awaken in the masses of the population a tendency to listen to anti-Soviet 'gossips' – that is, to anyone who, albeit in a whisper, criticizes the greedy and capricious bosses. It is a question, therefore, not of spectres of the past, not of the remnants of what no longer exists, not, in short, of the snows of yesteryear, but of new, mighty, and continually reborn tendencies to personal accumulation. The first still very meagre wave of prosperity in the country, just because of its meagreness, has not weakened, but strengthened, these centrifugal tendencies. On the other hand, there has developed simultaneously a desire of the unprivileged to slap the grasping hands of the new gentry. The social struggle again grows sharp. Such are the sources of the power of the bureaucracy. But from those same sources comes also a threat to its power . . .

To define the Soviet regime as transitional, or intermediate, means to abandon such finished social categories as *capitalism* (and therewith 'state capitalism') and also *Socialism*. But besides being completely inadequate in itself, such a definition is capable of producing the mistaken idea that from the present Soviet regime a transition *only* to Socialism is possible. In reality a backslide to capitalism is wholly possible. A more complete definition will of necessity be complicated and ponderous.

The Soviet Union is a contradictory society, halfway between capitalism and Socialism, in which:

1. The productive forces are still far from adequate to give the state property a Socialist character.
2. The tendency towards primitive accumulation created by want breaks out through innumerable pores of the planned economy.
3. Norms of distribution preserving a bourgeois character lie at the basis of a new differentiation of society.
4. The economic growth, while slowly bettering the situation of the toilers, promotes a swift formation of privileged strata.
5. Exploiting the social antagonisms, a bureaucracy has converted itself into an uncontrolled caste alien to Socialism.
6. The social revolution, betrayed by the ruling party, still exists in property relations and in the consciousness of the toiling masses.
7. A further development of the accumulating contradictions can as well lead to Socialism as back to capitalism.
8. On the road to capitalism the counter-revolution would have to break the resistance of the workers.
9. On the road to Socialism the workers would have to overthrow the

bureaucracy. In the last analysis, the question will be decided by a struggle of living social forces, in both the national and the world arenas.

•

GEORGE ORWELL
1937

'The miner'

The old Etonian Eric Blair (1903–50) used the pseudonym George Orwell for his essays and novels, which included Animal Farm *and* 1984, *two of the outstanding books of the century. For his semi-documentary study of unemployment,* The Road to Wigan Pier, *Orwell travelled widely in the north of England, lodged in working-class homes and observed an area of the country that was utterly foreign to literary London.*

By experiencing working-class life at first hand, he developed his own brand of Socialism which was contemptuous of intellectualism – as shown in this eloquent protest at the establishment's ignorance of the miner's backbreaking daily toil.

When I am digging trenches in my garden, if I shift two tons of earth during the afternoon, I feel that I have earned my tea. But earth is tractable stuff compared with coal, and I don't have to work kneeling down, a thousand feet underground, in suffocating heat and swallowing coal dust with every breath I take; nor do I have to walk a mile bent double before I begin. The miner's job would be as much beyond my power as it would be to perform on the flying trapeze or to win the Grand National. I am not a manual labourer and please God I never shall be one, but there are some kinds of manual work that I could do if I had to. At a pinch I could be a tolerable road-sweeper or an inefficient gardener or even a tenth-rate farm hand. But by no conceivable amount of effort or training could I become a coal-miner; the work would kill me in a few weeks.

Watching coal-miners at work, you realize momentarily what different universes different people inhabit. Down there where coal is dug it is a sort of world apart which one can quite easily go through life without ever hearing about. Probably a majority of people would even prefer not to hear about it. Yet it is the absolutely necessary counterpart of our world above. Practically everything we do, from eating an ice to crossing the Atlantic, and from baking a loaf to writing a novel, involves the use of coal, directly or indirectly. For all the arts of peace coal is needed; if war breaks out it is needed all the more. In time of revolution the miner must go on working or the revolution must stop, for revolution as much as reaction needs coal. Whatever may be happening on the surface, the hacking and shovelling have got to continue without a pause, or at any rate without pausing for more than a few weeks at the most. In order that Hitler may march the goosestep, that the Pope may denounce Bolshevism, that the cricket crowds may assemble at Lord's, that the Nancy poets may scratch one another's backs, coal has got to be forthcoming. But on the whole we are not aware of it; we all know that we 'must have coal', but we seldom or never remember what coal getting involves. Here am I, sitting writing in front of my comfortable coal fire. It is April but I still need a fire. Once a fortnight the coal cart drives up to the door and men in leather jerkins carry the coal indoors in stout sacks smelling of tar and shoot it clanking into the coal-hole under the stairs. It is only very rarely, when I make a definite mental effort, that I connect this coal with that far-off labour in the mines. It is just 'coal' – something that I have got to have; black stuff that arrives mysteriously from nowhere in particular, like manna except that you have to pay for it. You could quite easily drive a car right across the north of England and never once remember that hundreds of feet below the road you are on the miners are hacking at the coal. Yet in a sense it is the miners who are driving your car forward. Their lamp-lit world down there is as necessary to the daylight world above as the root is to the flower.

It is not long since conditions in the mines were worse than they are now. There are still living a few very old women who in their youth worked underground, with a harness round their waists and a chain that passed between their legs, crawling on all fours and dragging tubs of coal. They used to go on doing this even when they were pregnant. And even now, if coal could not be produced without pregnant women dragging it to and fro, I fancy we should let them do it rather than deprive ourselves of coal. But most of the time, of course, we should prefer to forget that they were doing it. It is so with all types of manual work; it keeps us alive, and we are oblivious of its existence. More than anyone else, perhaps, the miner can stand as the type of the manual worker, not only because his work is so exaggeratedly awful, but also because it is so vitally necessary and yet so remote from our experience, so invisible, as it were, that we are capable of forgetting it as we forget the blood in our veins. In a way it is even humiliating to watch coal-miners working. It raises in you a momentary doubt about your own status as an 'intellectual' and a superior person generally. For it is brought home to you, at least while you are watching, that it is only because miners sweat their guts out that superior persons can remain superior. You and I and the editor of the *Times Lit. Supp.*, and the Nancy poets and the Archbishop of Canterbury and Comrade X, author of *Marxism for Infants* – all of us *really* owe the comparative decency of our lives to poor drudges underground, blackened to the eyes, with their throats full of coal dust, driving their shovels forward with arms and belly muscles of steel.

•

WINSTON CHURCHILL
1938

'A total and unmitigated defeat'

A prolonged four-day debate in the House of Commons followed the signing of the Munich Pact. Chamberlain was so popular that his majority was never in doubt.

Nevertheless, several powerful speeches lamenting British humiliation and weakness were made by prominent Conservatives, including Anthony Eden, who had resigned as Chamberlain's Foreign Secretary because of his policy of appeasement, and Duff Cooper, First Lord of the Admiralty, who resigned after declaring that Britain should have gone to war to prevent one country dominating the continent by 'brute force'.

Speaking on the third day, Churchill (1874–1965) made the most damning indictment of all of Chamberlain's policies.

What I find unendurable is the sense of our country falling into the power, into the orbit and influence of Nazi Germany, and of our existence becoming dependent upon their good will or pleasure. It is to prevent that that I have tried my best to urge the maintenance of every bulwark of defence – first, the timely creation of an Air Force superior to anything within striking distance of our shores; secondly, the gathering together of the collective strength of many nations; and thirdly, the making of alliances and military conventions, all within the Covenant, in order to gather together forces at any rate to restrain the onward movement of this power. It has all been in vain. Every position has been successfully undermined and abandoned on specious and plausible excuses.

We do not want to be led upon the high road to becoming a satellite of the German Nazi system of European domination. In a very few years, perhaps in a very few months, we shall be confronted with demands with which we shall no doubt be invited to comply. Those demands may affect the surrender of territory or the surrender of liberty. I foresee and foretell that the policy of submission will carry with it restrictions upon the freedom of speech and debate in Parliament, on public platforms, and discussions in the press, for it will be said – indeed, I hear it said sometimes now – that we cannot allow the Nazi system of dictatorship to be criticized by ordinary, common English politicians. Then, with a press under control, in part direct but more potently indirect, with every organ of public opinion doped and chloroformed into acquiescence, we shall be conducted along further stages of our journey . . .

I have been casting about to see how measures can be taken to protect us from this advance of the Nazi power, and to secure those forms of life which are so dear to us. What is the sole method that is open? The sole method that is open for us is to regain our old island independence by acquiring that supremacy in the air which we were promised, that security in our air defences which we were assured we had, and thus to make ourselves an island once again. That, in all this grim outlook, shines out as the overwhelming fact. An effort at rearmament the like of which has not been seen ought to be made forthwith, and all the resources of this country and all its united strength should be bent to that task . . .

I do not begrudge our loyal, brave people, who were ready to do their duty no matter what the cost, who never flinched under the strain of last week – I do not grudge them the natural spontaneous outburst of joy and relief when they learned that the hard ordeal would no longer be required of them at the moment; but they should know the truth. They should know that there has been gross neglect and deficiency in our defences; they should know that we have sustained a defeat without a war, the consequences of which will travel far with us along our road; they should know that we have passed an awful milestone in our history, when the whole equilibrium of Europe has been deranged, and that the terrible words have for the time being been pronounced against the Western democracies: 'Thou art weighed in the balance and found wanting.' And do not suppose that this is the end. This is only the beginning of the reckoning. This is only the first sip, the first foretaste of a bitter cup which will be proffered to us year by year unless by a supreme recovery of moral health and martial vigour, we arise again and take our stand for freedom as in the olden time.

•

JOMO KENYATTA
1938

'Emancipation'

During the Mau Mau rebellion in Kenya in the 1950s many atrocities were committed against British settlers, and Jomo Kenyatta (c. 1889–1978) was imprisoned as a terrorist. Yet Kenyatta (who was to become the first president of independent Kenya in 1963) had been challenging the racist assumptions of colonial rule for three decades, especially in Facing Mount Kenya, *a series of essays he had written on the tribal life of the Kikuyu for Bronislaw Malinowski's anthropology seminar at the London School of Economics. He argued that the Kikuyu tribe's social order had been ruined and its members reduced to serfdom.*

The average European observer, not being trained in comparative sociology, takes his own fundamental assumptions for granted without realizing that he is doing so. He thinks of the tribe as if it must be analogous to the European sovereign state, and draws the conclusion that the executive authority for that sovereignty must be vested in the Chief, as if he were a prime minister or a president. In doing so he makes a huge mistake, which makes it impossible for him to enter into intelligible relations with the Kikuyu people. They simply do not know where he gets his ideas from, since to them the family rather than the larger unit is the primary reality on which power is based.

The visible symbol of this bond of kinship is the family land, which is the source of livelihood and the field of labour. In an agricultural community the whole social organization must derive from the land, and without understanding the system on which it is held and worked it will be impossible to see the meaning of other aspects of life. In Kikuyu society the system of land tenure can only be understood by reference to the ties of kinship. It is no more true to say that the land is collectively owned by the tribe than that it is privately owned by the individual. In relation to the tribe, a man is the owner of his land, and there is no official and no committee with authority to deprive him of it or to levy a tax on his produce. But in so far as there are other people of his own flesh and blood who depend on that land for their daily bread, he is not the owner, but a partner, or at the most a trustee for the others. Since the land is held in trust for the unborn as well as for the living, and since it represents his partnership in the common life of generations, he will not lightly take upon himself to dispose of it. But in so far as he is cultivating a field for the maintenance of himself and his wives and children, he is the undisputed owner of that field and all that grows in it. In the same way a woman is the owner of her land and her hut as far as outside people, even her husband's other wives, are concerned, and in her management of her property she expresses her initiative as well as contributing to the family budget. But her ownership is not irresponsible; her chief function in the group is the bringing up of her own children, and it would not occur to her that the land was hers for any other purpose . . .

A culture has no meaning apart from the social organization of life on which it is built. When the European comes to the Kikuyu country and robs the people of their land, he is taking away not only their livelihood, but the material symbol that holds family and tribe together. In doing this he gives one blow which cuts away the foundations from the whole of Kikuyu life, social, moral and economic. When he explains, to his own satisfaction and after the most superficial glance at the issues involved, that he is doing this for the sake of the Africans, to 'civilize' them, 'teach them the disciplinary value of regular work', and 'give them the benefit of European progressive ideas', he is adding insult to injury, and need expect to convince no one but himself.

There certainly are some progressive ideas among the Europeans. They include the ideas of material prosperity, of medicine, and hygiene, and literacy which enables people to take part in world culture. But so far the Europeans who visit Africa have not been conspicuously zealous in imparting these parts of their inheritance to the Africans, and seem to think that the only way to do it is by police discipline and armed force. They speak as if it was somehow beneficial to an African to work for them instead of for himself, and to make sure that he will receive this benefit they do their best to take away his land and leave him with no alternative. Along with his land they rob him of his government, condemn his religious ideas, and ignore his fundamental conceptions of justice and morals, all in the name of civilization and progress.

If Africans were left in peace on their own lands, Europeans would have to offer them the benefits of white civilization in real earnest before they could obtain the African labour which they want so much. They would have to offer the African a way of life which was really superior to the one his forefathers lived before him, and a share in the prosperity given them by their command of science. They would have to let the African choose what parts of European culture could be beneficially transplanted, and how they could be adapted. He would probably not choose the gas bomb or the armed police force, but he might ask for some other things of which he does not get so much today. As it is, by driving him off his ancestral lands, the Europeans have robbed him of the material foundations of his culture, and reduced him to a state of serfdom incompatible with human happiness. The African is conditioned, by the cultural and social institutions of centuries, to a freedom of which Europe has little conception, and it is not in his nature to accept serfdom for ever. He realizes that he must fight unceasingly for his own complete emancipation; for without this he is doomed to remain the prey of rival imperialisms, which in every successive year will drive their fangs more deeply into his vitality and strength.

•

G. E. R. GEDYE
1939

'The march of the swastika'

The British journalist G. E. R. Gedye (1890–1970) was in Vienna when the Nazis marched on Austria. His account of Nazi rule, Fallen Bastions, *was published for the Left Book Club by the socialist publisher Victor Gollancz who described it as a 'classic denunciation'.*

A few days after the Nazi triumph I passed through the Taborstrasse in the Jewish quarter of Vienna. Outside a big Jewish store stood a long string of lorries into which storm-troopers were pitching all kinds of millinery goods as they took them from the shop. Police stood by to see that they were not interfered with in the work of plunder and moved on the curious. There was nothing remarkable in this – it was just one incident which I happened to see myself among thousands. This was private plunder – for some reason considered more reprehensible than the systematic plundering by the Nazi organization as such which stole Jewish businesses, some of which had been built up slowly for generations, and ruined some of them in a few months. Amidst all the horrors to which Austrian Jews, Austrian patriots and Austrian democrats – in fact, all non-Nazis – have been exposed ever since 11 March, the loss of every remedy against theft and plunder is the least. After a few days I do not think I heard any complaints or anxieties expressed by Jews on this score; it was just accepted as inevitable.

Much more terrible was the acceptance of suicide as a perfectly normal and natural incident by every Jewish household. It is quite impossible to convey to anyone outside Austria in how matter-of-fact a way the Jews of

Austria today refer to this way out of their agony. When I say one's Jewish friends spoke to one of their intention to commit suicide with no more emotion than they had formerly talked of making an hour's journey by train, I cannot expect to be believed. Nevertheless, the fact must be recorded. It is not your fault that you cannot believe me, because it is impossible for you to conceive of the diseased and degenerate mentality which lies behind the pathological anti-Semitism of the Nazis. Therefore it is impossible for you to imagine what it means for one-sixth of the population of Vienna to be made pariahs overnight, deprived of all civil rights, including the right to retain property large or small, the right to be employed or to give employment, to exercise a profession, to enter restaurants, cafés, bathing beaches, baths or public parks, to be faced daily and hourly, without hope of relief, with the foulest insults which ingenious and vicious minds can devise, to be liable always to be turned overnight out of house and home, and at any hour of every day and every night to arrest without the pretence of a charge or hope of a definite sentence, however heavy – and with all this to find every country in the world selfishly closing its frontiers to you when, after being plundered of your last farthing, you seek to escape. For most of the non-Jewish victims of the Nazis, many of whom are now sharing the punishment of the Jews, there is a hope that one day the nightmare may pass. For the Jews there is none while the Nazis rule.

It is no fault of yours, but your very good fortune, that you cannot believe that one after another families are being turned out of their houses and herded into a ghetto merely because they are not of undiluted Teutonic blood, that in their thousands men and women are still being arrested, held in crowded cells for months without the suggestion of any guilt or charge, and then called upon to sign a promise to leave the country forthwith or go to Dachau – knowing full well that there is not a country they can enter. You cannot believe the stories you read in your newspapers of Jewish families, after living for generations in Burgenland villages, being taken out to an island breakwater – children, old men and women, cripples of eighty and more, and very sick persons – and abandoned in the midst of a raging storm in the Danube, whose swirling, muddy brown waters lap their feet. It cannot make any real impression on your consciousness as things which are really happening daily and hourly – yes, at the very moment that you read these words in such comfort as they may leave you, a little less than you are accustomed to feel, I hope – to hear that these peasant or shop-keeping families were rescued, refused anywhere an asylum, and are to this day huddled together on an ancient vessel in mid-stream – as are others in filthy, desolate Alpine huts in a triangle of no-man's-land between three countries and in the dank fields of Bohemia outside the new German frontiers – without a hope in the world of ever getting back to life. You will shrug your comfortable shoulders and say 'Bogey tales' when I tell you of women whose husbands had been arrested a week before without any charge, receiving a small parcel from the Viennese postman with the curt intimation: 'To pay, 150 Marks, for the cremation of your husband – ashes enclosed from Dachau.' The usual intimation is just a printed slip, a copy of which lies before me: 'The relatives of — are informed herewith that he died today at Dachau Concentration Camp. (*Signed*) STAPO HEADQUARTERS.' Or if I tell you of a professional man coming with ashen face and loose, quivering lips to the journalist he had often attended and babbling out: 'Hide my son, hide him – last week they took my cousin's boy to Dachau and sent back the ashes in an urn four days later.' I envy you, because you have not known any of these people as I have – they are not to you human beings as they are to me, but just part of a picture drawn in a book. You have never seen Nazis gloating over the daily suicide lists, you have not looked into the indescribably bestial pages of Julius Streicher's *Der Stürmer*, or seen the slavering mouth of this scarlet-faced, bald-headed vulture beside whom I have more than once drunk beer in Munich and read his headlines above the stories of the suicides in Vienna: 'Recommended as an Example to Others.' And so you do not need to feel the horror which I cannot escape as I remember that in all this we acquiesce, and soothe our consciences with a bottle of Evian water and a few more committees. I envy you – believe me, I envy you. But yesterday I was asked by an Englishman for the address of a cheap hotel in Vienna where he could spend his holidays – *holidays* in Austria, amidst all this! Him I did not envy.

Some of the horrors I saw at very close quarters. Hurrying down the stairs of my flat to hear Hitler make his first speech on his arrival in Vienna, I was delayed by men carrying out the bodies of a young Jewish doctor and his mother, who had lived, quiet, decent and hard-working neighbours for years, two floors below. The man had been dismissed from his hospital overnight without a hope of ever being allowed to earn another penny. Nazis had forced their way into his flat and thrust a great swastika banner out of his window. Being a doctor, escape was easier for him and his mother than for most; they had found it through a hypodermic syringe. The SS guards in the basement premises, who had replaced Schuschnigg's Sturmkorps, stood around grinning their satisfaction as the bodies came out. From my window I could watch for many days how they would arrest Jewish passers-by – generally doctors, lawyers or merchants, for they preferred their victims to belong to the better educated classes – and force them to scrub, polish and beat carpets in the flat where the tragedy had taken place, insisting the while that the non-Jewish maid should sit at ease in a chair and look on. My street, the Habsburgergasse, was made a park for stolen Jewish cars, on which the SS had painted their dreaded insignia, ' *ℋ* '. I could not enter or leave my house all the time I was in Vienna without having to witness the degrading spectacle of Jewish men of all social ranks and ages and Jewish ladies and young girls collected at random on the streets – every non-Jew wore the swastika, so that they were easily recognized – doing press-gang labour, washing the cars stolen from their co-racials.

•

ELLEN WILKINSON
1939

'Jarrow'

After losing her seat as Member of Parliament for Middlesbrough East in 1931, Ellen Wilkinson (1891–1947) returned to Parliament as MP for Jarrow in 1935. Only 4 feet 10 inches tall and with striking red hair, Wilkinson was a charismatic politician who was determined to bring the plight of Jarrow, where two-thirds of the men were permanently unemployed, to national attention. On 5 October 1936, she set out from Jarrow with 200 men to march to London – the march of the forgotten men. The impact the march made on public opinion was revived three years later when Wilkinson published The Town That Was Murdered *in the Left Book Club. 'This town is an illustrated footnote to British working-class history,' she wrote. 'Every stage of the class struggle in Britain has been fought out there in turn.'*

The story of Jarrow's industries, the fight in shipping and steel, reveal the weakness of British capitalism in its old unchallenged strongholds. The way is no longer easy and open. Other countries have developed to share the markets. But that is not the chief or the most anxious problem for the British manufacturer. The Anglo-Saxon technique in finance is old-established and clever in its developed ways. Britain still has advantages in material and in personnel, in her stable forms of government and the sense of security that until very recently has been a characteristic of these islands. Chairmen of directors are continually reported as saying in their shareholders' meetings that 'given equal conditions British industry has nothing to fear from its competitors'. But the central fact is just that conditions are no longer 'equal'. For that matter they never were, but while Britain had the advantage that fact was not stressed. British capitalists with their individualistic traditions and their gospel of *laissez-faire* are now facing competitors highly organized into national units.

Germany and Britain thus face each other in 1939, as they did in 1914, for a struggle for the economic mastery of the world, and each of the protagonists has taken measures in its own way to prepare for the day. Germany has put her industry on a war footing. Her whole equipment has been modernized, the trade unions and democratic movements smashed, and her whole economy placed under the control of the armaments ring and the army high command. There are no able-bodied unemployed. Nor are private interests allowed to interfere with the dominant interest of war-preparation. This highly centralized economy, of course, is not intended only for war purposes. The idea is to win for Germany that economic self-sufficiency in raw materials which Britain enjoys because of her Empire. If this can be achieved without actual physical warfare – as the munitions and highly organized industries of Czechoslovakia, the oil and wheat of Romania, the metals, vegetables and meat of Yugoslavia and the ores of Spain have been taken without war – then Germany proceeds to an economic dominance of Europe and displaces Britain.

British capitalism has felt the effects of this direct challenge and has reacted in its own way. In place of the violent methods of the German high command in war and trade, the British have tried to make the transition slowly. With much the same end as the German Nazis they have been more concerned with preserving the position and increasing the share of the private capitalist. For instance, it is quite inconceivable that had they had a country so vulnerable as Britain, so dependent on sea-borne food, the Germans would have allowed a private company to rationalize the shipping industry to danger point. That one-third of the shipbuilding berths should be sterilized for forty years – some of them, like Jarrow, the finest sites in the world for the work – by the very year that war seemed most likely, is fantastic enough. But that when subsidies have to be hastily arranged to bring up the shipping strength, that the Board of Trade should confess itself helpless to prevent ships being sold to the ostensible enemy until fresh legislation had been passed, and then allow so long a time to elapse before obtaining the necessary powers, can only be explained by this government's intense reluctance to interfere with private profit-making . . .

Jarrow's plight is not a local problem. It is the symptom of a national evil.

Anyone who takes the trouble to study the new forces at work in our urban civilization cannot deny the dangerous trend towards over-centralization that cheap power and quick transport have brought into this tiny country. London, already the biggest market, tends to draw wealth and initiative to the capital city, and thus become the prestige centre for commerce, for governmental activity, for art and literature, for political and social life.

Every industry which comes to London creates new consuming power, a new market for other industries. Every cultural organization, every trade union which wants headquarters in London, every employers' federation which insists on being at the centre though its main industry is in the North all helps the pull. It is a problem which a Labour Government would have to face straightaway, for a lot of its strength would come from the older industrial areas. It would have to balance their demand to be allowed to live with the new interests of the vast and growing mass of London workers.

This island is too small, its economic life too precariously balanced, its geographical situation too vulnerable, for its fate to be left to the casual workings of chance, or the insatiable unheeding drive of the profit-makers. Jarrow is an object lesson of what happens then. The profiteers, having ravaged a town or a country, can take themselves and their gains elsewhere. The workers have the main stake in their homeland, for in it they must remain. They have built it, and worked in it, fought for it. On their skill and their toil has been built England's industrial reputation. They were crowded into hovels, their children starved and died, and on their sacrifice great capital has been accumulated. It is time now that the workers took control of this country of ours. It is time that they planned it, organized it, and developed it so that all might enjoy the wealth which we can produce. In the interest of this land we love that is the next job which must be done.

•

DAILY MIRROR
1940

'How many more failures?'

After the British setback in Norway, the Daily Mirror *started to campaign against the 'vain, disastrous' prime minister Neville Chamberlain, particularly in the editorials written by Richard Jennings, son of a leader writer on* The Times, *who always signed his articles W. M. Chamberlain was an expert at the art of explaining away failure – he had so much practice at it, Jennings wrote. On the day of the historic debate on Norway, he wrote this leading article on 'The Real Issue'.*

A good many readers have written to us, in plaintive style, to lament that it is useless to point out blunders or delays in the government's conduct of the war.

Why is it useless?

Because (moan these defeatists) we can't find another, or a renovated, government! There isn't one on the map.

This is hard on those able men, in or out of Parliament, who have not yet been given an opportunity of showing what they could do, if they were allowed to try.

It is hard on those men who dissociated themselves from the government because they doubted the wisdom of its policy, in earlier days.

It is hard on the fighting forces, the public, the nation – thus invited to believe that it is better to lose a war than to change or reconstruct a Cabinet.

And this fatuous argument would plainly have lost us the last war – during which one government crashed and another took its place.

So much for the sillies who think we can muddle through.

We shall see if the House of Commons agrees with them today.

But today – let us press this point – the sole issue, the real issue, is not the failure in Norway; with its repercussions in Italy and in America and in the Balkans: in fact, all over the world.

Let us, if you like, wipe out the Norwegian episode, which is not a side-show – though what it is we have not yet been told.

The questions for MPs of any patriotism, the questions for Conservatives who have the strength of mind and character not to quail at the crack of the Margesson whip, are these:

What of the next phase? What of the next possible failure? What excuses are ready for the next crash in the prolonged 'too late' campaign? Have we been warned? Have partial or local failures taught us their lessons? Or will the technique, the 'sickening technique', of muddle have to be exemplified again and again, till its disasters rouse even those poor mutts who moan that it is better to drift to defeat under the men who muddle than to call upon new men to pull the war machine together in good time . . .

Whatever may be said in excuse of the Norwegian failure today is said too late.

Moreover, what may be said comes after many such apologies or justifications or explanations. We know the style and the tone of these utterances. We know only too well the sycophantic cheers that greet them from the government back benches.

Today the real issue is: How many more failures – followed by 'assurance of victory'?

•

LEO AMERY
1940

'In the name of God, go'

By 1940, Leo Amery (1873–1955) was almost at the end of his political career, during which he had been First Lord of the Admiralty, colonial secretary and Dominions secretary in the 1920s. Now a distinguished elder statesman, he was a fierce critic of Chamberlain's vacillation and weak leadership.

On 7 May 1940, Chamberlain opened a debate on the disastrous Norwegian campaign. Among the younger Conservative MPs, there were many territorial officers who spoke for the units which had suffered in Norway.

Then Amery, a friend and colleague of Chamberlain's for many years and a fellow Birmingham MP, stood up to speak. He was called during the dinner hour but the House quickly filled up as he moved the target of Chamberlain's critics from the navy towards the prime minister and his conduct of the war. Sensing the mood of the Commons, and with devastating effect, he ended his speech with the angry words used by Oliver Cromwell to the Long Parliament in the seventeenth century. As he uttered them, he pointed at the prime minister and delivered his pitiless attack. It was one of the most dramatic moments in the tumultuous two-day debate.

Believe me, as long as the present methods prevail, all our valour and all our resources are not going to see us through. Above all, so long as they prevail, time is not going to be on our side, because they are methods which, inevitably and inherently, waste time and weaken decisions. What we must have, and have soon, is a supreme war directorate of a handful of men free from administrative routine, free to frame policy among themselves, and with the task of supervising, inspiring and impelling a group of departments clearly allocated to each one of them. That is the only way. We learned that in the last war. My right hon. Friend the Member for Carnarvon Boroughs (Mr Lloyd George) earned the undying gratitude of the nation for the courage he showed in adopting what was then a new experiment. The experiment worked, and it helped to win the war. After the war years, the Committee of Imperial Defence laid it down as axiomatic that, while in a minor war you might go on with an ordinary Cabinet, helped perhaps by a War Committee, in a major war you must have a War Cabinet – meaning precisely the type of Cabinet that my right hon. Friend introduced then. The overwhelming opinion of this House and of the public outside has been demanding that for a long while. We are told that there would be no particular advantage in it at the present time. I ask: Is this or is this not a major war?

We must have, first of all, a right organization of government. What is no less important today is that the government shall be able to draw upon the whole abilities of the nation. It must represent all the elements of real political power in this country, whether in this House or not. The time has come when hon. and right hon. Members opposite must definitely take their share of the responsibility. The time has come when the organization, the power and influence of the Trades Union Congress cannot be left outside. It must, through one of its recognized leaders, reinforce the strength of the national effort from inside. The time has come, in other words, for a real National Government . . .

Just as our peacetime system is unsuitable for war conditions, so does it tend to breed peacetime statesmen who are not too well fitted for the conduct of war. Facility in debate, ability to state a case, caution in advancing an unpopular view, compromise and procrastination are the natural qualities – I might almost say, virtues – of a political leader in time of peace. They are fatal qualities in war. Vision, daring, swiftness and consistency of decision are the very essence of victory. In our normal politics, it is true, the conflict of party did encourage a certain combative spirit. In the last war we Tories found that the most perniciously aggressive of our opponents, the right hon. Member for Carnarvon Boroughs, was not only aggressive in words, but was a man of action. In recent years the normal weakness of our political life has been accentuated by a coalition based upon no clear political principles. It was in fact begotten of a false alarm as to the disastrous results of going off the Gold Standard. It is a coalition which has been living ever since in a twilight atmosphere between protection and free trade and between unprepared collective security and unprepared isolation. Surely, for the government of the last ten years to have bred a band of warrior statesmen would have been little short of a miracle. We have waited for eight months, and the miracle has not come to pass. Can we afford to wait any longer?

Somehow or other we must get into the government men who can match our enemies in fighting spirit, in daring, in resolution and in thirst for victory. Some 300 years ago, when this House found that its troops were being beaten again and again by the dash and daring of the Cavaliers, by Prince Rupert's Cavalry, Oliver Cromwell spoke to John Hampden. In one of his speeches he recounted what he said. It was this:

> I said to him, 'Your troops are most of them old, decayed serving men and tapsters and such kind of fellows . . . You must get men of a spirit that are likely to go as far as they will go, or you will be beaten still.'

It may not be easy to find these men. They can be found only by trial and by ruthlessly discarding all who fail and have their failings discovered. We are fighting today for our life, for our liberty, for our all; we cannot go on being led as we are. I have quoted certain words of Oliver Cromwell. I will quote certain other words. I do it with great reluctance, because I am speaking of those who are old friends and associates of mine, but they are words which, I think, are applicable to the present situation. This is what Cromwell said to the Long Parliament when he thought it was no longer fit to conduct the affairs of the nation:

> You have sat too long here for any good you have been doing. Depart, I say, and let us have done with you. In the name of God, go.

•

MICHAEL FOOT, FRANK OWEN, PETER HOWARD
1940

'Guilty Men'

On the cover, the author of Guilty Men *was given, anonymously, as 'Cato'. The book's searing indictment of Chamberlain, Baldwin, MacDonald, Halifax, Simon, Hoare and the other ministers who ruled Britain before the Second World War was in fact written by three left-wing journalists who worked for Lord Beaverbrook – Michael Foot, Frank Owen and Peter Howard. It was a 'polemic of genius' which gave the indictment of Chamberlain and his associates its classic form, says Cambridge historian Peter Clarke.*
This is Chapter 23: 'Missing the Bus. Cast: Mr Chamberlain'.

It will be seen from the account of events here set out that the British Government did not exert itself to any great extent in the arming of our country, even after we had clashed into war with the most tremendous military power of all times.

The pressure on the government not to do so came from Sir John Simon at the Treasury. His views were reinforced by the Banks, representing Big Business. The case for lethargy presented by these people was as follows:

'Do not disorganize industry by turning the whole country into an arms factory. Let us continue to manufacture pins and bicycles and films and vacuum cleaners so that we can make profits, contribute to taxation and pay for the war.'

Tens of thousands of people in Britain became angry and indignant at this state of affairs. Young men, who wanted to fight, could not get called up. There were no guns for them. Young women who wanted to work at munition making could not do so. There were no new munition factories to absorb them.

Meanwhile, millions of tons of raw materials which could have been converted into instruments of war were manufactured into perambulators.

In order to quieten the apprehensions of the citizens, ministers and generals began to make a series of speeches calculated to encourage the public in the belief that the war was already won.

On 3 April 1940, Mr Chamberlain, still Prime Minister, declared that he was ten times as confident of victory as he was when the war began.

'Whether it was that Hitler thought he might get away with what he had got without fighting for it, or whether it was that, after all, his preparations were not sufficiently complete, one thing is certain – *he missed the bus*,' said Mr Chamberlain.

The Prime Minister added, 'When war broke out German preparations were far ahead of our own. It was natural then to expect that the enemy would take advantage of his initial superiority, to make an endeavour to overwhelm us and France before we had time to make good our deficiencies. Is it not a very extraordinary thing that no such attempt was made? Those seven months that we have had have enabled us to make good and remove our weaknesses; to consolidate and tune up every arm, offensive and defensive, and so enormously to add to our fighting strength that we can face the future with a calm and steady mind, whatever it brings.'

On 4 April General Ironside joined the chorus. General Ironside was at that time Chief of the Imperial General Staff.

'Frankly we could welcome an attack,' ejaculated that old warrior. 'We are sure of ourselves. We have no fears. Our army has at last turned the corner. I was sure of this for the first time a fortnight ago. We started with very little. The Germans gave us these months to build a real fighting force. If they had launched a full attack at the very start when we were unprepared, they might possibly have got us. It's too late now. We are ready for anything they may start. As a matter of fact we'd welcome a go at them.'

Within a week, the Germans overran Norway. So little did Mr Chamberlain know of this invasion that he hinted to the expectant House of Commons that they must take with a grain of salt the tales that the Germans were in Narvik. Mr Chamberlain himself took the view that the place in German hands might well be Larvik (a port 1,000 miles south down the coast of Norway).

'I have no doubt,' added the ex-Prime Minister of Britain, 'that this further rash and cruel act of aggression will redound to Germany's disadvantage and contribute to her ultimate defeat.'

Two months later the last British troops were hurried home from Norway, and bombed as they departed by the Germans, who now possess the whole Norwegian coastline, with airfields for their planes and deep water harbours for their ships, so providing themselves with a first-rate opportunity to slip in and out through Britain's blockade, or to launch attacks on the Scottish coast.

Mr Chamberlain added to his pep talks with this sentence spoken on 15 April 1940 to the National Free Church Council:

'Only a short while ago I declared that I felt ten times as confident as at the beginning of the war of ultimate victory. I repeat that confidence now.'

On the morning of 10 May with a roar which drowned the futile boasts and foolish brags of Britain's Prime Minister and Chief of General Staff, the Nazi hordes streamed over the frontiers of Holland, Belgium and Luxemburg, with tanks, planes, guns and motorized infantry in endless columns.

Within three weeks the tragedy of the Dunkirk beaches was enacted before the staring eyes of a trembling world.

•

GEORGE ORWELL
1941

'The ruling class'

'I believe in England, and I believe that we shall go forward,' George Orwell (1903–50) wrote in the concluding sentence of 'The Lion and the Unicorn', a prophetic essay on Socialism and the English Genius published four years before the Labour victory in 1945. Yet England could only advance by a revolution from below, he argued, with a Socialist movement that actually had the mass of the people behind it. That 'sleepy, unwilling' revolution had gathered momentum when the troops returned from Dunkirk, recognized that 'something was wrong'. England was a family with the wrong members in control.

England is a family with the wrong members in control. Almost entirely we are governed by the rich, and by people who step into positions of command by right of birth. Few if any of these people are consciously treacherous, some of them are not even fools, but as a class they are quite incapable of leading us to victory. They could not do it, even if their material interests did not constantly trip them up.

As soon as one considers any problem of this war – and it does not matter whether it is the widest aspect of strategy or the tiniest detail of home organization – one sees that the necessary moves cannot be made while the social structure of England remains what it is. Inevitably, because of their position and upbringing, the ruling class are fighting for their own privileges, which cannot possibly be reconciled with the public interest. It is a mistake to imagine that war aims, strategy, propaganda and industrial organization exist in watertight compartments. All are interconnected. Every strategic plan, every tactical method, even every weapon will bear the stamp of the social system that produced it. The British ruling class are fighting against Hitler, whom they have always regarded and whom some of them still regard as their protector against Bolshevism. That does not mean that they will deliberately sell out; but it does mean that at every decisive moment they are likely to falter, pull their punches, do the wrong thing.

Internally, England is still the rich man's paradise. All talk of 'equality of sacrifice' is nonsense. At the same time as factory-workers are asked to put up with longer hours, advertisements for 'Butler. One in family, eight in staff' are appearing in the press. The bombed-out populations of the East End go hungry and homeless while wealthier victims simply step into their cars and flee to comfortable country houses. The Home Guard swells to a million men in a few weeks, and is deliberately organized from above in such a way that only people with private incomes can hold positions of command. Even the rationing system is so arranged that it hits the poor all the time, while people with over £2,000 a year are practically unaffected by it. Everywhere privilege is squandering good will. In such circumstances even propaganda becomes almost impossible. As attempts to stir up patriotic feeling, the red posters issued by the Chamberlain Government at the beginning of the war broke all depth-records. Yet they could not have been much other than they were, for how could Chamberlain and his followers take the risk of rousing strong popular feeling *against Fascism*? Anyone who was genuinely hostile to Fascism must also be opposed to Chamberlain himself and to all the others who had helped Hitler into power.

It is only by revolution that the native genius of the English people can be set free. Revolution does not mean red flags and street fighting, it means a fundamental shift of power. Whether it happens with or without bloodshed is largely an accident of time and place. Nor does it mean the dictatorship of a single class. The people in England who grasp what changes are needed and are capable of carrying them through are not confined to any one class, though it is true that very few people with over £2,000 a year are among them. What is wanted is a conscious open revolt by ordinary people against inefficiency, class privilege and the rule of the old. It is not primarily a question of change of government. British governments do, broadly speaking, represent the will of the people, and if we alter our structure from below we shall get the government we need. Ambassadors, generals, officials and colonial administrators who are senile or pro-Fascist are more dangerous than Cabinet ministers whose follies have to be committed in public. Right through our national life we have got to fight against privilege, against the notion that a half-witted public schoolboy is better for command than an intelligent mechanic. Although there are gifted and honest *individuals* among them, we have got to break the grip of the moneyed class as a whole. England has got to assume its real shape. The England that is only just beneath the surface, in the factories and the newspaper offices, in the aeroplanes and the submarines, has got to take charge of its own destiny.

•

CASSANDRA (WILLIAM CONNOR)
1941

'Keep it in the family'

When this Cassandra column by William Connor (1909–67) appeared in January 1941, Churchill was upset and wrote to Cecil King, director of the Daily Mirror, *accusing the paper of being inspired by a spirit of 'hatred and malice' against the government. Cassandra had a vitriolic style, King replied, but his attitude to Churchill was not in any way malevolent – and loyalty to England meant loyalty to the future as well as the past.*

By the time these words appear in print, Mr R. A. Butler, who is Under-Secretary of State for Foreign Affairs, may be President of the Board of Education, which should not worry you a great deal and doesn't hurt me either.

If this has occurred, it is because Mr Butler has been faithful and loyal and not markedly inept.

If it has not occurred, it may still occur.

If it never occurs, it will be because the system has broken down.

It is a remarkable system because it presumes that the whole of the talent of the British Empire is contained within the number of people who comprise a cricket team.

This cricket team is so good that all the batsmen can bowl and all the bowlers can bat. The wicket keeper is excellent at mid-on and the lads in the slips are grand in the outfield.

Why anybody like Mr Butler, who has been working on Foreign Affairs should be given a job in education as a promotion, beats me.

Is a painter a better man when he becomes a plumber?

And more important, is the plumbing improved?

But to return to this remarkable flexibility and versatility of the men who are running the war.

See how they play ball among themselves.

See how the great closed-shop works.

Meet Sir John Anderson, Lord President of the Council, ex-Home Secretary, ex-Minister of Security, ex-Lord Privy Seal, ex-Governor of Bengal, ex-Under-Secretary at the Home Office, ex-Permanent Under-Secretary of State, ex-Secretary to the Ministry of Shipping.

Meet Sir Kingsley Wood, Chancellor of the Exchequer, ex-Secretary of State for Air, ex-Minister of Health, ex-Postmaster-General, ex-Parliamentary Secretary to the Board of Education, ex-Parliamentary Secretary to the Ministry of Health, ex-Parliamentary Private Secretary to the Minister of Health.

Meet Mr Anthony Eden, Secretary for Foreign Affairs, ex-Secretary of State for War, ex-Secretary for Foreign Affairs, ex-Secretary of State for Dominion Affairs, ex-Lord Privy Seal, ex-Minister Without Portfolio for the League of Nations.

And meet all the rest of the gang. Ex-this and ex-that – but never ex a job!

Everybody has done everybody else's business.

Everybody knows everybody.

Keep it in the family!

Scratch my back and I'll scratch yours!

Talk about musical chairs!

The trouble is that this particular game is being played to a funeral march. Ours.

•

JEANNETTE RANKIN
1941

'The mothers of America'

Jeannette Rankin (1880–1973) was the only American politician who voted against American participation in both world wars. A pacifist, she voted against war with Germany in 1917 (when she was elected to Congress for Montana – its first woman member) and then again twenty-four years later after the Japanese attack on Pearl Harbor.

Next Sunday will be Mother's Day. There is a great deal of sentiment about mothers and wanting to give mothers what they wish. There is nothing in the world the mothers of this country would like on this Mother's Day so much as assurance that their sons are not going to be taken to war. [Applause.]

This is an entirely new experience for the mothers of America. Never before have they been presented with a situation such as this. The men who are potential fighters in this war were little children in the last war, and the mothers have had twenty years to contemplate their sons being sacrificed as the sons in the past have been sacrificed. I am, therefore, going to offer a resolution, although I know there is little probability of getting it before the House for consideration, but I feel it represents the sentiments of the great majority of the men and women in this House. This is a concurrent resolution which reads:

> Congress hereby declares that it is the policy of the United States not to send the armed forces of the United States to fight in any place outside the Western Hemisphere or insular possessions of the United States.

It seems to me a resolution of this kind would bring more comfort to the women of America at this time than any action this House can take.

I have confidence in the mothers. The mothers are not going to have their sons sent to war if they can prevent it – and they can. You may think this Congress can declare war and send the men to Europe, but if the mothers of this country say 'No,' no matter what Congress wishes those men will not be sent to war. The mothers of America have the courage to stand up and protect their lifework. They are not going to have their sons sacrificed needlessly for issues that cannot be solved by violence. This is not the war of the mothers. The mothers of America are perfectly willing to protect our shores.

For years I have insisted that we state our military policy and have it conform to a national policy representing the convictions of the American people. The American mothers want to protect our shores from invasion, but they do not believe the war method can be used to settle disputes. The women must refuse to have the mothers' work sacrificed for the profits of a few or because some wish to decide the problems of Europe by the war method.

•

GEORGE VLACHOS
1941

'How to live, how to die'

When Hitler issued an ultimatum to Greece in 1941, George Vlachos, editor of I Kathimerini, *published this open letter to the German führer. It is mentioned in Louis de Bernières's bestselling novel* Captain Corelli's Mandolin. *Moved by its 'noble, grandiloquent exposition of the right to national independence', Dr Iannis, the village doctor, cuts the letter from the paper and sticks it on the wall – 'unaware that every other literate man in Greece had done the same'.*

We cannot believe that a mighty nation of eighty-five million people will make a flanking attack on a small nation struggling for its freedom and already fighting against an empire of forty-five million.

What would your army do, Mr Chancellor, if, instead of infantry, artillery and divisions, Greece sends as sentries to her frontiers 20,000 invalids, with no legs, with no arms, with blood and bandages to confront it? Would there be an army to attack such soldiers? But no, that cannot be. The many or few Greek soldiers who can be sent there will stand in Thrace as they stood in Epirus. There, too, they will fight. There, too, they will die. And they will await from Berlin the runner who came five years ago to receive the light from Olympia, now, with the same torch, to set on fire this small in size yet great country, which once taught mankind how to live and now will teach it how to die.

•

A. PHILIP RANDOLPH
1942

'Jim Crow'

The labour leader A. Philip Randolph (1889–1978) organized the Brotherhood of
Sleeping Car Porters and Maids, the first successful black labour union, in 1925. He
won his most spectacular success, however, in 1941 when he announced that unless the
colour bar against the employment of blacks was lifted he would lead a march on Washington
on 1 July. It was a date near the Glorious Fourth and an event calculated to draw the
greatest possible attention to racial oppression in the leading Western democracy – and a
propaganda gift to Goebbels.

America's blacks responded enthusiastically – 20,000 attended a meeting at New
York's Madison Square Garden in June. Randolph refused to call off the march in spite
of entreaties from President Roosevelt – who eventually issued an executive order forbidding
racial discrimination in defence contracts between the government and industry. Randolph
explained the aims of his protest in this subsequent article.

Though I have found no Negroes who want to see the United Nations lose
this war, I have found many who, before the war ends, want to see the
stuffing knocked out of white supremacy and of empire over subject peoples.
American Negroes, involved as we are in the general issues of the conflict,
are confronted not with a choice but with the challenge both to win democracy
for ourselves at home and to help win the war for democracy the world over.

There is no escape from the horns of this dilemma. There ought not to
be escape. For if the war for democracy is not won abroad, the fight for
democracy cannot be won at home. If this war cannot be won for the white
peoples, it will not be won for the darker races.

Conversely, if freedom and equality are not vouchsafed the peoples of
color, the war for democracy will not be won. Unless this double-barreled
thesis is accepted and applied, the darker races will never wholeheartedly
fight for the victory of the United Nations. That is why those familiar with
the thinking of the American Negro have sensed his lack of enthusiasm,
whether among the educated or uneducated, rich or poor, professional or
nonprofessional, religious or secular, rural or urban, north, south, east or
west.

That is why questions are being raised by Negroes in church, labor
union and fraternal society; in poolroom, barbershop, schoolroom, hospital,

hairdressing parlor; on college campus, railroad, and bus. One can hear such questions asked as these: What have Negroes to fight for? What's the difference between Hitler and that 'cracker' Talmadge of Georgia? Why has a man got to be Jim Crowed to die for democracy? If you haven't got democracy yourself, how can you carry it to somebody else?

What are the reasons for this state of mind? The answer is: discrimination, segregation, Jim Crow. Witness the navy, the army, the air corps; and also government services at Washington. In many parts of the South, Negroes in Uncle Sam's uniform are being put upon, mobbed, sometimes even shot down by civilian and military police, and on occasion lynched. Vested political interests in race prejudice are so deeply entrenched that to them winning the war against Hitler is secondary to preventing Negroes from winning democracy for themselves. This is worth many divisions to Hitler and Hirohito. While labor, business and farm are subjected to ceilings and doors and not allowed to carry on as usual, these interests trade in the dangerous business of race hate as usual.

When the defense program began and billions of the taxpayers' money were appropriated for guns, ships, tanks and bombs, Negroes presented themselves for work only to be given the cold shoulder. North as well as South, and despite their qualifications, Negroes were denied skilled employment. Not until their wrath and indignation took the form of a proposed protest march on Washington, scheduled for July 1, 1941, did things begin to move in the form of defense jobs for Negroes. The march was postponed by the timely issuance (June 25, 1941) of the famous Executive Order No. 8802 by President Roosevelt. But this order and the President's Committee on Fair Employment Practice, established thereunder, have as yet only scratched the surface by way of eliminating discriminations on account of race or color in war industry. Both management and labor unions in too many places and in too many ways are still drawing the color line.

The March on Washington Movement is essentially a movement of the people. It is all-Negro and pro-Negro, but not for that reason anti-white or anti-Semitic, or anti-Catholic, or anti-foreign, or anti-labor. Its major weapon is the non-violent demonstration of Negro mass power. Negro leadership has united back of its drive for jobs and justice. 'Whether Negroes should march on Washington, and if so, when?' will be the focus of a forthcoming national conference. For the plan of a protest march has not been abandoned. Its purpose would be to demonstrate that American Negroes are in deadly earnest, and all out for their full rights. No power on earth can cause them today to abandon their fight to wipe out every vestige of second-class citizenship and the dual standards that plague them.

A community is democratic only when the humblest and weakest person can enjoy the highest civil, economic and social rights that the biggest and most powerful possess. To trample on these rights of both Negroes and poor whites is such a commonplace in the South that it takes readily to anti-social, anti-labor, anti-Semitic and anti-Catholic propaganda. It was because of laxness in enforcing the Weimar constitution in republican Germany that Nazism made headway. Oppression of the Negroes in the United States, like suppression of the Jews in Germany, may open the way for a fascist dictatorship.

By fighting for their rights now, American Negroes are helping to make America a moral and spiritual arsenal of democracy. Their fight against the poll tax, against lynch law, segregation and Jim Crow, their fight for economic, political and social equality, thus becomes part of the global war for freedom.

•

HANS SCHOLL, SOPHIE SCHOLL, CHRISTOPH PROBOST
1943

'Tyranny'

The German town of Munich was shocked in 1943, shortly after the defeat at Stalingrad, when the words 'Down with Hitler' were daubed in large white letters on the walls of the university. Leaflets were found calling for resistance to Hitler. A few days later, garish red placards were posted throughout the town announcing that Hans and Sophie Scholl and Christoph Probost had been sentenced to death for high treason. The sentences had already been carried out. Three co-conspirators, Willi Graf, Professor Kurt Huber and Alexandra Schmerell, were also executed soon afterwards.

As Inge Scholl, whose brother and sister were executed, explained in her 1955 book, Six Against Tyranny, *they were six students and teachers who decided to oppose the Nazi state. They set to work producing thousands of leaflets and then took trains to distribute them in such cities as Frankfurt, Stuttgart and Vienna. This was the last leaflet they wrote before they were seized.*

Fellow students!

The nation is horrified by the fate of the men of Stalingrad. Three hundred and thirty thousand Germans have been driven to death and destruction needlessly, irresponsibly, by the brilliant strategy of a corporal of the First World War. *Führer*, we thank thee!

The German people are in a state of ferment: shall we continue to entrust the fate of our armies to a dilettante? Shall we continue to sacrifice what is left of German youth to the base lust for power of a party gang? No, never! The day of reckoning is here, when German youth will settle accounts with the foulest tyranny that our country has ever endured. In the name of German youth we claim from Adolf Hitler's government the restoration of personal freedom, the Germans' most precious possession, filched from us by the basest deception.

We have grown up in a country where all free expression of opinion is ruthlessly suppressed. The Hitler Youth, the Brown Shirts, the Black Shirts have tried, in the most fruitful and receptive years of our lives, to regiment us, to revolutionize us, to stupefy us. The despicable routine by which germinating individual thought was choked in a fog of empty phrases, was called 'Philosophic Training'. Chosen leaders, inconceivably depraved and mentally undeveloped, train the future Party bosses to be godless, shameless, unscrupulous exploiters and killers, and to give blind, unreasoning obedience to those above them. We 'brain-workers' would be clearly destined to be the whipping-boys of this new aristocracy. Front-line soldiers are ordered about like schoolboys by *Studentenführer* and aspirants to the rank of *Gauleiter*. *Gauleiters* besmirch the honour of German girl students with their obscene witticisms. German girl students at the Munich *Hochschule* have given a proper answer to such defilement, and the men students have supported them and refused to yield. This is a first step towards the reconquest of our right of free self-determination, a precondition to the re-creation of spiritual values. Our thanks are due to brave fellow-students of both sexes who have set us a shining example.

There is only one watchword for us: War against the Party. Come out of the Party organizations where they still try to suppress all political discussion. Come out of the lecture halls of the SS under-leaders and over-leaders and party sycophants! We need genuine science and genuine intellectual freedom. No threats can intimidate us, not even that of closing the universities. Each one of us must join in the struggle for our future – a future of freedom and honour under a government conscious of its moral responsibility.

Freedom and honour! For ten long years Hitler and his fellows have crushed, worn out and perverted these two words, the finest in the German language. They have done so as only dilettantes can, who throw the nation's treasures to the swine. In ten years they have eliminated all material and intellectual freedom, the moral substance of the German people, and have shown in doing so what freedom and honour mean to them. The eyes of even the dullest German have been opened by the fearful blood-bath perpetrated all over Europe and daily renewed in the name of the freedom and honour of the German people. The name of Germany will remain for ever blackened unless the youth of Germany at last arises, avenges and atones, crushes our tormentors and founds a new, spiritual Europe. Students! The eyes of the German people are upon us. Germany awaits from us the breaking of the National Socialist terror of 1943, as the Napoleonic terror was broken in 1813, by the might of the spirit. Beresina and Stalingrad are aflame in the east. The dead of Stalingrad adjure us!

Awake, my people, the beacons are aflame!

Our nation, inspired by a new outburst of faith in freedom and honour, is on the move against the enslavement of Europe by National Socialism.

•

SHMUEL ZYGIELBOJM
1943

'I cannot be silent'

Shmuel Zygielbojm, a prominent member of the pre-war Jewish Social Democrat Party (the Bund) and the Jewish Council in Lodz and Warsaw, left Poland in 1940 for London, where he became a leading speaker and broadcaster on the fate of the Jews.

His wife and child perished in the Warsaw Ghetto, and Zygielbojm's distress became so great that he committed suicide in London. He left behind in his Paddington flat a letter in Polish addressed to the president and the prime minister of Poland which was published in Britain and the United States.

I take the liberty of addressing to you my last words, and through you the Polish Government and people, the governments and people of the Allied States and the conscience of the world.

From the latest information received from Poland, it is evident that without doubt the Germans with ruthless cruelty are now murdering the few remaining Jews in Poland. Behind the walls of the ghettos the last act of a tragedy unprecedented in history is being performed.

The responsibility for the crime of murdering all the Jewish population in Poland falls in the first instance on the perpetrators, but indirectly also it weighs on the whole of humanity, the peoples and governments of the Allied States, which so far have made no effort towards a concrete action for the purpose of curtailing this crime. By passive observation of this murder of defenceless millions and the maltreatment of children and women, the men of those countries have become accomplices of criminals.

I have also to state that although the Polish Government has in a high degree contributed to stirring the opinion of the world, yet it did so insufficiently, for it did nothing extraordinary enough to correspond to the magnitude of the drama now being enacted in Poland.

Out of the nearly 350,000 Polish Jews and about 700,000 Jews deported to Poland from other countries, there still lived in April of this year, according to the official information of the head of the underground Bund organization sent to the United States through a delegate of the government, about 300,000. And the murders are still going on incessantly.

I cannot be silent and I cannot live while the remnants of the Jewish people of Poland, of whom I am a representative, are perishing.

My comrades in the Warsaw ghetto perished with weapons in their hands in their last heroic impulse.

It was not my destiny to perish as they did, together with them, but I belong to them, and their mass graves.

By my death I wish to express my strongest protest against the inactivity with which the world is looking on and permitting the extermination of Jewish people. I know how little human life is worth, especially today. But as I was unable to do anything during my life, perhaps by my death I shall contribute to destroying the indifference of those who are able and should act in order to save now, maybe at the last moment, this handful of Polish Jews who are still alive from certain annihilation.

My life belongs to the Jewish people in Poland and, therefore, I give it to them. I wish that this handful that remains of the several million Polish Jews could live to see with the Polish masses the day of liberation – that it could breathe in Poland and in a world of freedom and in the justice of socialism in return for all its tortures and inhuman sufferings. And I believe that such a Poland will arise and that such a world will come.

I trust that the President and Prime Minister will direct my words to all of those for whom they are destined and that the Polish Government will immediately begin appropriate action in the diplomatic and propaganda fields in order to save from extermination the Polish Jews who are still alive.

I bid farewell to all and everything dear to me and loved by me.'

S. Zygielbojm

I. F. STONE
1944

'Save the Jews'

The investigative journalist I. F. Stone (1907–89) was outraged at the indecision of President Roosevelt in his treatment of Jewish refugees from Europe. Roosevelt announced that he would consider creating 'free ports' for the internment of refugees but no action was taken. In this article in The Nation, *Stone appealed to fellow editors for help: 'Anything newspapermen can write about this in their own papers will help. It will save lives, the lives of people like ourselves.'*

The essence of tragedy is not the doing of evil by evil men but the doing of evil by good men, out of weakness, indecision, sloth, inability to act in accordance with what they know to be right. The tragic element in the fate of the Jews of Europe lies in the failure of their friends in the West to shake loose from customary ways and bureaucratic habit, to risk inexpediency and defy prejudice, to be wholehearted, to care as deeply and fight as hard for the big words we use, for justice and for humanity, as the fanatic Nazi does for his master race or the fanatic Jap for his Emperor. A reporter in Washington cannot help seeing this weakness all about him. We are half-hearted about what little we could do to help the Jews of Europe as we are half-hearted about our economic warfare, about blacklisting those who help our enemies, about almost everything in the war except the actual fighting.

There is much we could have done to save the Jews of Europe before the war. There is much we could have done since the war began. There are still things we could do today which would give new lives to a few and hope to many. The hope that all is not black in the world for his children can be strong sustenance for a man starving in a camp or entering a gas chamber. But to feel that your friends and allies are wishy-washy folk who mean what they say but haven't got the gumption to live up to it must brew a poisonous despair. When Mr Roosevelt established the War Refugee Board in January, he said it was 'the policy of this government to take all measures within its power . . . consistent with the successful prosecution of the war . . . to rescue the victims of enemy oppression.'

The facts are simple. Thanks to the International Red Cross and those good folk the Quakers, thanks to courageous non-Jewish friends in the occupied countries themselves and to intrepid Jews who run a kind of underground railway under Nazi noses, something can still be done to alleviate the suffering of the Jews in Europe and some Jews can still be got out.

Even under the White Paper there are still 22,000 immigration visas available for entry into Palestine. The main problem is to get Jews over the Turkish border without a passport for transit to Palestine. 'Free ports' in Turkey are needed, but the Turks, irritated by other pressures from England and the United States, are unwilling to do for Jewish refugees what we our-selves are still unwilling to do, that is, give them a temporary haven. Only an executive order by the President establishing 'free ports' in this country can prove to the Turks that we are dealing with them in good faith; under present circumstances they cannot but feel contemptuous of our pleas. And the longer we delay the fewer Jews there will be left to rescue, the slimmer the chances to get them out. Between 4,000,000 and 5,000,000 European Jews have been killed since August 1942, when the Nazi extermination campaign began.

There are people here who say the President cannot risk a move of this kind before election. I believe that an insult to the American people. I do not believe any but a few unworthy bigots would object to giving a few thousand refugees a temporary breathing spell in their flight from oppression. It is a question of Mr Roosevelt's courage and good faith. All he is called upon to do, after all, is what Franco did months ago, yes, *Franco*. Franco established 'free ports,' internment camps, months ago for refugees who fled across his border, refugees, let us remember, from his own ally and patron, Hitler. Knowing the Führer's maniacal hatred for Jews, that kindness on Franco's part took considerably more courage than Mr Roosevelt needs to face a few sneering editorials, perhaps from the *Chicago Tribune*. I say 'perhaps' because I do not know that even Colonel McCormick would in fact be hostile.

Official Washington's capacity for finding excuses for inaction is endless, and many people in the State and War departments who play a part in this matter can spend months sucking their legalistic thumbs over any problem. So many things that might have been done were attempted too late. A little more than a year ago Sweden offered to take 20,000 Jewish children from occupied Europe if Britain and the United States guaranteed their feeding and after the war their repatriation. The British were fairly rapid in this case, but it took three or four months to get these assurances from the American Government, and by that time the situation had worsened to a point that seems to have blocked the whole project. In another case the Bulgarian Government offered visas for 1,000 Jews if arrangements could be made within a certain time for their departure. A ship was obtained at once, but it took seven weeks for British officials to get clearance for the project from

London, and by that time the time limit had been passed. The records, when they can be published, will show many similar incidents.

The news that the United States had established 'free ports' would bring hope to people who have now no hope. It would encourage neutrals to let in more refugees because we could take out some of those they have already admitted. Most important, it would provide the argument of example and the evidence of sincerity in the negotiations for 'free ports' in Turkey, last hope of the Balkan Jews. I ask fellow-newspapermen to show the President by their expressions of opinion in their own papers that if he hesitates for fear of an unpleasant political reaction he badly misconstrues the real feelings of the American people.

•

MARIE CLAUDE VAILLANT-COUTURIER
1944

'*Auschwitz*'

Marie Claude Vaillant-Couturier was a veteran of the French resistance who survived more than three years of torture in Nazi concentration camps, mainly the infamous Auschwitz (and went on to become a Deputy in the French constituent Assembly in 1946 and a decorated heroine). She described the horror of Auschwitz when she was cross-examined by Charles Dubost, the deputy French prosecutor, at the Nuremberg War Crimes Tribunal. Silence fell on the courtroom as she gave her testimony. Some of the defendants were so moved by her account of the atrocities that they had to take off their headphones.

We saw the unsealing of the cars and the soldiers letting men, women and children out of them. We then witnessed heart-rending scenes: old couples forced to part from each other, mothers made to abandon their young daughters, since the latter were sent to the camp, whereas mothers and children were sent to the gas chambers. All these people were unaware of the fate awaiting them. They were merely upset at being separated, but they did not know that they were going to their death. To render their welcome more pleasant at this time – June–July 1944 – an orchestra composed of internees, all young and pretty girls dressed in little white blouses and navy blue skirts, played during the selection, at the arrival of the trains, gay tunes such as 'The Merry Widow', the 'Barcarolle' from *The Tales of Hoffman*, and so forth. They were then informed that this was a labour camp and since they were not brought into the camp they saw only the small platform surrounded by flowering plants. Naturally, they could not realize what was in store for them. Those selected for the gas chamber, that is, the old people, mothers and children, were escorted to a red-brick building which bore the letters 'Baden', that is to say 'Baths'. There, to begin with, they were made to undress and given a towel before they went into the so-called shower room. Later on, at the time of the large convoys from Hungary, they had no more time left to play-act or to pretend; they were brutally undressed, and I know these details as I knew a little Jewess from France who lived with her family at the 'Republique' district.

She was called 'little Marie' and she was the only one, the sole survivor of a family of nine. Her mother and her seven brothers and sisters had been gassed on arrival. When I met her she was employed to undress the babies before they were taken into the gas chamber. Once the people were undressed they took them into a room which was somewhat like a shower room, and gas capsules were thrown through an opening in the ceiling. An SS man would watch the effect produced through a porthole. At the end of five or seven minutes, when the gas had completed its work, he gave the signal to open the doors; and men with gas masks – they too were internees – went into the room and removed the corpses. They told us that the internees must have suffered before dying, because they were closely clinging to one another and it was very difficult to separate them.

After that a special squad would come to pull out gold teeth and dentures; and again, when the bodies had been reduced to ashes, they would sift them in an attempt to recover the gold.

At Auschwitz there were eight crematories but, as from 1944, these proved insufficient. The SS had large pits dug by the internees, where they put branches, sprinkled with gasoline, which they set on fire. Then they threw the corpses into the pits. From our block we could see after about three-quarters of an hour or an hour after the arrival of a convoy, large flames coming from the crematorium, and the sky was lighted up by the burning pits.

One night we were awakened by terrifying cries. And we discovered, on the following day, from the men working in the Sonderkommando – the 'Gas Kommando' – that on the preceding day, the gas supply having run out, they had thrown the children into the furnaces alive.

During Christmas 1943 – when we were in quarantine, we saw, since we lived opposite Block 25, women brought to Block 25 stripped naked. Uncovered trucks were then driven up and on them the naked women were piled, as many as the trucks could hold. Each time a truck started, the infamous Hessler ... ran after the truck and with his bludgeon repeatedly struck the naked women going to their death. They knew they were going to the gas chamber and tried to escape. They were massacred. They attempted to jump from the truck and we, from our own block, watched the trucks pass by and heard the grievous wailing of all those women who knew they were going to be gassed. Many of them could very well have lived on, since they were suffering only from scabies and were, perhaps, a little too undernourished . . .

Since the Jewesses were sent to Auschwitz with their entire families and since they had been told that this was a sort of ghetto and were advised to bring all their goods and chattels along, they consequently brought considerable riches with them. As for the Jewesses from Salonika, I remember that on their arrival they were given picture postcards bearing the post office address of 'Waldsee', a place which did not exist; and a printed text to be sent to their families, stating, 'We are doing very well here; we have work and we are well treated. We await your arrival.' I myself saw the cards in question; and the Schreiberinnen, that is, the secretaries of the block, were instructed to distribute them among the internees in order to post them to their families. I know that whole families arrived as a result of these postcards.

•

WILLIAM BEVERIDGE
1944

'The six giant evils'

The Beveridge Report of 1942 and R. A. Butler's Education Act of 1944 laid the foundations of the welfare state created by the reforming Labour government elected in 1945.

William Beveridge (1879–1963) had been social reformer, civil servant, director of the London School of Economics and Master of University College, Oxford, when he was recalled to Whitehall in 1940 to become chairman of the Committee on Social Insurance. Its report proposed a programme of universal social security, a war, as Beveridge put it in this speech two years later, against six unnecessary evils. Although Churchill's coalition government was initially lukewarm – there was still a war to be won – the report became a bestseller.

When it was debated in Parliament, Labour demanded stronger commitment from the government and revolted for the only time in the war. The rebellion was a political watershed. Afterwards support for a postwar coalition fell away and opinion polls showed Labour ahead of the Conservatives.

My case is that this is very far from being the best of all possible worlds, but that it might be a very good world, because most of the major evils in it are unnecessary – either wholly so or to the extent to which they exist today. The evils which are wholly unnecessary and should be abolished are Want, Squalor, Idleness enforced by unemployment, and War. The evils which are unnecessary to the extent to which they exist today and which should be reduced drastically are Disease and Ignorance.

The six Giant Evils of Want, Squalor, Disease, Ignorance, Idleness and War as they exist in the modern world, are six needless scandals. The Radical Programme which I propose to you is a war on these six giants. As a Liberal I propose it as a programme for the Liberal Party. Let me take the giants in turn, beginning with the easiest to attack.

Want means not having enough money income to buy the necessaries of life for oneself and one's family. Want in Britain just before this was utterly unnecessary. The productive power of the community was far more than enough to provide the bare necessaries of life to everyone (that, of course, is something quite different from satisfying the desires of everyone). Want arose because income – purchasing power to buy necessaries – was not properly distributed, between different sections of the people and between different periods in life, between times of earning and not earning, between times of no family responsibilities and large family responsibilities.

Before this war, as is said in the Beveridge Report, 'want was a needless scandal due to not taking the trouble to prevent it'. After this war, if want persists, it will be even more of a scandal. It is contrary to reason and experience to suppose that, with all that we have learned in war, we shall be less productive after it than before. And we know also just how to prevent want – by adopting Social Security in full as set out in the Beveridge Report. This means guaranteeing to every citizen through social insurance that, on condition of working while he can and contributing from his earnings, he shall, when he is unable to work through sickness, accident, unemployment or old age, have a subsistence income for himself and his family, an income as of right without means test, and not cut down because he has other means . . .

Squalor means the conditions under which so many of our people are compelled to live, in houses ill-built, too small, too close together, either too far from work or too far from country air, with the air around them polluted by smoke, impossible to keep clean, with no modern equipment to save the housewife's toil, wasting the life and energy of the wage-earner in endless crowded travel to and from his job. Squalor is obviously unnecessary, because the housing which leads to squalor is made by man, and that which is made by man can by man be prevented.

The time has come for a revolution in housing, but an essential condition of good housing is town and country planning; to stop the endless growth of the great cities; to control the location of industry so that men can live both near their work and near country air; to manage transport in the national interest, so as to bring about the right location of industry.

Only on the basis of town and country planning should we build our houses and they must be built not just shells, but fully equipped with every modern convenience, with water, light, power, model kitchens for clean cooking, refrigerators, mechanical washers for clothes. As is said in the Beveridge Report: 'In the next thirty years housewives as mothers have vital work to do to ensure the adequate continuance of the British race and of British ideals in the world.' They must be set free from needless endless toil, so that they may undertake this vital service and rear in health and happiness the larger families that are needed.

A revolution in housing is the greatest contribution that can be made to raising the standard of living throughout this country, for differences of housing represent the greatest differences between various sections of our people today, between the comfortable and the uncomfortable classes.

Disease cannot be abolished completely, but is needless to anything like its present extent. It must be attacked from many sides by measures for prevention and for cure. The housing revolution, of which I have spoken, is perhaps the greatest of all the measures for prevention of disease. It has been estimated that something like 45,000 people die each year because of bad housing conditions. Scotland – your country and my country – used to be a healthier land than England – with a lower death rate – till about fifty years ago. Now it has a higher death rate, because in the past fifty years its health has not improved nearly as much as that of England. The big difference between the two countries lies in housing, which in many ways is worse here. Let us put that right for our country. Next to better housing as a means of preventing disease ranks better feeding. Experience of war has shown how much can be done to maintain and improve health under the most unfavourable conditions by a nutrition policy carried out by the state on the basis of science. It is essential for the future to make good food available for all, at prices within the reach of all, and to encourage, by teaching and by price policy good nutrition instead of mere eating and drinking.

Ignorance cannot be abolished completely, but is needless to anything like its present extent. Lack of opportunity to use abilities is one of the greatest causes of unhappiness. A revolution in education is needed, and the recent

Education Act should be turned into the means of such a revolution. Attacking ignorance means not only spending money on schools and teachers and scholars in youth, but providing also immensely greater facilities for adult education. The door of learning should not shut for anyone at eighteen or at any time. Ignorance to its present extent is not only unnecessary, but dangerous. Democracies cannot be well governed except on the basis of understanding.

With these measures for prevention must go also measures for cure, by establishing a national health service which secures to every citizen at all times whatever treatment he needs, at home or in hospital, without a charge at the time of treatment. It should be the right and the duty of every British citizen to be as well as science can make him. This, too, was included in my report more than two years ago. Let us get on with it!

Unemployment, as we have had it in the past, is needless. The way to abolish unemployment is not to attack it directly by waiting until people are unemployed and then to make work for them, but to plan to use the whole of our manpower in the pursuit of vital common objectives.

The Radical Programme for attacking the five giants of Want, Squalor, Disease, Ignorance and Idleness through unemployment is all one programme. We abolish unemployment in war because we are prepared to spend up to the limit of our manpower in abolishing Hitler. We can equally abolish unemployment in peace by deciding to spend up to the limit of our manpower in abolishing social evils.

The last and the greatest of the giant evils of the world is War. Unless we can win freedom from war and from fear of war, all else is vain. The way to abolish murder and violence between nations is the same as that by which we abolish murder and violence between individuals, by establishing the rule of law between nations. This is a task beyond the power of any nation but it is within the power of the three great victorious nations of this war – the United States, Soviet Russia and the British Commonwealth. If those three nations wish to abolish war in the future they can do so, by agreeing to accept impartial justice in their own case and to enforce justice in all other cases, by respecting the freedom and independence of small nations and the right of each nation to have its own institutions so long as these do not threaten harm to its neighbours. By doing so, they will accomplish something far more glorious than any victory in war. In the past statesmen have prided themselves in getting 'Peace with honour'. The formula of the future – the only one that can give us lasting peace – should be 'Peace with justice'. Honour is national, justice is international.

•

VICTOR KRAVCHENKO
1944

'*I Chose Freedom*'

On a Saturday night in March 1944, Victor Kravchenko (1905–66), son of a Soviet revolutionary, a former director of industry with an office in the Kremlin and a captain in the Red Army, resigned his post with the Soviet Purchasing Commission in Washington and fled to New York. A few days later, he issued this statement, published in the New York Times, *accusing the Soviet government of a 'double-faced' foreign policy, denouncing the Stalin regime and forecasting the postwar aims of Stalin that led to the Cold War.*

His book I Chose Freedom, *published in 1946, was a bestseller.*

I have taken this action only after considerable thought and hesitation, having in mind, first and foremost, the interests of the war effort of my people, of the United Nations, and the larger war aims of the peoples arrayed against the Axis powers.

For many years I have worked loyally for the people of my country in the service of the Soviet Government and have followed closely the development of Soviet policy in its various stages. For the sake of the Soviet Union's interests and her people I tried hard to overlook many aspects of the situation which were repugnant and alarming. But I cannot keep silent any longer. The interests of the war effort and of my suffering, tortured people compel me to keep silent on many things, but they demand that I speak out on fundamentals of the policy pursued today by the Soviet Government and its leaders affecting the war and the hopes of all peoples for a new international order of peace and reconstruction.

I can no longer support the double-faced political maneuvers directed at one and the same time toward collaboration with the United States and Britain while pursuing aims incompatible with such collaboration. Collaboration with the democratic countries cannot be pursued while the Soviet Government and its leaders are in reality following a concealed policy of their own designed to accomplish purposes at variance with their public professions.

The Soviet Government has dissolved the Communist International but only in form; in reality Moscow has continued to support its Communist Party affiliates in many countries. The new democratic terminology being utilized by Moscow is only a maneuver. Intelligent and informed people in Russia and abroad are not deceived by the new Soviet terminology of nationalism, the object of which is to conceal the substance and purposes of real Soviet policy. These purposes have guided also the formation of the All-Slav Committee in Moscow and of the so-called Union of Polish Patriots, with their alleged national programs.

The latest maneuvers directed toward the formation of a Polish Government that would be obedient to the Soviet Government have provoked consternation and protests, which I fully share. The Soviet Government rightly objects to the interference of outsiders in the internal affairs of Russia. Why, then, do the Soviet rulers consider it proper to force their brand of 'democracy' upon Poland?

The Soviet policy in the Balkans and Czechoslovakia is pictured to the world as a guarantee of the future welfare and co-operation of the peoples of Europe – in reality it has quite different practical ends.

Officially the Soviet Government has proclaimed its desire to support the establishment of democratic regimes in Italy, Austria and other countries. In reality this is but another attempt to adapt its own aims to the purposes of the Allies and to promote the inclusion of Communists, obedient to the Kremlin, in the future governments of these countries. The real plans and aims of the Soviet Government, as distinct from its public professions, are in contradiction with the interests and needs of the Russian people and of the cause for which the peoples of the United Nations are fighting. While professing to seek the establishment of democracy in countries liberated from fascism, the Soviet Government at home has failed to take a single serious step toward granting elementary liberties to the Russian people.

The Russian people are subjected, as before, to unspeakable oppression and cruelties, while the NKVD [Soviet secret police], acting through its thousands of spies, continues to wield its unbridled domination over the peoples of Russia. In the territories cleared of the Nazi invaders, the Soviet Government is re-establishing its political regime of lawlessness and violence, while prisons and concentration camps continue to function, as before.

The hopes of political and social reforms cherished by the Russian people at the beginning of the war have proved to be empty illusions.

This war is not yet ended, but already the rulers in the Kremlin are preparing a new generation for the next war. An enduring and genuine peace after the conclusion of the present war and the interests of my people require a different policy from that now pursued by the Soviet Government.

I maintain that more than any other people the Russian people require that they be granted elementary political liberties – genuine freedom of press and speech, freedom from want and freedom from fear. What the Russian people have had from their government has been only lip service to these freedoms. For years they have lived in constant dread and want. The Russian people have earned a new deal by their immeasurable sacrifices, which have saved the country as well as the existing regime itself, and through which they have dealt such decisive blows to fascism and have determined the course of the war.

Being aware of the methods of struggle employed by the Soviet rulers against political opponents I fully expect that they will now be used against me – the methods of slander, provocation and possibly worse.

I declare that I have never committed any acts detrimental to my people, the ruling party and the Soviet Government, and have always tried to perform my duties to my country, my party and my people honestly and conscientiously.

I hope to have the opportunity of continuing to devote my experience and energy to the war effort in this country.

I, therefore, place myself now under the protection of American public opinion.

•

BISHOP GEORGE BELL
1944

'Obliteration is not a justifiable act of war'

The Anglican churchman George Bell (1893–1958) was Dean of Canterbury and then Bishop of Chichester from 1929 to 1958. Bell was a bishop with an international outlook and moral courage. That courage was demonstrated when he exposed the anti-Christian trend of Hitlerism at its beginnings, for which he was sharply criticized. It was shown again during the Second World War when he attacked the Allied policy of bombing cities and civilian homes in Germany, as in this House of Lords speech. His criticism made him deeply unpopular but he did not flinch from his moral position.

I turn to the situation in February 1944, and the terrific devastation by Bomber Command of German towns. I do not forget the Luftwaffe, or its tremendous bombing of Belgrade, Warsaw, Rotterdam, London, Portsmouth, Coventry, Canterbury and many other places of military, industrial and cultural importance. Hitler is a barbarian. There is no decent person on the Allied side who is likely to suggest that we should make him our pattern or attempt to be competitors in that market. It is clear enough that large-scale bombing of enemy towns was begun by the Nazis. I am not arguing that point at all. The question with which I am concerned is this. Do the government understand the full force of what area bombardment is doing and is destroying now? Are they alive not only to the vastness of the material damage, much of which is irreparable, but also to the harvest they are laying up for the future relationships of the peoples of Europe as well as to its moral implications? The aim of Allied bombing from the air, said the Secretary of State for Air at Plymouth on 22 January, is to paralyse German war industry and transport. I recognize the legitimacy of concentrated attack on industrial and military objectives, on airfields and air bases, in view especially of the coming of the Second Front. I fully realize that in attacks on centres of war industry and transport the killing of civilians when it is the result of bona fide military activity is inevitable. But there must be a fair balance between the means employed and the purpose achieved. To obliterate a whole town because certain portions contain military and industrial establishments is to reject the balance.

Let me take two crucial instances, Hamburg and Berlin. Hamburg has a population of between one and two million people. It contains targets of immense military and industrial importance. It also happens to be the most democratic town in Germany where the anti-Nazi opposition was strongest. Injuries to civilians resulting from bona fide attacks on particular objectives are legitimate according to international law. But owing to the methods used the whole town is now a ruin. Unutterable destruction and devastation were wrought last autumn. On a very conservative estimate, according to the early German statistics, 28,000 persons were killed. Never before in the history of air warfare was an attack of such weight and persistence carried out against a single industrial concentration. Practically all the buildings, cultural, military, residential, industrial, religious – including the famous University Library with its 800,000 volumes, of which three-quarters have perished – were razed to the ground.

Berlin, the capital of the Reich, is four times the size of Hamburg. The offices of the government, the military, industrial, war-making establishments in Berlin are a fair target. Injuries to civilians are inevitable. But up to date half Berlin has been destroyed, area by area, the residential and the industrial portions alike. Through the dropping of thousands of tons of bombs, including fire-phosphorus bombs, of extraordinary power, men and women have been lost, overwhelmed in the colossal tornado of smoke, blast and flame. It is said that 74,000 persons have been killed and that three million are already homeless . . .

If we wish to shorten the war, as we must, then let the government speak a word of hope and encouragement both to the tortured millions of Europe and to those enemies of Hitler to whom in 1939 Mr Churchill referred as 'millions who stand aloof from the seething mass of criminality and corruption constituted by the Nazi Party machine'.

Why is there this blindness to the psychological side? Why is there this inability to reckon with the moral and spiritual facts? Why is there this forgetfulness of the ideals by which our cause is inspired? How can the War Cabinet fail to see that this progressive devastation of cities is threatening the roots of civilization? How can they be blind to the harvest of even fiercer warring and desolation, even in this country, to which the present destruction will inevitably lead when the members of the War Cabinet have long passed to their rest? How can they fail to realize that this is not the way to curb military aggression and end war? This is an extraordinarily solemn moment. What we do in war – which, after all, lasts a comparatively short time – affects the whole character of peace, which covers a much longer period. The sufferings of Europe, brought about by the demoniac cruelty of Hitler and his Nazis, and hardly imaginable to those in this country who for the last five years have not been out of this island or had intimate association with Hitler's victims, are not to be healed by the use of power only, power exclusive and unlimited. The Allies stand for something greater than power. The chief name inscribed on our banner is 'Law'. It is of supreme importance that we who, with our Allies, are the liberators of Europe should so use power that it is always under the control of law. It is because the bombing of enemy towns – this area bombing – raises this issue of power unlimited and exclusive that such immense importance is bound to attach to the policy and action of His Majesty's Government.

•

ANEURIN BEVAN
1944

'The Tory'

With the end of the war in sight in 1944, and the prospect of a general election in 1945, Aneurin Bevan (1897–1960) knew that Churchill would be the Tories' chief asset. Labour must destroy his image, he argued. He wrote Why Not Trust the Tories? *for the Left Book Club. It sold 80,000 copies, and, as his biographer Michael Foot says, provided a 'powerful prophylactic against the Tory virus'.*

It is not possible for anyone to understand the recent history of this country, its present situation, nor its future trends, unless they grasp firmly on to this fundamental conflict between the primitive disposition of the Tory character and mentality, and the practice of democracy to which he is compelled to conform by historical circumstance. It explains both the stultification of British democracy between the wars, and the apparent dishonesty and deceitfulness of Tory political conduct. The Tory feels no guilt because he is conscious of no fealty. When he betrays democracy, when he cheats it and debilitates it, he is not capable of remorse nor even of contrition, because he has no kinship with it. It is another world of alien values, into which by the very laws of his nature he is never capable of entering. Surely, you may retort, this cannot be the whole truth. After all, the Tory displayed all the arts of parliamentary government for centuries. True, but there were Parliaments in Britain long before there was a democracy. The Tories looked upon Parliament as a means by which they could settle differences among themselves, without resort to armed conflict. They never looked upon it as a place where they shared power with the masses, much less yielded power to them. When Keir Hardie went to Parliament in his cap they looked on it as funny before they grew angry with it as a portent. The most popular Labour Members of Parliament, with the Tories, have always been those who plead for mercy for the poor. They have never shown anything but bare-fanged hatred for those Labour Members who want political power for the masses.

It must be obvious that the pre-requisite for the successful practice of an idea is that you should believe in it. How absurd therefore it is to expect democracy to be successful under the Tories. Democracy is poison to the Tory's whole conception of life. Is it reasonable to expect him to make his poison stronger? It is more reasonable and natural for him to do what he does, that is, weaken, undermine and deride democratic government in every way he can and then to blame its failure on the incapacity of the people for government. It is here the danger to the ordinary man and woman arises. With the twentieth century the ordinary man stepped into history. You have only to read the history books to see he had little to do with the making of history before that. He was never allowed a say in choosing his place. The rise of political democracy changed all that. Although he is still in a subordinate position he has won the right to be taken into consultation. His present position is, therefore, a dangerous one for him. He is charged with the responsibility for events, but not with the power to shape them. The real power is still in the hands of those who have held it all along. You have only to look at the composition of the House of Commons to see that. The same families are represented there today who have ruled Britain for centuries. At each election power passes to the people, and each time they hand it back again to the same people who held it before. The ordinary man is therefore in a double peril. He accepts the responsibility for government but denies himself the power to exercise it. Up to the twentieth century he was the drudge of history. He is now the scapegoat as well. His fault consists in not assuming the power which alone can give meaning to the responsibility which political democracy confers upon him.

Instead of this, he is still content to give democratic sanction to those property institutions, ideas and values which belong not to a democratic but to an authoritarian regime. In the past the ordinary man was a compulsory helot. Under our political democracy he is a voluntary one. The change is profoundly important; but it is a transitory stage. He either steps back to the shadows of history once more or into the light of full social maturity. Property now rules with his permission. At any moment he can withhold it. But he must be brought to realize that he must either make the threat good or withdraw it altogether. It is perfectly true that property cannot rule effectively, in accordance with its own tenets, under a perpetual threat of expropriation. The threat must either pass into action or be removed. A static democracy must die, if only because the people are blamed for the resultant nervelessness of government. Stalemate between contending forces in the state usually ends in the defeat of the people. It was so in Germany and Italy. There the people were persuaded to give away their power precisely because they hesitated to fully employ it . . .

The economic structure of Britain is the domain of private adventure. The prime motivator in industry and finance is the property owner, and/or his hirelings. It is he who employs and dismisses. It is he whose wishes direct industrial enterprise and the use of credit. The mass of the people are the creatures of his private plans, they are never privy to them, but are the victims of their consequences. Parliament, therefore, legislates in a framework formed for it by the decisions of individuals who consult no one and nothing but their private interests. Parliament is therefore always after the fact, conditioned by what the City or some great captain of industry decides.

The situation thus created is one of sustained frustration. Parliament debates unemployment when at the same time the instruments of employment are left in private hands. In short, responsibility rests with the people and power with private property. Parliament washes in public the linen which property dirties in private. It is a division of labour ultimately fatal to representative democratic government. It makes the public representative the scapegoat for the bandits of industry and finance, over whose actions he is denied effective control. Parliament is the professional public mourner for private economic crimes.

The divorcement of parliamentary discussion from action brings discussion itself into contempt. If the deed lags too far behind the word then the word itself turns sour. This is the psychological basis of Fascism. Fascism is not a new social order in the strict sense of the term. It is the future refusing to be born. It is the fruit of an aborted democracy. Representative institutions cannot stand by helpless spectators of mass unemployment, preventable poverty and economic anarchy without losing prestige, and eventually their own life. Nevertheless, this is the inevitable fate of a Parliament which denies itself the instruments of action, which are the industries and services of society. By refusing the state effective intervention in the economic activities of society, the Tory is a potential Fascist element in the community. By denying Parliament a vigorous economic life he condemns it to death. It is true he does not always, in his own person, perform the execution, but he prepares the way for the executioners who, at a certain stage, appear in the form of political assassins, now familiarized to us by events on the continent. These assassins, once in power, are compelled by the laws of their being to keep power by feverishly stirring up the nationalist passions of their people, and by using the surplus production of their industries in the making of war machines. So far, it is true, the British Tory has not brought that fate upon us in this country yet, in all its phases. But he did make a considerable contribution to it abroad, and helped to bring the war upon us. The important thing to bear in mind is that all the phases are implicit in the Tory conception of politics.

•

F. A. HAYEK
1944

'The Road to Serfdom'

F. A. Hayek (1899–1992) had been professor of economics at the London School of Economics since the 1930s when his classic polemic against socialist planning and the welfare state was published in 1944. Most economists had been silenced by their official positions in the war machine, he wrote in his Preface: 'In consequence public opinion is to an alarming extent guided by amateurs and cranks, by people who have an axe to grind or a pet panacea to sell.'

He set out his belief in capitalism, individualism and free markets against the serfdom of socialism in The Road to Serfdom, *a book which deeply influenced Margaret Thatcher, who became prime minister in 1979 and started to dismantle socialist nationalization. This extract is on 'The Totalitarians in Our Midst.'*

The problem of monopoly would not be as difficult as it is if it were only the capitalist monopolist whom we have to fight. But, as has already been said, monopoly has become the danger that it is, not through the efforts of a few interested capitalists, but through the support they have obtained from those whom they have let share in their gains, and from the many more whom they have persuaded that in supporting monopoly they assist in the creation of a more just and orderly society. The fatal turning point in the modern development was when the great movement which can serve its original ends only by fighting all privilege, the Labour Movement, came under the influence of anti-competition doctrines and became itself entangled in the strife for privilege. The recent growth of monopoly is largely the result of a deliberate collaboration of organized capital and organized labour where the privileged groups of labour share in the monopoly profits at the expense of the community and particularly at the expense of the poorest, those employed in the less well organized industries and the unemployed.

It is one of the saddest spectacles of our time to see a great democratic movement support a policy which must lead to the destruction of democracy and which meanwhile can benefit only a minority of the masses who support it. Yet it is this support from the left of the tendencies towards monopoly which make them so irresistible and the prospects of the future so dark. So long as Labour continues to assist in the destruction of the only order under which at least some degree of independence and freedom has been secured to every worker, there is indeed little hope for the future. The Labour leaders who now proclaim so loudly that they have 'done once and for all with the mad competitive system' are proclaiming the doom of the freedom of the individual. There is no other possibility than either the order governed by the impersonal discipline of the market or that directed by the will of a few individuals; and those who are out to destroy the first are wittingly or unwittingly helping to create the second. Even though some workmen will perhaps be better fed, and all will no doubt be more uniformly dressed in that new order, it is permissible to doubt whether the majority of English workmen will in the end thank the intellectuals among their leaders who have presented them with a socialist doctrine which endangers their personal freedom.

To anyone who is familiar with the history of the major continental countries in the last twenty-five years, the study of the recent programme of the Labour Party, now committed to the creation of a 'planned society' is a most depressing experience. To 'any attempt to restore traditional Britain' there is opposed a scheme which not only in general outline but also in detail and even wording is indistinguishable from the socialist dreams which dominated German discussion twenty-five years ago. Not only demands, like those of the resolution, adopted on Professor Laski's motion, which requires the retention in peace time of the 'measures of government control needed for mobilizing the national resources in war', but all the characteristic catch words, such as the 'balanced economy' which Professor Laski now demands for Great Britain, or the 'community consumption' towards which production is to be centrally directed, are bodily taken over from the German ideology. Twenty-five years ago there was perhaps still some excuse for holding the naive belief 'that a planned society can be a far more free society than the competitive *laissez-faire* order it has come to replace'. But to find it once more held after twenty-five years of experience and the re-examination of the old beliefs to which this experience has led, and at a time when we are fighting the results of those very doctrines, is tragic beyond words. That the great party which in Parliament and public opinion has largely taken the place of the progressive parties of the past, should have ranged itself with what, in the light of all past development, must be regarded as a reactionary movement, is the decisive change which has taken place in our time and the source of the mortal danger to everything a liberal must value. That the advances of the past should be threatened by the traditionalist forces of the right is a phenomenon of all ages which need not alarm us. But if the place of the opposition, in public discussion as well as in Parliament, should become lastingly the monopoly of a second reactionary party, there would indeed be no hope left.

•

LABOUR PARTY
1945

'Let Us Face the Future'

The war in Europe was over but the war in the Pacific had still to be won when Churchill called a general election in July 1945. He had led the nation to victory over Hitler and was cheered by the voters even as they voted decisively against him. Some still recalled the broken promises after 1918, many remembered the unemployment of the thirties and wanted the welfare state promised in the Beveridge Report. 'Let Us Face the Future' was the title of Labour's manifesto. Labour won 393 seats against 213 for the Conservatives and proceeded to fulfil its promises under Clement Attlee, who had been Churchill's deputy throughout the war.

Victory is assured for us and our allies in the European war. The war in the East goes the same way. The British Labour Party is firmly resolved that Japanese barbarism shall be defeated just as decisively as Nazi aggression and tyranny. The people will have won both struggles. The gallant men and women in the Fighting Services, in the Merchant Navy, Home Guard and Civil Defence, in the factories and in the bombed areas – they deserve and must be assured a happier future than faced so many of them after the last war. Labour regards their welfare as a sacred trust.

So far as Britain's contribution is concerned, this war will have been won by its people, not by any one man or set of men, though strong and greatly valued leadership has been given to the high resolve of the people in the present struggle. And in this leadership the Labour ministers have taken their full share of burdens and responsibilities. The record of the Labour ministers has been one of hard tasks well done since that fateful day in May 1940, when the initiative of Labour in Parliament brought about the fall of the Chamberlain Government and the formation of the new War Government which has led the country to victory.

The people made tremendous efforts to win the last war also. But when they had won it they lacked a lively interest in the social and economic problems of peace, and accepted the election promises of the leaders of the anti-Labour parties at their face value. So the 'hard-faced men who had done well out of the war' were able to get the kind of peace that suited themselves. The people lost that peace. And when we say 'peace' we mean not only the treaty, but the social and economic policy which followed the fighting.

In the years that followed, the 'hard-faced men' and their political friends kept control of the government. They controlled the banks, the mines, the big industries, largely the press and the cinema. They controlled the means by which the people got their living. They controlled the ways by which most of the people learned about the world outside. This happened in all the industrialized countries.

Great economic blizzards swept the world in those years. The great inter-war slumps were not acts of God or of blind forces. They were the sure and certain result of the concentration of too much economic power in the hands of too few men. These men had only learned how to act in the interest of their own bureaucratically run private monopolies which may be likened to totalitarian oligarchies within our democratic state. They had and they felt no responsibility to the nation.

Similar forces are at work today. The interests have not been able to make the same profits out of this war as they did out of the last. The determined propaganda of the Labour Party, helped by other progressive forces, had its effect in 'taking the profit out of war'. The 100 per cent Excess Profits Tax, the controls over industry and transport, the fair rationing of food and control of prices – without which the Labour Party would not have remained in the government – these all helped to win the war. With these measures the country has come nearer than ever before in its history to making 'fair shares' the national rule.

But the war in the East is not yet over. There are grand pickings still to be had. A short boom period after the war, when savings, gratuities and postwar credits are there to be spent, can make a profiteer's paradise. But Big Business knows that this will happen only if the people vote into power the party which promises to get rid of the controls and so let the profiteers and racketeers have that freedom for which they are pleading eloquently on every Tory platform and in every Tory newspaper.

They accuse the Labour Party of wishing to impose controls for the sake of control. That is not true, and they know it. What is true is that the anti-controllers and anti-planners desire to sweep away public controls, simply in order to give the profiteering interests and the privileged rich an entirely free hand to plunder the rest of the nation as shamelessly as they did in the nineteen-twenties.

Does freedom for the profiteer mean freedom for the ordinary man and woman, whether they be wage-earners or small business or professional men or housewives? Just think back over the depressions of the twenty years between the wars, when there were precious few public controls of any kind and the Big Interests had things all their own way. Never was so much injury done to so many by so few. Freedom is not an abstract thing. To be real it must be won, it must be worked for.

The Labour Party stands for order as against the chaos which would follow the end of all public control. We stand for order, for positive constructive progress as against the chaos of economic do-as-they-please anarchy.

The Labour Party makes no baseless promises. The future will not be easy. But this time the peace must be won. The Labour Party offers the nation a plan which will win the peace for the people.

Britain's coming election will be the greatest test in our history of the judgement and common sense of our people.

The nation wants food, work and homes. It wants more than that – it wants good food in plenty, useful work for all, and comfortable, labour-saving homes that take full advantage of the resources of modern science and productive industry. It wants a high and rising standard of living, security for all against a rainy day, an educational system that will give every boy and girl a chance to develop the best that is in them.

These are the aims. In themselves they are no more than words. All parties may declare that in principle they agree with them. But the test of a political programme is whether it is sufficiently in earnest about the objectives to adopt the means needed to realize them. It is very easy to set out a list of aims. What matters is whether it is backed up by a genuine workmanlike plan conceived without regard to sectional vested interests and carried through in a spirit of resolute concentration.

Point by point these national aims need analysis. Point by point it will be found that if they are to be turned into realities the nation and its postwar governments will be called upon to put the nation above any sectional interest, above any cheap slogan about so-called free enterprise. The problems and pressures of the postwar world threaten our security and progress as surely as – though less dramatically than – the Germans threatened them in 1940. We need the spirit of Dunkirk and of the Blitz sustained over a period of years.

•

DAILY MIRROR
1945

'Vote for Him'

The Nuffield College study of newspaper influence in the 1945 election said that the 'Vote for Him' campaign in the Daily Mirror _might well have won more votes for the Labour Party than any other journalistic enterprise. It gave political expression to the discontent of serving soldiers and political ambition to many women who had never before voted._

The keynote of the Mirror _was set by a war correspondent in Germany who reported that soldiers had decided to write home to their wives and mothers to tell them to 'vote the soldiers' way'. The slogan 'I'll Vote for Him!' appeared on the front page accompanied by this letter._

Mrs Gardiner's letter, described by one clergyman as 'The Cry of Mother England', expressed something more than the intention of one woman, the Mirror _stated. It offered advice to all women._

My husband won't be home to vote. He is in the CMF. He has fought against the Fascist enemy in Italy and North Africa for a better Britain – now he is denied the chance of hearing candidates give their views for a better Britain.

I shall vote for him. I know what he wants.

He wants a good house with a bit of garden. He wants a job at a fair wage, however hard the work may be. He wants a good education for the children. He wants to feel they won't have to go through what he has gone through in this war. So he wants a Parliament that will be faithful to our alliance with Russia and America.

How my husband would despise these politicians who are trying to scare us and stir up our fears. I can hear him laughing at those who think the world holds no promise for Great Britain unless we return to the bad old pre-war days.

If he and all his pals had not had the courage to laugh and have faith in each other after Dunkirk where would we be now?

My husband would say, 'Vote for Courage'. I shall. I shall vote for him.

(Mrs) C. Gardiner, Ilford, Essex

•

PAN-AFRICAN CONGRESS
1945

'Imperialist control'

The 200 delegates to the fifth Pan-African Congress in Manchester in 1945 included Kwame Nkrumah, who became the first president of Ghana, and Jomo Kenyatta, the first president of Kenya. The chairman was W. E. Du Bois. Their meeting was hardly noticed (although it was covered by Picture Post*) but it was a historic landmark in the story of African liberation.*

Among the resolutions passed were two declarations – to the colonial powers and to the colonial peoples – which some of the founders of modern Africa assembled in Manchester returned to implement in their own countries over the next two decades.

The delegates believe in peace. How could it be otherwise, when for centuries the African peoples have been the victims of violence and slavery? Yet if the Western world is still determined to rule mankind by force, then Africans, as a last resort, may have to appeal to force in the effort to achieve freedom, even if force destroys them and the world.

We are determined to be free. We want education. We want the right to earn a decent living; the right to express our thoughts and emotions, to adopt and create forms of beauty. We demand for Black Africa autonomy and independence, so far and no further than it is possible in this one world for groups and peoples to rule themselves subject to inevitable world unity and federation.

We are not ashamed to have been an age-long patient people. We continue willingly to sacrifice and strive. But we are unwilling to starve any longer while doing the world's drudgery, in order to support by our poverty and ignorance a false aristocracy and a discarded imperialism.

We condemn the monopoly of capital and the rule of private wealth and industry for private profit alone. We welcome economic democracy as the only real democracy.

Therefore, we shall complain, appeal and arraign. We will make the world listen to the facts of our condition. We will fight in every way we can for freedom, democracy and social betterment.

We affirm the right of all colonial peoples to control their own destiny. All colonies must be free from foreign imperialist control, whether political or economic.

The peoples of the colonies must have the right to elect their own governments, without restrictions from foreign Powers. We say to the peoples of the colonies that they must fight for these ends by all means at their disposal.

The object of imperialist Powers is to exploit. By granting the right to colonial peoples to govern themselves that object is defeated. Therefore, the struggle for political power by colonial and subject peoples is the first step towards, and the necessary prerequisite to, complete social, economic and political emancipation. The Fifth Pan-African Congress therefore calls on the workers and farmers of the colonies to organize effectively. Colonial workers must be in the front of the battle against imperialism. Your weapons – the strike and the boycott – are invincible.

We also call upon the intellectuals and professional classes of the colonies to awaken to their responsibilities. By fighting for trade union rights, the right to form co-operatives, freedom of the press, assembly, demonstration and strike, freedom to print and read the literature which is necessary for the education of the masses, you will be using the only means by which your liberties will be won and maintained. Today there is only one road to effective action – the organization of the masses. And in that organization the educated colonials must join. Colonial and subject peoples of the world, unite!

•

ROBERT H. JACKSON
1945

'War crimes'

The International Military Tribunal established by Britain, France, the Soviet Union and the United States to judge the war crimes of the Nazis met at the Palace of Justice in Nuremberg. The Nuremberg trial was the first trial in history in which the accused were charged with crimes against humanity. There were eight judges and twenty-one defendants, including Hermann Goering and Rudolf Hess, both of whom had been Hitler's deputy, as well as Karl Donitz, Hitler's designated successor, von Ribbentrop, Julius Streicher and Martin Bormann. The case against the Nazis was opened by Robert Jackson (1892–1954), the chief American prosecutor.

The privilege of opening the first trial in history for crimes against the peace of the world imposes a grave responsibility. The wrongs which we seek to condemn and punish have been so calculated, so malignant, and so devastating, that civilization cannot tolerate their being ignored, because it cannot survive their being repeated. That four great nations, flushed with victory and stung with injury, stay the hand of vengeance and voluntarily submit their captive enemies to the judgment of the law is one of the most significant tributes that power has ever paid to reason.

This inquest represents the practical effort of four of the most mighty of nations, with the support of seventeen more, to utilize international law to meet the greatest menace of our times – aggressive war. The common sense of mankind demands that law shall not stop with the punishment of petty crimes by little people. It must also reach men who possess themselves of great power and make deliberate and concerted use of it to set in motion evils which leave no home in the world untouched. It is a cause of that magnitude that the United Nations will lay before Your Honors.

In the prisoners' dock sit twenty-odd broken men . . .

What makes this inquest significant is that these prisoners represent sinister influences that will lurk in the world long after their bodies have returned to dust. We will show them to be living symbols of racial hatreds, of terrorism and violence, and of the arrogance and cruelty of power. They are symbols of fierce nationalisms and of militarism, of intrigue and war-making which have embroiled Europe generation after generation, crushing its manhood, destroying its homes, and impoverishing its life. They have so identified themselves with the philosophies they conceived and with the forces they directed that any tenderness to them is a victory and an encouragement to all the evils which are attached to their names. Civilization can afford no compromise with the social forces which would gain renewed strength if we deal ambiguously or indecisively with the men in whom those forces now precariously survive.

Some general considerations which may affect the credit of this trial in the eyes of the world should be candidly faced. There is a dramatic disparity between the circumstances of the accusers and of the accused that might discredit our work if we should falter, in even minor matters, in being fair and temperate.

Unfortunately, the nature of these crimes is such that both prosecution and judgment must be by victor nations over vanquished foes. The world-wide scope of the aggressions carried out by these men has left but few real neutrals. Either the victors must judge the vanquished or we must leave the defeated to judge themselves. After the First World War, we learned the futility of the latter course. The former high station of these defendants, the notoriety of their acts, and the adaptability of their conduct to provoke retaliation make it hard to distinguish between the demand for a just and measured retribution, and the unthinking cry for vengeance which arises from the anguish of war. It is our task, so far as humanly possible, to draw the line between the two. We must never forget that the record on which we judge these defendants today is the record on which history will judge us tomorrow. To pass these defendants a poisoned chalice is to put it to our own lips as well. We must summon such detachment and intellectual integrity to our task that this trial will commend itself to posterity as fulfilling humanity's aspirations to do justice.

If these men are the first war leaders of a defeated nation to be prosecuted in the name of the law, they are also the first to be given a chance to plead for their lives in the name of the law. Realistically, the charter of this tribunal, which gives them a hearing, is also the source of their only hope. It may be that these men of troubled conscience, whose only wish is that the world forget them, do not regard a trial as a favor. But they do have a fair opportunity to defend themselves – a favor which these men, when in power, rarely extended to their fellow countrymen. Despite the fact that public opinion already condemns their acts, we agree that here they must be given a presumption of innocence, and we accept the burden of proving criminal acts and the responsibility of these defendants for their commission.

Our case will disclose these defendants all uniting at some time with the Nazi Party in a plan which they well knew could be accomplished only by an outbreak of war in Europe. Their seizure of the German state, their subjugation of the German people, their terrorism and extermination of dissident elements, their planning and waging of war, their calculated and planned ruthlessness in the conduct of warfare, their deliberate and planned criminality toward conquered peoples – all these are ends for which they acted in concert; and all these are phases of the conspiracy, a conspiracy which reached one goal only to set out for another and more ambitious one. We shall also trace for you the intricate web of organizations which these men formed and utilized to accomplish these ends. We will show how the entire structure of offices and officials was dedicated to the criminal purposes and committed to the use of the criminal methods planned by these defendants and their co-conspirators, many of whom war and suicide have put beyond reach.

The case as presented by the United States will be concerned with the brains and authority back of all the crimes. These defendants were men of a station and rank which does not soil its own hands with blood. They were men who knew how to use lesser folk as tools. We want to reach the planners and designers, the inciters and leaders without whose evil architecture the world would not have been for so long scourged with the violence and lawlessness, and wracked with the agonies and convulsions, of this terrible war . . .

•

THE FRANCK REPORT
1945

'A fateful decision'

When President Harry Truman succeeded Roosevelt, a committee of experts was convened to advise him on the employment of the bomb. It recommended that it should be used against Japan as soon as possible. As the news filtered through to scientists at Los Alamos and the University of Chicago, the university in turn set up a committee on the 'social and political consequences' of atomic energy under the chairmanship of 1925 Physics Nobel Prize-winner James Franck (1882–1964). Its members included Leo Szilard and biochemist Eugene Rabinowitch and their report was forwarded to the Secretary for War Henry Stimson in the form of a solemn petition on 11 June.

Rabinowitch recalled that he was overwhelmed by a vision of crashing skyscrapers under a flaming sky as he walked the streets of Chicago that summer: 'Something had to be done to warn humanity.'

Truman's scientific panel, meeting at Los Alamos five days later, decided to ignore the Franck Report. They argued that American lives would be saved. The postwar world would also be more stable if America had demonstrated its power.

The scientists on this Project do not presume to speak authoritatively on problems of national and international policy. However, we found ourselves, by the force of events, during the last five years, in the position of a small group of citizens cognizant of a grave danger for the safety of this country as well as for the future of all the other nations, of which the rest of mankind is unaware. We therefore feel it our duty to urge that the political problems arising from the mastering of nuclear power be recognized in all their gravity, and that appropriate steps be taken for their study and the preparation of necessary decisions. We hope that the creation of the Committee by the Secretary of War to deal with all aspects of nucleonics indicates that these implications have been recognized by the government. We believe that our acquaintance with the scientific elements of the situation and prolonged preoccupation with its world-wide political implications, imposes on us the obligation to offer to the Committee some suggestions as to the possible solution of these grave problems.

Scientists have often before been accused of providing new weapons for the mutual destruction of nations, instead of improving their well-being. It is undoubtedly true that the discovery of flying, for example, has so far brought much more misery than enjoyment and profit to humanity. However, in the past, scientists could disclaim direct responsibility for the use to which mankind had put their disinterested discoveries. We feel compelled to take a more active stand now because the success which we have achieved in the development of nuclear power is fraught with infinitely greater dangers than were all the inventions of the past. All of us, familiar with the present state of nucleonics, live with the vision before our eyes of sudden destruction visited on our own country, of a Pearl Harbor disaster repeated in thousand-fold magnification in every one of our major cities.

In the past, science has often been able to provide also new methods of protection against new weapons of aggression it made possible, but it cannot promise such efficient protection against the destructive use of nuclear power. This protection can come only from the political organization of the world. Among all the arguments calling for an efficient international organization for peace, the existence of nuclear weapons is the most compelling one. In the absence of an international authority which would make all resort to force in international conflicts impossible, nations could still be diverted from a path which must lead to total mutual destruction, by a specific international agreement barring a nuclear armaments race.

The development of nuclear power not only constitutes an important addition to the technological and military power of the United States, but also creates grave political and economic problems for the future of this country.

Nuclear bombs cannot possibly remain a 'secret weapon' at the exclusive disposal of this country for more than a few years. The scientific facts on which construction is based are well known to scientists of other countries. Unless an effective international control of nuclear explosives is instituted, a race for nuclear armaments is certain to ensue following the first revelation of our possession of nuclear weapons to the world. Within ten years other countries may have nuclear bombs, each of which, weighing less than a ton, could destroy an urban area of more than ten square miles. In the war to which such an armaments race is likely to lead, the United States, with its agglomeration of population and industry in comparatively few metropolitan districts, will be at a disadvantage compared to nations whose populations and industry are scattered over large areas.

We believe that these considerations make the use of nuclear bombs for an early unannounced attack against Japan inadvisable. If the United States were to be the first to release this new means of indiscriminate destruction upon mankind, she would sacrifice public support throughout the world, precipitate the race for armaments and prejudice the possibility of reaching an international agreement on the future control of such weapons.

Much more favorable conditions for the eventual achievement of such an agreement could be created if nuclear bombs were first revealed to the world by a demonstration in an appropriately selected uninhabited area.

In case chances for the establishment of an effective international control of nuclear weapons should have to be considered slight at the present time, then not only the use of these weapons against Japan, but even their early demonstration, may be contrary to the interests of this country. A postponement of such a demonstration will have in this case the advantage of delaying the beginning of the nuclear armaments race as long as possible.

If the government should decide in favor of an early demonstration of nuclear weapons, it will then have the possibility of taking into account the public opinion of this country and of the other nations before deciding whether these weapons should be used against Japan. In this way, other nations may assume a share of responsibility for such a fateful decision.

•

ALBERT EINSTEIN
1945

'A menace'

It was Albert Einstein (1879–1955), perhaps the greatest scientist of the century, who warned President Roosevelt in 1940 that Germany might try to make an atom bomb – a warning which helped bring about the Manhattan Project. In an interview in Atlantic Monthly *soon after the bomb was dropped on Hiroshima, Einstein advocated the creation of a world government responsible for atomic control in order to prevent war.*

The release of atomic energy has not created a new problem. It has merely made more urgent the necessity of solving an existing one. One could say that it has affected us quantitatively, not qualitatively. As long as there are sovereign nations possessing great power war is inevitable. That statement is not an attempt to say when war will come, but only that it is sure to come. That fact was true before the atomic bomb was made. What has been changed is the destructiveness of war.

I do not believe that the secret of the bomb should be given to the United Nations Organization. I do not believe that it should be given to the Soviet Union. Either course would be like the action of a man with capital who, wishing another man to work with him on some enterprise, should start out by simply giving his prospective partner half of his money. The second man might choose to start a rival enterprise, when what was wanted was his cooperation.

The secret of the bomb should be committed to a World Government, and the United States should immediately announce its readiness to give it to a World Government. This government should be founded by the United States, the Soviet Union and Great Britain – the only three powers with great military strength. The fact that there are only three nations with great military power should make it easier rather than harder to establish such a government.

Since the United States and Great Britain have the secret of the atomic bomb and the Soviet Union does not, they should invite the Soviet Union to prepare and present the first draft of a constitution for the proposed World Government.

That action should help to dispel the distrust which the Russians already feel because the bomb is being kept a secret, chiefly to prevent their having it. Obviously the first draft would not be the final one, but the Russians should be made to feel that the World Government would assure them their security.

After the three great powers have drafted a constitution and adopted it, the smaller nations should be invited to join the World Government. They should be free to stay out; and though they would be perfectly secure in staying out, I am sure they would wish to join. Naturally they should be entitled to propose changes in the constitution as drafted by the Big Three. But the Big Three should go ahead and organize the World Government whether the smaller nations join or not.

The World Government would have power over all military matters and need have only one further power: the power to intervene in countries where a minority is oppressing a majority and creating the kind of instability that leads to war. Conditions such as exist in Argentina and Spain should be dealt with. There must be an end to the concept of non-intervention, for to end it is part of keeping the peace.

The establishment of the World Government must not have to wait until the same conditions of freedom are to be found in all three of the great powers. While it is true that in the Soviet Union the minority rules, I do not consider that internal conditions there are of themselves a threat to world peace.

One must bear in mind that the people in Russia did not have a long political education . . . and changes to improve Russian conditions had to be carried through by a minority for the reason that there was no majority capable of doing it. If I had been born a Russian, I believe I could have adjusted myself to this condition.

It is not necessary, in establishing a world organization with a monopoly of military authority, to change the structure of the three great powers. It would be for the three individuals who draft the constitution to devise ways for the different structures to be fitted together for collaboration.

Do I fear the tyranny of a World Government? Of course I do. But I fear still more the coming of another war or wars. Any government is certain to be evil to some extent. But a World Government is preferable to the far greater evil of wars, particularly with their intensified destructiveness. If a World Government is not established by agreement, I believe it will come in another way and in a much more dangerous form. For war or wars will end in one power being supreme and dominating the rest of the world by its overwhelming military strength.

Now that we have the atomic secret, we must not lose it, and that is what we should risk doing if we should give it to the United Nations Organization or to the Soviet Union. But we must make it clear, as quickly as possible, that we are not keeping the bomb a secret for the sake of our power, but in the hope of establishing peace in a World Government, and that we will do our utmost to bring this World Government into being.

Since I do not foresee that atomic energy is to be a great boon for a long time, I have to say that for the present it is a menace. Perhaps it is well that it should be. It may intimidate the human race into bringing order into its international affairs, which, without the pressure of fear, it would not do.

•

NIELS BOHR
1945

'The crisis of humanity'

The Danish physicist Niels Bohr (1885–1962), who had won the Nobel Prize for Physics in 1922, escaped through Sweden to England in 1943 before moving on to America. Leo Szilard, Niels Bohr and Albert Einstein separately lobbied President Roosevelt, urging that the bomb should not be used as a military weapon – or that Japan should be warned before it was used. After the Second World War was over, Leo Szilard recalled that the greatest worry of the scientists working at Los Alamos on the Manhattan Project, the making of the atom bomb, had been that Germany would perfect the bomb before the Allies invaded Europe. 'In 1945, when we ceased worrying about what the Germans might do to us, we began to worry about what the government of the United States might do to other countries.'

Their protests were ignored and the citizens of Hiroshima and Nagasaki soon discovered the deadly new power that had been unleashed upon the world and which dominated the international political agenda for the next forty years.

This article appeared in The Times *after the bomb had been used on Japan.*

The possibility of releasing vast amounts of energy through atomic disintegration, which means a veritable revolution of human resources, cannot but raise in the mind of everyone the question whither the advance of physical science is leading civilization. While the increasing mastery of the forces of nature has contributed so prolifically to human welfare, and holds out even greater promises, it is evident that the formidable power of destruction which has come within reach of man may become a mortal menace unless human society can adjust itself to the exigencies of the situation. Civilization is presented with a challenge more serious, perhaps, than ever before, and the fate of humanity will depend on its ability to unite in averting common dangers and jointly to reap the benefit from the immense opportunities which the progress of science offers.

Indeed, not only have we left the time far behind when each man, for self-protection, could pick up the nearest stone, but we have even reached the stage when the degree of security offered to the citizens of a nation by collective defence measures is entirely insufficient. Against the new destructive powers no defence may be possible, and the issue centres on world-wide cooperation to prevent any use of the new sources of energy which does not serve mankind as a whole. The possibility of international regulation for this purpose should be ensured by the very magnitude and the peculiar character of the efforts which will be indispensable for the production of the new formidable weapon. It is obvious, however, that no control can be effective without free access to full scientific information and the granting of the opportunity of international supervision of all undertakings which, unless regulated, might become a source of disaster.

Such measures will, of course, demand the abolition of barriers hitherto considered necessary to safeguard national interests but now standing in the way of common security against unprecedented dangers. Certainly the handling of the precarious situation will demand the good will of all nations, but it must be recognized that we are dealing with what is potentially a deadly challenge to civilization itself. A better background for meeting such a situation could hardly be imagined than the earnest desire to seek a firm foundation for world security, so unanimously expressed from the side of all those nations which only through united efforts have been able to defend elementary human rights. The extent of the contribution which an agreement about this vital matter would make to the removal of obstacles to mutual confidence and to the promotion of a harmonious relationship between nations can hardly be exaggerated.

In the great task lying ahead, which places upon our generation the gravest responsibility towards posterity, scientists all over the world may offer most valuable services. Not only do the bonds created through scientific intercourse form some of the firmest ties between individuals from different nations, but the whole scientific community will surely join in a vigorous effort to induce in wider circles an adequate appreciation of what is at stake and to appeal to humanity at large to heed the warning which has been sounded. It need not be added that every scientist who has taken part in laying the foundation for the new development, or has been called upon to participate in work which might have proved decisive in the struggle to preserve a state of civilization where human culture can freely develop, is prepared to assist in any way

open to him in bringing about an outcome of the present crisis of humanity
worthy of the ideals for which science through the ages has stood.

●

VICTOR GOLLANCZ
1946

'Our Threatened Values'

*As soon as the war ended, leaving Germany devastated, the publisher Victor Gollancz
(1893–1967), founder of the Left Book Club, worked to relieve starvation in Germany.
He opposed the view that all Germans should share in collective guilt for the crimes
committed by the Nazis.*

In his book Our Threatened Values, *he protested at the manner in which Germans
were being treated in the British Zone.*

We non-fraternized with the Germans in the summer of 1945: we are starving
them in the spring of 1946. And we are starving them, not deliberately in the
sense that we definitely want them to die, but wilfully in the sense that we
prefer their death to our own inconvenience: by which I mean that we prefer
utter misery for them, with death as an often inevitable consequence, to any
serious reduction in our own relatively very high standard of living, or even
to the possibility that at some future date such a reduction might have to be
effected. The only qualification we admit is that their misery must stop short
at the point below which any semblance of orderly administration would
become impossible.

This is our real policy; but its true nature is largely concealed by the three
propositions with which the government defends its world food policy as a
whole. They are as follows: (1) We have all along been making every possible
sacrifice for the relief of distress wherever it may occur. (2) In the general
share-out our first duty is to fight for the interests of our Empire (which means
chiefly India) and our Allies, towards whom we have a special responsibility. (3)
The Germans properly come at the end of the queue.

What have we done – we, with our Potsdam Conference, for which we
cannot evade our due share of responsibility?

First, we have lopped off from Germany, and handed over to Poland,
some of the richest of her food-producing territories; secondly, we have
divided her into four more or less watertight zones; and thirdly, by the policy
of mass expulsions we have so increased the population in the British Zone

that today there are at least 2,000,000 more mouths to feed than there were in 1939. After producing famine by our own acts, just or unjust – and for my part I think them abominably unjust – and a famine over and above what would in any case have resulted from war or acts of God, can we decently refuse to alleviate it?

Other suffering countries have independent governments which can bargain to some degree at least in the world markets, and some can also draw assistance from Unrra, far too meagre though it is. Germany has no government, and Unrra is strictly forbidden to operate there, except for displaced persons.

A special obligation is involved in the relation as such of a liberal or Christian conqueror to his enemy. It is a matter of spiritual *noblesse oblige*. But I will not labour the point, for people who do not understand why St Paul said, 'If thine enemy hunger, feed him' will certainly not listen to a feeble re-echo from me. The degree of need, I repeat, is the final criterion: to prefer a suffering enemy to an equally suffering friend would be wickedness: but, with that proviso, an enemy's enmity is something additionally compulsive, or would be if his hunger were not already compulsive absolutely.

The position in Germany remains unchanged. Normal consumers in our zone still officially get only 1,000 calories; and though some may be able to supplement this ration by a few extra calories, millions have to live or die on it, and many of these millions get in practice even a hundred or two hundred calories less – in other words, the Belsen ration of eight or nine hundred calories. A high official of military government, on leave in this country, has just told me that the girls in his office are daily fainting at their desks. The ration will, I believe, be maintained; indeed the government is probably now fighting to maintain it, not from humanitarian motives – does Mr Attlee realize, I wonder, what it means for a socialist to have to write like this? – but because otherwise our administrative task would become totally impossible. There is so far, however, no sign of any intention to increase the ration. Now there are around 45 million civilians in this country, and there are 10 million 'normal consumers' in the British Zone.

It therefore follows that a reduction of our 2,850 calories – or 2,750 or whatever it may be – by an average of no more than 100 a day would lift these Germans from starvation to the level of about 1,500 calories, which is still far below the essential minimum as generally recognized. Unless by this cut in our consumption, by release of stocks (not necessarily of wheat) or by any other method you may prefer we raise them to that still wretched level, then we lose for western civilization even such parts of Germany as can still be saved: and, what is more, there will be something in our own lives from which we can never escape, and it will not be a blessing.

If we treat these Germans kindly, kindness will stir in them. If we show them mercy, they will know, by the immediacy of contact, how 'delightful' mercy is. If we, the enemy, act justly to them when we could have acted unjustly – if we give them the rights that we might so easily have withheld – then they will understand what rights mean, just because we had the power to withhold them. And if we respect them – all of them, whatever some may be or may have done, for such considerations cannot modify respect in the sense I am insisting on – respect, by some process of mutuality, will be born in them, not only for us but for themselves and others. Martin Büber tells somewhere how, as he was looking into his dog's eyes, there was suddenly, for the fraction of a second, complete and immediate – unmediated – recognition, not the one of the other, but between them. That is how these things work. I do not mean, of course, that a change in the temper of the German people can be a matter of days or weeks: a boy who has been indoctrinated for twelve years with Nazism does not become a liberal or a Christian overnight. Nor can it be accomplished easily or by the way. The very depth of the moral wound requires a corresponding intensity in the effort to reach and cure it. Only if we feel the same passionate devotion to our ethic as Hitler felt for his and the communists feel for theirs, and only if we apply it with complete integrity and sustained consistency where in human weakness we might fail to apply it but where by the same token its application is the criterion of our sincerity – only so can we win the heart of Germany and ultimately, perhaps, of the whole world. And why should we lack passion? Isn't it as good, this way of life that has produced so much gentleness and so many freedoms, as the barbarism of Hitler and the ruthless expediency of what is now called communism?

•

FERENC NAGY
1948

'The new tyranny'

The prime minister of Hungary, Ferenc Nagy, was forced to resign in 1947 while on holiday in Switzerland after being charged with complicity in a plot to overthrow Stalin's Hungarian regime. He was given asylum in the United States. A year later he published his account of the terror behind the Iron Curtain, particularly in his native land, as the Soviet steamroller crushed all opposition.

The struggle behind the Iron Curtain has come to an end. The patriots who had struggled have died or ended in prison.

The first to flee Hungary was Béla Varga, the President of the Parliament and much beloved Catholic prelate. He was to have been arrested or carried off by the Russians.

Members of Parliament who dared to give the faintest voice to the desires of their constituents have either fled or been imprisoned.

Countless are the thousands of the poor and wealthy, the prominent and nameless, who, leaving behind their homes, their land, their social roots, took the hard trek to the safety of the West, to lands where freedom is realized, to await – sometimes in dire privation – the coming of a brighter dawn and the liberation of the Hungarian people from Soviet dictatorship.

Hungary is engulfed in the silence of death. Only the caw of the raven, the Communist political police, can be heard as it strikes another victim.

My country, sinking into the mire of destruction and decline, is not alone: all the long-suffering peoples of Eastern Europe cry for peace, quiet and the chance to live their lives undisturbed.

The struggle has come to an end in Poland, too. The leader of the peasants, the voice of the God-fearing and patriotic Polish people, former Prime Minister Stanislav Mikolajczyk, is in exile, and there is no other Polish statesman to take up the banner. Reymont's peasants are deep in the apathy of hopelessness and political impotence. Is it for this that the freedom-loving Poles bled and suffered? . . .

The blood of the silent Serbs and Croats waters the grave of their dead liberty. Yugoslav Communism is more dreaded than Russian. Tito won from the Kremlin the honor of directing the suppressed countries of southeastern Europe as a reward for introducing the most efficient, inconceivable terror in his own land.

Czechoslovakian democracy has been dealt its death blow; President Beneš and more particularly the Czech people are paying for the secret treaty they signed with the Soviets while still enjoying the fruits of American and British support. Jan Masaryk, bearer of one of the greatest names in the history of liberty, took his own life; Eduard Beneš is a living wraith . . .

In Hungary, the Soviet Union was forced to sound every note in the discordant symphony composed by the Comintern. With the removal of the stalwart guards of Hungarian self-determination, the last stage of penetration has now been reached; it is enlightening to observe the methods Moscow employs.

The government *coup d'état* in Hungary created the possibility of completely liquidating the democratic political institutions . . .

Soviet generals ordered the first so-called Parliament convened according to their own design, and all but appointed the first Cabinet. Their troops gorged themselves at the expense of a starving people. The Soviet Union turned the Allied Control Commission into its own agency, denying a voice to the two great Western powers sharing control.

It swallowed blameless leaders, statesmen and officers in dead of night, never to be heard from again. Its trained agents barnacled the nation as leaders of the Communist Party. It interfered constantly with the creation of national defense and forced the army to become a Communist unit. It forged the Potsdam agreement into chains for our economic slavery; and forced Hungary, by this stranglehold, into unequal economic collaboration. It coerced the democratic parties, through these economic claims, to yield to the Communists. It tried to force a common ticket on the chosen political parties, to still the voice of democracy. It ordered the all-powerful portfolio of the Minister of the Interior granted to the Communists. It interfered with tranquil government within the Cabinet by giving secret support to the Communist ministers. It decided who could be appointed in the Cabinet and who must be dismissed. Its armed terror dictated the direction and pace of agrarian reform. It ordered hundreds of thousands of citizens uprooted and expelled because of their ancestry. It barred us from establishing desirable diplomatic relations. It prevented Hungary from giving insight into its economic affairs to the great Western powers which were desirous of helping. Its insistence resulted in the dissolution of the religious organizations. It always forced through the desires of the Communist Party during political crises. It prevented humane laws from going into effect. Its direct inspiration and support prevented the so-called conspiracy from having a fair day in court. It abducted the revered Béla Kovács. It at last perpetrated the putsch which eliminated me from the premiership of my country and forced me into exile.

Thus events themselves indict the Union of Soviet Socialist Republics; the world must pass judgment. Penetration completed, today there is no breath, no motion, no life in Hungary without Soviet direction or approval.

These appearances have been duplicated in all of Eastern Europe, a part of the world has become dark, impenetrable; where, behind the outward quiescence, a bitter ideological struggle rages against the new tyranny.

Were this the end of the black story, there would be no need to spotlight it. But Communist imperialism is an advancing process of penetration, not content with constricting the countries nearest its borders; shrouded in a pseudo ideology, the red snake inches from its pit in the East in a deadly attempt to poison the emotions of the civilized world.

By its very nature, it cannot stop. It has been said that a dictator is like a bicyclist: he may only move forward, if he stops, he falls. The course of dictatorship is irreversible – it must continue on the road of conquest paved by its agents in every country.

Only those who have fled before lava, prairie fire and flood can convey their terror. I too have had to seek shelter from a dynamic force which threatens the concord of humanity and its highly developed form of life; threatens that political structure which, through the struggles and vicissitudes of thousands of years of human society, has developed into the highest form of social expression – democracy.

I stand on free soil. But unless I voice the warning that weighs on the hearts of people everywhere I shall not regard my obligation to those less fortunate than I, as discharged.

By the grace of destiny, democracy shall yet embrace the world.

•

HUBERT H. HUMPHREY
1948

'Civil rights'

As the 1948 election approached, Harry Truman's Democrats had already lost their left wing when Harry Wallace formed the Progressive Party. Meanwhile, at the Convention, Strom Thurmond from the right threatened to take the old South out of the party if civil rights were included in the Democratic manifesto.

Undaunted, Hubert Humphrey (1911–78), mayor of Minneapolis and a senatorial candidate, called for confrontation – not compromise – on the civil rights issue in a speech that was the defining moment of his career (he was later vice-president to Lyndon Johnson). The Democrats were not rushing the issue of civil rights, he declared: 'I say we are 172 years late.' Truman went on to victory.

We are here as Democrats. But more important, as Americans – and I firmly believe that as men concerned with our country's future, we must specify in our platform the guarantees which I have mentioned.

Yes, this is far more than a party matter. Every citizen has a stake in the emergence of the United States as the leader of the free world. That world is being challenged by the world of slavery. For us to play our part effectively, we must be in a morally sound position.

We cannot use a double standard for measuring our own and other people's policies. Our demands for democratic practices in other lands will be no more effective than the guarantees of those practiced in our own country.

We are God-fearing men and women. We place our faith in the brotherhood of man under the fatherhood of God.

I do not believe that there can be any compromise of the guarantees of civil rights which I have mentioned.

In spite of my desire for unanimous agreement on the platform, there are some matters which I think must be stated without qualification. There can be no hedging – no watering down.

There are those who say to you we are rushing this issue of civil rights. I say we are 172 years late.

There are those who say this issue of civil rights is an infringement on states' rights. The time has arrived for the Democratic Party to get out of the shadow of states' rights and walk forthrightly into the bright sunshine of human rights.

People – human beings – this is the issue of the twentieth century. People – all kinds and all sorts of people – look to America for leadership, for help, for guidance.

My friends, my fellow Democrats, I ask you for a calm consideration of our historic opportunity. Let us forget the evil passions, the blindness of the past. In these times of world economic, political and spiritual – above all, spiritual – crisis, we cannot, we must not, turn from the path so plainly before us.

That path has already led us through many valleys of the shadow of death. Now is the time to recall those who were left on that path of American freedom.

For all of us here, for the millions who have sent us, for the whole 2 billion members of the human family, our land is now, more than ever, the last best hope on earth. I know that we can – I know that we shall – begin here the fuller and richer realization of that hope, that promise of a land where all men are free and equal, and each man uses his freedom and equality wisely and well.

●

SIMONE DE BEAUVOIR
1949

'*The Second Sex*'

Simone de Beauvoir's The Second Sex, *published in France in 1949, has become a twentieth-century feminist classic, one of the most important books ever written about the oppression of women. De Beauvoir (1908–86) challenged the sexual conservatism of the late 1940s. 'One is not born, but rather becomes, a woman,' she wrote in a phrase which found resonance with a new generation. This extract is from the opening section, 'Re-awakening'.*

Women have no past, no history, no religion of their own; and they have no such solidarity of work and interest as that of the proletariat. They are not even promiscuously herded together in the way that creates community feeling among the American Negroes, the ghetto Jews, the workers of Saint-Denis or the factory hands of Renault. They live dispersed among the males, attached through residence, housework, economic condition, and social standing to certain men – fathers or husbands – more firmly than they are to other women. If they belong to the bourgeoisie, they feel solidarity with men of that class, not with proletarian women; if they are white, their allegiance is to white men, not to Negro women. The proletariat can propose to massacre the ruling class, and a sufficiently fanatical Jew or Negro might dream of getting sole possession of the atomic bomb and making humanity wholly Jewish or black; but woman cannot even dream of exterminating the males. The bond that unites her to her oppressors is not comparable to any other. The division of the sexes is a biological fact, not an event in human history. Male and female stand opposed within a primordial *Mitsein*, and woman has not broken it. The couple is a fundamental unity with its two halves riveted together, and the cleavage of society along the line of sex is impossible. Here is to be found the basic trait of woman: she is the Other in a totality of which the two components are necessary to one another ...

   Woman has always been man's dependent, if not his slave; the two sexes have never shared the world in equality. And even today woman is heavily handicapped, though her situation is beginning to change. Almost nowhere is her legal status the same as man's, and frequently it is much to her disadvantage. Even when her rights are legally recognized in the abstract, long-standing custom prevents their full expression in the mores. In the economic sphere men and women can almost be said to make up two castes; other things being equal, the former hold the better jobs, get higher wages, and have more opportunity for success than their new competitors. In industry and politics men have a great many more positions and they monopolize the most important posts. In addition to all this, they enjoy a traditional prestige that the education of children tends in every way to support, for the present enshrines the past – and in the past all history has been made by men. At the present time, when women are beginning to take part in the affairs of the world, it is still a world that belongs to men – they have no doubt of it at all and women have scarcely any. To decline to be the Other, to refuse to be a party to the deal – this would be for women to renounce all the advantages conferred upon them by their alliance with the superior caste. Man-the-sovereign will provide woman-the-liege with material protection and will undertake the moral justification of her existence; thus she can evade at once both economic risk and the metaphysical risk of a liberty in which ends and aims must be contrived without assistance. Indeed, along with the ethical urge of each individual to affirm his subjective existence, there is also the temptation to forgo liberty and become a thing. This is an inauspicious road, for he who takes it – passive, lost, ruined – becomes henceforth the creature of another's will, frustrated in his transcendence and deprived of every value . . .

Many men will affirm as if in good faith that women *are* the equals of man and that they have nothing to clamor for, while *at the same time* they will say that women can never be the equals of man and that their demands are in vain. It is, in point of fact, a difficult matter for man to realize the extreme importance of social discriminations which seem outwardly insignificant but which produce in woman moral and intellectual effects so profound that they appear to spring from her original nature. The most sympathetic of men never fully comprehend woman's concrete situation. And there is no reason to put much trust in the men when they rush to the defence of privileges whose full extent they can hardly measure. We shall not, then, permit ourselves to be intimidated by the number and violence of the attacks launched against women, nor to be entrapped by the self-seeking eulogies bestowed on the 'true woman', nor to profit by the enthusiasm for woman's destiny manifested by men who would not for the world have any part of it . . .

•

MARGARET CHASE SMITH
1950

'McCarthyism'

Republican Senator Joe McCarthy of Wisconsin (1909–57) launched a witch-hunt in February 1950 when he announced that he had in his possession a list of Communists known to the Secretary of State who were still working and making policy in the State Department. McCarthy's 'Red Scare' inflicted fear on America, particularly among actors, authors, scientists and scholars – and destroyed many careers.

Senator Margaret Chase Smith led seven Republican senators in a Declaration of Conscience dissociating them from McCarthy and attacking McCarthyism – but only four years later was McCarthy finally censured by the Senate that she had addressed in June 1950.

Mr President, I speak as a Republican. I speak as a woman. I speak as a United States senator. I speak as an American.

The United States Senate has long enjoyed worldwide respect as the greatest deliberative body in the world. But recently that deliberative character has too often been debased to the level of a forum of hate and character assassination sheltered by the shield of congressional immunity.

It is ironical that we senators can in debate in the Senate, directly or indirectly, by any form of words, impute to any American who is not a senator any conduct or motive unworthy or unbecoming an American – and without that nonsenator American having any legal redress against us – yet if we say the same thing in the Senate about our colleagues we can be stopped on the grounds of being out of order.

It is strange that we can verbally attack anyone else without restraint and with full protection, and yet we hold ourselves above the same type of criticism here on the Senate floor. Surely the United States Senate is big enough to take self-criticism and self-appraisal. Surely we should be able to take the same kind of character attacks that we 'dish out' to outsiders.

I think that it is high time for the United States Senate and its members to do some real soul-searching and to weigh our consciences as to the manner in which we are performing our duty to the people of America and the manner in which we are using or abusing our individual powers and privileges.

I think it is high time that we remembered that we have sworn to uphold and defend the Constitution. I think it is high time that we remembered that the Constitution, as amended, speaks not only of the freedom of speech but also of trial by jury instead of trial by accusation.

Whether it be a criminal prosecution in court or a character prosecution in the Senate, there is little practical distinction when the life of a person has been ruined.

Those of us who shout the loudest about Americanism in making character assassinations are all too frequently those who, by our own words and acts, ignore some of the basic principles of Americanism – the right to criticize; the right to hold unpopular beliefs; the right to protest; the right of independent thought.

The exercise of these rights should not cost one single American citizen his reputation or his right to a livelihood, nor should he be in danger of losing his reputation or livelihood merely because he happens to know someone who holds unpopular beliefs. Who of us does not? Otherwise none of us could call our souls our own. Otherwise thought control would have set in.

The American people are sick and tired of being afraid to speak their minds lest they be politically smeared as Communists or Fascists by their opponents. Freedom of speech is not what it used to be in America. It has been so abused by some that it is not exercised by others.

The American people are sick and tired of seeing innocent people smeared and guilty people whitewashed. But there have been enough proved cases to cause nationwide distrust and strong suspicion that there may be something to the unproved, sensational accusations.

As a Republican, I say to my colleagues on this side of the aisle that the Republican Party faces a challenge today that is not unlike the challenge which it faced back in Lincoln's day. The Republican Party so successfully met that challenge that it emerged from the Civil War as the champion of a united nation – in addition to being a party which unrelentingly fought loose spending and loose programs.

Today our country is being psychologically divided by the confusion and the suspicions that are bred in the United States Senate to spread like cancerous tentacles of 'know nothing, suspect everything' attitudes. Today we have a Democratic administration which has developed a mania for loose spending and loose programs. History is repeating itself – and the Republican Party again has the opportunity to emerge as the champion of unity and prudence . . .

As a United States senator, I am not proud of the way in which the Senate has been made a publicity platform for irresponsible sensationalism. I am not proud of the reckless abandon in which unproved charges have been hurled from this side of the aisle. I am not proud of the obviously staged, undignified countercharges which have been attempted in retaliation from the other side of the aisle.

I do not like the way the Senate has been made a rendezvous for vilification, for selfish political gain at the sacrifice of individual reputations and national unity. I am not proud of the way we smear outsiders from the floor of the Senate and hide behind the cloak of congressional immunity and still place ourselves beyond criticism on the floor of the Senate.

As an American, I am shocked at the way Republicans and Democrats alike are playing directly into the Communist design of 'confuse, divide, and conquer.' As an American, I do not want a Democratic administration whitewash or cover up any more than I want a Republican smear or witch-hunt.

As an American, I condemn a Republican Fascist just as much as I condemn a Democrat Communist. I condemn a Democrat Fascist just as much as I condemn a Republican Communist. They are equally dangerous to you and me and to our country. As an American, I want to see our nation recapture the strength and unity it once had when we fought the enemy instead of ourselves . . .

•

WHITTAKER CHAMBERS
1953

'Screams in the night'

Whittaker Chambers (1901–61) achieved notoriety when he denounced Alger Hiss as a Soviet agent. Chambers joined the Communist Party in 1925. He went underground in Washington in 1931, although he later claimed he spied for only a year and a half from 1936. He was Secretary General of the 1945 San Francisco Conference which set up the United Nations, and a senior editor at Time *magazine until 1948.*

Chambers broke from the Communist Party in the 1940s and confessed his activities to the government, although he was not investigated until 1945. He described his conversion from Communism to Christianity in his book Witness. *This extract is from 'A Letter to My Children'.*

There is one experience which most sincere ex-Communists share, whether or not they go only part way to the end of the question it poses. The daughter of a former German diplomat in Moscow was trying to explain to me why her father, who, as an enlightened modern man, had been extremely pro-Communist, had become an implacable anti-Communist. It was hard for her because, as an enlightened modern girl, she shared the Communist vision without being a Communist. But she loved her father and the irrationality of his defection embarrassed her. 'He was immensely pro-Soviet,' she said, 'and then – you will laugh at me, but you must not laugh at my father – and then, one night, in Moscow, he heard screams. That's all. Simply one night he heard screams.'

A child of Reason and the twentieth century, she knew that there is a logic of the mind. She did not know that the soul has a logic that may be more compelling than the mind's. She did not know at all that she had swept away the logic of the mind, the logic of history, the logic of politics, the myth of the twentieth century, with five annihilating words: one night he heard screams.

What Communist has not heard those screams? They come from husbands torn forever from their wives in midnight arrests. They come, muffled, from the execution cellars of the secret police, from the torture chambers of the Lubianka, from all the citadels of terror now stretching from Berlin to Canton. They come from those freight cars loaded with men, women and children, the enemies of the Communist state, locked in, packed in, left on remote sidings to freeze to death at night in the Russian winter. They come from minds driven mad by the horrors of mass starvation ordered and enforced as a policy of the Communist state. They come from the starved skeletons, worked to death, or flogged to death (as an example to others) in the freezing filth of sub-arctic labor camps. They come from children whose parents are suddenly, inexplicably, taken away from them – parents they will never see again.

What Communist has not heard those screams? Execution, says the Communist code, is the highest measure of social protection. What man can call himself a Communist who has not accepted the fact that terror is an instrument of policy, right if the vision is right, justified by history, enjoined by the balance of forces in the social wars of this century? Those screams have reached every Communist's mind. Usually they stop there. What judge willingly dwells upon the man the laws compel him to condemn to death – the laws of nations or the laws of history?

But one day the Communist really hears those screams. He is going about his routine Party tasks. He is lifting a dripping reel of microfilm from a developing tank. He is justifying to a Communist fraction in a trade union an extremely unwelcome directive of the Central Committee. He is receiving from a trusted superior an order to go to another country and, in a designated hotel, at a designated hour, meet a man whose name he will never know, but who will give him a package whose contents he will never learn. Suddenly, there closes around that Communist a separating silence, and in that silence he hears screams. He hears them for the first time. For they do not merely reach his mind. They pierce beyond. They pierce to his soul. He says to himself: 'Those are not the screams of man in agony. Those are the screams of a soul in agony.' He hears them for the first time because a soul in extremity has communicated with that which alone can hear it – another human soul.

Why does the Communist ever hear them? Because in the end there persists in every man, however he may deny it, a scrap of soul. The Communist who suffers this singular experience then says to himself: 'What is happening to me? I must be sick.' If he does not instantly stifle that scrap of soul, he is lost. If he admits it for a moment, he has admitted that there is something greater than Reason, greater than the logic of mind, of politics, of history, of economics, which alone justifies the vision. If the Party senses his weakness, and the Party is peculiarly cunning at sensing such weakness, it will humiliate him, degrade him, condemn him, expel him. If it can, it will destroy him. And the Party will be right. For he has betrayed that which alone justifies its faith – the vision of Almighty Man. He has brushed the only vision that has force against the vision of Almighty Mind. He stands before the fact of God.

•

KENNETH TYNAN
1954

'Loamshire'

As theatre critic of the Observer *from 1954 to 1963, Kenneth Tynan (1929–80) was the most influential cultural commentator of his era. He shocked, provoked and dazzled in equal measure, according to the age of his readers, and championed new and original dramatists.*

In this early review, he contrasted the excitement of the cinema with the apathy he deplored in the theatre.

'And how,' ask my friends, having debated the opera, the ballet, politics and the Italian cinema, 'how is the theatre getting along?' The very set of their features, so patiently quizzical, tells me I am being indulged; after the serious business of conversation, they are permitting themselves a lapse into idleness. I shrug cheerily, like a martyr to rheumatism. A wan, tingling silence ensues. Then: 'De Sica's new film is superb,' says somebody, and talk begins again, happy and devout. I stew, meanwhile, in what Zelda Fitzgerald once called 'the boiling oil of sour grapes'.

The bare fact is that, apart from revivals and imports, there is nothing in the London theatre that one dares discuss with an intelligent man for more than five minutes. Since the great Ibsen challenge of the nineties, the English intellectuals have been drifting away from drama. Synge, Pirandello and O'Casey briefly recaptured them, and they will still perk up at the mention of Giraudoux. But – cowards – they know Eliot and Fry only in the study; and of a native prose playwright who might set the boards smouldering they see no sign at all. Last week I welcomed a young Frenchwoman engaged in writing a thesis on contemporary English drama. We talked hopefully of Mr John Whiting; but before long embarrassment moved me to ask why she had not chosen her own theatre as a subject for study. She smiled wryly. 'Paris is in decline,' she said, 'apart from Sartre, Anouilh, Camus, Cocteau, Aymé, Claudel, Beckett and Salacrou, we have almost nobody.'

If you seek a tombstone, look about you; survey the peculiar nullity of our drama's prevalent *genre*, the Loamshire play. Its setting is a country house in what used to be called Loamshire but is now, as a heroic tribute to realism, sometimes called Berkshire. Except when someone must sneeze, or be murdered, the sun invariably shines. The inhabitants belong to a social class derived partly from romantic novels and partly from the playwright's vision of the leisured life he will lead after the play is a success – this being the only effort of imagination he is called on to make. Joys and sorrows are giggles and whimpers: the crash of denunciation dwindles into 'Oh, stuff, Mummy!' and 'Oh, really, Daddy!' And so grim is the continuity of these things that the foregoing paragraph might have been written at any time during the last thirty years.

Loamshire is a glibly codified fairy-tale world, of no more use to the student of life than a doll's house would be to a student of town planning. Its vice is to have engulfed the theatre, thereby expelling better minds. Never believe that there is a shortage of playwrights; there are more than we have ever known; but they are all writing the same play. Nor is there a dearth of English actors; the land is alive with them; but they are all playing the same part. Should they wish to test themselves beyond Loamshire's simple major thirds, they must find employment in revivals, foreign plays or films. Perhaps Loamshire's greatest triumph is the crippling of creative talent in English directors and designers. After all, how many ways are there of directing a tea-party? And how may a designer spread his wings in a mews flat or 'The living room at "Binsgate", Charles Trevannion's country house near Dymsdyke'? Assume the miracle: assume the advent of a masterpiece. There it crouches, a pink-eyed, many-muscled, salivating monster. Who shall harness it? We have a handful of directors fit to tame something less malleable than a mouse; and a few designers still capable of dressing something less submissive than a clothes-horse. But they are the end, not the beginning, of a tradition.

Some of us need no miracles to keep our faith; we feed it on memories and imaginings. But many more – people of passionate intellectual appetites – are losing heart, falling away, joining the queues outside the Curzon. To lure them home, the theatre must widen its scope, broaden its horizon so that Loamshire appears merely as the play-pen, not as the whole palace of drama. We need plays about cabmen and demi-gods, plays about warriors, politicians and grocers – I care not, so Loamshire be invaded and subdued. I counsel aggression because, as a critic, I had rather be a war correspondent than a necrologist.

•

PETER WILDEBLOOD
1955

'Against the law'

Peter Wildeblood, a London journalist, was one of five men charged with homosexual acts in what became known as the 'Montagu Case' (after Lord Montagu, one of the accused). Three of the men were sent to prison, the other two were set free after turning Queen's Evidence. Wildeblood's courageous book, Against the Law, *describing the plight of homosexuals, was addressed to the Wolfenden Committee which was investigating homosexual law reform. 'The right which I claim for myself, and for all those like me, is the right to choose the person whom I love,' Wildeblood wrote. (The Wolfenden Report recommended in 1957 that homosexual acts between consenting adults in private should be legalized – but its proposal was not implemented until 1967.)*

I am a homosexual. It is easy for me to make that admission now, because much of my private life has already been made public by the newspapers. I am in the rare, and perhaps privileged, position of having nothing left to hide. My only concern is that some good may come at last out of so much evil, and with that end in view I shall set down what happened to me as faithfully and fairly as I can. I do not pity myself, and I do not ask for pity. If there is bitterness in this book, I hope it will be the bitterness of medicine, not of poison.

I am no more proud of my condition than I would be of having a glass eye or a hare-lip. On the other hand, I am no more ashamed of it than I would be of being colour-blind or of writing with my left hand. It is essentially a personal problem, which only becomes a matter of public concern when the law makes it so. For many years I kept it a secret from my family and friends, not so much from choice as from expediency, and I tried privately to resolve my own struggle in a way as consistent as possible with the moral law. During that time I do not believe I ever did any harm to anyone else; if any harm has been done since, I do not think the fault lies with me, but rather with those who dragged out into the merciless light of publicity things which would have been better left in darkness. When the searchlights of the law were turned on to my life, only a part of it was illuminated. I am not proud of what was exposed; most people, if they were honest, would admit that their private lives would not bear such a relentless scrutiny. It will be my task, therefore, to turn on more lights, revealing, in place of the blurred and shadowy figure of the newspaper photographs, a man differing from other men only in one respect.

I must begin by trying to show what this difference is. The whole question is so surrounded by ignorance, moral horror and misunderstanding that it is not easy to approach it with an open mind. I shall not try, at this stage, either to explain or to excuse it, but simply to describe my condition. Briefly, it is that I am attracted towards men, in the way in which most men are attracted towards women. I am aware that many people, luckier than myself, will read this statement with incredulity and perhaps with derision; but it is the simple truth. This peculiarity makes me a social misfit from the start; I know that it cannot ever be entirely accepted by the rest of the community, and I do not ask that it should. It is up to me to come to terms, first with my own condition, and secondly with other people whose lives quite rightly centre upon the relationship between a man and a woman. If it was possible for me to become like them I should do so, and nothing would be easier for me than to assume a superficial normality, get married and perhaps have a family. This would, however, be at best dishonest, because I should be running away from my own problem, and at worst it would be cruel, because I should run the risk of making two people unhappy instead of one.

I think it is more honest, and less harmful, for a man with homosexual tendencies to recognize himself for what he is. He will always be lonely; he must accept that. He will never know the companionship that comes with marriage or the joy of watching his children grow up, but he will at least have the austere consolations of self-knowledge and integrity. More than that he cannot have, because the law, in England, forbids it. A man who feels an attraction towards other men is a social misfit only; once he gives way to that attraction, he becomes a criminal.

The truth is that an adult man who has chosen a homosexual way of life has done so because he knows that no other course is open to him. It is easy to preach chastity when you are not obliged to practise it yourself, and it must be remembered that, to a homosexual, there is nothing intrinsically shameful or sinful in his condition. Everywhere he goes, he sees other men like himself, forbidden by the law to give any physical expression to their desires. It is not surprising that he should seek a partner among them, so that together they may build a shelter against the hostile world. One of the charges often levelled against homosexuals is that they tend to form a compact and exclusive group. They can hardly be expected to do anything else, since they are legally excluded from the rest of the community.

The view of the law – and it is shared by many sincere men and women – is that homosexuality is a monstrous perversion deliberately chosen, and that the men who make that choice deserve to be punished for it. The very words of the law are impregnated with emotion on this subject; murder is merely murder, but homosexual acts are 'the abominable crime' and 'gross indecency'. The upholders of the law will claim that homosexuality has always been a symptom of a nation's decadence, forgetting that it is widespread and tolerated in such respectable and progressive places as Switzerland and Scandinavia. They will say that it is inseparable from effeminacy, ignoring the fact that it has been practised among the most warlike communities, from the Samurai of medieval Japan to the present-day Pathans of the Northwest Frontier, and that men like Julius Caesar, Frederick the Great and Lawrence of Arabia are known to have been homosexuals. They will argue that homosexuals are by nature vicious and depraved, because they cannot know that this minority group, branded by them as 'immoral', has an austere and strict morality of its own . . .

It seems to me very important to discriminate between the pederast, or lover of boys, and the homosexual, or lover of men. I am not convinced that a boy can be turned into a permanent homosexual by an isolated, early experience, but this risk must at all costs be avoided. Furthermore, it seems fundamentally immoral to me for a man to take advantage of his greater age and experience to seduce a child, whether a boy or girl. Sexual experiences of any kind play such an important part in a person's development that they should not be allowed to take place until he or she is physically and mentally ready for them.

Homosexuality between adults presents a very different moral problem. There are thousands of men in this condition, who are forbidden by the law to seek any sexual outlet, even with one another. To the homosexual, this seems unjust. He does not wish to seduce children, not only because it seems to him basically immoral to do so, but because he is not attracted towards them. He is unlikely to make advances to 'normal' adults, because he knows that such men, even if he finds them attractive, will not want to have anything to do with him. Even if it were possible, he would not wish to take a 'normal' man away from his wife and family and persuade him to take up a way of life which he would always regret. On the other hand, he cannot see why he should be condemned to perpetual continence, when there are so many other men like himself with whom it would be possible to enter into a relationship which would do no harm to anyone.

That is the morality of the homosexual, and it is my own. It is not endorsed by the law of the country, as the best kind of relationship between a man and a woman is endorsed; in fact, as I shall show, the present state of the law actually goes far to discourage homosexual relationships of the more sincere and 'moral' kind. Nor is it much encouraged by the community: when all homosexual acts, whether between adult men or between men and boys, are treated by the law with equal severity, it is difficult for the general public to discriminate between them.

There is another misconception which I should like to dispel. This concerns the appearance and manner of the homosexual. Everyone has seen the pathetically flamboyant pansy with the flapping wrists, the common butt of music-hall jokes and public-house stories. Most of us are not like that. We do our best to look like everyone else, and we usually succeed. That is why nobody realizes how many of us there are. I know many hundreds of homosexuals and not more than half a dozen would be recognized by a stranger for what they are. If anything, they dress more soberly and behave more conventionally in public than the 'normal' men I know; they have to, if they are to avoid suspicion.

When I ask for tolerance, it is for men like these. Not the corrupters of youth, not even the effeminate creatures who love to make an exhibition of themselves, although by doing so they probably do no harm; I am only concerned with the men who, in spite of the tragic disability which is theirs, try to lead their lives according to the principles which I have described. They cannot speak for themselves, but I shall try to speak for them. Although I have been to prison and most of them have not, it is they who are the captives of circumstance, not I.

•

SOMERSET MAUGHAM
1955

'Scum'

Even as Kenneth Tynan deplored 'Loamshire', a new generation of young writers who came to be known as the 'Angry Young Men' was emerging in British literature – and, soon, the theatre. The first was John Wain, with his 1953 novel Hurry On Down. *The second was Kingsley Amis with* Lucky Jim *in 1954, a comic novel which satirized life at a provincial university (Amis was teaching at University College Swansea). When the novelist Somerset Maugham (1874–1965), then eighty-one, was asked to select his book of the year by the* Sunday Times, *he chose* Lucky Jim. *He explained why.*

Lucky Jim is a remarkable novel. It has been greatly praised and widely read, but I have not noticed that any of the reviewers have remarked on its ominous significance. I am told that today rather more than 60 per cent of the men who go to the universities go on a government grant. This is a new class that has entered upon the scene. It is the white-collar proletariat. Mr Kingsley Amis is so talented, his observation is so keen, that you cannot fail to be convinced that the young men he so brilliantly describes truly represent the class with which his novel is concerned.

They do not go to the university to acquire culture, but to get a job, and when they have got one, scamp it. They have no manners and are woefully unable to deal with any social predicament. Their idea of a celebration is to go to a public house and drink six beers. They are mean, malicious and envious. They will write anonymous letters to harass a fellow undergraduate and listen in to a telephone conversation that is no business of theirs. Charity, kindliness, generosity are qualities which they hold in contempt. They are scum. They will in due course leave the university. Some will doubtless sink back, perhaps with relief, into the modest class from which they emerged; some will take to drink, some to crime and go to prison. Others will become schoolmasters and form the young, or journalists and mould public opinion. A few will go into Parliament, become Cabinet ministers and rule the country. I look upon myself as fortunate that I shall not live to see it.

•

AFRICAN NATIONAL CONGRESS
1955

'The Freedom Charter'

When the African National Congress set up a Congress of the People to create a set of conditions for the foundation of a new South Africa it invited all the participating organizations to send suggestions – if you could make the laws, what would you do? Three thousand delegates braved police intimidation to attend the Congress at Kliptown near Johannesburg in June 1955. On the second day, when the charter had been adopted by acclamation, police brandishing sten guns swarmed on to the platform, announcing that treason was suspected. All the delegates had their names taken.

'The charter became a great beacon for the liberation struggle,' says Nelson Mandela. 'It captured the hopes and dreams of the people and acted as a blueprint for the liberation struggle and the future of the nation'.

We, the people of South Africa, declare for all our country and the world to know:

that South Africa belongs to all who live in it, black and white, and that no government can justly claim authority unless it is based on the will of all the people;

that our people have been robbed of their birthright to land, liberty and peace by a form of government founded on injustice and inequality;

that our country will never be prosperous or free until all our people live in brotherhood, enjoying equal rights and opportunities;

that only a democratic state, based on the will of all the people, can secure to all their birthright without distinction of colour, race, sex or belief.

And therefore, we, the people of South Africa, black and white together – equals, countrymen and brothers – adopt this Freedom Charter. And we pledge ourselves to strive together, sparing neither strength nor courage, until the democratic changes here set out have been won.

THE PEOPLE SHALL GOVERN!

Every man and woman shall have the right to vote for and to stand as a candidate for all bodies which make laws;

All people shall be entitled to take part in the administration of the country;

The rights of the people shall be the same, regardless of race, colour or sex;

All bodies of minority rule, advisory boards, councils and authorities shall be replaced by democratic organs of self-government.

ALL NATIONAL GROUPS SHALL HAVE EQUAL RIGHTS!

There shall be equal status in the bodies of state, in the courts and in the schools for all national groups and races;

All people shall have equal right to use their own languages, and to develop their own folk culture and customs;

All national groups shall be protected by law against insults to their race and national pride;

The preaching and practice of national, race or colour discrimination and contempt shall be a punishable crime;

All apartheid laws and practices shall be set aside.

THE PEOPLE SHALL SHARE IN THE COUNTRY'S WEALTH!

The national wealth of our country, the heritage of all South Africans, shall be restored to the people;

The mineral wealth beneath the soil, the banks and monopoly industry shall be transferred to the ownership of the people as a whole;

All other industry and trade shall be controlled to assist the well-being of the people;

All people shall have equal rights to trade where they choose, to manufacture and to enter all trades, crafts and professions.

THE LAND SHALL BE SHARED AMONG THOSE WHO WORK IT!

Restrictions of land ownership on a racial basis shall be ended, and all the land redivided amongst those who work it, to banish famine and land hunger;

The state shall help the peasants with implements, seed, tractors and dams to save the soil and assist the tillers;

Freedom of movement shall be guaranteed to all who work on the land;

All shall have the right to occupy land wherever they choose;

People shall not be robbed of their cattle, and forced labour and farm prisons shall be abolished.

ALL SHALL BE EQUAL BEFORE THE LAW!

No one shall be imprisoned, deported or restricted without a fair trial;

No one shall be condemned by the order of any government official;

The courts shall be representative of all the people;

Imprisonment shall be only for serious crimes against the people, and shall aim at re-education, not vengeance;

The police force and army shall be open to all on an equal basis and shall be the helpers and protectors of the people;

All laws which discriminate on grounds of race, colour or belief shall be repealed.

ALL SHALL ENJOY EQUAL HUMAN RIGHTS!

The law shall guarantee to all their right to speak, to organize, to meet together, to publish, to preach, to worship and to educate their children;

The privacy of the house from police raids shall be protected by law;

All shall be free to travel without restriction from countryside to town, from province to province, and from South Africa abroad;

Pass Laws, permits and all other laws restricting these freedoms shall be abolished.

THERE SHALL BE WORK AND SECURITY!

All who work shall be free to form trade unions, to elect their officers and to make wage agreements with their employers;

The state shall recognize the right and duty of all to work, and to draw full unemployment benefits;

Men and women of all races shall receive equal pay for equal work;

There shall be a forty-hour working week, a national minimum wage, paid annual leave, and sick leave for all workers and maternity leave on full pay for all working mothers;

Miners, domestic workers, farm workers and civil servants shall have the same rights as all others who work;

Child labour, compound labour, the tot system and contract labour shall be abolished.

THE DOORS OF LEARNING AND OF CULTURE SHALL BE OPENED!

The government shall discover, develop and encourage national talent for the enhancement of our cultural life;

All the cultural treasures of mankind shall be open to all, by free exchange of books, ideas and contact with other lands;

The aim of education shall be to teach the youth to love their people and their culture, to honour human brotherhood, liberty and peace;

Education shall be free, compulsory, universal and equal for all children;

Higher education and technical training shall be opened to all by means of state allowances and scholarships awarded on the basis of merit;

Adult illiteracy shall be ended by a mass state education plan;

Teachers shall have all the rights of other citizens;

The colour bar in cultural life, in sport and in education shall be abolished.

•

TREVOR HUDDLESTON
1956

'White supremacy'

The Anglican missionary Father Trevor Huddleston (1913–1998) entered the Community of the Resurrection after ordination and went to Johannesburg in 1943, where he was provincial of the order from 1949 to 1955. As a passionate believer in the universal brotherhood of man in Christ, he was appalled by South Africa's apartheid, the policy of separate development for blacks and whites.

On his return to England, he wrote Naught for Your Comfort, *one of the first books to alert the rest of the world to the plight of South Africa's blacks.*

I am not trying to fight the religious convictions of the Calvinist Afrikaner by any other means than the proclamation of the Catholic faith. But I do not, for that reason, believe it to be wrong, or foolish, or un-Christian to try to strike from the hand of white South Africa the weapons which not only hurt and wound the African every day, but must also ultimately destroy civilization on this sub-continent. I would, in fact, deny absolutely that 'political weapons' are not to be used by Christians, for I believe that the Christian is bound to act politically, wherever he may be: that if the Church refuses to accept responsibility in the political sphere as well as in the strictly theological sphere, then she is guilty of betraying the very foundation of her faith: the Incarnation. It is when the Church has so abdicated her position of political trust that the state, freed from any absolute higher than itself, has assumed a totalitarian shape and a dictatorial attitude. That is a matter of history, not of opinion . . .

To allow democracy to lose all Christian content, or to refuse to fight for democratic rights in the interests of theology – and of converting one's opponents to a more Christian theological outlook – that is to court disaster. So at least it seems to me. I believe, with Father Wood, that Calvinistic theology is largely to blame for the present tragedy in South Africa: I would wish with all my heart that a 'conversion' might be achieved. But I am certainly not prepared to wait for that conversion while, at every level, political weapons are being used to create a condition of permanent servitude for the African in his own country. I am reminded of the kind of opposition from 'good' men (including bishops of the Established Church) which William Wilberforce had to fight continuously. I am reminded, too, of the kind of arguments used by Pétain to justify, on a religious and theological basis, his collaboration with the Nazis. Slavery would have endured a great deal longer if Wilberforce had used no political weapons: thousands of refugees from Nazism, including some of the most honourable men in Europe, might be alive today if Pétain had refused to sign Article Nineteen in the Armistice Treaty which Hitler presented to him. And in South Africa, if we wait to impress Afrikaners with the truth of Catholic theology, and English-speaking South Africans with the need for religion, we might as well give up the struggle for human rights altogether. They will have vanished into the night.

The Director of the South African Church Institute, the Rev. C. T. Wood, in a sermon preached at Chester Cathedral in February 1955, said: 'I hold that by far the most important factor in our approach to the vital problems that are confronting South Africa today is the theological one. That what really matters, that what really influences the Afrikaner, is what he thinks about God and God's purpose for him and his race. We make the greatest possible mistake in trying to fight his convictions with political weapons. Broad cries about democracy are not the answer to the theocracy which he has built up and which he jealously guards – we must fight him and convict him on his own grounds and not on arbitrary grounds of our own choosing . . .'

I have quoted this passage from an Anglican sermon, preached by one who knows South Africa, because it seems to me to express a point of view and an attitude widely representative of intelligent 'ecclesiastical' opinion both in the Union and outside it. It also seems to me to state a truth – the primacy of theology – and to draw totally wrong conclusions from that truth. And it assumes what I am not prepared to assume – that the tragedy of the present situation in South Africa can be blamed upon one section of the white population, the Afrikaner, and upon his religion. The whole purpose of this book has been an attempt to demonstrate, out of my personal, day-to-day experience, the effect of a policy upon a people: of a policy which I believe to be basically sub-Christian, and imposed by a government whose motives are clearly and unmistakably racial. But this policy could not be imposed, neither could the government which imposes it remain in power, if the majority of white South African Christians did not approve of it. The doctrine of white supremacy is common to both Afrikaner and 'English' sections of the population. If it derives from the theological presuppositions of the Afrikaner and from the Calvinism which is their source, it derives equally from the failure of Anglicans, of Roman Catholics and of Methodists to live by the faith which they profess. To deny this is both dishonest and absurd.

Father Wood says that we make the greatest possible mistake in trying 'to fight his convictions with political weapons'. This is a most interesting and significant statement: for it is almost exactly what the Archbishop of Canterbury said to me when we met for a brief few hours in Southern Rhodesia not many months ago. As we stood in our small community parlour after supper, waiting for our African guests to arrive for the reception, the archbishop turned to me and said: 'You are entirely wrong in the methods you are using to fight this situation . . . The Christian must never use force . . . must never use the same weapons as his opponent.' We had a fierce but wholly friendly argument, which lasted until the reception began and which continued in correspondence afterwards. I was not convinced by the archbishop, and I am not convinced by Father Wood. For what does this statement really mean?

Afrikaner theology and English apathy have together created a situation in which men, made in the image and likeness of God, are treated as inferior because they are of a different race and colour from their rulers. The weapons used to impose a racial discrimination policy upon the African people are, of course, political. Prejudice and fear are doubtless the motive forces behind the policy, but it is such measures as the Native Urban Areas Act, the Native Resettlement Act, the Group Areas Act and the Bantu Education Act which translate that prejudice and that fear into hard reality. It is the propaganda put forth by the State Information Office: it is the speeches made, and reported at length, by Cabinet ministers (and often enough by Opposition leaders too): it is the notices, 'Slegs vir Blankes', 'Europeans only', displayed on public buildings: it is the daily police raids for passes, or for determining the racial group to which you belong, or for just reminding you that you are a kaffir . . . It is these things which are the weapons of the white race, weapons as prominent as the revolver which hangs on every policeman's belt. They are not just 'the convictions' of the Afrikaner. They are the expression of 'baasskap': of white domination. And, certainly, they are 'political weapons'.

•

OBSERVER
1956

'Eden must go'

*There was a huge outcry in Britain – and a major rift in Anglo-American relations –
when Anthony Eden, the British prime minister, decided to invade Suez after General
Nasser, the Egyptian president, nationalized the Suez Canal.*

But only two newspapers, the Manchester Guardian *and the* Observer, *consistently
opposed Eden and his ill-fated invasion and called for his resignation. Some of the most
faithful readers of both were outraged. This* Observer *leading article, drafted by the
Labour politician Dingle Foot (brother of Michael) but revised by the editor, David Astor
(especially the first paragraph), provoked 1,227 letters, of which 866 were hostile. More
than half of those who wrote in announced that they were giving up the paper.*

We wish to make an apology. Five weeks ago we remarked that, although *we*
knew our government would not make a military attack in defiance of its
solemn international obligations, people abroad might think otherwise. The
events of last week have proved us completely wrong: if we misled anyone,
at home or abroad, we apologize unreservedly. We had not realized that our
government was capable of such folly and such crookedness.

Whatever the government now does, it cannot undo its air attacks on
Egypt, made after Egypt had been invaded by Israel. It can never live down
the dishonest nature of its ultimatum, so framed that it was certain to be
rejected by Egypt. Never since 1783 has Great Britain made herself so
universally disliked. That was the year in which the Government of Lord
North, faced with the antagonism of almost the whole civilized world, was
compelled to recognize the independence of the American Colonies. Sir
Anthony Eden's eighteenth-century predecessors succeeded in losing us an
Empire. Sir Anthony and his colleagues have already succeeded in losing us
incalculable political assets. So long as his government represents this country,
we cannot expect to have a good standing in the councils of the nations. It
has attempted to prove those councils futile by rendering them futile. This
it has done by, first, frustrating the Security Council of the United Nations
through the use of the veto, and then by defying an overwhelming vote in
the General Assembly. The Eden Government has become internationally
discredited.

Ever since 1945, there have been two cardinal features of British external policy. The first has been to uphold the rule of law with special reference to the United Nations. The second has been the steady progress away from imperialism, exemplified in the full emancipation of Burma, India, Pakistan, Ceylon, West Africa and the West Indies. Neither of these cardinal features of our national policy was sincerely endorsed by the leaders of the Conservative Party, as we now see. In the eyes of the whole world, the British and French Governments have acted, not as policemen, but as gangsters. It will never be possible for the present government to convince the peoples of the Middle East and of all Asia and Africa that it has not been actively associated with France in an endeavour to reimpose nineteenth-century imperialism of the crudest kind.

Is there any way of retrieving, in some degree, the errors of the last six days? There is one essential. Sir Anthony Eden must go. His removal from the Premiership is scarcely less vital to the prospects of this country than was that of Mr Neville Chamberlain in May 1940.

The Eden administration has shown that it does not understand the sort of world we live in. It is no longer possible to bomb countries because you fear that your trading interests will be harmed. Nowadays, a drowning man on a raft is the occasion for all shipping to be diverted to try to save him; this new feeling for the sanctity of human life is the best element in the modern world. It is the true distinction of the West. Our other distinction is our right of personal independence and responsibility in politics – a right that must be exercised.

Nations are said to have the governments they deserve. Let us show that we deserve better.

●

IMRE NAGY
1956

'The dream of Hungary'

As Britain prepared to invade Egypt and seize the Suez Canal, the Soviet Union invaded Hungary, where the veteran Communist Imre Nagy (1895–1958) was once again prime minister.

When the Hungarian people rose against Soviet domination in October 1956, Nagy promised free elections and a Russian military withdrawal. In a broadcast speech on the evening of 1 November, Nagy declared Hungarian neutrality. As he finished he already knew that Russian troops had reached central Hungary.

Three days later, as the tanks arrived in Budapest, he used the radio again to appeal to the world to save Hungary. (Nagy was deposed, replaced by the Soviet puppet János Kádár and executed – but he was given a hero's reburial in 1989.)

People of Hungary! The Hungarian National Government, imbued with profound responsibility towards the Hungarian people and history, and giving expression to the undivided will of the Hungarian millions, declares the neutrality of the Hungarian People's Republic. The Hungarian people, on the basis of independence and equality and in accordance with the spirit of the United Nations Charter wishes to live in true friendship with its neighbours, the Soviet Union and all the peoples of the world.

The Hungarian people desire the consolidation and further development of the achievements of their national revolution without joining any power blocks. The century-old dream of the Hungarian people is now being fulfilled. The revolutionary trouble fought by the Hungarian people and heroes has at last carried the cause of freedom and independence to victory. Our heroic struggle has made possible the enforcement, in international relations of our people, of their fundamental national interest: neutrality. We appeal to our neighbours, countries near and far, to respect the unalterable decision of our people.

This is Imre Nagy speaking, Chairman of the Council of Ministers of the Hungarian People's Democracy. In the early hours of this morning, Soviet troops launched an attack against our capital city with the obvious intention of overthrowing the lawful, democratic Hungarian Government. Our troops are fighting. The government is in its place. I hereby inform the people of Hungary and world opinion of the situation.

•

PETER FRYER
1956

'The petty Stalins of British Communism'

Peter Fryer had been a journalist on the Daily Worker, *the newspaper of the British Communist Party, for eight years when he went to Hungary to report the uprising against the Soviet Union. At least 20,000 Hungarians were killed. He watched appalled as Hungary's newly-won freedom was crushed by Soviet guns and tanks and as he saw the fear, poverty and suffering of the people under Communist rule.*

His reports to the Daily Worker *were suppressed, he resigned and was subsequently expelled from the party. His experience in Budapest was a 'bitter awakening', he wrote in* Hungarian Tragedy, *a mass uprising against tyranny crushed by the army of the world's first socialist state.*

Most Hungarians, while they do not want capitalism back or the landowners back, today detest, and rightly so, the regime of poverty, drabness and fear that has been presented to them as Communism. The responsibility for this lies squarely on the shoulders of the Communist leaders, and principally on those of Rákosi, Farkas and Gerö, who promised the people an earthly paradise and gave them a police state as repressive and as reprehensible as the pre-war fascist dictatorship of Admiral Horthy. The workers were exploited and bullied and lied to. The peasants were exploited and bullied and lied to. The writers and artists were squeezed into the most rigid of ideological strait-jackets – and bullied and lied to. To speak one's mind, to ask an awkward question, even to speak about political questions in language not signposted with the safe, familiar monolithic jargon, was to run the risk of falling foul of the ubiquitous secret police. The purpose of this highly-paid organization was ostensibly to protect the people from attempts at the restoration of capitalism, but in practice it protected the power of the oligarchy. To this end it used the most abominable methods, including censorship, thought control, imprisonment, torture and murder. The tragedy was that such a regime was presented as a Socialist society, as a 'people's democracy', as a first step on the road to Communism.

The honest rank-and-file Communists, inside whose party the reign of terror was in full force, saw their ideals and principles violated, their sacrifices abused, their faith in human beings rejected in favour of a soulless bureaucracy which mechanically copied the Soviet model and which stifled the creative initiative of a people that wanted to build Socialism. The honest Communists, inside and outside Rákosi's jails, saw their party brought into disrepute, their ideology made to stink in the nostrils of the common people to whose elevation they had dedicated their lives. No wonder they joined in the people's revolution; no wonder they helped to resist the Soviet invasion . . .

Look at the hell that Rákosi made of Hungary and you will see an indictment, not of Marxism, not of Communism, but of Stalinism. Hypocrisy without limit; medieval cruelty; dogmas and slogans devoid of life or meaning; national pride outraged; poverty for all but a tiny handful of leaders who lived in luxury, with mansions on Rózsadomb, Budapest's pleasant Hill of Roses (nicknamed by people 'Hill of Cadres'), special schools for their children, special well-stocked shops for their wives – even special bathing beaches at

Lake Balaton, shut off from the common people by barbed wire. And to protect the power and privileges of this Communist aristocracy, the AVH – and behind them the ultimate sanction, the tanks of the Soviet Army. Against this disgusting caricature of Socialism our British Stalinists would not, could not, dared not protest; nor do they now spare a word of comfort or solidarity or pity for the gallant people who rose at last to wipe out the infamy, who stretched out their yearning hands for freedom, and who paid such a heavy price.

Hungary was Stalinism incarnate. Here in one small, tormented country was the picture, complete in every detail: the abandonment of humanism, the attachment of primary importance not to living, breathing, suffering, hoping human beings but to machines, targets, statistics, tractors, steel mills, plan fulfilment figures . . . and, of course, tanks. Struck dumb by Stalinism, we ourselves grotesquely distorted the fine Socialist principle of international solidarity by making any criticism of *present* injustices or inhumanities in a Communist-led country taboo. Stalinism crippled us by castrating our moral passion, blinding us to the wrongs done to men if those wrongs were done in the name of Communism. We Communists have been indignant about the wrongs done by imperialism; those wrongs are many and vile; but our one-sided indignation has somehow not rung true. It has left a sour taste in the mouth of the British worker, who is quick to detect and condemn hypocrisy.

Stalinism is Marxism with the heart cut out, de-humanized, dried, frozen, petrified, rigid, barren. It is concerned with 'the line', not with the tears of Hungarian children. It is preoccupied with abstract power, with strategy and tactics, not with the dictates of conscience and common humanity. The whole future of the world Communist movement depends on putting an end to Stalinism. The whole future of the British Communist Party depends on a return to Socialist principles.

That I am ostracized by the petty Stalins in the British Communist Party is of no consequence. What is important, and what must be stopped without delay, is their dragging Socialism in the mud. The writing is on the wall for them. Once too often they have lost an opportunity to speak out in ringing words against oppression. This time their shame is so obvious that anyone who has not retired into a fantasy world can recognize it. Thousands of British Communists in these past few weeks have seen this sickening betrayal of Socialism by leaders who put their faith in T54 tanks rather than in the Hungarian people, who are prepared to spit on a nation's agony and grief rather than venture even the mildest doubt about the infallibility of Soviet policy. For many Communists this tragic betrayal by their leaders has brought a poignant personal dilemma, and they have resolved it by leaving the Party. Their decision is regrettable, for it strengthens the Stalinist hard core at a moment when the chance of removing them has never been so strong.

The British Communist Party will be able to hold up its head before the British people only when it has settled accounts with the dark heritage of Stalinism which still fetters it, which makes its leaders walk by on the other side while Hungary lies bleeding. Then we shall witness the flourishing of a real Communist Party, dedicated to the principles of Socialist humanism. Marx called revolution 'a human protest against an inhuman life'. The Hungarian revolution was precisely that. It has shown the way forward. In our own small way we British Communists, too, can become freedom fighters.

•

KENNETH TYNAN
1956

'Jimmy Porter'

The 'Loamshire' plays about which Kenneth Tynan (1929–80), the Observer's *theatre critic, had protested in 1954, were swept from the stage after John Osborne's first play,* Look Back in Anger, *was put on at London's Royal Court Theatre in 1956. It was the best young play of its decade, declared Tynan: 'I doubt if I could love anyone who did not wish to see* Look Back in Anger.'

Its main character, Jimmy Porter, was a genuinely angry young man.

'They are scum,' was Mr Maugham's famous verdict on the class of state-aided university students to which Kingsley Amis's *Lucky Jim* belongs; and since Mr Maugham seldom says anything controversial or uncertain of wide accept-ance, his opinion must clearly be that of many. Those who share it had better stay well away from John Osborne's *Look Back in Anger*, which is all scum, and a mile wide.

Its hero is a provincial graduate who runs a sweet-stall. With his flair for introspection, his gift for ribald parody, his contempt for 'phoneyness', his weakness for soliloquy and his desperate conviction that the time is out of joint, Jimmy Porter is the completest young pup in our literature since Hamlet, Prince of Denmark. His wife, whose Anglo-Indian parents resent him, is persuaded by an actress friend to leave him: Jimmy's prompt response is to go to bed with the actress. Mr Osborne's picture of a certain kind of modern marriage is hilariously accurate: he shows us two attractive young animals engaged in competitive martyrdom, each with its teeth sunk deep in the other's neck, and each reluctant to break the clinch for fear of bleeding to death.

The fact that he writes with charity has led many critics into the trap of supposing that Mr Osborne's sympathies are wholly with Jimmy. Nothing could be more false. Jimmy is simply and abundantly alive; that rarest of dramatic phenomena, the act of original creation, has taken place: and those who carp were better silent. Is Jimmy's anger justified? Why doesn't he *do* something? These questions might be relevant if the character had failed to come to life; in the presence of such evident and blazing vitality, I marvel at the pedantry that could ask them. Why don't Checkhov's people *do* something? Is the sun justified in scorching us? There will be time enough to debate Mr Osborne's moral position when he has written a few more plays. In the present one he certainly goes off the deep end, but I cannot regard this as a vice in a theatre that seldom ventures more than a toe into the water.

Look Back in Anger presents postwar youth as it really is, with special emphasis on the non-U intelligentsia who live in bed-sitters and divide the Sunday papers into two groups, 'posh' and 'wet'. To have done this at all would be a signal achievement; to have done it in a first play is a minor miracle. All the qualities are there, qualities one had despaired of ever seeing on the stage – the drift towards anarchy, the instinctive leftishness, the automatic rejection of 'official' attitudes, the surrealist sense of humour (Jimmy describes a pansy friend as 'a female Emily Brontë'). The casual promiscuity, the sense of lacking a crusade worth fighting for and, underlying all these, the determination that no one who dies shall go unmourned.

One cannot imagine Jimmy Porter listening with a straight face to speeches about our inalienable right to flog Cypriot schoolboys. You could never mobilize him and his kind into a lynching mob, since the art he lives for, jazz, was invented by Negroes: and if you gave him a razor, he would do nothing with it but shave. The Porters of our time deplore the tyranny of 'good taste' and refuse to accept 'emotional' as a term of abuse; they are classless, and they are also leaderless. Mr Osborne is their first spokesman in the London theatre. He has been lucky in his sponsors (the English Stage Company), his director (Tony Richardson), and his interpreters: Mary Ure, Helena Hughes and Alan Bates give fresh and unforced performances, and in the taxing central role Kenneth Haigh never puts a foot wrong.

That the play needs changes I do not deny: I agree that *Look Back in Anger* is likely to remain a minority taste. What matters is the size of the minority. I estimate it at roughly 6,733,000, the number of people in this country between the ages of twenty and thirty. And this figure will doubtless be swelled by refugees from other age-groups who are curious to know precisely what the contemporary young pup is thinking and feeling. I doubt if I could love anyone who did not wish to see *Look Back in Anger*. It is the best young play of its decade.

•

ARTHUR KOESTLER
1956

'Hanging'

Until 1965, when the death penalty was abolished by the Labour government, convicted murderers were sentenced to death by hanging. Apart from hanging being irreversible if the hanged person was later found innocent, the method employed – being hanged by the neck on a gallows – aroused horror among liberals. At the culmination of the long campaign against capital punishment, Arthur Koestler (1905–83) stood alongside the Labour MP Sidney Silverman as its most effective critic, as this chilling extract from his book Reflections on Hanging *demonstrates.*

Dostoievsky says somewhere that if in the last moment before being executed, a man, however brave, were given the alternative of spending the rest of his days on the top of a bare rock with only enough space to sit on it, he would choose it with relief. There is indeed a Kafkaesque horror attached to an execution, which goes beyond the mere fear of death or pain or indignity. It is connected not with the brutality but with the macabre, cold-blooded politeness of the ceremony, in which the person whose neck is going to be broken is supposed to collaborate in a nice, sensible manner, as if it were a matter of a minor surgical operation. It is symbolized in the ceremonial handshake with the executioner; it is present in the delinquent's knowledge that in the embarrassed stares of the officials he is already mirrored as a dead man with a blue face and ruptured vertebrae; and that what for him is the final, violent termination of life is for them merely an unpleasant duty, followed by a sigh of relief and a plate of bacon and eggs. The Romans deprived their victim of the dignity of death by throwing him to the beasts in the arena with a clown's mask attached to his face; we put a white cap over his head, and if the victim is a woman she is made to put on waterproof underwear on the morning of the execution.

Officialdom wishes to make us believe that the operation itself is always quick and expeditious. This is not true. A confidential Home Office instruction to Prison Governors dated 10 January 1925 runs in part as follows:

> Any reference to the manner in which an execution has been carried out should be confined to as few words as possible, e.g., 'it was carried out expeditiously and without a hitch'. No record should be taken as to the number of seconds and, if pressed for details of this kind, the Governor should say he cannot give them, and he did not time the proceedings, but 'a very short interval elapsed', or some general expression of opinion to the same effect.

When the Home Secretary was subsequently asked in the House of Commons whether he would not publish the whole instruction, he answered:

> It would be most undesirable and entirely contrary to established practice to make the terms of such instructions public ... the less said at the inquest either by Governors or anyone else, the better ... it is preferable to draw a veil over these cases.

The truth is that some prisoners struggle both in the condemned cell and under the noose, that some have to be carried tied to a chair, others dragged to the trap, limp, bowels open, arms pinioned to the back, like animals; and that still other things happen which should only happen in nightmare dreams. In the Commons debate of 1948, the then Mr Beverley Baxter mentioned one case which the Home Office did not succeed in hushing up, the case of a sick woman of twenty-eight whose insides fell out before she vanished through the trap:

> After her execution two of the warders who had taken part in that execution came to my office, and their faces were not human. I can assure you, Sir, they were like people of another world. Edith Thompson had disintegrated as a human creature on her way to the gallows, and yet somehow they had to get her there ... Those two warders who took part in that execution said to me, 'Use your influence; never again must a woman be hanged.'

Everybody who took part in that scene suffered some damage to their nervous system. The executioner, Ellis, attempted suicide a few weeks later. The Governor of Holloway, Dr Morton, was described a few days later by a visiting magistrate: 'I think I have never seen a person look so changed in appearance by mental suffering as the Governor appeared to me to be.' The prison chaplain, the Rev. Glanville Murray, said of the scene of the execution: 'When we were all gathered together there, it seemed utterly impossible to believe what we were there to do ... My God, the impulse to rush in and save her by force was almost too strong for me.' When it was over, the Deputy Governor of Holloway, Miss Cronin, who was 'not at all a sensitive or easily moved person', remarked of the hanged woman: 'I think if she had been spared she could have become a very good woman.'

These nightmare scenes are not exceptional. When Pierrepoint was asked by the Royal Commission, 'You must in so many executions have had things go wrong occasionally?' he had at first lied: 'Never.' Pressed further whether he had had any 'awkward moments', he climbed down and said that he had had one awkward moment 'with a foreign spy who had to be carried to the gallows strapped to a chair'. Pressed even further, he said he had 'probably three more' such cases 'like a faint at the last minute or something like that, but it has not been anything to speak about'. It may not be much for Pierrepoint to speak about, but it should be enough for the nation to think about. For if it is proper that these things should be done in its name, then it is proper that it should hear about them.

The horror of the operation remains even if there is no struggle or dementedness in the condemned cell. The preparations on the previous day when executioner and assistant discreetly take the measure and weight of the victim to determine the length of the drop; the dress rehearsal of dropping a stuffed sack of the same weight to make sure that the estimated length of rope will neither strangle the victim too slowly nor tear his head off; the jolly domino game in the condemned cell while the preparations go on and the hour draws nearer; the stratagems to make him sit with his back to the door through which the executioner will enter; the brisk, businesslike opening of that door, the pinioning of the hands behind the back and the walking or dragging him in solemn procession to the execution shed and on to the white chalk mark on the trap; the tying of his legs while two officers stand at his sides on planks thrown across the trap, to hold him up; the fixing of the white cap and the noose with its sliding brass ring – in a few years' time, when Lord Goddard and Mr Pierrepoint have, with God's help, been defeated, all this will appear as unthinkable as drawing, quartering and pressing to death appear to us today.

JOHN OSBORNE
1957

'The gold filling'

Declaration, a collection of essays whose authors included Doris Lessing, Kenneth Tynan and Lindsay Anderson, was an attempt to cash in on the Angry Young Men – a literary gunpowder prank, as it was described by another contributor, John Osborne (1929–96). 'A number of young and widely opposed writers have burst upon the scene and are striving to change many of the values which have held good in recent years,' its publisher Tom Maschler said in the introduction.

It was this contribution by Osborne, with its attack on the monarchy, which captured the headlines. The governor of the English Stage Company banned a party for Declaration *at the Royal Court Theatre, where* Look Back in Anger *had opened a year earlier. 'My own piece, written hastily over a weekend punctuated by Maschler's deadline calls, deserved some if not most of the scorn heaped upon it,' Osborne wrote in his autobiography,* Almost a Gentleman.

I can't go on laughing at the idiocies of the people who rule our lives. We have been laughing at their gay little madnesses, my dear, at their point-to-points, at the postural slump of the well-off and mentally under-privileged, at their stooping shoulders and strained accents, at their waffling cant, for too long. They are no longer funny, because they are not merely dangerous, they are murderous. I don't think I want to make people laugh at them any more, because they are stupid, insensitive, unimaginative beyond hope, uncreative and murderous. I, too, have done nothing. I was furious with unbelief, but I went on going to work, answering my correspondence and talking to my friends. I behaved like any other 'intellectual' of my generation. We sat at home, well fed, with our reputations and our bank accounts intact, and left it to some hard-up little Unitarian who was over sixty to hitch-hike all the way, making the only gesture on his own. Nobody laughed at us, we made quite sure of that. 'H-Bomb Harold' the brave lads of Fleet Street called him. No doubt he was a crank, or he may not have been very smart or intelligent, but he was the only one of us who had the decency or the courage to leave his wife and children, take his savings out of the bank and make his comical little protest that was certain to fail. The liars in Westminster saw to that, the liars in Fleet Street saw to it. We 'intellectuals' saw to it, with our 'campaigns' and our signatures. During the

Suez Crisis I had collected signatures to a letter to *The Times*! That was the limit of my imagination then. True, it was a very militant letter, possibly seditious even, which may have been the reason why it was not published. This time I didn't even send a letter to *The Times*. A writer can demonstrate feeling. It takes an extraordinary human being to demonstrate action as well. Most weeks my own courage allowance doesn't last beyond Monday lunchtime . . .

I have called royalty religion the 'national swill' because it is poisonous, what an old vegetarian I used to know would call 'foodless food', or, as Orwell might have put it, the leader-writers and the bribed gossipmongers have only to rattle their sticks in the royalty bucket for most of their readers to put their heads down in this trough of Queen-worship, their tails turned against the world. It just doesn't seem so funny any more . . .

My objection to the royal symbol is that it is dead; it is the gold filling in a mouthful of decay. While the cross symbol represented *values*, the crown simply represents a *substitute* for values. When the Roman crowds gather outside St Peter's, they are taking part in a moral *system*, however detestable it may be. When the mobs rush forward in the Mall they are taking part in the last circus of a civilization that has lost faith in itself, and sold itself for a splendid triviality, for the 'beauty of the ceremonial' and the 'essential spirituality of the rite'. We may not create any beauty or exercise much spirituality, but by God! we've got the finest ceremonial and rites in the world! Even the Americans haven't got that.

Ever since a generation thrilled to an announcer intoning the lines about its king's life moving peacefully to its close, the BBC has produced a staff of highly-trained palace lackeys with graveyard voices, and a ponderous language stuffed with Shakespearian and semi-biblical echoes. It is all as nourishing and useful as wax fruit under a glass case. But to a nation that finds her most significant myths in the idiot heroes of *Reach for the Sky* and *Battle of the River Plate* and longs for aggrandizement but cannot afford a new set of teeth or a breast plate that will save her from humiliation, it is about the one wholly satisfying thing left.

Because royalty is deprived of active political power, and therefore of the necessity to make moral, or any other, decisions, it is presented with a staggering power that gives it a greater grip on the public imagination than any other single institution. While commanding a unique position, it is protected from ever having to solve a problem or make a choice. It is not mercly above criticism, it is above the necessity of having to justify its existence. It is unhealthy because it encourages a peculiarly sloppy-cynical attitude to politics.

Nobody can seriously pretend that the royal round of gracious boredom, the protocol of ancient fatuity, is politically useful or morally stimulating: the state visits to countries like France and Portugal which successfully fulfil the monarchy function of disguising important political issues – such as the barbarity of the French Government's policy in Algeria, and the openly anti-democratic constitution of Portugal – in a sludge of generalized patriotic feelings. As for the ship launchings, the visits to 'establishments', the polo games, the night-clubs with well-bred nobodies, the TV appearances, the endless concentration at the racecourse, the Christmas Day set-cant: are these the crowning interests of a rich, healthy culture? Is no one aghast at the thought of a lifetime of reading about the first day at prep-school, the measles, the first dance, the wedding, and finally the beauty of the ceremonial?

It bores me, it distresses me that there should be so many empty minds, so many empty lives in Britain to sustain this fatuous industry; that no one should have had the wit to laugh it into extinction, or the honesty to resist it. I don't believe that there can be one intellectual in the Labour Party who doesn't find it hilarious or contemptible. Naturally they would never dream of losing all those votes by saying so, but as long as they encourage people to revel in the political and literal horseplay of a meaningless symbol, they need not expect the masses to start discovering meanings in a serious political idea like socialism. A socialist party that is not republican is not crediting its potential followers with reason or intelligence. By suggesting to a man that fatuity, as long as it is hallowed by tradition, is acceptable and admirable, you cannot expect him to treat a complex social concept with any seriousness. He is not conditioned to seriousness but to totem worship. While a ridiculous anachronism is reverenced as a serious institution the road to socialism will be bedevilled by regard for implicit ruling-class ideals like 'restraint', 'good taste', 'healthy caution' and so on.

•

JOSIAH MWANGI KARIUKI
1957

'A British beating'

Josiah Mwangi Kariuki wrote A Kikuyu Tells His Story *in 1963 when Kenya was an independent state and he was the Member of Parliament for the Aberdares, voted in by 25,000 farm workers and following two Old Etonians. Eleven years earlier he had taken two Mau Mau oaths during the Kikuyu rebellion against British rule and spent seven years in detention camps, where he was victimized by British prison officers because of his habit of smuggling out letters of complaint to British MPs and senior Kenyan officials about the prisoners' treatment. He was kept in a 6ft by 4ft prison cell on half rations and in one six-month period received 200 strokes of the cane.*

'Rochester' is a pseudonym disguising the name of a former army officer.

After a while Rochester and Buxton realized that I was not going to confess voluntarily, and, more dangerous still, that I had begun to collect a following which was like-minded. So they decided to use their ultimate weapon – force. One day they called me and told me they now wished me to confess. As usual I refused and I also told them clearly that they could only rehabilitate someone when he decided to be rehabilitated, and that any confessions extracted under force were not binding. At this point I was given a strong blow by Rochester which knocked me down.

Slowly I rose to my feet and I was then taken to another open place near the ration stores where three other men were called to come and help screen me. They were Jonah and Elijah, both from Nyeri, and a clerk from Kiambu. Four Europeans were also present, Rochester, Buxton and two prison officers. They said that this was my last chance to confess. I gave the same reply as before. Slowly and significantly they started on me. Europeans only; the African screeners took no part in what happened: people said that the Europeans thought they could do it without going too far and that they were frightened the Africans would deliver a fatal blow. Many of the detainees working nearby could see what was happening and after what seemed a long while, just before I mercifully fell unconscious, I saw Kiragu Wamugure, a great friend from Lodwar, standing among a group with tears streaming down their cheeks at my extreme suffering. My face was puffed up and split open, my right knee was fractured just below the kneecap by a club, and my chest was pierced by a strange instrument like a black truncheon with nails in it. I failed to die but the scars on my knees and chest will always be with me and I still suffer from severe attacks of pain in my abdomen and thorax. I was shaved completely, the blood flowing from that operation too. The screeners eventually carted me away, my clothes splotched red with blood, and paraded me in triumph past the barbed-wire compounds, telling my friends to come and see what their leader looked like now. I was thrown into a small cell and for two days no food was brought near me; even if it had been I should not have been able to open my mouth to put it in. The evening of my beating-up a detainee hanged himself in Compound 4. His sleeping companion, Jimmy from Embu, told me that he had seen my treatment and had said that he could not stand living in this hell any longer. He had used the rope which was issued by the government to tie up our shorts.

The third day some detainees brought gruel to me. They said that the people in the camp were very worried that I would be beaten to death and they had been sent by the others to beg me to go and make a confession of some sort, remembering that it was forced and could therefore be retracted later. They also felt that this would then give me a chance of writing a letter to the authorities telling them what was going on. They did not want me to die, they wanted me to stay with them, even if I was now going to be a cripple for life.

•

LORD ALTRINCHAM
1957

'A pain in the neck'

It was the newspaper 'silly season' in Britain when the thirty-three-year-old Lord Altrincham (now John Grigg) published a critique of the monarchy in The National and English Review. *It provoked an outcry, perhaps because he was an Old Etonian and former Guards officer. He was assaulted in the street and threatened with shooting or a horse-whipping by opponents who failed to appreciate the strongly monarchist nature and motivation of his protest.*

Altrincham's essay was followed within weeks by another making similar criticisms, though in a more journalistic manner than Altrincham, from Malcolm Muggeridge. Both were critics who were ahead of their times.

When she has lost the bloom of youth the Queen's reputation will depend, far more than it does now, upon her personality. It will not then be enough for her to go through the motions; she will have to say things which people can remember, and do things on her own initiative which will make people sit up and take notice. As yet there is little sign that such a personality is emerging. But time, though no longer clearly on her side, is not yet her enemy.

If it is vital that the monarchy should transcend race, it is hardly less necessary that it should transcend class. Social distinctions are bound to exist in any large community. To pretend that they do not exist is naive or hypocritical, and to seek to eliminate them by state action may become a dire threat to liberty and to other civilized values which must at all costs be protected. Yet the crown must not seem to be identified with any particular social group. The relatively classless character of George V unfortunately is not to be seen in his grand-daughters. The Queen and Princess Margaret still bear the debutante stamp.

Why is this? The most likely reason is that they were given a conventional upper-class education. This is, perhaps, the price which had to be paid for the Queen Mother's many services, and for the matchless charm which she has brought to her high position. 'Crawfie', Sir Henry Marten, the London season, the racecourse, the grouse moor, canasta, and the occasional Royal tour – all this would not have been good enough for Queen Elizabeth I! It says much for the Queen that she has not been incapacitated for her job by this woefully inadequate training. She has dignity, a sense of duty and (so far as one can judge) goodness of heart – all precious assets. But will she have the wisdom to give her children an education very different from her own? Will she, above all, see to it that Prince Charles is equipped with all the knowledge he can absorb without injury to his health, and that he mixes during his formative years with children who will one day be bus drivers, dockers, engineers, etc. – not merely with future landowners or stockbrokers? These are crucial questions.

The Queen's private choice of friends may or may not be inspiring, but in any case it is not a legitimate matter for public comment. On the other hand, it is quite in order to criticize public functions, such as the Presentation Parties, which are a grotesque survival from the monarchy's hierarchical past. These parties should certainly have been quietly discontinued in 1945. They pander to snobbishness and give the Queen the appearance of standing at the apex of an aristocratic and plutocratic pyramid. People have a right to 'bring out' their daughters in whatever way they please, but the crown's benison should be reserved for those who have qualified for it by public service.

The present composition of the court emphasizes the social lopsidedness to which the monarchy is still prone. The Queen's entourage – those who serve her from day to day, who accompany her when she travels and sit with her when she eats – are almost without exception people of the tweedy sort. Such people may be shrewd, broad-minded and thoroughly suitable for positions at court, but the same is true of many who are not tweedy; and the fact that the Queen's personal staff represents almost exclusively a single social type creates an unfortunate impression. Worse still, courtiers are nearly always citizens of one Commonwealth country – the United Kingdom. In other words, the court has lamentably failed to move with the times; while the monarchy has become popular and multi-racial, the court has remained a tight little enclave of British 'ladies and gentlemen'. This cannot be right.

The Queen should surely now be surrounded by advisers and companions with as many different backgrounds as possible. A truly classless and Commonwealth court would not only bear eloquent witness to the transformed nature of the monarchy, but would also give the Queen and her family the advantage of daily contact with an interesting variety of personalities and points of view. It would not, of course, be desirable to appoint courtiers on any strict rationing principle – so many Canadians, so many Africans, so many trade unionists, so many aesthetes, so many Socialists, so many Tories, and so on. This would be an absurdity. But granted the fitness of someone for a post at court, political and social considerations should also be taken into account before an appointment is made. Thus there would be no sudden or artificial change, but over a period of time the composition of the court would gradually become more catholic and more representative . . .

The advent of broadcasting gave a new importance to the spoken word, and George V, as has been said, made excellent use of the opportunity so provided. George VI did his best, but was handicapped by an impediment in his speech and by being a rather less imposing version of his father. The Duke of Edinburgh, who is a first-rate speaker, has recently moved, not without success, into the domain of television. To this the Royal Family, like all others who are engaged in public life, will have to pay increasing attention, and in fact the Queen's Christmas broadcast will this year, for the first time, be televised.

She will not, however, achieve good results with her present style of speaking, which is frankly a pain in the neck. Like her mother, she appears to be unable to string even a few sentences together without a written text – a defect which is particularly regrettable when she can be seen by her audience. Courtiers are apt to justify this failure to speak spontaneously with the argument that she must first and foremost guard against the danger of indiscretion or misunderstanding. But this is humbug. The occasional lapse – even if it were to occur – would do very little harm by comparison with the immense good which would be done if the Queen appeared to speak from the heart. Phrases such as 'I am deeply moved' sound very hollow when they are read from a typescript. But even if the Queen feels compelled to read all her speeches, great and small, she must at least improve her method of reading them. With practice even a prepared speech can be given an air of spontaneity.

The subject-matter also must be endowed with a more authentic quality. George V, for instance, did not write his own speeches, yet they were always in character; they seemed to be a natural emanation from, and expression of, the man. Not so the present Queen's. The personality conveyed by the utterances which are put into her mouth is that of a priggish schoolgirl, captain of the hockey team, a prefect, and a recent candidate for Confirmation. It is not thus that she will be enabled to come into her own as an independent and distinctive character.

•

J. B. PRIESTLEY
1957

'Nuclear madness'

Although he is best known as a novelist, author of Angel Pavement *and* The Good Companions, *J. B. Priestley (1894–1984) was also a playwright (*An Inspector Calls*), broadcaster (especially during the Second World War) and essayist. When Priestley wrote this article for the* New Statesman *in 1957, Aneurin Bevan had shaken his supporters on the left by opposing unilateral nuclear disarmament. A British Foreign Secretary could not go 'naked into the conference chamber', Bevan had declared. The Soviet Union had also launched its first two satellites, the Sputniks.*

It was this article – and another by Bertrand Russell – which inspired the meetings which led to the formation of the Campaign for Nuclear Disarmament. According to Michael Foot, Priestley's argument that the British should lead the way to nuclear sanity infused the whole CND campaign.

We ended the war high in the world's regard. We could have taken over its moral leadership, spoken and acted for what remained of its conscience; but we chose to act otherwise – with obvious and melancholy consequences both abroad, where in power politics we cut a shabby figure, and at home, where we shrug it all away or go to the theatre to applaud the latest jeers and sneers at Britannia. It has been said we cannot send our ministers naked to the conference table. But the sight of a naked minister might bring to the conference some sense of our human situation. What we do is something much worse: we send them there half-dressed, half-smart, half-tough, half-apologetic, figures inviting contempt. That is why we are so happy and excited when we can send abroad a good-looking young woman in a pretty new dress to represent us, playing the only card we feel can take a trick – the Queen.

It is argued, as it was most vehemently by Mr Bevan at Brighton, that if we walked out of the nuclear arms race then the world would be 'polarized' between America and the Soviet Union, without any hope of mediation between the two fixed and bristling camps. 'Just consider for a moment,' he cried, 'all the little nations running, one here and one there, one running to Russia, the other to the US, all once more clustering under the castle wall . . .' But surely this is one of those 'realistic' arguments that are not based on reality. The idea of the Third Force was rejected by the very party Mr Bevan was addressing. The world was polarized when, without a single protest from all the noisy guardians of our national pride, parts of East Anglia ceased to be under our control and became an American air base. We cannot at one and the same time be both an independent power, bargaining on equal terms, and a minor ally or satellite. If there are little nations that do not run for shelter to the walls of the White House or the Kremlin because they are happy to accept Britain as their nuclear umbrella, we hear very little about them. If it is a question of brute power, this argument is unreal.

It is not entirely stupid, however, because something more than brute power is involved. There is nothing unreal in the idea of a third nation, especially one like ours, old and experienced in world affairs, possessing great political traditions, to which other and smaller nations could look while the two new giants mutter and glare at each other. But it all depends what the nation is doing. If it is still in the nuclear gamble, without being able to control or put an end to the game, then that nation is useless to others, is frittering away its historical prestige, and the polarization, which Mr Bevan sees as the worst result of our rejection of nuclear warfare, is already an accomplished fact. And if it is, then we must ask ourselves what we can do to break this polarity, what course of action on our part might have some hope of changing the world situation. To continue doing what we are doing will not change it. Even during the few weeks since Mr Bevan made his speech the world is becoming more rigidly and dangerously polarized than ever, just because the Russians have sent a metal football circling the globe. What then can Britain do to de-polarize the world?

The only move left that can mean anything is to go into reverse, decisively rejecting nuclear warfare. This gives the world something quite different from the polarized powers: there is now a country that can make H-bombs but decides against them. Had Britain taken this decision some years ago the world would be a safer and saner place than it is today. But it is still not too late. And such a move will have to be 'unilateral'; doomsday may arrive before the nuclear powers reach any agreement; and it is only a decisive 'unilateral' move that can achieve the moral force it needs to be effective.

It will be a hard decision to take because all habit is against it. Many persons of consequence and their entourages of experts would have to think fresh thoughts. They would have to risk losing friends and not influencing people. For example, so far as they involve nuclear warfare, our commitments to Nato, Seato and the rest, and our obligations to the Commonwealth, would have to be sharply adjusted. Anywhere from Brussels to Brisbane, reproaches would be hurled, backs would be turned. But what else have these countries to suggest, what way out, what hope for man? And if, to save our souls and this planet, we are willing to remain here and take certain risks, why should we falter because we might have complaints from Rhodesia and reproaches from Christchurch, NZ? And it might not be a bad idea if the Nato peoples armed themselves to defend themselves, taking their rifles to the ranges at the weekend, like the Swiss.

American official and service opinion would be dead against us, naturally. The unsinkable (but expendable) aircraft carrier would have gone. Certain Soviet bases allotted to British nuclear attack would have to be included among the targets of the American Strategic Air Service. And so on and so forth. But though service chiefs and their staffs go on examining and marking the maps and planning their logistics, having no alternative but resignation, they are as fantastic and unreal in their way as their political and diplomatic colleagues are in theirs. What is fantastic and unreal is their assumption that they are traditionally occupied with their professional duties, attending in advance to the next war, Number Three in the world series. But what will happen – and one wrong report by a sleepy observer might start it off – will not be anything recognizable as a war, an affair of victories and defeats, something that one side can win or that you can call off when you have had enough. It will be universal catastrophe and apocalypse, the crack of doom into which Communism, Western democracy, their way of life and our way of life, may disappear for ever. And it is not hard to believe that this is what some of our contemporaries really desire, that behind their photogenic smiles and cheerful patter nothing exists but the death wish.

We live in the thought of this prospect as if we existed in a permanent smog. All sensible men and women – and this excludes most of those who are in the *VIP-Highest-Priority-Top-Secret-Top-People Class*, men now so conditioned by this atmosphere of power politics, intrigue, secrecy, insane invention, that they are more than half-barmy – have no illusions about what is happening to us, and know that those responsible have made two bad miscalculations. First, they have prostituted so much science in their preparations for war that they have completely changed the character of what they are doing, without any equivalent change in the politics of and relations between states. Foreign affairs, still conducted as if the mobilization of a few divisions might settle something, are now backed with push-button arrangements to let loose earthquakes and pestilences and pronounce the death sentences of continents. This leaves us all in a worse dilemma than the sorcerer's apprentice. The second miscalculation assumed that if the odds were only multiplied fast enough, your side would break through because the other side would break down. And because this has not happened, a third illusion is being welcomed, namely, that now, with everything piling up, poker chips flung on the table by the handful, the tension obviously increasing, now at last we are arriving at an acknowledged drawn game, a not-too-stale stale-mate, a cosy old balance of power. This could well be the last of our illusions.

The risk of our rejecting nuclear warfare, totally and in all circumstances, is quite clear, all too easy to understand. We lose such bargaining power as we now possess. We have no deterrent to a nuclear threat. We deliberately exchange 'security' for insecurity. (And the fact that some such exchange is recommended by the major religions, in their earlier and non-establishment phases, need not detain us here.) But the risk is clear and the arguments against running it quite irrefutable, only if we refuse, as from the first too many of us here have refused, to take anything but short-term conventional views, only if we will not follow any thought to its conclusion. Our 'hard-headed realism' is neither hard-headed nor realistic just because it insists on our behaving in a new world as if we were still living in an old world, the one that has been replaced.

Britain runs the greatest risk by just mumbling and muddling along, never speaking out, avoiding any decisive creative act. For a world in which our deliberate 'insecurity' would prove to be our undoing is not a world in which real security could be found. As the game gets faster, the competition keener, the unthinkable will turn into the inevitable, the weapons will take command, and the deterrents will not deter. Our bargaining power is slight; the force of our example might be great. The catastrophic antics of our time have behind them men hag-ridden by fear, which explains the neurotic irrationality of it all, the crazy disproportion between means and ends. If we openly challenge this fear, then we might break the wicked spell that all but a few uncertified lunatics desperately wish to see broken, we could begin to restore the world to sanity and lift this nation from its recent ignominy to its former grandeur. Alone, we defied Hitler; and alone we can defy this nuclear madness into which the spirit of Hitler seems to have passed, to poison the world. There may be other chain-reactions besides those leading to destruction; and we might start one. The British of these times, so frequently hiding their decent, kind faces behind masks of sullen apathy or sour, cheap cynicism, often seem to be waiting for something better than party squabbles and appeals to their narrowest self-interest, something great and noble in its intention that would make them feel good again. And this might well be a declaration to the world that after a certain date one power able to engage in nuclear warfare will reject the evil thing for ever.

•

EDWARD R. MURROW
1958

'Television'

It was Ed Murrow (1908–65) who reported on the Blitz to America during the Second World War, always with the words – and a dramatic pause after the first – 'This is London.'

He returned to the United States but, having angered the powerful CBS chairman William Paley by attacking Senator McCarthy and departing from the CBS policy of strict objectivity, he was relegated to a minor role on the next election night. At the 1958 Chicago Convention, when asked to speak to the Radio and Television News Directors Association, Murrow said: 'Somebody ought to make a speech on one of these occasions which would outrage all our employers.' His protest, delivered in 'accents of despair' according to one observer, certainly shortened his career.

This nation is now in competition with malignant forces of evil who are using every instrument at their command to empty the minds of their subjects and fill those minds with slogans, determination and faith in the future. If we go on as we are, we are protecting the mind of the American public from any real contact with the menacing world that squeezes in upon us. We are engaged in a great experiment to discover whether a free public opinion can devise and direct methods of managing the affairs of the nation. We may fail. But we are handicapping ourselves needlessly.

Let us have a little competition. Not only in selling soap, cigarettes and automobiles, but in informing a troubled, apprehensive, but receptive public. Why should not each of the twenty or thirty big corporations which dominate radio and television decide that they will give up one or two of their regularly scheduled programs each year, turn the time over to the networks, and say in effect: 'This is a tiny tithe, just a little bit of our profits. On this particular night we aren't going to try to sell cigarettes or automobiles; this is merely a gesture to indicate our belief in the importance of ideas.' The networks should, and I think would, pay for the cost of producing the program. The advertiser, the sponsor, would get name credit but would have nothing to do with the content of the program. Would this blemish the corporate image? Would the stockholders object? I think not. For if the premise upon which our pluralistic society rests, which as I understand it is that if the people are given sufficient undiluted information, they will then somehow, even after long, sober second thoughts, reach the right decision – if that premise is wrong, then not only the corporate image but the corporations are done for.

There used to be an old phrase in this country, employed when someone talked too much. It was: 'Go hire a hall.' Under this proposal the sponsor would have hired the hall; he has bought the time; the local station operator, no matter how indifferent, is going to carry the program – he has to. Then it's up to the networks to fill the hall. I am not here talking about editorializing but about straightaway exposition as direct, unadorned and impartial as fallible human beings can make it. Just once in a while let us exalt the importance of ideas and information. Let us dream to the extent of saying that on a given Sunday night the time normally occupied by Ed Sullivan is given over to a clinical survey of the state of American education, and a week or two later the time normally used by Steve Allen is devoted to a thoroughgoing study of American policy in the Middle East. Would the corporate image of their respective sponsors be damaged? Would the stockholders rise up in their wrath and complain? Would anything happen other than that a few million people would have received a little illumination on subjects that may well determine the future of this country, and therefore the future of the corporations? . . .

It may be that the present system, with no modifications and no experiments, can survive. Perhaps the money-making machine has some kind of built-in perpetual motion, but I do not think so. To a very considerable extent the media of mass communications in a given country reflect the political, economic and social climate in which they flourish. That is the reason ours differ from the British and French, or the Russian and Chinese. We are currently wealthy, fat, comfortable and complacent. We have currently a built-in allergy to unpleasant or disturbing information. Our mass media reflect this. But unless we get up off our fat surpluses and recognize that television in the main is being used to distract, delude, amuse and insulate us, then television and those who finance it, those who look at it and those who work at it, may see a totally different picture too late.

I do not advocate that we turn television into a twenty-seven-inch wailing wall, where longhairs constantly moan about the state of our culture and our defense. But I would just like to see it reflect occasionally the hard, unyielding realities of the world in which we live. I would like to see it done inside the existing framework, and I would like to see the doing of it redound to the credit of those who finance and program it. Measure the results by Nielsen, Trendex, or Silex – it doesn't matter. The main thing is to try. The responsibility can be easily placed, in spite of all the mouthings about giving the public what it wants. It rests on big business, and on big television, and it rests at the top. Responsibility is not something that can be assigned or delegated. And it promises its own reward: good business and good television.

Perhaps no one will do anything about it. I have ventured to outline it against a background of criticism that may have been too harsh only because I could think of nothing better. Someone once said – I think it was Max Eastman – that 'that publisher serves his advertiser best who best serves his readers.' I cannot believe that radio and television, or the corporations that finance the programs, are serving well or truly their viewers or listeners, or themselves.

Our history will be what we make it. If we go on as we are, then history will take its revenge, and retribution will not limp in catching up with us.

We are to a large extent an imitative society. If one or two or three corporations would undertake to devote just a small fraction of their advertising appropriation along the lines that I have suggested, the procedure would grow by contagion; the economic burden would be bearable, and there might ensue a most exciting adventure – exposure to ideas and the bringing of reality into the homes of the nation.

To those who say people wouldn't look; they wouldn't be interested; they're too complacent, indifferent and insulated, I can only reply: There is, in one reporter's opinion, considerable evidence against that contention. But even if they are right, what have they got to lose? Because if they are right, and this instrument is good for nothing but to entertain, amuse and insulate, then the tube is flickering now and we will soon see that the whole struggle is lost.

This instrument can teach, it can illuminate; yes, and it can even inspire. But it can do so only to the extent that humans are determined to use it to those ends. Otherwise it is merely wires and lights in a box. There is a great and perhaps decisive battle to be fought against ignorance, intolerance and indifference. This weapon of television could be useful.

Stonewall Jackson, who knew something about the use of weapons, is reported to have said, 'When war comes, you must draw the sword and throw away the scabbard.' The trouble with television is that it is rusting in the scabbard during a battle for survival.

•

J. K. GALBRAITH
1958

The Affluent Society

When the American economist J. K. Galbraith (1908–) was writing his onslaught on the affluent society, he wondered if his timing was right: 'The premature prophet shares the precise fate of the crackpot.' Then, in autumn 1957, the Soviet Union launched the first Sputnik, 'the result of a much more purposeful use of a much less productive economy'. Galbraith knew he would be heard. As he explains in this extract, amidst America's affluence, there was also grim, degrading poverty.

An affluent society, that is also both compassionate and rational, would, no doubt, secure to all who needed it the minimum income essential for decency and comfort. The corrupting effect on the human spirit of a small amount of unearned revenue has unquestionably been exaggerated as, indeed, have the character-building values of hunger and privation. To secure to each family a minimum standard, as a normal function of the society, would help ensure that the misfortunes of parents, deserved or otherwise, were not visited on their children. It would help ensure that poverty was not self-perpetuating. Most of the reaction, which no doubt would be almost universally adverse, is based on obsolete attitudes. When poverty was a majority phenomenon, such action could not be afforded. A poor society had to enforce the rule that the person who did not work could not eat. And possibly it was justified in the added cruelty of applying the rule to those who could not work or whose efficiency was far below par. An affluent society has no similar excuse for such rigour. It can use the forthright remedy of providing for those in want. Nothing requires it to be compassionate. But it has no high philosophical justification for callousness.

None the less any such forthright remedy for poverty is beyond reasonable hope. Also, as in the limiting case of the alcoholic or the mental incompetent, it involves difficulties. To spend income requires a minimum of character and intelligence even as to produce it. By far the best hope for the elimination, or in any case the minimization, of poverty lies in less direct but, conceivably, almost equally effective means.

The first and strategic step in an attack on poverty is to see that it is no longer self-perpetuating. This means ensuring that the investment in children from families presently afflicted be as little below normal as possible. If the children of poor families have first-rate schools and school attendance is properly enforced; if the children, though badly fed at home, are well nourished at school; if the community has sound health services, and the physical well-being of the children is vigilantly watched; if there is opportunity for advanced education for those who qualify regardless of means; and if, especially in the case of urban communities, law and order are well enforced and recreation is adequate – then there is a very good chance that the children of the very poor will come to maturity without grave disadvantage. In the case of insular poverty this remedy requires that the services of the community be assisted from outside. Poverty is self-perpetuating because the poorest communities are poorest in the services which would eliminate it. To eliminate poverty efficiently we should invest more than proportionately in the children of the poor community. It is there that high-quality schools, strong health services, special provision for nutrition and recreation are most needed to compensate for the very low investment which families are able to make in their own offspring.

The effect of education and related investment in individuals is to enable them either to contend more effectively with their environment, or to escape it and take up life elsewhere on more or less equal terms with others. The role of education as an antidote to the homing instinct which crowds people into the areas of inadequate opportunity and frustration is also clear. However, in the strategy of the attack on insular poverty a place remains for an attack on the frustrations of the environment itself. This is particularly clear in the case of the slum. Slum clearance and expansion of low- and middle-income housing removes a comprehensive set of frustrations and greatly widens opportunity. There is a roughly parallel opportunity in the rural slum. By identifying a land use which is consistent with a satisfactory standard of living, and by assisting with the necessary reorganization of land and capital, public authority can help individuals to surmount frustrations to which they are now subject. The process promises to be expensive and also time-consuming. But the question is less one of feasibility than of will.

Nor is poverty in the contemporary generation wholly intransigent. Much can be done to treat those characteristics which cause people to reject or be rejected by the modern industrial society. Educational deficiencies can be overcome. Mental deficiencies can be treated. Physical handicaps can be remedied. The limiting factor is not knowledge of what can be done. Overwhelmingly it is our failure to invest in people. The myopic preoccupation with production and material investment has diverted our attention from the more urgent questions of how we are employing our resources and, in particular, from the greater need and opportunity for investing in persons.

Here is a paradox. When we begin to consider the needs of those who are now excluded from the economic system by accident, inadequacy or misfortune – we find that the normal remedy is to make them or their children productive citizens. This means that they add to the total output of goods. We see once again that even by its *own terms* the present preoccupation with material as opposed to human investment is inefficient. The parallel with investment in the supply of trained and educated manpower will be apparent.

No one would be called upon to write at such length on a problem so easily solved as that of increasing production. The main point lies elsewhere. Poverty – grim, degrading and ineluctable – is not remarkable in India. For few the fate is otherwise. But in the United States the survival of poverty is remarkable. We ignore it because we share with all societies at all times the capacity for not seeing what we do not wish to see. Anciently this has enabled the nobleman to enjoy his dinner while remaining oblivious to the beggars around his door. In our own day it enables us to travel in comfort through south Chicago and the South. But while our failure to notice can be explained, it cannot be excused. 'Poverty', Pitt exclaimed, 'is no disgrace but it is damned annoying.' In the contemporary United States it is not annoying but it is a disgrace.

•

ALEX COMFORT
1958

'Ban the Bomb'

The Campaign for Nuclear Disarmament, founded in 1958, two years after Suez and Hungary, became the most celebrated pressure group in Britain. Its supporters included Bertrand Russell, A. J. P. Taylor, Canon John Collins, J. B. Priestley (see page 243), Michael Foot and Trevor Huddleston. Eight thousand people took part in a fifty-mile march to the Atomic Weapons Research Establishment at Aldermaston. Subsequently the march from Aldermaston to Trafalgar Square became an annual Easter event, supported by thousands.

CND's protest, 'Ban the Bomb,' was simple to understand and it attracted the support of middle-class activists and students in search of a cause. Its aims were set out in this speech by Alex Comfort at the inaugural meeting in London's Conway Hall.

For many years now, and most evidently since last year, the salient new factor in the politics of Europe has been the growing discontent of ordinary men and women with the policies of inhumanity; of anger and disillusion with compromises, double talk and cruelty, and with the complete lack of principle which has become the rule in government since Hitler.

In Russia, and in the other Communist countries, reason has been genuinely in revolt; and scientists there have rebelled, and rebelled effectively, against the abuse of science, as the younger generation is rebelling against Stalinism. The atomic scientist Kapitza spent years under house arrest for refusing to work on atomic bombs.

In Germany, physicists have declared that they will not lend themselves to the development of nuclear weapons.

I choose scientists as examples, not because they have any greater moral duty to rebel against folly than others, but because in Britain and America they have been culpably slow to do so; among the public at large there is growing anger and apprehension all over Europe at the risks which are being run, and the absence of good faith among those who are running them.

However much this discontent is exploited for electoral purposes, I do not see the parties today giving an answer to the hundreds of people, of all persuasions, who are asking what they, individually, can do to reassert the rule of sanity. That is the function of the campaign which we are launching here tonight: to make every individual reassume the moral responsibility for opposing public insanity. The issue is one for direct action by every one of us.

We are not at the mercy of the government, nor of events, nor of the policy of other nations, nor of the world situation, if we are prepared as a public to be sufficiently combative . . .

Within the coming weeks we intend to raise throughout the country a solid body of opposition to the whole strategy of moral bankruptcy and ceremonial suicide which the hydrogen bomb epitomizes, to all the mentally under-privileged double-talk by which it has been justified.

I would urge every one of us at this meeting to go home determined to become a living focus of that opposition. Some of us are going to march to Aldermaston on Good Friday, whether the Minister of Works likes it or not. Some of us live in areas which have been selected to receive American guided missile bases.

The government is intensely anxious about public reaction to those bases, and is trying to keep their location secret.

If there are no local committees in your area, keeping their eyes open for base-building activity, form one. If there is no focus for public opposition to nuclear tests and nuclear weapons in your district, in your church, among your neighbours, become one. If you are not already exerting pressure on your Member, on the Prime Minister, on the press, on any scientists involved in unethical projects whose addresses you can get, begin to do so now, by letter and by lobbies.

It is high time we held some atomic tests of our own – in Downing Street.

Much has been said about a summit conference. Sanity is always hardest to restore at the summit – the air there is rarefied. It seems to affect the brain. We can reassert it at the base.

The people must take over – you must take over. The leaders of all the parties are waiting, as they always wait on any issue of principle, to follow public opinion. We can coerce them.

Gaitskell and Bevan say they will not abandon the H-bomb unilaterally. If they were here tonight, they would see that in this issue their party is abandoning them unilaterally.

We can make Britain offer the world something which is virtually forgotten – moral leadership. Let us make this country stand on the side of human decency and human sanity – alone if necessary. It has done so before. If it does so again I do not think we need fear the consequences.

•

ENOCH POWELL
1959

'Hola Camp'

Enoch Powell (1912–98) was one of the most gifted, principled and controversial Conservative politicians of his era, who achieved notoriety in 1968 when he delivered an inflammatory speech attacking Kenyan Asian immigrants in which he used the phrase: 'I seem to see the River Tiber foaming with much blood.' (See The Penguin Book of Twentieth-Century Speeches.)

Once a professor of Greek (and a future Minister of Health), Powell was still a backbencher when an official inquiry confirmed allegations of brutality at the Kenyan detention camp at Hola, where batons and rifle butts had been used on Mau Mau detainees and eleven men had died (allegedly after drinking dirty water). His coruscating speech, insisting on ministerial responsibility, and made at 1 a.m., was remembered by many MPs on both sides of the House as the best they ever heard. As Powell ended, he sat down and cried. He said later: 'One of the exhilarations of being a member of the House of Commons, if you experience it, are the moments when you actually have it in your hand, in which you play upon it like an instrument.'

The speech remains the most powerful memory of his long career.

I am as certain of this as I am of anything, that my right hon. Friend the Secretary of State from the beginning to the end of this affair is without any jot or tittle of blame for what happened in Kenya, that he could not be expected to know, that it could not be within the administrative conventions that these matters should be brought to his attention before or during the execution. When I say my right hon. Friend was in this matter utterly and completely blameless, that is of a piece with his administration of his high office generally, which has been the greatest exercise of the office of Colonial Secretary in modern times. It is in the name of that record, it is in the name of his personal blamelessness, that I beg of him to ensure that the responsibility is recognized and carried where it properly belongs, and is seen to belong.

I have heard it suggested that there were circumstances surrounding this affair at Hola Camp which, it is argued, might justify the passing over of this responsibility – which might justify one in saying, 'Well, of course, strictly speaking, that is quite correct: but then here there were special circumstances.'

It has been said – and it is a fact – that these eleven men were the lowest of the low; sub-human was the word which one of my hon. Friends used. So be it. But that cannot be relevant to the acceptance of responsibility for their death. I know that it does not enter into my right hon. Friend's mind that it could be relevant, because it would be completely inconsistent with his whole policy of rehabilitation, which is based upon the assumption that whatever the present state of these men, they can be reclaimed. No one who supports the policy of rehabilitation can argue from the character and condition of these men that responsibility for their death should be different from the responsibility for anyone else's death. In general, I would say that it is a fearful doctrine, which must recoil upon the heads of those who pronounce it, to stand in judgement on a fellow human being and to say, 'Because he was such-and-such, therefore the consequences which would otherwise flow from his death shall not flow.'

It is then said that the morale of the Prison Service, the morale of the whole Colonial Service, is above all important and that whatever we do, whatever we urge, whatever we say, should have regard to that morale. 'Amen' say I. But is it for the morale of the Prison Service that those who executed a policy should suffer – whether inadequately or not is another question – and those who authorized it, those to whom they appealed, should be passed over? I cannot believe that that supports the morale of a service.

Going on beyond that, my hon. Friend the Member for Leicester, South-East (Mr Peel) reminded the House how proud the Colonial Service is of the integrity of its administration and its record. Nothing could be more damaging to the morale of such a service than that there should be a breath of a blemish left upon it. No, sir; that argument from the morale of the Prison Service and the Colonial Service stands on its head if what we mean is that therefore the consequences of responsibility should not follow in this case as they would in any other similar case.

Finally it is argued that this is Africa, that things are different there. Of course they are. The question is whether the difference between things there and here is such that the taking of responsibility there and here should be upon different principles. We claim that it is our object – and this is something which unites both sides of the House – to leave representative institutions behind us wherever we give up our rule. I cannot imagine that it is a way to plant representative institutions to be seen to shirk the acceptance and the assignment of responsibility, which is the very essence of responsible Government.

Nor can we ourselves pick and choose where and in what parts of the world we shall use this or that kind of standard. We cannot say, 'We will have African standards in Africa, Asian standards in Asia and perhaps British standards here at home.' We have not that choice to make. We must be consistent with ourselves everywhere. All government, all influence of man upon man, rests upon opinion. What we can do in Africa, where we still govern and where we no longer govern, depends upon the opinion which is entertained of the way in which this country acts and the way in which Englishmen act. We cannot, we dare not, in Africa of all places, fall below our own highest standards in the acceptance of responsibility.

•

ANTHONY CROSLAND
1960

'A contempt for ordinary people'

Anthony Crosland's The Future of Socialism, *published in 1956, was the most important theoretical treatise written from the moderate left of British politics in the twenty-five postwar years, according to his friend and political rival Roy Jenkins. It assumed the triumph of Keynesianism, disputed the importance of nationalization, and challenged the bureaucratic socialism of the Webbs.*

The article that Crosland (1918–77) wrote for Encounter *four years later was described by Christopher Booker, in* The Neophiliacs, *his study of the sixties, as the first full-dress statement of the new political mood, even as Harold Macmillan was riding high, that swept Labour to power in 1964.*

Complacent, stagnant, obsolete, modernization, innovation, change – all the key words used by the pacemakers of the English revolution appeared in Crosland's reflections on the future of the left.

A dogged resistance to change now blankets every segment of our national life. A middle-aged conservatism, parochial and complacent, has settled over the country; and it is hard to find a single sphere in which Britain is pre-eminently in the forefront. Our production and export performance is almost the poorest of any advanced industrial country; and in individual industries one constantly finds that the only dynamic firm is controlled by an American, a Canadian, an Irishman or a refugee. The Trade Union and Co-operative Movements share with the Labour Party a profound conservatism of outlook. Our Parliament and Civil Service, brilliantly adapted to the needs of a by-gone age, and which we still seek to export unmodified to ex-colonial territories, are in fact in need of drastic modernization. Oxford and Cambridge are the last universities in the world to recognize the newer social sciences. Much of our technical education is equally backward.

We cling to every outmoded scrap of national sovereignty, continue to play at the obsolete role of imperial power, and fail to adjust to the new, dynamic Europe; Commonwealth fanatics on the Right and nuclear disarmers on the Left share an equal blindness to our changed position in the world. Our deplorable postwar architecture and city planning demonstrate a failure of nerve in the face of contemporary cultural problems. We are the last country to build a flyover or a motorway; yet our transport system is no more antiquated than our licensing laws, our attitude to homosexuality, British football or the Labour Party Constitution.

No doubt we still lead the world in certain traditional spheres – merchant banking, classical scholarship, trooping the colour, sailing the Atlantic single-handed. But wherever innovation is required, we see a frightful paralysis of the will. The cause is partly our oppressive, traditional pattern of class relations, partly the psychological difficulty of adapting from great power to second-rate international status, partly the complacent ignorance bred by an insular tradition. Eventually, one hopes, a rebellious younger generation, aided by much increased intercourse with the outside world, will shatter the present mood. Meanwhile, radical reformers everywhere will meet tenacious opposition from conservative 'stand-patters'.

This conservatism is particularly marked within the Labour Party, which manifests a colossal resistance to change. In my original *Encounter* article I argued that the party's defeat was due to its failure to recognize and welcome the transformation of our society – not to ill-chance or sudden prosperity or the machinations of Colman, Prentice & Varley. This diagnosis has since been abundantly confirmed, notably by the Nuffield study of the general election and by Dr Mark Abram's survey in *Socialist Commentary*. The steady upgrading of the working class, both occupationally and still more in terms of social aspirations, renders Labour's one-class image increasingly inappropriate. Some of the party's old-style policies are thought (rightly) to be often irrelevant to present-day conditions. And younger voters react especially strongly against both Labour's class image and its identification with the problems and attitudes of a past generation – with the fantastic consequence that the young now see the complacent, sluggish, hidebound Conservatives as the party of change and opportunity!

Evidently the Labour Party must adapt itself to these new realities. This problem has faced every Socialist party in every developed country. Some have faced it successfully, others not. The majority (notably the Dutch, Swedish, German, Austrian, Swiss and New Zealand parties) have both broadened their appeal and thoroughly overhauled their basic programmes. A minority (notably the French, Japanese and Australian parties) have clung obstinately either to outworn Marxist dogma (especially ludicrous in France) or to a purely sectional, class appeal. The 'revisionist' parties have been markedly more successful in maintaining or improving their position; indeed, the three 'fundamentalist' parties mentioned above have all suffered from damaging splits.

Yet the Labour Party shows some signs (to put it mildly) of drifting into the fundamentalist category. No doubt this is partly due to the absence of really effective reforming leadership. A high proportion of the party's leaders have seen fit, at a moment of historic party crisis, to maintain a deafening silence on the entire question of the party's future; while those few leaders who have spoken out for change have (with the notable exception of Mr Morgan Phillips) not only shown a most imperfect sense of tactics, but have also conducted their campaign in a singularly fitful, unplanned and dilettante manner – adequate, no doubt, to the country-house politics of pre-1914, but wholly inappropriate in a modern mass party. We may note the contrast with the concerted, systematic campaign for modernization which the quartet Brandt–Schmid–Erler–Wehner conducted so successfully in the German *SPD*.

But the resistance to change of course has deeper causes. Plainly Labour suffers seriously from the national vice of conservatism. But there are also factors internal to the party itself. The first is a tendency to blame the voters for their new prosperity, and to explain, smugly and self-righteously, that we were defeated because (in the words of Mrs Barbara Castle) 'our ethical reach was beyond the mental grasp of the average person'. The second is an ostrich-like reluctance to admit the evidence of what people are thinking; it arises from the extraordinary fear that a party which tries to deal with the real problems of real men and women will become immoral, power-centred, 'indistinguishable from the Tories'. The third is the conviction of the 'millennialists' that Labour need only wait, uncompromising and uncontaminated, for the inevitable capitalist crisis. All three betray a priggish self-satisfaction, a contempt for the judgement of ordinary people and an indifference to their interests, which is wholly alien to the party's tradition and, in itself, enough to condemn it to opposition and sterility.

•

KINGSLEY AMIS
1960

'More will mean worse'

The author of Lucky Jim *started his contribution to* Encounter's *views of the fifties in characteristic style by saying that the 'sociologizing generalization' was swelling in volume and variety. Kingsley Amis (1922–96) was not as he had been dubbed an angry young man but an old-fogey with distinctly right-wing views. As a university lecturer at Swansea (later at Cambridge), he was convinced that university expansion was wrong. His phrase 'More will mean worse' was constantly recalled as seven new universities were created in the 1960s. By the 1990s, when there were more than ninety and student numbers had increased threefold, Amis was even more convinced he had been right.*

Nobody who has not seen it in all its majesty – I speak as a university lecturer – can imagine the pit of ignorance and incapacity into which British education has sunk since the war. It is a pretty good pit not only in depth but laterally, for it takes in everyone from the kindergarten to the House of Lords, assuming these as opposite poles. Here at last I feel I have come up with a really man-sized fifties trend, one which justifies the utmost dis– oops: one which disquiets and vexes me.

The trouble is not just illiteracy, even understanding this as including unsteady grasp of the fundamentals of a subject as well as unsteadiness with hard words like *goes* and *its*. But for the moment I want to drum the fact of that illiteracy into those who are playing what I have heard called the university numbers racket, those quantitative thinkers who believe that Britain is *falling behind* America and Russia by not producing as many university graduates per head, and that she must *catch up* by building *more* colleges which will turn out *more* graduates and so give us *more* technologists (especially them) and *more* schoolteachers. I wish I could have a little tape-and-loudspeaker arrangement sewn into the binding of this magazine, to be triggered off by the light reflected from the reader's eyes on to this part of the page, and set to bawl out at several decibels: MORE WILL MEAN WORSE.

I do not know whether it is better to have three really bad schoolteachers where formerly there were two mediocre ones, and I have no information about what can be expected to happen to technologists, but I am quite sure that a university admissions policy demanding even less than it now demands – for that is what a larger intake means – will wreck academic standards beyond repair. Already a girl who has literally never heard of metre (I found this out last week) can come to a university to study English literature; what will her successors never have heard of if the doors are opened wider – rhyme, poem, sentence? Not only will examining standards have to be lowered to enable worse and worse people to graduate – you cannot let them all in and then not allow most of them to pass – but the good people will be less good than they used to be: this has been steadily happening ever since I started watching in 1949. Please do not think that I am resenting the prospect of being tugged into the hurly-burly and away from the little circle of devotees with whom I am currently exploring the niceties of Pope's use of the caesura. What I explore with the chaps already tends to be far more the niceties of who Pope was.

My personal stake in this is twofold. I do not fancy teaching in something that is called a university but is really a rather less glamorous and authentic training college. And I do not fancy living in a society which has abandoned the notion of the university as a centre of learning. Powerful forces, both inside and outside its walls, are bringing this notion under ever more intense attack. The mere acceptance of expansion (we are promised a 50 per cent increase in students by 1970) is itself, I have argued, equivalent to such attack.

More will mean worse. The delusion that there are thousands of young people about who are capable of benefiting from university training, but have somehow failed to find their way there, is of course a necessary component of the expansionist case. It means that one can confidently mention a thing called *quality* and say it will be *maintained*. University graduates, however, are like poems or bottles of hock, and unlike cars or tins of salmon, in that you cannot *decide* to have more good ones. All you can decide to have is more. And MORE WILL MEAN WORSE.

Many university teachers work hard at *not* stereotyping their students. If many of these enter the great world in fuddled and temporary possession of tutorial opinions, this is because, after the most dedicated probing, they have shown no sign of forming any of their own.

The demand for expansion is frequently coupled with the demand for more science, and therefore less arts, in the university. We live in a scientific age, you see. It might be thought that this is just when you want more arts, but no. We are to have more 'general courses' of mixed, i.e. diluted, science and arts, more science for the arts students – oh, and arts for the scientists too, naturally. If any policy-making educational body should ever turn away for a moment from its corps of nodding vice-chancellors and go so far as to consult someone actually engaged in teaching, they will be told (unless indeed they pick, as they will tend to and be encouraged to, one of the growing body of numbers-racketeers) that it is already hard enough to turn out an arts graduate who knows something about arts, without eating into his time at the university, and at school, in order to provide him with a smattering of biology or physics. What they will almost certainly not be told is that the humanities are in danger and must be defended. That case, to the permanent shame of those engaged in the humanities, is going by default. Last March I wrote to the *Observer* to attack some vulgar TV boost for technology, and inquired whether there was anybody who was prepared to 'refute the phantom dichotomy of "the two cultures", repudiate the ever more widely accepted view of the humanities as behind the times, vague, decorative, marginal, contemplative, postponable, while science (which in this context usually means technology) is seen as up with the times, precise, essential, central, active, urgent'. I had answer enough. There was nobody. Why are there no voices, lone or otherwise, in our arts faculties?

•

COLIN WELCH
1960

'Dear little Noddy'

Enid Blyton's books can be almost as big a subject of everyday protest among parents of young children as the profounder issues of war and peace – as this Encounter *essay by the* Daily Telegraph *journalist Colin Welch (1924–97) published in* The Odd Thing About The Colonel, *a collection of his journalism, demonstrates.*

If you have small children and they don't like Noddy, you are very lucky. I have; they do; I am not. This insipid wooden doll, with its nodding head crowned with cap and bell, with its taxi and its friend Big Ears, has opened a rift between parents and children which time alone may heal. They love it; we don't. And we can't agree to differ, live and let live, because we parents have to sit and read the stuff to them.

The Noddy business has by now taken its place among Britain's major non-warlike industries, along with sauce-bottling, the Pools, cheesecake photography and the manufacture of ice-lollies, righteous indignation and plastic pixies. The business is founded on the mass-production of Noddy books, of which 12 million had been sold two years ago: twelve titles, that is to say, and about a million sold of each. The export branch produces Noddy books in countless foreign languages, including Tamil, Hebrew and Swahili. By-products, controlled by five separate companies, include Noddy soap and Noddy chocolates, Noddy pyjamas and nighties, Noddy painting books, jigsaws, Christmas annuals, cut-outs on cereal packets and models ('smashing fun modelling Noddy and his friends: all easily made from Sculptorcraft Rubber Moulds'). Noddy has also appeared on television and the West End stage, though not yet at the Royal Court.

Noddy's onlie begetter is a former schoolmistress called Enid Blyton. The really outstanding thing about her is her industry. In the five years 1948–52 inclusive, she managed to fill nearly four close-printed columns of Whitaker's Cumulative Book List – 261 titles by my count. In 1955 she clocked up fifty-nine titles, more than a book a week (not all of them about Noddy, of course). Last year, flagging slightly, she only managed twenty-eight. She also produces a fortnightly magazine ('the only magazine I write'), runs four children's clubs (the Famous Five Club, the Busy Bees, the Sunbeam Society and the Magazine Club), and personally answers a thousand or more fan-letters a week. Miss Blyton is, by Johnson's definition, no blockhead. Even two years ago, the royalties on Noddy alone totalled £400,000. With an income estimated at £50,000 a year, she must be about the highest-paid woman in the British Isles.

The essence of a children's classic – perhaps of any classic – is that it can be enjoyed at a number of different levels. The *Adventures of Alice in Wonderland* and *Through the Looking-Glass*; the tales of Grimm and Andersen; the wistful nonsense of Edward Lear; Beatrix Potter's strange stories, in which the matter-of-fact surface half conceals a sort of mysterious poetry; *The Wind in the Willows*, *Doctor Dolittle* and *Winnie the Pooh* – all these books have delighted generations of children. They have also delighted generations of grown-ups. And when parents read them to their children, it is to experience a complex harmony of pleasures: they find delight in the book itself; they recapture the delight it once brought them as children; and they see awakened that same delight in a new generation. These books thus form a most precious link between the generations, binding them together, part of the family, for ever part of the life of each member of it.

To compare say, Winnie the Pooh with Noddy is not really unfair. Both appeal primarily to the same age group, both with complete success. In other respects, the difference is startling. The Pooh stories are written with wit, taste and economy of means, and with an almost magical felicity of form. For sheer craftsmanship take the story 'in which Pooh and Piglet go hunting and nearly catch a woozle'. The mounting suspense as these two enchanting fools plod round and round the tree in the snow, tracking first one woozle, then two, three and four, and the effortless way in which the illusion is finally pricked, make this in miniature a perfect short story. Compared with such happy mastery, Noddy is mere drooling, shapeless meandering – 'cotton from a reel'.

If children enjoy Noddy, is that all that matters? Miss Blyton, of course, wouldn't think so; neither would I. By writing ruthlessly *down* to children, she does not merely bore and antagonize grown-ups. Her Noddy books also fail to stretch the imagination of children, to enlarge their experience, to kindle wonder in them or awaken their delight in words. They contain nothing incomprehensible even to the dimmest child; nothing mysterious or stimulating. They have no 'contact with nescience'; they never suggest new and exciting fields to conquer. By putting everything within reach of the child mind, they enervate and cripple it.

In this witless, spiritless, snivelling, sneaking doll the children of England are expected to find themselves reflected. From it they are to derive 'ethical and moral' edification. But Noddy is not merely an example: he is a symbol. Noddy, according to Miss Blyton, 'is completely English, and stands for the English way of life. He's very popular in Germany. It's interesting to think that a generation of young Germans is absorbing English standards and English morals.' The Russians, it seems, have pirated some of Miss Blyton's books, but not yet Noddy. 'I wish they would,' says Miss Blyton. 'I don't care about the royalties – I should like the Russian children to read English stories. It might help them to understand our way of life.' It is disquieting to reflect that they might indeed.

RICHARD HOGGART
1960

'One fucks'

Regina v *Penguin Books, the Lady Chatterley trial of 1960, added greatly to public entertainment. It followed the publication of an unexpurgated paperback edition of D. H. Lawrence's notorious novel by Penguin which distributed 200,000 copies in a direct challenge to the prevailing censorship laws. The prosecuting counsel, Mr Mervyn Griffith Jones, provoked great derision when he asked the jury, 'Is it a book you would wish your wife or servants to read?'*

Many distinguished witnesses appeared for Penguin including Dame Rebecca West, the Bishop of Woolwich, C. V. Wedgwood, Cecil Day Lewis and Roy Jenkins (who subsequently became a reforming Home Secretary). Another was Richard Hoggart, author of The Uses of Literacy *and senior lecturer in English literature at Leicester University. This account of his defence of Lawrence is from the Penguin edition of* The Trial of Lady Chatterley, *edited by C. H. Rolph.*

Lawrence's descriptions of 'sexual intercourse' (itself a ponderous euphemism that grew more irritating as the trial went on) were again referred to by Mr Hutchinson in a question about their alleged monotony – 'varying only in the *locus in quo*'. He asked for Mr Hoggart's view about that. 'I would deny that absolutely,' replied Mr Hoggart. 'Again, it is a gross misreading of the whole book. I don't know how many times sexual intercourse takes place in the book, perhaps eight or ten times; and any good reading of the book, I don't mean a highbrow's reading, a good decent person's reading of the book, shows there is no one the same as the next; each one is a progression of greater honesty and a greater understanding. If one reads them as being a series of acts of sexual intercourse, one is doing violence to Lawrence's whole intention, and not reading what is in the text.'

'By the time you have reached the end of the book, have those two persons, in your view of the reading of it, found some true and real contact, as opposed to all the contacts at the beginning of the book?' – 'Yes, I think the ending of the book has a result which one can hardly find in literature now. He is able to say things in the letter he writes at the end, the very last page, "Now is the time to be chaste, it is so good to be chaste, like a river of cool water in my soul." This is the writing of a pure man. "I love the chastity now that it flows between us. It is like fresh water and rain. How can men want wearisomely to philander," that is, to be promiscuous. This seems to me a resolution which establishes that the book has moved through the whole cycle.'

'It is quite obvious, of course, that this relationship is between two people who in fact are married. Would you say this book advocates – it obviously describes – but would you say it advocates adultery?' – 'I think the book advocates marriage, not adultery. It takes a difficult and distressing human situation which we know exists. A marriage which has gone wrong, which had never started right. It doesn't burk the issue by saying they went on somehow, and this is very much to the point. He could have made this analysis of the realization of the solution through sex by a wife who did not love her husband. He stacked the cards against himself. He was talking about the nature of a true marriage relationship between people. We know there are bound to be occasions in human beings, sometimes for very bad reasons and sometimes for reasons that are unavoidable, when there is friction between our formal state of marriage and the relationship we meet with, the genuine relationship he is talking about. He did not say, if you want to enjoy yourself in sex you should leave your wife or husband, but the thing to do in a marriage was to work hard at every level. When you get up in the morning and cook the breakfast, don't lose your temper with the children. Having gone through all this they will get married. He tells us so; they are waiting for it.'

'In your view is there anything more in this book than, at the end, two people finding a state of satisfactory sexual relationship?' – 'There is not only more in it than that, but one could say – although it sounds paradoxical – one could say the physical sexual side is subordinate. I am sure it was for Lawrence. He said more than once that really he is not interested, not unduly interested, in sexual acts. He is interested in a relationship between people which is in the deepest sense spiritual. This includes a due and proper regard for our sexual and physical side. I believe in this book what he said is, "I must face this problem head on, even at the risk of having people think I am obsessed by sex." But one realizes from this last letter that, between Mellors and Lady Chatterley, there will be periods of extraordinary chasteness; there will be moments of coming together in love which will be all the better because they are not using one another like creatures for enjoyment. It is a kind of sacrament for him.'

'I want to pass now to the four-letter words. You told the jury yesterday you were educated at an elementary school. Where was it?' – 'Leeds.'

'How did you start your life?' – 'I was born into the working class and I was orphaned at the age of eight and brought up by my grandmother.'

'What is your view as to the genuineness and necessity in this book of the use of these four-letter words in the mouth of Mellors?' – 'They seem to me totally characteristic of many people, and I would like to say not only working-class people, because that would be wrong. They are used, or seem to me to be used, very freely indeed, far more freely than many of us know. Fifty yards from this Court this morning I heard a man say "fuck" three times as he passed me. He was speaking to himself and he said "fuck it, fuck it, fuck it" as he went past. If you have worked on a building site, as I have, you will find they recur over and over again. The man I heard this morning and the men on building sites use the words as words of contempt, and one of the things Lawrence found most worrying was that the word for this important relationship had become a word of vile abuse. So one would say "fuck you" to a man, although the thing has totally lost its meaning; it has become simply derision, and in this sense he wanted to re-establish the meaning of it, the proper use of it.'

'What do you say about the use of these words as they have been used in this book?' – 'The first effect, when I first read it, was some shock, because they don't go into polite literature normally. Then as one read further on one found the words lost that shock. They were being progressively purified as they were used. We have no word in English for this act which is not either a long abstraction or an evasive euphemism, and we are constantly running away from it, or dissolving into dots, at a passage like that. He wanted us to say "This is what one does. In a simple, ordinary way, one fucks," with no sniggering or dirt.'

•

FRANTZ FANON
1960

'*The Wretched of the Earth*'

Frantz Fanon (1925–61) was born in Martinique, trained as a psychiatrist in France and became an activist in the Algerian revolution. He criticized African élites for their narrow nationalism and bourgeois tendencies and called on African intellectuals to identify with the aspirations of their people. Using his experience of treating Algerian mental patients, he praised the therapeutic effect of revolutionary violence on the minds of the colonized – an idea which was embraced by America's Black Panthers, who rejected the non-violent methods advocated by Martin Luther King.

Fanon's book The Wretched of the Earth *has been named by the journal* Foreign

Affairs *as one of the most significant books of the century. This extract is from the conclusion.*

Come, then, comrades; it would be as well to decide at once to change our ways. We must shake off the heavy darkness in which we were plunged, and leave it behind. The new day which is already at hand must find us firm, prudent and resolute.

We must leave our dreams and abandon our old beliefs and friendships of the time before life began. Let us waste no time in sterile litanies and nauseating mimicry. Leave this Europe where they are never done talking of Man, yet murder men everywhere they find them, at the corner of every one of their own streets, in all the corners of the globe. For centuries they have stifled almost the whole of humanity in the name of a so-called spiritual experience. Look at them today swaying between atomic and spiritual disintegration.

And yet it may be said that Europe has been successful in as much as everything that she has attempted has succeeded.

Europe undertook the leadership of the world with ardour, cynicism and violence. Look at how the shadow of her palaces stretches out ever farther! Every one of her movements has burst the bounds of space and thought. Europe has declined all humility and all modesty; but she has also set her face against all solicitude and all tenderness.

She has only shown herself parsimonious and niggardly where men are concerned; it is only men that she has killed and devoured.

So, my brothers, how is it that we do not understand that we have better things to do than to follow that same Europe?

That same Europe where they were never done talking of Man, and where they never stopped proclaiming that they were only anxious for the welfare of Man: today we know with what sufferings humanity has paid for every one of their triumphs of the mind.

Come, then, comrades, the European game has finally ended; we must find something different. We today can do everything, so long as we do not imitate Europe, so long as we are not obsessed by the desire to catch up with Europe.

Europe now lives at such a mad, reckless pace that she has shaken off all guidance and all reason, and she is running headlong into the abyss; we would do well to avoid it with all possible speed.

Yet it is very true that we need a model, and that we want blueprints and examples. For many among us the European model is the most inspiring. We have seen to what mortifying setbacks such an imitation has led us.

European achievements, European techniques and the European style ought no longer to tempt us and to throw us off our balance.

When I search for Man in the technique and the style of Europe, I see only a succession of negations of man, and an avalanche of murders.

The human condition, plans for mankind and collaboration between men in those tasks which increase the sum total of humanity are new problems, which demand true inventions.

Let us decide not to imitate Europe; let us combine our muscles and our brains in a new direction. Let us try to create the whole man, whom Europe has been incapable of bringing to triumphant birth.

•

CHE GUEVARA
1961

'A million hands'

The face of Che Guevara (1928–67), the Argentinian Communist revolutionary leader, was posted on the walls of hundreds of thousands of students' rooms in the sixties. As the architect with Fidel Castro of the Cuban revolution against 'American imperialism', he became a student activist hero, especially after he was executed by government troops in the presence of a CIA agent in 1967 as he tried to foment revolt in Bolivia.

President Kennedy pushed through bills imposing sanctions against countries that bought Cuban sugar with American loans and cut off security assistance to nations that gave any aid to Cuba. An indignant Castro responded with his first Havana Declaration. The reason for his protest was described by Che Guevara in this speech in Uruguay.

In May 1960, the conflict with imperialism became open and acute. The oil companies operating in Cuba, invoking the right of might and ignoring the laws of the republic that clearly specified their obligations, refused to refine the petroleum we had purchased from the Soviet Union, in the exercise of our free right to trade with the whole world and not with one part thereof.

Everybody knows how the Soviet Union responded, sending us, with real effort, hundreds of ships to carry 3,600,000 tons per year – our total imports of crude petroleum – to keep in operation all of the industrial machinery which works on the basis of petroleum today.

In July 1960 there was the economic aggression against Cuban sugar, which some governments have not yet perceived. The differences became more acute, and the OAS meeting took place in Costa Rica in August of 1960. There the meeting [of Ministers of Foreign Affairs] declared that it 'Condemns energetically the intervention or threat of intervention, even when conditional, by an extracontinental power in the affairs of the American republics' and declared that 'the acceptance of a threat of extracontinental intervention by any American state endangers American solidarity and security, and that this obliges the Organization of American States to disapprove it and reject it with equal vigour.'

That is to say, the American republics, meeting in Costa Rica, denied us the right to defend ourselves. This is one of the strangest denials ever made in the history of international law. Naturally, our people are a little refractory with respect to the voice of technical meetings and they met in the Assembly of Havana and approved unanimously – more than a million hands raised to the skies, one-sixth of the country's total population – the Declaration of Havana, which states in part as follows:

The People's National General Assembly reaffirms – and is sure that in doing so it is expressing the common criterion of the peoples of Latin America – that democracy is incompatible with financial oligarchy, with the existence of discrimination against the Negro and the excesses of the Ku Klux Klan, and with the persecution that deprived scientists such as Oppenheimer of their jobs, that for years prevented the world from hearing the wonderful voice of Paul Robeson, a prisoner in his own country, and that led the Rosenbergs to their death, in the face of the protests and the horror of the whole world and despite the appeals of the leaders of various countries and of Pope Pius XII.

The People's National General Assembly of Cuba expresses the Cuban conviction that democracy cannot consist merely in the exercise of an electoral vote which is nearly always fictitious and is directed by large landowners and professional politicians, but rather in the right of the citizens to decide their own destinies, as this People's Assembly is now doing. Furthermore, democracy will exist in Latin America only when its peoples are really free to choose, when the humble are no longer reduced – by hunger, by social inequality, by illiteracy and by the judicial systems – to the most hopeless impotence.

And further, the People's National General Assembly of Cuba condemned 'the exploitation of man by man, and the exploitation of the underdeveloped countries by imperialist financial capital'.

That was a declaration of our people, made before the world, to show our determination to defend with arms, with blood, with our lives, our freedom and our right to control the destinies of the country, in the way that our people deem most advisable.

•

STUDENTS FOR A DEMOCRATIC SOCIETY
1962

'A new left'

Students for a Democratic Society was founded in 1960 in the United States but did not hold its first convention until 1962 when it set out its manifesto in the seminal Port Huron statement which led to the rise of the New Left. The statement attacked nuclear deterrence, capitalism and the paternalist welfare state, the military industrial complex, the university in loco parentis, the Soviet Union (for suppressing dissent) and the United States (for supporting right-wing dictatorships) – all the themes that inspired the student protests which reached their climax in 1968 – the year of the barricades.

We are people of this generation, bred in at least modest comfort, housed now in universities, looking uncomfortably to the world we inherit.

When we were kids the United States was the wealthiest and strongest country in the world; the only one with the atom bomb, the least scarred by modern war, an initiator of the United Nations that we thought would distribute Western influence throughout the world. Freedom and equality for each individual, government of, by and for the people – these American values we found good, principles by which we could live as men. Many of us began maturing in complacency.

As we grew, however, our comfort was penetrated by events too troubling to dismiss. First, the permeating and victimizing fact of human degradation, symbolized by the Southern struggle against racial bigotry, compelled most of us from silence to activism. Second, the enclosing fact of the Cold War, symbolized by the presence of the Bomb, brought awareness that we ourselves, and our friends, and millions of abstract 'others' we knew more directly because of our common peril, might die at any time. We might deliberately ignore, or avoid, or fail to feel all other human problems, but not these two, for these were too immediate and crushing in their impact, too challenging in the demand that we as individuals take the responsibility for encounter and resolution.

While these and other problems either directly oppressed us or rankled our consciences and became our own subjective concerns, we began to see complicated and disturbing paradoxes in our surrounding America. The declaration 'All men are created equal . . .' rang hollow before the facts of Negro life in the South and the big cities of the North. The proclaimed peaceful intentions of the United States contradicted its economic and military investments in the Cold War status quo . . .

Our work is guided by the sense that we may be the last generation in the experiment with living. But we are a minority – the vast majority of our people regard the temporary equilibriums of our society and world as eternally functional parts. In this is perhaps the outstanding paradox: we ourselves are imbued with urgency, yet the message of our society is that there is no viable alternative to the present. Beneath the reassuring tones of the politicians, beneath the common opinion that America will 'muddle through', beneath the stagnation of those who have closed their minds to the future, is the pervading feeling that there simply are no alternatives, that our times have witnessed the exhaustion not only of utopias, but of any new departures as well. Feeling the press of complexity upon the emptiness of life, people are fearful of the thought that at any moment things might be thrust out of control.

They fear change itself, since change might smash whatever invisible framework seems to hold back chaos for them now. For most Americans, all crusades are suspect, threatening. The fact that each individual sees apathy in his fellows perpetuates the common reluctance to organize for change. The dominant institutions are complex enough to blunt the minds of their potential critics, and entrenched enough to swiftly dissipate or entirely repel the energies of protest and reform, thus limiting human expectancies. Then, too, we are a materially improved society, and by our own improvements we seem to have weakened the case for further change.

Some would have us believe that Americans feel contentment amidst prosperity – but might it not be better called a glaze above deeply felt anxieties about their role in the new world? And if these anxieties produce a developed indifference to human affairs, do they not as well produce a yearning to believe there *is* an alternative to the present, that something *can* be done to change circumstances in the school, the workplaces, the bureaucracies, the government? It is to this latter yearning, at once the spark and engine of change, that we direct our present appeal. The search for truly democratic alternatives to the present, and a commitment to social experimentation with them, is a worthy and fulfilling human enterprise, one which moves us and, we hope, others today . . .

We regard *men* as infinitely precious and possessed of unfulfilled capacities for reason, freedom, and love. In affirming these principles we are aware of countering perhaps the dominant conceptions of man in the twentieth century: that he is a thing to be manipulated, and that he is inherently incapable of directing his own affairs. We oppose the depersonalization that reduces human beings to the status of things – if anything, the brutalities of the twentieth century teach that means and ends are intimately related, that vague appeals to 'posterity' cannot justify the mutilations of the present. We oppose, too, the doctrine of human incompetence because it rests essentially on the modern fact that men have been 'competently' manipulated into incompetence – we see little reason why men cannot meet with increasing skill the complexities and responsibilities of their situation, if society is organized not for minority, but for majority, participation in decision-making . . .

Human relationships should involve fraternity and honesty. Human interdependence is contemporary fact; human brotherhood must be willed, however, as a condition of future survival and as the most appropriate form of social relations. Personal links between man and man are needed, especially to go beyond the partial and fragmentary bonds of function that bind men only as worker to worker, employer to employee, teacher to student, American to Russian . . .

We would replace power rooted in possession, privilege or circumstance by power and uniqueness rooted in love, reflectiveness, reason and creativity. As a *social system* we seek the establishment of a democracy of individual participation, governed by two central aims: that the individual share in those social decisions determining the quality and direction of his life; that society be organized to encourage independence in men and provide the media for their common participation.

Any new left in America must be, in large measure, a left with real intellectual skills, committed to deliberativeness, honesty, reflection as working tools. The university permits the political life to be an adjunct to the academic one, and action to be informed by reason.

A new left must be distributed in significant social roles throughout the country. The universities are distributed in such a manner.

A new left must consist of younger people who matured in the postwar world, and partially be directed to the recruitment of younger people. The university is an obvious beginning point.

A new left must include liberals and socialists, the former for their relevance, the latter for their sense of thoroughgoing reforms in the system. The university is a more sensible place than a political party for these two traditions to begin to discuss their differences and look for political synthesis.

A new left must start controversy across the land, if national policies and national apathy are to be reversed. The ideal university is a community of controversy, within itself and in its effects on communities beyond.

A new left must transform modern complexity into issues that can be understood and felt close-up by every human being. It must give form to the feelings of helplessness and indifference, so that people may see the political, social and economic sources of their private troubles and organize to change society. In a time of supposed prosperity, moral complacency and political manipulation, a new left cannot rely only on aching stomachs to be the engine force of social reform. The case for change, for alternatives that will involve uncomfortable personal efforts, must be argued as never before. The university is a relevant place for all of these activities.

But we need not indulge in illusions: the university system cannot complete a movement of ordinary people making demands for a better life. From its schools and colleges across the nation, a militant left might awaken its allies, and by beginning the process towards peace, civil rights and labor struggles, reinsert theory and idealism where too often reign confusion and political barter. The power of students and faculty united is not only potential; it has shown its actuality in the South, and in the reform movements of the North.

The bridge to political power, though, will be built through genuine cooperation, locally, nationally and internationally between a new left of young people, and an awakening community of allies. In each community we must look within the university and act with confidence that we can be powerful, but we must look outwards to the less exotic but more lasting struggles for justice.

To turn these possibilities into realities will involve national efforts at university reform by an alliance of students and faculty. They must wrest control of the educational process from the administrative bureaucracy. They must make fraternal and functional contact with allies in labor, civil rights and other liberal forces outside the campus. They must import major public issues into the curriculum – research and teaching on problems of war and peace is an outstanding example. They must make debate and controversy, not dull pedantic cant, the common style for educational life. They must consciously build a base for their assault upon the loci of power.

As students for a democratic society, we are committed to stimulating this kind of social movement, this kind of vision and program in campus and community across the country. If we appear to seek the unattainable, as it has been said, then let it be known that we do so to avoid the unimaginable.

FIDEL CASTRO
1962

The duty of a revolutionary

After leading an unsuccessful armed revolt against the Moncada Barracks in 1953, the Cuban revolutionary leader Fidel Castro (1927–) was sentenced to fifteen years' imprisonment but released under an amnesty within a year. He fled to the United States and then Mexico, but landed back in Cuba with a small band of insurgents in 1956. Fidel succeeded in ousting President Batista in 1958, became prime minister in 1959 and proclaimed a Marxist-Leninist state. In 1966 he routed an invasion inspired by the United States at the Bay of Pigs.

The defiant speech he delivered in Havana after Cuba was expelled from the Organization of American States is regarded by sympathizers as one of the great political documents of the time. It became the Second Declaration of Havana, was translated into the major languages and distributed throughout the world.

The duty of every revolutionary is to make the revolution. It is known that the revolution will triumph in America and throughout the world, but it is not for revolutionaries to sit in the doorways of their houses waiting for the corpse of imperialism to pass by. The role of Job doesn't suit a revolutionary. Each year that the liberation of America is speeded up will mean the lives of millions of children saved, millions of intelligences saved for culture, an infinite quantity of pain spared the people. Even if the Yankee imperialists prepare a bloody drama for America, they will not succeed in crushing the peoples' struggles, they will only arouse universal hatred against themselves. And such a drama will also mark the death of their greedy and carnivorous system.

No nation in Latin America is weak – because each forms part of a family of 200 million brothers, who suffer the same miseries, who harbour the same sentiments, who have the same enemy, who dream about the same better future and who count upon the solidarity of all honest men and women throughout the world.

Great as was the epic of Latin American Independence, heroic as was that struggle, today's generation of Latin Americans is called upon to engage in an epic which is even greater and more decisive for humanity. For that struggle was for liberation from Spanish colonial power, from a decadent Spain invaded by the armies of Napoleon. Today the call for struggle is for liberation from the most powerful world imperialist centre, from the strongest force of world imperialism and to render humanity a greater service than that rendered by our predecessors.

But this struggle, to a greater extent than the earlier one, will be waged by the masses, will be carried out by the people; the people are going to play a much more important role now than then, the leaders are less important and will be less important in this struggle than in the one before.

This epic before us is going to be written by the hungry Indian masses, the peasants without land, the exploited workers. It is going to be written by the progressive masses, the honest and brilliant intellectuals, who so greatly abound in our suffering Latin American countries. Struggles of masses and ideas. An epic which will be carried forward by our people, despised and maltreated by imperialism, our people, unreckoned with till today, who are now beginning to shake off their slumber. Imperialism considered us a weak and submissive flock; and now it begins to be terrified of that flock; a gigantic flock of 200 million Latin Americans in whom Yankee monopoly capitalism now sees its gravediggers.

This toiling humanity, inhumanly exploited, these paupers, controlled by the whip and overseer, have not been reckoned with or have been little reckoned with. From the dawn of independence their fate has been the same: Indians, gauchos, mestizos, zambos, quadroons, whites without property or income, all this human mass which formed the ranks of the 'nation', which never reaped any benefits, which fell by the millions, which was cut into bits, which won independence from the mother country for the bourgeoisie, which was shut out from its share of the rewards, which continued to occupy the lowest step on the ladder of social benefits, which continued to die of hunger, curable diseases and neglect, because for them there were never enough essentials of life – ordinary bread, a hospital bed, the medicine which cures, the hand which aids – their fate has been all the same.

But now from one end of the continent to the other they are signalling with clarity that the hour has come – the hour of their redemption. Now this anonymous mass, this America of colour, sombre, taciturn America, which all over the continent sings with the same sadness and disillusionment, now this mass is beginning to enter conclusively into its own history, is beginning to write it with its own blood, is beginning to suffer and die for it . . .

Because now in the fields and mountains of America, on its slopes and prairies and in its jungles, in the wilderness or in the traffic of cities, this world is beginning with full cause to erupt. Anxious hands are stretched forth, ready to die for what is theirs, to win those rights which were laughed at by one and all for 500 years. Yes, now history will have to take the poor of America into account, the exploited and spurned of Latin America, who have decided to begin writing history for themselves for all time. Already they can be seen on the roads, on foot, day after day, in endless marches of hundreds of kilometres to the governmental 'eminences', to obtain their rights.

Already they can be seen armed with stones, sticks, machetes, in one direction and another, each day, occupying lands, sinking hooks into the land which belongs to them and defending it with their lives. They can be seen carrying signs, slogans, flags; letting them flap in the mountain or prairie winds. And the wave of anger, of demands for justice, of claims for rights, which is beginning to sweep the lands of Latin America, will not stop. That wave will swell with every passing day. For that wave is composed of the greatest number, the majorities in every respect, those whose labour amasses the wealth and turns the wheels of history. Now, they are awakening from the long, brutalizing sleep to which they had been subjected.

For this great humanity has said 'enough!' and has begun to march. And their giant march will not be halted until they conquer true independence – for which they have vainly died more than once. Today, however, those who die will die like the Cubans at Playa Girón. They will die for their own true and never-to-be-surrendered independence.

Patria o Muerte! Venceremos!

•

RACHEL CARSON
1962

'The Silent Spring'

Two years after The Silent Spring *was published, the United States banned the domestic use of DDT and other chemical pesticides. Rachel Carson (1907–64), a former marine biologist with the US Fish and Wildlife Service, wrote one of the most influential books of the century, a polemic written in often poetic prose. Carson beat the formidable forces ranged against her by showing the deadly fall-out from indiscriminate crop-spraying and the dangers of pesticides – both to man and the natural environment.*

Only within the moment of time represented by the present century has one species – man – acquired significant power to alter the nature of his world.

During the past quarter-century this power has not only increased to one of disturbing magnitude but it has changed in character. The most alarming of all man's assaults upon the environment is the contamination of air, earth, rivers, and sea with dangerous and even lethal materials. This pollution is for the most part irrecoverable; the chain of evil it initiates not only in the world that must support life but in living tissues is for the most part irreversible. In this now universal contamination of the environment, chemicals are the sinister and little-recognized partners of radiation in changing the very nature of the world – the very nature of its life. Strontium 90, released through nuclear explosions into the air, comes to earth in rain or drifts down as fallout, lodges in soil, enters into the grass or corn or wheat grown there, and in time takes up its abode in the bones of a human being, there to remain until his death. Similarly, chemicals sprayed on croplands or forests or gardens lie long in soil, entering into living organisms, passing from one to another in a chain of poisoning and death. Or they pass mysteriously by underground streams until they emerge and, through the alchemy of air and sunlight, combine into new forms that kill vegetation, sicken cattle, and work unknown harm on those who drink from once pure wells.

It took hundreds of millions of years to produce the life that now inhabits the earth – eons of time in which that developing and evolving and diversifying life reached a state of adjustment and balance with its surroundings. The environment, rigorously shaping and directing the life it supported, contained elements that were hostile as well as supporting. Certain rocks gave out dangerous radiation; even within the light of the sun, from which all life draws its energy, there were short-wave radiations with power to injure. Given time – time not in years but in millennia – life adjusts, and a balance has been reached. For time is the essential ingredient; but in the modern world there is no time.

The rapidity of change and the speed with which new situations are created follow the impetuous and heedless pace of man rather than the deliberate pace of nature. Radiation is no longer merely the background radiation of rocks, the bombardment of cosmic rays, the ultraviolet of the sun that have existed before there was any life on earth; radiation is now the unnatural creation of man's tampering with the atom. The chemicals to which life is asked to make its adjustment are no longer merely the calcium and silica and copper and all the rest of the minerals washed out of the rocks and carried in rivers to the sea; they are the synthetic creations of man's inventive mind, brewed in his laboratories, and having no counterparts in nature.

To adjust to these chemicals would require time on the scale that is nature's; it would require not merely the years of a man's life but the life of generations. And even this, were it by some miracle possible, would be futile, for the new chemicals come from our laboratories in an endless stream; almost 500 annually find their way into actual use in the United States alone. The figure is staggering and its implications are not easily grasped – 500 new chemicals to which the bodies of men and animals are required somehow to adapt each year, chemicals totally outside the limits of biologic experience.

Among them are many that are used in man's war against nature. Since the mid-1940s over 200 basic chemicals have been created for use in killing insects, weeds, rodents, and other organisms described in the modern vernacular as 'pests'; and they are sold under several thousand different brand names.

These sprays, dusts and aerosols are now applied almost universally to farms, gardens, forests, and homes – nonselective chemicals that have the power to kill every insect, the 'good' and the 'bad,' to still the song of birds and the leaping of fish in the streams, to coat the leaves with a deadly film, and to linger on in soil – all this though the intended target may be only a few weeds or insects. Can anyone believe it is possible to lay down such a barrage of poisons on the surface of the earth without making it unfit for all life? They should not be called 'insecticides,' but 'biocides.' . . .

Along with the possibility of the extinction of mankind by nuclear war, the central problem of our age has therefore become the contamination of man's total environment with such substances of incredible potential for harm – substances that accumulate in the tissues of plants and animals and even penetrate the germ cells to shatter or alter the very material of heredity upon which the shape of the future depends.

Some would-be architects of our future look towards a time when it will be possible to alter the human germ plasm by design. But we may easily be doing so now by inadvertence, for many chemicals, like radiation, bring about gene mutations. It is ironic to think that man might determine his own future by something so seemingly trivial as the choice of an insect spray.

All this has been risked – for what? Future historians may well be amazed by our distorted sense of proportion. How could intelligent beings seek to control a few unwanted species by a method that contaminated the entire environment and brought the threat of disease and death even to their own kind? . . .

These insecticides are not selective poisons; they do not single out the one species of which we desire to be rid. Each of them is used for the simple reason that it is a deadly poison. It therefore poisons all life with which it comes in contact: the cat beloved of some family, the farmer's cattle, the rabbit in the field, and the horned lark out of the sky. These creatures are innocent of any harm to man. Indeed, by their very existence they and their fellows make his life more pleasant. Yet he rewards them with a death that is not only sudden but horrible. Scientific observers at Sheldon described the symptoms of a meadow lark found near death: 'Although it lacked muscular coordination and could not fly or stand, it continued to beat its wings and clutch with its toes while lying on its side. Its beak was held open and breathing was labored.' Even more pitiful was the mute testimony of the dead ground squirrels, which 'exhibited a characteristic attitude in death. The back was bowed, and the forelegs with the toes of the feet tightly clenched were drawn close to the thorax . . . The head and neck were outstretched and the mouth often contained dirt, suggesting that the dying animal had been biting at the ground.'

By acquiescing in an act that can cause such suffering to a living creature, who among us is not diminished as a human being?

•

NELSON MANDELA
1962

'Penalties do not deter men when their conscience is aroused'

The 1962 trial of Nelson Mandela (1918–) at the Old Synagogue in Johannesburg, when he was accused of inciting African workers to strike as leader of the African National Congress, marked the start of his international reputation. Mandela turned the trial into a scathing indictment of white domination and challenged the court's moral jurisdiction (as he was to do in the more famous Rivonia trial of 1964 which led to his twenty-two-year imprisonment). (See The Penguin Book of Twentieth-Century Speeches.*)*

Before he was sentenced (to three years for incitement and two for travelling abroad without a passport, the stiffest sentence ever imposed for a political offence) he made an hour-long address to the court which was a declaration of his political testament.

Why is it that in this courtroom I am facing a white magistrate, confronted by a white prosecutor, escorted by white orderlies? Can anybody honestly and seriously suggest that in this type of atmosphere the scales of justice are evenly balanced? Why is it that no African in the history of this country has ever had the honour of being tried by his own kith and kin, by his own flesh and blood? I will tell Your Worship why: the real purpose of this rigid colour bar is to ensure that the justice dispensed by the courts should conform to the policy of the country, however much that policy might be in conflict with the norms of justice accepted in judiciaries throughout the civilized world . . . Your Worship, I hate racial discrimination most intensely and in all its manifestations. I have fought it all my life. I fight it now, and I will do so until the end of my days. I detest most intensely the set-up that surrounds me here. It makes me feel that I am a black man in a white man's court. This should not be.

Many years ago, when I was a boy brought up in my village in the Transkei, I listened to the elders of the tribe telling stories about the good old days before the arrival of the white man. Then our people lived peacefully, under the democratic rule of their kings and their *amapakati* [literally 'insiders', but meaning those closest in rank to the king], and moved freely and confidently up and down the country without let or hindrance. The country was our own, in name and right. We occupied the land, the forests, the rivers; we extracted the mineral wealth beneath the soil and all the riches of this beautiful country. We set up and operated our own government, we controlled our own arms and we organized our trade and commerce. The elders would tell tales of the wars fought by our ancestors in defence of the Fatherland, as well as the acts of valour by generals and soldiers during these epic days . . .

The structure and organization of early African societies in this country fascinated me very much and greatly influenced the evolution of my political outlook. The land, then the main means of production, belonged to the whole tribe and there was no individual ownership whatsoever. There were no classes, no rich or poor and no exploitation of man by man. All men were free and equal and this was the foundation of government. Recognition of this general principle found expression in the constitution of the council, variously called 'Imbizo' or 'Pitso' or 'Kgotla', which governs the affairs of the tribe. The council was so completely democratic that all members of the tribe could participate in its deliberations. Chief and subject, warrior and medicine man, all took part and endeavoured to influence its decisions. It was so weighty and influential a body that no step of any importance could ever be taken by the tribe without reference to it.

There was much in such a society that was primitive and insecure and it certainly could never measure up to the demands of the present epoch. But in such a society are contained the seeds of revolutionary democracy in which none will be held in slavery or servitude, and in which poverty, want and insecurity shall be no more. This is the history which, even today, inspires me and my colleagues in our political struggle.

I would say that the whole life of any thinking African in this country drives him continuously to a conflict between his conscience on the one hand and the law on the other. This is not a conflict peculiar to this country. The conflict arises for men of conscience, for men who think and who feel deeply in every country. Recently in Britain, a peer of the realm, Earl [Bertrand]

Russell, probably the most respected philosopher of the Western world, was sentenced and convicted for precisely the type of activities for which I stand before you today – for following his conscience in defiance of the law, as a protest against the nuclear weapons policy being pursued by his own government. He could do no other than to oppose the law and to suffer the consequences for it. Nor can I. Nor can many Africans in this country. The law as it is applied, the law as it has been developed over a long period of history, and especially the law as it is written and designed by the Nationalist government is a law which, in our views, is immoral, unjust and intolerable. Our consciences dictate that we must protest against it, that we must oppose it and that we must attempt to alter it . . . Men, I think, are not capable of doing nothing, of saying nothing, of not reacting to injustice, of not protesting against oppression, of not striving for the good society and the good life in the ways they see it.

I was made, by the law, a criminal, not because of what I had done, but because of what I stood for, because of what I thought, because of my conscience. Can it be any wonder to anybody that such conditions make a man an outlaw of society? Can it be wondered that such a man, having been outlawed by the government, should be prepared to lead the life of an outlaw, as I have led for some months, according to the evidence before this court?

It has not been easy for me during the past period to separate myself from my wife and children, to say goodbye to the good old days when, at the end of a strenuous day at an office, I could look forward to joining my family at the dinner-table, and instead to take up the life of a man hunted continuously by the police, living separated from those who are closest to me, in my own country, facing continually the hazards of detection and of arrest. This has been a life infinitely more difficult than serving a prison sentence. No man in his right senses would voluntarily choose such a life in preference to the one of normal, family, social life which exists in every civilized community.

But there comes a time, as it came in my life, when a man is denied the right to live a normal life, when he can only live the life of an outlaw because the government has so decreed to use the law to impose a state of outlawry upon him. I was driven to this situation, and I do not regret having taken the decisions that I did take. Other people will be driven in the same way in this country, by this very same force of police persecution and of administrative action by the government, to follow my course, of that I am certain.

I do not believe, Your Worship, that this court, in inflicting penalties on me for the crimes for which I am convicted should be moved by the belief that penalties will deter men from the course that they believe is right. History shows that penalties do not deter men when their conscience is aroused, nor will they deter my people or the colleagues with whom I have worked before.

I am prepared to pay the penalty even though I know how bitter and desperate is the situation of an African in the prisons of this country. I have been in these prisons and I know how gross is the discrimination, even behind the prison wall, against Africans . . . Nevertheless these considerations do not sway me from the path that I have taken nor will they sway others like me. For to men, freedom in their own land is the pinnacle of their ambitions, from which nothing can turn men of conviction aside. More powerful than my fear of the dreadful conditions to which I might be subjected in prison is my hatred for the dreadful conditions to which my people are subjected outside prison throughout this country . . .

Whatever sentence Your Worship sees fit to impose upon me for the crime for which I have been convicted before this court, may it rest assured that when my sentence has been completed I will still be moved, as men are always moved, by their conscience; I will still be moved by my dislike of the race discrimination against my people when I come out from serving my sentence, to take up again, as best I can, the struggle for the removal of those injustices until they are finally abolished once and for all . . .

I have done my duty to my people and to South Africa. I have no doubt that posterity will pronounce that I was innocent and that the criminals that should have been brought before this court are the members of the government.

•

MARTIN LUTHER KING
1963

' "Wait" means "never" '

The remarkable American Negro leader Martin Luther King (1929–68) first captured America's attention when he defied the segregation laws on the buses in Montgomery, Alabama, and the Supreme Court ruled that segregation was unconstitutional. It was a famous victory for King, who was inspired by the non-violent tactics of Gandhi which he believed could be employed to overthrow white supremacy. In 1963 he led the great march on Washington where he delivered one of the most memorable speeches of the century – 'I Have a Dream' (see The Penguin Book of Twentieth-Century Speeches*). Five years later he was assassinated.*

Shortly before the Washington march, King addressed this letter from Birmingham city jail to fellow clergymen who had criticized his activities as 'unwise and untimely'.

We know through painful experience that freedom is never voluntarily given by the oppressor; it must be demanded by the oppressed. Frankly, I have yet to engage in a direct-action campaign that was 'well timed' in the view of those who have not suffered unduly from the disease of segregation. For years now I have heard the word 'Wait!' It rings in the ear of every Negro with piercing familiarity. This 'Wait' has almost always meant 'Never.' We must come to see, with one of our distinguished jurists, that 'justice too long delayed is justice denied.'

We have waited for more than 340 years for our constitutional and God-given rights. The nations of Asia and Africa are moving with jetlike speed toward gaining political independence, but we still creep at horse-and-buggy pace toward gaining a cup of coffee at a lunch counter. Perhaps it is easy for those who have never felt the stinging darts of segregation to say, 'Wait.' But when you have seen vicious mobs lynch your mothers and fathers at will and drown your sisters and brothers at whim; when you have seen hate-filled policemen curse, kick and even kill your black brothers and sisters; when you see the vast majority of your 20 million Negro brothers smothering in an airtight cage of poverty in the midst of an affluent society; when you suddenly find your tongue twisted and your speech stammering as you seek to explain to your six-year-old daughter why she can't go to the public amusement park that has just been advertised on television, and see tears welling up in her eyes when she is told that Funtown is closed to colored children, and see ominous clouds of inferiority beginning to form in her little mental sky, and see her beginning to distort her personality by developing an unconscious bitterness toward white people; when you have to concoct an answer for a five-year-old son who is asking: 'Daddy, why do white people treat colored people so mean?'; when you take a cross-country drive and find it necessary to sleep night after night in the uncomfortable corners of your automobile because no motel will accept you; when you are humiliated day in and day out by nagging signs reading 'white' and 'colored'; when your first name becomes 'nigger,' your middle name becomes 'boy' (however old you are) and your last name becomes 'John,' and your wife and mother are never given the respected title 'Mrs'; when you are harried by day and haunted by night by the fact that you are a Negro, living constantly at tiptoe stance, never quite knowing what to expect next, and are plagued with inner fears and outer resentments; when you are forever fighting a degenerating sense of 'nobodiness' – then you will understand why we find it difficult to wait. There comes a time when the cup of endurance runs over, and men are no longer willing to be plunged into the abyss of despair. I hope, sirs, you can understand our legitimate and unavoidable impatience.

You express a great deal of anxiety over our willingness to break laws. This is certainly a legitimate concern. Since we so diligently urge people to obey the Supreme Court's decision of 1954 outlawing segregation in the public schools, at first glance it may seem rather paradoxical for us consciously to break laws. One may well ask: 'How can you advocate breaking some laws and obeying others?' The answer lies in the fact that there are two types of laws: just and unjust. I would be the first to advocate obeying just laws. One has not only a legal but a moral responsibility to obey just laws. Conversely, one has a moral responsibility to disobey unjust laws. I would agree with St Augustine that 'an unjust law is no law at all.'

Now, what is the difference between the two? How does one determine whether a law is just or unjust? A just law is a man-made code that squares with the moral law or the law of God. An unjust law is a code that is out of harmony with the moral law. To put it in the terms of St Thomas Aquinas: An unjust law is a human law that is not rooted in eternal law and natural law. Any law that uplifts human personality is just. Any law that degrades human personality is unjust. All segregation statutes are unjust because segregation distorts the soul and damages the personality. It gives the segregator a false sense of superiority and the segregated a false sense of inferiority. Segregation, to use the terminology of the Jewish philosopher Martin Buber, substitutes an 'I – it' relationship for an 'I – thou' relationship and ends up relegating persons to the status of things. Hence segregation is not only politically, economically and sociologically unsound, it is morally wrong and sinful. Paul Tillich has said that sin is separation. Is not segregation an existential expression of man's tragic separation, his awful estrangement, his terrible sinfulness? Thus it is that I can urge men to obey the 1954 decision of the Supreme Court, for it is morally right; and I can urge them to disobey segregation ordinances, for they are morally wrong . . .

Oppressed people cannot remain oppressed for ever. The yearning for freedom eventually manifests itself, and that is what has happened to the American Negro. Something within has reminded him of his birthright of freedom, and something without has reminded him that it can be gained. Consciously or unconsciously, he has been caught up by the *Zeitgeist*, and with his black brothers of Africa and his brown and yellow brothers of Asia, South America and the Caribbean, the United States Negro is moving with a sense of great urgency toward the promised land of racial harmony.

I wish you had commended the Negro sit-inners and demonstrators of Birmingham for their sublime courage, their willingness to suffer and their amazing discipline in the midst of great provocation. One day the South will recognize its real heroes. They will be the James Merediths, with the noble sense of purpose that enables them to face jeering and hostile mobs, and with the agonizing loneliness that characterizes the life of the pioneer. They will be old, oppressed, battered Negro women, symbolized in a seventy-two-year-old woman in Montgomery, Alabama, who rose up with a sense of dignity and with her people decided not to ride segregated buses, and who responded with ungrammatical profundity to one who inquired about her weariness: 'My feets is tired, but my soul is at rest.' They will be the young high school and college students, the young ministers of the gospel and a host of their elders, courageously and nonviolently sitting in at lunch counters and willingly going to jail for conscience's sake. One day the South will know that when these disinherited children of God sat down at lunch counters, they were in reality standing up for what is best in the American dream and for the most sacred values in our Judaeo-Christian heritage, thereby bringing our nation back to those great wells of democracy which were dug deep by the founding fathers in their formulation of the Constitution and the Declaration of Independence.

•

THE TIMES
1963

'*It* is *a moral issue*'

When John Profumo, Secretary of State for War, was forced to resign in June 1963 after lying to the House of Commons about his affair with a call-girl, Christine Keeler (who was simultaneously sleeping with a Russian diplomat), the scandal was yet another blow to the fading reputation of the prime minister Harold Macmillan. His inept handling of the affair suggested that he was out of touch as Britain moved into the swinging sixties.

The damage to the fortunes of the Tory Party (swept from office the following year when Harold Wilson led Labour to power) became even greater when William Haley, editor of The Times, *wrote a critical leading article. The main issue was not security, he argued, but morality.*

Mr Harold Wilson also is a shrewd politician and his immediate reaction was to stress that Labour's concern was about security, not about morals. (It will be interesting to see how he can deploy his attack on the government's security arrangements without the question of Mr Profumo's morals coming in.) Everyone has been so busy assuring the public that the affair is not one of morals, that it is time to assert that it is. Morals have been discounted too long. A judge may be justified in reminding a jury 'This is not a court of morals.' The same exemption cannot be allowed public opinion, without rot setting in and all standards suffering in the long run. The British are not by and large an immoral nation, but through their pathetic fear of being called smug they make themselves out to be one.

No one would wish the security aspects of the matter to be ignored. There is no danger of this. Many questions have already been aired about it in public and they touch the Prime Minister both as the minister ultimately responsible for the security services and as the head of an administration the conduct of one of whose members has been questioned. Yesterday it was revealed that before he went on his holiday, and before the House rose, Mr Macmillan asked the Lord Chancellor to conduct an inquiry into the security side of the affair. (Why this should have been kept secret for five days after the announcement of Mr Profumo's resignation is yet another thing to be explained.) The outcome must at latest be told to the House of Commons in next Monday's debate. Beforehand the point must be stressed that even if the Prime Minister confirms what has so far been accepted, that there was no security risk, and even if the Opposition force a vote and for one reason or another the government gets its usual majority, that will not be the end of the business. For the Conservative Party – and, it is to be hoped, for the nation – things can never be quite the same again.

The hope must be that they will become better. There is plenty of room for this. However multifarious and ingenious the causes to which the Conservative Central Office ascribe the desperate state of the party's present fortunes as shown by the opinion polls, the overriding reason is that eleven years of Conservative rule have brought the nation psychologically and spiritually to a low ebb. The Conservatives came to power a few months before the present reign opened. They have been in office so far throughout the whole of it. The ardent hopes and eager expectations that attended its beginning have been belied. They gibed at austerity, and in all truth the British people deserved some easement after their historic and heroic exertions, although history is never a nicely balanced business of rewards and penalties. They declared they had the right road for Britain. They would set the people free. Change, they declared, was their ally. Nothing else, they seemed later to think, mattered, compared with the assertion that the nation had never had it so good. Today they are faced with a flagging economy, an uncertain future, and the end of the illusion that Britain's greatness could be measured by the so-called independence of its so-called deterrent. All this may seem far from Mr

Profumo, but his admissions could be the last straw. It remains strange that not a single member of the government resigned when the affair broke in March and he did not himself resign.

What the Conservatives need now, and what they have needed ever since Churchill was in his heyday, is courage. One of the paradoxes of modern war is that defeat is more likely to restore a nation's fibre than victory. There is no hiding place from the tidal wave of overthrow and disaster. All too dangerously comfortable is the slow, insidious, almost imperceptible but inexorable ebb tide. Appeal after appeal has been made to immediate self-interest. The professional politicians will assert that these have worked. Has not the pendulum been stopped? Have not the Conservatives won three elections in a row? Granting that politics is mainly the pursuit of power, this is not its only purpose. The Prime Minister and his colleagues can cling together and be still there a year hence. They will have to do more than that to justify themselves.

Whether in the next few days some heads fall or none, damage has been done. It may be a caricature for the *Washington Post* to say that 'a picture of widespread decadence beneath the glitter of a large segment of stiff-lipped society is emerging'. But the essence of caricature is to exaggerate real traits. There are plenty of earnest and serious men in the Conservative Party who know that all is not well. It is time they put first things first, stopped weighing electoral chances, and returned to the starker truths of an earlier day. Popularity by affluence is about played out, especially when it rests on so insecure a basis. Even if the call had metaphorically to be for 'blood, sweat and tears' instead of to the fleshpots, they might be surprised by the result. The British are always at their best when they are braced.

•

BETTY FRIEDAN
1963

'Is this all?'

The 'problem that had no name' was uncovered by Betty Friedan (1921–) when she was working on an article for McCalls *magazine about her Smith College class reunion and asked that group of educated middle-class women: 'What do you wish you had done differently?' Their answers led to* The Feminine Mystique, *which exposed the myth of the happy housewife. Friedan went on to found the National Organization of Women and to help form the National Women's Political Caucus and the Women's Bank.*

The problem that has no name is described in this first chapter of The Feminine Mystique.

The problem lay buried, unspoken, for many years in the minds of American women. It was a strange stirring, a sense of dissatisfaction, a yearning that women suffered in the middle of the twentieth century in the United States. Each suburban wife struggled with it alone. As she made the beds, shopped for groceries, matched slipcover material, ate peanut butter sandwiches with her children, chauffeured Cub Scouts and Brownies, lay beside her husband at night – she was afraid to ask even of herself the silent question – 'Is this all?' . . .

The suburban housewife – she was the dream image of the young American women and the envy, it was said, of women all over the world. The American housewife – freed by science and labor-saving appliances from the drudgery, the dangers of childbirth and the illnesses of her grandmother. She was healthy, beautiful, educated, concerned only about her husband, her children, her home. She had found true feminine fulfillment. As a housewife and mother, she was respected as a full and equal partner to man in his world. She was free to choose automobiles, clothes, appliances, supermarkets; she had everything that women ever dreamed of.

In the fifteen years after World War II, this mystique of feminine fulfillment became the cherished and self-perpetuating core of contemporary American culture. Millions of women lived their lives in the image of those pretty pictures of the American suburban housewife, kissing their husbands goodbye in front of the picture window, depositing their stationwagonsful of children at school, and smiling as they ran the new electric waxer over the spotless kitchen floor. They baked their own bread, sewed their own and their children's clothes, kept their new washing machines and dryers running all day. They changed the sheets on the beds twice a week instead of once, took the rug-hooking class in adult education, and pitied their poor frustrated mothers, who had dreamed of having a career. Their only dream was to be perfect wives and mothers; their highest ambition to have five children and a beautiful house, their only fight to get and keep their husbands. They had no thought for the unfeminine problems of the world outside the home; they wanted the men to make the major decisions. They gloried in their role as women, and wrote proudly on the census blank: 'Occupation: housewife.' . . .

But on an April morning in 1959, I heard a mother of four, having coffee with four other mothers in a suburban development fifteen miles from New York, say in a tone of quiet desperation, 'the problem.' And the others knew, without words, that she was not talking about a problem with her husband, or her children, or her home. Suddenly they realized they all shared the same problem, the problem that has no name. They began, hesitantly, to talk about it. Later, after they had picked up their children at nursery school and taken them home to nap, two of the women cried, in sheer relief, just to know they were not alone.

Just what was this problem that has no name? What were the words women used when they tried to express it? Sometimes a woman would say, 'I feel empty somehow . . . incomplete.' Or she would say, 'I feel as if I don't exist.' Sometimes she blotted out the feeling with a tranquilizer. Sometimes she thought the problem was with her husband, or her children, or that what she really needed was to redecorate her house, or move to a better neighborhood, or have an affair, or another baby. Sometimes, she went to a doctor with symptoms she could hardly describe: 'A tired feeling . . . I get so angry with the children it scares me . . . I feel like crying without any reason.' (A Cleveland doctor called it 'the housewife's syndrome.') A number of women told me about great bleeding blisters that break out on their hands and arms. 'I call it the housewife's blight,' said a family doctor in Pennsylvania. 'I see it so often lately in these young women with four, five and six children who bury themselves in their dishpans. But it isn't caused by detergent and it isn't cured by cortisone.'

It is no longer possible to ignore that voice, to dismiss the desperation of so many American women. This is not what being a woman means, no matter what the experts say. For human suffering there is a reason; perhaps the reason has not been found because the right questions have not been asked, or pressed far enough. I do not accept the answer that there is no problem because American women have luxuries that women in other times and lands never dreamed of; part of the strange newness of the problem is that it cannot be understood in terms of the age-old material problems of man: poverty, sickness, hunger, cold. The women who suffer this problem have a hunger that food cannot fill.

It is easy to see the concrete details that trap the suburban housewife, the continual demands on her time. But the chains that bind her in her trap are chains in her own mind and spirit. They are chains made up of mistaken ideas and misinterpreted facts, of incomplete truths and unreal choices. They are not easily seen and not easily shaken off.

How can any woman see the whole truth within the bounds of her own life? How can she believe that voice inside herself, when it denies the conventional, accepted truths by which she has been living? And yet the women I have talked to, who are finally listening to that inner voice, seem in some incredible way to be groping through to a truth that has defied the experts.

I think the experts in a great many fields have been holding pieces of that truth under their microscopes for a long time without realizing it. I found pieces of it in certain new research and theoretical developments in psychological, social and biological science whose implications for women seem never to have been examined.

I became aware of a growing body of evidence, much of which has not been reported publicly because it does not fit current modes of thought about women – evidence which throws into question the standards of feminine normality, feminine adjustment, feminine fulfillment, and feminine maturity by which most women are still trying to live.

I began to see in a strange new light the American return to early marriage and the large families that are causing the population explosion; the recent movement to natural childbirth and breastfeeding; suburban conformity, and the new neuroses, character pathologies, and sexual problems being reported by the doctors. I began to see new dimensions to old problems that have long been taken for granted among women: menstrual difficulties, sexual frigidity, promiscuity, pregnancy fears, childbirth depression, the high incidence of emotional breakdown and suicide among women in their twenties and thirties, the menopause crises, the so-called passivity and immaturity of American men, the discrepancy between women's tested intellectual abilities in childhood and their adult achievement, the changing incidence of adult sexual orgasm in American women, and persistent problems in psychotherapy and in women's education.

If I am right, the problem that has no name stirring in the minds of so many American women today is not a matter of loss of femininity or too much education, or the demands of domesticity. It is far more important than anyone recognizes. It is the key to these other new and old problems which have been torturing women and their husbands and children, puzzling their doctors and educators for years. It may well be the key to our future as a nation and a culture. We can no longer ignore that voice within women that says: 'I want something more than my husband and my children and my home.'

•

JAMES BALDWIN
1963

'The black God'

James Baldwin (1924–87) was born and brought up in Harlem but lived in Europe (mainly in France) from 1948 until 1957 when he returned to America as an activist for civil rights. He joined John Griffin, author of Black Like Me, *and Ralph Ellison, who wrote* Invisible Man, *as one of the three most influential writers in the cause of Negro rights, especially with his books* Notes of a Native Son, The Fire Next Time *and* Nobody Knows My Name. *'He's so brilliant,' said the black leader Malcolm X, 'he confuses the white man with words on paper. He's upset the white man more than anybody except The Honourable Elijah Muhammad.'*

In this extract from The Fire Next Time, *Baldwin derides the Negro's treatment by white America.*

White men in America do not behave toward black men the way they behave toward each other. When a white man faces a black man, especially if the black man is helpless, terrible things are revealed. I know. I have been carried into precinct basements often enough, and I have seen and heard and endured the secrets of desperate white men and women, which they knew were safe with me, because even if I should speak, no one would believe me. And they would not believe me precisely because they would know that what I said was true.

The treatment accorded the Negro during World War II marks, for me, a turning point in the Negro's relation to America. To put it briefly, and somewhat too simply, a certain hope died, a certain respect for white Americans faded. One began to pity them, or to hate them. You must put yourself in the skin of a man who is wearing the uniform of his country, is a candidate for death in its defence, and who is called a 'nigger' by his comrades-in-arms and his officers; who is almost always given the hardest, ugliest, most menial work to do; who knows that the white GI has informed the Europeans that he is sub-human (so much for the American male's sexual security); who does not dance at the USO the night white soldiers dance there, and does not drink in the same bars white soldiers drink in; and who watches German prisoners of war being treated by Americans with more human dignity than he has ever received at their hands. And who, at the same time, as a human being, is far freer in a strange land than he has ever been at home. *Home!*

The very word begins to have a despairing and diabolical ring. You must consider what happens to this citizen, after all he has endured, when he returns home: search, in his shoes, for a job, for a place to live; ride, in his skin, on segregated buses; see, with his eyes, the signs saying 'White' and 'Colored,' and especially the signs that say 'White Ladies' and 'Colored *Women*'; look into the eyes of his wife; look into the eyes of his son; listen, with his ears, to political speeches, North and South; imagine yourself being told to 'wait.' And all this is happening in the richest and freest country in the world, and in the middle of the twentieth century. The subtle and deadly change of heart that might occur in you would be involved with the realization that a civilization is not destroyed by wicked people; it is not necessary that people be wicked but only that they be spineless.

But, in the end, it is the threat of universal extinction hanging over all the world today that changes, totally and for ever, the nature of reality and brings into devastating question the true meaning of man's history. We human beings now have the power to exterminate ourselves; this seems to be the entire sum of our achievement. We have taken this journey and arrived at this place in God's name. This, then, is the best that God (the white God) can do. If that is so, then it is time to replace him – replace him with what? And this void, this despair, this torment is felt everywhere in the West, from the streets of Stockholm to the churches of New Orleans and the sidewalks of Harlem.

God is black. All black men belong to Islam; they have been chosen. And Islam shall rule the world. The dream, the sentiment is old; only the color is new.

•

MALCOLM X
1964

'Ballot or bullet'

Born in Nebraska but raised in Michigan and Boston, the son of a radical Baptist minister, Malcolm X (1925–65) became a pimp and hustler nicknamed Detroit Red. He was jailed for burglary in 1946, discovered the Nation of Islam and its leader Elijah Muhammad in prison in 1952 and became a disciple and Black Muslim minister preaching vengeance against the 'white devil'. He advocated violence and black separation and often described himself as the angriest black man in America. After a conflict with Muhammad, he was suspended from the Black Muslims in 1963 and travelled to Mecca. When he

realized that orthodox Muslims preached racial equality, he abandoned his attacks on the
'white devils' and founded the Organization of Afro-American Unity. He was assassinated
by a Black Muslim at an OAAU rally in 1965.

Malcolm X co-operated with Alex Haley in writing his autobiography which was
subsequently filmed. The chapter on the Black Muslims explained the roots of his hatred
of the whites – the Ku Klux Klan killed his father – why he despised the contemporary
Uncle Toms, and the reaction to a television documentary on the Black Muslims.

In late 1959, the television program was aired. 'The Hate That Hate Produced'
– the title – was edited tightly into a kaleidoscope of 'shocker' images . . . Mr
Muhammad, me, and others speaking . . . strong-looking, set-faced black
men, our Fruit of Islam . . . white-scarved, white-gowned Muslim sisters of
all ages . . . Muslims in our restaurants, and other businesses . . . Muslims and
other black people entering and leaving our mosques . . .

Every phrase was edited to increase the shock mood. As the producers
intended, I think people sat just about limp when the program went off.

In a way, the public reaction was like what happened back in the 1930s
when Orson Welles frightened America with a radio program describing, as
though it was actually happening, an invasion by 'men from Mars.'

'Mr Malcolm X, why do you teach black supremacy, and hate?' A red flag
waved for me, something chemical happened inside me, every time I heard
that. When we Muslims had talked about 'the devil white man' he had been
relatively abstract, someone we Muslims rarely actually came into contact
with, but now here was that devil-in-the-flesh on the phone – with all of his
calculating, cold-eyed, self-righteous tricks and nerve and gall. The voices
questioning me became to me as breathing, living devils.

And I tried to pour on pure fire in return. 'The white man so guilty of
white supremacy can't hide *his* guilt by trying to accuse The Honorable Elijah
Muhammad of teaching black supremacy and hate! All Mr Muhammad is
doing is trying to uplift the black man's mentality and the black man's social
and economic condition in this country.

'The guilty, two-faced white man can't decide *what* he wants. Our slave
foreparents would have been put to death for advocating so-called "integration" with the white man. Now when Mr Muhammad speaks of "separation," the white man calls us "hate-teachers" and "fascists"!

'The white man doesn't *want* the blacks! He doesn't *want* the blacks that
are a parasite upon him! He doesn't *want* this black man whose presence and
condition in this country expose the white man to the world for what he is!
So why do you attack Mr Muhammad?'

I'd have *scathing* in my voice; I *felt* it.

'For the white man to ask the black man if he hates him is just like the rapist asking the *raped*, or the wolf asking the *sheep*, "Do you hate me?" The white man is in no moral *position* to accuse anyone else of hate!

'Why, when all of my ancestors are snake-bitten, and I'm snake-bitten, and I warn my children to avoid snakes, what does that *snake* sound like accusing *me* of hate-teaching?'

'Mr Malcolm X,' those devils would ask, 'why is your Fruit of Islam being trained in judo and karate?' An image of black men learning anything suggesting self-defense seemed to terrify the white man. I'd turn their question around: 'Why does judo or karate suddenly get so ominous because black men study it? Across America, the Boy Scouts, the YMCA, even the YWCA, the CYP, PAL – they *all* teach judo! It's all right, it's fine – until *black men* teach it! Even little grammar school classes, little girls, are taught to defend themselves –'

'How many of you are in your organization, Mr Malcolm X? Right Reverend Bishop T. Chickenwing says you have only a handful of members –'

'Whoever tells you how many Muslims there are doesn't know, and whoever does know will never tell you –'

The Bishop Chickenwings were also often quoted about our 'anti-Christianity'. I'd fire right back on that:

'Christianity is the white man's religion. The Holy Bible in the white man's hands and his interpretations of it have been the greatest single ideological weapon for enslaving millions of non-white human beings. Every country the white man has conquered with his guns, he has always paved the way, and salved his conscience, by carrying the Bible and interpreting it to call the people "heathens" and "pagans;" then he sends his guns, then his missionaries behind the guns to mop up –'

White reporters, anger in their voices, would call us 'demagogues,' and I would try to be ready after I had been asked the same question two or three times.

'Well, let's go back to the Greek, and maybe you will learn the first thing you need to know about the word "demagogue." "Demagogue" means, actually, "teacher of the people." And let's examine some demagogues. The greatest of all Greeks, Socrates, was killed as a "demagogue." Jesus Christ died on the cross because the Pharisees of his day were upholding their law, not the spirit. The modern Pharisees are trying to heap destruction upon Mr Muhammad, calling him a demagogue, a crackpot and fanatic. What about Gandhi? The man that Churchill called "a naked little fakir," refusing food in a British jail? But then a quarter of a billion people, a whole subcontinent, rallied behind Gandhi – and they twisted the British Lion's tail! What about Galileo, standing before his inquisitors, saying "The earth *does* move!" What about Martin Luther, nailing on a door his thesis against the all-powerful Catholic church which called him "heretic"? We, the followers of The Honorable Elijah Muhammad, are today in the ghettoes as once the sect of Christianity's followers were like termites in the catacombs and the grottoes – and they were preparing the grave of the mighty Roman Empire!'

•

IAIN MACLEOD
1964

'The magic circle'

The sudden death of Iain Macleod (1913–70) robbed the Conservative Party of its greatest and most charismatic personality of that generation. He invested politics with a colour, warmth and wit none of his colleagues could rival, says Robert Blake, historian of the Conservative Party.

When Harold Macmillan resigned as prime minister in 1963, Macleod, joint chairman of the party after being colonial secretary, supported R. A. Butler as Macmillan's successor – but Sir Alec Douglas-Home 'emerged' as the victor over both Butler and Lord Hailsham, the other contender.

Macleod refused to serve under Douglas-Home and went to edit the Spectator. *He gave his account of the critical day when Douglas-Home was chosen in a review of Randolph Churchill's* The Fight for the Tory Leadership – *and used a phrase which has resounded ever since.*

The key day was Thursday, 17 October [1963], a day which for me began as an ordinary working day and ended with my firm decision that I could not serve in the administration that I knew Lord Home was to be invited to form. The first indication that the day was going to be unusual came at breakfast. My wife came back from a long telephone conversation with one of our oldest friends (mainly concerning the affairs of a voluntary society in which they are both interested) to say that the succession was to be decided that afternoon. The information was third-hand, but the links were strong, and the original source the one man who would certainly know. I was surprised, but not disturbed. To me it seemed clear that if the situation was going to gell swiftly, the choice must be Butler: if there was deadlock, it would surely come back to the Cabinet. I had not, of course, appreciated then that it was in fact an essential part of the design that the Cabinet should have no such opportunity. Churchill's book makes this plain.

My only important engagement in the morning was a meeting at No. 10 called by Butler to consider the difficult closing stages of the Kenya conference. Both Maudling and I attended as ex-Secretaries of State for the Colonies. I walked away with Maudling to his rooms at the Treasury. I had always held Maudling in high and warm regard and throughout considered him a possible Prime Minister. Alone in the Chancellor's room over a drink I told him of my wife's telephone conversation. He had heard nothing, and had in general reached a similar conclusion to mine. Naturally his own chances (which he recognized were now slim) depended on the issue being protracted. A decision today, he thought, could only be for Butler. And with this he was more than content. He spoke on the telephone to Lord Dilhorne, and the Lord Chancellor confirmed that he and others were to present their collective views that afternoon. They had already been separately to see Macmillan that morning. To all suggestions that the Cabinet (or the Cabinet less the chief contenders) should meet, Dilhorne was deaf; as he had been, I have since learned, to at least one more similar request. No doubt he thought he was acting wisely.

Curiouser and curiouser it seemed, and Maudling and I decided to stay in touch. I joined him and Mrs Maudling for lunch. Butler we discussed a good deal. Hailsham we mentioned once, but we both knew that his bandwagon had long ago stopped rolling: indeed, the opposition to Hailsham (not, of course, on personal grounds) was and was known to be so formidable that it remains astonishing that he was not given clear warning of it in advance of his declaration that he would disclaim his peerage. Home we never mentioned in any connection. Neither of us thought he was a contender, although for a brief moment his star seemed to have flared at Blackpool. It is some measure of the tightness of the magic circle on this occasion that neither the Chancellor of the Exchequer nor the Leader of the House of Commons had any inkling of what was happening.

After lunch I returned to Central Office to clear some papers. In mid-afternoon the telephone rang. It was an important figure in Fleet Street. He told me the decision had been made, and that it was for Home. He himself found this incredible, but he was utterly sure of his source. I telephoned Maudling and Powell and arranged to meet as soon as we could at my flat. Powell's views I knew coincided with mine and both at Blackpool and in the days following the conference we had been closely in touch. Almost at once the phone calls started from the leading newspaper political correspondents. Each of them had the same story. Someone, I presume, thought it proper even before the Prime Minister had resigned to prepare the press for the (unexpected) name that was to emerge. News management can be taken too far.

•

WILLIAM REES-MOGG
1965

'Doing the right thing'

The result of the 1964 general election, in which the Tory prime minister, Scottish aristocrat Sir Alec Douglas-Home, fought the modernizing and eventually victorious Labour leader Harold Wilson, was much closer than commentators had assumed. When the Tories made gains in the local elections nearly a year later, Douglas-Home, who had considered resignation, was persuaded to stay, but his position changed when Wilson, who had a small majority, announced there would be no general election in 1965. A new Tory leader would therefore have time to establish himself. Douglas-Home's decision to go was confirmed when he read this powerful article on the opinion page of the Sunday Times, *the most influential Sunday newspaper in Tory circles, written by its deputy editor William Rees-Mogg (1928–), who went on to become editor of* The Times *eighteen months later. Four days after Rees-Mogg's article appeared, Douglas-Home announced his resignation.*

Having been strongly opposed to Sir Alec Douglas-Home becoming leader of the Conservative Party I find myself in some difficulty in writing about his position now. It is obvious that he has not been as bad a leader as I and others feared, and that ought to be said. Equally he has not been anything like as good a leader as his original supporters hoped.

He has in fact played the sort of captain's innings one used to see in county cricket before the war. There were then in most counties good club players, often fresh from university, who were appointed captain because they were amateurs. They lacked the professional skills and they never had very high averages. But occasionally, when the wicket was taking spin at Canterbury or Weston-super-Mare, they would come in when their side had scored thirty-seven for six and by dint of concentration and a well-coached forward prod survive to make twenty runs or so and see their side past the follow-on.

Sir Alec will always be able to claim that he stopped the rot. Whether or not the Conservatives would have won under another leader, they were, in the circumstances of October 1963, facing the political equivalent of an innings defeat. The rally was achieved for a number of reasons, but Sir Alec's personal confidence and optimism played an important part.

On the other hand, the main criticism which was made on his appointment has also proved true. In his period as Prime Minister Sir Alec Douglas-Home never managed to be at all convincing about economic affairs or modernization, nor did his administration actually handle the economy well. The nation was in a state of uncertainty and almost at times of despair. He did not know what to say and, though he never did anything very foolish, he did not know what to do. At a time when bad leadership would have been disastrous and even great leadership might not have been successful, Sir Alec was only able to provide decent leadership. It was something, but it was not enough.

In opposition he has been very sensible but not very effective. Again he has shown qualities of steadiness and shrewdness, he has on the whole made good appointments and the Conservative Party has recovered part of its morale. Yet he has not been able to make a national impact himself. A leader of an Opposition must present an alternative image to government; he does not have the sounding board of a great administration behind him or the power of initiative of a Prime Minister. A decent capable man can make something of leading a country, but in opposition can almost disappear as a figure of importance.

For the whole of the period since the election Sir Alec must have been pondering when and whether he should go, and what to do for the best. I do not wholly share the view that he was a reluctant Prime Minister, only dragged into the job by the call of duty. I distrust the *nolo episcopari* of bishops, let alone of statesmen. Yet I am certain that he is now quite genuinely concerned with doing the right thing, and not at all concerned with hanging on to power, if it is best for his party that he should go.

Until the last fortnight the balance of advice has just rested with Sir Alec staying. That balance has now decisively shifted the other way, and it has been shifted by two events. The first and more important is that Sir Alec no longer commands the preponderant support in the Conservative Party in Parliament that he used to have.

The second event was the publication of the *Daily Mail* National Opinion Poll which showed that the Labour lead was again increasing, and also showed that public opinion rated Mr Wilson as superior to Sir Alec in every quality of political character and a majority of issues of policy. It can of course be argued that this shows that public opinion is an ass. Anyone who shares the public view that Sir Alec is virtually as intelligent but considerably less straightforward than Mr Wilson must be a poor judge of intelligence and a preposterously bad judge of character. Nevertheless the poll is there, and it confirms previous polls and most people's common observation that the public has much more confidence in Mr Wilson than in Sir Alec.

The situation has been reached when the leadership problem cannot be settled without a change. Many commentators this year have wanted to let it settle itself, and Sir Alec has had a favourable period and a fair run of luck.

Yet at the end of that period the Labour Party is regaining its lead and Sir Alec's position is weaker than at any time since he became leader. If his support crumbles in good times, it will scarcely hold together in bad.

The question obviously has to be faced of which contender ought to succeed. This is more difficult because Mr Heath's and Mr Maudling's qualities are so very different. Mr Maudling is a large, tolerant, quick-minded and good-natured man. He would be a good Prime Minister for his Cabinet and would approach with cautious good sense the problems he had to deal with. Mr Heath is a much more intensely purposeful man, active and dynamic by disposition, with a greater interest in detail, less willingness to delegate and less easy-going a manner.

The question must be decided in terms of the needs of the present situation. The Conservative Party has to be translated into a fighting opposition, which the constituencies want. The only really effective Conservative fighting in this Parliament has been on the Finance Bill and that obviously counts in Mr Heath's favour. Others, including Mr Macleod, are born fighters who have had little Parliamentary chance to show it.

The second requirement is that the Conservative Party should offer a serious prospect of being an effective reforming administration if it is returned. The Labour Party could not have won the election if there had not been some faith in its promise as a modernizing party and an utter lack of faith in the Conservative ability to fit that role. Yet the need is still there – the need to use all the power and resources of government and industry to make Britain fully competitive and effective in terms of the 1960s and 1970s. We must be governed by men who feel it is an affront that new designs are invented in Britain and developed abroad, that Britain and Austria are the back-markers of Europe in the use of computers, or that it takes twenty-five men to produce in British industry what ten men produce in the United States. These are facts which require an emotional as well as an intellectual response.

If this is one's view of the real character of the political problem then it seems to me that one will prefer to see Mr Heath rather than Mr Maudling as the next Conservative leader. We are in a national situation which demands that we should take risks – we cannot avoid them – and we should take our risks on the side of energy.

What is certain however is that the Conservative Party is not going to be able to play either role so long as the leadership crisis is postponed. If there is to be another crisis at Conference time and another at Christmas, a third next Easter and a fourth next July, then there can be no recovery. Much more important than that it is clear that Sir Alec cannot tell the nation what it ought to do at a very dark and critical moment. Others may not have the right answer. He does not have an answer at all. A man cannot lead a party successfully who does not in his heart of hearts feel absolutely convinced that he knows what ought to be done. It is hard to resist the very widespread view that the Conservatives, unless after a national disaster will not now win a general election while Sir Alec remains their leader.

•

VIETNAM

Apart from the struggle by America's blacks for civil rights (which culminated in President Lyndon Johnson's Great Society programme of 1964), no single issue so convulsed the United States in the twentieth century as the Vietnam War – in which American soldiers and bombers were engaged for nine years.

Still obsessed by the Cold War, the prospect of a 'Red Victory' and the domino theory – if Indo-China fell to the Communists, Thailand and Malaysia would follow – Johnson sent American troops to the aid of Saigon in 1965 and the war was eventually also carried, under President Richard Nixon, to Cambodia.

Some 58,000 Americans lost their lives and nearly 200,000 were wounded as the United States was routed by Ho Chi Minh, leader of North Vietnam, and his Vietcong soldiers. The horror of the war was brought home nightly to the American people by television, and the ferocity of the protest across the nation, especially by students threatened by the draft, eventually ended Johnson's presidency – he decided not to run in 1968.

Some of the most famous and eloquent protests against the Vietnam War follow.

•

HO CHI MINH
1965

'A heroic people'

Many great successes had been achieved by the North Vietnamese on both sides of the North–South border, Ho Chi Minh (1892–1969) proclaimed to his National Assembly, as he said that the movement to oppose the United States was 'seething'.

Over the past ten years, the US imperialists and their henchmen have carried out an extremely ruthless war and have caused much grief to our compatriots in South Vietnam. Over the past few months, they have frenziedly expanded the war to North Vietnam. In defiance of the 1954 Geneva Agreements and international law, they have sent hundreds of aircraft and dozens of warships to bomb and strafe North Vietnam repeatedly. Laying bare themselves their piratical face, the US aggressors are blatantly encroaching upon our country. They hope that by resorting to the force of weapons they can compel our 30 million compatriots to become their slaves. But they are grossly mistaken. They will certainly meet with ignominious defeat.

Our Vietnamese people are a heroic people. Over the past ten years or more, our 14 million compatriots in the South have overcome all hardships, made every sacrifice and struggled very valiantly. Starting with their bare hands, they have seized guns from the enemy to fight against the enemy, have recorded victory after victory, and are launching a continual attack inflicting upon the US aggressors and the traitors ever greater defeats and causing them to be bogged down more and more deeply. The greater their defeats, the more frantically they resort to the most cruel means, such as using napalm bombs and toxic gas to massacre our compatriots in the South. It is because they are bogged down in South Vietnam that they have furiously attacked North Vietnam.

As the thief crying 'stop, thief!' is a customary trick of theirs, the US imperialists, who are the aggressors, have impudently slandered North Vietnam as committing 'aggression' in South Vietnam. The US imperialists are precisely the saboteurs of the Geneva Agreements, yet they have brazenly declared that because they wished to 'restore peace' and 'defend the Geneva Agreements' they brought US troops to our country to carry out massacres and destruction. The US imperialists are precisely those who are devastating our country and killing our people, yet they hypocritically declared that they would give $1 billion to the people in Vietnam and the other Southeast Asian countries to 'develop their countries and improve their life'.

US President Johnson has also loudly threatened to resort to violence to subdue our people. This is a mere foolish illusion. Our people will definitely never be subjugated.

•

BERTRAND RUSSELL
1966

'How many women and children died at your hands today?'

At the age of ninety-four, Bertrand Russell (1872–1970) was actively opposed to the Vietnam War and set up a War Crimes Tribunal to pass judgement on the United States. He made this broadcast to American soldiers on the South Vietnam Liberation Front radio station.

When the United States first began to intervene militarily in South Vietnam, the pretence was made that the United States was merely helping a government in Saigon put down subversion from outside. But you American soldiers have seen for yourselves what kind of governments have existed in Saigon. They are brutal, corrupt, dictatorial and completely despised by the people. Why is it that these governments have been able to continue, one after another, in Saigon, despite the fact that the students, the women, the villagers, everyone risks life itself to overthrow them? The sole answer is that the United States is using its enormous military force to impose on the people of Vietnam puppet governments which do not represent them.

Let us now consider together why the US Government does this. The excuse that they are protecting the Vietnamese against the Vietcong or the North Vietnamese can be seen by all of you to be the disgusting lie it is. Vietnam is one country. Even the Geneva Agreements acknowledge that it is one country. The North Vietnamese and the South Vietnamese are not merely the same people, but the wives and children of men living in the North are in the South and many of those who live in the South were born in the North.

You may not know that between 1954 and 1960 more Vietnamese died than since 1960. Think hard about that. The Vietcong had not taken up arms until 1960, and yet more Vietnamese died in the six years before that time than since the National Liberation Front began to struggle. The reason is simple. The Government of Ngo Dinh Diem killed, tortured, imprisoned and mutilated hundreds of thousands of Vietnamese and was able to do this solely because of the military support and direction of the United States. Can any of you forget the brutality of Ngo Dinh Diem, which moved Buddhist priests to burn themselves in protest?

It ought to be clear that the National Liberation Front, which you know as the Vietcong, took up arms to defend their people against a tyranny more brutal than the Japanese occupation itself, for more died under Diem than under the Japanese. This is the responsibility of the United States Government.

The reason why you American soldiers are in Vietnam is to suppress the people of Vietnam, who are trying to free themselves from economic strangulation and foreign military rule. You are sent to protect the riches of a few men in the United States.

Do you know that the United States controls 60 per cent of the resources of the world, but has only 6 per cent of the world's population, and yet one out of three Americans lives in poverty? Do you know that the United States has over 3,300 military bases in the world, almost all of which are used against the population of the country in which the bases exist?

Your Air Force is flying 650 sorties a week in the North and the tonnages used in the South are higher than those used during the Second World War or the Korean War. You are using napalm, which burns everything it touches. You are using phosphorus, which eats like an acid into those who are in its path. You are using fragmentation bombs and 'lazy dogs', which cut up in pieces and lacerate women and children in the villages hit without discrimination. You are using poison chemicals which cause blindness, affect the nervous system and paralyse. You are using poison gases which are listed in army manuals of the Second World War as poisons, and other gases which are so deadly that even soldiers with gas masks have been killed by their own gas.

When you return from battle, ask yourselves who are these people you are killing? How many women and children died at your hands today? What would you feel if these things were happening in the United States to your wives, parents and children? How can you bear the thought of what is taking place around you, day after day and week after week? I ask these questions of you because you bear the responsibility and within your hands lies the choice of whether this criminal war is to continue.

•

MARY McCARTHY
1967

'The military establishment'

The novelist and critic Mary McCarthy (1912–89), whose most famous novels are The
Groves of Academe *and* The Group, *wrote two denunciations of the war. One was*
Hanoi *(1968). The other, from which this extract is taken, was* Vietnam, *described by*
Alastair Cooke in one of his Letters from America *as 'another whanging knife between*
the shoulder-blades of Our Leader . . . Her Vietnam is a Hieronymus Bosch bedlam run
by the Pentagon.'

The generals are sure they could win the war if they could only bomb the
port of Haiphong and the Ho Chi Minh trail in Laos. They blame politics
for their failure to win it, and by politics is meant the existence of counter-forces
in the theater: China, Russia, the Pathet Lao, and simply people, civilians, a
weak counter-force, but still an obstacle to total warfare under present
conditions. It used to be said that the balance of terror would give rise to a
series of limited wars. Up to now, this has been true, so far as geographical
scale goes, but the abstention from the use of atomic arms, in Vietnam, has
not exactly worked to moderate the war.

On the contrary, the military establishment, deprived for the time being
of tactical atomic weapons (toys being kept in the closet) and held back from
bombing the port of Haiphong and the Ho Chi Minh trail, has compensated
for these limitations by developing other weapons and devices to the limit:
antipersonnel bombs; a new, more adhesive napalm; a twenty-pound gadget,
the E-63 manpack personnel detector, made by General Electric, replacing
British-trained bloodhounds, to sniff out Vietcong; a battery-powered blower
that raises the temperature in a V C tunnel network to 1,000 degrees Fahrenheit
(loudspeakers, naturally, exhort the Vietcong in the tunnels to surrender);
improved tear gases; improved defoliants. The classic resistance offered by
climate and terrain to armies of men, one of the ancient limitations on warfare,
will doubtless be all but eliminated as new applications for patents pour into
the US Patent Office. The jungle will be leafless and creeperless, and the
mangrove swamps dried out; the weather will be controlled, making bombing
possible on a 365-day-a-year basis, exclusive of Buddha's birthday, Christmas,
and Tet. The diseases of the jungle and tropical climates are already pretty
well confined to the native population, thanks to pills and immunization. In

other words, for an advanced nation, practically no obstacles remain to the exercise of force except 'politics.'

US technology is bent on leaving nothing to chance in the Vietnamese struggle, on taking the risk out of war (for ourselves, of course, while increasing the risk for the enemy). Whatever cannot be controlled scientifically – shifts of wind, rain – is by-passed by radar and electronics. Troop performance is fairly well guaranteed by the Selective Service system and by rotation; the 'human element,' represented by the Arvin, prone to desert or panic, is despised and feared. And if chance can be reduced to a minimum by the 'miracle' of American technology, there is only one reality-check on American *hubris*: the danger of Chinese or Russian intervention, which computers in the Pentagon are steadily calculating, to take the risk out of *that*.

•

A YOUNG NEGRO
1967

'No Vietnamese'

The briefest protest at the march on the Pentagon – and perhaps the most telling – appeared on a placard carried, in Norman Mailer's description, by a handsome young Negro.

'No Vietnamese Ever Called Me A Nigger.'

•

NORMAN MAILER
1968

'Leave Asia to the Asians'

Norman Mailer (1923–), one of America's most celebrated writers and author of The Naked and the Dead, *a novel about his experiences in the Second World War, was a prominent protester throughout the 1960s. He was arrested at the great 1967 march on the Pentagon and was the only protester given a prison sentence (thirty days, twenty-five suspended).*

The march was the subject of his book Armies of the Night, *which won the Pulitzer Prize and from which this extract is taken.*

Mailer was a Left Conservative. So he had his own point of view. To himself he would suggest that he tried to think in the style of Marx in order to attain certain values suggested by Edmund Burke. Since he was a Conservative, he would begin at the root. He did not see all wars as bad. He could conceive of wars which might be noble. But the war in Vietnam was bad for America because it was a bad war, as all wars are bad if they consist of rich boys fighting poor boys when the rich boys have an advantage in the weapons. He recollected a statistic: it was droll if it was not obscene. Next to every pound of supplies the North Vietnamese brought into South Vietnam for their soldiers, the Americans brought in 1,000 pounds. Yes, he would begin at the root. All wars were bad which undertook daily operations which burned and bombed large numbers of women and children; all wars were bad which relocated populations (for the root of a rich peasant lore was then destroyed); all wars were bad which had no line of battle or discernible climax (an advanced notion which supposes that wars may be in part good because they are sometimes the only way to define critical conditions rather than blur them); certainly all wars were bad which took some of the bravest young men of a nation and sent them into combat with outrageous superiority and outrageous arguments: such conditions of combat had to excite a secret passion for hunting other humans. Certainly any war was a bad war which required an inability to reason as the price of retaining one's patriotism; finally any war which offered no prospect of improving itself as a war – so complex and compromised were its roots – was a bad war. A good war, like anything else which is good, offers the possibility that further effort will produce a determinable effect upon chaos, evil or waste. By every Conservative measure (reserving to Conservatism the right to approve of wars) the war in Vietnam was an extraordinarily bad war.

Since he was also a *Left* Conservative, he believed that radical measures were sometimes necessary to save the root. The root in this case was the welfare of the nation, not the welfare of the war. So he had an answer to the hawks. It was: pull out of Vietnam completely. Leave Asia to the Asians. What then would happen?

If the Communists absorbed those countries, and succeeded in building splendid nations that made the transition to technological culture without undue agony, one would be forced to applaud; it seemed evident on the face of the evidence in Vietnam, that America could not bring technology land to Asia without bankrupting itself in operations ill-conceived, poorly comprehended, and executed in waste. But the greater likelihood was that if the Communists prevailed in Asia they would suffer in much the same fashion. Divisions, schisms and sects would appear. An endless number of collisions between primitive custom and Marxist dogma, a thousand daily pullulations of intrigue, a heritage of cruelty, atrocity and betrayal would fall upon the Communists. It was not difficult to envision a time when one Communist nation in Asia might look for American aid against another Communist nation. Certainly Russia and China would be engaged in a cold war with each other for decades. Therefore, to leave Asia would be precisely to gain the balance of power. The answer then was to get out, to get out any way one could. Get out. There was nothing to fear – perhaps there never had been. For the more Communism expanded, the more monumental would become its problems, the more flaccid its preoccupations with world conquest. In the expansion of Communism was its own containment. The only force which could ever defeat Communism was Communism itself.

Yet there was no likelihood America would ever withdraw from Asia. Rather there was the covert and unhappy intimation that we were in Vietnam because we had to be. Such was the imbalance of the nation that war was its balance. The burning of villages by napalm might be the index of our collective instability.

Mailer had been going on for years about the diseases of America, its oncoming totalitarianism, its oppressiveness, its smog – he had written so much about the disease he had grown bored with his own voice, weary of his own petulance; the war in Vietnam offered therefore the grim pleasure of confirming his ideas. The disease he had written about existed now in open air: so he pushed further in his thoughts – the paradox of this obscene unjust war is that it provided him new energy – even as it provided new energy to the American soldiers who were fighting it.

He came at last to the saddest conclusion of them all for it went beyond the war in Vietnam. He had come to decide that the center of America might be insane. The country had been living with a controlled, even fiercely controlled, schizophrenia which had been deepening with the years. Perhaps the point had now been passed. Any man or woman who was devoutly Christian and worked for the American Corporation, had been caught in an unseen vise whose pressure could split their mind from their soul. For the center of Christianity was a mystery, a son of God, and the center of the corporation was a detestation of mystery, a worship of technology. Nothing was more intrinsically opposed to technology than the bleeding heart of Christ. The average American, striving to do his duty, drove further every day into working for Christ, and drove equally further each day in the opposite direction – into working for the absolute computer of the corporation. Yes and no, 1 and 0. Every day the average American drove himself further into schizophrenia; the average American believed in two opposites more profoundly apart than any previous schism in the Christian soul. Christians had been able to keep some kind of sanity for centuries while countenancing love against honor, desire versus duty, even charity opposed in the same heart to the lust for power – that was difficult to balance but not impossible. The love of the Mystery of Christ, however, and the love of no Mystery whatsoever, had brought the country to a state of suppressed schizophrenia so deep that the foul brutalities of the war in Vietnam were the only temporary cure possible for the condition – since the expression of brutality offers a definite if temporary relief to the schizophrenic. So the average good Christian American secretly loved the war in Vietnam. It opened his emotions. He felt compassion for the hardships and the sufferings of the American boys in Vietnam, even the Vietnamese orphans. And his view of the war could shift a little daily as he read his paper, the war connected him to his newspaper again: connection to the outside world, and the small shift of opinions from day to day are the two nostrums of that apothecary where schizophrenia is treated. America needed the war. It would need a war so long as technology expanded on every road of communication, and the cities and corporations spread like cancer; the good Christian Americans needed the war or they would lose their Christ.

•

THE TIMES
1967

'The law against marijuana is immoral'

'Who breaks a butterfly on a wheel?' The Times *thundered when Mick Jagger, lead singer of the Rolling Stones, was sentenced to three months' imprisonment and fined £100 for being in possession of four amphetamine tablets.*

The Times, *still regarded as an establishment newspaper, had a new editor, William Rees-Mogg, and the shock he caused by questioning the sentence on Jagger ensured that it was quashed on appeal. Three weeks after the original sentence – and a week before the Appeal Court hearing – a full-page advertisement in* The Times *put the case for changing the law.*

The herb *Cannabis sativa*, known as 'Marihuana' or 'Hashish', is prohibited under the Dangerous Drugs Act (1965). The maximum penalty for smoking cannabis is ten years' imprisonment and a fine of £1,000. Yet informed medical opinion supports the view that cannabis is the least harmful of pleasure-giving drugs, and is, in particular, far less harmful than alcohol. Cannabis is non-addictive, and prosecutions for disorderly behaviour under its influence are unknown.

The use of cannabis is increasing, and the rate of increase is accelerating. Cannabis smoking is widespread in the universities and the custom has been taken up by writers, teachers, doctors, businessmen, musicians, scientists and priests. Such persons do not fit the stereotype of the unemployed criminal dope fiend. Smoking the herb also forms a traditional part of the social and religious life of hundreds of thousands of immigrants to Britain.

A leading article in *The Lancet* (9 November 1963) has suggested that it is 'worth considering . . . giving cannabis the same status as alcohol by legalizing its import and consumption . . . Besides the undoubted attraction of reducing, for once, the number of crimes that a member of our society can commit, and of allowing the wider spread of something that can give pleasure, a greater revenue would certainly come to the state from taxation than from fines . . . Additional gains might be the reduction of inter-racial tension, as well as that between generations.'

The main justification for the prohibition of cannabis has been the contention that its use leads to heroin addiction. This contention does not seem to be supported by any documented evidence, and has been specifically refuted by several authoritative studies. It is almost certainly correct to state that the risk to cannabis smokers of becoming heroin addicts is far less than the risk to drinkers of becoming alcoholics.

Cannabis is usually taken by normal persons for the purpose of enhancing sensory experience. Heroin is taken almost exclusively by weak and disturbed individuals for the purpose of withdrawing from reality. By prohibiting cannabis Parliament has created a black market where heroin could occasionally be offered to persons who would not otherwise have had access to it. Potential addicts, having found cannabis to be a poor escape route, have doubtless been tempted to try heroin; and it is probable that their experience of the harmlessness and non-addictive quality of cannabis has led them to underestimate the dangers of heroin. It is the prohibition of cannabis, and not cannabis itself, which may contribute to heroin addiction.

The present system of controls has strongly discouraged the use of cannabis preparations in medicine. It is arguable that claims which were formerly made for the effectiveness of cannabis in psychiatric treatment might now bear re-examination in the light of modern views on drug therapy; and a case could also be made out for further investigation of the antibiotic properties of cannabidiolic acid, one of the constituents of the herb. The possibility of alleviating suffering through the medical use of cannabis preparations should not be dismissed because of prejudice concerning the social effects of 'drugs'.

The government ought to welcome and encourage research into all aspects of cannabis smoking, but according to the law as it stands no one is permitted to smoke cannabis under any circumstances, and exceptions cannot be made for scientific and medical research. It is a scandal that doctors who are entitled to prescribe heroin, cocaine, amphetamines and barbiturates risk being sent to prison for personally investigating a drug which is known to be less damaging than alcohol or even tobacco.

A recent leader in *The Times* called attention to the great danger of the 'deliberate sensationalism' which underlies the present campaign against 'drugs' and cautioned that 'Past cases have shown what can happen when press, police and public all join in a manhunt at a moment of national anxiety.' In recent months the persecution of cannabis smokers has been intensified. Much larger fines and an increasing proportion of unreasonable prison sentences suggest that the crime at issue is not so much drug abuse as heresy.

The prohibition of cannabis has brought the law into disrepute and has demoralized police officers faced with the necessity of enforcing an unjust law. Uncounted thousands of frightened persons have been arbitrarily classified as criminals and threatened with arrest, victimization and loss of livelihood. Many of them have been exposed to public contempt in the courts, insulted by uninformed magistrates and sent to suffer in prison. They have been hunted down with Alsatian dogs or stopped on the street at random and improperly searched. The National Council for Civil Liberties has called attention to instances where drugs have apparently been 'planted' on suspected cannabis smokers. Chief Constables have appealed to the public to inform on their neighbours and children. Yet despite these gross impositions and the threat to civil liberties which they pose the police freely admit that they have been unable to prevent the spread of cannabis smoking.

Abuse of opiates, amphetamines and barbiturates has become a serious national problem, but very little can be done about it so long as the prohibition of cannabis remains in force. The police do not have the resources or the manpower to deal with both cannabis and the dangerous drugs at the same time. Furthermore prohibition provides a potential breeding ground for many forms of drug abuse and gangsterism. Similar legislation in America in the twenties brought the sale of both alcohol and heroin under the control of an immensely powerful criminal conspiracy which still thrives today. We in Britain must not lose sight of the parallel.

The signatories to this petition suggest to the Home Secretary that he implement a five-point programme of cannabis law reform:

1. THE GOVERNMENT SHOULD PERMIT AND ENCOURAGE RESEARCH INTO ALL ASPECTS OF CANNABIS USE, INCLUDING ITS MEDICAL APPLICATIONS.

2. ALLOWING THE SMOKING OF CANNABIS ON PRIVATE PREMISES SHOULD NO LONGER CONSTITUTE AN OFFENCE.

3. CANNABIS SHOULD BE TAKEN OFF THE DANGEROUS DRUGS LIST AND CONTROLLED, RATHER THAN PROHIBITED BY A NEW *AD HOC* INSTRUMENT.

4. POSSESSION OF CANNABIS SHOULD EITHER BE LEGALLY PER-MITTED OR AT MOST BE CONSIDERED A MISDEMEANOUR, PUNISH-ABLE BY A FINE OF NOT MORE THAN £10 FOR A FIRST OFFENCE AND NOT MORE THAN £25 FOR ANY SUBSEQUENT OFFENCE.

5. ALL PERSONS NOW IMPRISONED FOR POSSESSION OF CANNABIS OR FOR ALLOWING CANNABIS TO BE SMOKED ON PRIVATE PREM-ISES SHOULD HAVE THEIR SENTENCES COMMUTED.

Jonathan Aitken
Tariq Ali
David Bailey
Humphry Berkeley
Anthony Blond
Derek Boshier
Sidney Briskin
Peter Brook
Dr David Cooper
Dr Francis Crick, FRS
David Dimbleby
Tom Driberg, MP
Dr Ian Dunbar
Brian Epstein
Dr Aaron Esterson
Peter Fryer
John Furnival
Tony Garnett
Clive Goodwin

Graham Greene
dsh
Richard Hamilton
George Harrison, MBE
Michael Hastings
Dr J. M. Heaton
David Hockney
Jeremy Hornsby
Dr S. Hutt
Francis Huxley
Dr Brian Inglis
The Rev Dr Victor
    E. S. Kenna, OBE
George Kiloh
Herbert Kretzmer
Dr R. D. Laing
Dr Calvin Mark Lee
John Lennon, MBE
Dr D. M. Lewis

Paul McCartney, MBE	John Pudney
David McEwen	Alastair Reid
Alasdair MacIntyre	L. Jeffrey Selznick
Dr O. D. Macrae-Gibson	Nathan Silver
Tom Maschler	Tony Smythe
Michael Abdul Malik	Michael Schofield
George Melly	Dr David Stafford-Clark
Dr Jonathan Miller	Richard Starkey, MBE
Adrian Mitchell	Dr Anthony Storr
Dr Ann Mully	Kenneth Tynan
P. H. Nowell-Smith	Dr W. Grey Walter
Dr Christopher Pallis	Brian Walden, MP
John Piper	Michael White
Patrick Procktor	Pat Williams

•

MARIO VARGAS LLOSA
1968

'Czechoslovakia'

*The Western world rose in protest when the Soviet Union crushed the hopes raised by the
Czech leader Alexander Dubček of 'socialism with a human face' after the 'Prague spring'.
Dubček was deposed and another Soviet puppet regime restored.*

*A different perspective to the protest was offered by the Peruvian novelist Mario Vargas
Llosa (1936–) whose first novel,* The Time of the Hero, *was a powerful social satire
published in 1962. In a newspaper article, 'Socialism and the Tanks', from London,
Llosa viewed the tragedy unfolding in Prague from the Latin American standpoint which
considered Americans equally guilty of super-power tyranny in crushing the uprising by the
people of Santo Domingo.*

The military intervention in Czechoslovakia by the Soviet Union and its four
allies in the Warsaw Pact is, purely and simply, an imperialist aggression
which is a dishonour to the country of Lenin, a political blunder of dizzying
proportions and an irreparable setback for the cause of socialism in the world.
Its most obvious antecedent is not so much Hungary as the Dominican
Republic. The sending of Soviet tanks into Prague to suppress a movement
of socialist democratization is as much to be condemned as the despatching

of American marines to Santo Domingo to stamp out by violence a popular uprising against a military dictatorship and an unjust social system.

The violation of the sovereignty of the Czech people by the USSR has been less bloody but no less immoral than that committed against the people of Santo Domingo. In both cases, the justifications used by Washington and Moscow – the famous argument that the interventions had been requested by the victims themselves and were intended to save 'democracy' or 'socialism' threatened by an outside power – reveal the same cynical contempt for the truth. The truth, in both cases, is that a great power, protected by the right of military superiority, has decided to trample over a small nation because the political direction that this nation has taken does not fit within its strategic global interests, and then it hides the intervention behind an ideological smoke-screen. What is at stake in the dramatic events that Czechoslovakia is living through today is not the struggle between capitalism and communism, but rather the destiny of those countries that make up the Third World. A terrible future seems to be darkening their historical horizon: to have to live perpetually at the mercy of the two great colossuses, alienated between two forms of colonial servitude, never really to be independent and free.

What was threatened in Czechoslovakia was not 'socialism', nor was 'freedom' threatened in the Dominican Republic. What was in jeopardy in the Dominican Republic when the military intervention took place was the power of the large landowners, the plunder of the country's wealth by foreign companies and the greed of the local caste system. What was threatened in Czechoslovakia was a robot socialism, remote-controlled by Moscow, press censorship, police abuse, the lack of internal criticism and a cancerous bureaucracy which had suffocated individual initiatives and allowed immorality to proliferate in its shadow. When they inform Dubček, Svoboda and Cernik that the presence of occupying troops, the destruction of freedom of expression and the banning of political organizations are the conditions of their survival, the Soviet leaders are not thinking of socialism but of preventing the development of any popular internal movement in East Germany, Bulgaria or the USSR itself that might seek to give socialism back a human face.

When the events in Hungary took place, divisions, uncertainty and confusion were still possible: it was the high point of the Cold War, the activities of counter-revolutionary forces could not be discounted and the Hungarian people seemed divided. None of this justified military intervention, but it was at least possible to have doubts, to think that this was a mistake that would later be corrected as far as it was possible. In the case of Czechoslovakia there can be no doubt, because all the elements with which we can judge the situation are crystal clear and none of them excuses the USSR, all of them instead accuse her.

Ten days after the intervention, Moscow cannot offer a shred of evidence to the world to show that the Dubček regime was endangering internal security or was about to leave the socialist camp to become part of the capitalist world. No factory had been seized from the workers, no international consortium had been undermining the socialist economy, the half a million occupying troops have not been able to capture one single 'agent of German militarism'. Furthermore, not even the most conservative elements of the Communist Party have dared to play the role of quislings and no one has ventured to claim authorship of this imaginary manifesto which purportedly asked the countries of the Warsaw Pact to carry out the invasion. Rather, the foreign occupation has shown the world the extraordinary unity of the Czech people behind their leaders, and their dignity and serenity in the face of the humiliation that has been inflicted on them. Whatever the outcome of this tragedy, and even if the outcome is the one that political morality and common sense dictate – the withdrawal of the occupying forces, to allow the Czech people the freedom to direct their socialism along whatever path they might choose, compensation for the damages sustained – one does not need to be a fortune-teller to know that the wound inflicted so disloyally by the USSR on Czechoslovakia will take a long time to heal and that, paradoxically, this action will only serve to sharpen and to strengthen precisely what it intended to snuff out: the Czech desire for national independence and freedom.

•

ELDRIDGE CLEAVER
1968

'Soul on Ice'

Eldridge Cleaver (1935–98), minister of information of the Black Panthers, the militant black liberation group, chose exile in 1968 rather than return to jail after a violent confrontation between the Panthers and the police in which one Panther was killed. He went to Cuba, Algeria and France before returning to the United States seven years later when he repudiated his earlier views. 'People with grievances must find political methods for obtaining redress,' he wrote.

Cleaver wrote Soul on Ice *in Fulsom Prison between 1957 and 1966, and it was originally published in monthly instalments in the mass-selling new left magazine* Ramparts.

The Negro revolution at home and national liberation movements abroad have unceremoniously shattered the world of fantasy in which the whites have been living. It is painful that many do not yet see that their fantasy world has been rendered uninhabitable in the last half of the twentieth century. But it is away from this world that the white youth of today are turning. The 'paper tiger' hero, James Bond, offering the whites a triumphant image of themselves, is saying what many whites want desperately to hear reaffirmed: *I am still the White Man, lord of the land, licensed to kill, and the world is still an empire at my feet.* James Bond feeds on that secret little anxiety, the psychological white backlash, felt in some degree by most whites alive. It is exasperating to see little brown men and little yellow men from the mysterious Orient, and the opaque black men of Africa (to say nothing of these impudent American Negroes!) who come to the UN and talk smart to us, who are scurrying all over *our* globe in their strange modes of dress – much as if they were new, unpleasant arrivals from another planet. Many whites believe in their ulcers that it is only a matter of time before the Marines get the signal to round up these truants and put them back securely in their cages. But it is away from this fantasy world that the white youth of today are turning.

In the world revolution now under way, the initiative rests with people of color. That growing numbers of white youth are repudiating their heritage of blood and taking people of color as their heroes and models is a tribute not only to their insight but to the resilience of the human spirit. For today the heroes of the initiative are people not usually thought of as white: Fidel Castro, Che Guevara, Kwame Nkrumah, Mao Tse-tung, Gamal Abdel Nasser, Robert F. Williams, Malcolm X, Ben Bella, John Lewis, Martin Luther King Jr, Robert Parris Moses, Ho Chi Minh, Stokeley Carmichael, W. E. B. Du Bois, James Forman, Chou En-lai.

The white youth of today have begun to react to the fact that the 'American Way of Life' is a fossil of history. What do they care if their old baldheaded and crew-cut elders don't dig their caveman mops? They couldn't care less about the old, stiffassed honkies who don't like their new dances: Frug, Monkey, Jerk, Swim, Watusi. All they know is that it feels good to swing to way-out body-rhythms instead of dragassing across the dance floor like zombies to the dead beat of mind-smothered Mickey Mouse music. Is it any wonder that the youth have lost all respect for their elders, for law and order, when for as long as they can remember all they've witnessed is a monumental bickering over the Negro's place in American society and the right of people around the world to be left alone by outside powers?

They have witnessed the law, both domestic and international, being spat upon by those who do not like its terms. Is it any wonder, then, that they feel justified, by sitting-in and freedom riding, in breaking laws made by lawless men? Old funny-styled, zipper-mouthed political night riders know nothing but to haul out an investigating committee *to look into the disturbance* to find the cause of the unrest among the youth. Look into a mirror! The cause is you, Mr and Mrs Yesterday, you with your forked tongues.

A young white today cannot help but recoil from the base deeds of his people. On every side, on every continent, he sees racial arrogance, savage brutality toward the conquered and subjugated people, genocide; he sees the human cargo of the slave trade; he sees the systematic extermination of American Indians; he sees the civilized nations of Europe fighting in imperial depravity over the lands of other people – and over possession of the very people themselves. There seems to be no end to the ghastly deeds of which his people are guilty. GUILTY. The slaughter of the Jews by the Germans, the dropping of atomic bombs on the Japanese people – these deeds weigh heavily upon the prostrate souls and tumultuous consciences of the white youth. The white heroes, their hands dripping with blood, are dead.

The young whites know that the colored people of the world, Afro-Americans included, do not seek revenge for their suffering. They seek the same things the white rebel wants: an end to war and exploitation. Black and white, the young rebels are free people, free in a way that Americans have never been before in the history of their country. And they are outraged.

•

MICHAEL ROSEN
1968

'Exams'

The student revolt which spread throughout the Western world in 1968 was partly inspired by Vietnam but was also a rebellion against 'paternalistic' university rules and regulations.

Michael Rosen has subsequently become a successful poet, performer and broadcaster, but is known above all as an author of children's books. In 1968 he was a student at Oxford and the essay he wrote for the undergraduate newspaper Isis *encapsulated several of the issues that led to student occupations of university buildings.*

For years and years people like us have conditioned their whole lives to passing exams. We took exams because that would help us to 'get on'. To bigger and better facts and bigger and better jobs. And there were people called teachers who did two things: they knew the facts and gave them to us in exam-question-shaped bundles – and they told us that we couldn't piddle on the school field because that would be letting the name of the school down.

Watching people take finals this summer in lunatic sub-fusc is like some grisly *déjà-vu* nightmare to me. For three years we accept syllabuses devised by reactionary old men fifty years ago; eating conditions devised 500 years ago; deans, dons (they look like headmasters) inventing their own little rules and fines (there was a dean in Magdalen who fined someone for going home without collecting the exeat he'd given him); proctors acting as judge, jury, defending and prosecuting counsels in order to ruin someone's career and/or life by chucking him out. But this is sickening – not simply because this is a gang of reactionary old men and women putting the screws on. I wouldn't want a gang of *nice* men and women, old or young, putting nice screws on me.

I want to make my own decisions about how I run my life. And I want to reach those decisions by co-operating with a lot of other people doing the same thing. On equal terms. That's student participation in the academic sphere and student control in discipline. To abdicate one's right to participate in the decision-making process is abdicating one's basic right to be.

And in discipline. The whole 'loco parentis' matter is absurd. Forcing people to live in landlady-ridden digs and the pretence that, 'Oh, no we don't know that people f—k but by god we'll make it difficult for them if they do.'

So how? Quite simply you start by saying to the authorities: 'We don't like it. Get rid of it.' They say, 'No. You're too young. It doesn't foster the spirit of inquiry. Let's have a commission. Send your leaders to us and we'll have sherry and a chat.' This just won't do. Students can and must be executors. Not consultants to wary little authoritarians fighting off the spectre of the Sorbonne. Before last Monday at the Clarendon they had us by the short and curlies. If a proctor decided he wanted to punish anyone he just went ahead and did it. If that person felt victimized he had no way of protecting himself. They tried it on Tony Hodges and leafleting. We made them stage at least two big climb-downs because we were united. Victimize one – victimize ninety. If you can't – then remove the rule. That victory means that they'll never be able to behave like that again. The proctors had to argue with us on equal terms that day as they've never had to do before. What we do now is turn to the rest of the university authority and say: do the same. The whole thing has been a massive education to me – reaching decisions in groups, no bureaucracy, no executive committees.

The difficulty getting things going here is of course enormous. The collegiate system fragments opinion. A union which is everything except a union, summer aesthetes' freak-out, success-chasing up at Bush House. Very few people seem to realize before the third year that one of the main causes for their moments of misery in this place comes from segregated submissive living and studying. By the time they do – they're neck-deep in the exam ritual all over again.

•

JEAN-JACQUES LEBEL
1968

'The night of the barricades'

When the students of Paris took to the streets in 1968 they were not only protesting against the Vietnam War but also against overcrowded conditions and irrelevant courses at their universities. When the students of Nanterre and the Sorbonne joined forces, the university rector summoned the state security police. The direct result was the 'événements' leading to the night of the barricades when France teetered on the brink of revolution.

No single speech or manifesto can capture the spirit of Paris in May 1968, but this description of what happened on 10 May, published in Black Dwarf *in 1968 and reprinted by Tariq Ali and Susan Watkins in* 1968 Marching in the Streets *(Bloomsbury), is a vivid report on the biggest student protest of the century.*

'We circle the Santé prison which is defended by thousands of armed police, then turn towards the Right Bank and the ORTF. But the route has been blocked off by the police. The enormous demonstration is halted in Boulevard St Michel by gigantic forces: we are encircled.

'The decision is taken to occupy the Latin Quarter, peacefully – not to provoke the police, but to defend ourselves if they attack.'

The huge crowd spreads through the labyrinthine streets, heaping up cobblestones, traffic signs, scaffolding and rubble from the building sites – anything that comes to hand to build up defences against the *flics*. The atmosphere is exhilarating, electric: a night-time carnival, thirty thousand strong. 'It's the Commune,' they say. The Commune: the insurrectionary power that arose in Paris during the French Revolution, and again during the revolutionary attempt of 1871. The power that consists only of the people in the act of governing themselves.

For Daniel Cohn-Bendit, the student leader at Nanterre, 'It's a moment I shall never forget. Suddenly, spontaneously, barricades were being thrown up in the streets. People were piling up the cobblestones because they wanted, many for the first time, to throw themselves into a collective, spontaneous activity. People were releasing all their repressed feelings, expressing them in a festive spirit. Thousands felt the need to communicate with each other, to love one another. That night has made me for ever optimistic about history. Having lived through it, I can't ever say, "It will never happen."'

By 10 p.m. the students hold the Latin Quarter. A few hours later Jean-Jacques Lebel pens this dispatch from Paris:

'1 a.m.: Our group organizes the barricade at the corner of Rue Gay Lussac and St Jacques. We are composed of six students, ten workers, some Italians, bystanders and four artists who joined later. Most have never seen the others before. We never even knew each other's names.

'A hundred people help carry the stuff and pile it across the street. From then on I was so busy co-ordinating work at our barricade that I don't know what happened elsewhere. Witnesses say it all happened at the same time and more or less in the same way all over the Latin Quarter.

'Our barricade is double: one 3 foot high row of cobblestones, an empty space of about 20 yards, then a 9 foot high pile of wood, cars, metal posts, dustbins. Our weapons are stones, metal, etc. found in the street.

'A great deal of spontaneous help is given from inhabitants of nearby houses who offer water, sugar and cloth as protection against gases and warn us of police movements. It is their support which keeps our enthusiasm from flagging in the seemingly endless time of waiting for the inevitable police attack.'

Negotiations are going on. From the back of a mobile radio van, student leaders are conducting a discussion with the rector, live on air on Radio Luxembourg. The students are refusing to disperse until their comrades are freed, the *flics* are withdrawn and the Sorbonne reopened.

The radios report heavy *flic* reinforcements flooding into the Quarter.

Shortly after midnight Cohn-Bendit speaks to the press: 'We told the rector that what is happening on the street tonight is a whole generation rising against a certain sort of society. We told him blood would flow if the police did not leave the Latin Quarter. We know the demonstrators will stay behind the barricades until our three demands have been met.'

The rector telephones the Ministry of the Interior, pleading for permission for more talks. His hands are tied: in an inner sanctum at the ministry, de Gaulle's hard-line security and intelligence adviser, Jacques Foccart, and Bernard Tricot, the President's key aide from the Élysée Palace, are urging on the Education and Interior Ministers the necessity of taking a firm stand. This is insurrection. It must be crushed. The Defence Minister is also present.

Lines of armoured black CRS vans glimmer in the dark streets. The massed ranks of the security police seem barely human in their insectoid, goggle-eyed masks and helmets. They are sheathed in black leather, armed with batons, shields and tear-gas grenades. This is the naked face of the power wielded by the Fifth Republic. Lebel reports:

'2 a.m.: It is now obvious that the police are preparing a powerful attack. The radio announces that we are surrounded and the government has ordered the police to attack. We continue building up barricades, organizing a supply of rocks and medical centres every 100 yards. I try to co-ordinate runners between different barricades near ours but we lack time and are caught by attacks before we can get it together. Practically no news comes from other points of our territory.

'Someone finds a French flag – we tear off the blue and white parts: the red flag now flies over our barricade. I am told many red and black flags flew on other barricades. In front of us we turn over cars to prevent police from charging with their buses and tanks. (The radio said tanks were coming but we never saw any.)

'The police attack Place de Luxembourg. Their tactics are simple: at 100 yards distance they launch gas grenades which blind, suffocate and knock us out. The gas is mace (Vietnam and Detroit mace), tear-gas and phosphorus grenades which set fire to the cars. Also small explosive grenades: one student near us picked one up to throw it back and it tore his whole hand off.

'We defend as best we can and later we find out that practically every barricade withstood the police at least an hour, sometimes four hours, regardless of blinding and suffocating gases. The police are slowly advancing up Gay Lussac (crowds are running away, we have a hard time calming them down and channelling them towards the exit down Gay Lussac where the police are fewer).

'Then the police attack at three points simultaneously: at two extremities of Gay Lussac, at our barricade and at Rue d'Ulm. Casualties are heavy on our side, mostly people knocked unconscious by gas, some temporarily blinded. Thousands of voices shout together: "De Gaulle assassin", "*Libérez nos camarades*", "Revolution". Some make Molotov cocktails. I try to dissuade them for fear of police massacre, not so much of us but of thousands of onlookers, just standing there, fascinated. The general feeling is of a trance. We feel liberated. Suddenly, we have turned into human beings and we are shouting "WE EXIST, WE ARE HERE."

'One boy, in an incredibly heroic gesture, grabs a red flag and leads us towards the cops, through the gas and grenades. To our utter surprise we outnumber the enemy and they retreat. Crowds behind us cheer wildly. We come back behind our barricade, only one slightly wounded. But gases are our worst enemy, we can't breathe, we can't see.

'Finally we are forced back. Our barricade burns. At this point all I can remember is that I fainted from lack of air. I come to in a corridor with two girls slapping my face and putting wet cloths on my eyes. Water is the only thing that helps. They tell me that a student carried me there.

'I look outside: police are everywhere, our barricade across the street is burning. Yellow gas fumes are so thick you can't see.

'I try to run out, thinking to rejoin our forces further down, but police are charging from both sides with grenades and big lethal truncheons: we are cornered.

'We organize inside the apartment building: there are at least sixty students, some wounded, others fainting. We try to barricade the street doors. Some desperately ring doorbells of the flats; nobody dares answer. We crowd staircases. The police arrive, break down the door, grab a few and beat them to pulp, then throw in three gas grenades which are murder to our lungs and eyes. They go on down the street.

'A girl on the second floor tells us to come in. We crowd into her flat and she gives us water. Outside: explosions, explosions, explosions.'

A well-known French football commentator is sent to the Latin Quarter to cover the night's events for one of the radio stations. He reports:

'Now the CRS are charging, they're storming the barricade – oh, my God! There's a battle raging. The students are counter-attacking, you can hear the noise – the CRS are retreating . . . Now they're regrouping, getting ready to charge again. The inhabitants are throwing things from their windows at the CRS – oh! The police are retaliating, shooting grenades into the windows of apartments . . .'

The producer interrupts: 'This can't be true, the CRS don't do things like that!'

'I'm telling you what I'm seeing . . .' His voice goes dead. They have cut him off.

(At 5 a.m. university students in Strasbourg who have been following the street fighting in Paris all night on their radios, take over and occupy the university's administrative building.)

At 6 a.m., exhausted and unshaven, security boss Foccart and the three ministers leave the Interior Ministry and drive to the Élysée to report to President de Gaulle that the insurrection has been crushed.

Lebel carries on writing:

'6 a.m.: Still fighting outside. We all vote to call the Red Cross anyway because one of us is bleeding badly. The police are searching house by house, room by room. Anybody with black bands or wounds or gas spots on clothes (gas attacks leather) is beaten and arrested. We sixty decide to leave together in case we have to fight our way down the street. Helmets are given to the girls. The sun is up.

'We run into the open in a body: fantastic: what a sight! Smoking barricades everywhere, overturned cars, streets unpaved, for half a mile. Painted words on walls: *Viva la Commune du 8 Mai, À BAS L'ÉTAT POLICIER* . . .

'I can't help it, I run over to see our barricade. It still stands, deserted; some onlookers, stunned, the unbelievable sight of the empty battlefield. This Rue Gay Lussac was ours all night till about 4.30 a.m.

'I ask a student for a piece of his dirty red shirt, we tie it to a stick, put it back on our barricade and run: police are charging on the other side of the street.

'I can hardly walk from pain. We circle round to Rue d'Ulm, to find police arresting everybody, including those in the medical centre. Barricades and cars are smoking in every street, on every corner. Passers-by warn us where the police are. Many people in cars and taxis volunteer to take us out of the police zone. Everywhere we see enormous police buses full of our people: tired, beaten, bloody prisoners.

'The revolution has begun. If you want to help us there is one way. 'DO THE SAME THING.'

In a broken voice, Daniel Cohn-Bendit goes on the radio and calls for a general strike in protest against the state's behaviour on this night.

•

BERNADETTE DEVLIN
1969

'Stark human misery'

The Ulster civil rights activist Bernadette Devlin was only twenty-one when she was elected to the House of Commons as MP for Mid-Ulster in 1969. Her victory was followed by a weekend of unrest: there was a bomb explosion at a reservoir, an electricity pylon was sabotaged and nine post offices were set on fire. A thousand police in military formation marched into Derry to stop street-fighting. As the Ulster prime minister Terence O'Neill asked for British military units to safeguard key installations, Harold Wilson, the British prime minister, called an emergency debate on the breakdown of order in the province, at which Devlin's maiden speech was a sensation.

She spoke immediately after Robin Chichester-Clark, MP for Londonderry and leader of the Ulster Unionist MPs. 'I didn't need any notes because everything I detested about the system was written on his Tory face,' she wrote later. 'It was a bitter speech that stated that the situation was medieval . . . and the time for Westminster's action had almost passed.'

I had never hoped to see the day when I might agree with someone who represents the bigoted and sectarian Unionist Party which uses a deliberate policy of dividing the people in order to keep the oppressed people of Ulster oppressed. I never thought that I should see the day where I should agree with any phrase uttered by the representative of such a party but the hon. Gentleman summed up the situation 'to a t'. He referred to stark human misery. That is what I saw in Bogside. It has been there for fifty years – and the same stark human misery is to be found in the Protestant Fountain area, which the hon. Gentleman would claim to represent.

These are the people the hon. Gentleman [Mr Chichester-Clark] would claim do want to join society. Because they are equally poverty-stricken they are equally excluded from the society which the Unionist Party represents – the society of landlords who, by ancient charter of Charles II, still hold the rights of the ordinary people of Northern Ireland over such things as fishing and as paying the most ridiculous and exorbitant rents, although families have lived for generations on their land. But this is the ruling minority of landlords who, for generations, have claimed to represent one section of the people and, in order to maintain their claim, divide the people into two sections and stand up in this House and say that there are those who do not wish to join the society.

The people in my country who do not wish to join the society which is represented by the hon. Member for Londonderry are by far the majority. There is no place in society for us, the ordinary 'peasants' of Northern Ireland. There is no place for us in the society of landlords because we are the 'have-nots' and they are the 'haves' . . .

The situation with which we are faced in Northern Ireland is one in which I feel I can no longer say to the people, 'Don't worry about it. Westminster is looking after you.' Westminster cannot condone the existence of this situation. It has on its benches Members of that party who by deliberate policy keep down the ordinary people. The fact that I sit on the Labour benches and am likely to make myself unpopular with everyone on these benches . . . [hon. Members: 'No'] Any socialist government worth its guts would have got rid of them long ago.

There is no denying that the problem and the reason for this situation in Northern Ireland is social and economic, because the people of Northern

Ireland are being oppressed not only by a Tory Government, a misruling Tory Government and an absolutely corrupt, bigoted and self-interested Tory Government, but by a Tory Government of whom even the Tories in this House ought to be ashamed and from which they should dissociate themselves.

I should like in conclusion to take a brief look at the future. This is where the question of British troops arises. The question before this House, in view of the apathy, neglect and lack of understanding which this House has shown to these people in Ulster which it claims to represent, is how in the shortest space it can make up for fifty years of neglect, apathy and lack of understanding. Short of producing miracles, such as factories overnight in Derry and homes overnight in practically every area in the North of Ireland, what can we do? If British troops are sent in I should not like to be either the mother or sister of an unfortunate soldier stationed there. The point in common among Ulstermen is that they are not very fond of Englishmen who tell them what to do.

Possibly the most extreme solution, since there can be no justice while there is a Unionist Party, because while there is a Unionist Party they will by their gerry-mandering control Northern Ireland and be the Government of Northern Ireland, is to consider the possibility of abolishing Stormont and ruling from Westminster. Then we should have the ironical situation in which the people who once shouted 'Home rule is Rome rule' were screaming their heads off for home rule, so dare anyone take Stormont away? They would have to ship every government member out of the country for his own safety because only the 'rank' defends, such as the Prime Minister and the Minister of Agriculture.

Another solution which the government may decide to adopt is to do nothing but serve notice on the Unionist Government that they will impose economic sanctions on them if true reforms are not carried out. The interesting point is that the Unionist Government cannot carry out reforms. If they introduce the human rights bill and outlaw sectarianism and discrimination what will the party which is based on, and survives on, discrimination do? By introducing the human rights bill, it signs its own death warrant. Therefore, the government can impose economic sanctions but the Unionist Party will not yield. I assure you Mr Speaker, that one cannot impose economic sanctions on the dead.

●

GEORGE MANGAKIS
1969

'The fate of a victim'

When a military coup in 1967 ousted the Greek government and imposed a right-wing dictatorship by the 'Greek Colonels' on the nation where democracy was born, George Mangakis (1906–91) was dismissed from his chair of penal law at the University of Athens for his open defiance. He was accused by the junta of a 'lack of spirit of conformity' with the regime, arrested on charges of terrorism, imprisoned and tortured (but after the restoration of democracy served as a minister). This 'Letter to Europeans' appeared in the first issue of Index on Censorship.

The dimensions of my cell are approximately 10 feet by 10 feet. You gradually become accustomed to this space and even grow to like it, since, in a way, it is like a lair in which you lie hidden, licking your wounds. But in reality its object is to annihilate you. On one side of it there is a heavy iron door, with a little round hole in the upper part. Prisoners hate this little hole; they call it the 'stool pigeon'. It is through this hole that the jailer's eye appears every now and then – an isolated eye, without a face. There is also a peculiar lock, on the outside only; it locks with a dry, double sound. That is one thing you never get used to, no matter how much time goes by. It gives you the daily, tangible sensation of the violence that is being done to you. Before I came here, I didn't know that violence could be expressed so completely by the dry sound of a double lock.

On the other side of my cell there is a little window with bars. From this window you can see part of the city. And yet a prisoner rarely looks out of the window. It is too painful. The prisoner, of course, has a picture of life outside the prison constantly in his mind. But it is dim, colourless, like an old photograph; it is soft and shapeless. It is bearable. So you don't dare look out of the window. Its only use is to bring you some light. That is something I have studied very carefully. I have learned all the possible shades of light. I can distinguish the light that comes just before daybreak, and the light that lingers on after nightfall.

We turned in despair to Europe, and the people of Europe did not forsake us. Now all those of us who have entered upon this ordeal, in the prisons of the dictatorship, say 'Europe' as we would say 'our country'. And we mean exactly that: this fusion, in depth, of common historical experiences, cultural value and human solidarity which we call 'country', 'fatherland'. We clutch the bars of our narrow windows, we look at the world outside, and we think of those millions of people walking the streets, and we know that if they could see us, they would raise their hands in greeting, they would give us a sign. In those moments, with our mind's eye, we embrace the whole of Europe. It is a place which includes all our own people, all the ones who would raise their hands in greeting. The headhunters have locked us up in this narrow place in order to make us shrink, like those hideous human scalps which are their trophies. But what they haven't realized is that our country has widened; it has become a whole continent. They have isolated us so as to turn us into solitary, forsaken creatures, lost in a purely individual fate. But we now live in the immense human community of European solidarity. Their power is helpless in the face of this knowledge.

We often talk about the dignity of man. It is not an abstraction; it is a thing which I have actually experienced. It exists in our very depths, like a sensitive steel spring. It has absolutely nothing to do with personal dignity. Its roots lie much deeper. Throughout the nightmare of the interrogation sessions, I lost my personal dignity; it was replaced by pure suffering. But human dignity was within me, without my knowing it. There came a moment when they touched it; the questioning had already been going on for some time. They cannot tell when this moment comes, and so they cannot plan their course accordingly. It functioned suddenly, like a hidden spring that made my scattered spiritual parts jerk upright, all of a piece. It wasn't really me who rose to my feet then, it was Everyman. The moment I began to feel this, I began to overcome the questioning ordeal. The effort was no longer only for myself. It was for all of us. Together we stood our ground.

I have experienced the fate of a victim. I have seen the torturer's face at close quarters. It was in a worse condition than my own bleeding, livid face. The torturer's face was distorted by a kind of twitching that had nothing human about it. He was in such a state of tension that he had an expression very similar to those we see on Chinese masks: I am not exaggerating. It is not an easy thing to torture people. It requires inner participation. In this situation, I turned out to be the lucky one. I was humiliated. I did not humiliate others. I was simply bearing a profoundly unhappy humanity in my aching entrails. Whereas the men who humiliate you must first humiliate the notion of humanity within themselves. Never mind if they strut around in their uniforms, swollen with the knowledge that they can control the suffering, sleeplessness, hunger and despair of their fellow human beings, intoxicated with the power in their hands. Their intoxication is nothing other than the degradation of humanity. The ultimate degradation. They have had to pay very dearly for my torments. I wasn't the one in the worst position. I was simply a man who moaned because he was in great pain. I prefer that. At this moment I am deprived of the joy of seeing children going to school or playing in the parks. Whereas they have to look their own children in the face. It is their own humiliation that I cannot forgive the dictators.

•

JOHN ARLOTT
1970

'Why I'm off the air'

The question of whether, by playing against South Africa, English cricket was condoning apartheid aroused heated controversy, especially when Basil D'Oliveira, a coloured South African who had settled in England, was selected for the English team to tour South Africa. He was refused admission and British teams refused to go to South Africa. When a South African tour of England was arranged in 1970, John Arlott (1914–91), the voice of cricket as a renowned commentator for the BBC, refused to broadcast on the matches.

For personal reasons, I shall not broadcast on the matches of the South African cricket tour of England arranged for 1970. The BBC has accepted my decision with understanding and an undertaking that my standing with them will not be affected by it.

This course of action has not been dictated by mass influences. Apartheid is detestable to me, and I would always oppose it. On the other hand, I am not satisfied that the cricket tour is the aspect of apartheid which should have been selected as the major target for attack. It would have seemed to me more justifiable, more tactically simple, and more effective, to mount a trade embargo or to picket South Africa House. Surely the Nationalist South African Ambassador is a thousand times more guilty of the inhuman crime of apartheid than Graeme Pollock who, throughout the English summer of 1969, played cricket for the International Cavaliers XI with eight or nine West Indians and, before he went home, said: 'What great chaps – there couldn't have been a better bunch to play with.'

Jack Plimsoll, the manager of this touring team, was an intimate friend of mine on the South African tour of England in 1947, before the election of the first – Malan – Nationalist Government, and the introduction of apartheid.

Every one of the South African players of my acquaintance has already played with, and against, non-white cricketers. Indeed, only a multi-racial match, played in South Africa before the Vorster (Verwoerd) Government banned such fixtures for ever, provided the expert assessment of Basil D'Oliveira's ability which enabled me to persuade Middleton to give him a contract to play in England. Not all South Africans are pro-apartheid.

Crucially, though, a successful tour would offer comfort and confirmation to a completely evil regime. To my mind, the Cricket Council, acting on behalf of British cricket, has failed fairly to represent those British people – especially cricketers – who genuinely abominate apartheid. The council might have determined – and been granted – terms which would have demonstrated its declared disapproval of apartheid. It did not do so; nor give the slightest indication of a will to do so. To persist with the tour seems to me a social, political, and cricketing error. If I were a supporter of apartheid I would feel the same. It seems to me destined to failure on all levels, with the game of cricket the ultimate and inevitable sufferer. If it should 'succeed' to the extent of being completed, what is the outcome to be – a similarly contentious tour four years hence?

It is my limitation, an advantage, that I can only broadcast as I feel. Commentary on any game demands, in my professional belief, the ingredient of pleasure; it can only be satisfactorily broadcast in terms of shared enjoyment. This series cannot, to my mind, be enjoyable. There are three justifiable reasons for playing cricket – performance, pleasure, and profit – and I do not believe that this tour will produce any of them.

The terms of the BBC's charter do not permit expression of editorial opinion. It would not be professional or polite to disagree with my fellow commentators on the significance of the tour within the hearing of listeners. It therefore seems to me unfair, on both sides, for me to broadcast about the tour in a manner uncritical of its major issues, while retaining the right to be critical of them in this newspaper.

It is my hope to write and talk about cricket in which the minor issue of a game is not overshadowed by the major issue of principle.

•

GERMAINE GREER
1970

'The Female Eunuch'

For the generation of women born in the 1950s Germaine Greer's The Female Eunuch *was as significant as Simone de Beauvoir's* The Second Sex *had been for their mothers. It became a bestseller in Britain and the United States, at the time when the pill was new and the age of sexual emancipation was beginning. Greer (1939–), a feminist, university teacher of English and Shakespeare scholar, was delightedly heterosexual and enjoyed outraging social conventions. As the feminist historian Sheila Rowbotham observes, Greer was one of the crusaders calling for sex to be brought out into the open, as an all-pervasive element of daily life – more sex, better sex, different sex.*

Unhappily we have accepted, along with the reinstatement of the clitoris after its proscription by the Freudians, a notion of the utter passivity and even irrelevance of the vagina. Love-making has become another male skill, of which women are the judges. The skills that the Wife of Bath used to make her husbands swink, the athletic sphincters of the Tahitian girls who can keep their men inside them all night, are alike unknown to us. All the vulgar linguistic emphasis is placed upon the *poking* element; *fucking, screwing, rooting, shagging* are all acts performed upon the passive female: the names for the penis are all *tool* names . . .

Women will have to accept part of the responsibility for their own and their partners' enjoyment, and this involves a measure of control and conscious co-operation. Part of the battle will be won if they can change their attitude towards sex, and embrace and stimulate the penis instead of *taking* it. Enlightened women have long sung the praises of the female superior position, because they are not weighted down by the heavier male body, and can respond more spontaneously. It is after all a question of communication, and communication is not advanced by the *he talk, me listen* formula.

The banishment of the fantasy of the vaginal orgasm is ultimately a service, but the substitution of the clitoral spasm for genuine gratification may turn out to be a disaster for sexuality. Masters and Johnson's conclusions have produced some unlooked for side-effects, like the veritable clitoromania which infects Mette Ejlersen's book, *I accuse!* While speaking of women's orgasms as resulting from the 'right touches on the button', she condemns sexologists who recommend . . . the stimulation of the clitoris as part of the prelude to intercourse, to that which most men consider to be the 'real thing'. What is in fact the 'real thing' for them is *completely devoid of sensation* for the woman.

This is the heart of the matter! Concealed for hundreds of years by humble, shy and subservient women.

Not all the women in history have been humble and subservient to such an extent. It is nonsense to say that a woman feels nothing when a man is moving his penis in her vagina: the orgasm is qualitatively different when the vagina can undulate around the penis instead of vacancy. The differentiation between the simple inevitable pleasure of men and the tricky responses of women is not altogether valid. If ejaculation meant release for all men, given the constant manufacture of sperm and the resultant pressure to have intercourse, men could copulate without transport or disappointment with anyone. The process described by the experts, in which man dutifully does the rounds of the erogenous zones, spends an equal amount of time on each nipple, turns his attention to the clitoris (usually too directly), leads through the stages of digital or lingual stimulation, and then politely lets himself into the vagina, perhaps waiting until the retraction of the clitoris tells him that he is welcome, is laborious and inhumanly computerized. The implication that there is a statistically ideal fuck which will always result in satisfaction if the right procedures are followed is depressing and misleading. There is no substitute for excitement: not all the massage in the world will insure satisfaction, for it is a matter of psychosexual release. Real satisfaction is not enshrined in a tiny cluster of nerves but in the sexual involvement of the whole person. Women's continued high enjoyment of sex, which continues after orgasm, observed by men with wonder, is not based on the clitoris, which does not respond particularly well to continued stimulus, but in a general sensual response. If we localize female response in the clitoris we impose upon women the same limitation of sex which has stunted the male's response. The male sexual idea of virility without languor or amorousness is profoundly desolating: when the release is expressed in mechanical terms it is sought mechanically. Sex becomes masturbation in the vagina.

Many women who greeted the conclusions of Masters and Johnson with cries of 'I told you so!' and 'I am normal!' will feel that this criticism is a betrayal. They have discovered sexual pleasure after being denied it but the fact that they have only ever experienced gratification from clitoral stimulation is evidence for my case, because it is the index of the desexualization of the whole body, the substitution of genitality for sexuality. The ideal marriage as measured by the electronic equipment in the Reproductive Biology Research Foundation laboratories is enfeebled – dull sex for dull people. The sexual personality is basically anti-authoritarian. If the system wishes to enforce complete suggestibility in its subjects, it will have to tame sex. Masters and Johnson supplied the blueprint for standard, low-agitation, cool-out monogamy. If women are to avoid this last reduction of their humanity, they must hold out not just for orgasm but for ecstasy.

•

JAMES EVANS/HAROLD EVANS
1972

'Thalidomide'

After their mothers took the thalidomide sleeping pill during pregnancy, more than 450 British children were born deformed, some without arms, some without legs and some as limbless trunks. Only sixty-two claims against Distillers, whose subsidiary Distillers Biochemicals made the drug under licence from Chemie Grumenthal of Germany, had been settled by 1965, at an average of £16,000.

By then Harold Evans, the campaigning editor of the Sunday Times*, had been waiting three years to publish articles on how thalidomide was made. James Evans, the* Sunday Times *lawyer, found the solution when, on the instruction of Harold Evans, he drafted a leading article which enabled the* Sunday Times *to publish by making a distinction between moral and legal liability. The campaign, which began with this leading article 'Children on our Conscience', ended six years later with victory in the European Court.*

The thalidomide babies have grown up. It is eleven years since the deformities they suffer shocked the world. Some 8,000 mothers who took the drug bore deformed children, 400 or so in Britain. Many people must long ago have assumed that society had paid its debt to the children and the parents; few can fail to recall the wave of compassion and anger that followed their birth. Yet even now the bulk of the compensation claims in Britain are not settled, and the peculiar agony of this saga is that no one should feel a sense of relief that at last a settlement may be in sight. One should feel only a sense of shame.

First, it shames our society that a decade should have passed. No money can ever compensate for being born a limbless trunk, but at least a generous compensation can give the glimmer of a normal life. One thinks also of the parents who for so long have had added to their sorrows the anxieties of protracted litigation.

Secondly, it shames the law that the compensation proposed should be so low. Essentially Mr Justice Hinchcliffe fixed the level when, in two test cases in 1968, he assessed what the damages would be if the drug's sellers, Distillers Biochemicals, lost a suit for negligence. Distillers agreed to pay 40 per cent of the assessment if the allegations of negligence were withdrawn. Clearly, if the full sum was judged 'sufficient' to compensate the victims, the 40 per cent must be judged 60 per cent insufficient to human need at the time, to say nothing of the effects of future inflation. Even the full sum exposes the crudeness of the rule-of-thumb assessments of the law. As the Law Commissioners say, the legal method of fixing damages lacks any mathematical, actuarial, statistical or other scientific basis. What is stopping the government immediately bringing in an Act to make evidence of this kind crucial?

Thirdly, the thalidomide children shame Distillers. It is appreciated that Distillers have always denied negligence and that if the cases were pursued, the children might end up with nothing. It is appreciated that Distillers' lawyers have a professional duty to secure the best terms for their clients. But at the end of the day what is to be paid in settlement is the decision of Distillers, and they should offer much, much more to every one of the thalidomide victims. It may be argued that Distillers have a duty to their shareholders and that, having taken account of skilled legal advice, the terms are just. But the law is not always the same as justice. There are times when to insist on the letter of the law is as exposed to criticism as infringement of another's legal rights. The figure in the proposed settlement is to be £3.25 million spread over ten years. This does not shine as a beacon against pre-tax profits last year of £64.8 million and company assets worth £421 million. Without in any way surrendering on negligence, Distillers could and should think again.

And the government must act. The adversarial system will not do. Compassion after disaster requires a state insurance scheme for compensation, as some have long advocated for personal injury cases. But even the wisest reform will be a sham if society does not now insist on justice for the victims of an enduring tragedy.

•

BERNARD LEVIN
1973

'The Gas Board'

When The Times *columnist Bernard Levin (1928–) devoted one of his columns to a furious denunciation of the North Thames Gas Board and its treatment of his mother, he received one of his biggest ever postbags from readers who had also suffered from its incompetence. The Gas Board stood as a symbol of the uncaring, unaccountable face of nationalized industry.*

An elderly widowed lady of whom I am rather fond was notified some time ago that she was about to undergo the full horrors of conversion to natural gas. Resigning herself to a future of uncontrollably fluctuating gas pressure, burnt saucepans and higher bills, she awaited the coming of the convertors. The day dawned.

Two men came; they converted her stove, her kitchen water-heater, her refrigerator and her gas fires. She also has, however, in her bathroom, a geyser of ancient design and dilapidated condition (I suppose we had better pause here for the one that goes 'Mornin' lady; 'ave you got an old geyser 'ere what won't work?' – 'Yes, 'e's just gone down to the Labour Exchange to draw the dole'), but which – mark these words, and mark them well – has operated adequately and served her well.

Obstinate in its faith, the geyser resisted conversion. The two gasmen explained that it needed a device that they did not have with them, but which they would bring; meanwhile, the geyser was out of action. The lady bore her bathless state with as much fortitude as she could muster, and awaited their return.

They did not return, of course. Nor, of course, did she hear from anybody at all on the subject. So she telephoned the office from which the men had come; they had left a form with its address and telephone number. (It was the Conversion Report Centre, Oakington Road, London, W9, telephone 349 3171, and I put these details in so that whoever is in what is laughably known as charge of the enterprise in question shall know exactly where the finger is pointing.) She explained that she had now been without a bath for a week, that a promise had been made and broken, and what was going to be done about it? The reply was that action would be taken. About a week later (nobody, of course, had told her anything at all in the interim), two more men turned up. They, too, tinkered with the geyser; they, too, said that it needed an extra device that they had not got with them; they, too, said that they would return with it; they, too, of course, did no such thing. Nor, of course, did anybody at all get in touch with her.

The lady in question, I will have you know, likes to bath regularly and often; moreover, she is not accustomed, or for that matter able, to take a bath in a kettle. So when another week had gone by, she telephoned the Gas Board. The office for the district in which she lives is North Thames Gas Board Area 5, telephone number 328 1717, address not given in the telephone-book (I suppose they are afraid of violence from their customers, and well they might be). An official of the Gas Board came round (she cannot remember how long after her call, though she doubts if it was immediately, and so, by God, do I); he explained that the Gas Board and the conversion programme are independently run (if 'run' is the right word, and my own opinion is that it is most emphatically not the right word), but that he would inspect the geyser. He did so, told her that he knew exactly what was needed, and left with the memorable words 'Leave it to me, Mrs Levin.' The reason he addressed her thus was that Levin is her name, and this seems as good a moment as any to reveal that the fact that it is the same name as mine is not a coincidence; she is my mother.

She did indeed leave it to him; she is a patient and trusting soul, and – rather more to the point – she had no option. He did not return, of course; nor, of course, did anybody get in touch with her. So she rang the Gas Board again. She was assured that action would be taken. It was; another man arrived (this made six she had actually seen, plus several more she had spoken to on the telephone). Had he, she asked, brought the necessary device? 'I have brought nothing,' he replied with candour; nor had he. (He also explained that he knew nothing of any extra and needed part.) He would, however, go back to the office and report the situation. He went; that was on Monday. Not long after he left an official (female) telephoned from the Gas Board to ask if he had been. Yes, said my mother, grinding her teeth, he had, but he had not brought the magic device, and had therefore gone away. In that case, said the official, I will see what the situation is, and ring you back and let you know. She didn't, of course, and at the time of writing this (Wednesday afternoon), my mother had heard nothing more from anybody.

I now want three things to happen. First, I want my mother's bathroom water-heater fixed, and at once. Second, I want a written apology to my mother to be sent from both the Natural Gas Conversion office and from the Gas Board.

That will satisfy my mother. But I also want a third thing on my own behalf;

or rather, on behalf of the public in general, who have to put up with the kind of behaviour I have just described. I want a public answer to this question: what is wrong with a national organization which gives its customers not the service they pay for but, instead, incompetence and a string of broken promises?

•

E. F. SCHUMACHER
1973

'Small is Beautiful'

'A study of economics as if people mattered' was the subtitle of the seminal book Small is Beautiful *published in 1973 by Dr E. F. Schumacher, who had been economics adviser to the National Coal Board for twenty years. Schumacher (1911–77) founded the concept of intermediate technology for developing countries and was president of the Soil Association, Britain's largest organic farming organization. His plea that small is beautiful maintained that the pursuit of profit and progress results in inhumane working conditions, pollution of the environment and gross economic inefficiency. It became a rallying cry of the environment movement.*

As Gandhi said, the poor of the world cannot be helped by mass production, only by production by the masses. The system of *mass production*, based on sophisticated, highly capital-intensive, high energy-input dependent, and human labour-saving technology, presupposes that you are already rich, for a great deal of capital investment is needed to establish one single workplace. The system of *production by the masses* mobilizes the priceless resources which are possessed by all human beings, their clever brains and skilful hands, *and supports them with first-class tools*. The technology of *mass production* is inherently violent, ecologically damaging, self-defeating in terms of non-renewable resources, and stultifying for the human person. The technology of *production by the masses*, making use of the best of modern knowledge and experience, is conducive to decentralization, compatible with the laws of ecology, gentle in its use of scarce resources, and designed to serve the human person instead of making him the servant of machines. I have named it *intermediate technology* to signify that it is vastly superior to the primitive technology of bygone ages but at the same time much simpler, cheaper and freer than the super-technology of the rich. One can also call it self-help technology, or democratic or people's technology – a technology to which everybody can gain admittance and which is not reserved to those already rich and powerful.

Strange to say, the Sermon on the Mount gives pretty precise instructions on how to construct an outlook that could lead to an Economics of Survival.

How blessed are those who know that they are poor:
the Kingdom of Heaven is theirs.
How blessed are the sorrowful;
they shall find consolation.
How blessed are those of a gentle spirit;
they shall have the earth for their possession.
How blessed are those who hunger and thirst to see right prevail;
they shall be satisfied;
How blessed are the peacemakers;
God shall call them his sons.

It may seem daring to connect these beatitudes with matters of technology and economics. But may it not be that we are in trouble precisely because we have failed for so long to make this connection? It is not difficult to discern what these beatitudes may mean for us today:

We are poor, not demigods.
We have plenty to be sorrowful about, and are not emerging into a
    golden age.
We need a gentle approach, a non-violent spirit, and small is beautiful.
We must concern ourselves with justice and see right prevail.
And all this, only this, can enable us to become peacemakers.

The home-comers base themselves upon a different picture of man from that which motivates the people of the forward stampede. It would be very superficial to say that the latter believe in 'growth' while the former do not. In a sense, everybody believes in growth, and rightly so, because growth is an essential feature of life. The whole point, however, is to give to the idea of growth a qualitative determination; for there are always many things that ought to be growing and many things that ought to be diminishing . . .

In the excitement over the unfolding of his scientific and technical powers, modern man has built a system of production that ravishes nature and a type of society that mutilates man. If only there were more and more wealth, everything else, it is thought, would fall into place. Money is considered to be all-powerful; if it could not actually buy non-material values, such as justice, harmony, beauty or even health, it could circumvent the need for them or compensate for their loss. The development of production and the acquisition of wealth have thus become the highest goals of the modern world in relation to which all other goals, no matter how much lip-service may still be paid to them, have come to take second place. The highest goals require no justification; all secondary goals have finally to justify themselves in terms of the service their attainment renders to the attainment of the highest.

This is the philosophy of materialism, and it is this philosophy – or metaphysic – which is now being challenged by events.

We shrink back from the truth if we believe that the destructive forces of the modern world can be 'brought under control' simply by mobilizing more resources – of wealth, education and research – to fight pollution, to preserve wildlife, to discover new sources of energy, and to arrive at more effective agreements on peaceful coexistence. Needless to say, wealth, education, research and many other things are needed for any civilization, but what is most needed today is a revision of the ends which these means are meant to serve. And this implies, above all else, the development of a life-style which accords to material things their proper, legitimate place, which is secondary and not primary.

•

ALEXANDER SOLZHENITSYN
1973

The Gulag Archipelago

Although accounts of Stalin's gulags had filtered out to the West in the 1930s, it was Alexander Solzhenitsyn (1918–) who exposed their full horror to the postwar generation in The Gulag Archipelago. *His book, published in the West after it had been seized by Soviet State Security, arguably did more than any other to undermine the moral claims of Communism throughout the world. It was based on evidence from 227 witnesses, as well as what Solzhenitsyn took away from the Archipelago – 'on the skin of my back, and with my eyes and tears'. 'I dedicate this to all those who did not live to tell it,' he wrote. 'And may they please forgive me for not having seen it all nor remembered it all, for not having divined all of it.' Solzhenitsyn was deported to Germany in 1974 and later settled in the United States.*

In this extract from the penultimate chapter, 'Our Muzzled Freedom', Solzhenitsyn tries to summarize the 'full loathsomeness' of the state in which he lived.

1. *Constant Fear.* The roster of the waves of recruitment into the Archipelago is not exhausted with 1935, or 1937, or 1949. The recruitment went on *all the time.* Just as there is no minute when people are not dying or being born,

so there was no minute when people were not being arrested. Sometimes this came close to a person, sometimes it was further off; sometimes a person deceived himself into thinking that nothing threatened him, and sometimes he himself became an executioner, and thus the threat to him diminished. But any adult inhabitant of this country, from a collective farmer up to a member of the Politburo, always knew that it would take only one careless word or gesture and he would fly off irrevocably into the abyss.

Just as in the Archipelago beneath every trusty lay the chasm (and death) of general work, so beneath every inhabitant lay the chasm (and death) of the Archipelago. In appearance the country was much bigger than its Archipelago, but all of it and all its inhabitants hung phantomlike above the latter's gaping maw . . .

Peace of mind is something our citizens have never known.

2. *Servitude.* If it had been easy to change your place of residence, to leave a place that had become dangerous for you and thus shake off fear and refresh yourself, people would have behaved more boldly, and they might have taken some risks. But for long decades we were shackled by that same system under which no worker could quit work of his own accord. And the passport regulations also fastened everyone to particular places. And the housing, which could not be sold, nor exchanged, nor rented. And because of this it was an insane piece of daring *to protest* in the place where you lived or worked.

3. *Secrecy and Mistrust.* These feelings replaced our former open-hearted cordiality and hospitality (which had still not been destroyed in the twenties). These feelings were the natural defence of any family and every person, particularly because no one could ever quit work or leave, and every little detail was kept in sight and within earshot for years. The secretiveness of the Soviet person is by no means superfluous, but is absolutely necessary, even though to a foreigner it may at times seem superhuman.

4. *Universal Ignorance.* Hiding things from each other, and not trusting each other, we ourselves helped implement the *absolute secrecy*, absolute misinformation, among us which was *the cause of causes* of everything that took place – including both the millions of arrests and the mass approval of them also. Informing one another of nothing, neither shouting nor groaning, and learning nothing from one another, we were completely in the hands of the newspapers and the official orators. Every day they pushed in our faces some new piece of incitement, like a photograph of a railway wreck (sabotage) somewhere 3,000 miles away. And what we really needed to learn about, which was what had happened on our apartment landing that day, we had no way of finding out.

How could you become a citizen, knowing nothing about life around you?

Only when you yourself were caught in the trap would you find out – too late.

5. *Squealing* was developed to a mind-boggling extent. Hundreds of thousands of security officers in their official offices, in the innocent rooms of official buildings, and in prearranged apartments, sparing neither paper nor their unoccupied time, tirelessly recruited and summoned stool pigeons to give reports, and this in such enormous numbers as they could never have found necessary for collecting information.

Secretiveness spread its cold tentacles throughout the whole people. It crept between colleagues at work, between old friends, students, soldiers, neighbours, children growing up – and even into the reception room of the NKVD, among the prisoners' wives bringing food parcels.

6. *Betrayal as a Form of Existence.* Given this constant fear over a period of many years – for oneself and one's family – a human being became a vassal of fear, subjected to it. And it turned out that the least dangerous form of existence was constant betrayal.

The mildest and at the same time most widespread form of betrayal was not to do anything bad directly, but just not to notice the doomed person next to one, not to help him, to turn away one's face, to shrink back. They had arrested a neighbour, your comrade at work, or even your close friend. You kept silence. You acted as if you had not noticed. (For you could not afford to lose your current job!) And then it was announced at work, at the general meeting, that the person who had disappeared the day before was . . . an inveterate enemy of the people. And you, who had bent your back beside him for twenty years at the same desk, now by your noble silence (or even by your condemning speech!), had to show how hostile you were to his crimes.

7. *Corruption.* In a situation of fear and betrayal over many years people survive unharmed only in a superficial, bodily sense. And inside . . . they become corrupt.

So many millions of people agreed to become stool pigeons. And, after all, if some 40 to 50 million people served long sentences in the Archipelago during the course of the thirty-five years up to 1953, including those who died – and this is a modest estimate, being only three or four times the population of Gulag at any one time, and, after all, during the war the death rate there was running at *1 per cent per day* – then we can assume that at least every third or at least every fifth case was the consequence of somebody's denunciation and that somebody was willing to provide evidence as a witness! All of them, all those murderers with ink, are still among us today. Some of them brought about the arrest of their neighbours out of fear – and this was only the first step. Others did it for material gain. And still others, the youngest at the time, who are now on the threshold of a pension, betrayed with inspiration, out of ideological considerations, and sometimes even openly; after all, it was considered a service to one's class to expose the enemy! And all these people are among us. And most often they are prospering. And we still rejoice that they are 'our ordinary Soviet people.'

8. *The Lie as a Form of Existence.* Whether giving in to fear, or influenced by material self-interest or envy, people can't none the less become stupid so swiftly. Their souls may be thoroughly muddied, but they still have a sufficiently clear mind. They cannot believe that all the genius of the world has suddenly concentrated itself in one head with a flattened, low-hanging forehead. They simply cannot believe the stupid and silly images of themselves which they hear over the radio, see in films, and read in the newspapers. Nothing forces them to speak the truth in reply, but no one allows them to keep silent! They have to *talk*! And what else but a lie? They have to applaud madly, and no one requires honesty of them.

The permanent lie becomes the only safe form of existence, in the same way as betrayal. Every wag of the tongue can be overheard by someone, every facial expression observed by someone. Therefore every word, if it does not have to be a direct lie, is none the less obliged not to contradict the general, common lie.

9. *Cruelty.* And where among all the preceding qualities was there any place left for kindheartedness? How could one possibly preserve one's kindness while pushing away the hands of those who were drowning? Once you have been steeped in blood, you can only become more cruel. And, anyway, cruelty ('class cruelty') was praised and instilled, and you would soon lose track, probably, of just where between bad and good that trait lay. And when you add that kindness was ridiculed, that pity was ridiculed, that mercy was ridiculed – you'd never be able to chain all those who were drunk on blood!

And one could go on enumerating further. One could name in addition:

10. *Slave Psychology.* That same unfortunate Babich in his declaration to the prosecutor: 'I understand that wartime places more serious obligations and duties on the organs of government than to sort out the charges against individual persons.'

And much else.

But let us admit: if under Stalin this whole scheme of things did not just come into being *on its own* – and if, instead, he himself worked it all out for us point by point – he really was a genius!

So there in that stinking damp world in which only executioners and the most blatant of betrayers flourished, where those who remained honest became drunkards, since they had no strength of will for anything else, in which the bodies of young people were bronzed by the sun while their souls putrefied inside, in which every night the grey-green hand reached out and collared someone in order to pop him into a box – in that world millions of women wandered about lost and blinded, whose husbands, sons or fathers had been torn from them and dispatched to the Archipelago. They were the most scared of all. They feared shiny nameplates, office doors, telephone rings, knocks on the door, the postman, the milkwoman and the plumber. And everyone in whose path they stood drove them from their apartments, from their work and from the city.

In various parts of our country we find a certain piece of sculpture: a plaster guard with a police dog which is straining forward in order to sink its teeth into someone. In Tashkent there is one right in front of the NKVD school, and in Ryazan it is like a symbol of the city, the one and only monument to be seen if you approach from the direction of Mikhailov.

And we do not even shudder in revulsion. We have become accustomed to these figures setting dogs on to people as if they were the most natural things in the world.

Setting the dogs on to us.

•

IRISH TIMES
1974

'The shame of Britain'

Under the Sunningdale Agreement of 1973, Ulster's Catholics were given, for the first time since 1920, a direct role in government with the Unionists in a Northern Ireland Assembly. Six months later, after an illegal strike by the Protestant Ulster Workers' Council and collusion between the security forces and Loyalist paramilitaries, the agreement became moribund as the Labour Government found itself powerless against industrial action. The power-sharing Executive collapsed when Brian Faulkner resigned as its head. As this leading article in the Irish Times *demonstrated, moderate nationalist opinion was outraged by the 'bigots of Belfast'.*

A former Prime Minister of Britain was described as the boneless wonder. That was Ramsay MacDonald. The Dublin Government's opinion of the present incumbent of the post would be no more flattering.

The Labour lads on the other side of the water are no match for the corner-boys of Belfast; those who held hands and sang 'The Red Flag' at the end of their party conference have been routed by genuine proletarians; of all the shame that Britain has suffered at the hands of her departing colonials, this lying down to the bigots of Belfast ranks high in infamy: for it has been accompanied by deception of the government in Dublin.

The British Army and the British Government have been routed almost without a shot being fired; a few hoods and masks and clubs and the UDA men put the Tommies in their place.

The world of Dublin politics, a world which has not had to face up to anything much in fifty years, is now agog with fateful predictions for the North: Sunningdale is finished, it never had much chance, etc. There is no evidence that Dublin used much muscle on Britain in recent weeks when some disquiet was expressed over London's delaying tactics.

The Executive has largely been held in these last days by the tenacity of the SDLP. If partnership means anything it means bringing the other fellow with you. The SDLP have faced reality and have done just this. They have brought Faulkner and his party along with them. It is a sad day for them that Sunningdale has to be chopped into bits. But they are realists. They have fought. They have lived through not only political strife but a hail of bullets and bombs.

When, it might be asked, has any Dublin Government ever given to the North – a real give that had to be sold hard to their followers? What political figure in Dublin has risked his political life over the North? Daily Northern politicians like the SDLP and their Unionist colleagues too – risk not just their political life but their own skin.

This could do without too much wailing from Dublin.

For all the woe-sayers, there is one thing to be pointed out, if the SDLP had pulled out on Wednesday there would have been bonfires throughout the North, there would have been jubilation in every Loyalist quarter and the war-lords could well have gone on the rampage.

The SDLP is still there, the gains for the former minority are being defended, the partnership with the Unionists and Alliance maintained.

The out-of-date people in all of Ireland today are those who hold for total victory only. They include leaders like Bill Craig and clerical toughs like Ian Paisley. They include, need it be said, the Provisionals.

The thing that matters is how the people of this island are to live together; never mind shouts about sell-out or betrayal, to live together is to compromise and compromise is still a dirty word in Irish politics.

If the churches were more clear-minded and even more Christian one of their great themes might be that compromise is a good and a holy thing. They are too busy, many of them, looking after their own empires – making sure that too much compromise does not enter their own domain. So it is left to the few good politicians we have.

The day has been largely with the Loyalists. It is not the end of the story. The North in its fifty years of life never had politics. It is learning slowly and it is learning a good deal from politicians which were formerly those of the minority.

The men out in front of the Loyalists are saying quite simply: 'We alone will rule.' This is what Carson preached sixty years ago. Historians have seen in this earlier eruption within what was then the British Empire, the first examples of fascism in the century.

Some of the classical elements for a coup are present in the North today – most important being very limited communications. But it is not just the British Government which will no doubt waver at the last minute that the Ulster Workers' Council faces. It is the rock-like sense of the vast majority of the people of Northern Ireland.

•

BERNARD LEVIN
1977

'The fuse of revolution'

When Bernard Levin (1928–) laid down his pen after nearly thirty years as a columnist on The Times, *a rival journalist, Barbara Amiel of the* Daily Telegraph, *saluted him as a profoundly spiritual and moral writer in an age of moral relativism. Levin was a staunch anti-Communist who wrote constantly about the plight of the Soviet dissidents. No article was more prophetic than this column in August 1977. The name Levin did not, could not, know was Gorbachev.*

As we contemplate the Soviet Union today, her leaders faced with a perpetually growing dissident movement (growing in diversity as well as in numbers) and quite unable to devise a strategy for dealing with the threat it poses to their future, we have to ask ourselves why they seem so helpless in the face of what is, after all, still only a tiny minority, with no access to publication or dissemination of their views in any official or widespread form. (Millions of Russians, I am sure, have never so much as heard of any dissident movement, and must be considerably bewildered by the incomprehensible attacks of their press and radio on individuals and groups whose activities are not described and whose ideas are never expounded.) Why do I believe that Brezhnev and his colleagues have seen the writing on the wall, and know that the message it conveys is exactly the same, word for word, as the original slogan that gave us the metaphor? Why do I believe that a new Russian Revolution is inevitable, and that it may come much sooner than anyone would now dare to hope?

It is because I do not believe it possible that the thirst for freedom and decency in the countries of the Soviet Empire can remain much longer unslaked, and that any attempt either to quench it by total repression or to satisfy it by real reforms, will be cataclysmically destructive of the eroded foundations of the entire state system. If it is to be repression, the economic consequences will be appalling, and even more appalling will be the resistance it will provoke. And if it is to be reform, there will be no stopping the tide once the first sluice has been opened. Memories of the Czech tragedy of 1968 will still be fresh (except, of course, in the minds of the British Foreign Office and present government); the most significant element of the Prague Spring was the way in which, once Mr Dubček had shown that he supported the Czech desire for liberation, no attempt by him and his equally brave colleagues to go slowly proved availing – the scent of freedom in the nostrils of his people was too strong.

But, it will be objected, Czechoslovakia was an occupied and enslaved land; what the Czechs wanted was what the Dutch and the Belgians and the French wanted in 1943 – liberation from their hated conquerors. How can that be said to apply to the Soviet Union herself?

In the first place, it applies to a considerable extent in exactly the same way. Perhaps the most powerful of all the dissident movements has been the one fuelled by nationalist feeling: Ukrainians, Lithuanians, Uzbeks, Estonians, and other national minorities there are struggling, their national pride all the stronger for decades of repression, for what they see as their birthright (though they should not expect the United Nations Sub-Committee on Colonialism to sympathize). Released from its iron bottle, the force of this feeling could be devastating – indeed, could not be otherwise, which is why the Soviet authorities have for so long feared it most and treated it most cruelly. But although it is expressed only through the mouths of a few exceptionally brave individuals, the feeling lies dormant in millions, like an underground reservoir of oil, only waiting for the bore to come through from the surface to erupt in a roaring fountain.

But even apart from the latent pressure of nationalism there are latent pressures, similarly given form and a voice only by an exceptionally courageous few, which must similarly gush forth if the rock is ever struck. Is it seriously to be believed that the only Christians in Russia are the ones we know about? Will anyone maintain that the only seekers after elementary human rights there are the ones whose names are familiar here? Can anyone think that the only people who would like to get out of that vast prison are the ones who ask for permission to do so? What do you suppose Christianity *is*, what do you imagine freedom *means*, what do you think emigration *represents*, that it can be confined to a few? It is simply not credible that forces which have moved men and women in countless millions throughout the ages exist only in sketchy form in the Soviet Union, in the hearts of the few who speak openly of them. The charge is there, packed tight, tamped down and waiting. The fuse is laid. All that remains is the match.

Nor, as it happens, is it particularly difficult to see who will strike it, and why. I do not know his name or what he looks like, but I know he is there. For do you seriously suppose – now we extend the same questions into another area – that Mr Dubček and President Svoboda and Mr Pelikan and Mr Goldstuecker and Professor Sik and the rest of the Czech liberationists who led the doomed revolt came up one night like mushrooms, or arrived in a rocket from outer space? They came up through the system, through the system installed and maintained in Czechoslovakia, and most carefully monitored, by the Soviet authorities. But no Soviet tracker-dog could pick up the scent of the contraband they carried, for they carried it in their souls, where no dog's nose is sensitive enough to detect it.

And if you tell me that no such figures exist in the Soviet Union, even more completely unknown outside (or for that matter inside) than the Czech heroes were, I shall tell you in return that it simply cannot be so. The odds against such an extraordinary aberration of the human spirit are so preposterously high that the chance can be ignored with impunity. They are there, all right, at this very moment, obeying orders, doing their duty, taking the official line against dissidents not only in public but in private. They do not conspire, they are not in touch with Western intelligence agencies, they commit no sabotage. They are in every respect model Soviet functionaries. Or rather, in every respect but one: they have admitted the truth about their country to themselves, and have vowed, also to themselves, to do something about it.

That is how it will be done. There will be no gunfire in the streets, no barricades, no general strikes, no hanging of oppressors from lamp-posts, no sacking and burning of government offices, no seizure of radio stations or mass defections among the military. But one day soon, some new faces will appear in the Politburo – I am sure they have already appeared in municipal and even regional administrative authorities – and gradually, very gradually, other, similarly new, faces will join them. Until one day they will look at each other and realize that there is no longer any need for concealment of the truth in their hearts. And the match will be lit.

There is nothing romantic or fantastic about this prognosis – it is the most sober extraposition from known facts and tested evidence. That, or something like it, *will* happen. *When* it will happen it is neither possible nor useful to guess; but I am sure it will be within the lifetime of people much older than I. And when it does happen – let us suppose for neatness' sake, on 14 July 1989 – you must, in all eventuality, allow me to be the first to repeat Charles James Fox's words on their 200th anniversary: How much the greatest event it is that ever happened in the world! And how much the best!

•

DONALD WOODS
1977

'Steve Biko'

South Africa's Black Consciousness leader Steve Biko (1946–77) died in police custody, almost certainly after being beaten to death by his white jailers. With Nelson Mandela in jail, he was South Africa's most important political leader, but had constantly been silenced, imprisoned without trial and put in solitary confinement.

As editor of the Daily Dispatch, *Donald Woods (1933–) campaigned against apartheid and became a friend of Biko. He also wrote the most widely read syndicated column in the country. A week after Biko's funeral, attended by 20,000 blacks, Woods made this speech at the University of Natal in Pietmaritzburg. Shortly afterwards, he was placed under a banning order. A year later he escaped to Britain, as depicted in the film* Cry Freedom.

South Africa today is ruled by fear – the fear of the ruled and the fear of the rulers.

The rulers are fearful because they are a minority, and their fear is increasing because they perceive that the hatred of them by the majority is increasing.

As always, fear breeds hatred and hatred in turn breeds more fear. Increasingly, voices of warning are seen as voices of incitement. Voices of dissent are seen as voices of treachery and treason. Increasingly, moderation is being seen as extremism and the peacemakers are being portrayed as the advocates of violence.

South Africa today is heading for civil war, and we who warn of this endanger ourselves by doing so, because what we intend as a warning motivated by love of all our fellow citizens is seen as a kind of advocacy of the very thing we are trying to prevent.

The danger lies in actually speaking out loud the things the people don't want to think about. The people hate such thoughts because they fear all the implications behind them. They would rather push the whole subject into the depths of the subconscious and pretend that today's pleasant sunshine reflects the wishful reality.

Steve Biko foresaw violence and bloodshed in South Africa. Don't we all? He could see it looming ahead. Don't we all? But to suggest that he advocated it or desired it is a despicable lie. The main issue is that a key political figure in this country was detained in good health and within three weeks became the forty-fifth South African to die mysteriously in Security Police custody, and that it is the duty of all free men to question this mysterious death until those responsible have given adequate reply.

I am aware of the physical danger involved in calling for justice in the matter of Steve Biko's death. I am also aware that beyond certain sensible precautions nothing further can be done to minimize such danger, but I want to take this opportunity of saying this: if anything happens to people like myself to silence our voice in this matter, I ask the hundreds of thousands of South Africans who feel as we do to ensure that such a silencing would not succeed in diminishing the chorus of demands for justice but would rather add to it in volume and intensity.

It is highly unpleasant to live under threat, but circumstances have made this necessary at this time and there cannot be the remotest possibility of turning back. But, for the climate of hysteria and hatred that has created these dangers I blame this government and in particular Prime Minister Vorster and Justice and Police Minister Kruger as well as their lackey newspapers.

They are the ones who have not only created the conditions causing violent unrest but have on several occasions by their words lent encouragement to excesses by white extremists, who mysteriously have access to tear gas canisters and unlisted telephone numbers. More than this, they have presided over a system of detention under whose dispensation helpless people can be seized, tortured and assaulted without ever having had access to lawyers or friends or family – access not even denied to a criminal. Yet the government can see no reason for a judicial inquiry into deaths in detention.

There are several reasons: the numerous complaints of torture in detention. Whether or not Mr Vorster regards these allegations as untrue, I can tell him that literally millions of South Africans believe that Security Police interrogation is often accompanied by torture, including torture by shocks with electrical apparatus and including beating up and tightening of material about necks until a point of near-suffocation is reached. It is also believed that that point has on occasion been exceeded – hence the number of alleged hangings in detention. Surely this matter is more important than several other matters that became the subject of inquiries.

If Mr Vorster and Mr Kruger want the Biko tragedy to stop harming this country's image, then several things must be done, and done quickly:

Prosecutions indicated as necessary by inquest evidence must be initiated as soon as possible thereafter.

A judicial commission of inquiry into all detainee deaths and all allegations of torture in detention must be set up as soon as possible.

Detention without trial must be stopped.

Minister Kruger must either resign or be sacked for his grossly inept and callous handling of the entire matter.

And let [Afrikaner] Nationalists stop trying to find scapegoats for black unrest. The unrest is not due to agitators, it is due to apartheid. They can lock up every single alleged agitator, but lasting peace will come to South Africa only when apartheid is scrapped.

Let me say this to all [Afrikaner] Nationalists: believe it or not, we, your open critics, do not wish to hate you. We wish to share this country with you as loved fellow citizens with a full appreciation of your culture and your identity. These need not be sacrificed.

But in God's name turn back from the madness of apartheid before it is too late, and honestly learn to see yourselves now as others see you. After thirty years in power you have succeeded in turning everyone against your policies – the blacks, the Indians, the Coloreds and many whites. You have succeeded in turning the whole continent of Africa against you, and indeed the whole world. Is everyone out of step but you? Are all Christian churches out of step but yours?

You pronounce yourselves ready to fight the whole world – yet not even the majority of your own citizens will be your allies in such a fight. It is not your known courage and your sterling qualities that are in dispute – it is your racism. It is your insistence that only you can decide what is good for most of us in this country. But this country isn't your house – it is a house you share with all of us, and the rights you are entitled to exercise in it are by no standard the dominant ones. Yet nobody wants to put you out. There is nobody who disputes your right to be here – there are only multimillions who dispute your right to be here *only on your terms*.

These are dangerous days, and I am saying here all the things I want to say while I can say them and I am saying them in conscious fear of a number of terrible possibilities that may eventuate in this climate of excessive recrimination by the agents of hatred.

But these things must be said, because there is no fear that can outweigh the need for them to be said.

•

DAVID GWYN
1977

'*Idi Amin*'

Idi Amin ousted Milton Obote as Ugandan prime minister in 1971 and established one of the most notorious African military dictatorships until he was deposed in 1979.

He expelled all Ugandan Asians with British passports, seized foreign businesses and butchered thousands of his opponents. One was Archbishop Janani Luwum, head of the Anglican Church. In his book Idi Amin, *David Gwyn, who said that for Amin murder was a legitimate instrument of government, described how Amin rid himself of a meddlesome cleric.*

The facts of the death of Archbishop Janani Luwum, head of the Anglican Church in Uganda, are now clear. The usual hot-season tension had, as usual, been compounded by the coup anniversary celebrations and by at least one assassination plot, timed for late January 1977, which misfired because a football match was cancelled. Some firearms were found in a truck moving through the country – probably being sent in by yet another outside resistance group. There is not the remotest possibility that Archbishop Luwum or any church leaders, Protestant or Catholic, knew anything about these incidents. But Amin was nervous.

On 5 February 1977, Luwum's house was searched for arms. Nothing was found. The Anglican bishops of Uganda, appalled, made this incident the peg on which to hang a letter of protest to Amin, drawing attention yet again to the shootings, killings and disappearances. On 14 February Luwum delivered to Amin his copy of this public letter signed by the archbishop himself and by fifteen of the eighteen bishops. Amin retaliated, after an interval for a diversionary cup of tea with his next victim, by issuing a Radio Uganda accusation that arms had been found 'near' the archbishop's house.

There was about twenty-four hours of further softening-up by Uganda's radio and government-controlled press. Then, on the morning of 16 February, Luwum was subjected to a five-hour mock trial. A main feature of the proceeding was a long forgery read by a previously tortured, and later killed, friend of Luwum. The assembled troops were packed with Amin's Nubians and black mercenaries. In a horrifying and perhaps unconscious parody of the crowd assembled before Pilate to accuse Christ, they bellowed: 'Kill him, kill him!' Within four hours, Amin had done just that. Luwum was shot. A truck was driven over his body and those of the two ministers, Oryema and Oboth Ofumbi, who were murdered at the same time. The bodies were never recovered for burial.

The background to Luwum's death illustrates many of the main characteristics of Amin's abuse of power and some of his motivations. The sudden and brutal killing is typical, showing the complete lack of restraint and the abandonment of any normal human reaction.

The crude attempts to blame someone else thereafter have been a constant feature of the six years of Amin. There is madness there, but also sufficient awareness of the normal consequences of murder to want to cover up the crime. Like so many others, the archbishop was 'ambushed by guerrillas' one moment and 'trying to escape' the next.

The attempt to destroy the evidence is a third constant pattern of Amin's behaviour. If there is no mangled body he cannot so easily be accused, whether of eating the liver or of the actual death. Normal burial ceremonies, a vital part of most tribes' culture, are denied to the relatives.

The pursuit of anyone who could give any evidence of Amin's complicity is a fourth theme. For Amin the group is responsible – and the group must suffer, whether it be the race, the tribe, the profession or the church. In only three months after Luwum's murder, seven of Uganda's eighteen Anglican bishops had been forced to leave the country as an alternative to almost certain death. Luwum's fellow tribesmen and worshippers, with less mobility, were less fortunate. About 10,000 may have reached Kenya by June 1977. God knows how many thousand others failed to do so and died in the towns, in the villages and in the bush.

What motivated Amin to kill Luwum? Luwum had emerged to counter, in himself and by his actions, all the twisted evils carried out by Amin and to bring out each last obsession and fear in Amin's mind.

Luwum was a Christian and leader of the second largest group of Christians in Uganda. There is no longer any reasonable doubt that Amin is determined, if he can, to destroy the Christian churches. He may, or may not, be 'inspired' to proselytise for Islam by instructions given him by another head of state or by a miraculous thunderstorm said to have descended at Mecca when Amin did the Haj.

It seems probable that Amin views the Christian churches in Uganda as associations of reasonable men and women consistently opposed to killing and wishes to destroy them for that entirely secular reason. Or perhaps the two germs of ideas join with others in his mind. In any event, to be a Christian was dangerous, and Luwum was Christian. So were the two ministers who were murdered at the same time; one, Erinayo Oryema, had been chairman of the committee which arranged the lay celebrations when Luwum first became a bishop in 1969. All three were vulnerable.

Luwum's next 'crime' was that he was an Acholi, Amin's least-favoured tribe. The killing of members of this tribe started on 25 January 1971, and has not stopped since. Amin fears and hates them. He fears their tall carelessness, their capacity to absorb punishment and still come back for more. He hates their pre-coup dominance in the army and resents the fact that they were one of the tribes most liked by the British before independence. They have long memories and, despite Amin, they will outlive him. For this, too, he fears and hates them.

Then Luwum, supported by his bishops, attempted, as others had tried and failed before him, to stop the senseless killings and disappearances. He tried openly and in writing. That, alone, was sufficient cause for Amin to kill him. Others had long since learned that to ask Amin to stop the killing of any group had only two results: you were immediately under suspicion yourself, and the killings escalated. There was no way out of the irrational dilemma – you just kept on trying. Luwum tried again. But there are, for Amin, no widows and no orphans; to suggest that there may be is an excuse to kill more husbands and fathers . . .

Luwum, in his last hours, prayed openly and aloud. This, for Amin, was sacrilege. Only Amin has a direct line to God. (He attributes to it a whole series of 'dreams', 'visions', and 'guidance'.) It is surprising that he has not already had himself entitled 'the shadow of God upon earth' in much the same casual way that he awarded himself a chestful of medals and decorations. Whatever else, Amin is terrified at the thought that someone else, through prayer, may have contact with God.

Amin knows he has done wrong, is desperately afraid of the future, and hates to be reminded of it. One of the few things known to have shut him up temporarily was a challenge from the father of a murdered and grossly mutilated ex-wife: 'I cannot punish you, but God will.' For this Luwum prayed and died.

The list is long – the evil balanced against the good with the evil controlling the gun. Amin wants to sweat consistently at the focus of all the spotlights. The year 1977 is the centenary of the Anglican Church in Uganda, and, as archbishop, Luwum would have perhaps taken a little of the national stage. The centenary celebrations, planned for 30 June, were cancelled one month after Luwum's murder. In typically misinformative fashion, Amin let it be known, shortly after the cancellation was decided, that he would take a full part in the celebration. But he knew by then that he was safe to bask alone in his notoriety. To achieve that, too, Luwum had died.

●

GLORIA STEINEM
1978

'*If men could menstruate*'

When Gloria Steinem (1934–) started Ms. Magazine *in 1972, its subscription list quickly reached 300,000. She was a journalist, educated (like Betty Friedan) at Smith College, politically active and a feminist. One of her most celebrated essays of protest was this one on men and menstruation, from which this is an excerpt.*

So what would happen if suddenly, magically, men could menstruate and women could not?

Clearly, menstruation would become an enviable, boast-worthy masculine event.

Men would brag about how long and how much.

Young boys would talk about it as the envied beginning of manhood.

Gifts, religious ceremonies, family dinners, and stag parties would mark the day.

To prevent monthly work loss among the powerful, Congress would fund a National Institute of Dysmenorrhea. Doctors would research little about heart attacks, from which men were hormonally protected, but everything about cramps.

Sanitary supplies would be federally funded and free. Of course, some men would still pay for the prestige of such commercial brands as Paul Newman Tampons, Muhammad Ali's Rope-a-Dope Pads, John Wayne Maxi Pads, and Joe Namath Jock Shields – 'For Those Light Bachelor Days.'

●

VACLAV HAVEL
1978

'The system'

A year after the 'Prague spring' of 1968, Vaclav Havel (1936–) was arrested for subversion. He had signed a petition opposing the 'normalization' imposed on Czechoslovakia after the downfall of Dubček. His books and plays were banned and removed from libraries – but read and performed in the West where he won a growing reputation as the leading Czech dissident. In his famous essay 'The Power of the Powerless', from which this extract is taken, Havel wrote of the responsibility each Czech bore for perpetuating the dictatorship by their daily compliance with it. (Havel spent four years in jail from 1979 but became president of Czechoslovakia after Communism collapsed throughout Eastern Europe in 1989.)

The manager of a fruit and vegetable shop places in his window, among the onions and carrots, the slogan: 'Workers of the World, Unite!' Why does he do it? What is he trying to communicate to the world? Is he genuinely enthusiastic about the idea of unity among the workers of the world? Is his enthusiasm so great that he feels an irrepressible impulse to acquaint the public with his ideals? Has he really given more than a moment's thought to how such a unification might occur and what it would mean?

I think it can safely be assumed that the overwhelming majority of shop-keepers never think about the slogans they put in their windows, nor do they use them to express their real opinions. That poster was delivered to our greengrocer from the enterprise headquarters along with the onions and carrots. He put them all into the window simply because it has been done that way for years, because everyone does it, and because that is the way it has to be. If he were to refuse, there could be trouble. He could be reproached for not having the proper 'decoration' in his window; someone might even accuse him of disloyalty. He does it because these things must be done if one is to get along in life. It is one of the thousands of details that guarantee him a relatively tranquil life 'in harmony with society', as they say.

Obviously the greengrocer is indifferent to the semantic content of the slogan on exhibit; he does not put the slogan in his window from any personal desire to acquaint the public with the ideal it expresses. This, of course, does not mean that his action has no motive or significance at all, or that the slogan communicates nothing to anyone. The slogan is really a *sign*, and as such it contains a subliminal but very definite message. Verbally, it might be expressed this way: 'I, the greengrocer XY, live here and I know what I must do. I behave in the manner expected of me. I can be depended upon and am beyond reproach. I am obedient and therefore I have the right to be left in peace.' This message, of course, has an addressee: it is directed above, to the greengrocer's superior, and at the same time it is a shield that protects the greengrocer from potential informers. The slogan's real meaning, therefore, is rooted firmly in the greengrocer's existence. It reflects his vital interests. But what are those vital interests?

Let us take note: if the greengrocer had been instructed to display the slogan, 'I am afraid and therefore unquestioningly obedient,' he would not be nearly as indifferent to its semantics, even though the statement would reflect the truth. The greengrocer would be embarrassed and ashamed to put such an unequivocal statement of his own degradation in the shop window, and quite naturally so, for he is a human being and thus has a sense of his own dignity. To overcome this complication, his expression of loyalty must take the form of a sign which, at least on its textual surface, indicates a level of disinterested conviction. It must allow the greengrocer to say, 'What's wrong with the workers of the world uniting?' Thus the sign helps the greengrocer to conceal from himself the low foundations of his obedience, at the same time concealing the low foundations of power. It hides them behind the façade of something high. And that something is *ideology* . . .

The post-totalitarian system touches people at every step, but it does so with its ideological gloves on. This is why life in the system is so thoroughly permeated with hypocrisy and lies: government by bureaucracy is called popular government; the working class is enslaved in the name of the working class; the complete degradation of the individual is presented as his or her ultimate liberation; depriving people of information is called making it available; the use of power to manipulate is called the public control of power, and the arbitrary abuse of power is called observing the legal code; the repression of culture is called its development; the expansion of imperial influence is presented as support for the oppressed; the lack of free expression becomes the highest form of freedom; farcical elections become the highest form of democracy; banning independent thought becomes the most scientific of world views; military occupation becomes fraternal assistance. Because the regime is captive to its own lies, it must falsify everything. It falsifies the past. It falsifies the present, and it falsifies the future. It falsifies statistics. It pretends not to possess an omnipotent and unprincipled police apparatus. It pretends to respect human rights. It pretends to persecute no one. It pretends to fear nothing. It pretends to pretend nothing.

Individuals need not believe all these mystifications, but they must behave as though they did, or they must at least tolerate them in silence, or get along well with those who work with them. For this reason, however, they must *live within a lie*. They need not accept the lie. It is enough for them to have accepted their life with it and in it. For by this very fact, individuals confirm the system, fulfil the system, make the system, *are* the system . . .

•

JOHN PILGER
1979

'Year Zero'

With his reports for the Daily Mirror *and the* Guardian *and his television documentaries, John Pilger (1939–) became the outstanding campaigning journalist of his generation. He was twice named Journalist of the Year for his work in Vietnam and Cambodia. His reports from Cambodia were first published over eleven pages of the* Daily Mirror *in 1979. They were later published in* Heroes, *an anthology of his journalism.*

At 7.30 on the morning of 17 April 1975, they entered Phnom Penh. They marched in Indian file along the boulevards, through the still traffic. They wore black and were mostly teenagers, and people cheered them nervously, naively, as people do when war seems to be over. Phnom Penh then had a swollen population of about 2 million people. At one o'clock the 'men in black' decreed that the city be abandoned by all except for a few thousand who would maintain its skeleton. According to witnesses interviewed later and journalists in Phnom Penh at the time, the sick and wounded were ordered and dragged at gunpoint from their hospital beds; surgeons were forced to leave patients in mid-operation. On the road out through the suburbs a procession of mobile beds could be seen, with their drip-bottles swinging at the bedpost; a man whose throat and mouth had been torn away by a rocket explosion was pushed along by his aged father. The old and crippled fell beside the road and their families were forced to move on. Crippled and dying children were carried in plastic bags. Women barely out of childbirth staggered forward, supported by parents. Orphaned babies, forty-one by one estimate, were left in their cradles at the Phnom Penh paediatric centre without anybody to care for them.

'Don't take anything with you,' broadcast the young troops through loud-speakers. 'The Angkar is saying that you must leave the city for just three hours so that we can prepare to defend you against bombing by American aircraft.'

The prospect of bombing was believed by many, but even among those on the road who knew it to be a lie, defeatism, fear and exhaustion seemed to make them powerless. The haemorrhage lasted two days and two nights, then Cambodia fell into shadow. When, on 7 January 1979, the Vietnamese Army came up the Mekong and drove into Phnom Penh, they found the city virtually as it had been left on the first day of 'Year Zero'.

This was how I found it when I arrived with photographer Eric Piper, film director David Munro, cameraman Gerry Pinches and sound recordist Steve Phillips of Associated Television (ATV). In the silent, airless humidity it was like entering a city the size of Manchester or Brussels in the wake of a nuclear cataclysm which had spared only the buildings. Houses, flats, office blocks, schools, hotels stood empty and open, as if vacated by their occupants that day. Personal possessions lay trampled on a front path, a tricycle crushed and rusted in the gutter, the traffic lights jammed on red. There was electricity in the centre of the city; elsewhere there was neither power nor a working sewer nor water to drink. At the railway station trains stood empty at various stages of interrupted departure. Pieces of burned cloth fluttered on the platform, and when we enquired about this it was explained that on the day they fled before the Vietnamese Army the Khmer Rouge had set fire to carriages in which as many as 200 wounded people lay.

When the afternoon monsoon broke, the gutters of the city were suddenly awash with paper; but this was not paper, it was money. The streets ran with money, much of it new and unused banknotes whose source was not far away. The modern concrete building of the National Bank of Cambodia looked as if it had sustained one mighty punch. As if to show their contempt for the order they replaced, the Khmer Rouge had blown it up and now with every downpour a worthless fortune sluiced from it into the streets. Inside, cheque books lay open on the counter, one with a cheque partly filled out and the date 17 April 1975. A pair of broken spectacles rested on an open ledger; money seemed to be everywhere; I slipped and fell hard on a floor brittle with coins; boxes of new notes were stacked where they had been received from the supplier in London five years ago.

In our first hours in Phnom Penh we shot no film and took no photographs; incredulity saw to that. I had no sense of people, of even the remnants of a population; the few human shapes I glimpsed seemed incoherent images, detached from the city itself. On catching sight of us, they would flit into the refuge of a courtyard or a cinema or a filling station. Only when I pursued several, and watched them forage, did I see that they were children. One child about ten years old – although age was difficult to judge – ran into a wardrobe lying on its side which was his or her refuge. In an Esso station an old woman and three emaciated children squatted around a pot containing a mixture of roots and leaves, which bubbled over a fire fuelled with paper money: thousands of snapping, crackling brand new *riel*: such a morbid irony, for these were people in need of everything money no longer could buy.

The first person we stopped and spoke to was a man balancing a load on his head and an arm on his son's shoulder. He was blind and his face was pitted from what might have been smallpox. His son was fifteen years old, but so skeletal that he might have been nine. The man spoke some French and said his name was Khim Kon and his son was Van Sok and that 'before Pol Pot' he had been a carpenter. 'This boy,' he said, touching his son with affection, 'is my only child left. Because we came from the city, we were classified "new people". We had to work from three in the morning until eleven at night; the children, too. My wife and three others are all dead now.' I asked him how he had lost his sight. 'I was always blind in one eye,' he said. 'When my family started to die I cried, so they took out my other eye with a whip.' Of all the survivors I would talk to in the coming weeks, that man and his son, who had lost four members of their immediate family, were the least damaged.

My memory of Phnom Penh from twelve years before now told me where I was; I was in the middle of Monivong Avenue, facing the Roman Catholic cathedral. But there was no cathedral. In the constitution of Pol Pot's 'Democratic Kampuchea', article twenty stated that all Khmers had 'the right to worship according to any religion and the right not to worship according to any religion', but religion that was 'wrong' and 'reactionary' and 'detrimental' was prohibited. So the Gothic cathedral of Phnom Penh, a modest version of the cathedral at Rheims, a place where the 'wrong' religion was practised, was dismantled, stone by stone. Only wasteland is left now . . .

Two months earlier Eric Piper and I had followed Pope John Paul on his return to Poland, where we had seen Auschwitz for the first time. Now, in South-East Asia, we saw it again. On a clear, sunny day with flocks of tiny swifts, the bravest of birds, rising and falling almost to the ground, we drove along a narrow dirt road at the end of which was a former primary school, called Tuol Sleng. During the Pol Pot years this school was run by a Khmer gestapo, 'S-21', which divided the classrooms into an 'interrogation unit' and a 'torture and massacre unit'. People were mutilated on iron beds and we found their blood and tufts of their hair still on the floor. Between December 1975 and June 1978 at least 12,000 people died slow deaths here: a fact not difficult to confirm because the killers, like the Nazis, were pedantic in their sadism. They photographed their victims before and after they tortured and killed them and horrific images now looked at us from walls; some had tried to smile for the photographer, as if he might take pity on them and save them. Names and ages, even height and weight, were recorded. We found, as at Auschwitz, one room filled to the ceiling with victims' clothes and shoes, including those of many children.

However, unlike Auschwitz, Tuol Sleng was primarily a political death centre. Leading members of the Khmer Rouge Army, including those who formed an early resistance to Pol Pot, were murdered here, usually after 'confessing' that they had worked for the CIA, the KGB or Hanoi. Whatever its historical model, if any, the demonic nature of Tuol Sleng was its devotion to human suffering. Whole families were confined in small cells, fettered to a single iron bar. They were kept naked and slept on the stone floor, without blanket or mat, and on the wall was a school blackboard, on which was written:

1. Speaking is absolutely forbidden
2. Before doing something, the authorization of the warden must be obtained.

'Doing something' might mean only changing position in the cell, but without authorization the prisoner would receive twenty to thirty strokes with a whip. Latrines were small ammunition boxes left over from Lon Nol's Army, labelled 'Made in USA'. For upsetting a box of excrement the punishment was licking the floor with your tongue, torture or death, or all three.

When the Vietnamese discovered Tuol Sleng they found nineteen mass graves within the vicinity of the prison and eight survivors, including four children and a month-old baby. Tem Chan was one of them. He told me, 'For a whole week I was filled with water, then given electric currents. Finally, I admitted anything they wanted. I said I worked for the KGB. It was so ridiculous. When they found out I was a sculptor the torture stopped and I was put to work making busts of Pol Pot. That saved my life.'

Two concerns preoccupied us. Was it possible, we asked ourselves, to convey the evidence of what we had seen, which was barely credible to us, in such a way that the *enormity* of the crime committed in Cambodia might be recognized internationally and the survivors helped? And, on a personal level, how could we keep moving *away* from the sounds which pursued us? The initial silence had broken and now the cries of fleshless children tormented us almost everywhere.

This was especially so when we reached the town of Kompong Speu where 150,000 people were said to be 'missing'. Where there had been markets, houses and schools, there was bare land. Substantial buildings had been demolished, *erased* like the cathedral. The town's hospital had disappeared; Vietnamese engineers had erected a temporary one and supplied a doctor and some drugs. But there were few beds and no blankets and antiseptic was splashed urgently on our hands every few yards we walked; many of the people lying on the stone floor were dying from plague and anthrax, which is passed through the meat of diseased cattle and takes about a month to kill. It can be cured by penicillin, but there was no penicillin, except that brought by two French doctors, Jean Yves Follezou and Jean Michel Vinot, who had travelled down from Phnom Penh with us. The human sounds here, I recall vividly, had a syncopation, a terrible prosody: high and shrill, then deep and unrelenting, the rhythm of approaching death. In the 'orphan's war', the children sat and leaned and lay on mats, impassive, looking directly at us and at the camera lens. When a young girl died after begging us for help, I felt the depths of shame and rage.

Similarly, in the 'hospital' of an orphanage in Phnom Penh, laid out like a First World War field station in the Gothic shell of an abandoned chapel, there were children who had been found wandering in the forest, living off treebark, grass and poisonous plants. Their appearance denied their humanity; rows of opaque eyes set in cloth-like skin. Here Gerry put his camera on the ground, walked away and cried.

One of several adults in charge at the orphanage was Prak Sarinn, a former teacher, who had survived the Pol Pot years by disguising himself as a peasant. 'It was the only acceptable class,' he said. 'I changed my personality, and I shall not be the same again. I can no longer teach; my head is filled with death and worry.' I asked him what had happened on 17 April 1975. He said, 'I was in my classroom when they burst in. They looked like boys, not even thirteen. They put their guns on us and told us all to march north into the countryside. The children were crying. I asked if we could first go home to join our families. They said no. So we just walked away, and most of the little ones died from exhaustion and hunger. I never saw my family again.'

•

MARGARET THATCHER
1979

'Time for a change'

After winning the 1979 general election, Margaret Thatcher (1925–) became the first woman prime minister in British history. The election had been called after she had won – by a single vote – a motion of no confidence in James Callaghan's Labour government, whose reputation had been severely dented by union militancy during the 1978 winter of discontent.

Thatcher's manifesto emphasized law and order, less state intervention, lower taxation and getting government 'off our backs'. The first part of this extract from the manifesto is by Mrs Thatcher, the rest states the five main tasks the Conservative Party set for government.

For me, the heart of politics is not political theory, it is people and how they want to live their lives.

No one who has lived in this country during the last five years can fail to be aware of how the balance of our society has been increasingly tilted in favour of the state at the expense of individual freedom.

This election may be the last chance we have to reverse that process, to restore the balance of power in favour of the people. It is therefore the most crucial election since the war.

Together with the threat to freedom there has been a feeling of helplessness, that we are a once great nation that has somehow fallen behind and that it is too late now to turn things round.

I don't accept that. I believe we not only can, we must. This manifesto points the way.

It contains no magic formula or lavish promises. It is not a recipe for an easy or a perfect life. But it sets out a broad framework for the recovery of our country, based not on dogma, but on reason, on common sense, above all on the liberty of the people under the law.

The things we have in common as a nation far outnumber those that set us apart.

It is in that spirit that I commend to you this manifesto.

OUR FIVE TASKS

This election is about the future of Britain – a great country which seems to have lost its way. It is a country rich in natural resources, in coal, oil, gas, and fertile farmlands. It is rich, too, in human resources, with professional and managerial skills of the highest calibre, with great industries and firms whose workers can be the equal of any in the world. We are the inheritors of a long tradition of parliamentary democracy and the rule of law.

Yet today, this country is faced with its most serious problems since the Second World War. What has happened to our country, to the values we used to share, to the success and prosperity we once took for granted?

During the industrial strife of last winter, confidence, self-respect, common sense, and even our sense of common humanity were shaken. At times this society seemed on the brink of disintegration.

Some of the reasons for our difficulties today are complex and go back many years. Others are more simple and more recent. We do not lay all the blame on the Labour Party: but Labour have been in power for most of the fifteen years and cannot escape the major responsibility.

They have made things worse in three ways. First, by practising the politics of envy and by actively discouraging the creation of wealth, they have set one group against another in an often bitter struggle to gain a larger share of a weak economy.

Second, by enlarging the role of the state and diminishing the role of the individual, they have crippled the enterprise and effort on which a prosperous country with improving social services depends.

Third, by heaping privilege without responsibility on the trade unions, Labour have given a minority of extremists the power to abuse individual liberties and to thwart Britain's chances of success. One result is that the trade union movement, which sprang from a deep and genuine fellow-feeling for the brotherhood of man, is today more distrusted and feared than ever before.

It is not just that Labour have governed Britain badly. They have reached a dead-end. The very nature of their party now prevents them from governing successfully in a free society and mixed economy.

Divided against themselves; devoid of any policies except those which have led to and would worsen our present troubles; bound inescapably by ties of history, political dogma and financial dependence to a single powerful interest group, Labour have demonstrated yet again that they cannot speak and dare not act for the nation as a whole.

Our country's relative decline is not inevitable. We in the Conservative

Party think we can reverse it, *not* because we think we have all the answers but because we think we have the one answer that matters most. We want to work *with the grain* of human nature, helping people to help themselves – and others. This is the way to restore that self-reliance and self-confidence which are the basis of personal responsibility and national success.

Attempting to do too much, politicians have failed to do those things which *should* be done. This has damaged the country and the authority of government. We must concentrate on what should be priorities for *any* government. They are set out in this manifesto.

Those who look in these pages for lavish promises or detailed commitments on every subject will look in vain. We may be able to do more in the next five years than we indicate here. We believe we can. But the Conservative government's first job will be to rebuild our economy and reunite a divided and disillusioned people.

Our five tasks are:

1. To restore the health of our economic and social life, by controlling inflation and striking a fair balance between the rights and duties of the trade union movement.
2. To restore incentives so that hard work pays, success is rewarded and genuine new jobs are created in an expanding economy.
3. To uphold Parliament and the rule of law.
4. To support family life, by helping people to become home-owners, raising the standards of their children's education, and concentrating welfare services on the effective support of the old, the sick, the disabled and those who are in real need.
5. To strengthen Britain's defences and work with our allies to protect our interests in an increasingly threatening world.

This is the strategy of the next Conservative Government.

•

WEI JINGSHENG
1979

'The people's prerogative'

Wei Jingsheng (1950–), one of the bravest Chinese dissidents, was convicted in 1979 of 'a serious counter-revolutionary crime of a most heinous nature' – supplying a foreigner with state military information, agitation and writing reactionary articles – and was sentenced to fifteen years' imprisonment. He was kept in isolation and denied family visits.

He became a hero to the democracy movement in China, which was crushed in Tiananmen Square in 1989. This is an extract from the speech he made in his defence at his trial.

To a considerable extent the theoretical core of original Marxism is in part centred around a description of a proper society, an idealistic state which is by no means unique in its conception to Marxism alone. For such a society was a widespread aspiration, shared by the working classes and intellectuals alike in their hope for liberty and equality, public ownership of property and social justice. The method Marxism advocated for the achievement of this ideal society was the fusing of common democracy with a dictatorship in which power had been centralized. It is this fusion which is the most striking characteristic of the Marxist tenets.

Following a hundred years of actual practice, those governments which have emerged from this method of dictatorship, where power has been concentrated – such as those of the Soviet Union, Vietnam and China before the smashing of the 'Gang of Four' – have without exception deteriorated into fascist regimes, where a small leading faction imposes its autocracy over the large mass of ordinary labouring people. Moreover, the fascist dictators, in whose grasp the government has come to rest, have long since ceased to use the dictatorship of the proletariat as a tool of implementing the old ideals of Communism itself. Precisely the opposite is the case. For without exception these rulers have used the ideals of Communism to reinforce the so-called dictatorship of the proletariat so that it may function as a tool for the benefit of those in power.

Thus, Marxism's fate is common to that of several religions. After the second or third generation of transmission, its revolutionary substance is quietly removed, while its doctrinal ideals are partially taken over by the rulers, to be used as an excuse to enslave the people and as a tool to deceive and fool them. By this stage, the nature of its teachings has also undergone a basic change, in that the ideals become, respectively, the excuse and tool of enslavement and deception. Thus, the nature of the teachings has been fundamentally changed. I call the practice of using ideals to mislead and enslave people 'idealism'. (Others think of it as a matter of faith.) The feudal fascist dictatorship of the 'Gang of Four' represented the culmination of such a development. When these forms of fascism make use of fine and glorious ideals to set up a blind faith in some modern superstition, so that the people may be the easier cheated and deceived, is this not a modern form of charlatanism? Is it not an even more brilliant panacea or poultice than those of the old nostrum-mongering pox-doctor?

The constitution grants citizens the right to criticize their leaders, because these leaders are not gods. It is only through the people's criticism and supervision that those leaders will make fewer mistakes, and only in this way that the people will avoid the misfortune of having their lords and masters ride roughshod over them. Then, and only then, will the people be able to breathe freely. Secondly, if we wish to carry out the reform of our nation's socialist system we must base this on the entire population using the methods of criticism and discussion to find out the defects in the present system; otherwise reforms cannot be successfully carried out. It is the people's prerogative, when faced by unreasonable people and unacceptable matters, to make criticisms. Indeed, it is also their unshirkable duty so to do and this is a sovereign right with which no individual or government organization has a right to interfere.

Criticism may not be beautiful or pleasant to hear, nor can it always be completely accurate. If one insists on criticism being pleasant to hear, and demands its absolute accuracy on pain of punishment, this is as good as forbidding criticism and banning reforms. In such a situation one might just as well deify the leadership outright. Surely we are not expected to retread that old path of blind faith in the leadership advocated by the 'Gang of Four'?

•

E. P. THOMPSON
1980

'Protest and Survive'

The Marxist historian E. P. Thompson (1924–93) is most widely known for his classic study of eighteenth-century politics and protest, The Making of the English Working Class. *He left the Communist Party after the Soviet invasion of Hungary in 1956. Thompson was a leading proponent of nuclear disarmament and was one of the editors of 'Protest and Survive', a series of essays arguing against the deployment of cruise missiles in Britain.*

His own essay was written in reaction to a letter in The Times *from the Oxford professor Michael Howard, which argued that civil defence on a scale sufficient to give protection to a substantial number of the population in the event of a limited nuclear strike was an indispensable element of deterrence. This is an edited extract.*

It has never been true that nuclear war is 'unthinkable'. It has been thought and the thought has been put into effect. This was done in 1945, in the name of allies fighting for the Four Freedoms (although what those Freedoms were

I cannot now recall), and it was done upon two populous cities. It was done by professing Christians, when the Western allies had already defeated the Germans, and when victory against the Japanese was certain, in the longer or shorter run. The longer run would have cost some thousands more of Western lives, whereas the short run (the bomb) would cost the lives only of enemy Asians. This was perfectly thinkable. It was thought. And action followed on.

What is 'unthinkable' is that nuclear war could happen to *us*. So long as we can suppose that this war will be inflicted only on *them*, the thought comes easily. And if we can also suppose that this war will save 'our' lives, or serve our self-interest, or even save us (if we live in California) from the tedium of queuing every other day for gasoline, then the act can easily follow on. We *think* others to death as we define them as the Other, the enemy: Asians: Marxists: non-people. The deformed human mind is the ultimate doomsday weapon – it is out of the human mind that the missiles and the neutron warheads come.

For this reason it is necessary to enter a remonstrance against those who use this kind of language and adopt these mental postures. They are preparing our minds as launching platforms for exterminating thoughts. The fact that Soviet ideologists are doing much the same (thinking us to death as 'imperialists' and 'capitalists') is no defence. This is not work proper to scholars.

Academic persons have little influence upon political and military decisions, and less than they suppose. They do, however, operate within our culture, with ideas and language, and, as we have seen, the deformation of culture is the precedent condition for nuclear war.

It is therefore proper to ask such persons to resist the contamination of our culture with those terms which precede the ultimate act. The death of fifteen millions of fellow-citizens ought not to be described as 'disagreeable consequences'. A war confined to Europe ought not to be given the euphemisms of 'limited' or 'theatre'. The development of more deadly weapons, combined with menacing diplomatic postures and major new political and strategic decisions (the siting of missiles on our own territory under the control of alien personnel), ought not to be concealed within the anodyne technological term of 'modernization'. The threat to erase the major cities of Russia and East Europe ought not to trip easily off the tongue as 'unacceptable [*sic*] damage'.

I am thinking of that great number of persons who very much dislike what is going on in the actual world, but who dislike the vulgarity of exposing themselves to the business of 'politics' even more. They erect both sets of dislikes around their desks or laboratories like a screen, and get on with their work and their careers. I am not asking these, or all of them, to march around the place or to spend hours in weary little meetings. I am asking them to examine the deformities of our culture and then, in public places, to demur . . .

I have come to the view that a general nuclear war is not only possible but probable, and that its probability is increasing. We may indeed be approaching a point of no-return when the existing tendency or disposition towards this outcome becomes irreversible.

I ground this view upon two considerations, which we may define (to borrow the terms of our opponents) as 'tactical' and 'strategic'.

By tactical I mean that the political and military conditions for such war exist now in several parts of the world; the proliferation of nuclear weapons will continue, and will be hastened by the export of nuclear energy technology to new markets; and the rivalry of the superpowers is directly inflaming these conditions.

Such conditions now exist in the Middle East and around the Persian Gulf, will shortly exist in Africa, while in south-east Asia, Russia and China have already engaged in wars by proxy with each other, in Cambodia and Vietnam.

Such wars might stop just short of general nuclear war between the superpowers. And in their aftermath the great powers might be frightened into better behaviour for a few years. But so long as this behaviour rested on nothing more than mutual fear, then military technology would continue to be refined, more hideous weapons would be invented, and the opposing giants would enlarge their control over client states. The strategic pressures towards confrontation will continue to grow.

These *strategic* considerations are the gravest of the two. They rest upon a historical view of power and of the social process, rather than upon the instant analysis of the commentator on events.

In this view it is a superficial judgement, and a dangerous error, to suppose that deterrence 'has worked'. Very possibly it may have worked, at this or that moment, in preventing recourse to war. But in its very mode of working, and in its 'postures', it has brought on a series of consequences within its host societies.

'Deterrence' is not a stationary state, it is a degenerative state. Deterrence has repressed the export of violence towards the opposing bloc, but in doing so the repressed power of the state has turned back upon its own author. The repressed violence has backed up, and has worked its way back into the economy, the polity, the ideology and the culture of the opposing powers. This is the deep structure of the Cold War.

Within the logic of 'deterrence', millions are now employed in the armed services, security organs and military economy of the opposing blocs, and corresponding interests exert immense influence within the counsels of the great powers. Mystery envelops the operation of the technological 'alchemists'. 'Deterrence' has become normal, and minds have been habituated to the vocabulary of mutual extermination. And within this normality, hideous cultural abnormalities have been nurtured and are growing to full girth.

The menace of nuclear war reaches far back into the economies of both parties, dictating priorities, and awarding power. Here, in failing economies, will be found the most secure and vigorous sectors, tapping the most advanced technological skills of both opposed societies and diverting these away from peaceful and productive employment or from efforts to close the great gap between the world's north and south. Here also will be found the driving rationale for expansionist programmes in unsafe nuclear energy, programmes which cohabit comfortably with military nuclear technology whereas the urgent research into safe energy supplies from sun, wind or wave are neglected because they have no military pay-off. Here, in this burgeoning sector, will be found the new expanionist drive for 'markets' for arms, as 'capitalist' and 'socialist' powers compete to feed into the Middle East, Africa and Asia more sophisticated means of killing.

The menace of this stagnant state of violence backs up also into the polity of both halves of the world. Permanent threat and periodic crisis press the men of the military-industrial interests, by differing routes in each society, towards the top. Crisis legitimates the enlargement of the security functions of the state, the intimidation of internal dissent, and the imposition of secrecy and the control of information. As the 'natural' lines of social and political development are repressed, and affirmative perspectives are closed, so internal politics collapses into squabbling interest groups, all of which interests are subordinated to the overarching interests of the state of perpetual threat.

All this may be readily observed. It may be observed even in failing Britain, across whose territory are now scattered the bases, airfields, camps, research stations, submarine depots, communications-interception stations, radar screens, security and intelligence HQ, munitions works – secure and expanding employment in an economic climate of radical insecurity.

What we cannot observe so well – for we ourselves are the object which must be observed – is the manner in which three decades of 'deterrence', of mutual fear, mystery and state-endorsed stagnant hostility, have backed up into our culture and our ideology. Imagination has been numbed, language and values have been fouled, by the postures and expectations of the 'deterrent' state. But this is matter for a close and scrupulous inquiry.

These, then, are among the strategic considerations which lead me to the view that the probability of great power nuclear warfare is strong and increasing. I do not argue from this local episode or that: what happened yesterday in Afghanistan and what is happening now in Pakistan or North Yemen. I argue from a general and sustained historical process, an accumulative logic, of a kind made familiar to me in the study of history. The episodes lead in this direction or that, but the general logic of process is always towards nuclear war.

The local crises are survived, and it seems as if the decisive moment – either of war or of peace-making and reconciliation – has been postponed and pushed forward into the future. But what has been pushed foward is always worse. Both parties change for the worse. The weapons are more terrible, the means for their delivery more clever. The notion that a war might be fought to 'advantage', that it might be 'won', gains ground. There is even a tremor of excitement in our culture as though, subconsciously, humankind has lived with the notion for so long that expectations without actions have become boring. The human mind, even when it resists, assents more easily to its own defeat. All moves on its degenerative course, as if the outcome of civilization was as determined as the outcome of this sentence: in a full stop.

I am reluctant to accept that this determination is absolute. But if my arguments are correct, then we cannot put off the matter any longer. We must throw whatever resources still exist in human culture across the path of this degenerative logic. We must protest if we are to survive. *Protest is the only realistic form of civil defence.*

•

SOCIAL DEMOCRATIC PARTY
1981

'A realignment of British politics'

The left had consolidated their control of the Labour Party at its conference in 1980. Three months later, at a special party conference in London on 24 January, it was decided that the leader of the party would no longer be chosen only by Labour MPs but also by the unions and constituencies, with the unions having 40 per cent of the votes and the constituencies and the parliamentary party 30 per cent each. All sitting MPs, moreover, would have to be reselected between elections.

Next day the three MPs who had been the leading opponents of the changes – David Owen, Shirley Williams and William Rodgers – were joined at Owen's home in London's

Limehouse by Roy Jenkins, whose term as president of the European Community had just ended. They issued the Declaration for Social Democracy which led two months later to the founding of the Social Democratic Party.

The calamitous outcome of the Labour Party Wembley Conference demands a new start in British politics. A handful of trade union leaders can now dictate the choice of a future prime minister. The Conference disaster is the culmination of a long process by which the Labour Party has moved steadily away from its roots in the people of this country and its commitment to parliamentary government.

We propose to set up a Council for Social Democracy: Our intention is to rally all those who are committed to the values, principles and policies of social democracy. We seek to reverse Britain's economic decline. We want to create an open, classless and more equal society, one which rejects ugly prejudices based upon sex, race or religion.

A first list of those who have agreed to support the Council will be announced at an early date. Some of them have been actively and continuously engaged in Labour politics. A few were so engaged in the past, but have ceased to be so recently. Others have been mainly active in spheres outside party politics. We do not believe the fight for the ideals we share and for the recovery of our country should be limited only to politicians. It will need the support of men and women in all parts of our society.

The Council will represent a coming together of several streams: politicians who recognize that the drift towards extremism in the Labour Party is not compatible with the democratic traditions of the Party they joined and those from outside politics who believe that the country cannot be saved without changing the sterile and rigid framework into which the British political system has increasingly fallen in the last two decades.

We do not believe in the politics of an inert centre merely representing the lowest common denominator between two extremes. We want more, not less, radical change in our society, but with a greater stability of direction.

Our economy needs a healthy public sector and a healthy private sector without frequent frontier changes. We want to eliminate poverty and promote greater equality without stifling enterprise or imposing bureaucracy from the centre. We need the innovating strength of a competitive economy with a fair distribution of rewards. We favour competitive public enterprise, co-operative ventures and profit sharing.

There must be more decentralization of decision-making in industry and government, together with an effective and practical system of democracy at work. The quality of our public and community services must be improved and they must be made more responsive to people's needs. We do not accept that mass unemployment is inevitable. A number of countries, mainly those with social democratic governments, have managed to combine high employment with low inflation.

Britain needs to recover its self-confidence and be outward looking, rather than isolationist, xenophobic or neutralist. We want Britain to play a full and constructive role within the framework of the European Community, NATO, the United Nations and the Commonwealth. It is only within such a multilateral framework that we can hope to negotiate international agreements covering arms control and disarmament and to grapple effectively with the poverty of the Third World.

We recognize that for those people who have given much of their lives to the Labour Party, the choice that lies ahead will be deeply painful. But we believe that the need for a realignment of British politics must now be faced.

•

DAVID TINKER
1982

'The Falklands'

When the British expeditionary force sailed to recapture the Falkland Islands, after the invasion by Argentinian troops, Lieutenant David Tinker was on board HMS Glamorgan. The leader of the Labour Party, Michael Foot, supported Margaret Thatcher's decision and there was hardly any protest in Britain until American attempts to broker a peace deal were constantly scuppered. Yet there were many who believed that Britain did not need to go to war for the Falklands. One was Tinker, whose growing disillusion was chronicled in his letters home to his father Hugh, and to Jonathan and Helena, his brother and sister-in-law.

When Hugh Tinker published a collection of his son's poems and letters after the war was won, David (who died when Glamorgan was hit by an Exocet) was described as the nearest Britain would get to a Falklands Wilfred Owen (the greatest poet of the First World War).

I sometimes wonder if I am totally odd in that I utterly oppose all this killing that is going on over a flag. Wilfred Owen wrote that 'There'll come a day when men make war on death for lives, not men for flags,' but it has been the reverse here – 'nations trek from progress' still.

It is quite easy to see how the war has come about; Mrs Thatcher imagined she was Churchill defying Hitler, and the Navy advised a quick war before the winter set in, the Navy chiefs also wanted maximum use made of the Navy for maximum publicity to reverse the Navy cuts: which has happened. For [utmost] worth, victory or defeat would have the same result: publicity and popular support, either congratulations or sympathy. The Navy thus overlooked the fact that we were fighting without all the necessary air cover which is provided by the USA in the Atlantic and by the RAF in the North Sea and Icelandic Sea. Although the Harrier is a marvellous little aircraft it is not a proper strike aircraft, and the best the Navy could get when carriers were 'abolished'. Consequently, we have no proper carriers which can launch early-warning aircraft fitted with radar as strike aircraft. From the fifties onwards these two were absolute essentials.

However, the Navy felt that we were British and they [the Argentinians] were wogs, and that would make all the difference. The Admiral said as much to us on [the task force] TV. Consequently, we have no way of spotting low-level attacks beyond twenty miles, which is how *Sheffield* was sunk.

Apart from the military fiasco the political side is even more disgraceful. Even if Britain does reconquer the Falklands we still have to talk to the Argentinians and come to some arrangement, so why not settle before a war has devastated the Falklanders' island? However, if Britain is going to turn the Falklands into a garrison island (in direct contravention of the Antarctic treaty?) it will show the complete hypocrisy of the British Government which was going to leave the islands totally undefended and take away the islanders' British citizenship! I suppose Mrs Thatcher will have to let them become British again – if so, will we provide them with a proper British health service, money for development, etc.? The garrison alone, with married quarters, NAAFI, hospital, barracks, air base, naval base, repair facilities, etc., bringing in, say, 3,000 people at the minimum (including dependants) will have to be taken out of NATO – so more defence spending when the RN is to be cut by a third! Or, maybe, not cut the RN after all this publicity, and increase defence spending by, say, a third. The forces will have an immense mill stone around their necks; people will not want to go there (going to Scotland is hated enough) and the NCOs and Senior Ratings will simply leave the forces. The whole business is absolute nonsense.

I read that Argentina was prepared to accept a deal which involved

Argentinian sovereignty and British administration and way of life. Those, to me, sound fair terms to avoid bloodshed. Now that war has started, neither side can give way until the other is exhausted. This is not a war between civilized countries. It is not fought for any good reason (trade, survival, top-nation status, etc.) but is fought on a 'principle' by two dictatorships. It is a dangerous state of affairs in Britain when the Prime Minister can tell the forces to go to war without consulting even Parliament. If that is the case, it is time the forces were cut so that it is impossible to use them for anything but the defence of Britain, and [that] they were placed under NATO control. Thinking of wars fought on 'principle' alone I can only think of religious wars of bigotry, and the Thirty Years War which destroyed Germany. Thinking of enormous expenditure, I can only think of the Spanish Armada, the Dutch Wars of Independence – and Suez! A classicist on board also quoted an example of another dying power having a last fling. I only hope that the Falklands do not become our Vietnam, but so long as this government is in power they will be . . . Mrs Thatcher, and our Admiral (he more understandably) seem to have no compunction about casualties at all – the initial shock of *Sheffield* has worn off, and now they are accepted willingly – twenty yesterday in a helicopter, and twenty in *Ardent*. And they will not end until one side surrenders.

The pity for us is that there is no cause for this war; and, to be honest, the Argentinians are more patriotic about the Malvinas than we are about the Falklands. And the iniquitous thing is that we trained and equipped them! Their carrier, Type 42 destroyers, submarines and aircraft are all European. Britain even sold Argentina the maps of the Falklands a month before the invasion so that there were no maps for our own troops when we needed them. We were about to train their Lynx helicopter crews to use the Sea Skua missile (in May). That's the only advantage we have over their ships at present. And we even gave them an official cocktail party when one of their Type 42 destroyers was training in Portsmouth last year! I suppose we didn't think that we'd have a warmonger in charge.

I cannot think of a single war in Britain's history which has been so pointless. They have always been either for trade, survival, maintaining the balance of power, world (economic?) growth, etc. This one is to recapture a place which we were going to leave undefended from April, and to deprive its residents of British citizenship in October. And to recapture it, having built up *their* forces with the most modern Western arms (not even *we* have the air-launched Exocet which is so deadly). And fighting ourselves without the two prerequisites of naval warfare: air cover, and airborne early warning, which have been essential since the Second World War . . .

Not only has Mrs Thatcher survived a political fiasco; she has covered up the military cost to Britain (ten times what it will cost the Argentinians) and sent a fleet to do a job it should never have been sent to do: because of no air cover resulting in four ships sunk, four written off, and more damaged. She has become a complete dictator, ordering war without consulting Parliament, and she is dragging the masses, shouting and cheering, behind her. The newspapers just see it as a real-life 'War Mag', and even have drawings of battles, and made-up descriptions, entirely from their own imagination! If some of the horrible ways that people have died occurred in *their* offices maybe they would change their tone.

•

ARTHUR SCARGILL
1983

'Why the miners must fight'

Within four weeks of the 1983 election in which Margaret Thatcher was re-elected, with a sweeping majority of 144, Arthur Scargill (1938–), president of the National Union of Mineworkers, threw down the gauntlet to the government. Addressing the union's annual conference, he said that the fight against pit closures would require 'extra-parliamentary action'.

A year-long strike started the following year, but Scargill was decisively defeated by Thatcher and the NUM lost half its membership.

The re-election of a Tory administration is a severe setback to the Labour Party, a catastrophe for Britain and the British people. We should not forget that despite their record number of seats, the Tories were re-elected with a reduced vote compared to 1979. Nor should we forget that nearly 60 per cent of the British people voted against Thatcher's monetarist philosophy . . .

When the NUM obtained approximately 40 per cent of the votes cast in support of our recommendation for industrial action in our two ballots over the past year, we were told (especially by the media) that we were out of touch with our members, and the result was a landslide defeat for the Union's leaders, many of whom should resign.

Yet, Mrs Thatcher gets elected with a 40 per cent vote, and the media hails this as a landslide *victory*, a vote of confidence. She is thus able to form a government, and if necessary take this nation to war, even though she has obtained only a minority of our support.

For that injustice, our outmoded and undemocratic electoral system is to blame – it has yet again failed to reflect popular will. I have argued and fought for thirty years – in line with what was once Labour Party policy – that proportional representation is essential to electoral justice. Its introduction would in my opinion lead to a polarization of views, eventually electing a Labour Government with a clear majority of votes behind it. I hope this election result stirs our movement in that direction . . .

We have re-elected a government which is intent on heightening international tensions and increasing the likelihood of war – a government which, although it represents a minority of feeling in the country, will attempt to dismantle our health service, close down our schools, and destroy our basic industries – including coal.

We have two choices. We can give in, as many German people did in the 1930s, and allow the worst to happen – we can watch social destruction and repression on a truly horrific scale, and wait for the inevitable holocaust. Or we can fight back.

A fight-back against this government's policies will inevitably take place outside rather than inside Parliament. When I talk about 'extra-parliamentary action', there is a great outcry in the press, and from leading Tories about my refusal to accept the democratic will of the people.

I am not prepared to accept policies proposed by a government elected by a minority of the British electorate. I am not prepared to quietly accept the destruction of the coal-mining industry, nor am I willing to see our social services utterly decimated.

This totally undemocratic government can now easily push through whatever laws it chooses. Faced with possible parliamentary destruction of all that is good and compassionate in our society, extra-parliamentary action will be the only course open to the working class and the Labour movement.

As for us – miners will have to take direct action if we are to save our industry, our jobs, our self-respect and dignity. That action will, however, only be effective if it is infused with the ideals, the hopes and aspirations upon which our movement was founded. We have inherited the dreams of Wat Tyler, the Chartists, of Keir Hardie and the suffragettes, of our own early leaders such as A. J. Cook.

To carry out those dreams we must fight for a social framework in which all people can live and grow, work, learn and create. I ask this Conference to raise its eyes and look to a new horizon. Be prepared to stand and fight for our industry, and alongside our fellow workers in other industries.

We must face the fact that the hearts and minds of Britain's trade unionists, among them our members, have not yet been moved by the vision of a socialist future.

It is my contention that we need to put *politics* back into the centre of trade union activity. That does not mean altering our priorities. On the contrary, we must fight even harder for wages, jobs and good conditions. But we must infuse that fight with an understanding of how our claims and battles affect other sections of the community, and find new ways of working together wherever possible.

Our Union is already part of a framework moving towards a spirit of co-operation within the Triple Alliance. Over the past year, the savage dismantling of the British steel industry has continued unchecked. Only industrial action such as that taken by steel workers in South Yorkshire a few months ago has forced any concessions, as the Tories continue to decimate not only the public steel sector, but the private one as well.

As for the railways, the government is now ready to move in and take apart our nation's railway network, destroy jobs and turn entire communities throughout Britain into semi-ghettos without access to public transport by train.

I must warn, however, that time is not on our side. Our economy is in danger, our national future in jeopardy, and our planet itself faces a countdown to destruction.

The Tory victory last month was a victory for the war-mongers who have the full support of Mrs Thatcher and her nuclear-obsessed Cabinet.

Let us begin to practise those passionate socialist beliefs our movement preaches. If we dedicate ourselves to this end, we shall not only save our industry – we will pave the way towards a caring and truly democratic socialist system of society.

•

RONALD REAGAN
1983

'An evil empire'

As president of the United States from 1981 to 1988, the Hollywood actor turned politician Ronald Reagan (1911–) deserved his final credit as the man who won the Cold War. Although dubbed a hawk by critics of his unyielding opposition to the Soviet dictatorship, he was vindicated at the very end of his presidency when the Soviet empire collapsed in the era of Mikhail Gorbachev (after which Reagan said that he could no longer in good conscience call the Soviet Union an 'evil empire'). It was that epithet which became one of Reagan's most famous pronouncements.

He made several major speeches on the morality of the Soviet Union during his presidency, but it was this one, to the National Association of Evangelicals at Orlando, Florida, which remains the best known.

A number of years ago, I heard a young father, a very prominent young man in the entertainment world, addressing a tremendous gathering in California. It was during the time of the Cold War, and Communism and our own way of life were very much on people's minds. And he was speaking to that subject. And suddenly, though, I heard him saying, 'I love my little girls more than anything –' And I said to myself, 'Oh, no, don't. You can't – don't say that.' But I had underestimated him. He went on: 'I would rather see my little girls die now, still believing in God, than have them grow up under Communism and one day die no longer believing in God.'

There were thousands of young people in that audience. They came to their feet with shouts of joy. They had instantly recognized the profound truth in what he had said, with regard to the physical and the soul and what was truly important.

Yes, let us pray for the salvation of all of those who live in that totalitarian darkness – pray they will discover the joy of knowing God. But until they do, let us be aware that while they preach the supremacy of the state, declare its omnipotence over individual man, and predict its eventual domination of all peoples on the earth, they are the focus of evil in the modern world.

It was C. S. Lewis who, in his unforgettable *Screwtape Letters*, wrote: 'The greatest evil is not done now in those sordid "dens of crime" that Dickens loved to paint. It is not even done in concentration camps and labor camps. In those we see its final result. But it is conceived and ordered (moved, seconded, carried and minuted) in clean, carpeted, warmed, and well-lighted offices, by quiet men with white collars and cut fingernails and smooth-shaven cheeks who do not need to raise their voice.'

Well, because these 'quiet men' do not 'raise their voices,' because they sometimes speak in soothing tones of brotherhood and peace, because, like other dictators before them, they're always making 'their final territorial demand,' some would have us accept them at their word and accommodate ourselves to their aggressive impulses. But if history teaches anything, it teaches that simpleminded appeasement or wishful thinking about our adversaries is folly. It means the betrayal of our past, the squandering of our freedom.

While America's military strength is important, let me add here that I've always maintained that the struggle now going on for the world will never be decided by bombs or rockets, by armies or military might. The real crisis we face today is a spiritual one; at root, it is a test of moral will and faith.

Whittaker Chambers, the man whose own religious conversion made him a witness to one of the terrible traumas of our time, the Hiss–Chambers case, wrote that the crisis of the Western world exists to the degree in which the West is indifferent to God, the degree to which it collaborates in Communism's attempt to make man stand alone without God. And then he said, for Marxism-Leninism is actually the second-oldest faith, first proclaimed in the Garden of Eden with the words of temptation, 'Ye shall be as gods.'

The Western world can answer this challenge, he wrote, 'but only provided that its faith in God and the freedom He enjoins is as great as Communism's faith in Man.'

I believe we shall rise to the challenge. I believe that Communism is another sad, bizarre chapter in human history whose last pages even now are being written. I believe this because the source of our strength in the quest for human freedom is not material, but spiritual. And because it knows no limitation, it must terrify and ultimately triumph over those who would enslave their fellow man. For in the words of Isaiah: 'He giveth power to the faint; and to them that have no might He increased strength ... But they that wait upon the Lord shall renew their strength; they shall mount up with wings as eagles; they shall run, and not be weary ...'

•

CHURCH OF ENGLAND
1985

'*Acute human misery*'

Dr Robert Runcie (1921–), Archbishop of Canterbury, set up a commission of churchmen and lay people in 1983 to examine the conditions of urban life in Britain and how the Church and the government could improve them. When the commission's report was published two years later, 'Faith in the City' caused an immediate political uproar and was denounced by government spokesmen as 'Marxist'. There were no recommendations about individuals and families, the source of all standards in society, said an 'absolutely shocked' Margaret Thatcher. What so angered the Thatcher government were the report's attacks on aspects of government policy, some of which were set out in the introduction.

A serious situation has developed in the major cities of this country.

This is not a new situation: there have been other occasions in the last 200 years when urban poverty has presented an acute challenge to society. But the recent dramatic reduction and redistribution of employment in the manufacturing industries around which so many of our great cities were built, and the decentralization of the new and growing industries to smaller towns and even rural areas, have speeded the process of decay in parts of once-flourishing industrial cities to an unprecedented degree. This observation does not depend on any particular theoretical or political stance. The social, political and economic factors can be described and analysed in many different ways; different sets of indicators can be used to identify poverty and deprivation. But whatever method or framework is used to establish and to present the facts, the same message of acute human misery is received.

We have to report that we have been deeply disturbed by what we have seen and heard. We have been confronted with the human consequences of unemployment, which in some urban areas may be over 50 per cent of the labour force, and which occasionally reaches a level as high as 80 per cent – consequences which may be compounded by the effects of racial discrimination. We have seen physical decay, whether of Victorian terraced housing or of inferior system-built blocks of flats, which has in places created an environment so degrading that some people have set fire to their own homes rather than be condemned to living in them indefinitely. Social disintegration has reached a point in some areas that shop windows are boarded up, cars cannot be left on the street, residents are afraid either to go out themselves or to ask others in, and there is a pervading sense of powerlessness and despair . . .

People in Britain are not actually starving. But many residents of UPAs [Urban Priority Areas] are deprived of what the rest of society regard as the essential minimum for a decent life; they live next door to, but have little chance to participate in a relatively affluent society; by any standards theirs is a wretched condition which none of us would wish to tolerate for ourselves or to see inflicted on others.

Poverty is at the root of *powerlessness*. Poor people in UPAs are at the mercy of fragmented and apparently unresponsive public authorities. They are trapped in housing and in environments over which they have little control. They lack the means and opportunity – which so many of us take for granted – of making choices in their lives.

One way of seeking to understand these phenomena is as signs of an evident and apparently increasing *inequality* in our society. It can of course be said that there will always be inequality, just as there will always be poverty. But there are degrees of inequality, just as there are degrees of poverty. What we have seen exceeds the limits that would be thought acceptable by most of our fellow citizens . . .

'Unemployment,' said Archbishop William Temple in the 1930s, 'is the most hideous of our social evils.' The effects of unemployment in the 1980s have been all too clear to us on our visits to Britain's UPAs. We have been confronted time and time again with the deep human misery – coupled in some cases with resentment, in others with apathy and hopelessness – that is its result. The absence of regular paid work has eroded self-respect. 'Give me back my dignity' was the heartfelt plea from one man – made redundant, and with no prospect of a job – at one of our public meetings in the North-west.

Unemployment for most people is not a liberating experience. Although unemployed people clearly have more time for leisure pursuits, their financial situation makes it more difficult or impossible for them to indulge in leisure activities. The cheapest form of entertainment available – television – can be a constant and painful reminder of the opportunities of a consumer society that is beyond their reach.

What has most astonished (and depressed) us has been a widespread feeling among those we have talked to in the UPAs that 'nothing can be done' about unemployment. Not, however, that nothing *should* be done – the feeling is more that the 'social evil' is so widespread and unchanging, the problem so baffling, and the authorities apparently so unresponsive, that hope has been abandoned. We wonder whether some politicians really understand the despair which has become so widespread in many areas of our country.

We must make it perfectly clear that we believe there is no instant, dogmatic or potent solution to the problem of unemployment. Certainly the Church of England cannot 'solve' the problem of unemployment. It possesses neither the mandate nor the competence to do so. Yet as it is in the position of being the national Church, it has a particular duty to act as the conscience of the nation. It must question all economic philosophies, not least those which, when put into practice, have contributed to the blighting of whole districts, which do not offer the hope of amelioration, and which perpetuate the human misery and despair to which we have referred. The situation requires the Church to question from its own particular standpoint the *morality* of these economic philosophies.

The main assumption on which present economic policies are based is that prosperity can be restored if individuals are set free to pursue their own economic salvation. The appeal is to economic self-interest and individualism, and freeing market mechanisms through the removal of 'unnecessary' governmental interference and restrictive trade union practice.

Individual responsibility and self-reliance are excellent objectives. The nation cannot do without them. But pursuit of them must not damage a collective obligation and provision for those who have no choice, or whose choices are at best forced ones. *We believe that at present too much emphasis is being given to individualism, and not enough to collective obligation.* In the absence of a spirit of collective obligation, or the political will to foster it, there is no guarantee that the pursuit of innumerable individual self-interests will add up to an improvement in the common good . . .

We must not fall into the trap of letting economics suffocate morality by taking decisions for us: economic determinism is an insidious philosophy. The role of economic science is to tell us the likely effects of choices we make on moral grounds.

If it is by their *outcomes* that macro-economic policies must be judged, we are united in the view that the costs of present policies, with the continuing growth of unemployment, are unacceptable in their effect on whole communities and generations. A degree of hardship may be needed to attain longer-term objectives, but it is unacceptable that the costs of transition should fall hardest on those least able to bear them.

•

SARAH HIPPERSON
1986

'Greenham Common'

There were thirty people, mostly women and children, on the march from Cardiff to the American base at Greenham Common to protest at Margaret Thatcher's agreement that cruise missiles could be used from Britain. As they arrived at Greenham in 1981, they decided to chain themselves to the gates in a suffragette-style defiance of the military.

'This was to be the engine of the Greenham Camp, a new kind of protest which refused to go away,' Sheila Rowbotham says in A Century of Women. *'They evoked old freedoms to use the common land and sent out schoolgirl-style chain letters inviting women to embrace the base.'* Women responded in their thousands and the camp survived until 1995. Fences were regularly cut as campaigners tried to force their way inside the airbase and their all-women protest was seen on television around the world.*

One of the women was Sarah Hipperson. In the poet Beth Junor's history of the Greenham Camp, Greenham Common Women's Peace Camp: A History of Non-Violent Resistance 1984–1995, *Ms Hipperson describes why she joined the protest.*

Each of us recognizes the anger and helplessness that rises in us when confronted with denial of rights, oppression, loss of liberty. The horrendous occurrences of the concentration camps, the dropping of nuclear bombs on

Hiroshima and Nagasaki, the inhuman apartheid laws of South Africa, the segregation of black people in the US, the Vietnam War, the present-day war in Northern Ireland (the list is endless) – fill us with a sense of urgency, a need to find some power, to counteract the evil that lies at the very root of the thinking which makes these crimes against humanity possible.

As we reach for some effective way to channel our abhorrence and anger, in an attempt to stop these happening, we often just thrash around in self-destructive behaviour, and become powerless in the face of the 'steam road roller' of the state. Feeling helpless and disillusioned, we end up apathetic and indifferent to suffering. In this condition we easily become encompassed in the corruption of the state.

Some believe the solution can be found in political theories and practice – but on their own, without a conversion to non-violence and justice, these end up creating the same injustices and crimes against humanity that they genuinely set out to correct. Unless there is true respect for humanity and the life force, all the energy put into overcoming evil will be squandered. We will fail in our defence of those who are immediately in the path of the particular evil we hope to overcome.

The women who live at Yellow Gate choose the power of non-violence to counteract the power of evil, generated from inside the base by genocidal nuclear weapons. There are 101 cruise missiles – each with the explosive power of sixteen Hiroshima bombs – held in six silos on Greenham Common in Berkshire in the lush green countryside of rural England. The base can best be described as a nuclear concentration camp, where preparations for mass murder are carried out daily. This is accepted as normal behaviour by most people in Britain, but not by the small group of women who protest vociferously all attempts to normalize, and make acceptable, this nuclear concentration camp. Each month when the cruise missile convoy leaves the base to go to Salisbury Plain we resist strongly but non-violently this practice for mass murder – the consequence of taking this action is that we will serve prison sentences.

Non-violence is neither an easy nor a soft option, it is a clearly chosen path of confrontation with the state and the military. It is not a posture to be struck in an attempt to avoid human responsibilities or the risk of losing privileges. Not taking stands in order to appear non-judgemental is not non-violent, it is a clear dereliction of responsibility, as is rhetoric without practical commitment. Direct action becomes non-violent with the acceptance of the full consequences – the willingness to choose to go to prison even when given the corrupting choice to pay fines by the court. The non-violent action remains non-violent only by the refusal to make deals, financial or otherwise (e.g. the promise of 'good' behaviour).

We work non-violently in faith because we know it works. We believe it is realistic and practicable, also, its results are measurable.

Non-violence is an energy that gives you the power to overcome power-lessness. Whatever the occurrence, you know that there is some action you can take to interrupt, disrupt or stop deliberately, so that the 'occurrence' does not work as it was intended to do. Evil depends on being thorough and efficient; non-violent direct action makes it unworkable at the time. It also gives a chance to change the thinking behind the ideas that promote these crimes against humanity.

The women's peace camp on Greenham Common provides the perfect place for women to develop non-violent skills, as a living experience, twenty-four hours a day. Learning to dwell on the land amidst nature, your senses become heightened. You become like a receiver, ready to pick up signals in the constantly changing daily patterns, and ready to take non-violent direct action when it is called for.

I believe that non-violence is a spiritual energy – a primitive response of resistance to events and circumstances that we find intolerable. It is a precious resource and has an infinite life, if treated with respect.

•

PAUL FOOT
1986

'The Birmingham Six'

Twenty-one people were killed and 162 injured when the main railway station in Birmingham was bombed by the IRA in 1974. It was the biggest killing of civilians in Britain's postwar history. Three days later six Irishmen were charged and later sent to prison. The 'Birmingham Six' always protested their innocence. It was only when the journalist Chris Mullin (now a Labour MP) started investigating their case with Granada Television's World in Action *team that doubts began to arise about the case for the prosecution.*

In this article for the London Review of Books, *Paul Foot reviews Mullin's book* Error of Judgement: The Truth about the Birmingham Bombings *and argues that the six men were wrongly imprisoned. Five years later, after sixteen years in jail, they were freed.*

There appears to be a link between the enormity of a crime and the ignominy which attaches to any journalist or investigator who publicly questions the guilt of those convicted for it. This has been especially true in the case of

Irish people convicted of bombings in Britain. Anyone who questions the verdict against an Irish bomber is assumed to be a bomber himself. As a result of this extraordinary logic, the authorities have been able to get away with mistakes, inconsistencies and far worse. No praise is too high, then, for Chris Mullin and the way he has pursued the Birmingham bombings case over the past eight years. He has tried to influence other journalists with access to larger circulations than he had when he was editor of *Tribune*. From most of them (including me) he got every encouragement short of help. Most of us felt that there was so much injustice in the world that to concentrate on the Birmingham bombings case was eccentric to the point of perversity. There was one exception. Granada Television's *World in Action* gave Chris Mullin the resources he needed. They furnished him with forensic experts who alone could tackle the complicated evidence about nitroglycerine. With the help of *World in Action* and Chatto and Windus, Mullin has destroyed the case against the six men which seemed so powerful in 1974 and 1975.

What has happened to the Greiss tests for explosives on three of the men which was so important to the prosecution case at Lancaster? Dr Skuse told the court that a positive Greiss test had only one meaning: contact with nitroglycerine. Since the trial, Mr David Baldock, former head of the Home Office forensic laboratories at Nottingham, carried out exactly the same test on a series of quite different substances – on nitrocellulose lacquer, for instance, on nitrocellulose chips and nitrocellulose aerosol spray. Tests on all three proved positive. Dr Brian Caddy, head of the Forensic Science Unit at Strathclyde University, carried out exactly the same tests and found positive readings on a varnished wooden surface, a cigarette packet, a picture postcard and two packs of old playing-cards. The convicted Irishmen had been playing cards in the train just before their arrest. Mr Caddy gave the cards to a *World in Action* producer, who shuffled them for a few minutes. Then Mr Caddy did the Greiss test on the producer's hands. The test proved positive. If the *World in Action* producer had been at Lancaster Crown Court, a Home Office scientist would have said it was 99 per cent certain he had been handling nitroglycerine.

Every single one of the positive tests which played such a crucial part in the trial has been utterly discredited by subsequent research, and there is now no evidence whatever that any of the men had ever handled an explosive. 'I've never touched a bomb in my life,' one of them, Paddy Hill, has said. There is now nothing to contradict him. There are signs that the authorities have since recognized the weakness of the Greiss tests. Poor Dr Skuse, the Home Office scientist who carried out the tests, was retired early, at the age of fifty, only three weeks after the *World in Action* programme discredited his efforts. No one in authority, certainly not Dr Skuse himself, has explained why. At the Court of Appeal, the Lord Chief Justice – Widgery – made light of the forensic evidence, asserting that 'this was not a point of great importance'. It was, of course, as the trial judge put it, 'absolutely critical' to the prosecution case. If the Greiss tests had not proved positive, the five men would, almost certainly, have been allowed to continue their journey to Belfast. Before the Greiss tests, they were treated courteously by their arresting officers. After the tests the whole atmosphere changed.

What happened to the five men at Morecambe police station on the morning the tests proved positive – the morning after the bombings – and at Queen's Road police station, Birmingham, where they were taken the next day and joined by their mate Hughie Callaghan? That is the most important question in this important book. The men have alleged throughout that they were savagely beaten. Billy Power says he was led into a darkened room where he reckons about half a dozen policemen waited for him. They systematically beat his body – his testicles, especially – until he agreed to sign a confession. His screams were heard by the others, who were then taken in turn for their beatings. Special savagery was reserved for Paddy Hill, who refused, then or ever, to make a statement implicating himself in the bombings. Johnny Walker said he had a lighted cigarette pushed into a blister in his foot; Richard McIlkenny said that he was suffocated under a blanket. The brutality, the men alleged, continued as they were driven, barefoot and terrified, to Birmingham on the day after the bombings. At Queen's Road station, they all said, the violence continued. The men were kept awake all that night, and given next to nothing to eat and drink. All except Power, who had already confessed, were beaten up again and again. More sophisticated methods were brought into play. The men were threatened with guns. A gun was fired at Richard McIlkenny, and he thought he was dead. When he opened his eyes he saw threads of black material coming out of the barrel and floating down to the floor. Again and again the men were told that they would be killed if they did not confess: they had 'gelly on their hands' and no one could care less if they were found dead. McIlkenny, Walker and Callaghan signed confessions though Hill and Hunter did not.

There is a word for all this: torture. The allegations of each of the six men, though they were made quite separately when the men were not in contact with one another, read like a training manual in deep interrogation techniques for use in time of war. The systematic 'breaking down' of a suspect depends, above all, on terror, and fear of pain. A common myth is that 'beating up' is old-fashioned and counter-productive. It is not. Violence and pain are crucial to such techniques. It is only when the violence fails, as it did in the first instance with four of the five men at Morecambe, that more 'subtle' methods, such as shooting with wax bullets, taking suspects to open windows and starting to throw them out, threats to the suspects' families, enforced sleeplessness and so on are introduced. When Gerry Hunter admitted that he did not like dogs, he said, a snarling Alsatian was brought into the room and told to 'get him, get him'. They let it come within six inches of Hunter, and then took it away. This was the torture immortalized in George Orwell's *1984*, after Winston Smith admitted he didn't like rats. Indeed, there is nothing in the allegations which could not have fitted neatly into the two great British novels about torture in a totalitarian state – Orwell's *1984* and Koestler's *Darkness at Noon*, both of which have been used ever since they were written as justifications for the 'Western way of life'.

Did all this happen? The police vigorously denied that there was any violence at all, either at Morecambe, or on the journey to Birmingham or at Queen's Road. Their denials were at once accepted by judge and jury at the Lancaster trial. Since then, not one policeman has told a different story, though Chris Mullin and Charles Tremayne of *World in Action* appear to have tracked down every policeman who was involved, even those who have since retired. It would indeed be comforting if we could dismiss the allegations of violence as the fantasies of desperate men who had committed foul murders, confessed to them, and had somehow to explain their confessions in court.

What has happened since the trial, however, suggests that this isn't possible. There can now be no doubt that all six men were savagely beaten in the week after their arrest. The evidence of their bodies proved that incontestably. The West Midlands Police have an explanation for it. They say that the men were beaten up at Winson Green prison on their arrival there. Accordingly, in 1976, fourteen prison officers from Winson Green were charged with assaulting the Irish prisoners. They did not give evidence at their trial. Their defence relied on attacking the prosecution witnesses, who were, in the main, the six convicted men. The jury found all the officers not guilty. The result is that although everyone agrees the men were beaten up, no one has yet been punished.

In the course of the case, the accused prison officers were persuaded to make secret statements to their solicitors about what happened in the prison. Chris Mullin has had access to them, and the result is the two most chilling chapters in his book. The statements describe the most awful assaults on the men in the prison corridors and bathrooms. On occasion the accounts read like records from the torture chambers of the secret police in Russia or in Chile. But the statements also allege that the men were beaten before they got to Winson Green. Prison Officer Brian Sharpe declared, for instance: 'I saw bruises on many parts of Walker's body. His torso was more or less covered. They were all colours: black, blue, yellow, purple, and most of them looked oldish.' There was only one credible source for such injuries: the interrogating police officers.

There is other recent evidence that some of the men's stories might not be as far-fetched as had been assumed at the trial. There is, for instance, a firing range at Queen's Road police station where guns are used with wax bullets: bullets which leave precisely the residue which Richard McIlkenny describes. He could not possibly ever have seen a wax bullet fired elsewhere. This evidence enabled the six men to get legal aid to sue the West Midlands Police for assaulting them at Morecambe and at Queen's Road. The police applied for the action to be struck out. Mr Justice Cantley turned them down. The police appealed, and the Court of Appeal obligingly struck the action out. The judgment of Lord Denning in that hearing needs to be read carefully by anyone who still believes that the judiciary is 'independent'. He spoke as follows:

> If the six men win, it will mean that the police were guilty of perjury, that they were guilty of violence and threats, that the confessions were involuntary and were improperly admitted in evidence and that the convictions were erroneous. That would mean the Home Secretary would either have to recommend they be pardoned or he would have to remit the case to the Court of Appeal. This is such an appalling vista that every sensible person in the land would say: 'It cannot be right that these actions should go any further.'

If the six men won, in other words, it would be clear that the fantasy world of *1984* and *Darkness at Noon* had emerged in the real world, at Morecambe and at Queen's Road police stations. In a free society, such a possibility could best be avoided by not allowing the legal action to proceed . . .

We should not have to wait until Chris Mullin becomes MP for Sunderland South before a campaign is launched to discover the truth, and if the truth is half as bad as he suggests, to punish those responsible.

•

PRIMO LEVI
1986

'We must be listened to'

The Italian writer Primo Levi (1919–87) was haunted for the rest of his life by the ten months he spent at Auschwitz. If This Is a Man, published in Italy in 1958, is the most eloquent and moving testimony to the 'German hell on earth' – as the American novelist Philip Roth put it – that was created at Auschwitz. Shortly after he completed The Drowned and Saved *in 1986, Levi committed suicide. He could not forgive the Germans. Nor, however, could he hate them.*

The question addressed in his conclusion was whether younger generations would remember the lessons Levi's generation had learned from the Holocaust – or whether they would be 'extraneous'. It could happen again. Would-be tyrants are always waiting in the wings.

For us to speak with the young becomes ever more difficult. We see it as a duty, and at the same time as a risk: the risk of appearing anachronistic, of not being listened to. We must be listened to: above and beyond our personal experiences, we have collectively been the witnesses of a fundamental, unexpected event, fundamental precisely because unexpected, not foreseen by anyone. It took place in the teeth of all forecasts; it happened in Europe. Incredibly, it happened that an entire civilized people, just issued from the fervid cultural flowering of Weimar, followed a buffoon whose figure today inspires laughter, and yet Adolf Hitler was obeyed and his praises were sung right up to the catastrophe. It happened, therefore it can happen again: this is the core of what we have to say.

It can happen, and it can happen everywhere. I do not intend to nor can I say that it will happen; it is not very probable that all the factors that unleashed the Nazi madness will again occur simultaneously but precursory signs loom before us. Violence, 'useful' or 'useless', is there before our eyes: it snakes either through sporadic and private episodes, or government lawlessness, both in what we call the first and the second worlds, that is to say, the parliamentary democracies and countries in the Communist area. In the Third World it is endemic or epidemic. It only awaits its new buffoon (there is no dearth of candidates) to organize it, legalize it, declare it necessary and mandatory and so contaminate the world. Few countries can be considered immune to a future tide of violence generated by intolerance, lust for power, economic difficulties, religious or political fanaticism, and racialist attritions. It is therefore necessary to sharpen our senses, distrust the prophets, the enchanters, those who speak and write 'beautiful words' unsupported by intelligent reasons.

It has obscenely been said that there is a need for conflict: that mankind cannot do without it. It has also been said that local conflicts, violences in the streets, factories and stadiums, are equivalent of generalized war and preserve us from it, as *le petit mal*, the epileptic equivalent, preserves from *le grand mal*. It has been observed that never before in Europe did forty years go by without a war: such a long European peace is supposedly an historical anomaly.

These are captious and suspect arguments. Satan is not necessary: there is no need for wars and violences, under any circumstances. There do not exist problems that cannot be solved around a table, provided there is good will and reciprocal trust: or even reciprocal fear, as the present interminable stalled situation seems to demonstrate, a situation in which the greatest powers confront each other with cordial or threatening faces, but have no restraint when it comes to unleashing (or allow the unleashing) of bloody wars among those 'protected' by them, supplying sophisticated weapons, spies, mercenaries and military advisers instead of arbiters of peace.

Nor is the theory of preventive violence acceptable: from violence only violence is born, following a pendular action that becomes more frenzied as time goes by rather than dying down. In actuality, many signs lead us to think of a genealogy of today's violence that branches out precisely from the violence that was dominant in Hitler's Germany. Certainly it was not absent before, in the remote and recent past: nevertheless, even in the midst of the insensate slaughter of the First World War there survived the traits of a reciprocal respect between the antagonists, a vestige of humanity towards prisoners and unarmed citizens, a tendential respect for treaties, a believer might say 'a certain fear of God'. The adversary was neither a demon nor a worm. After the Nazi *Gott mit uns*, everything changed. Goering's terrorist bombings were answered by the 'carpet' bombings of the Allies. The destruction of a people and a civilization was proved to be possible, and desirable both in itself and as an instrument of rule. The massive exploitation of slave labour was learned by Hitler in the school of Stalin, but in the Soviet Union it was brought back again, multiplied at the end of the war. The exodus of brains from Germany and Italy, together with the fear of being surpassed by Nazi scientists, gave birth to the nuclear bombs. Desperate, the Jewish survivors, in flight from Europe after the great shipwreck, have created in the bosom of the Arab world an island of Western civilization, a portentous palingenesis of Judaism, and the pretext for renewed hatred. After the defeat, the silent Nazi diaspora has taught the art of persecution and torture to the military and the political men of a dozen countries, on the shores of the Mediterranean, the Atlantic and Pacific. Many new tyrants have kept in their drawer Adolf Hitler's *Mein Kampf*: with a few changes perhaps, and the substitution of a few names, it can still come in handy.

•

HELEN STEEL/DAVE MORRIS
1987

'McDonald's'

When Helen Steel and Dave Morris helped distribute a London Greenpeace leaflet about the hamburger chain McDonald's, they became involved in the longest libel trial in British history. It lasted 313 days.

For the best part of two years (1995 and 1996), the two defendants, who represented themselves, fought McDonald's over allegations that the company was responsible for the deforestation of Central and South America, that it was cruel in the rearing and slaughter of animals, that it was lying over its claim to use recycled paper and that there was a real risk of customers getting heart disease and cancer of the breast or bowel from hamburgers. The court also had to decide if McDonald's were misleading the public through their advertising campaigns, exploiting children, paid their staff badly and whether the company was generally 'wrecking the planet'. The judge decided that the company was not 'wrecking the planet', that McDonald's could not be blamed for the destruction of any rainforest, that they were not lying over their claim to use recycled paper and that it was not right to say that 'eating McDonald's' food brought a very real risk of heart disease, cancer, etc'. But while McDonald's won on most of the allegations levelled against them, they were found to have misled the public in some of their advertising, they did exploit children's love of fast food, they did not pay their staff well and they were cruel in the way that they treated some of their animals. The defendants were ordered to pay McDonald's damages of £60,000 – they have since appealed the judge's ruling.

This is part of the leaflet that the London Greenpeace campaigners put out after McDonald's pyrrhic victory.

McDonald's spend over $1.8 billion every year worldwide on advertising and promotions, trying to cultivate an image of being a 'caring' and 'green' company that is also a fun place to eat. Children are lured in (dragging their parents behind them) with the promise of toys and other gimmicks. But behind the smiling face of Ronald McDonald lies the reality – McDonald's only interest is *money*, making profits from whoever and whatever they can, just like all multinational companies. McDonald's Annual Reports talk of 'global domination' – they aim to open more and more stores across the globe – but their continual worldwide expansion means more uniformity, less choice and the undermining of local communities.

PROMOTING UNHEALTHY FOOD   McDonald's promote their food as 'nutritious', but the reality is that it is junk food – high in fat, sugar and salt, and low in fibre and vitamins. A diet of this type is linked with a greater risk of heart disease, cancer, diabetes and other diseases. Their food also contains many chemical additives, some of which may cause ill-health, and hyperactivity in children. Don't forget too that meat is the cause of the majority of food poisoning incidents. In 1991 McDonald's were responsible for an outbreak of food poisoning in the UK, in which people suffered serious kidney failure. With modern intensive farming methods, other diseases – linked to chemical residues or unnatural practices – have become a danger to people too (such as BSE).

EXPLOITING WORKERS   Workers in the fast-food industry are paid low wages. McDonald's do not pay overtime rates even when employees work very long hours. Pressure to keep profits high and wage costs low results in understaffing, so staff have to work harder and faster. As a consequence, accidents (particularly burns) are common. The majority of employees are people who have few job options and so are forced to accept this exploitation, and they're compelled to 'smile' too! Not surprisingly staff turnover at McDonald's is high, making it virtually impossible to unionize and fight for a better deal, which suits McDonald's who have always been opposed to unions.

ROBBING THE POOR   Vast areas of land in poor countries are used for cash crops or for cattle ranching, or to grow grain to feed animals to be eaten in the West. This is at the expense of local food needs. McDonald's continually promote meat products, encouraging people to eat meat more often, which wastes more and more food resources. Seven million tons of grain fed to livestock produces only 1 million tons of meat and by-products. On a plant-based diet and with land shared fairly, almost every region could be self-sufficient in food.

DAMAGING THE ENVIRONMENT   Forests throughout the world – vital for all life – are being destroyed at an appalling rate by multinational companies. McDonald's have at last been forced to admit to using beef reared on ex-rainforest land, preventing its regeneration. Also, the use of farmland by multinationals and their suppliers forces local people to move on to other areas and cut down further trees.

McDonald's are the world's largest user of beef. Methane emitted by cattle reared for the beef industry is a major contributor to the 'global warming' crisis. Modern intensive agriculture is based on the heavy use of chemicals which are damaging to the environment.

Every year McDonald's use thousands of tons of unnecessary packaging, most of which ends up littering our streets or polluting the land buried in landfill sites.

MURDERING ANIMALS   The menus of the burger chains are based on the torture and murder of millions of animals. Most are intensively farmed, with no access to fresh air and sunshine, and no freedom of movement. Their deaths are barbaric – 'humane slaughter' is a myth. We have the choice to eat meat or not, but the billions of animals massacred for food each year have no choice at all.

●

EDWARD NORMAN
1988

'Gay Christians'

The Lesbian and Gay Christian Movement were prosecuted in the ecclesiastical courts by the Archdeacon of London for taking possession of offices at St Botolph's Church in the City of London. 'I am all in favour of them existing,' he said, 'but it is different when the organization gains credence from being on church property.'

The Archdeacon's statement involved a familiar distinction between personal homosexual orientation and homosexual practice, said Edward Norman, Dean of Peterhouse at Cambridge University. 'Goings-on once too terrible to be contemplated but which in these more spacious days are known in some detail even to widows and orphans.'

The general synod of the Church of England had stated that homosexuality 'fell short' of the Christian ideal, but had not declared it evil or sinful. Dr Norman wrote this protest at the Church's position for The Times.

Actual experience of life in liberal society suggests that the moral and spiritual accompaniments of human love are as capable of germinating and flowering in relationships once called deviant as they are in sexual associations which, for all their apparent orthodoxy and normality, in reality disclose an enormous range of experiences – some of which are certainly rather far from what the bishops, calling upon their own doubtless well-stocked reminiscences, can suppose to be 'the Christian ideal'.

The truth, surely, is that just as Christianity has abandoned the dietary laws which once occupied a prominent position in religion, so now it can shed its adhesion to exclusive views of human sexuality. Those views took their origin in distant societies where the frail existence of semi-nomadic peoples required that sexual energy should never be expended on anything that did not potentially add to their numbers. They are scarcely needed when an over-crowded planet, and a desiccated culture, yearn for human affection. Christianity is committed to human culture and advances in a dynamic relationship with it.

For all that, there may be all kinds of sexual expressions which Christianity would wish to warn its adherents against: bestiality, sexual consort with minors and so forth. And it needs to be freely admitted that the lines of definition are very difficult to draw.

It is surely right, however, to be agnostic in relation to homosexual practice – just as it should be in relation to the huge variations of practice grouped together in conventional understandings of conventional sexuality. Sin has a way of leaking into all human enterprises, and even God's gifts of love and affection are not left unsullied by our use of them. It is, indeed, precisely because that is the case that inclusive condemnations of homosexual practice are inappropriate.

But the notion, as enunciated by the bishops, that individuals are put together by God, who fills them with sexual urges and then sends them indelibly celibate into a world in which their contemporaries – because of a shade of difference in their body chemistry or their early environment – achieve a kind of fulfilment which they are not allowed to, can hardly be compatible with Christianity.

If the Church is not to have a place where practising gay Christians can meet and exchange information, and where, in an antipathetic culture, they can find mutual understanding, then the Church will itself be the loser. Gay Christians have a faith which will not evaporate away because they are spurned by others. It will, on the contrary, find its expression in separatist organizations. An Anglican equivalent of the row in the Labour Party about black sections is in prospect.

Is not that an unnecessary additional burden to have to carry around? However distasteful homosexuality is, the fact is that the lives of very many homosexual Christians down the centuries have disclosed spiritual gifts in astonishing abundance.

•

ROSALIND MILES
1988

'All About Eve'

The English feminist Rosalind Miles has devoted much of her life to writing women back into the history books, particularly in her pioneering The Women's History of the World. *Women's exclusion from the annals of history represents 'a million stifled voices', she argues. Women are the greatest race of underdogs the world has ever known. In this extract her main target is Hollywood.*

The recent experience of many women in their own countries suggests that freedom may be coming – but 'not here, not yet, and not for us', in the Iranian women's phrase. There the enforced Westernization of the late Shah gave way to the fundamentalist fanaticism of the Ayatollah Khomeini without a momentary interruption in the tyranny of men over women. A Western observer summed up the contradictions inflicted on Iranian women from both sides of the religious and political spectrum:

> In 1978–9, educated women donned the *chador* as a protest against the Shah, while Ayatollah Khomeini denounced the Shah's attitude to women . . . 'The Shah declared that women should only be objects of sexual attraction. It is this concept which leads women to prostitution and reduces them to the status of sexual objects.'
>
> Today, women who expose too much hair can be sent to camps for 'corrective moral re-education'. The veil is seen as the symbol of independence from the Western values that the Shah used merely to consolidate his family's power. Failure to observe correct wearing of 'hejab' (correct religious dress) is counter-revolutionary.

This attack on the 'romanticization of Islam', though made by a Western male, is abundantly supported by the testimony of Iranian women themselves. Writer Mashid Amir Shahi has publicly attacked Khomeini's decree that women are 'unequal, and biologically, naturally and intellectually inferior to men'. What this has meant in practice was illustrated by an anonymous speaker at a London conference:

> Wedding day, well, is compulsory. Political women are tortured and raped before execution. Especially young women. They rape nine-year-

old women in the prison because it is against God if they execute a
virgin woman. Women are attacked in various horrific ways, such as
acid being thrown in their faces, their hair being burnt if it is not
covered. It means that just to be a woman in Iran is a political crime.

Plus ça change. . . In the course of history, to be a woman had been a sin against
nature and a crime against God. Now it has become an ideological deviance
into the bargain. Under this system, the woman who dared to question the
ideology by which she was judged would find herself among the 'daughters of
the Devil' whom the men of God, or the God of men, had determined to
destroy. For the woman who argued, questioned, challenged, was not a woman.
Woman was designed by nature to please and complement man, to love and
serve her lord and master. After all, what else are women for?

In this baseline demand lurks the eternal myth of womanhood, and the
eternal unsatisfied fantasy of the self-deluded male. To them, the answer was
simple – women were for men, and should be grateful. Nowhere has this
egregious exaction been more visibly expressed, nor more extensively fostered,
than in the world's dream factory of the twentieth century, the Hollywood
film industry. Hollywood's idiosyncratic vice and overriding obsession, the
sexualizing of the female, in fact is wholly characteristic of all the other mass
media, and indeed the secret of their commercial success. But although
advertising has now taken over as the prime site of sexual stereotyping in the
Western industrialized societies, Hollywood led the way. Whatever ideas the
inhabitants of the postwar world nurse about male and female, love and
work, they will have derived a high proportion of them from the dream-world
of Hollywood fiction.

And what did Hollywood have to tell a breathless world through the
undying magic of the silver screen? What was the message of the moguls
who knew All About Eve, how women became Notorious, feared a Psycho
and longed for King Kong and a grapefruit in the face? What else but that
there were bad girls and good girls, girls you fucked and girls you married,
little women and good wives, and the birth of a nation was man's work (tell
the women to boil some water, lots of it). Study on this, sister, Gentlemen
Prefer Blondes. Without knowing how, for it was always very respectful
towards religion (Jesus of Nazareth, the Man Born To Be Box-Office),
Hollywood became the Church of America, every film the new covenant,
every picture told a story and the story was the greatest, oldest, cruellest,
dumbest story ever told, the man born to be man.

For boys will be boys, and nowhere more so than in the all-American
playground of the Hollywood movie. As film after film rolled off the cameras

under the beady scrutiny of the first generation movie-moguls, patriarchs of the purest water to the last man, the father gods must have been hugging themselves with glee. For who needed physical restraints, savage laws, exclusion from education, from work and from society to keep women in their second-rate 'sphere', when you could show them a film that did the same job, *and* sent them away happy into the bargain?

The extent to which the mass media of the twentieth century have served to replace the older instruments of dominance and restraint in the perennial patriarchal work of keeping women subordinate has yet to be fully acknowledged. But in its groping, voyeuristic response to the female, its tireless recycling of the same old female archetypes of mother, maiden, whore, its unreeling of ideal scenarios contrasted with the threatening accounts of the 'girls who went wrong', Hollywood has to take its proud place alongside the 'morals police' of the Ayatollah Khomeini for its valuable work in keeping women in line and training them to be everything a regular guy could ever hope for as his wife and the mother of his children.

As these pseudo-modern industries, the mass media, lead us firmly by the genitals backwards into the future, we can recognize the new arena in which the next stage for the freedom and equality of women will be fought out. Over the millennia of civilization, the source and site of women's inferiority has been located in nature, biology, religion, physiology, brain size and the female psyche. Women have fought back, for the right to read, to own money, to vote. One by one those oppressions have gone down in some parts of the world, thereby undermining the 'natural' and inevitable status of those that remain. But underlying patterns change slowly. This is in no way to belittle the fruits of the struggle to date. It is simply to insist that in the deeper struggle which feminists worldwide now realize that they face, changing the world takes longer.

For there is much to do, amounting in fact to a remaking of modern society. *All democratic experiments, all revolutions, all demands for equality have so far, in every instance, stopped short of sexual equality.* Every society has in its prestige structures a series of subtle, interacting codes of dominance which always, everywhere, finally rank men higher than women. Nowhere has any society successfully dispensed with the age-old sex-role division of labour and the rewards in goods and power that accompany it. Nowhere do women enjoy the rights, privileges, possibilities and leisure time that men do. Everywhere men still mediate between women and power, women and the state, women and freedom, women and themselves.

•

CHARTER 88
1988

'Our endangered freedom'

When the formidable Tory minister Michael Heseltine stormed out from a Cabinet meeting in 1986 and resigned after a clash with Margaret Thatcher, he accused the prime minister of having a 'dictatorial style'. As other ministers also made coded criticisms of dictatorial tendencies, there was a revival of the civil liberties movement, especially when the government used the Official Secrets Act against civil servants, abolished free trade unionism at GCHQ security establishment and tried to suppress the memoirs of a retired member of MI5.

The most enduring expression of the rising public disquiet was Charter 88, inspired by the radical political thinker Anthony Barnett, and published on the 300th anniversary of the 'Glorious Revolution'.

We have been brought up in Britain to believe that we are free: that our Parliament is the mother of democracy; that our liberty is the envy of the world; that our system of justice is always fair; that the guardians of our safety, the police and security services, are subject to democratic, legal control; that our civil service is impartial; that our cities and communities maintain a proud identity; that our press is brave and honest.

Today such beliefs are increasingly implausible. The gap between reality and the received ideas of Britain's 'unwritten constitution' has widened to a degree that many find hard to endure. Yet this year we are invited to celebrate the third centenary of the 'Glorious Revolution' of 1688, which established what was to become the United Kingdom's sovereign formula. In the name of freedom, our political, human and social rights are being curtailed while the powers of the executive have increased, are increasing and ought to be diminished.

A process is underway which endangers many of the freedoms we have had. Only in part deliberate, it began before 1979 and is now gathering momentum. Scotland is governed like a province from Whitehall. More generally, the government has eroded a number of important civil freedoms: for example, the universal rights to habeas corpus, to peaceful assembly, to freedom of information, to freedom of expression, to membership of a trade union, to local government, to freedom of movement, even to the birthright itself. By taking these rights from some, the government puts them at risk for all.

A traditional British belief in the benign nature of the country's institutions encourages an unsystematic perception of these grave matters; each becomes an 'issue' considered in isolation from the rest. Being unwritten the constitution also encourages a piecemeal approach to politics; an approach that gives little protection against a determined, authoritarian state. For the events of 1688 only shifted the absolute power of the monarch into the hands of the parliamentary oligarchy.

The current administration is not an un-English interruption in the country's way of life. But while the government calls upon aspirations for liberty, it also exploits the dark side of a constitutional settlement which was always deficient in democracy.

The 1688 settlement had a positive side. In its time the Glorious Revolution was a historic victory over Royal tyranny. Britain was spared the rigours of dictatorship. A working compromise between many different interests was made possible at home, even if, from Ireland to India, quite different standards were imposed by Empire abroad. No criticism of contemporary developments in Britain should deny the significance of past democratic achievements, most dramatically illuminated in May 1940 when Britain defied the fascist domination of Europe.

But the eventual victory that liberated Western Europe preserved the paternalist attitudes and institutions of the United Kingdom. These incorporated the popular desire for work and welfare into a postwar national consensus. Now this had broken down. So, too, have its conventions of compromise and tolerance: essential components of a free society. Instead, the inbuilt powers of the 1688 settlement have enabled the government to discipline British society to its ends: to impose its values on the civil service; to menace the independence of broadcasting; to threaten academic freedom in the universities and schools; to tolerate abuses committed in the name of national security. The break with the immediate past shows how vulnerable Britain has always been to elective dictatorship. The consequence is that today the British have fewer legal rights and less democracy than many other West Europeans.

The intensification of authoritarian rule in the United Kingdom has only recently begun. The time to reverse the process is now, but it cannot be reversed by an appeal to the past. Three hundred years of unwritten rule from above are enough. Britain needs a democratic programme that will end unfettered control by the executive of the day. It needs to reform a Parliament in which domination of the lower house can be decided by fewer than 40 per cent of the population; a Parliament in which a majority of the upper house is still determined by inheritance.

We have had less freedom than we believed. That which we have enjoyed has been too dependent on the benevolence of our rulers. Our freedoms have remained their possession, rationed out to us as subjects rather than being our own inalienable possession as citizens. To make real the freedoms we once took for granted means for the first time to take them for ourselves.

The time has come to demand political, civil and human rights in the United Kingdom. The first step is to establish them in constitutional form, so that they are no longer subject to the arbitrary diktat of Westminster and Whitehall.

We call, therefore, for a new constitutional settlement which would:

Enshrine, by means of a Bill of Rights, such civil liberties as the right to peaceful assembly, to freedom of association, to freedom from discrimination, to freedom from detention without trial, to trial by jury, to privacy and to freedom of expression.

Subject executive powers and prerogatives, by whomsoever exercised, to the rule of law.

Establish freedom of information and open government.

Create a fair electoral system of proportional representation.

Reform the upper house to establish a democratic, non-hereditary second chamber.

Place the executive under the power of a democratically renewed Parliament and all agencies of the state under the rule of law.

Ensure the independence of a reformed judiciary.

Provide legal remedies for all abuses of power by the state and the officials of central and local government.

Guarantee an equitable distribution of power between local, regional and national government.

Draw up a written constitution, anchored in the idea of universal citizenship, that incorporates these reforms.

Our central concern is the law. No country can be considered free in which the government is above the law. No democracy can be considered safe whose freedoms are not encoded in a basic constitution.

We, the undersigned, have called this document Charter 88. First, to mark our rejection of the complacency with which the tercentenary of the

Revolution of 1688 has been celebrated. Second, to reassert a tradition of demands for constitutional rights in Britain, which stretches from the barons who forced the Magna Carta on King John, to the working men who drew up the People's Charter in 1838, to the women at the beginning of this century who demanded universal suffrage. Third, to salute the courage of those in Eastern Europe who still fight for their fundamental freedoms.

Like the Czech and Slovak signatories of Charter 77, we are an informal, open community of people of different opinions, faiths and professions, united by the will to strive, individually and collectively, for the respect of civil and human rights in our own country and throughout the world. Charter 77 welcomed the ratification by Czechoslovakia of the UN International Covenant on Political and Civil Rights, but noted that it 'serves as a reminder of the extent to which basic human rights in our country exist, regrettably, on paper only'.

Conditions here are so much better than in Eastern Europe as to bear no comparison. But our rights in the United Kingdom remain unformulated, conditional upon the goodwill of the government and the compassion of bureaucrats. To create a democratic constitution at the end of the twentieth century, however, may extend the concept of liberty, especially with respect to the rights of women and the place of minorities. It will not be a simple matter: part of British sovereignty is shared with Europe; and the extension of social rights in a modern economy is a matter of debate everywhere. We cannot foretell the choices a free people may make. We are united in one opinion only, that British society stands in need of a constitution which protects individual rights and of the institutions of a modern and pluralist democracy.

The inscription of laws does not guarantee their realization. Only people themselves can ensure freedom, democracy and equality before the law. None the less, such ends can be far better demanded, and more effectively obtained and guarded, once they *belong to everyone by inalienable right.*

•

VIKTOR ORBAN
1989

'End the Communist dictatorship'

There was a crowd of about 200,000 in Heroes' Square in Budapest on 16 June 1989, for the funeral, thirty-one years after his death, of Imre Nagy, the Hungarian leader of 1956. Ceremonial flames burned beside the six coffins – five for Nagy and his closest associates, the sixth a symbolic coffin of the Unknown Insurgent. The academic and journalist Timothy Garton Ash, in his book We the People, *described the great neo-classical columns wrapped in black cloth, the huge red, green and white national flags each with a hole in the middle – a reminder of how the insurgents of 1956 cut out the hammer and sickle – the first speeches.*

When the last speaker, Viktor Orban, at twenty-six the youngest, took the stand for the militant student group the Young Democrats, the crowd was still subdued. When he finished, there was fierce and prolonged applause. Within six months, Hungary was a free nation. Orban's speeches helped to light the pyre under Communist rule.

Citizens!

In the forty years since the beginning of the Communist dictatorship and the Soviet occupation, Hungary has only once had the chance, only once had the strength and the courage, to attain her ambitions of 1848: national independence and political liberty. Our aims haven't changed; we will not renounce any of the goals of 1848, as we cannot renounce 1956, either.

The young Hungarians now struggling for democracy bow their heads before the Communist Imre Nagy and his companions for two reasons.

We appreciate that these statesmen identified themselves with the wishes of the Hungarian nation, that they broke with the sacred tenets of Communism – that is, with blind obedience to the Russian Empire and with the dictatorship of a single party.

In 1956, the Hungarian Socialist Workers' Party (MSZMP) seized our future. Thus, there in the sixth coffin, alongside the massacred youth, lay our prospects for years to come.

Friends! We young people fail to understand many things that are obvious to the older generations. We are puzzled that those who were so eager to slander the Revolution and Imre Nagy have suddenly become the greatest supporters of the former prime minister's policies. Nor do we understand why the party leaders who saw to it that we were taught from books that falsified the Revolution are now rushing to touch the coffins as if they were good-luck charms. We need not be grateful for their permission to bury our martyrs after thirty-one years; nor do we have to thank them for allowing our political organizations to function. Hungary's leaders are not to be praised because they have refrained from using weapons against those striving for democracy and free elections, because they have not adopted, as well they could, the methods of Li Peng, Pol Pot, Jaruzelski and Rákosi.

Citizens! Thirty-three years after the Hungarian Revolution was crushed and thirty-one years after the execution of the last legitimate prime minister, we may now have a chance to achieve peacefully the goals that the revolutionaries briefly attained through bloody combat. If we trust our souls and our strength, we can put an end to the Communist dictatorship; if we are determined enough, we can force the party to submit to free elections; and if we do not lose sight of the ideals of 1956, then we will be able to elect a government that will immediately begin negotiations on the swift withdrawal of the Russian troops. We can fulfill the will of the Revolution if – and only if – we are brave enough. We cannot trust the party-state to change of its own accord. Remember: on 6 October 1956, on the very day Lászlo Rajk was reburied, the party's daily declared in bold letters: 'Never Again!' Three weeks later, the Communist Party ordered its security forces to shoot and kill defenceless people. Before two years had passed, the MSZMP had hundreds of innocent people, even party members, sentenced to death on trumped-up charges. We will never accept the empty promises of Communist leaders; our goal is to prevent the ruling party from ever using force against us again. This is the only way to avoid new coffins – new burials like today's. Imre Nagy, Miklós Gimes, Géza Losonczy, Pál Maléter, and József Szilágyi gave their lives for Hungarian independence and liberty. These values are still cherished by Hungary's youth: we bow to your memory. *Requiescant in pacem!*

•

ROBERT HARRIS
1989

'Mad'

By 1989 Margaret Thatcher had won three elections and had been prime minister for ten years, but her style of leadership created increasing tensions between her and her Cabinet ministers, particularly Nigel Lawson, the Chancellor, and Sir Geoffrey Howe, whom she had removed as Foreign Secretary and appointed deputy prime minister. John Major had taken his place.

In this column for the editorial page of the Sunday Times, *the journalist and political commentator Robert Harris (who has since written the two bestselling novels* Fatherland *and* Enigma*) declared that the prime minister was fussy, bossy, deluded and 'mad' – a protest at the Thatcher style which provoked his biggest postbag. A year later, Howe's resignation precipitated a challenge to Margaret Thatcher's leadership and she resigned.*

It is a sobering thought to realize that one is living in a country in which the prime minister is mad. 'Mad', I appreciate, is a vulgar adjective, properly frowned upon by the medical profession, but in the sense that it means unbalanced judgement, delusions of grandeur, an inability to distinguish between reality and unreality, paranoia and general mental instability, I submit that 'mad' is not an unfair description of the present occupant of 10 Downing Street.

Margaret Thatcher has always seemed (how shall we put it?) a slightly manic and obsessive person. Previously, these traits could be dismissed as the usual characteristics of an ambitious politician. Perhaps, in her case, they were present to an unusual degree. But then, Britain, as her supporters used to argue, was in need of a revolution, and revolutionaries are not always congenial, or even 'normal', characters.

But, over the past six months, things seem to have been getting a little out of hand. Some of the evidence, admittedly, has been trivial, such as the revelation that she consults a lady in Shepherd's Bush who passes a few volts through her bath water each morning. Similarly, her proclamation that 'we have become a grandmother' strengthened the impression that she comports herself like a monarch.

But that was followed by the announcement that palace gates were to be installed at the end of Downing Street. Work on this particular monument to her *folie de grandeur* has begun: shaken ministers were obliged to pass the excavations during last Thursday night's excitements.

On a more serious level, it has become clear lately that Mrs Thatcher sees herself not as the premier of a middle-ranking European power, but as the inspiration for some millennial victory of world capitalism.

She has dismissed the French and Russian revolutions as no great shakes and substituted her own election as a turning-point in planetary history. She told her party conference this month: 'In 1979, we knew that we were starting a British revolution; in fact, we were the pioneers of a world revolution.'

Many rulers, in the past, have been aware of the dangers of such epic delusions. Roman emperors used to employ slaves to walk one pace behind them, whispering timely reminders in their ear that they were only human, not gods. In our own age, this vital function used to be performed by Lord Whitelaw. Now he is gone, there is nobody to tell Mrs Thatcher she is mortal.

The result has been a series of disastrous misjudgements. First came the European election campaign, directly run from Number 10, with its baffling posters about 'staying at home and living on a diet of Brussels'. The result was the first national electoral defeat for the Tory Party since 1974.

The reshuffle débâcle was next. Even the most elementary understanding of human nature should have warned Mrs Thatcher that, before offering Sir Geoffrey Howe the home secretaryship, she should first have told him what was coming and alerted Douglas Hurd to her plan. As it was, an opportunity to strengthen and freshen her government was transformed into a series of elephantine blunders: an unknown and inexperienced court favourite rocketed to prominence; two loyal colleagues kicked in the teeth; a squalid public dispute over houses and titles. The government fell ten points behind Labour in the polls.

After the traumas of July, what should any sane ruler have done? The answer is easy. She should have stood back to allow her Foreign Secretary to establish his position, and mollified her disgruntled senior ministers by leaving them alone to get on with their jobs. This was, after all, as we were endlessly told at the party conference, 'the right team for Britain's future'.

Mrs Thatcher did precisely the opposite. She publicly undermined John Major at the Commonwealth conference by issuing a statement repudiating the agreement he had just reached. And, on her return, rather than dismissing (as she should have done) her loose-tongued economic adviser, she forced, instead, the resignation of her Chancellor of the Exchequer.

This is a catalogue of folly almost unmatched in recent political history, the work of someone who has long since parted company with reality. Perhaps, after more than a decade in office, she is simply too exhausted to think properly. At question time on Thursday, shortly before the Chancellor resigned, she was asked her opinion of the engineering union's claim for a thirty-five-hour week. She replied, scornfully, that she worked thirty-five hours in two days. If that is true, it is no wonder that her judgement has gone awry.

All the signs of crankiness are there. She has no friends, apart from a few cronies in her private office. There are no senior advisers to whom she turns. Instead, she has set herself up as a one-woman opposition within the government, hectoring, arguing and interfering in the smallest details of ministers' work. Presumably, she imagines this is 'strong' leadership. It is not. It is a recipe for weak government.

Thanks to her fussy, bossy, argumentative style of doing business, Britain is now the odd one out in virtually every international organization to which we belong: Nato, the European Community and the Commonwealth. As long as she is there, the conflict and uncertainty that have come to characterize this government will go on. She may reform for a time, as she did after Westland in 1986, but sooner or later she will be back to her old tricks.

The last senior Tory who went mad in office, as far as I know, was Lord Castlereagh who, as Foreign Secretary, stabbed himself to death with a penknife. That was in 1822 and is probably not much of a precedent for the present situation. The Conservative Party is thus moving into uncharted waters.

There is one guide we can follow: the law of reverse probability. We know that most of Mrs Thatcher's statements in the past few weeks meant the exact opposite of what they said. 'There is no disagreement on economic policy' actually meant 'I hate Nigel Lawson's guts'. 'I back the Chancellor totally' meant 'I really listen to Sir Alan Walters'. 'I have always had every confidence in the Chancellor' should have been 'he is writing his letter of resignation'.

So when Conservative MPs proclaim that 'there is no question of a change in the leadership', I suspect that what they really mean is 'we'll give her another year'. If, at the end of that time, the government is still lurching from crisis to crisis, my bet is that she will be out, leaving her successor eighteen months to establish himself before the next election. The big question will be: who tells her to go? Sir Geoffrey? The men from the 1922 Committee? Or the men in white coats?

•

LIU XIAOBO, ZHOU DUO, HOU DEJIAN, GAO XIN
1989

'Hunger strike'

The massacre in Beijing's Tiananmen Square in June 1989, when 2,000 protesters for democracy were killed by the tanks of the People's Army, was seen on television in the West. Its brutality shocked the world. The four student leaders of the demonstration issued this declaration shortly before the massacre.

We are on hunger strike. We protest, we appeal, we repent. We are not in search of death; we are looking for real life. In the face of irrational and violent pressure from the Li Peng government, the Chinese intellectuals must cure their soft-boned disease of being vocal but of never being active for thousands of years. We must act to protest against martial law, to call for the birth of a new political culture, to make up for our past mistakes of being soft and weak for so long.

We all share responsibility for the Chinese nation being left behind many others.

During this movement the government and the students have both made mistakes. The mistakes of the government are dominated by the old mode of class struggle, of a way of political thinking which places them in opposition to the students and citizens.

The mistakes of the students are mainly the crudity of the students' own organization. There appeared to be a lot of undemocratic elements in the process of seeking democracy. So we appeal both to the government and to the students; they should calmly question and examine themselves. It is our view that as a whole the mistakes of this movement are mainly with the government. Marches, hunger strikes and actions of that kind are democratic methods. They are entirely legitimate and reasonable and do in no way constitute unrest.

But the government has ignored the basic rights endowed to every citizen by the constitution and has declared this movement to be a form of unrest. This stems from their thinking in terms of dictatorial politics and has led to a series of mistaken decisions and to confrontation. Therefore the real creator of the unrest is the government's error. The seriousness of its mistakes is no less than of those taken during the Cultural Revolution. It was only due to the self-restraint of students and citizens and due to the strong appeals of society, including the wise people in the Party, the government and the army that massive bloodshed was then avoided. The government must admit its mistakes. A correction now would not be too late.

The government should draw the painful lessons from this massive movement to democracy. It should learn to listen to the voice of the people.

We think the true realization of democratic politics is the democratization of the procedures, the methods and the operation. So we appeal to the Chinese: Get rid of the tradition of pure ideology making, of sloganeering, of objectifying. These are empty democracy. They must start the process of turning a democracy movement centred on the enlightenment of thought into that of an actual operation.

The major errors by the government in decision-making are shown in the phrase they have used to describe the movement: they have called us 'the very, very few'. Through our hunger strike we want to show public opinion in China and abroad that the so-called 'very, very few' are people who are not merely students. Those who actively took part in this nationwide movement to democracy, led by students, are citizens with a sense of political responsibility.

It must be acknowledged that to govern a country democratically is a strange concept for every Chinese citizen. So all citizens of China must learn from the very beginning – and in this way we must include the top leaders of the Party and the state. In the process mistakes by the government and by the people are inevitable. The key lies in acknowledging their mistakes when they occur, and in correcting them when they occur, in learning from mistakes so that they can be turned into a positive asset and, in the process of correcting mistakes, to learn to govern our country democratically.

The rules of the hunger strike:

a) Location: under the monument to the People's Heroes in Tiananmen Square.

b) Duration: 72 hours, from 14.00 2 June to 14.00 5 June.

c) Rules: boiled water only, no food, no nutritious drinks (such as glucose, fat or protein).

•

RICHARD DAVENPORT-HINES
1990

'AIDS is a tragedy'

The first person in Britain to die of AIDS was Terrence Higgins, in 1982. Within a year AIDS was recognized as a medical crisis, as dangerous as cholera in the 1840s or tuberculosis in the early twentieth century, particularly for homosexuals. A national government campaign was launched to promote 'safe sex' and the use of condoms.

In his book, Sex, Death and Punishment, *the writer and critic Richard Davenport-Hines attacked the AIDS scares promoted in the press and argued that the panic they created led to an attack on pleasure for its own sake.*

AIDS is a cruel and silly neologism, as Bruce Chatwin wrote. 'Aid' connotes succour and comfort: yet the word becomes a horror once a hissing sibilant is added to it (rather as the serpentine sibilance of the word 'syphilis' has seemed so apt through the ages). HIV are far preferable initials: AIDS excites panic and despair, emotions which can only facilitate the spread of disease. HIV will kill millions of people, but fear of its contagion is spoiling the lives of millions more. In reality it is infectious but not contagious; but whether transmitted accidentally or deliberately, intimately or indirectly, its micro-organisms are fearful because like the spirochaete of syphilis they seem invincible, invisible and ubiquitous. The virus has been depicted (particularly by commentators who equate hedonism with national weakness) not only as attacking the body of individuals, but as an invasion of society itself. HIV, which cannot be transmitted by casual contact and need not be transmitted by sexual contact, has provoked a contagion panic disproportionate to the risk of contraction. It has excited the destructive terror that festers when our troubles are attributable to infection spread by other people: the rank belief that patients must be punished or eradicated has erupted in consequence.

The first person known to have died as a result of AIDS in Britain was Terrence Higgins, in July 1982, and for perhaps a year after that it was possible to deny that anything significant was occurring, as people tend to do in the first stage of an epidemic. But once the existence of a medical crisis was recognized, as with cholera in the 1840s or tuberculosis in the early twentieth century, groups or individuals were identified as blameworthy, traduced as dirty or contagious, and punished as miscreants. In Britain, as a consequence,

HIV has been perceived less as a virus that must be conquered than as an affliction of the undisciplined. Blame, in all its forms, has only negative results: it spreads confusion and victimizes the weak. Blame helps no one and nothing except the spread of the virus.

Readers can imagine the sheer sadness of AIDS: the exhausting rage against the meaninglessness of the syndrome, its swathe of destruction and the cruelty that it has provoked. 'A tragedy,' wrote Thomas Hardy, 'exhibits a state of things in the life of an individual which unavoidably causes some natural aim or desire of his to end in catastrophe when carried out.' AIDS is a tragedy.

In Britain contagion fears have been politicized in order to attempt to frighten people into accepting a regime in which sexual appetite is regulated, eroticism is repressed, social conformity equated with health and conspicuous people of all sorts are treated as undesirable. All those individuals for whom social controls are not just a necessary evil to keep society intact, but a bulwark against personal disintegration, or a pleasure when exercised aggressively against the weak, have been aroused to a fervent pitch. Chiliasts who relish crises and drastic restrictions have been granted their heart's desire as we career towards the end of another millennium.

There has been an attack on pleasure for its own sake, a vindictive sanctimony about other people's ills has flourished, with a chorus of triumphant censure unknown in this country since the swansong of the pleasure-haters around the time of the First World War. 'The Church should condemn both those who catch this fatal disease and those who transmit it to others,' wrote a Kensington man in 1987: 'Christianity without morality is nothing.' People with AIDS are condemned, and told to go away and die without expending anyone else's time or money. 'I am fed up being continually bombarded with the AIDS problem,' as a correspondent of the *Daily Express* declared in 1988. 'The majority of victims have only themselves to blame because of their sexual activities and needle sharing. I abhor the amount of money being spent on them and feel no sympathy for them whatsoever.'

The context for these ideas, and for this outburst of human unkindness, has been set by journalists. As few people in Britain have experience of AIDS, perceptions have been nurtured by press coverage which offers inflammatory phrases like 'Gay Plague', 'Gay Menace' and 'Gay Killer Bug', even though the transmission of HIV both from male to female and female to male has been demonstrated since 1983.

One explanation for this insistent depiction, against the evidence, of gay men as killers, the only possible cause and source of HIV, may be a displaced desire to kill them. The people whom one accuses of wanting to destroy oneself are the people one wishes to destroy.

Since the stereotyping of the molly began in the eighteenth century, there has been an extraordinary regime of self-deception and denial among men. Enclosed groups like the army or police force have had to maintain ridiculous pretences about the nature of male mentorship and gender. Throughout British society there have been pressures never to recognize or admit one's own feelings, to separate one's actions from one's emotions, to repudiate one's desires and to punish other people who seem to practise their own freely. Homosexuality has to be rendered recognizably extraordinary – invested with terrifying 'Otherness' – so as to help people forget or ignore the potential for it in themselves. It needs to be feared as a spreading scourge – a myth sustained by the pretence that the habit is the result of contamination during teenage seduction. People whose behaviour threatens to explode all these fantasies and self-inflicted untruths – bisexuals for example – seem particularly dangerous and have become special targets of abuse.

AIDS is not merely a vile syndrome which has occasioned physical and verbal attacks on scapegoats; it also provides a pretext to undermine personal privacy and to regulate an individual's imagination. Under the dizzying rush of contagion fears, people are discouraged from thinking for themselves, or from fulfilling their own wishes: such conduct is dubbed 'selfish', and perceived as a national peril. AIDS has created a retinue of fears. It has created counsels of expedient self-deception: thus fidelity enforced by the threat of illness poses as proof of true emotional commitment; desires are not only to remain unconsummated, but the reality of their existence is to be denied. In the cause of saving lives endangered by AIDS both the essence and variety of human life can be tragically denied. To fear sex is to fear our shared humanity.

•

GEOFFREY HOWE
1990

'A conflict of loyalty'

Geoffrey Howe (1927–) served throughout the eleven years of Margaret Thatcher's three administrations, first as Chancellor of the Exchequer, then as Foreign Secretary and finally as Leader of the Commons. By 1990 he was the sole survivor from her first Cabinet. Yet their relationship, which had never been founded on mutual admiration, had sharply deteriorated, mainly because of Mrs Thatcher's distrust of the instincts of the Foreign Office,

*and her frequent humiliations of Howe, who was also her deputy. The apparently faithful
and imperturbable Howe finally snapped and he resigned on 1 November, saying he could
no longer serve her with honour.*

*Howe's pedestrian style was once memorably summed up. Being attacked by him was
like being savaged by a dead sheep, said his opponent Denis Healey. Yet in his resignation
speech the dead sheep became a lion, drawing audible gasps of surprise from fellow
Conservatives (who included Mrs Thatcher). It was 'an act of brilliantly executed matricide,'
says Sir Ronald Millar, Mrs Thatcher's principal speechwriter, 'each word honed with
Aesculapian skill for maximum effect.'*

We have done best when we have seen the [European] Community not as a
static entity to be resisted and contained, but as an active process which we
can shape often decisively provided we allow ourselves to be fully engaged
in it with confidence and enthusiasm and in good faith.

We must at all costs avoid presenting ourselves yet again with an over-
simplified choice, a false antithesis, a bogus dilemma, between one alternative
starkly labelled 'co-operation between independent sovereign states' and a
second equally crudely labelled alternative 'a centralized federal super-state'
as if there were no middle way in between.

We commit a serious error if we think always in terms of 'surrendering'
sovereignty and seek to stand pat for all time on a given deal by proclaiming,
as the prime minister did two weeks ago, that we have 'surrendered enough'.
The European enterprise is not and should not be seen like that, as some
kind of zero sum gain.

Sir Winston Churchill put it much more positively forty years ago
when he said: 'It is also possible and not less agreeable to regard [this
sacrifice or merger of national sovereignty] as the gradual assumption by all
the nations concerned of that larger sovereignty which can alone protect
their diverse and distinctive customs and characteristics and their national
traditions.'

I find Winston Churchill's perception a good deal more convincing and
encouraging for the interests of our nation than the nightmare image sometimes conjured up by the prime minister who sometimes seems to look out
on a continent that is positively teeming with ill-intentioned people scheming,
in her words, to 'extinguish democracy', to 'dissolve our national identities',
to lead us 'through the back door into a federal Europe'.

What kind of vision is that for our business people who trade there each day,
for our financiers who seek to make London the money capital of Europe, or
for all the young people of today? These concerns are especially important as
we approach the crucially important topic of EMU. We must be positively and

centrally involved in this debate and not fearfully and negatively detached. The cost of disengagement here could be very serious indeed . . .

The tragedy is – and it is for me personally, for my party, for our whole people, for the prime minister herself a very real tragedy – that the prime minister's perceived attitude towards Europe is running increasingly serious risks for the future of our nation. It risks minimizing our influence and maximizing our chances of being once again shut out.

We have paid heavily in the past for late starts and squandered opportunities in Europe. We dare not let that happen again. If we detach ourselves completely as a party or as a nation from the middle ground of Europe, the effects will be incalculable and very hard ever to correct.

In my letter of resignation, which I tendered with the utmost sadness and dismay, I said: 'Cabinet government is about trying to persuade one another from within.' That was my commitment to government by persuasion, persuading colleagues and the nation.

I have tried to do that as Foreign Secretary and since, but I realize now that the task has become futile, of trying to stretch the meaning of words beyond what was credible, and trying to pretend there was a common policy when every step forward risked being subverted by some casual comment or impulsive answer.

The conflict of loyalty, of loyalty to my right hon. Friend the prime minister – and, after all, in two decades together that instinct of loyalty is still very real – and of loyalty to what I perceive to be the true interests of the nation, has become all too great. I no longer believe it possible to resolve that conflict from within this government. That is why I have resigned. In doing so, I have done what I believe to be right for my party and my country. The time has come for others to consider their own response to the tragic conflict of loyalties with which I have myself wrestled for perhaps too long.

•

AUGUST WILSON
1990

'I want a black director'

In his critique of the cult of ethnicity, The Disuniting of America *(see page 434), the American historian Arthur M. Schlesinger criticized the doctrine that only blacks could teach or write black history and only women write women's history.*

That was 'voodoo' and the voodoo principle was being extended from scholarship to the arts, he argued — singling out this article for the New York Times, *originally written for* Spin *magazine, in which the black playwright August Wilson insists on a black director for the film of his play* Fences.

'I don't want to hire nobody just 'cause they're black.'

Eddie Murphy said that to me. We were discussing the possibility of Paramount Pictures purchasing the rights to my play *Fences*. I said I wanted a black director for the film. My response to his remark was immediate. 'Neither do I,' I said.

What Mr Murphy meant I am not sure. I meant I wanted to hire somebody talented, who understood the play and saw the possibilities of the film, who would approach my work with the same amount of passion and measure of respect with which I approach it, and who shared the cultural responsibilities of the characters.

That was more than three years ago. I have not talked to Mr Murphy about the subject since. Paramount did purchase rights to make the film in 1987. What I thought of as a straightforward, logical request has been greeted by blank, vacant stares and the pious shaking of heads as if in response to my unfortunate naivety.

I usually have had to repeat my request, 'I want a black director,' as though it were a complex statement in a foreign tongue. I have often heard the same response: 'We don't want to hire anyone just because they are black.' What is being implied is that the only qualification any black has is the color of his skin.

In the film industry, the prevailing attitude is that a black director couldn't do the job, and to insist upon one is to make the film 'unmakeable,' partly because no one is going to turn a budget of $15 million over to a black director. That this is routinely done for novice white directors is beside the point.

The ideas of ability and qualification are not new to blacks. The skills of black lawyers, doctors, dentists, accountants and mechanics are often greeted with skepticism, even from other blacks. 'Man, you sure you know what you doing?'

At the time of my last meeting with Paramount, in January 1990, a well-known, highly respected white director wanted very much to direct the film. I don't know his work, but he is universally praised for sensitive and intelligent direction. I accept that he is a very fine film director. But he is not black. He is not a product of black American culture – a culture that was honed out of the black experience and fired in the kiln of slavery and survival – and he does not share the sensibilities of black Americans.

I have been asked if I am not, by rejecting him on the basis of his race, doing the same thing Paramount is doing by not hiring a black director. That is a fair, if shortsighted, question which deserves a response.

I am not carrying a banner for black directors. I think they should carry their own. I am not trying to get work for black directors. I am trying to get the film of my play made in the best possible way.

As Americans of various races, we share a broad cultural ground, a commonality of society that links its diverse elements into a cohesive whole that can be defined as 'American.'

We share certain mythologies. A history. We share political and economic systems and a rapidly developing, if suspect, ethos. Within these commonalities are specifics. Specific ideas and attitudes that are not shared on the common cultural ground. These remain the property and possession of the people who develop them, and on that 'field of manners and rituals of intercourse' (to use James Baldwin's eloquent phrase) lives are played out.

At the point where they intercept and link to the broad commonality of American culture, they influence how that culture is shared and to what purpose.

White American society is made up of various European ethnic groups which share a common history and sensibility. Black Americans are a racial group which do not share the same sensibilities. The specifics of our cultural history are very much different.

We are an African people who have been here since the early seventeenth century. We have a different way of responding to the world. We have different ideas about religion, different manners of social intercourse. We have different ideas about style, about language. We have different esthetics.

Someone who does not share the specifics of a culture remains an outsider, no matter how astute a student or how well-meaning their intentions.

I declined a white director not on the basis of race but on the basis of culture. White directors are not qualified for the job. The job requires someone who shares the specifics of the culture of black Americans.

Webster's *Third New International Dictionary* gives the following character definitions listed under black and white:

White: free from blemish, moral stain or impurity: outstandingly righteous; innocent; not marked by malignant influence; notably pleasing or auspicious; fortunate; notably ardent; decent; in a fair upright manner; a sterling man; etc.

Black: outrageously wicked; a villain; dishonorable; expressing or indicating disgrace, discredit or guilt; connected with the devil; expressing menace; sullen; hostile; unqualified; committing a violation of public regulation, illicit, illegal; affected by some undesirable condition; etc.

No wonder I had been greeted with incredulous looks when I suggested a black director for *Fences*. I sat in the offices of Paramount suggesting that someone who was affected by an undesirable condition, who was a violator of public regulations, who was sullen, unqualified and marked by a malignant influence, direct the film.

While they were offering a sterling man, who was free from blemish, notably pleasing, fair and upright, decent and outstandingly righteous – with a reputation to boot!

Despite such a linguistic environment, the culture of black Americans has emerged and defined itself in strong and effective vehicles that have become the flag-bearers for self-determination and self-identity.

In the face of such, those who are opposed to the ideas of a 'foreign' culture permeating the ideal of an American culture founded on the icons of Europe seek to dilute and control it by setting themselves up as the assayers of its value and the custodians of its offspring.

Therein lies the crux of the matter as it relates to Paramount and the film *Fences* – whether we as blacks are going to have control over our own culture and its products.

Some Americans, black and white, do not see any value to black American lives that do not contribute to the leisure or profit of white America. Some Americans, black and white, would deny that a black American culture even exists. Some Americans, black and white, would say that by insisting on a black director for *Fences* I am doing irreparable harm to the efforts of black directors who have spent the last fifteen years trying to get Hollywood to ignore the fact that they are black. The origins of such ideas are so very old and shallow that I am amazed to see them so vividly displayed in 1990.

What to do? Let's make a rule. Blacks don't direct Italian films. Italians don't direct Jewish films. Jews don't direct black American films. That might account for about 3 percent of the films that are made in this country. The other 97 percent – the action-adventure, horror, comedy, romance, suspense, western, or any combination thereof, that the Hollywood and independent mills grind out – let it be every man for himself.

•

AUNG SAN SUU KYI
1991

'Fear is not the natural state of civilized man'

Aung San Suu Kyi, daughter of Aung San, Burma's national hero who was assassinated when she was two, has become the symbol of resistance to the dictatorship which rules Burma (now renamed Myanmar). The National League for Democracy Party she founded on her return from England in 1988 won the election in 1990 but she had been put under house arrest in 1989 and the military junta refused to release her or to transfer power to a civilian government as it had promised. She was released in 1995. The junta remains in power.

In 1990 the European Parliament awarded Aung San Suu Kyi the Sakharov Prize for Freedom of Thought but she could not attend the award ceremony at Strasbourg in 1991. 'Freedom from Fear', the essay she wrote to mark the award, was published throughout the world. This is a slightly abridged version.

It is not power that corrupts but fear. Fear of losing power corrupts those who wield it and fear of the scourge of power corrupts those who are subject to it. Most Burmese are familiar with the four *a-gati*, the four kinds of corruption. *Chanda-gati*, corruption induced by desire, is deviation from the right path in pursuit of bribes or for the sake of those one loves. *Dosa-gati* is taking the wrong path to spite those against whom one bears ill will, and *moha-gati* is aberration due to ignorance. But perhaps the worst of the four is *bhaya-gati*, for not only does *bhaya*, fear, stifle and slowly destroy all sense of right and wrong, it so often lies at the root of the other three kinds of corruption.

Just as *chanda-gati*, when not the result of sheer avarice, can be caused by fear of want or fear of losing the goodwill of those one loves, so fear of being surpassed, humiliated or injured in some way can provide the impetus for ill will. And it would be difficult to dispel ignorance unless there is freedom to pursue the truth unfettered by fear. With so close a relationship between fear and corruption it is little wonder that in any society where fear is rife corruption in all forms becomes deeply entrenched.

Public dissatisfaction with economic hardships has been seen as the chief cause of the movement for democracy in Burma, sparked off by the student demonstrations of 1988. It is true that years of incoherent policies, inept official measures, burgeoning inflation and falling real income had turned the country into an economic shambles. But it was more than the difficulties of eking out a barely acceptable standard of living that had eroded the patience of a traditionally good-natured, quiescent people – it was also the humiliation of a way of life disfigured by corruption and fear. The students were protesting not just against the death of their comrades but against the denial of their right to life by a totalitarian regime which deprived the present of meaning-fulness and held out no hope for the future. And because the students' protests articulated the frustrations of the people at large, the demonstrations quickly grew into a nationwide movement. Some of its keenest supporters were businessmen who had developed the skills and the contacts necessary not only to survive but to prosper within the system. But their affluence offered them no genuine sense of security or fulfilment, and they could not but see that if they and their fellow citizens, regardless of economic status, were to achieve a worthwhile existence, an accountable administration was at least a necessary if not a sufficient condition. The people of Burma had wearied of a precarious state of passive apprehension where they were 'as water in the cupped hands' of the powers that be.

> Emerald cool we may be
> As water in cupped hands
> But oh that we might be
> As splinters of glass
> In cupped hands.

Glass splinters, the smallest with its sharp, glinting power to defend itself against hands that try to crush, could be seen as a vivid symbol of the spark of courage that is an essential attribute of those who would free themselves from the grip of oppression. Bogyoke Aung San regarded himself as a revolutionary and searched tirelessly for answers to the problems that beset Burma during her times of trial. He exhorted the people to develop courage: 'Don't just depend on the courage and intrepidity of others. Each and every one of you must make sacrifices to become a hero possessed of courage and intrepidity. Then only shall we all be able to enjoy true freedom.'

The effort necessary to remain uncorrupted in an environment where fear is an integral part of everyday existence is not immediately apparent to those fortunate enough to live in states governed by the rule of law. Just laws do not merely prevent corruption by meting out impartial punishment to offenders. They also help to create a society in which people can fulfil the basic requirements necessary for the preservation of human dignity without recourse to corrupt practices. Where there are no such laws, the burden of upholding the principles of justice and common decency falls on the ordinary people. It is the cumulative effect of their sustained effort and steady endurance which will change a nation where reason and conscience are warped by fear into one where legal rules exist to promote man's desire for harmony and justice while restraining the less desirable destructive traits in his nature.

In an age when immense technological advances have created lethal weapons which could be, and are, used by the powerful and the unprincipled to dominate the weak and the helpless, there is a compelling need for a closer relationship between politics and ethics at both the national and international levels. The Universal Declaration of Human Rights of the United Nations proclaims that 'every individual and every organ of society' should strive to promote the basic rights and freedoms to which all human beings regardless of race, nationality or religion are entitled. But as long as there are governments whose authority is founded on coercion rather than on the mandate of the people, and interest groups which place short-term profits above long-term peace and prosperity, concerted international action to protect and promote human rights will remain at best a partially realized ideal. There will continue to be arenas of struggle where victims of oppression have to draw on their own inner resources to defend their inalienable rights as members of the human family.

The quintessential revolution is that of the spirit, born of an intellectual conviction of the need for change in those mental attitudes and values which shape the course of a nation's development. A revolution which aims merely at changing official policies and institutions with a view to an improvement in material conditions has little chance of genuine success. Without a revolution of the spirit, the forces which produced the iniquities of the old order would continue to be operative, posing a constant threat to the process of reform and regeneration. It is not enough merely to call for freedom, democracy and human rights. There has to be a united determination to persevere in the struggle, to make sacrifices in the name of enduring truths, to resist the corrupting influences of desire, ill will, ignorance and fear.

Saints, it has been said, are the sinners who go on trying. So free men are the oppressed who go on trying and who in the process make themselves fit to bear the responsibilities and to uphold the disciplines which will maintain a free society. Among the basic freedoms to which men aspire that their lives might be full and uncramped, freedom from fear stands out as both a means and an end. A people who would build a nation in which strong, democratic institutions are firmly established as a guarantee against state-induced power must first learn to liberate their own minds from apathy and fear . . .

Fearlessness may be a gift but perhaps more precious is the courage acquired through endeavour, courage that comes from cultivating the habit of refusing to let fear dictate one's actions, courage that could be described as 'grace under pressure' – grace which is renewed repeatedly in the face of harsh, unremitting pressure.

Within a system which denies the existence of basic human rights, fear tends to be the order of the day. Fear of imprisonment, fear of torture, fear of death, fear of losing friends, family, property or means of livelihood, fear of poverty, fear of isolation, fear of failure. A most insidious form of fear is that which masquerades as common sense or even wisdom, condemning as foolish, reckless, insignificant or futile the small, daily acts of courage which help to preserve man's self-respect and inherent human dignity. It is not easy for a people conditioned by the iron rule of the principle that might is right to free themselves from the enervating miasma of fear. Yet even under the most crushing state machinery courage rises up again and again, for fear is not the natural state of civilized man.

•

EDWARD W. SAID
1991

'Ignorant armies'

So which side was guilty in the Gulf War – the Arabs or the United States? In this article for The Nation*, the Palestinian-American Edward W. Said, professor of humanities at New York's Columbia University and a critic of Western imperialism and racism, protested that it was not only the Americans who were guilty of ignorance of the Middle East. Self-pitying Arabs had created a largely fictional image of a monolithic West.*

It is curious, but profoundly symptomatic of the present conflict, that the one word that should be tediously pronounced and repronounced and yet left unanalyzed is 'linkage,' an ugly solecism that could have been invented only in late twentieth-century America. 'Linkage' means not that there is but that there is no connection. Things that belong together by common association, sense, geography, history, are sundered, left apart for convenience' sake and for the benefit of US imperial strategists. Everyone his own carver,

Jonathan Swift said. That the Middle East is linked by all sorts of ties, that is irrelevant. That Arabs might see a connection between Saddam in Kuwait and Israel in Lebanon, that too is futile. That US policy itself is the linkage, this is a forbidden topic to broach . . .

Seen from the Arab point of view, the picture of America is just as constricted . . . To my knowledge there is still no institute or major academic department in the Arab world whose main purpose is the study of America, although the United States is by far the largest outside force in the Arab world. It is still difficult to explain even to well-educated and experienced fellow Arabs that US foreign policy is not in fact run by the CIA, or a conspiracy, or a shadowy network of key 'contacts.' Many Arabs I know believe the United States plans virtually every event of significance in the Middle East, including, in one mind-boggling suggestion made to me last year, the intifada.

This mix of long familiarity, hostility and ignorance pertains to both sides of a complex, variously uneven and quite old cultural encounter now engaging in very unmetaphorical warfare. From early on there has been an overriding sense of inevitability, as if George Bush's apparent need to get down there and, in his own sporty argot, 'kick ass' had to run up against Saddam Hussein's monstrous aggressiveness, now vindicating the Arab need to confront, talk back to, stand unblinkingly before the United States. The public rhetoric, in other words, is simply undeterred, uncomplicated by any considerations of detail, realism or cause and effect.

Perhaps the central unanalyzed link between the United States and the Arabs in this conflict is nationalism. The world can no longer afford so heady a mixture of patriotism, relative solipsism, social authority, unchecked aggressiveness and defensiveness toward others. Today the United States, triumphalist internationally, seems in a febrile way anxious to prove that it is Number One, perhaps to offset the recession; the endemic problems posed by the cities, poverty, health, education, production; and the Euro-Japanese challenge. On the other side, the Middle East is saturated with a sense that Arab nationalism is all-important, but also that it is an aggrieved and unfulfilled nationalism, beset with conspiracies, enemies both internal and external, obstacles to overcome for which no price is too high. This was especially true of the cultural framework in which I grew up. It is still true today, with the important difference that this nationalism has resolved itself into smaller and smaller units. In the colonial period as I was growing up, you could travel overland from Lebanon and Syria through Palestine to Egypt and points west. That is now impossible. Each country places formidable obstacles at its borders. For Palestinians, crossing is a horrible experience, since countries

that make the loudest noises in support of Palestine treat Palestinians the
worst . . .

•

MARTIN WOOLLACOTT
1991

'The valleys of death'

*Once the Gulf War was over, Saddam Hussein sent a force of 10,000 men and 250
tanks to crush the Kurds who had rebelled against his persecution of Kurdistan. The*
Guardian *devoted the whole of its front page to this despatch from its veteran foreign
correspondent Martin Woollacott.*

A monstrous crime is being perpetrated in Kurdistan. As the Kurdish people's
brief springtime of freedom ends, they are, and will be, subject not only to
the effects of a war waged in their own cities and towns without restraint or
morality, but to the reimposition of Saddam Hussein's brutal rule and his
revenge on those who have challenged him . . .

Turkey's National Security Council said that more than 200,000 people
fleeing Iraq, mostly women and children, were in danger of death near the
Turkish border. 'Where is Bush?' was a question we must have heard a
thousand times as we toiled up the slopes of the 8,000-foot mountain passes
that separate Iraq from Turkey. 'Why did he start if he was not going to
finish?' or 'Why has he not finished Saddam?'

Sometimes all the bitterness and despair are compressed into the single
word Bush, pronounced with a terrible resignation. The name of a man who
was a hero to the Kurds only a few days ago has become almost a curse . . .

There is no doubt that after he has re-established control, President Saddam
will take a terrible revenge on those who rose against him and effaced his
image from every corner of their land. This is the man who gassed a whole
town and who took hostage thousands of Kurds who disappeared, almost
certainly dead, in 1983.

You have only to visit one of the torture palaces which exist in every city
and town in Kurdistan to realize how brutal his rule has been. And not just
brutal; the tactics of his intelligence services go beyond brutality to the most
ingenious refinements of cruelty. There is the raping room, for instance – a
sort of hut off the main interrogation room, with a bloodied mattress inside
and a pile of discarded women's clothes outside. And there are persistent

tales of naked men being thrown to dogs trained to bite their private parts. In other countries you might discount such tales: in Iraq, the chances are that they are true.

The Kurdish response to the revolution was so wholehearted and so widespread that it could be said that virtually everybody has committed offences that would have warranted imprisonment, torture, and execution in the old Iraq. When the security services get back into their burned and blasted headquarters, the list-making will begin and the arrests will soon follow. Their revenge will be the more ferocious because of the evidence that in some towns Iraqi security men were done to death after the fighting was over. In the Sulaymaniyah security centre, the severed forearm of one was still stuck on a hook on the wall.

There were not many such deaths, because on the whole the Kurdish revolution tried to be magnanimous even towards its worst enemies. One middle-class Kurd, who tried to stop the killing of a security man, was shouted at by a woman: 'Have you had a sister who was raped and tortured? If you have, then you can speak. If you haven't, you have nothing to say.'

Another man pushed him away from the scene, telling the story of losing three sons, of whose fate at the hands of the security services he learned only when curt demands for seventy dinars 'burial charges' came through the post. Everybody involved in the revolution, even in a minor way, is potentially on the death list . . .

Kurdistan's brief freedom began three weeks ago when a tentative push at the structure of oppression in a town called Rania was so brilliantly successful that it led to a chain reaction throughout Kurdistan. There was an extraordinary euphoria, a feeling that after many betrayals and disasters the Kurdish people's moment had finally come.

It all turned to dust in two days, from the fall of Kirkuk last Thursday to the collapse of Kurdish defences in the last few days. The problem was that the Kurds had won in the north by guile, not by main force. They had persuaded the government mercenaries to change sides, and organized the surrender of President Saddam's unsteady units in many places. The people had done the rest and only in a few towns did the guerrillas have to fight hard battles.

President Saddam proved to have more resources of men and equipment than was believed, and more political control at the centre than had been expected. Only ten days ago Massoud Barzani, the leader of the Kurdish Democratic Party, was talking confidently of establishing a temporary government for all Iraq in free Kurdistan.

The Kurdish military leaders were over-confident, inexperienced in conventional war, and disorganized. They believed too readily that a collapse in

Baghdad would come soon and that, if things did by some mischance go wrong, the United States would rescue the situation.

These were their faults. But what of ours? The US, which to the Kurds is shorthand for all of the West, failed to make the intervention that the Kurds are convinced might have tipped the balance their way. Its reconnaissance planes circled lazily over Kurdish towns as Iraqi helicopters bombed the civil population with terrible results. If just one or two of those helicopters had been shot down, like the fixed-wing aircraft that were downed earlier by US planes, it just might have made the difference. It would have had a tremendous effect on Kurdish morale, and it might have convinced President Saddam that further military moves in the north would attract serious American military intervention.

Why didn't the US and the allies do it? God knows, we bent international law and the UN Charter whenever we wanted to in the effort to free Kuwait. We spent millions and killed many thousands to punish President Saddam's aggression and, bluntly, to bring him down. Why then this sudden excess of legalism, this prating about internal affairs, these oh-so-wise thoughts about the undesirability of a divided Iraq?

Saddam Hussein has no more right to Kurdistan than he had to Kuwait. He has forfeited any such right by a vicious record of oppression of the Kurds worse even than his treatment of Iraq's Arab population. When he gets back full control he will kill, and kill, and kill.

•

STEPHEN SACKUR
1991

'Mutla Ridge'

The Gulf War began in 1991 when Operation Desert Storm was launched by the American president George Bush, supported by John Major, the British prime minister, to free Kuwait which had been invaded by the Iraqi dictator Saddam Hussein. A million Allied troops routed the Iraqis. There was controversy, however, about Allied tactics as the war ended, particularly the bombing of the fleeing Iraqi troops at Mutla Ridge. Several journalists questioned whether 'maximum force' – the term used by Major-General Rupert Smith, commander of the British 1st Armoured Division, to describe how war was prosecuted – was really necessary. One was the BBC correspondent Stephen Sackur, who wrote this report for the London Review of Books.

'Maximum force' was the phrase that stuck in my mind long after I took my leave of General Smith. Was it an approach, I wondered, that remained legitimate against an enemy patently beaten and retreating in disarray? Does warfare of its nature require the application of 'maximum force' from the opening of hostilities to their cessation?

By a quirk of fate my doubts were intensified the very next day. Instead of heading back into Iraq, I took a seat in an army Land Rover heading for Kuwait City. After bumping along a desert track for no more than five minutes we turned on to the main highway – Route 80 – which runs north from Kuwait City to the Iraqi border, and the southern Iraqi city of Basra. As we continued to head south we passed dozens of wrecked civilian and military vehicles, many gutted by fire. Now and again bodies, sometimes covered in rough blankets, sometimes not, could be seen on the side of the road. It was clear that allied aircraft had attacked the highway with cluster bombs – the spent casings were lying all over the area. Cluster bombs are designed to break up into hundreds of little 'bomblets' to saturate the target area, spewing out specially formulated metal shrapnel to maximize damage to both man and machine. They leave tell-tale pockmarks in the area of impact. The Basra road, needless to say, was covered in pockmarks.

Our Land Rover continued on its way towards Kuwait City, skirting round the torn metal and the abandoned corpses. But only two miles ahead the highway was blocked in an altogether more thorough fashion. We had reached the Mutla Ridge, an escarpment perhaps a couple of hundred feet high, from which, on a clear day, you can see Kuwait City itself, some twenty miles away. On the crest of the ridge were a group of buildings, including a petrol station and a police station. The Iraqis had, we were told, established heavily fortified defences on the ridge, on both sides of the highway, during the allied offensive. The Land Rover could go no further, so I got out and walked. To my left was the police station, badly damaged, but still standing. Close by, on the other side of the road, was a grotesque collection of charred bodies, forty in all, some frozen in mid-scream, others so badly burnt that it was impossible to distinguish their sex. In many instances the human form had been reduced to nothing more than a shapeless black lump, the colour of coal, the texture of ash.

Over the ridge, down the highway, this was where they had been incinerated. Across all six lanes of the road, and as far as the low grey cloud would allow me to see, there was nothing but devastation – saloon cars, tanks, military vehicles sitting nose-to-tail in a stalled procession. This was an escape convoy stopped in its tracks. Iraqi soldiers in Kuwait City, and some civilians too, though God knows how many, had realized on the Tuesday of the ground offensive that the game was up – allied soldiers were already approaching the outskirts of the city. They had panicked, seizing any vehicle that looked capable of taking them to Iraq before the allies could close in. The evidence of their desperation was still to be seen on the highway some sixty hours later. Some had commandeered Kuwaiti police cars and fire engines; others had climbed aboard a milk delivery van; somebody had even chosen a civilian bulldozer. Mostly, though, the fleeing thousands had stolen luxury saloons of which Kuwait City could offer a plentiful supply. In their last panic stricken minutes many found time to stuff these cars with useless trinkets and consumer goods looted from Kuwaiti homes. But Mercedes, BMW or Range Rover, it mattered little: nothing offered much protection from the American bombs and shells which rained down on the convoy that night.

How did it happen? Why did it happen? The only answers I got were from an American major, Bob Williams, who had been part of the tank battalion charged with cutting off the Iraqi line of retreat from Kuwait City. Major Williams, his men and their M-1 tanks – collectively known as 'The Hounds of Hell' – were still on the scene some three days later. According to the major, his tanks had been involved in what he called a 'five-hour fire-fight' with Iraqi troops dug in around the police station at the top of the ridge. As the fight continued the highway became blocked, causing a huge tailback of traffic to build up. There were tanks, military vehicles and thousands of armed troops in the trapped convoy – it was, in short, a legitimate military target, he said. American aircraft bombed the convoy while Major Williams and his men maintained a heavy barrage on the ground. The result, he agreed, was 'apocalyptic' . . .

As to the number of Iraqis who lost their lives, the Americans would say only that they had recovered more than 150 bodies. But numerous blackened corpses remained inside the twisted metal of their vehicles, and it seemed obvious to me that many hundreds of people must have been obliterated under the sustained American fire. It's hard to imagine how the doctrine of 'maximum force' could have been given a more forcible illustration. Within the international regulations which are supposed to govern the conduct of warfare the American actions on the Mutla Ridge were legitimate. Iraqi soldiers were retreating, but they were armed and (as far as we know) they offered no formal surrender. It was the scale of the American attack that took my breath away. Was it necessary to bomb the entire convoy? What threat could these pathetic remnants of Saddam Hussein's beaten army have posed? Wasn't it obvious that the people of the convoy would have given themselves up willingly without the application of such ferocious weaponry? The hundreds who, by some miracle, did survive were duly taken prisoner.

They included two women and a child. Further evidence suggests that Palestinian and Indian civilians were killed, along with other Iraqis and some Kuwaitis who were being taken back to Iraq as prisoners.

When I asked Major Williams to justify what had happened he said: 'As you look at the vehicles down in this area you'll find they are all filled with booty . . . these were thieves, not professional soldiers . . . our cause was just.' A few yards away, American and British troops were rooting around the wrecked vehicles looking for Iraqi military souvenirs to take home and hang on their walls . . .

•

JOHN KEEGAN
1991

'Television grandees'

John Keegan, who received the OBE in the Gulf War Honours List, is the outstanding military historian of his generation. After many years as senior lecturer at Sandhurst Military Academy, he became Defence Editor of the Daily Telegraph *and reported the war in the Gulf, the first fought in the glare of the electronic global village created by satellite television news stations such as* CNN. *When the war was won, he wrote this philippic for the* Daily Telegraph *expressing his contempt for some of the television commentators.*

On one side stood a country of 18 million Third World people, without a defence industry and with an armoury of second-hand Soviet equipment which could not be replaced if lost in combat. On the other stood three of the strongest states in the First World, with a combined population of 350 million, which are respectively the first, third and fourth international suppliers of advanced military equipment.

Their armed forces are at the peak of world military efficiency and, by the time the United Nations' deadline ran out on 15 January, the army they had assembled in the Gulf equalled in numbers that which Saddam had deployed in Kuwait, while their air forces outnumbered his by four times. The facts were so stark that the layman could conclude that once battle was joined the Iraqis would be overwhelmed in a few days of fighting. Have the television grandees told us any such thing? They have not.

On the contrary: for day after day they have strung us along, turning an open-and-shut case into a cliffhanger. Sober, responsible military experts, many of them retired officers of high rank, have been brought to the studio

to state facts and opinions similar to those I have outlined above, only to
hear, in the familiar way, their considered advice being chipped away in the
condescending, imperious, incredulous tone which is now the received style
wherever the television grandees hold sway. In an earlier article I called the
refusal of the grandees to listen 'the higher ignorance'. But now I think it is
worse than that. It is a petulant determination not to learn, lest learning
interfere with the right they have established for themselves over the years
to know better than anyone they interview.

If what they were offering were 'just television', as most transmissions are,
that would not matter. But a whole nation has necessarily had to hang on
the narcissistic grandees' words for the last months. Worse, tens of thousands
of viewers who are relatives and friends of our servicemen in the Gulf have
had their anxieties stretched day after day by the relentless expression of
professional doubt that the grandees have turned on anyone who dared to
utter the simple truth that the allies were bound to win and to win without
serious loss among the ranks of the soldiers, sailors and airmen who had
gone to the Gulf to do their duty.

I do not know Jeremy Paxman, either of the Dimblebys or any of the
other television grandees. I do know many of the soldiers. Some I taught as
cadets at Sandhurst, many were my colleagues there or at the Staff college. I
know their wives and families. I know the lives they have lived during the
twenty years when the Cold War reached its climax. I know that they have
scraped, on salaries which would not cover a television grandee's lunches, to
keep up appearances, pay their debts and educate their children. I know they
have spent months of each year living on cold rations in bleak training areas
on the North German plain to wear down the will of the Soviet Union in its
confrontation with democracy.

I know that they have lived under a code of behaviour that the television
world would regard as an intolerable restriction of individual liberty. I know
that their professional lives have been governed by standards of efficiency
so rigorous that a single uncomplimentary report can blight a whole career.
I know, in short, that they are people of a quality scarcely to be found
anywhere in the kingdom today. What is more, I know that the kingdom
values them for what they are.

We may well recognize with hindsight that the most successful national
institution of the post-1945 years is the British Army – a title that the BBC
perhaps deserved when it was the most respected broadcasting institution in
the world, but which it has now lost. The army has stoically kept order in
Northern Ireland for twenty years without suffering the least taint of political
involvement. It has efficiently performed any essential service – fire-fighting,

ambulance driving, rubbish collection – left undone by public employees on strike. It won the Falklands war with a despatch that the American Army has clearly been at pains to emulate ever since. With the American Army, it garrisoned the Iron Curtain until the Soviet Union dismantled it in despair.

This wonderful national institution lies under the threat of returning from a historic, just and necessary victory, which will benefit the whole world for decades to come, to face heavy demobilizations under the programme of budgetary reductions known as Options for Change. The British Army, 150,000 strong, probably costs some £4.5 billion a year to maintain. The BBC, which employs 23,000 people, costs £1.5 billion a year. Each BBC employee, in short, costs about twice as much as a soldier.

If, from our pockets, we have to choose between paying taxes for the army or licences for the BBC, which do we think better deserves the outlay? Is *Newsnight* worth more than the 7th Armoured Brigade? Do the smooth men of our screens better deserve their livelihoods than the quiet and unassuming friends of my youth who have led their soldiers to victory on the Euphrates?

•

HAIDAR ABDUL SHAFI
1991

'Palestine'

The cause of the Palestinians has preoccupied world leaders since 1948 when the state of Israel was created from Palestine, leaving the Palestinians dispossessed. As leader of the Palestine Liberation Organization, Yassir Arafat was dedicated to establishing an independent Palestinian state. In 1994 Israel agreed to withdraw from Jericho, the Gaza strip and later the West Bank and he began to realize his aim of creating a Palestine homeland, but the Israelis and Palestinians are still fighting over the terms.

The grievances of the Palestinians were described in this speech to the Madrid Peace Conference of 1991 by the leader of the Palestinian delegation Haidar Abdul Shafi.

We, the people of Palestine, stand before you in the fullness of our pain, our pride, and our anticipation, for we long harboured a yearning for peace and a dream of justice and freedom. For too long, the Palestinian people have gone unheeded, silenced and denied. Our identity negated by political expediency; our right for struggle against injustice maligned; and our present existence subdued by the past tragedy of another people. For the greater part of this century we have been victimized by the myth of a land without a people and described with impunity as the invisible Palestinians. Before such wilful blindness, we refused to disappear or to accept a distorted identity. Our Intifada is a testimony to our perseverance and resilience waged in a just struggle to regain our rights. It is time for us to narrate our own story, to stand witness as advocates of truth which has long lain buried in the consciousness and conscience of the world. We do not stand before you as supplicants, but rather as the torch-bearers who know that, in our world of today, ignorance can never be an excuse. We seek neither an admission of guilt after the fact, nor vengeance for past inequities, but rather an act of will that would make a just peace a reality.

We speak out, ladies and gentlemen, from the full conviction of the rightness of our cause, the verity of our history, and the depth of our commitment. Therein lies the strength of the Palestinian people today, for we have scaled walls of fear and reticence, and we wish to speak out with the courage and integrity that our narrative and history deserve. But even in the invitation to this peace conference, our narrative was distorted and our truth only partially acknowledged.

The Palestinian people are one, fused by centuries of history in Palestine, bound together by a collective memory of shared sorrows and joys, and sharing a unity of purpose and vision. Our songs and ballads, full of tales and children's stories, the dialect of our jokes, the image of our poems, that hint of melancholy which colours even our happiest moments, are as important to us as the blood ties which link our families and clans. Yet, an invitation to discuss peace, the peace we all desire and need, comes to only a portion of our people. It ignores our national, historical, and organic unity. We come here wrenched from our sisters and brothers in exile to stand before you as the Palestinian under occupation, although we maintain that each of us represents the rights and interests of the whole.

We have been denied the right to publicly acknowledge our loyalty to our leadership and system of government. But allegiance and loyalty cannot be censored or severed. Our acknowledged leadership is more than [the] justly democratically chosen leadership of all the Palestinian people. It is the symbol of our national unity and identity, the guardian of our past, the protector of our present, and the hope of our future. Our people have chosen to entrust it with their history and the preservation of our precious legacy. This leadership has been clearly and unequivocally recognized by the community of nations, with only a few exceptions who had chosen for so many years shadow over substance. Regardless of the nature and conditions of our oppression, whether the disposition and dispersion of exile or the brutality and repression of the occupation, the Palestinian people cannot be torn asunder. They remain united – a nation wherever they are, or are forced to be.

And Jerusalem, ladies and gentlemen, that city which is not only the soul of Palestine, but the cradle of three world religions, is tangible even in its claimed absence from our midst at this stage. It is apparent, through artificial exclusion from this conference, that this is a denial of its right to seek peace and redemption. For it, too, has suffered from war and occupation. Jerusalem, the city of peace, has been barred from a peace conference and deprived of its calling. Palestinian Jerusalem, the capital of our homeland and future state, defines Palestinian existence, past, present, and future, but itself has been denied a voice and an identity. Jerusalem defies exclusive possessiveness or bondage. Israel's annexation of Arab Jerusalem remains both clearly illegal in the eyes of the world community, and an affront to the peace that this city deserves.

We come to you from a tortured land and a proud, though captive people, having been asked to negotiate with our occupiers, but leaving behind the children of the Intifada, and a people under occupation and under curfew who enjoined us not to surrender or forget. As we speak, thousands of our brothers and sisters are languishing in Israeli prisons and detention camps, most detained without evidence, charge or trial, many cruelly mistreated and tortured in interrogation, guilty only of seeking freedom or daring to defy the occupation. We speak in their name and we say: Set them free. As we speak, the tens of thousands who have been wounded or permanently disabled are in pain. Let peace heal their wounds. As we speak, the eyes of thousands of Palestinian refugees, deportees and displaced persons since 1967 are haunting us, for exile is a cruel fate. Bring them home. They have the right to return. As we speak, the silence of the demolished homes echoes through the halls and in our minds. We must rebuild our homes in our free state.

•

KEN SARO-WIWA
1992

'The war against the Ogoni'

The Nigerian writer and political activist Ken Saro-Wiwa became the international spokesman for the rights of the Ogoni people. He accused the Nigerian government of genocide, and the multinational oil giants such as Shell of pillaging Ogoni land. He set out his plea for the Ogoni in this address to the Unrepresented Nations and Peoples Organization, set up to teach groups such as the Ogoni how to work with the United Nations and its Human Rights Commission. A year later Saro-Wiwa was detained by the Nigerian government, who executed him in November 1995.

Ogoni territory lies on 404 square miles of the coastal plains terraces to the north-east of the Niger River Delta. Inhabited by 500,000 people, its population density of about 1,500 per square mile is among the highest in any rural area of the world and compares with the Nigerian national average of 300.

The Ogoni people have settled in this area as farmers and fishermen since remembered time and had established a well-organized social system before the British colonialist invaded them in 1901. Within thirteen years, the British had destroyed the fabric of Ogoni society. British rule of the area was 'haphazard' and no treaties were signed with the Ogoni. By 1960, when colonial rule ended, the British had consigned the Ogoni willy-nilly to a new nation, Nigeria, consisting of 350 or so other peoples previously held together by force, violence and much argument in Britain's commercial and imperial interest.

The nation which the British left behind was supposed to be a federal democracy, but the federating ethnic nations were bound by few agreements and the peoples were so disparate, so culturally different, so varied in size, that force and violence seemed to be the only way of maintaining the nation. In the circumstances, the interests of the few and weak such as the Ogoni were bound to suffer and have suffered.

Petroleum was discovered in Ogoni in 1958 and since then an estimated 100 billion US dollars' worth of oil and gas has been carted away from Ogoni land. In return for this, the Ogoni people have received nothing.

Oil exploration has turned Ogoni into a wasteland: lands, streams and creeks are totally and continually polluted; the atmosphere has been poisoned, charged as it is with hydrocarbon vapours, methane, carbon monoxide, carbon dioxide and soot emitted by gas which has been flared twenty-four hours a day for thirty-three years in very close proximity to human habitation. Acid rain, oil spillages and oil blow-outs have devastated Ogoni territory. High-pressure oil pipelines crisscross the surface of Ogoni farmlands and villages dangerously.

The results of such unchecked environmental pollution and degradation include the complete destruction of the ecosystem. Mangrove forests have fallen to the toxicity of oil and are being replaced by noxious nypa palms; the rain forest has fallen to the axe of the multinational oil companies, all wildlife is dead, marine life is gone, the farmlands have been rendered infertile by acid rain and the once beautiful Ogoni countryside is no longer a source of fresh air and green vegetation. All one sees and feels around is death.

Environmental degradation has been a lethal weapon in the war against the indigenous Ogoni people.

Incidental to and indeed compounding this ecological devastation is the political marginalization and complete oppression of the Ogoni and especially the denial of their rights, including land rights. At independence Nigeria consisted of three regions. Since then, thirty states have been created largely for the ethnic majorities who rule the country. Most of the states so created are unviable and depend entirely on Ogoni resources for their survival. The demands of the Ogoni for autonomy and self-determination even within the Nigerian nation have been ignored. The Ogoni have been corralled into a multi-ethnic administrative state in which they remain a minority and therefore suffer several disabilities. Mining rents and royalties for Ogoni oil are not being paid to Ogoni people. In spite of the enormous wealth of their land the Ogoni people continue to live in pristine conditions in the absence of electricity, pipe-borne water, hospitals, housing and schools. The Ogoni are being consigned to slavery and extinction.

Faced by these terrible odds, the Ogoni people have continued courageously to demand social justice and equity. In October 1990 the Chiefs and leaders of Ogoni submitted a Bill of Rights to the Nigerian President and his council. The Bill called for (a) political control of Ogoni affairs by Ogoni people (b) the right to control and use a fair proportion of Ogoni economic resources for Ogoni development (c) adequate and direct representation as of right in all Nigerian national institutions (d) the use and development of Ogoni languages in Ogoni territory and (e) the right to protect the Ogoni environment and ecology from further degradation. The Ogoni are yet to receive a reply to these minimum demands.

The extermination of the Ogoni people appears to be policy. The Ogoni have suffered at the hands of the military dictatorships which have ruled Nigeria over the past decades. The new constitution, which is supposed to usher in a democratic government in 1993, does not protect the rights of the Ogoni. Indeed, it institutionalizes the expropriation of their land. A recently concluded national census omits all references to the ethnic origins of all citizens, which in a multi-ethnic state is a violation of community rights.

Nigeria has an external debt of over 30 billion dollars. None of that debt was incurred on any project in the Ogoni area or on any project remotely beneficial to the Ogoni. The International Monetary Fund and the World Bank, keen on the payment of the debt, are encouraging intensified exploitation of oil and gas, which constitute 94 per cent of Nigeria's Gross Domestic Product. Such exploitation is against the wishes of the Ogoni people as it only worsens the degradation of the Ogoni environment and the decimation of the Ogoni people. Studies have indicated that more Ogoni people are dying now than are being born. The Ogoni are faced by a powerful combination of titanic forces from far and near, driven by greed and cold statistics. Only the international community, acting with compassion and a sense of responsibility to the human race, can avert the catastrophe which is about to overtake the Ogoni. The Ogoni people are now appealing to that community . . .

National ideas of national independence, the fact of Africans ruling Africans in nations conceived by and for European economic interests have intensified, not destroyed, the propensity of man to subject weak peoples by force, violence and legal quibbling to slavery and extinction. I respectfully invite you to visit Nigeria, so that you can see for yourself that indigenous peoples abound there and that they suffer incredibly at the hands of rulers and the economic interests of other nations.

•

PETER TATCHELL
1992

'Call us queer'

The most articulate advocate of lesbian and gay rights in Britain is the activist Peter Tatchell, one of the leaders of the Queer Rights Group OutRage! He put the case for gay rights in this article for the Independent on Sunday.

'We're here! We're queer! Get used to it!' Some of us are quite happy to call ourselves queer. A once-despised word no longer makes us recoil in fear. Indeed, it is fast becoming a proud symbol of the angry and assertive New Queer Politics of the 1990s.

There have been no significant homosexual law reforms since the Sexual Offences Act partially decriminalized male homosexuality in England and Wales exactly twenty-five years ago.

A quarter of a century later, thousands of lesbians and gay men are still sacked from their jobs, convicted for consensual sex, beaten up by queer-bashers, denied custody of their children, and driven to attempt suicide.

The New Queer Politics is about seizing the vocabulary of oppression and transforming it into a language of liberation; appropriating a traditional term of homophobic abuse and redefining it as an expression of pride and defiance. By proclaiming ourselves queer, we subvert the derogatory meaning of the word and undermine its effectiveness as an insult. Responding to taunts with an unexpected 'Yes, I am queer, so what!' deflates the power of the abuse, disarms the abuser, and empowers the intended victim.

Adoption of the Q-word is also a conscious attempt to ditch the politeness of 'gay' in favour of the unpleasantness of 'queer', which reflects more accurately the way we are still perceived and treated by society. Whereas the term 'gay' masks the reality of homophobia, 'queer' forces people to face up to it. Queer is the brutal truth. However, the New Queer Politics is a battle over not just language but also the innovative and challenging ideas that go with it: the celebration of sexual diversity. In a democratic and multicultural society, sexual difference, like racial difference, ought to be respected and valued. Alas, it is not.

Some think queers should present a respectable image and emphasize that we are just the same, and just as good as, heterosexual men and women. But why should we have to lead blameless lives, or be able to pass as hetero, in order to win equal treatment?

Blurring the distinction between heterosexuals and homosexuals is profoundly dishonest. Queers are *not* the same as heterosexuals. Our sexuality gives many of us experiences and perspectives that are different. That difference is no bad thing, and certainly nothing to apologize for or hide.

The New Queer Politics rejects the stereotype of queers as victims. Being lesbian or gay is not just an endless story of discrimination and suffering. It has advantages. Compared with most heterosexuals we tend to have a wider range of sexual partners and to be more sexually adventurous. We've adapted better to safer sex. We find intimacy and openness with new partners easier. We generally have a broader network of friendships which cut across class and race. We're less compulsive about parenthood. We don't need marriage to sustain our relationships. We are likely to stay on friendlier terms with former partners. All these worthwhile aspects make me thankful to be queer.

Much of the lesbian and gay movement has traditionally argued that improving the lives of queers demands our integration into mainstream heterosexual society. The New Queer Politics questions that. Why should queers change to 'fit in' with the dominant sexual values, the morality of the majority? Surely it's prejudiced heterosexuals and homophobic social institutions that ought to change?

Unfortunately, the debate about equal rights is based on the assumption that equality for queers should be on heterosexual terms: extending the legislation governing heterosexuality to lesbians and gay men. That may be a desirable first step, but it has limitations. Heterosexuality is often 'strait-jacketed' by repressive laws, such as those governing prostitution, and sexually explicit imagery, and those that make it an offence against public decency for a couple to have sexual intercourse in lovers'-lane-type locations, when no one has actually been offended. Equality for homosexuals in these areas would merely mean equal victimization. We aim for the removal of all controls on sexual expression between consenting adults.

Likewise, queers do not aspire to equality with regard to the heterosexual age of consent. Yes, there should be safeguards against abuse of children. But the law criminalizes any seventeen-year-old who has sex with a consenting fifteen-year-old. It's just another example of a culture that is negative about sex, which hurts heterosexuals and homosexuals.

The New Queer Politics looks *beyond* equality, and challenges the assumption that lesbian and gay desire is an intrinsically minority sexual orientation. It argues that everyone is potentially homosexual (and heterosexual). While some biological factors may predispose individuals to a sexual preference, all the psychological and anthropological evidence suggests that sexuality is primarily culturally conditioned, and is not rigidly compartmentalized.

None of us is wholly attracted to one sex or the other. We are all a mixture of desires. Some we express, others we repress. 'Queer' emancipation is therefore in the interests of heterosexuals, too. They also are diminished by a system of homophobia that prevents them from relating sexually and emotionally to half of humanity: people of the same sex. In this sense, lesbian and gay rights are about the right of everyone to experience the joys of queer desire without guilt or discrimination.

•

ARTHUR M. SCHLESINGER
1992

'The disunited States'

Arthur M. Schlesinger (1917–), the son of a Harvard historian, himself in turn became associate professor of history at Harvard and then special adviser to President Kennedy. He wrote A Thousand Days, *the history of JFK's presidency, which won him his second Pulitzer Prize. His most recent book,* The Disuniting of America, *his reflections on a multicultural society, is a devastating critique of political correctness, especially Afrocentrism and other manifestations of radical multiculturalism. In this extract, he expounds European ideals as the inspiration that made America the refuge of the oppressed and persecuted of all nations and which made it from the start an experiment in a multiethnic society.*

No doubt Europe has done terrible things, not least to itself. But what culture has not? History, said Edward Gibbon, is little more than the register of the crimes, follies and misfortunes of mankind. The sins of the West are no worse than the sins of Asia or of the Middle East or of Africa.

There remains, however, a crucial difference between the Western tradition and the others. The crimes of the West have produced their own antidotes. They have provoked great movements to end slavery, to raise the status of women, to abolish torture, to combat racism, to defend freedom of inquiry and expression, to advance personal liberty and human rights.

Whatever the particular crimes of Europe, that continent is also the source – the *unique* source – of those liberating ideas of individual liberty, political democracy, the rule of law, human rights and cultural freedom that constitute our most precious legacy and to which most of the world today aspires. These are *European* ideas, not Asian, nor African, nor Middle Eastern ideas, except by adoption.

The freedoms of inquiry and of artistic creation, for example, are Western values. Consider the differing reactions to the case of Salman Rushdie: what the West saw as an intolerable attack on individual freedom the Middle East saw as a proper punishment for an evildoer who had violated the mores of his group. Individualism itself is looked on with abhorrence and dread by collectivist cultures in which loyalty to the group overrides personal goals – cultures that, social scientists say, comprise about 70 percent of the world's population.

There is surely no reason for Western civilization to have guilt trips laid on it by champions of cultures based on despotism, superstition, tribalism and fanaticism. In this regard the Afrocentrists are especially absurd. The West needs no lectures on the superior virtue of those 'sun people' who sustained slavery until Western imperialism abolished it (and, it is reported, sustain it to this day in Mauritania and the Sudan), who still keep women in subjection and cut off their clitorises, who carry out racial persecutions not only against Indians and other Asians but against fellow Africans from the wrong tribes, who show themselves either incapable of operating a democracy or ideologically hostile to the democratic idea, and who in their tyrannies and massacres, their Idi Amins and Boukassas, have stamped with utmost brutality on human rights.

Certainly the European overlords did little enough to prepare Africa for self-government. But democracy would find it hard in any case to put down roots in a tribalist and patrimonial culture that, long before the West invaded Africa, had sacralized the personal authority of chieftains and ordained the submission of the rest. What the West would call corruption is regarded through much of Africa as no more than the prerogative of power. Competitive political parties, an independent judiciary, a free press, the rule of law are alien to African traditions.

It was the French, not the Algerians, who freed Algerian women from the veil (much to the irritation of Frantz Fanon, who regarded deveiling as symbolic rape): as in India it was the British, not the Indians, who ended (or did their best to end) the horrible custom of suttee – widows burning themselves alive on their husbands' funeral pyres. And it was the West, not the non-Western cultures, that launched the crusade to abolish slavery – and in doing so encountered mighty resistance, especially in the Islamic world (where Moslems, with fine impartiality, enslaved whites as well as blacks). Those many brave and humane Africans who are struggling these days for decent societies are animated by Western, not by African, ideals. White guilt can be pushed too far.

The Western commitment to human rights has unquestionably been inter-mittent and imperfect. Yet the ideal remains – and movement toward it has been real, if sporadic. Today it is the *Western* democratic tradition that attracts and empowers people of all continents, creeds and colors. When the Chinese students cried and died for democracy in Tiananmen Square, they brought with them not representations of Confucius or Buddha but a model of the Statue of Liberty.

•

MILAN KUNDERA
1993

'Salman Rushdie'

After publication of his novel The Satanic Verses *Salman Rushdie was the first Western writer to become the victim of a fatwa, a death sentence issued by Ayatollah Khomeini of Iran, who decreed that his book was a blasphemy against the Muslim faith. The fatwa has not been rescinded and Rushdie has lived in hiding under twenty-four-hour-a-day protection by British Special Branch bodyguards since 1989.*

Writers across the world have risen to his defence. One was the Czech novelist Milan Kundera, who fled his country after the 1968 Soviet invasion and took French citizenship. In this essay from Testaments Betrayed, *the author of* The Unbearable Lightness of Being *argues that Rushdie did not blaspheme and did not attack Islam. He wrote a novel.*

Starting with his *Midnight's Children*, which in its time (in 1980) stirred unani-mous admiration, no one in the English-language literary world has denied that Rushdie is one of the most gifted novelists of our day. *The Satanic Verses*, appearing in English in September 1988, was greeted with the attention due a major writer. The book received these tributes with no anticipation of the storm that was to burst some months later, when the Imam Khomeini, the master of Iran, condemned Rushdie to death for blasphemy and sent killers after him on a chase whose end no one can predict.

That happened before the text could be translated. Thus everywhere except in the English-language world, the scandal arrived before the book. In France, the press immediately printed excerpts from the still unpublished novel to show the reasons for the condemnation. Completely normal behaviour, but fatal for a novel. Represented exclusively by its *incriminated* passages, it was, from the beginning, transformed from a work of art into a simple *corpus delicti*.

We should not denigrate literary criticism. Nothing is worse for a writer than to come up against its absence. I am speaking of literary criticism as meditation, as analysis; literary criticism that involves several readings of the book it means to discuss (like great pieces of music we can listen to time and again, great novels too are made for repeated readings); literary criticism that, deaf to the implacable clock of topicality, will readily discuss works a year, thirty years, 300 years old; literary criticism that tries to apprehend the originality of a work in order thus to inscribe it on historical memory. If such meditation did not accompany the history of the novel, we would know nothing today of Dostoyevsky, or Joyce, or Proust. For without it a work is surrendered to completely arbitrary judgements and swift oblivion. Now the Rushdie case shows (if proof is still needed) that such meditation is no longer practised. Imperceptibly, innocently, under the pressure of events, through changes in society and in the press, literary criticism has become a mere (often intelligent, always hasty) *literary news bulletin*.

About *The Satanic Verses*, the literary news was the death sentence on the author. In such a life-and-death situation, it seems almost frivolous to speak of art. What is art, after all, when great principles are under attack? Thus, throughout the world, all discussion concentrated on questions of principle: freedom of expression; the need to defend it (and indeed people did defend it, people protested, people signed petitions); religion; Islam and Christianity; but also this question: does a writer have the moral right to blaspheme and thereby wound believers? And even this problem: suppose Rushdie had attacked Islam only for publicity and to sell his unreadable book?

With mysterious unanimity (I noticed the same reaction everywhere in the world), the men of letters, the intellectuals, the salon initiates, snubbed the novel. They decided to resist all commercial pressure for once, and they refused to read a work they considered simply a piece of sensationalism.

They signed all the petitions for Rushdie, meanwhile deeming it elegant to say, with a supercilious smile: 'His book? Oh no, no, no! I haven't read it.' The politicians took advantage of this curious 'state of disgrace' of a novelist they didn't like. I'll never forget the virtuous impartiality they paraded at the time: 'We condemn Khomeini's verdict. Freedom of expression is sacred to us. But no less do we condemn this attack on religious faith. It is a shameful, contemptible attack that insults the soul of peoples.'

Of course, no one any longer doubted that Rushdie actually had *attacked* Islam, for only the accusation was real; the text of the book no longer mattered, it no longer existed.

A situation unique in history: Rushdie belongs by origin to a Muslim society that, in large part, is still living in the period before the Modern Era. He wrote his book in Europe, in the Modern Era – or, more precisely, at the end of that era.

Just as Iranian Islam was at the time moving away from religious moderation towards a combative theocracy, so, with Rushdie, the history of the novel was moving from the genteel, professorial smile of Thomas Mann to unbridled imagination drawn from the rediscovered wellspring of Rabelaisian humour. The antitheses collided, each in its extreme form.

From this viewpoint, the condemnation of Rushdie can be seen not as a chance event, an aberration, but as the most profound conflict between two eras: theocracy goes to war against the Modern Era and targets its most representative creation: the novel. For Rushdie did not blaspheme. He did not attack Islam. He wrote a novel. But that, for the theocratic mind, is worse than an attack: if a religion is attacked (by a polemic, a blasphemy, a heresy), the guardians of the temple can easily defend it on their own ground, with their own language; but the novel is a different planet for them; a different universe based on a different ontology; an *infernum* where the unique truth is powerless and where satanic ambiguity turns every certainty into enigma.

Let us emphasize this: not attack but ambiguity. The second part of *The Satanic Verses* (the incriminated part, which evokes Mohammed and the origin of Islam) is presented in the novel as a *dream* of Gibreel Farishta's, who then develops the dream into a cheap movie in which he himself will play the role of the archangel. The story is thus *doubly* relativized (first as a dream, then as a *bad* film that will flop) and presented not as a declaration but as a *playful invention*. A disagreeable invention? I say no: it showed me, for the first time in my life, the *poetry* of the Islamic religion, of the Islamic world.

We should stress this: there is no place for hatred in the relativistic universe of the novel: the author who writes a novel in order to settle scores (personal or ideological) is headed for total and certain aesthetic ruin. Ayesha, the girl who leads the hallucinating villagers to their deaths, is of course a monster, but she is also seductive, wondrous (haloed by the butterflies that accompany her everywhere), and often touching; even in the portrait of an émigré imam (an imaginary portrait of Khomeini), there is an almost respectful understanding; Western modernity is viewed with scepticism, never presented as superior to Oriental archaism; the novel 'historically and psychologically explores' sacred old texts, but it also shows how much they are *degraded* by TV, advertising, the entertainment industry; and the left-wing characters, who deplore the frivolity of this modern world – do they at least enjoy the author's full sympathy? No indeed, they are miserably ridiculous, and as frivolous as the frivolity around them; no one is right and no one entirely wrong in the immense *carnival of relativity* that is this work.

Therefore, with *The Satanic Verses*, the art of the novel as such is incriminated. That is why, in this whole sad story, the saddest thing is not Khomeini's verdict (which proceeds from a logic that is atrocious but consistent); rather, it is Europe's incapacity to defend and explain (explain patiently to itself and to others) that most European of the arts, the art of the novel; in other words, to explain and defend its own culture. The 'children of the novel' have abandoned the art that shaped them. Europe, the 'society of the novel', has abandoned its own self.

It does not surprise me that the Sorbonne theologians, the sixteenth-century ideological police who kindled so many stakes, should have made life so hard for Rabelais, forcing him often to flee and hide. What seems to me far more amazing and admirable is the protection provided him by the powerful men of his time, Cardinal du Bellay, for instance, and Cardinal Odet, and above all François I, the king of France. Were they seeking to defend principles? Freedom of expression? Human rights? They had a better motive: they loved literature and the arts.

I see no Cardinal du Bellay, no François I, in today's Europe. But is Europe still Europe? Is it still 'the society of the novel'? In other words, is it still living in the Modern Era? Or is it already moving into another era, as yet unnamed, for which its arts are no longer of much importance? If that is so, why be surprised that Europe was not disturbed beyond measure when, for the first time in its history, the art of the novel – *Europe's* art *par excellence* – was condemned to death? In this new age, after the Modern Era, has not the novel for some time already been living on death row?

•

DENNIS POTTER
1993

'The BBC'

The dramatist Dennis Potter (1935–94) was the most controversial playwright of his generation. He constantly tilted at convention in his plays for television, which included Brimstone and Treacle, The Singing Detective, Pennies from Heaven *and* Lipstick on Your Collar, *and challenged the authorities at the BBC to broadcast them.*

The most important speech of the year for the television industry is the James MacTaggart Memorial Lecture at the Edinburgh Film Festival. It was delivered in 1993, when he knew he was dying, by Dennis Potter. He used the occasion of addressing the television establishment to attack Rupert Murdoch, the newspaper and television mogul, and John Birt, director-general of the BBC.

Television could scarcely resist calling itself 'a window on the world', as it did in its early days, even using the subtitle on *Panorama*. But windows have frames, and the frames are part of a structure that has already been built. I have said, many years ago, that on the television screen it is often when the set is switched off that it actually picks up a direct or true reflection of its viewers, subdued into a glimmer on its dull grey tube. When the set is on, alive with images, the window analogy persists because, away from the expensive brilliance and often genuine sophistication of title sequences, logos and the commercials, most of television, most TV journalism, most of its decidedly over-long news programmes, all of its proliferating soaps, most of its dramas, pretend or assume or wish that the picture in the frame – adjusted for a laugh, a snigger, a gasp or a tear – is showing us things as they really are.

So-called naturalism is by far and away the dominant mode, and easily the most characteristic syntax of television grammar. But one of the troubles of supposedly showing things-as-they-really-are (the window problem) is how difficult it then becomes in the same grammar not to make people feel deep in their souls that this is also more or less the way things have to be. Hence the shock-horror-probe patterns, the inflated status of those bus conductors called news readers, the odd and only temporarily effective splashes of sensational indignation, the random violence, the unmediated sexuality, and the presence of critics who almost uniformly perceive their function to be joke-makers and snide-mongers. Who can blame them?

Our television has been ripped apart and falteringly reassembled by politicians who believe that value is a monetary term only, and that a cost-accountant is thereby the most suitable adjudicator of what we can and cannot see on our screens. And these accountants or their near clones are employed by new kinds of media owners who try to gobble up everything in their path. We must protect ourselves and our democracy, first by properly exercising the cross-ownership provisions currently in place, and then by erecting further checks and balances against dangerous concentrations of the media power which plays such a large part in our lives. No individual, group or company should be allowed to own more than one daily, one evening and one weekly newspaper. No newspaper should be allowed to own a television station, and vice versa. A simple act of public hygiene, tempering abuse, widening choice, and maybe even returning broadcasting to its makers.

The political pressures from market-obsessed radicals, and the huckster atmosphere that follows, have by degrees, and in confused self-defence, drawn the BBC so heavily into the dogma-coated discourses of so-called 'market efficiency' that in the end it might lose clear sight of why it, the BBC, is there in the first place.

I fear the time is near when we must save not the BBC from itself but public service broadcasting from the BBC. The old Titan should spawn smaller and more nimble offspring if its present controllers cannot be removed. Why not think about it anyway? Why not separate radio from television? Why not let BBC2 be a separate public service broadcaster? Let us begin to consider afresh how the thousands of millions of pounds of licence money could be apportioned between two, three or four successors to the currently misled Corporation. One of the successors could certainly be a publishing or commissioning authority on the model of Channel 4 . . .

Thirty years ago, under the personal pressures of whatever guilt, whatever shame and whatever remaining shard of idealism, I found or I made up what I may unwisely have termed a sense of vocation. I have it still. It was born, of course, from the already aborted dream of a common culture which has long since been zapped into glistening fragments by those who are now the real, if not always recognized, occupying powers of our culture. Look in the pink pages and see their mesh of connections. Open the *Sun* and measure their aspirations. Put Rupert Murdoch on public trial and televise every single second of it. Show us who is abusing us, and why. Ask your public library – if there is one left – to file the television franchise applications on the shelf hitherto kept for Fantasy, Astrology and Crime bracket Bizarre bracket.

I was exceptionally fortunate to begin my career in television at a time when the BBC was so infuriatingly confident about what public service broadcasting meant that the question itself was not even on what would now be called the agenda. The then ITV companies shared much more of this ethos than they were then willing to acknowledge. Our profession was then mostly filled with men and women who mostly cared about the programmes rather than the dividend. And the venomous hostilities of the small minority who are the political right – before its wholly ideological transformation into the type of venal, wet-mouthed radicalism which can even assert without a hint of shame that 'there is no such thing as society' – before those people had yet launched their poisoned arrows. Clunk! they go. Clunk! Clunk! And lo and behold we have in the fullness of such darkness sent unto us a Director-General who bares his chest to receive these arrows, a St Sebastian eager for their punishing stings.

The world has turned upside-down. The BBC is under governors who seem incapable of performing the public trust that is invested in them, under a Chairman who seems to believe he is heading a private fiefdom, and under a Chief Executive who must somehow or other have swallowed whole and unsalted the kind of humbug-punctuated pre-privatization manual which is being forced on British Rail or British Coal.

•

WILL HUTTON
1995

'The State We're In'

Only rarely does a political polemic feature in the hardback bestseller list for six months but The State We're In, *Will Hutton's impassioned critique of Thatcherism, was the surprise bestseller of 1995. Hutton obviously expressed the sense of rising national disquiet which swept the Tories from power two years later when Tony Blair's New Labour won the 1997 general election.*

Hutton, then economics editor of the Guardian, *started his career as a stockbroker before becoming economics editor of BBC2's* Newsnight. *He is now editor of the* Observer. *This extract is from his opening chapter.*

The British are accustomed to success. This is the world's oldest democracy. Britain built an empire, launched the Industrial Revolution and was on the winning side in the twentieth century's two world wars. The British believe that their civilization is admired all over the world. A Briton does not boast openly, but is possessed of an inner faith that he or she is special. To be born in these islands is still seen as a privilege.

Yet in the last decade of the twentieth century the record of success is tarnished and any sense of privilege is evaporating. The country's great industrial cities are decaying and listless, while in the new industries and technologies Britain is barely represented. Even its unique economic asset, the City of London, is sullied by malpractice and a reputation for commercial misjudgement.

The country is an inveterate consumer, but the rise in consumption has done little for indigenous industry. Production has stagnated while the inexorable tide of imports has steadily outpaced the growth of exports. No longer can the economy, with its ageing and inadequate stock of factories, machines and industrial infrastructure provide work for all those who want it.

For two decades unemployment has been a grim fact of British life, bearing particularly hard on men. As well as those included in the official count who want work and can't find it, there are millions more who are marginalized – prematurely retired or living off inadequate savings or sickness benefit. One in four of the country's males of working age is now either officially unemployed or idle, with incalculable consequences for our well-being and social cohesion. The numbers living in poverty have grown to awesome proportions, and the signs of social stress – from family breakdown to the growth of crime – mount almost daily.

As the economy weakens the country's international prestige is waning. Its capacity to cling on to its privileged position in the world pecking order – as a nuclear power with a permanent seat on the UN Security Council and at the centre of a web of special relationships with the US, Europe and the Commonwealth – is plainly ebbing . . .

Above all, we live in a new world of us and them. The sense of belonging to a successful national project has all but disappeared. Average living standards may have risen but have not generated a sense of well-being; if anything there is more discontent because the gains have been spread so unevenly and are felt to be so evanescent. The country is increasingly divided against itself, with an arrogant officer class apparently indifferent to the other ranks it commands. This privileged class is favoured with education, jobs, housing and pensions. At the other end of the scale more and more people discover they are the new working poor, or live off the state in semi-poverty. Their paths out of this situation are closing down as the world in which they are trapped becomes meaner, harder and more corrupting. In between there are growing numbers of people who are insecure, fearful for their jobs in an age of permanent 'down-sizing', 'cost-cutting' and 'casualization' and ever more worried about their ability to maintain a decent standard of living.

The rot starts at the top. The political system is malfunctioning, bringing politicians and civil servants into disrepute and discrediting the very notion of the public realm in which national renewal might be attempted. Instead the state is the handmaiden of the process of loss. The proud House of Commons regards itself as the cockpit of the nation, but it is no more than the creature of the government of the day. Once the courtesies of a nineteenth-century debating chamber have been observed, the government can make laws almost at will.

Yet this is only the tip of the iceberg. An unwritten constitution organized around the principle that the law is whatever the monarch assents to in Parliament has no clear democratic rules. Monarchical power has passed in effect to the majority party in the House of Commons. There are no limits to the centre's capacity to take power away from the regions and local authorities. The executive branch is held only nominally accountable to Parliament. There is no formal independence of the judiciary. There is no codified bill of rights. There is no presumption that the activity of the state should be open and transparent. There are no rules about the funding of political parties or the giving of honours. There aren't even rules governing the working of the House itself; there is 'custom and practice', but no formal code. The entire public realm can easily be captured by the partisans of the majority party in the House of Commons and its supporters outside.

The only formal check on executive power is the notion of a government-in-waiting – Her Majesty's Opposition – but four successive Conservative election victories have devalued even that threat. The Conservative Party has found itself in charge of a ruleless state, handed down virtually intact from the settlement of 1688 with universal suffrage bolted on, and has been willing to toss aside even unwritten custom and practice in pursuit of its objectives. In some respects the concentration and centralization of power resembles that of a one-party state.

But the incapacity of the constitution to offer any check to discretionary executive government has even corrupted the Conservative Party, with the contagion spreading to the state. Honours are routinely awarded to party contributors; funds are accepted from foreign donors of questionable character and motive in return for undeclared favours; defence contracts and the flotation of privatized public utilities are awarded to government supporters in industry and the City. What has been constructed in Britain, using the ancient and unfettered state, is a form of Conservative *hegemony* in the literal meaning of that word: a system of supremacy over others.

ROBERT HARRIS
1996

'Her Royal Highness'

After the Princess of Wales was divorced from Prince Charles, the Queen decided that she would no longer be styled Her Royal Highness. A strict interpretation of the decision required that she curtsy to her two young sons or to the minor royals. Robert Harris derided the absurdity of the decision in his weekly column for the Sunday Times.

One day, I guess, we'll know the full story of why the Queen decided to deny the style 'Her Royal Highness' to the Princess of Wales. We shall discover whether it was at Prince Philip's urging – as some rumours suggest – or Prince Charles's, or whether it was the Queen's own decision. For the moment it is enough to recognize that it was a disaster, yet another in the long catalogue of self-inflicted injuries which sometimes make one wonder whether Sir Robert Fellowes, the Queen's private secretary and closest adviser, isn't actually a secret republican.

All week I have been trying to put my finger on what it is about this business that is so peculiarly unpleasant. Even people who don't like Diana – who find her neurotic and publicity-hungry – seem to be uneasy about what's been done to her. Why, they wonder, does someone like HRH Princess Michael of Kent – a Catholic foreign divorcée, whose father was an officer in the SS – enjoy a status denied to the mother of the future king?

But there is more to it than mere unfairness. What really stinks is the obsession with status and protocol which the whole affair reveals, a canker which obviously infects the inner circle of the royal family almost completely. They really do think, apparently – they *must* think, otherwise why did they do it? – that all this stuff about HRHs, all this palaver about who precisely is supposed to bow and curtsy to whom, is *important*.

Prince Charles has claimed to find particular resonance in the lament of Shakespeare's *Henry V* (so much so that he recently recorded it on CD):

What infinite heart's ease
Must kings neglect, that private men enjoy!
And what have kings that privates have not too,
Save ceremony, save general ceremony?

But when push comes to shove, when separation turns to divorce, who is seen to be the most anxious to preserve his 'general ceremony' and status, even at the expense of his former wife? Why, none other than our dear old Prince of Wales, a man who has raised self-pity and hypocrisy to undreamt-of, indeed, to literally regal levels.

If this unseemly business has done nothing else, it has at least focused attention on just how many of these wretched HRHs there are for us to bow and scrape to. Setting to one side the Queen and the Queen Mother, who are both styled 'Her Majesty', there are no fewer than eighteen persons with the handle HRH, including the Duke and Duchess of Gloucester, the Duke and Duchess of Kent, the children of the Duke of York, and the elderly Princess Alice ('widow of the uncle of Her Majesty', as *Who's Who* puts it). When and if Prince Edward marries, his wife will also be HRH, and so will all their children. Poor old Diana had better get back to that gym: there seems no end to the amount of bobbing up and down she'll have to do the next time the family gets together. The strain on her calf muscles will be frightful.

Does any of this matter? Should we be concerned that the United States, a country with a population of a quarter of a billion, has just one president and commander-in-chief, while Britain, with a population of 58 million, supports this Himalayan range of highnesses? I cannot prove it, but somehow in my bones I feel it *does* matter, that all this snobbery and deference is, in its way, a symptom of national decline and decadence. One could almost frame it as a law, like Parkinson's or Gresham's: that a nation's preoccupation with titles and protocol is in inverse proportion to the importance of the country concerned.

Britain has not always been like this. If we take what was arguably our greatest half-century, 1840–1890, when British power, manufacturing, inventiveness and prestige were at their zenith, what is striking is the absence of deference – the scorn, almost, with which the royal family and all official flummery were treated. Sir Robert Peel spoke warmly of 'the distinction of an unadorned name', while Joseph Chamberlain, the first great industrialist-turned-politician, regarded the monarchy as an anachronism: 'I do not feel any great horror at the idea of the possible establishment of a republic in our country. I am quite certain that sooner or later it will come.'

There was nothing unpatriotic about this – certainly nobody could accuse Chamberlain, the most vociferous imperialist of his day, of not loving his country. But patriotism in those days was not bound up with homage. On the contrary: elaborate uniforms, fancy titles and royal pretensions were seen as essentially foreign and pathetic – the hot air with which less successful nations had to pump themselves up. The words of Isambard Kingdom Brunel, one of the greatest of all Victorians, ring even more loudly today than when he uttered them 140 years ago: 'I disapprove strongly of any introduction into England of the system of distinctions conferred by government upon individuals, whether engaged in professions, arts, or manufactures, whose merits can be so much better and more surely marked by public opinion.'

But then we come to our own, far less successful century, and what do we find? The classic story of boom to bust in two or three generations, as the descendants of the Victorians began devising and bestowing upon themselves a Ruritanian array of knighthoods, peerages and medals, usually in the name either of some outdated chivalrous order, or of a British Empire already slipping rapidly into decline. Shadow has replaced substance, ritual has taken over from reality.

Sometimes I sit and read the newspapers and think that I must be going mad. Surely it cannot be the case – tell me I am hallucinating – that in the final five years of the twentieth century, the Conservative and Unionist party, led by a man who proclaims his belief in a 'classless society', seriously intends to campaign for the hereditary principle being retained in the House of Lords? Yet it is! Not only that: Tory strategists apparently plan to put it at the heart of their manifesto. They believe it will be a 'vote-winner'.

And then, a few days later, in the same newspapers, I read that the mother of the heir to the throne is now technically required to curtsy to her own children, and also to various obscure royal dukes and duchesses I wouldn't recognize if they strolled in through my front door. And again, I think this must be a dream – a satire of some sort. But no: again, this is true! This is the state our country has reached in 1996.

And if these two stories are true, what reason is there to disbelieve a third? A report by young Treasury civil servants, leaked to the Opposition, has predicted that the British economy, by 2015, will have been overtaken by India, Brazil, Indonesia and Thailand, with Mexico and South Korea close behind.

This is no more improbable than the other two reports. Indeed, I don't think it's stretching things too far to suggest that they may be connected. Britain has become a bizarre country. Its rituals and traditions are inexplicable not only to most foreigners, but increasingly to a lot of the natives, too. We seem to have made a fetish of the past. The clarity of thought and robust individualism of earlier times have degenerated into absurd ritual and embarrassing obsequiousness. We are as curious as any jungle tribe, a suitable case for anthropological study.

Of course this affects the sort of people we are, which in turn shapes the nature of our democracy and our economy. How could it not be so? This is the significance of the royal divorce and the row over the Princess of Wales's style. Like a lightning flash over a darkened landscape, it has briefly illuminated our society, giving us a glimpse of the values that not only permeate our monarchy, but permeate our state.

•

MELANIE PHILLIPS
1996

'The de-education of Britain'

All Must Have Prizes, *the indictment of the flight from literacy in British education by the* Observer *columnist Melanie Phillips, won the 1996 Orwell Prize for Journalism. Britain would be courting disaster if her questions were fudged, said Professor Michael Barber, who became special adviser to the Secretary for Education in the 1997 Labour government. The book challenged the complacency and prejudice of educationalists, said Chris Woodhead, chief inspector of schools. This extract is from the opening chapter.*

The University of Oxford is one of the most prestigious universities in the world. Its undergraduates are some of the brightest in Britain and their A-level grades are among the highest. One might imagine, therefore, that these students had been educated.

In December 1993, however, Dr Richard Sheppard, a tutor in German at Oxford, expressed his despair at the standard of knowledge among undergraduates studying for their degrees. Students, he observed, could now only speak pidgin German. One candidate from an independent school didn't know about passive verb forms or past participles, and had never learned about the genders of German nouns or plural forms. One student spent the three years of his degree unable to learn that the word order in German was not a moveable feast and that word endings were not optional extras. At another university, he reported, a second year student with a B grade at A-level had demonstrated *after* a syntax revision course that he still didn't know the genders of common nouns, the basic rules of German orthography and punctuation, noun and adjectival endings, common strong verb forms, the passive, how to translate 'on' followed by a date from the calendar, what common prepositions took what cases and the position of verbs in subordinate clauses: 'the stuff', lamented Sheppard, 'of O-levels'. Nor was the general knowledge of undergraduates any better. At interviews with prospective candidates from 1991–3, he had had to explain who Homer was twice, what Buchenwald was three times and why Good Friday was not without significance for Western civilization . . .

Many university dons are in a state of utter despair about the low levels of knowledge presented by the young people turning up to read for their degrees. Alarm about education standards is by no means confined, however, to the universities. It extends throughout the education system and is reinforced almost with every official report that is published. There is evidence that something more significant and far-reaching has been happening than any politician has yet managed to identify, let alone address – and that it extends far beyond education.

There is now a yawning gap between the standards reached by British school-children and their counterparts in Europe or Japan. A report by the National Institute of Economic and Social Research, published in 1995, found that the bottom 40 per cent of English thirteen-year-olds lagged two years behind their German counterparts, while fewer than 30 per cent of Britain's workforce had vocational qualifications, compared to more than 60 per cent in Germany. In 1990–91, the proportion of sixteen-year-olds gaining the equivalent of three GCSE grades between A and C in maths, the national language and one science was 62 per cent in Germany, 66 per cent in France, 50 per cent in Japan and 27 per cent in England. In 1990, the proportion of young people obtaining a comparable school qualification at eighteen was 68 per cent in Germany, 48 per cent in France, 80 per cent in Japan and 29 per cent in England.

There is constant concern about standards of literacy and numeracy among the population at large. Employers consistently complain that many job applicants cannot even write a correctly spelled and punctuated letter. How can it be, in a modern, advanced economy which has had universal education since 1944, that so many of its citizens, including those who have been 'well educated', are so illiterate?

What's more, the problems appear to have been getting steadily worse. In 1995, secondary school head teachers reported a sharp and accelerating drop in standards, particularly in reading, among eleven-year-old pupils coming up from the primary schools. Certainly, the National Curriculum tests have revealed significant problems in the primary schools, particularly in the more senior classes. While a core of about 20 per cent of seven-year-olds have failed to reach the standard for their age since the first of these tests for their age group was held in 1991, eleven-year-olds have fared worse. The first tests for eleven-year-olds held in 1995 revealed that more than half were not up to scratch in English or maths. The poor results for eleven-year-olds produced a flood of excuses from primary teachers. The government drew comfort from the fact that the results at the ages of seven and fourteen had been better. But a report by the School Curriculum and Assessment Authority suggested that the malaise in education was very much deeper.

The report revealed that some teachers who marked the 1995 English tests for fourteen-year-olds had such a poor knowledge of Shakespeare's plays themselves that they gave pupils the wrong grades. Some markers were confused about who were Montagues and who were Capulets in *Romeo and Juliet*, marking wrong answers as right. Some gave pupils marks for naming figures of speech which were patent gobbledegook. One marker, for example, ticked one pupil's script when she wrote that Romeo used 'Simples and Metfords' instead of similes and metaphors. How can it possibly have come about that current or former English teachers can themselves be so ignorant of Shakespeare's plays – which, if they've forgotten, they only have to re-read before marking any scripts – and so indifferent to rank gibberish? What can be happening to British society?

Whatever reservations might be expressed about the curriculum tests, which have after all taken time to bed down, the evidence is overwhelming that standards throughout the education system, from infant classes right through to degree level, give cause for the most intense concern. Statistics are an erratic guide to any deterioration, since changes in criteria or collection methods make comparisons notoriously unreliable. What can be said with confidence, however, is that the standard of knowledge of many thousands of schoolchildren, adults and even teachers is lamentable. Reports by the national education inspectors identify about 30 per cent of lessons as unsatisfactory. But even 'satisfactory', by the inspectors' standards, is actually pretty mediocre. The unpalatable fact is that about two-thirds of British schools simply aren't good enough. There *are* good schools and good teachers; but they are fighting a cultural tide that washes well beyond the shores of their schools.

The rot sets in at primary school level and runs through the system. In 1990, a survey of 500 pupils in Cheshire primary schools found that one-fifth of them had difficulty forming their letters and writing legibly. But the difficulty wasn't confined to the children. Rhona Stainthorp, lecturer in education at Reading University, said: 'Some of our students have never been taught cursive script at school themselves, and they are very uncertain about it. We laid on handwriting workshops this term, but nobody turned up.' When even trainee teachers can't do joined-up writing, clearly something profound and disturbing has happened.

•

CHARLES MOORE
1996

'Europe'

When Britain was first considering joining the European Common Market (now the European Union), the Labour leader Hugh Gaitskell said it would mean the end of Britain as an independent European state: 'It means the end of a thousand years of history.' Since then 'Europe' has been the profoundest issue in British politics. It has divided the nation and divided the political parties.

By 1996 the Conservative Party, under the prime minister John Major, was so riven by the debate on Europe that it was effectively split into two rival camps and the split contributed significantly to the rout of the Tories in the 1997 general election. Both The Times *and the* Daily Telegraph, *the two newspapers most influential among Tory MPs, were in the Euro-sceptic camp. Charles Moore, editor of the* Telegraph, *set out his objections in this article published after the European Court ordered the British government to adopt a Brussels directive on the forty-eight-hour week. Whether judged in economic, political, legal, cultural or constitutional terms, it was a hostile ruling, a crushing defeat of Major's European policy, Moore declared in an accompanying leader.*

For someone of my generation, born in the mid-1950s, 'Europe' was not the romantically powerful ideal that it was for many who remembered the Second World War, but it was the apparently sensible course, the way of the future. The first vote I ever cast was in the 1975 referendum which confirmed Britain's membership of what was then the EEC. My father told me that wine would be cheaper if we stayed in (broadly speaking, he was right), and that was a serious incentive.

But my biggest reason for voting 'yes' was a vague one. It was that to vote 'no' was backward-looking or timorous or vainglorious. I was never a Euro-enthusiast, but I wanted my country to have a closer, more friendly relationship with France and Germany. Being a student, I was uninterested in arguments about open markets, but so far as I listened to them, I agreed with them. Pretty girls wore T-shirts that said 'Europe or bust', which seemed quite daring at the time. Going 'into Europe' represented a freer, more open approach to life than staying out of it. I think that is how most of my contemporaries felt, and voted.

When the referendum results came in, the Orkneys and Shetland, so far as I remember, were the only places where 'no' was in the majority. I felt a twinge of admiration for them which I couldn't quite explain at the time, but the fact that the remotest region stood alone served to confirm the reason the rest of us had voted 'yes'. To vote 'no' was to push yourself to the margin. The cost of voting 'yes' also seemed low, and not only because we were ratifying something that had already happened. It might be true that we were voting to undermine parliamentary sovereignty, but that did not seem too worrying since we believed (and were assured) that real power would stay with the British Parliament. Besides, there were no immediate proposals, except in agriculture and fishing, which changed anyone's life very much.

For quite a long time after the referendum Europe became a respectable but boring cause, and few of us paid much attention to it. Even the Single European Act of 1986 passed fairly quietly through a House of Commons lulled to sleep by the idea that these measures would simply improve market efficiency.

The Spectator, which I was editing at that time, was the only national publication to oppose the Act. By 1993, *all* the Conservative papers were against the Maastricht Treaty. It was in that period that feelings began to change. The overthrow of Mrs Thatcher in 1990 seemed at the time to mark the triumph of Euro-enthusiasm. In retrospect, it looks like its last clear victory.

In the summer of 1992, when I was writing weekly political columns for this paper and attacking British membership of the ERM, something happened which I had never known before, and have never seen since. I started to receive letters from members of the general public about economics. The effects of the policy were so clear, and so damaging, that people got interested and got angry. Thousands of them were being ruined and they wanted to know why. Ever since then, people have known that 'Europe' matters, and it is only when something does matter directly to them that people start to think about it.

Over these years, I often heard Euro-sceptics criticized on the grounds that, although they might talk about reform of the EEC, what they *really* wanted was to get out. In most cases, certainly in my own, the criticism was misplaced. We wanted what most centre-Right British politicians said they wanted – a politically friendly zone which provided for and policed the free movement of people, goods and services. Where we differed from, say, Mr Major, was not in what we wanted, but in what we thought we were getting. The ERM and Maastricht proved that things were not 'coming our way'.

The thought of getting out was always a frightening one, rather as the thought of the non-existence of God must be to someone whose religious faith is wavering or the thought of divorce must be to the man who gradually comes to see that he is not very happily married. It was too much to contemplate, too absolute, too final. Surely there must be something short of this, some way of continuing to go to church without paying much attention, some means of staying together for the sake of the children?

To me, at least, getting out still is frightening. I think it might give too much power to people who really do hate foreigners, or believe in a siege economy. 'Ourselves alone' is a slogan that makes me uneasy, even when it is not written in Irish. I fear our getting out might be part of a more general crisis for the EU in which peaceful habits of doing political business come under unbearable strain. I guess that, in the short term, several foreign investors in Britain would panic, and some businesses would go bust. I would still like to find an accommodation.

What has changed, though, is the balance of the argument. It has come to resemble those opinion polls about the 'fear factor' if Labour were to win the election: they now report an even greater fear at the idea that the Tories might win yet again. In the same way, getting out of Europe now looks less terrifying than going deeper in.

Different incidents trigger this thought in different minds. For some, it is the fact that we mayn't catch our own fish. For others, it is the regulations which Christopher Booker so painstakingly exposes in the *Sunday Telegraph*. It may be the beef cull. It may be the prospect of the abolition of the pound. It may be the idea that a foreign court can tell us how many hours we must work. The point is that these things make us feel less good about our country – less free and less proud. It adds up to this – we don't want any more; come to think of it, we want a good deal less.

The onus is now on the supporters of our membership to explain what is good about all these things, for they can no longer pretend that nothing serious is happening. I don't hear it. I hear a great deal of complaint about how vile the Euro-sceptics are, but I don't hear why what Helmut Kohl and Jacques Santer and the rest want is wonderful. After all, it is no longer the case that the continental economies are the models we need to follow. Our unemployment fell again yesterday and will probably go below 2 million next month; their unemployment rises. We are now the teacher, they the pupils.

British politicians still do not seem to understand what is happening. They have not adjusted to the change of feeling. They have their own party reasons for wanting the debate to go quiet. But it won't, because it can't, because Europe is now taking charge. That, it seems to me, is what we – most British people – really do not want. We shall vote for the first party that we believe will stop it.

●

PAUL FOOT
1996

'The public school flogger'

At Shrewsbury and Bradfield Anthony Chenevix-Trench was one of the most distinguished
headmasters in Britain. His career culminated in the glittering prize of Eton. Yet as the
radical journalist Paul Foot revealed when a biography of Chenevix-Trench by Mark Peel
was published in 1996, the headmaster who charmed parents was a drunkard and a child
abuser with a lust for flogging young boys – though he was not found out until he started
beating the sons of dukes and earls and viscounts. He was sacked from Eton but was still
able to become headmaster at Fettes.

It's rare to be able to test a book against one's own direct experience of its
subject-matter. I therefore make full use of mine, as a pupil at Shrewsbury
School in the fifties. In his Foreword to a new biography of Anthony
Chenevix-Trench, one-time headmaster of Eton, Sir William Gladstone writes
that Trench's 'interest was in drawing out the best from boys as individuals'.
Another interest, not mentioned by Sir William, lay in drawing down the
underpants of boys – as individuals – before ordering them to lie on his sofa
while he spanked their bare buttocks. In his Introduction, the author Mark
Peel pays tribute to Trench's 'common touch' without referring to his most
common touch of all: the sensuous fingering of his pupils' buttocks before
and during the interminable beatings.

At Shrewsbury, I was one of Trench's geese – he was my housemaster
from 1952 to 1955. When I first encountered him I was fourteen, underdeveloped, and utterly bored with the way I was being taught classics. Trench
closely followed reports from the classroom and suggested I could improve
my performance by regular visits to his study with my prepared work. He
seemed to have endless time for these encounters, and the reason quickly
became clear. He announced that if there were fewer than three mistakes in
the work, I would get a piece of chocolate; if more than three mistakes, a
beating. Beating on the backside with a cane was a common practice in the
house, but it was usually inflicted by senior boys on their juniors. A beating
by the housemaster was a serious and painful business. The prospect drove
me to approach some of the older Greek scholars in the house, who, in
solidarity with my predicament, helped all they could. The standard of my
Greek translations improved miraculously, but three mistakes could usually

be found. A beating was certain, but then, to my relief, the prospect of the cane diminished. Trench explained that I had a 'choice': the cane, with trousers on; or the strap, with trousers off. There was no choice, really, though Trench enormously enjoyed watching me make it.

When the relatively painless strap was nominated, he became extremely cheerful and excited. Clapping his hands in joyful anticipation, he would lead me out of the study to his upstairs sitting-room on the 'private side' of the house, where he locked the door, pulled down my trousers and pants, lowered me on to his sofa and laid into me with his belt. The blows hardly hurt at all, though the humiliation was excruciating. Trench was assaulting boys in his charge for one reason only: his own sexual gratification.

We boys all knew as much, and so, I suspect, did several other members of staff – but not the parents. The key to Trench's rise in the public schools was his mastery of public relations. He spent hours gushing to parents about the brilliance, wit and sporting prowess of their sons. The parents, kept in the dark by that instinctive solidarity with which adolescents protect each other against the adult world, adored him. Not one of us would have dreamt of 'sneaking' on Trench to our parents or to any other adult. In 1955, to the intense relief of everyone in School House, Trench, then only thirty-six, was appointed headmaster of Bradfield. His new position gave him even more power to indulge what Peel calls his 'foibles'. He won universal praise as a headmaster who continued to teach, but he carefully picked classes of fourteen-year-olds whom he could invite to his study for extra-curricular supervision.

After reading this book, I telephoned David Blackie, who now runs a computer language course in Bedfordshire, and who was unlucky enough to be patronized by Trench at Bradfield in the early sixties. Blackie is quoted by Peel as criticizing Trench's 'penchant for unrestricted and unsupervised corporal punishment of adolescent boys'. Our long conversation took us back more than three decades to the Trench study, and those tortuous conversations about punishment alternatives. 'I was once beaten on the marital bed,' Blackie reported in disgust. He reminded me of something I'd forgotten: Trench's habit of insisting before delivering each blow that his victim must not contract his buttocks in anticipation. 'Just relax' was the persistent growl from the great educationalist.

David Blackie was beaten over and over again during nocturnal visits to the headmaster's house to 'go over' his classical compositions. He was certainly not the only one at Bradfield who got the Trench treatment. Yet at Bradfield, too, there was universal ignorance of the abuse among parents and authorities. Sir Eric Faulkner, later chairman of Lloyds Bank, who sat on

456 Paul Foot: 'The public school flogger'

Bradfield's council and in 1964 became warden, is quoted here as saying: 'We were never worried by his use of corporal punishment.' Consequently, Peel records, the fact that Trench was a prolific and consistent abuser of young boys played no part in the discussions which shot him, in 1963, to the highest pinnacle of his profession: the headmastership of Eton.

The tone and style of Peel's book are admirably established in its opening sentence: 'As Britain awoke from the long, hard winter of 1962–3 the news that Anthony Chenevix-Trench had been appointed headmaster of Eton brought a spring to the step of all those who bemoaned the growing sense of drift and complacency in the country.' Never mind that Trench had been a crusted Tory ever since, at the age of nineteen, he had campaigned for Quintin Hogg in the 'appeasement' by-election in Oxford in 1938. Never mind that drift and complacency were two of Trench's most enduring characteristics. The arch-flogger, arch-creep and arch-hypocrite had somehow established himself as a wonderful teacher (which he was not: in the classroom as elsewhere he was discursive, reckless and self-obsessed) and a reformer (which he wasn't either). He was sycophantic enough to his superiors to survive for a long time at Eton. Even his increasing dependence on alcohol could have been overlooked in an environment where drunkenness was generally considered a sign of manliness. Only one thing cut short his career at Eton: the buttocks problem.

Again and again, his lust for flogging upset the delicate balance of control at Eton, where corporal punishment, though central to the culture, was traditionally a matter for housemasters and senior boys. The more difficult he found his job (he was a hopeless administrator), the more Trench lashed out at boys' bottoms. These boys were not, as at Shrewsbury and Bradfield, the sons of mere Northern manufacturers or Home Counties bourgeoisie. Their fathers were dukes, earls and viscounts who were not at all opposed to corporal punishment but who expected a modicum of consistency in its application to their own sons. When Trench turned down the advice of head boy James Mackay and flogged a couple of seniors for staying out late, Mackay told his father, the Earl of Inchcape. Rough treatment of the appropriately-named Viscount Brocas caused dismay in the household of his father, Earl Jellicoe. I recall the outraged indignation of the young Hume Shawcross, son of Lord Shawcross, who travelled to the offices of *Private Eye* to spill the beans. Also expelled was Caspar, son of Ann Fleming, whose influence in high society was legendary. In White's and Brooks's and at the Carlton the conversation turned invariably to 'the flogger they've got in charge of Eton'. There was only one thing for it: the bounder had to go.

•

MERRICK
1996

'Battle for the Trees'

The building of a bypass round the historic market town of Newbury in 1996 became the highpoint of the campaigns by eco-activists against the building of more and more new roads. The force of their argument, that new roads simply multiply traffic and destroy the countryside, was accepted even by supporters of the Conservative government which had sanctioned the bypass. Newbury became the last stand not of the protesters but of the roads lobby.

Between January and April protesters set up twenty-eight camps at Newbury and the drama of the treetops was seen nightly on TV news bulletins.

One of the protesters was Merrick who described why he went to Newbury in his booklet Battle for the Trees, *which is printed here using his own text indentations. At the front of his book he reproduced a fly poster from a Newbury wall, which prefaces this extract.*

We, the Road Protesters, have come to Newbury to do everything peacefully we can to stop the construction of the Newbury bypass. We may look different, our ways and lifestyle may seem strange, but we are all here because we love the countryside of merry England. We cannot sit back and let our heritage be destroyed in a fit of political madness. In the true spirit of England, in the true spirit of our mythic heroes, King Arthur and Robyn Hood, we are prepared to stand up for truth and justice.

We care enough to risk losing what little we have. We care enough to risk living outside in the depths of winter. We care enough to risk our own safety in the tree tops. We may seem like outlaws in the forest but the truth is that we are on your side. Not one of us would deny that Newbury has a horrific traffic problem, but we beg to differ on the proposed solution.

You, the people of Newbury, are the guardians of a noble heritage. History is written into the land around you. In ten years' time when the new road is full and once more you sit in traffic jams on your way to work you will think of us and remember everything you have lost. Ask yourselves now before it is too late, is it really worth it?

We believe that history will vindicate us. They will tell our story and sing our praise in song for many years to come. In times of great need England has always produced heroes and heroines to meet the challenge. Good people of Newbury, rise up, support us, and take your place in history!

The Road Protesters 1996

The whole idea is to do everything we can to make building this bypass as difficult, lengthy and expensive as possible, without risking anyone's safety but our own. The more expensive it is, the more they'll come away thinking NEVER AGAIN, and seek better solutions next time. They *know* it won't solve Newbury's traffic problem. The DoT's [Department of Transport's] own figures say that 70 per cent of traffic is local and will continue to go into the town even after the bypass is built. With the DoT's figures on expected traffic increase, this means that Newbury will have the same volume of traffic as today only five to seven years after the bypass opens, but instead of 10,000 trees to the west of the town, there'll be a band of pollution four lanes wide.

And not only do we lose the strip of land, we lose all the land around it to building development and pollution. And each new house will bring a new car, making new traffic to clog up this new road.

David Rendel [the local MP] says that pollution won't be as bad because bypass traffic will be moving at a more fuel-efficient speed. But even the DoT admit that *more roads encourages more road use*. That the town will be suffering the same pollution in seven years' time and be half encircled by more. Rendel's not an idiot. He can't believe this crap. It's worse. He's a liar and a mercenary.

It's all so fucking short-sighted – there's more road traffic, so make more roads. NOT 'Can we find ways to move people and goods just as well by reorganizing what we have already? We need to take a step back from catering for the demand (unhealthy, and ultimately impossible), to *managing* the demand. *Immediate* steps can be taken: a big part of Newbury's traffic problem is parents taking kids to and from school in the rush hour. A school bus could take fifty kids in the road space of two cars. The towns to the north and south of Newbury (Oxford and Winchester), both have effective Park & Ride schemes where everyone leaves the car *outside* the town and gets the bus in.

For bigger towns, get buses organized. In the early 1980s, David Blunkett's Sheffield City Council set a 5p flat fare on the buses. 'Cos they were so cheap, everyone wanted to use them, so more buses were put in service, and more routes made. Because the buses ran everywhere, all the time, for next to nothing, *everyone* used them. It took the traffic out of the city centre, making it cleaner and safer. Then Mrs Thatcher, with her belief in what she called 'the great car economy', scuppered local councils subsidising buses. *WHY?* A city with good public transport is a better city; non-drivers can get around, the air is cleaner, drivers don't get stuck in traffic, everyone's quality of life improves. *Isn't that good government?*

But Mrs Thatcher believed in making MONEY. The *only* thing that matters is economics. If a country's growing economically, then that is good. Nineteen-thirties Germany, therefore, is surely one of the great states of this century. There is a quality of life that isn't to do with economics: it's *people*, the people who the economy is supposed to be there *for*, with a feeling of their worth, of their potential, of opportunity to realize their potential and become the best they can. Not to be a slave to the Car Culture. And it *is* a slavery. Cars offer a kind of freedom, but their enslavement is far greater – they cost a lot of money to buy, a lot to maintain, and yet are worth *far less* to sell. They are the ultimate depreciating asset, they make owners stay in jobs they may well hate in order to get the money to pay for them, then give almost *no* return on this HUGE investment. If a car breaks down we're at the mercy of specialized manufacturers and suppliers for repairs, we can't do it ourselves. And even if they run fine, they need constant fuel, tax, insurance.

The Car Culture is foisted on us by the warmongering oil industry, own-nest feathering civil servants, and giant multinational corporations. We all know about what the oil industry do. Just ask the Saro-Wiwa family. And the insurance companies are big investors in money-making schemes: you don't make money by giving a shit for ANYTHING except making money. The biggest dividends come from the most destructive and tyrannical corporations This is where your insurance premium goes. *The Car Culture is not a necessity. It is the comparatively recent contrivance of certain powerful interests.* It's there to keep people in repetitious lives that keep the money flowing in. It's no freedom at all. It's slavery. One that's part of the consumerist worldview that the future will look back on with as much amazed horror as we do at colonialism and the rise of the Nazis.

I don't make these comparisons lightly. I know how everything we don't like gets called fascist and compared to the Nazis. I know that the way we do this says more about the Nazis than it does about Saddam Hussein, Colonel Qadaffi, General Galtieri, or whoever it is we think we're talking about. And I know that it also serves to belittle the enormity of what the Nazis did. I've spoken to several World War Two veterans here who have said that what they were doing fifty years ago was trying to save the world from fascism. It was getting out of hand, and to do nothing was to let it happen and condemn the next generation. If they hadn't acted decisively then, by 1950 we'd have been fucked. In the same way, environmental destruction is now the big threat to the next generation. In the last fifty years we've killed over half the world's rainforests, made 20 per cent of all species of plants and animals extinct or endangered, and human sperm count has dropped by 50 per cent. And the rate of destruction is *increasing*. If *we* don't do something, we're damning *every* future generation . . .

Just *WHAT* do they need to find on route before they'll stop? This whole thing amazes me. It's like they've taken a map of the Newbury area, marked all the great places, joined the dots, and called it the bypass route. They've got twelve archaeological sites of note from six distinct historic periods, mesolithic through to Civil War. The mesolithic one has been designated 'of national importance'. They've got rare rodents and beetles, they've got badgers, unspoilt woodland, unpolluted rivers, one of the densest populations of Desmoulins Whorl (mega-rare water snail) *ever*, three Sites of Special Scientific Interest, organic farmland (it takes five years to clear farmland of chemicals before it can be used for organic growing). *Anything* that makes a piece of land precious, special, worth saving, there's at least ONE on route.

Don't believe things can't change. They *will*, they *HAVE TO*, they can't do anything else. They'll get better or worse. We can determine which one.

Don't be afraid of 'unreasonableness' in society's eyes. It's always reactionary standards that they measure you with. To dare to see things differently is to bring you into conflict with the established order. Our heroes and pioneers have *always* been heretics hated by the establishment, and dismissed as dreamers, dangerous and/or mad. They have always started in a small way with no power against heavy odds. But a pure thirst for justice and hope for the future is enough. Martin Luther King, Charles Dickens, Emmeline Pankhurst, George Orwell, Nelson Mandela, oh I don't know; to name any is to exclude others, and reduce perennial principles to measurable deeds. These are our ideals. Anything less is a sell-out. No compromise, the future must be made the best it can be.

This isn't so much a battle between them and us, it's more of a battle between them and the earth. The Newbury bypass is just one manifestation of a destructive, greedy and corrupt system. Road protesters often get accused of being caught up in a single issue, but there is *no such thing* as a single issue, only a view that doesn't see the connections.

Our roads are full. Pollution damage, illnesses and deaths are rising and rising. Sooner or later, we ARE going to change that. Road protests are about making that change come sooner. We have to make it happen.

•

VERNON COLEMAN
1996

'Vivisection'

The veteran animal rights campaigner Vernon Coleman has been described as the Lone Ranger, Robin Hood and the Equalizer rolled into one. He has written more than fifty-six books and several novels but is most widely known for the columns he wrote for the Sunday People, *the national Sunday tabloid, exposing cruelty to animals. He has opposed vivisection since as a nineteen-year-old medical student he refused to conduct an experiment on a live rabbit.*

His book Fighting for Animals, *published by his own* European Medical Journal, *includes this harrowing description of animal experiments.*

Think of the animal you love most dearly. If he or she is close to you, reach out and touch him or her. Now, imagine the dog, cat or rabbit you love strapped – alive and alert – to the vivisector's laboratory bench. Imagine the vivisector approaching with scalpel raised. Imagine a tube implanted into the animal's brain and a scientist deliberately injecting an irritating chemical down the tube. Imagine the scientist sitting back and waiting to see what happens. Within a minute or two the animal you love begins to shiver. The shivering is mild at first but it quickly becomes vigorous and widespread. Then the animal begins to cry; loud and pitiful cries. He begins breathing rapidly and salivating. His ears twitch and his hair stands on end. He vomits, wets himself and empties his bowels. The white-coated, cold-blooded scientist who is watching all this dispassionately observes the animal's distress and carefully writes everything down in his notebook.

That is no fiction. It is real. It happens every day. In your name. With your money. And someone else's loved animal. Every thirty seconds that is exactly what happens to 1,000 animals. It could happen to your loved animal if the vivisectors get hold of him or her.

If you are uncertain about the nature of vivisection then try this simple exercise: imagine you are a 'guinea pig' taking part in a sensitization test for a new perfume.

First, scientists would shave a patch of your skin – removing every small hair – so that the perfume would make the best possible contact with your skin. Then they would put a large quantity of concentrated perfume on to your skin and leave it there. A plaster would be put over the test area to make sure that the perfume remained in the closest possible contact with your skin. You would be tied down to make sure that you didn't move about and disturb the experiment. Every few hours or so the test site would be inspected. And more of the concentrated perfume would be added until your skin went red and started to itch.

You would want to scratch but you wouldn't be able to. A thick dressing would be put over the test area and your hands would be tied to stop you interfering with the experiment. The itching would get worse and worse. But the scientists doing the experiment wouldn't give you anything to stop the itching. If they did they would mess up their results.

Even if you cried and begged for mercy they would ignore you. These scientists are trained to ignore such pleas. It is their job to cause suffering – and to record the consequences.

Gradually, the area of skin under test would become redder and redder. Eventually it would probably begin to blister. Fluids would ooze out of your skin and drip out from underneath your plaster. You would probably notice some blood oozing out as well. Before long your whole body would probably begin to react. You might start to wheeze and to have difficulty in breathing. Your skin would start to burn and to itch and your heart might well start to pound.

The aim of a sensitization experiment is deliberately to induce an allergy response by giving so much of the test product that the body responds violently. You would feel ill. You would probably feel nauseated and you might start to vomit. Still, the scientists would refuse to give you any treatment in case it interfered with the test. Instead they would simply write down your symptoms and make notes about the condition of your skin. When they had acquired enough information they would kill you.

Those who perform and support animal experiments are so embarrassed and ashamed of what they do that they frequently use euphemisms to disguise their activities. It is quite common, for example, for experimentalists to talk of animals 'taking part' in experiments and 'helping us with our research'. The word 'experiment' has been replaced by the word 'procedure', which is less evocative. Experimenters have their own language. Here are just a few choice phrases they use (and their meanings):

vocal response = crying
major airway embarrassment = choking
reacting to adverse stimulation with vigorous motor responses = trying
to escape
binocular deprivation = sewing the eyes up

decapitation = head removal
exhibiting lethal behaviour = dying
startle reflex = flinching
aversive electrical stimulation = electric shocks
thermal injury = burn or scald

Every thirty seconds vivisectors kill another 1,000 animals.

Vivisectors use cats, dogs, puppies, kittens, horses, sheep, rats, mice, guinea pigs, rabbits, monkeys, baboons and any other creature you can think of.

While waiting to be used in laboratory experiments animals are kept in solitary confinement in small cages. Alone and frightened they can hear the screams of the other animals being used.

Many of the animals used in laboratory experiments are 'pets' which have been kidnapped, taken off the streets and sold to the vivisectors.

Animals used in experiments are tortured, blinded, burned, shot, injected and dissected. They have their eyes sewn up or their limbs broken. Chemicals are injected into their brains and their screams of anguish are coldly recorded. If the animal lives through this torture it will then be killed.

Three-quarters of the experiments performed by vivisectors are done without any anaesthetic.

Most of the experimenters who torture and kill animals have no medical or veterinary training.

Most animal experiments are paid for with your money.

Animal experiments are now recognized to be of absolutely no value to patients or doctors or anyone else. Animal experiments are performed by companies wanting to put new products on to the market without doing more expensive tests and by second-rate scientists wanting to acquire academic status the easy way.

•

GRAHAM HARVEY
1997

'The grim reapers'

Nearly forty years after Rachel Carson's Silent Spring, *Graham Harvey, agricultural story editor of* The Archers, *British radio's everyday story of country folk, wrote an equally powerful and poetic polemic against the destruction of Britain's traditional landscape by modern methods of intensive farming. The more the farmer produced, the more subsidies he collected from the state, Harvey argued. A chemical company had only to show its new wonder product would yield more than its own value in extra output to be assured of a market. Not surprisingly the main thrust of agricultural research and development went into the production of fertilizers and pesticides.*

Harvey outlined his argument in 'The Grim Reapers,' the first chapter of The Killing of the Countryside.

On Salisbury Plain, close to where the holiday traffic thunders westward, the great Iron Age fortress of Yarnbury Castle stands sentinel over a rolling downland landscape. Scoured from the soil more than two millennia ago, its massive earth walls are now draped in chalk grassland, the tough mat of wild flowers, grasses and herbs that once formed the green mantle of all the chalk country. A summer haunt of bees and flickering butterflies, it is a living garment woven by centuries of grazing with sheep.

Beyond the earth walls there is precious little grassland left on the downs. The mantle of the chalk has all but disappeared along with the sheep flocks that produced it. Instead the landscape is engulfed in a tide of intensive wheat, dreary stands of identical plants stretching away to the far horizon. The flowers of the chalk survive only on the ancient earthwork where they are protected from the bite of the ploughshare. The fortress of a warrior people has become the refuge of a threatened and dwindling habitat.

For the farmers of the Plain have transformed this landscape on a scale that would have seemed unthinkable even a generation ago. Without public consultation they have obliterated a living heritage thousands of years old. Nor is the destruction confined to chalk downland. Across the length and breadth of Britain the countryside has been reconstructed in the sole interests of intensive agriculture. The very essence of a nation is drained away, yet it seems scarcely a voice is raised in protest.

For an urban people the British remain remarkably well disposed towards farmers. This is surprising since the only time most of us encounter them is in a traffic queue behind a crawling slurry wagon on the morning we are late for work. Even so we retain a sentimental attachment to them. We like to think of them as honest, well-meaning folk, kind to their animals and responsible in their care of the countryside . . .

Sadly our fond perceptions fail to square with reality. Dramatic changes have been taking place on Britain's farmland, changes that reveal farmers to be anything but the good custodians we like to think them. The numbers of a wide range of wildlife species have fallen dramatically. The skylark, the lapwing and the corn bunting; the barn owl and the grey partridge – birds that were once an everyday part of the farming scene – are now in steep decline.

Wild flowers, too, are disappearing from our countryside; species like shepherd's needle, cornflower and the exquisite pheasant's eye, along with a host of farmland butterflies – the adonis blue, the marbled white, the chequered skipper and the pearl-bordered fritillary – and several dozen species of invertebrates, little known most of them, yet each with its own place in the intricate lattice-work of Britain's farmland ecology.

The landscape they have shared for centuries has at once become hostile. Modern, intensive farming will no longer tolerate them. They are victims of the sprays, the fertilizers, the giant machines and the monocultures; of the sheer relentless pressure to maximize output from every hedge bank and field corner. We fondly imagine that agriculture allows wild species to flourish, if only at the margins – on the odd patch of rough grass, or the marshy patch at the bottom of the meadow. But there are few marginal areas left any more. For this is the age of farm support.

In the hot-house climate of state subsidies every last acre of marsh and rough grazing must be mobilized in the great drive for production. Out in the vanguard are the 100-horsepower tractor and the 40-foot spray boom. Everything must be sacrificed to them: the hedges and woods, the meadow-lands, the ponds and marshes, along with all the creatures that inhabit them. Since agriculture uses 80 per cent of the total land area, it's not just a part of our countryside that is affected. Farming doesn't merely shape the British countryside, it *is* the countryside. And with the industry gripped by a mania to produce regardless of the consequences, the outcome is inevitably a desert . . .

As a rule the British are zealously protective of their countryside. The threat of a by-pass through a stretch of ancient woodland is enough to bring out the middle classes in droves, setting them shoulder-to-shoulder with New Age eco warriors in a stand against the bulldozers. But the threat from agriculture is more insidious. Who is there to object when the sprayer moves across a flower-rich hedge bank or the plough buries a centuries-old meadow? There are no squadrons of earth-movers lining up to carve a swathe across a verdant hillside, no powerful images for the TV news crew. This enemy is within.

For those whose only view of the countryside is from a distance it's hard to appreciate just how much damage has already been done. The landscape still looks attractive enough. The hedges are neat and well-trimmed, the fields comfortingly green. Yet such things mean little. They tell us no more about the health of the countryside than a holiday brochure accurately portrays a foreign resort. To discover the reality it is necessary to take to the fields. Only then does it become apparent that this once 'living tapestry' is becoming a shroud.

Nowhere has the destruction been greater than on the chalk downs, those gently contoured slopes that ebb and flow across the south of England like an ocean swell. At Yarnbury Castle the downs are traversed by one of the great arterial routes to the west, the A303 trunk road. Crossing the Plain it skirts Stonehenge before dropping down into the Wylye Valley. This is a land of prehistory, of tumuli, hill forts and iron-age encampments. On these same bare hills the early Neolithic peoples began turning the first sods, setting Britain on a course for its farming destiny.

For the thousands of motorists who speed along the dual carriageway en route to their holiday destinations in the south-west, the transformation matters not one jot. This landscape of open skies and smooth-rounded peaks still has a lightness to lift the spirits. But for those choosing to strike out along one of the myriad droves or trackways there is no such refreshment for the soul. This is no living tapestry. It is a landscape of the dead.

The most striking feature is the silence. There is no sound in this rolling prairie land; no buzzing of bees, no rasping of crickets, no birdsong. Saddest of all, there is no joyous ripple from Shelley's 'blythe spirit', no 'silver chain of sound' from George Meredith's *Lark Ascending*. The skylarks have gone from this modern cornfield. Here the heavens are as devoid of life as the waving wheat beneath them.

Down below the ripening ears, on the bare earth, no bugs or insects are visible among the forest of stems. Nothing lives here; the pesticides have seen to that. Those that don't kill the insect predators directly destroy the smaller invertebrates on which they feed. They also wipe out the fungal life on which the smaller creatures feed in their turn. The end result is the same: a barren earth. And along with the invertebrates have gone the small mammals which lived on them. Finding a shrew or fieldmouse in this miserable monoculture is worth a letter to *The Times*. And because the ground is dead the skies are empty, too, save for the odd pigeon, or a sparrowhawk straying in from the roadside verges. Just as there is no food for the small mammals, there is none for the insect-eating birds. Shepherd Bawcombe would find neither corn bunting nor greenfinch were he to walk the lofty downland paths today.

This is no longer a farmed landscape. It has become an industrial site set in a rural location. Like a well-run factory, it is tidy and efficient. But in a landscape once vibrant, once teeming with life, its emergence is a catastrophe. And the greater tragedy is that it has all been unnecessary.

•

ANN MALLALIEU
1997

'Hunting is our music'

The first great protest addressed at Tony Blair's New Labour government occurred within ten weeks of the 1997 election after the Labour MP Michael Foster tabled a private member's bill to abolish hunting. Thousands of opponents of the bill gathered in London's Hyde Park for a Countryside Rally. They were brought to London by a thousand coaches, twelve trains, five aircraft and Eurostar. Many walked hundreds of miles.

Among more than thirty speakers, it was Ann Mallalieu, the Labour life peer, who most eloquently expressed the anger of the hunters and their supporters in the countryside.

All of us have given a part of our lives to be here in Hyde Park. We have come here for a reason. We cannot and will not stand by in silence and watch our countryside, our communities and our way of life destroyed for ever by misguided urban political correctness.

This rally is not just about hunting. Many perhaps most of those here today don't hunt themselves.

It is about freedom, the freedom of people to choose how they live their own lives. It is about tolerance of minorities, and sadly those who live in and work in the countryside are now a minority. It is about listening to and respecting the views of other people of which you may personally disapprove.

Many people don't want to fish or shoot or hunt – some dislike these things. Let them try and persuade those who disagree with them by reasoned argument but do not try to pass laws to make those you have failed to convince into criminals.

Many of you spend your lives living and working with animals. You see birth and death at close quarters. It is you who must take the hard decisions and bear the responsibilities day in and day out. It is an irony that this rally composed as it is of people who know, love and live among animals should be the target of abuse and vilification from those who claim to love animals but seldom have any knowledge of or direct responsibility for caring for them. The irresponsible seem to feel free and qualified to tell the responsible that they are barbaric sadists and perverts.

The simple truth is that those who hunt and shoot and fish and rear animals for food care for them greatly and probably understand them better than those who regard them sentimentally as quasi-human beings. It is also the simple truth that those who farm and those who take part in country sports control and maintain much of our countryside, preserve its wild places and wild things.

Without people like this how many of our wild animals would not exist today. The strong healthy herds of wild deer in the West Country, the finest in the land, are there because those who hunt have been their guardians and protectors over generations. Take away their protection and you sign their death warrant. The countryside faces a new and immediate threat. A very new MP will try to criminalize many of those here today. What a tragedy that a bill which is dismissive and damaging to our nation should be introduced at a time when its mood on having elected a new government is one of optimism and desire for co-operation, not confrontation.

Do those who support such legislation not know or care that a ban on hunting would result in more snaring, more wounding and more prolonged deaths which follow? That in some areas the hunt which is on call twenty-four hours a day provides the only quick and humane means of ending the suffering of casualty farm animals and horses?

That no one else will collect and dispose of carcasses free or at cost, that 16,500 jobs depend solely on hunting, 63,000 more rely in part on it?

That 50,000 horses and 20,000 hunts would become redundant overnight with consequences which need not be spelt out and £100,000,000 worth of business would be lost to the rural economy?

All these things are important but so is this.

Hunting is often described as a sport. But to those of us who have heard the music of the hounds and have loved it, it is far more than that.

Hunting is our music, it is our poetry, it is our art, it is our pleasure. It is where many of our best friendships are made, it is our community. It is our whole way of life. And we will fight for these things with all the strength and dedication we possess because we love them.

Tony Blair has said he will govern on behalf of the whole nation. That is what we want. Those present here today come from every political persuasion and I support Labour and I support hunting too. Our government has not given support to this pernicious bill and we hope it will never do so. Our quarrel is not with this government but with individual MPs.

We do not want this fight. It is not of our own making. We do not want conflict between the town and the country. We do not want a nation divided. We want others to share and enjoy the countryside with us.

To our newly elected Members of Parliament we say this: we elected you in the hope that you would provide more of our people with new and better opportunities to do more with their lives. We did not elect you to lecture us on morality or to criminalize hundreds and thousands of our decent law-abiding people.

Tonight this park will empty. We will be making our way home to all parts of our nation. We will go back and care for the animals and the countryside and its wildlife of which we have been the guardians for generations.

Don't forget us, or what we have done today. We have made history. The countryside has come to London to speak out for freedom. And many from the towns and cities who understand and share our fears have stood here with us today.

I hope we are not on the eve of a battle. We do not want one. But if there is one, the countryside will fight, and we will win.

•

ROYAL SOCIETY FOR THE PREVENTION OF CRUELTY TO ANIMALS
1997

'Death of a fox'

The new Labour government elected in May had promised that it would not obstruct a bill to abolish hunting. The lobbying in support of a private member's bill seeking to ban hunting with dogs intensified as the day set for the debate in November approached. The RSPCA published advertisements backing the bill – such as this one, written by Richard Foster of Abbott Mead Vickers – in several national newspapers.

Although the bill was subsequently talked out, the campaign continues.

'*Whatever you think about foxes, you have to admire their guts.*'
Most huntsmen will tell you that the death of a fox is swift and painless.

'A quick nip in the back of the neck,' they say, 'and he's dead.'

If only.

Foxhounds tend to go for the softer option.

The belly.

This brings the fox down, but doesn't immediately kill it. Death usually occurs by disembowelment.

There are those who would argue that this is no more than a fox deserves.

After all, they say, foxes are themselves killers and need to be controlled.

While it's true that foxes do occasionally take lambs, many of these are likely to be already dead.

(Twenty per cent of lambs born each year die from hypothermia, malnutrition or disease, or are stillborn.)

And the Ministry of Agriculture, Fisheries and Food estimates the number of lambs taken by foxes to be not significant.

The notion that hunting is necessary to control the fox population is equally unfounded.

At least 200,000 foxes are killed every year by shooting, snaring or in road accidents. Only about 15,000 are killed by hunting.

Where foxes are deemed a pest, it is more efficient and more humane for them to be shot by a marksman.

'It's hard to swim when you've been running for three hours.'

On average, a stag hunt lasts three hours and covers around twelve miles.

When the stag is finally caught by the hounds it is at the point of total exhaustion.

Scientific analysis of blood samples taken from hunted stags reveals a litany of suffering.

In the early stages of the chase, glycogen and blood sugar levels fall sharply.

As the hunt progresses, fatty acids in the blood rise, indicating high physiological stress levels.

Red pigment in blood plasma increases, caused by ruptured blood cells.

In the later stages of the hunt, high levels of muscle enzymes appear in the blood, indicating life-threatening muscle damage.

Despite its name, stag hunting is not confined to the male of the species.

Hinds are hunted too, sometimes when they are pregnant or with a calf at heel.

Stag or hind, the end is the same. A free wild animal is hunted to death.

The RSPCA has long campaigned against all hunting with dogs.

We believe that the hunting of wild animals is cruel and unacceptable in a civilized society.

•

EARL SPENCER
1997

'The most hunted person of the modern age'

People don't clap at funerals but they did – and inside Westminster Abbey – at the funeral of Diana, Princess of Wales, the divorced wife of Prince Charles, who had been killed with Dodi Fayed in a Paris car crash. The occasion was the tribute to his sister by Princess Diana's brother Earl Spencer.

He delivered a deeply felt attack on the press and then flung down a challenge to the royal family over the upbringing of the Princess's two sons, William and Harry. As he finished his oration, his voice broke. The masses outside, most of whom had been critical of the Queen's response to the Princess's death, started applauding. The sound of the applause penetrated the Abbey and the congregation joined in. It was utterly unprecedented and the Queen sat immobile as her subjects made their brief revolt.

I stand before you today the representative of a family in grief, in a country in mourning before a world in shock.

We are all united not only in our desire to pay our respects to Diana, but rather in our need to do so.

For such was her extraordinary appeal that the tens of millions of people taking part in this service all over the world, via television and radio, who never actually met her, feel that they, too, lost someone close to them in the early hours of Sunday morning. It is a more remarkable tribute to Diana than I can ever hope to offer her today.

Diana was the very essence of compassion, of duty, of style, of beauty. All over the world she was a symbol of selfless humanity. All over the world, a standard-bearer for the rights of the truly downtrodden, a very British girl who transcended nationality. Someone with a natural nobility who was classless and who proved in the last year that she needed no royal title to continue to generate her particular brand of magic.

Today is our chance to say thank you for the way you brightened our lives, even though God granted you but half a life. We will all feel cheated always that you were taken from us so young, and yet we must learn to be grateful that you came along at all. Only now that you are gone do we truly appreciate what we are now without and we want you to know that life without you is very, very difficult.

We have all despaired at our loss over the past week, and only the strength of the message you gave us through your years of giving has afforded us the strength to move forward.

There is a temptation to rush to canonize your memory. There is no need to do so. You stand tall enough as a human being of unique qualities not to need to be seen as a saint. Indeed, to sanctify your memory would be to miss out on the very core of your being, your wonderfully mischievous sense of humour with a laugh that bent you double.

Your joy for life transmitted wherever you took your smile and the sparkle in those unforgettable eyes. Your boundless energy, which you could barely contain.

But your greatest gift was your intuition, and it was a gift you used wisely. This is what underpinned all your other wonderful attributes, and if we look to analyse what it was about you that had such a wide appeal, we find it in your instinctive feel for what was really important in all our lives. Without your God-given sensitivity we would be immersed in greater ignorance at the anguish of AIDS and HIV sufferers, the plight of the homeless, the isolation of lepers, the random destruction of landmines.

Diana explained to me once that it was her innermost feelings of suffering that made it possible for her to connect with her constituency of the rejected.

And here we come to another truth about her. For all the status, the glamour, the applause, Diana remained throughout a very insecure person at heart, almost childlike in her desire to do good for others so she could release herself from deep feelings of unworthiness, of which her eating disorders were merely a symptom.

The world sensed this part of her character and cherished her for her vulnerability while admiring her for her honesty.

The last time I saw Diana was on 1 July, her birthday, in London, when typically she was not taking time to celebrate her special day with friends but was guest of honour at a special charity fund-raising evening.

She sparkled of course, but I would rather cherish the days I spent with her in March when she came to visit me and my children in our home in South Africa.

I am proud of the fact that, apart from when she was on display meeting President Mandela, we managed to contrive to stop the ever-present paparazzi from getting a single picture of her – that meant a lot to her.

These were days I will always treasure. It was as if we had been transported back to our childhood when we spent such an enormous amount of time together – the two youngest in the family.

Fundamentally, she had not changed at all from the big sister who mothered me as a baby, fought with me at school and endured those long train journeys between our parents' homes with me at weekends. It is a tribute to her level-headedness and strength that despite the most bizarre-like life imaginable after her childhood, she remained intact, true to herself.

There is no doubt that she was looking for a new direction in her life at this time. She talked endlessly of getting away from England, mainly because of the treatment she received at the hands of the newspapers. I don't think she ever understood why her genuinely good intentions were sneered at by the media, why there appeared to be a permanent quest on their behalf to bring her down. It is baffling.

My own and only explanation is that genuine goodness is threatening to those at the opposite end of the moral spectrum. It is a point to remember that of all the ironies about Diana, perhaps the greatest was this – a girl given the name of the ancient goddess of hunting was, in the end, the most hunted person of the modern age.

She would want us today to pledge ourselves to protecting her beloved boys William and Harry from a similar fate and I do this here, Diana, on your behalf. We will not allow them to suffer the anguish that used regularly to drive you to tearful despair.

And beyond that, on behalf of your mother and sisters, I pledge that we, your blood family, will do all we can to continue the imaginative way in which you were steering these two exceptional young men so that their souls are not simply immersed by duty and tradition but can sing openly as you planned.

We fully respect the heritage into which they have both been born, and will always respect and encourage them in their Royal role.

But we, like you, recognize the need for them to experience as many different aspects of life as possible to arm them spiritually and emotionally for the years ahead. I know you would have expected nothing less from us.

William and Harry, we all care desperately for you today. We are all chewed up with sadness at the loss of a woman who was not even our mother. How great your suffering is we cannot even imagine.

I would like to end by thanking God for the small mercies he has shown us at this dreadful time; for taking Diana at her most beautiful and radiant and when she had joy in her private life.

Above all, we give thanks for the life of a woman I am so proud to be able to call my sister: the unique, the complex, the extraordinary and irreplaceable Diana whose beauty, both internal and external, will never be extinguished from our minds.

•

GEORGE MONBIOT
1997

'Genetically modified food'

As George Monbiot notes in this protest in the Guardian, *a tiny handful of companies is coming to govern the global development, production, processing and marketing of mankind's most fundamental commodity: food.*

Monbiot, a former visiting fellow at Green College, Oxford, and visiting professor in environmental science at the University of East London, has been declared persona non grata *in seven countries for his campaigns, which include opposition to mahogany imports and road building. The target of this protest is Monsanto, the American multinational company at the forefront of genetically modified food.*

It's easy to miss even the biggest newspaper ads, when you're not looking out for them. The three pages in the middle of the *Financial Times* devoted to the corporate de-merger of a chemical company called Monsanto were not exactly riveting, even for many readers of the *FT*. But this was one advertisement we could ill-afford to ignore. It is one of the few public indications of the opening of a new chapter in the world's economic history.

The publicity, aimed at shareholders and corporate customers, announced that Monsanto is to split into two firms, to pursue 'applied chemistry' and 'life sciences'. The life-science division will 'provide better food, better nutrition, and better health for all people ... Hope for environmentally sustainable solutions. Hope for a healthier planet. That's how we'll be growing in the century to come.' Monsanto's claims about the environmental and human impacts of its produce are questionable, but one of these statements is surely beyond doubt: this company will be growing as fast as any firm on earth. For Monsanto has embarked on one of the most extraordinary and ambitious corporate strategies ever launched.

The story begins simply enough, with a single chemical. Glyphosate, sold to farmers and gardeners as 'Roundup', is the world's biggest-selling herbicide. Last year, it earned Monsanto nearly $1.5 billion. But the company's patent on Roundup runs out in the year 2000. Far from sowing corporate catastrophe, however, this event seems likely only to enhance Monsanto's market value. For the past ten years it has cleverly been developing a range of new crops, genetically engineered to resist glyphosate. Spraying them with Roundup does them no harm, but destroys all the weeds that compete. New patent legislation in Europe and the US allows Monsanto to secure exclusive rights to their production. The first 'Roundup-Ready' plant Monsanto released was a genetically engineered soya bean. Between 50 and 60 per cent of processed foods contain soya, so the potential market is enormous.

Alarmed at possible increases in the use of herbicides, as well as the health effects of genetically engineered crops in general, environmentalists and consumer groups in Europe started calling for products containing the new beans to be clearly labelled. But in the US – from which most of our soya comes – Monsanto insisted that it would be impossible to keep Roundup-Ready beans apart from ordinary ones. About 15 per cent of this year's US crop is Roundup-Ready: the chances are that nearly all of us will soon be consuming manipulated soya beans every week of the year.

As the new beans were snapped up by growers in the US, Monsanto began an extraordinary round of acquisitions, buying shares in seed and biotechnology companies worth nearly $2 billion in the past eighteen months alone. Among its purchases are companies which produce the famous 'Flavr-savr' tomato, own the US patent on all genetic manipulations of cotton, and control around 35 per cent of the germlines of American maize. Monsanto is now experimenting with new rice, maize, potato, sugarbeet, rape and cotton varieties. It has suggested that within a few years all the major staple crops on earth should be genetically engineered. The new products are so attractive to many farmers that the company has managed to get them to sign away their future rights to the seed they grow, and allow Monsanto to inspect their fields whenever it wants.

Monsanto's new crops could not have become commercially viable without major legislative change. As members of the trade lobby Europabio, Monsanto and the other big biotech companies have mastered the legal climate in which they operate. Despite significant public opposition, in July Europabio managed to persuade the European Parliament to adopt a new directive, allowing companies to patent manipulated plants and animals. Last week, the European Commission announced that it would force Austria, Italy and Luxembourg to repeal their laws banning the import of genetically engineered maize.

In the United States a Monsanto vice-president is, according to the *St Louis Post*, a 'top candidate' to become Commissioner of the Food and Drug Administration (FDA), which regulates the food industry. Researchers and lawyers from Monsanto already occupy important posts in the FDA. The administration has approved some of the company's most controversial products, including the artificial sweetener aspartame and an injectable growth hormone for cattle. Only the New York Attorney General's office has taken the company to task, forcing it to withdraw adverts claiming that Roundup is biodegradable and environmentally friendly.

But Monsanto has been most successful when appealing to multilateral bodies. Last month, the World Trade Organization confirmed its ruling that the European Union can no longer exclude meat and milk from cattle treated with bovine growth hormone, despite the protests of farmers, retailers and consumers. As *Scientific American* magazine claimed, Monsanto's clinical trials of the drug were incompletely analysed, obscuring the fact that it increases the number of infected udder cells in cows by about 20 per cent. Biotech firms are now trying to persuade the World Trade Organization to forbid the labelling of genetically engineered foods. Any country whose retailers tell consumers what they are eating would be subject to punitive sanctions.

With astonishing rapidity, a tiny handful of companies is coming to govern the global development, production, processing and marketing of our most fundamental commodity: food. The power and strategic control they are amassing will make the oil industry look like a cornershop.

More successfully than any other lobby, they are inhibiting the two remaining means of public restraint on their activities: government regulation and genuine consumer choice. All this will be a big pill for the public to swallow, which is why we'll be seeing a lot more of Monsanto over the next few weeks. It has just engaged an advertising agency for a major new 'consultative' campaign – aimed at us this time, not just the City. It deserves our full attention. This may be the first and the last chance we'll get to tell the biotechnology companies what we think about their re-engineering: of both the stuff of life itself and the means by which it reaches us.

•

COALITION AGAINST RUNWAY TWO
1997

'Air travel'

The campaign against a second runway at Manchester Airport, the third largest in Britain, was the first British airport protest which united 'vegans and Volvos', in which direct action protesters were accompanied by middle-class residents from the affluent villages south of Manchester in the Cheshire green belt.

The runway was given the go-ahead but delayed by eco-activists who obstructed the builders by living in tunnels and trees. There were 211 arrests and the cost of security rose to £6 million.

This is the protest against the second runway – similar to the case against the Newbury bypass – put by the Coalition Against Runway Two.

To those who say: 'What's the point, you'll never stop the runway,' we say: 'Noisy defeats, silent victories' – the campaigns to protect the environment are sometimes noisy defeats; the Newbury Bypass campaign, for instance. But silent victories follow in their wake, as politicians slash the Road Programme on the quiet, hoping no one will notice. That is why this campaign is also about plans for a third runway at Manchester, expansion plans at Heathrow and Air Transport in general.

We may not win this one, but we'll have put the issue on the agenda, and had fun doing it!

The principal argument put forward to convince the public that the second runway is a good idea is that employment would be created. However, with the same amount of investment in other areas many more jobs could be made, to improve quality of life *rather* than damage it through pollution and destruction.

Some air travel is beneficial, but much is extremely unnecessary. Seven-eighths of business passengers' flights from Manchester Airport are internal flights – why can't they use the train? Food is flown in when it can be grown here! Many foreign holiday journeys could also be made by train, or be taken in one of the many beautiful parts of the UK, if only we'd preserve them! These alternatives would benefit local economies, rather than flying money out of our already impoverished city.

Air pollution causes health problems. The growth in air transport will lead to increased problems of air pollution. A second runway with the projected extra passengers is estimated to increase road traffic by more than 100 per cent. That means more road building, more pollution and more accidents. 'Today one in seven children has asthma. In some inner city areas one child in three suffers' (Friends of the Earth, 1995). Many people are now recognizing that to preserve a future for ourselves and our children we must live more sustainably. One problem we must address is the impact of emissions from air transport on global climate change.

The Intergovernmental Panel on Climate Change (IPCC) says we must reduce carbon dioxide (CO_2) emissions by over 90 per cent in the UK to 'avoid potentially catastrophic consequences from climate change'.

Transport is the fastest-growing source of CO_2 emissions. Air transport is the fastest growing transport sector. 'Aircraft emit 35–65 per cent more CO_2 than even motor cars per passenger kilometre' (Dr John Rickard, chief economic adviser to the Department of Transport).

At a time when it is perhaps clearer than ever before that we must protect green spaces, conserve resources and develop more sustainable ways of living, Runway Two is obviously not the way forward. Manchester Airport itself admits that it is a 'major consumer of resources', and is '. . . simply not sustainable'.

The leader of Manchester City Council, Richard Leese, has said: 'Too much thinking in the region is backward looking and seeks to adopt policies and structures that might have been okay ten years ago, but don't meet the demands of the future.' Exactly: Runway Two jeopardizes the future. But then it is the sort of monolithic white elephant prestige project we've come to expect from Manchester's politicians.

It is obviously not the way forward. It is not responding to a need, but stimulating a demand that cannot safely be met. The previous leader of the Council, Graham Stringer, 'pledges that £1 million a week will be spent between now and 2005 on tarmac and terminals' . . . and in 2011 it could start all over again with a proposal for a THIRD runway . . .

Do you really want to see such vast amounts of money spent to destroy green belt, ponds, ancient woodlands, farmland and housing? 'The aviation industry has an obligation to the world's population, and to future generations, to act responsibly on environmental issues' (Director of International Civil Aviation Organization).

In what can only be seen as bad judgement, the two-mile-long second runway has officially been given permission. Before it is too late, Manchester Airport must be publicly challenged to recognize these important issues, and to live up to its own statement: 'to develop and refine its corporate environmental policies in order to minimize the environmental impact of the airport's operation'.

Species-rich ancient woodland in the Bollin Valley would be destroyed as a result of the proposed second runway. The River Bollin will be culverted, while miles of hedgerows and many ponds will also be destroyed or degraded. Translocation of species doesn't work. Biodiversity will decrease despite UK government commitments to protect it.

National Trust land in Styal Woods will be degraded, while other areas (for example, Arthur's Wood) will be devastated. Road-building and associated developments will further erode green belt land, leading to increased urbanization.

An estimated fifteen million extra car journeys per year on already congested roads.

The present road network will not be able to handle the forecast increases in car traffic. The M56 through Wythenshawe will have to handle 50,000 vehicles per day more – a third more – than the M62 or London's M25 already have to cope with. Road-building plans include a bypass of Stockport (the A6(M)) and a Stockport/Cheadle orbital trunk-road (the Manchester Airport Eastern Link Road).

The components of incompletely combusted gases produced by aircraft are toxic: there has been no independent study of human health impacts of such emissions. These act in combination with road traffic pollution.

Noise pollution will increase in proportion to the number of flights, and as a result of the increase in road traffic: night flights are set to increase by many thousands a year, to the gross inconvenience of nearby residents.

Expansion at Manchester Airport is linked to development of large areas of green land for office developments (e.g., Davenport Green), and retail parks. This will not only lead to the destruction of more precious green belt land, but will not aid regeneration of Manchester's depressed urban areas. Building office and retail developents in the countryside does nothing to promote the inner-urban regeneration that Manchester is so in need of.

What's wrong with air transport? The excessive use of air travel is a problem because: It is one of the principal contributors to global environmental problems such as climate change, ozone depletion and the wasteful use of scarce raw materials. It encourages unnecessary travel. The tourist industry encourages people who are able to travel to 'exotic' locations, which must exist on an unreliable tourist income. When the area has become overdeveloped, the tourists leave, to colonize the latest 'fashionable' resort.

The construction of the second runway would lead to: A largely unsustainable form of transport further encouraged. Higher emissions of global warming gases and other pollutants. Ozone layer destruction (in particular, from a new generation of supersonic airliners).

While the local effects of noise pollution and the destruction of irreplaceable tracts of countryside that will be lost for ever are well known, the global effects have received little publicity. This is a major problem as these are probably the most important issues surrounding air travel as we approach the twenty-first century.

The problem is as much to do with *where* the aircraft fly, as how much they emit. For example, nitrogen oxide emissions (NOx) from aircraft account for around 3 per cent of anthropogenic NOx emissions, yet 25–30 per cent of total NOx in the upper troposphere could be due to aircraft emissions [the troposphere extends to the tropopause at around 15 km, and above this lies the stratosphere].

Air travel consumes large quantities of untaxed non-renewable fossil fuels, and is a largely inappropriate form of internal travel. Air travel makes possible the ludicrous policy of transporting food thousands of miles, not only imposing the high environmental costs associated with air freight, but also increasing dependence on cash crop monoculture in poor countries.

Air travel has been estimated to contribute between 3–30 per cent of global warming. A study estimated that a single transatlantic return flight emits almost half the CO_2 emissions as from all other sources (lighting, heating, car use, etc.) consumed by an average person yearly. One recent study has estimated that 'if the airport grows as planned, CO_2 emissions by 2020 could be greater than from all other transport in the regional catchment'.

Aircraft are major sources of greenhouse gases, particularly carbon dioxide (CO_2), water vapour, and nitrogen oxides (NOx). We need to reduce our total carbon dioxide emissions by 60 per cent merely to stabilize atmospheric CO_2 at current levels – considering that we in the developed world already emit more than our fair share, this means that the UK has to reduce CO_2 emissions by 90 per cent.

Water vapour at high altitudes causes dual problems. Firstly it leads to an increase in cirrus cloud formation, which contributes to global warming, and secondly it reacts with NOx to destroy ozone in the stratosphere.

Nitrogen oxide in the troposphere (i.e., below the ozone layer), has a totally different effect from that in the stratosphere due to the complex nature of atmospheric processes. Here it contributes to ozone formation. Unfortunately this does not help replenish the ozone layer as it is in the wrong place, but instead acts as a greenhouse gas as well as contributing to smog around airports.

Plans for a new generation of supersonic airliners (following on from Concorde) which can travel higher in the earth's fragile atmosphere are causing concern: for example, *New Scientist*, 15 February 1997, 'Aircraft wreak havoc on ozone layer': 'A fleet of 500 supersonic aircraft . . . would have a direct effect on stratospheric ozone.' Similar effects are suspected from subsonic aircraft currently.

Nitrogen oxide (NOx) emissions from airliners are responsible for ozone depletion in the stratosphere, and many scientists are worried that this could negate the impact of the Montreal Protocol on CFC phase-out. With the next generation of supersonic airliners imminent (supersonics fly high in the stratosphere), and with subsonics flying in the upper troposphere as well as more and more in the lower stratosphere, this problem is likely to get much worse.

Recent research has also focused on the role of sulphur emissions (in the form of SO_2 and SO_3) leading to H_2SO_4 aerosol formation, and this may well prove as important in ozone layer depletion as the role of NOx.

It is becoming increasingly clear that the effects of aircraft on complex atmospheric processes are one of the major threats to our environment.

TONY BENN
1998

'War as a computer game'

Even his fiercest critics acknowledge that Tony Benn (1925–), the controversial dissident and populist guru of the left, is one of the most principled politicians in Britain. He is also one of its most powerful orators. Benn held several senior Cabinet posts in the Labour governments of Harold Wilson but, out of power, became leader of the party's left wing and campaigned for more democracy within the party over the election of the leader and the drafting of the manifesto. He narrowly failed to become deputy leader in 1981.

He was increasingly isolated by Tony Blair's New Labour but still spoke for the party's old principles. As a Labour government prepared to join the United States in a war against Iraq in 1998, Benn made this speech in the House of Commons – which he considers the best of his long career.

I regret that I shall vote against the government motion. The first victims of the bombing that I believe will be launched within a fortnight will be innocent people, many, if not most, of whom would like Saddam to be removed. The former Prime Minister, the right hon. Member for Huntingdon [John Major], talked about collateral damage. The military men are clever. They talk not about hydrogen bombs but about deterrence. They talk not about people but about collateral damage. They talk not about power stations and sewerage plants but about assets. The reality is that innocent people will be killed if the House votes tonight – as it manifestly will – to give the government the authority for military action.

The bombing would also breach the United Nations charter. I do not want to argue on legal terms. The charter says that military action can only be decided on by the Security Council and conducted under the military staffs committee. That procedure has not been followed and cannot be followed because the five permanent members have to agree. Even for the Korean War, the United States had to go to the general assembly to get authority because Russia was absent. That was held to be a breach, but at least an overwhelming majority was obtained.

Has there been any negotiation or diplomatic effort? Why has the Foreign Secretary not been in Baghdad, like the French Foreign Minister, the Turkish Foreign Minister and the Russian Foreign Minister? The time that the government said that they wanted for negotiation has been used to prepare public opinion for war and to build up their military position in the Gulf.

Saddam will be strengthened again. Or he may be killed. I read today that the security forces – who are described as terrorists in other countries – have tried to kill Saddam. I should not be surprised if they succeeded.

This second action does not enjoy support from elsewhere. There is no support from Iraq's neighbours. If what the Foreign Secretary says about the threat to the neighbours is true, why is Iran against, why is Jordan against, why is Saudi Arabia against, why is Turkey against? Where is that great support? There is no support from the opposition groups inside Iraq. The Kurds, the Shi'ites and the Communists hate Saddam, but they do not want the bombing. The Pope is against it, along with ten bishops, two cardinals, Boutros Boutros-Ghali and Perez de Cuellar. The Foreign Secretary clothes himself with the garment of the world community, but he does not have that support. We are talking about an Anglo-American preventive war. It has been planned and we are asked to authorize it in advance.

The House is clear about its view of history, but it does not say much about the history of the areas with which we are dealing. The borders of Kuwait and Iraq, which then became sacrosanct, were drawn by the British after the end of the Ottoman Empire. We used chemical weapons against the Iraqis in the 1930s. Air Chief Marshal Harris, who later flattened Dresden, was instructed to drop chemical weapons.

When Saddam came to power, he was a hero of the West. The Americans used him against Iran because they hated Khomeini, who was then the figure to be removed. They armed Saddam, used him and sent him anthrax. I am not anxious to make a party political point, because there is not much difference between the two sides on this, but, as the Scott report revealed, the previous government allowed him to be armed. I had three hours with Saddam in 1990. I got the hostages out, which made it worth going. He felt betrayed by the United States, because the American ambassador in Baghdad had said to him, 'If you go into Kuwait, we will treat it as an Arab matter.' That is part of the history that they know, even if we do not know it here.

In 1958, forty years ago, Selwyn Lloyd, the Foreign Secretary and later the Speaker, told Foster Dulles that Britain would make Kuwait a Crown colony. Foster Dulles said, 'What a very good idea.' We may not know that history, but in the Middle East it is known.

The Conservatives have tabled an amendment asking about the objectives. That is an important issue. There is no UN resolution saying that Saddam must be toppled. It is not clear that the government know what their objectives are. They will probably be told from Washington. Do they imagine that if we bomb Saddam for two weeks, he will say, 'Oh, by the way, do come in and inspect'? The plan is misconceived.

Some hon. Members – even Opposition Members – have pointed out the double standard. I am not trying to equate Israel with Iraq, but on 8 June 1981, Israel bombed a nuclear reactor near Baghdad. What action did either party take on that? Israel is in breach of UN resolutions and has instruments of mass destruction. Mordechai Vanunu would not boast about Israeli freedom. Turkey breached UN resolutions by going into northern Cyprus. It has also recently invaded northern Iraq and has instruments of mass destruction. Lawyers should know better than anyone else that it does not matter whether we are dealing with a criminal thug or an ordinary lawbreaker – if the law is to apply, it must apply to all. Governments of both major parties have failed in that.

Prediction is difficult and dangerous, but I fear that the situation could end in a tragedy for the American and British Governments. Suez and Vietnam are not far from the minds of anyone with a sense of history. I recall what happened to Sir Anthony Eden. I heard him announce the ceasefire and saw him go on holiday to Goldeneye in Jamaica. He came back to be replaced. I am not saying that that will happen in this case, but does anyone think that the House is in a position to piggy-back on American power in the Middle East? What happens if Iraq breaks up? If the Kurds are free, they will demand Kurdistan and destabilize Turkey. Anything could happen. We are sitting here as if we still had an empire – only, fortunately, we have a bigger brother with more weapons than us.

The British Government have everything at their disposal. They are permanent members of the Security Council and have the European Union presidency for six months. Where is that leadership in Europe which we were promised? It just disappeared. We are also, of course, members of the Commonwealth, in which there are great anxieties. We have thrown away our influence, which could have been used for moderation.

The amendment that I and others have tabled argues that the United Nations Security Council should decide the nature of what Kofi Annan brings back from Baghdad and whether force is to be used. Inspections and sanctions go side by side. As I said, sanctions are brutal for innocent people. Then there is the real question: when will the world come to terms with the fact that chemical weapons are available to anybody? If there is an answer to that, it must involve the most meticulous observation of international law, which I feel we are abandoning.

War is easy to talk about; there are not many people left of the generation which remembers it. The right hon. Member for Old Bexley and Sidcup [Edward Heath] served with distinction in the last war. I never killed anyone but I wore uniform. I was in London during the Blitz in 1940, living where the Millbank Tower now stands, where I was born. Some different ideas have come in there since. Every night, I went to the shelter in Thames House. Every morning, I saw docklands burning. Five hundred people were killed in Westminster one night by a landmine. It was terrifying. Are not Arabs and Iraqis terrified? Do not Arab and Iraqi women weep when their children die? Does not bombing strengthen their determination? What fools we are to live as if war is a computer game for our children or just an interesting little Channel 4 news item.

Every Member of Parliament who votes for the government motion will be consciously and deliberately accepting responsibility for the deaths of innocent people if the war begins, as I fear it will. That decision is for every hon. Member to take. In my parliamentary experience, this is an unique debate. We are being asked to share responsibility for a decision that we will not really be taking but which will have consequences for people who have no part to play in the brutality of the regime with which we are dealing.

On 24 October 1945 – the right hon. Member for Old Bexley and Sidcup will remember – the United Nations charter was passed. The words of that charter are etched on my mind and move me even as I think of them. It says:

> We the peoples of the United Nations determine to save succeeding generations from the scourge of war, which twice in our lifetime has brought untold sorrow to mankind.

That was that generation's pledge to this generation, and it would be the greatest betrayal of all if we voted to abandon the charter, take unilateral action and pretend that we were doing so in the name of the international community. I shall vote against the motion for the reasons that I have given.

•

COMPASSION IN WORLD FARMING
1998–9

'Battery hens'

It was Peter Singer's influential book Animal Liberation, *published in 1975, which first exposed the cruelty to chickens involved in the mass production of eggs for the breakfast tables of Britain and the United States. The cruelty continues although the European Commission is reviewing the battery cage system. Compassion in World Farming, the leading organization campaigning against factory farming and the live export trade, argued in this manifesto, 'How Do You Like Your Eggs?', that the commission had made no mention of a ban on the battery cage: 'Battery eggs mean cruelty and unfair competition that welfare driven systems find hard to beat. Only a ban on the cage can give us kinder eggs.'*

The second extract is the introduction to the CIWF 'Manifesto on Farm Animals' for the 1999 European elections.

Hens suffer in battery cages. Confined for a lifetime in a metal cage and standing on a wire floor with four other birds, the battery hen is treated solely as an egg-laying machine. Unable to move, her body deteriorates – her bones become so brittle they easily snap. Unhealthy, and suffering from anxiety and stress, she is kept alive until her high levels of egg production drop off. Then she is sent for slaughter.

Eighty-six per cent of our eggs are produced this way, despite repeated evidence that battery cages are cruel. The tiny floor space allotted to each bird is 450 square centimetres, or less than a sheet of A4 paper. With no room to exercise or nest, no earth to peck at, scratch, or use for a dust bath, and no perch to roost on securely at night, the birds are physically restrained from normal behaviour. Between 10,000 and 70,000 hapless hens are crammed together in one windowless shed, their cages piled high in long rows up to six tiers deep.

Study after study has confirmed that hens, like any living creatures, have basic behavioural needs. Foraging, exercising, dust bathing and nest building are natural activities for healthy hens but the battery cage prevents them all.

Scientists measured the space hens needed for specific movements. Up to a quarter of normal head movements were ruled out by the height of the cage. Standing took 475 sq. cms of space; wing flapping required 1,876 sq. cms. With only 450 sq. cms in the battery cage, *any* normal movement is severely restricted. Even the 600 sq. cms now recommended by FAWC [Farm Animal Welfare Charter] (to be achieved within five years) is not enough for a hen to stretch its wings, let alone to walk, run, or respond to a challenge.

Laying eggs in a nest is another instinctive need, crucial to the laying hen. Denying it and other natural instincts, causes stress for the hens. They show it by responding with abnormal behaviour, such as vacuum dust bathing. It's normal for hens to throw dust over their feathers to remove excess oil, but when no dust is available hens in cages go through the motions anyway . . . driven by a basic instinct.

No living creature can 'switch off' its instincts. In a cage, they are a constant cause of utter frustration.

Walking, running, wing flapping and flying are also forbidden by the confines of the cage. But, without this basic exercise, bone weaknesses, called 'cage layer fatigue', sets in. Hens given floor access have been found to have 41 per cent greater leg strength than those in cages, but without exercise the caged birds' bones simply deteriorate. Just as humans suffer osteoporosis – hens suffer the same kind of severe bone fragility. It can be fatal.

A recent study of caged hens found more than a third of all deaths during the laying cycle were due to osteoporosis. Dead hens were found to have broken bones in all parts of their bodies. Each one had at least one fracture in their ribs, sternum, humerus, radius, femur or tibia. Those that live are often so fragile they cannot withstand being mandhandled out of their cages. Up to 30 per cent end up with broken bones before reaching the slaughterhouse.

Lack of movement is accepted as the main cause of bone weakness, together with lack of minerals in the diet and the huge demand on the bird's calcium that high egg production (some 300 eggs per hen per year) demands. Lack of exercise, added to stress, also contributes to fatty liver haemorrhagic syndrome where a hen's liver ruptures, killing the bird.

Confined to the cage a hen is unable to forage or scratch around with its beak and claws. In natural conditions hens spend almost half their daytime foraging. Scratching at the ground wears down the claws, keeping them healthy. Denied this simple activity the hen's claws can grow long or twisted or be torn off. They can even grow around the wire mesh of the cage. Designed to reduce the risk of egg damage, this thin wire slopes downwards – putting painful pressure on the hen's toes, and causing damage to the bird's feet.

Even a hen's fundamental need for food is manipulated in the battery cage. The feed often contains a chemical colourant and is passed before the cages on a conveyor belt which often cannot be reached by all of the hens at once. Since their natural instinct is to feed simultaneously, the hens struggle to reach the food together, adding to their anxiety.

All in all a caged life is stressful, frustrating and very far from natural.

The majority of fattening pigs, chickens and turkeys continue to be factory farmed. They are kept indoors throughout their lives, crammed into over-crowded sheds or, in the case of hens, cages. They never experience fresh air or daylight until the day they are taken off to the slaughterhouse.

Animals' health has often been seriously impaired by the practice of selective breeding. Turkeys, bred to develop huge meaty breasts, have become so misshapen that they can no longer mate naturally and many adult males suffer from degenerative hip disorders. Each year millions of farm animals are mutilated. Piglets are tail-docked, hens and turkeys de-beaked and lambs castrated. These painful operations are nearly always carried out without anaesthetic. It cannot be right to cut bits off healthy animals for non-veterinary reasons simply to make them more amenable to our purpose.

All this pain and suffering is imposed on farm animals in the quest for ever cheaper food. Compassion in World Farming (CIWF) believes, however, that a responsible society should not treat animals as something placed in this world for our convenience, but should instead ensure that the animals it rears for food are treated humanely. Our well-being should not be founded on the suffering of other creatures who share this planet with us.

Moreover, we now know that there is a clear link between animal welfare and human health. If we want food that is safe to eat and high standards of animal health and welfare we must stop keeping animals in overcrowded, unhygienic conditions. Instead we must introduce much more humane and natural ways of rearing animals.

A major problem is now developing regarding antibiotics. The overuse of antibiotics in farming is leading to bacteria becoming resistant to some of the antibiotics used to treat disease in humans. Antibiotics are being used on farms on a routine basis both as growth promoters and to prevent the diseases which are inevitable in intensive farming systems. If the use of antibiotics as growth promoters is not banned and their prophylactic use to prevent disease severely restricted, we could see the antibiotics used in human medicine becoming increasingly less effective. (We have, of course, no objection to antibiotics being used therapeutically to treat disease in animals.)

The time has now come for a major change of thinking, for politicians of all parties to commit themselves to ending the cruelties systematically imposed on millions of animals in the name of cheap food and free trade.

•

EARTH FIRST!
1999

'The earth must come first'

The Earth First! movement was founded in 1979 to fight a 'lethargic, compromising and increasingly corporate environmental community'. It proclaims that Earth First! takes a 'decidedly different tack' towards environmental issues and its belief in direct action has won headlines across the world. 'We believe in using all the tools in the toolbox, ranging from grassroots organizing and involvement in the legal process to civil disobedience and monkeywrenching,' says the manifesto published on the Internet.

This is an edited extract.

Today is the most critical moment in the three-and-half-billion-year history of life on earth. Never before – not even since the end of the Cretaceous, 65 million years ago – has there been such an intense period of extinction as we are now witnessing, such a drastic reduction in the biological diversity of this planet.

Over the last several hundred years, human civilization has declared war on large mammals, leading some respected ecologists to assert that the only large mammals to survive the near future will be those we humans choose to allow to live.

Other prominent biologists, aghast at the wholesale devastation of tropical rainforests and temperate old-growth forests, rapidly accelerating desertification, and destruction of 'charismatic megafauna' due to habitat destruction and poaching, say that earth could lose one quarter to one third of all species within a very few years.

Not only is the blitzkrieg against the natural world destroying ecosystems and their associated species, but our activities are now beginning to have fundamental, systemic effects upon the entire life-support system of the planet – upsetting the world's climate, poisoning the oceans, destroying the ozone layer which protects us from excessive ultraviolet radiation, changing the CO_2 ratio in the atmosphere, and spreading acid rain, radioactive fallout, pesticides and industrial contamination throughout the biosphere.

Indeed, some biologists have warned that vertebrate evolution may be at an end due to the activities of humans.

Clearly, the conservation battle is not one of merely protecting outdoor recreation opportunities; neither is it a matter of elitist aesthetics, nor 'wise management and use' of natural resources. It is a battle for life itself, for the continuous flow of evolution.

We – this generation of humans – are at our most important juncture since we came out of the trees six million years ago. It is our decision, ours today, whether earth continues to be a marvellously living, diverse oasis in the blackness of space, or whether the charismatic megafauna of the future will consist of Norway rats and cockroaches . . .

We do not believe that it is enough to preserve some of our remaining wilderness. We need to preserve it all, and it is time to recreate vast areas of wilderness in all the planet's ecosystems: identify key areas, close roads, remove developments, and reintroduce extirpated wildlife.

It is not enough to oppose the construction of new dams. It is time to free our shackled rivers and tear down Hetch Hetchy, Glen Canyon, New Melones, Tellico and other concrete monstrosities.

While many environmental groups are members of the American political establishment and essentially adopt the anthropocentric (human-centred) world view of industrial civilization, we say the ideas and manifestations of industrial civilization are anti-earth, anti-woman, and anti-liberty. We are developing a new biocentric paradigm based on the intrinsic value of all natural things: Deep Ecology. Earth First! believes in wilderness for its own sake.

Lobbying, lawsuits, letter writing and research papers are important and necessary. But they are not enough. Earth First!ers also use confrontation, guerrilla theatre, direct action and civil disobedience to fight for wild places and life processes. And while we do not condone or condemn monkeywrenching, ecotage, or other forms of property destruction, we do present a forum for the exchange of ideas on creative opposition to the juggernaut of 'progress', including ideas about monkeywrenching.

To avoid co-option, we feel it is necessary to avoid the corporate organiz-ational structure so readily embraced by many environmental groups. Earth First! is a movement, not an organization. Our structure is non-hierarchical. We have no highly paid 'professional staff' or formal leadership. To put it simply, the earth must come first . . .

'Why wilderness?'

Is it because wilderness makes pretty picture postcards? Because it protects watersheds for downstream use by agriculture, industry and homes? Because it cleans the cobwebs out of our heads after a long week in the auto factory or over the video display terminal? Because it preserves resource extraction opportunities for future generations of humans? Because some unknown plant living in the wilds may hold a cure for cancer?

No. It is because wilderness is. Because it is the real world, the flow of life, the process of evolution, the repository of that three and a half billion years of shared travel.

All natural things have intrinsic value, inherent worth. Their value is not determined by what they will ring up on the cash register, nor by whether or not they are good. They are. They exist. For their own sake. Without consideration for any real or imagined value to human civilization.

Even more important than the individual wild creature is the wild intercon-nected community – the wilderness, the stream of life unimpeded by industrial interference or human manipulation . . .

Earth First!ers have 'cracked' Glen Canyon Dam on the Utah–Arizona border; climbed high into old-growth Douglas fir in Oregon, coast redwoods in California and the rainforests of the Canada coast, and sat on tiny platforms for days or even weeks; buried themselves up to their armpits in roads being cut into wilderness in Idaho, locked themselves to cement-filled barrels at a nuke plant under construction in Tennessee and snowshoed across treacherous terrain in British Columbia to videotape and oppose wolf hunting. Activists have occupied caves in Texas to save endangered species, occupied uranium mines on the north rim of the Grand Canyon in Arizona and have frequently shown up dressed as bears, owls, murrelets and trees in the offices of legislators and agencies to remind them of their jobs.

Through such tactics, for which thousands of EF!ers have been arrested around the world, the lethargic environmental movement has been re-energized and the news media have taken a new look at ecological issues. Earth First!ers, putting their bodies on the line, have given new definition to environmental activism and have shifted the spectrum of the conservation movement and raised the level of debate on the issues. The Earth First! Direct Action Fund has no fancy offices, no professional staff, and to avoid cumbersome and restricting regulations against free speech, has no nonprofit status. In this way, our meagre resources can be put where they will do the most good; on the front lines to defend the wild.

•

HUGO YOUNG
1999

'Europe'

As the principal political commentator of the Guardian *for nearly twenty years (and formerly the* Sunday Times*), Hugo Young is one of the most influential writers on British politics.*

In this essay for the Guardian, *based on his book* This Blessed Plot, *he starts by describing his esteem for Britishness and why his lack of zeal for 'Europe' has turned into a messianic belief that Britain's future lies in enthusiastic support of European union.*

The article by Charles Moore (see page 451) articulated the protest of the Euro-sceptics. Young's article represents the protest of those Britains who believe that Britain will become an offshore island without power or influence in the world if it does not enthusiastically embrace European union instead of constantly sniping at it.

I started work on *This Blessed Plot* as a Euro-agnostic, but completed it a few years later in a state of struggling incredulity at the demons and panics I had uncovered: the British exceptionalism that has seduced generations of our politicians into believing that 'Europe' is somewhere to escape from: the hallucinations, both positive and negative, that have driven so much of the British debate for so long. Having begun with the idea of writing a history that might call itself detached, I found myself in a process of self-instruction that now concludes, as the new currency gets under way, with the great simplicity of describing why I am a European.

The most obvious but least relevant part of this is cultural. It's easy to say how keenly I adore Schubert, and wallow in Proust, and am anticipating my next journey to consort with the shades of Virgil in the Roman Forum. But this is almost completely beside the point. European culture is the world's inheritance, absorbed on every continent, and the ability to appreciate the works of Johann Sebastian Bach, or even to speak his language, says nothing important about anyone's sense of 'being' a European.

Even Peter Lilley loves Michelangelo, as he and his colleagues never cease to explain, by way of proving that they are not anti-Europe, merely anti-'Europe': the European Union, the artefact of federalists, the dismal construct that has illicitly purloined the received identity of what Europe is held to mean these days. Lilley has a house in France, and Michael Portillo has roots in Spain, and there's a cross-party agreement that Umbro-Tuscany is where the British political classes most like to take their holidays. Does this not show their uninsular engagement with the continent, and expose the calumny that they might be Euro-phobic?

But the test cannot be who has heard more versions of 'The Ring' between Bayreuth and Covent Garden. As the boy becomes a man, the discovery that Shakespeare has a peer-group who write in different tongues may begin to broaden the mind. It is helpful to learn that these are not rival cultures, a zero-sum game of allegiance, but that they mingled and grew together. This discovery makes no demand on anyone's sense of belonging. Though the Conservative government proposed a ban on Beethoven's Ninth as the theme music for Euro 96, a football competition staged in England, it's safest to say that a taste for the Renaissance and Enlightenment is too universal to be significant. Like the travel, it proves nothing.

Very soon, therefore, what raises itself is the political question. About the culture, there is no issue. It may be important to many Euro-sceptics to be able to say that because they love Mozart, they love Europe, but this isn't what the argument is about. The division between the pro- and anti-Europeans is, in the real world, about nothing more or less than the European Union.

Everything else is sand in your eyes, an evasion. The EU, enlarged, or not: reformed, or not: with or without all its multiple imperfections; is the only item on the agenda.

It is not possible to be a European, in any meaningful sense, while opposing the EU. And it is not possible to support the EU without also supporting the success of the euro, and the belonging to the euro of every country that wants to call itself European.

I can think of many points which, added together, make a formidable critique of the EU. Its bureaucracy is strong, its democracy is weak, its accountability is seriously under-developed. The complexity of its tasks is always in danger of overwhelming the consensus needed to carry them out. Getting it to act demands formidable energy and patience and willpower from national leaders. Ensuring the singleness of the market it purports to be is work that is far from completed.

Equally, I can make the case against the euro, a project which fills those who support it with almost as much anxiety as it does excitement. Will this risk, which includes a repudiation of nationhood as traditionally understood, pay off? Will its hazards be sustainable? Is the closer political integration, which it undoubtedly foretells, something that the members with or without Britain, have the wit, will and wisdom to express in acceptable forms?

These questions don't fill me with horror. Their terrain awaits a long unfolding. They assume a process not voluntarily attempted anywhere in history: tampering by common agreement, with aspects of national identity, and working to create, in limited but significant aspects, a new kind of consciousness. To modify the nation-state throughout Europe is an extraordinary ambition, full of risks and difficulties. Yet if I'm ever tempted to despair of it, I need only remind myself of the alternative world summoned up by those, most ferociously in Britain, who devote passion to dismantling it.

They've had a long time to describe this non-European Britain, and the picture, where it is clear, is not persuasive. I conclude it is not meant to be. Portillo wrote not long ago that even to ask the question was 'extraordinary'. All the future has to satisfy, in the minds of many Euro-sceptics, is the need not to be 'European'. As long as it meets that test, the details hardly matter.

Thus, Little England (Scotland will be long gone from this) is, incorrigibly, a straitened place. Striving to define it, David Willetts, a Tory front-bencher, wrote a pamphlet, 'Who Do We Think We Are?', which, as well as saying our politics and economics were different from Europe, made much of the Changing of the Guard and Wensleydale cheese, calling in support some ancient paragraphs from T. S. Eliot and George Orwell to exalt the eternal time-warp in which England must be lodged. In all these tracts, the mystic chords of memory echo. Betraying history is most unimaginable, while predicting the future is subsumed into fantasy: the dream of an independent Britain, freed to assert her famous sovereignty, throwing herself on the mercy and markets of the non-European world.

So the anti-Europe cave is claustrophobic. It is also being re-filled (for we've been here before) with futile arrogance, making it obligatory not merely to criticize Brussels but abominate the Germans, laugh about the French, find nothing good to say about another European country, lest this betray our beleaguered sense of Britishness. A smart-ass headline writer in the *Sun* can get attention when the BBC finds an item for punning xenophobia so funny as to be worth a mention in the news.

At the heart of this is an impenetrable contradiction in the anti-Europe British mind. It cannot decide between terror and disdain. Britain is apparently so great, as well as so different, a place that she can afford to do without her continental hinterland. But she is so puny, so endangered, so destined to lose every argument with the continentals that she must fear for her identity if and when she makes the final commitment to belong among them. Studying the movements of sceptic thought, I see in their inability to provide a clear answer on this fundamental point a mirror of the vacillations, pro- and anti-Europe, that mark the personal histories of so many of the characters in the story. Either way, the conclusion points in the anti-Europe direction.

The same axiomatic outcome has penetrated every stage of Conservative Party thinking about the euro. While often purporting to be technical, the discussion has in fact been wholly political. First they said the euro wouldn't happen: 'a rain-dance', Major called it. Then they said it wouldn't work. Then they said it might well work. Now they say that even if it does work, it cannot work for Britain, as they edge into a position that bets their entire political future on its failure.

As each prediction is falsified the threshold for the euro's acceptance is raised. Shamelessly, the playing-field is tilted to make the game unwinnable, though most Tories still shrink from saying what they so plainly believe: that, as far as they're concerned, the British national identity as we know it can *never* coexist with membership of the European single currency. Thus the party that took Britain into Europe prepares to fight to the last in favour of excluding Britain from what 'Europe' any longer means.

My own odyssey has been quite different. The euro presents massive political challenges, but there seems no point in being outside it, since our future – the only future anyone has been able, with any respect for realism, to describe – is entirely bound up with its success or failure. Far from the development of 'Europe' being a conceptual barrier to belonging, it's the very reason why belonging ought soon to be seen as essential. I know the snags; and will argue for some radical political reform, but the European-ness of the euro is what makes it an exciting and benign adventure. We need to be a part. It should be Britain's own millennial leap, away from the century of nation-statehood, into a new time. All our neighbours are seeking a different way of bringing a better life to the continent and its regions.

What is so strange about Britain – so particular, so fearful, so other-worldly – that she should decide to withhold her unique wisdom from the enterprise? I can reject the premise of the question because I've grown up. Allegiance, to me, no longer has to be so exclusive. I still need it, as a psychic prop, a way of belonging. But the threat to the national identity now strikes me as bogus. This categorizing is what anti-Europe people insist on, but the best evidence of its falsity is to be found in the places that have been part of the new Europe for forty years, as against our twenty-five. Would anyone claim that Germany is less German as a result of the experience? We are all invaded by America. If cultural defences are needed, it's against transatlantic domination. But do I hear a single soul, on either side of the Channel, contend that France is less French than it ever was because of the EU?

So it will be with Britain. This reality won't come easy. Decades of propaganda defining national identity in the language of scorn for other nations can't be wiped out at a stroke. Persuading the British that they are allowed to be European should be the simplest task, yet the accretions of history, manipulated by frightened politicians, make it difficult. Though the Queen in parliament already looks like a bejewelled dot on the ocean of the global economy, there are voices that insist the only way of being British is by proclaiming her supremacy.

Redefining identity is not a task for the furtive. It cannot be done by the back door: another lesson of history. Nor will it be easily done by political leaders who still feel obliged to stand aside from the project they think they eventually want to join. But neither should the work be too alarming. In the twenty-first century, it will be exciting to escape from history into geography: from the prison of the past into a future that permits us at last the luxury of having it both ways: British *and* European.

•

SIMON JENKINS
1999

'Kosovo'

When Nato started to bomb Yugoslavia in April 1999 to stop the ethnic cleansing of Kosovo by the Serb president Slobodan Milosevic, Tony Blair's 'just war' was supported by most newspapers, and was at first not even debated in Cabinet or the House of Commons.

But there were a surprising number of critics of the bombing, particularly right-wing commentators who would be expected to support 'our boys' in a conflict overseas. One trenchant critic was Simon Jenkins in this column for The Times.

Am I completely wrong about Kosovo? Have I missed some vital point? Those who fight wars must banish doubt from their minds, since doubt is the enemy of courage. Those who criticize them enjoy no such security. If those who oppose Nato's bombing campaign in Yugoslavia are wrong, they are a menace to the war effort. Tony Blair this week put this war on a par with the 1939 fight against Hitler. We must not again appease dictators, he says. A line has been drawn in the sand. So stop blurring that line, Jenkins.

Such lines are indeed important. We drew them in the Falklands and in Kuwait. The essence of collective world action is that national boundaries should not be changed by force. Wars fought to restore the sovereign integrity of nations are thus just wars. The case against President Milosevic has been stated likewise, but with little conviction. President Clinton and Mr Blair have tried to portray Mr Milosevic as another Hitler, intent on destabilizing the whole Balkans and even dominating Europe, in order to justify Nato's aggressive bombing. But they have been ridiculed by a flurry of pundits. The real *casus belli* in Kosovo is different – the ruthlessness with which Mr Milosevic has treated his own separatists. The case, in essence, is that the man is a monster and 'must be stopped'.

So what is wrong with that? For evil to triumph, it is necessary only for good men to do nothing. Hamlet summoned us to 'find quarrel in a straw when honour's at the stake', and warned us against 'some craven scruple of thinking too precisely on the event'. Is Nato's honour not at stake in Kosovo?

Nato's leaders are certainly making it so. But whereas honour's stake was clear in the Falklands and Kuwait, in Kosovo it is wobbly. Every continent is awash in Kosovo-type conflicts. In former Yugoslavia, Britain recognized

Croatia and Bosnia as states, despite knowing that the outcome would be ethnic cleansing. President Tudjman of Croatia, supported by the Americans, did to his Serb population in 1994–5 exactly what Mr Milosevic is doing to his Kosovans: killing thousands and expelling hundreds of thousands. I do not recall shrill cries from Mr Blair for the bombing of Zagreb. Britain took no action in defence of the Krajina Serbs or the Bosnian minorities, at least until licensed by the UN at the end of the civil war. Why has it so ferociously espoused the Kosovo Albanians? The question can be answered by appeals to expediency, but Mr Blair said this was a war of 'moral purpose'. It is the apparent double-standard that enrages Serb opinion and gathers it, however reluctantly, behind Mr Milosevic.

Yet we are where we are. The gauntlet is down, Robin Cook talks of continuing with bombing 'until the job is done'. Anything less, he implies, would be nothing short of humiliation for Nato. Even Henry Kissinger, long an opponent of this intervention, is a convert to the argument. Now that American forces are engaged in combat, he tells the *Los Angeles Times*, 'victory is the only exit strategy' (an ominous phrase from Kissinger-of-Vietnam). But by victory he means ground assault, as the critics of the 'bombing alone' strategy have always claimed it would. And on this they are at odds with at least the public statements of Nato and the British Government.

What is now planned on Kosovo's border with Macedonia and Albania is a mystery wrapped in a horror. But a land assault on Kosovo has one virtue. It would close the gaping wound at the heart of Nato's present apologia. Mr Blair was near frantic to tell the world that the ethnic 'cleansing' of Kosovo had nothing to do with the Nato bombing. He said that Mr Milosevic planned it long ago and began it a week before the first bomb fell. Mr Milosevic, in other words, never intended only to crack down on the Kosovo Liberation Army but always meant to cleanse Kosovo of Albanians altogether. It is therefore a calumny against Nato to imply that the refugees are in any sense the result of the bombing.

The trouble with this explanation is that it implies an even greater calumny against Nato: that it was aware of the risk of humanitarian catastrophe and did nothing effective to stop it. It rejected as 'too costly' the one military option capable of stopping it, the swift insertion of a rapid reaction force before the main Serb army arrived, and resorted instead to the one option most likely to win Serb support for Mr Milosevic, bombing Belgrade. Mr Blair asks us to believe that his colleagues read intelligence warnings of what was about to happen, and then voted for 'bombing alone'. This was not 'doing something about Milosevic' but the opposite. If true, it was pure Munich.

For what it is worth, I cannot believe that Mr Blair and his colleagues were so cynical. I prefer to see them as victims of their own naive intervention in Yugoslavia's internal affairs and the consequent escalation of threats. Ministers who had never seen a gun fired in anger were mesmerized by military bombast about the political impact of 'pinpoint accurate, laser-guided weapons systems', despite their failure to move President Saddam Hussein in Iraq. Nato gambled that Mr Milosevic would not respond to bombing threats by a pre-emptive strike into Kosovo, but would agree some fudge as he did last October. The gamble failed. The refusal to deploy ground troops when Kosovo was largely undefended now seems cowardly and negligent. Mr Milosevic was invited to call the bluff of the mightiest armies in the world and he did.

I repeat, the war party has not 'done something about Milosevic'. It has done nothing about him. The only honourable thing to do now is properly to go to war with him, yet British politicians still cannot stomach this logical outcome of their posture. Nato has been witness to, if not party to, the disappointment of almost a million Kosovans. Its response is not to restore them to their land but to destroy the oil and power, the roads, factories, bridges, trains and radio stations of a sizeable European state. Mr Milosevic may be 'degraded' but he is politically impregnable, while the supposed beneficiary of this effort, Kosovo, is rendered a wasteland.

Having pulled Mr Milosevic on to the punch, the coherent policy would at least be to punch him properly – a policy to which gung-ho American opinion appears to be dragging the British Government. But such a policy must be mad. The most it could attain is some heavily fortified 'safe havens' in Kosovo. It would drag into the fight every Slav nationalist, not least from Russia. It would also send a signal to any separatist movement that if it can provoke enough mayhem to 'threaten a humanitarian disaster', bellicose Nato politicians will come rushing to its aid. A dozen such groups must be enviously watching the KLA's booming armouries at present. This is not 'world policing' but anarchy.

Nato had no business in half-heartedly sponsoring negotiations over Kosovan autonomy. It was not invited to do so, and made a hash of it. It has no more business in Romania or, for that matter, Basque Spain or Northern Ireland. Kosovo's autonomy remains where it was when Britain 'recognized' the new, truncated Yugoslavia: at the mercy of Mr Milosevic. To invade its deserted valleys and try to hold them against Serb forces would be costly and pointless. To subject Serbia to an indefinite, purely punitive blitz would be obscene.

My answer to the question 'What to do?' is that it is not to draw lines you have not the will to defend at proportionate cost. Non-intervention in foreign civil wars, coupled with generous aid to sufferers, has been normal British policy in the past. Most recently it has been policy in Ethiopia, Rwanda, Sudan, Palestine, Sri Lanka and Afghanistan. This is not a policy of cowardice or appeasement. Mr Milosevic is a nasty job of work but he is not Hitler to Stalin. He does not merit a third world war.

•

FRIENDS OF THE EARTH
1999

'Mahogany is Murder'

To walk in the deep peace of a tropical rainforest inspires a sense of awe at the insignificance of human life – and a sense of rage at their increasing destruction, notably in Brazil.

Friends of the Earth launched its campaign to protect the rainforests in 1985. This is part of the FoE manifesto, 'Mahogany is Murder – Don't Buy It'.

Could you kill another human being?

Could you shoot a woman or child in cold blood?

Of course not. But these things have happened as a result of the demand here in Britain for furniture and fittings made of mahogany.

Every time we buy a piece of Brazilian mahogany, we help to fund the destruction of the Amazon rainforest and the people who live there.

Britain is the world's second largest importer of Brazilian mahogany. Almost all of the mahogany sold here, about 80 per cent of it, is logged in Brazil's Amazon rainforest.

Most of this mahogany is stolen – illegally cut in Indian reserves – by gangs who plunder the forests, bringing disease and destruction with them. Those who get in their way are driven off their land and even shot.

Logging mahogany also seriously threatens the environment. Huge tracts of virgin rainforest are destroyed to extract one mahogany log.

The problem is not unique to Brazil. Forests across the world are under threat. In Ghana, for example, loggers will have exhausted some species of wood known as African mahogany in less than twenty years.

Tropical rainforests are the richest source of life on earth, home to over half the world's species of plants and animals. Yet, each year, an area covering the size of England and Wales is destroyed.

Time is running out, forests are disappearing, people are dying. Please help us to stamp out this murderous trade for ever.

The Bloody Facts

THE HUMAN COST   In 1988, over one hundred Ticuna Indians were attacked and gunned down by timber cutters. Fourteen Indians, children included, were killed and twenty-two wounded. Forced to flee their lands and suffering from imported diseases, the number of Arara Indians has fallen by 75 per cent.

SPECIES EXTINCTION   Rainforest destruction has already driven many species to extinction. An estimated fifty species of rainforest plants and animals become extinct each day.

ILLEGAL LOGGING   Campaigners in Brazil have had to obtain a Federal Court injunction, banning logging companies from cutting in legally protected Indian reserves. Four major suppliers to the UK have been caught logging illegally.

UNSUSTAINABLE LOGGING   The logging industry brings mass destruction into the heart of the forests, through road-building, the transportation of logs and construction of sawmills. Only 0.2 per cent of the world's tropical timber is sustainably produced.

Its time to get tough

Friends of the Earth is campaigning for:

A halt to the exploitation and trade in mahogany, until proper environmental and social safeguards are installed. Over one hundred environmental and human rights groups in Brazil support this demand.
The introduction of international legislation to control the timber trade. Consumers, industry and governments to reduce levels of consumption of timber from the world's natural forests.

Don't buy mahogany.
Since 1985 when we launched our campaign to protect the rainforests, UK imports of rainforest timber have fallen by over 50 per cent.

•

READ MORE IN PENGUIN

In every corner of the world, on every subject under the sun, Penguin represents quality and variety – the very best in publishing today.

For complete information about books available from Penguin – including Puffins, Penguin Classics and Arkana – and how to order them, write to us at the appropriate address below. Please note that for copyright reasons the selection of books varies from country to country.

In the United Kingdom: Please write to *Dept. EP, Penguin Books Ltd, Bath Road, Harmondsworth, West Drayton, Middlesex UB7 ODA*

In the United States: Please write to *Consumer Sales, Penguin Putnam Inc., P.O. Box 12289 Dept. B, Newark, New Jersey 07101-5289.* VISA and MasterCard holders call 1-800-788-6262 to order Penguin titles

In Canada: Please write to *Penguin Books Canada Ltd, 10 Alcorn Avenue, Suite 300, Toronto, Ontario M4V 3B2*

In Australia: Please write to *Penguin Books Australia Ltd, P.O. Box 257, Ringwood, Victoria 3134*

In New Zealand: Please write to *Penguin Books (NZ) Ltd, Private Bag 102902, North Shore Mail Centre, Auckland 10*

In India: Please write to *Penguin Books India Pvt Ltd, 11 Community Centre, Panchsheel Park, New Delhi 110017*

In the Netherlands: Please write to *Penguin Books Netherlands bv, Postbus 3507, NL-1001 AH Amsterdam*

In Germany: Please write to *Penguin Books Deutschland GmbH, Metzlerstrasse 26, 60594 Frankfurt am Main*

In Spain: Please write to *Penguin Books S. A., Bravo Murillo 19, 1° B, 28015 Madrid*

In Italy: Please write to *Penguin Italia s.r.l., Via Benedetto Croce 2, 20094 Corsico, Milano*

In France: Please write to *Penguin France, Le Carré Wilson, 62 rue Benjamin Baillaud, 31500 Toulouse*

In Japan: Please write to *Penguin Books Japan Ltd, Kaneko Building, 2-3-25 Koraku, Bunkyo-Ku, Tokyo 112*

In South Africa: Please write to *Penguin Books South Africa (Pty) Ltd, Private Bag X14, Parkview, 2122 Johannesburg*

READ MORE IN PENGUIN

POLITICS AND SOCIAL SCIENCES

The Unconscious Civilization   John Ralston Saul

In this powerfully argued critique, John Ralston Saul shows how corporatism has become the dominant ideology of our time, cutting across all sectors as well as the political spectrum. The result is an increasingly conformist society in which citizens are reduced to passive bystanders.

A Class Act   Andrew Adonis and Stephen Pollard

'Will Britain escape from ancient and modern injustice? A necessary first step is to read and take seriously this ... description of the condition of our country. Andrew Adonis and Stephen Pollard here destroy the myth that Britain is a classless society' *The Times Higher Education Supplement*

Accountable to None   Simon Jenkins

'An important book, because it brings together, with an insider's authority and anecdotage, both a narrative of domestic Thatcherism and a polemic against its pretensions ... an indispensable guide to the corruptions of power and language which have sustained the illusion that Thatcherism was an attack on "government"' *Guardian*

Structural Anthropology Volumes 1–2   Claude Lévi-Strauss

'That the complex ensemble of Lévi-Strauss's achievement ... is one of the most original and intellectually exciting of the present age seems undeniable. No one seriously interested in language or literature, in sociology or psychology, can afford to ignore it' George Steiner

Invitation to Sociology   Peter L. Berger

Without belittling its scientific procedures Professor Berger stresses the humanistic affinity of sociology with history and philosophy. It is a discipline which encourages a fuller awareness of the human world ... with the purpose of bettering it.

READ MORE IN PENGUIN

POLITICS AND SOCIAL SCIENCES

Anatomy of a Miracle   Patti Waldmeir

The peaceful birth of black majority rule in South Africa has been seen by many as a miracle – or at least political magic. 'This book is a brilliant, vivid account of this extraordinary transformation' *Financial Times*

A Sin Against the Future   Vivien Stern

Do prisons contribute to a better, safer world? Or are they a threat to democracy, as increasingly punitive measures are brought in to deal with rising crime? This timely account examines different styles of incarceration around the world and presents a powerful case for radical change.

The United States of Anger   Gavin Esler

'First-rate . . . an even-handed and astute account of the United States today, sure in its judgements and sensitive in its approach' *Scotland on Sunday*. 'In sharply written, often amusing portraits of this disconnected America far from the capital, Esler probes this state of anger' *The Times*

Killing Rage: Ending Racism   bell hooks

Addressing race and racism in American society from a black and a feminist standpoint, bell hooks covers a broad spectrum of issues. In the title essay she writes about the 'killing rage' – the intense anger caused by everyday instances of racism – finding in that rage a positive inner strength to create productive change.

'Just like a Girl'   Sue Sharpe

Sue Sharpe's unprecedented research and analysis of the attitudes and hopes of teenage girls from four London schools has become a classic of its kind. This new edition focuses on girls in the nineties and represents their views on education, work, marriage, gender roles, feminism and women's rights.

READ MORE IN PENGUIN

The Penguin Book of Twentieth-Century Speeches
Edited by Brian MacArthur

For better, for worse, the great orators have always had the power to change the world.

Whether it was Churchill rousing the British to war, Fidel Castro inspiring the Cuban revolution or Tony Blair leading New Labour out of the wilderness, great speakers have always had the power to stir hearts, uphold great ideals, and lead nations to new frontiers.

The dreams of Emmeline Pankhurst, John F. Kennedy, Martin Luther King and Nelson Mandela inspired millions. This anthology, newly revised to include speeches from the end of this century, including Earl Spencer's stirring philippic over the coffin of his sister, Princess Diana, contains the most famous or notorious speeches in English since 1899, as well as speeches in translation from world leaders, including Lenin, Hitler and Stalin. There are also lesser-known masterpieces from such speakers as Roger Casement, J. B. Priestley and Salman Rushdie. Many helped to change the history of the twentieth century.

'It would be hard to do better than MacArthur's selection, which is a tribute to the breadth of his knowledge' *The Times*

'Time and again, Mr MacArthur satisfies the reader's expectations. They are all here: Lloyd George's fit country for heroes, Woodrow Wilson's world made safe for democracy ... Enoch Powell's River Tiber foaming with much blood ... Those who hate the sound of public men may still find it hard to listen to Brian MacArthur's voices and not, now and then, be moved' *The Times Literary Supplement*

'A compelling read' *Observer*